MW00712473

The Higley Lesson Commentary 2005-2006

Based on the International Sunday School Lessons

New Larger Type
King James Version

73rd Annual Volume

Editor
Wesley C. Reagan

Contributing Writers
Ron Durham, Ph.D.
Doug deGraffenried
David Dietzel
Ralph W. Ford, D.Min.

The Higley Lesson Commentary, in this 73rd year of its life, renews its commitment to careful and reverent scholarship, clear and understandable language, practical and insightful application, and interesting and readable writing. We send it to you with a prayer that it will be a powerful resource for you.

© 2005 by **Higley Publishing Corp.**
1960 U.S. Highway 1 South, PMB 508
St. Augustine, Florida 32086
Toll Free Tel. 1-800-842-1093

Distributed by FaithWorks, a division of National Book Network,
15200 NBN Way, Blue Ridge Summit, PA 17214 / Tel. 1-877-323-4550

Printed in U.S.A.

Foreword

The Higley Commentary is an unusual combination of the work of several writers. Each draws on separate resources, training, and experiences. The result is, in some ways, more like a library than a single reference book.

Long before a reader approaches a single lesson, others have studied that text, researched their reference books, meditated on their experiences, and contemplated how to express their thoughts in the most concise and understandable way. These materials are put together in a single volume. They represent years of study and experience. They look at the text from different points of view. They draw illustrations from different backgrounds.

The reader, then, can have the benefit of hours of study and years of training condensed into a rich resource that can be accessed in only a brief period of time. He can look at the matter from different points of view. He can add his own perspective and experience. The result is a tapestry rich in knowledge and understanding.

Instead of having several sets of commentaries on his shelves and needing days to peruse them, he has that done for him. Instead of depending on a single point of view that could be biased or ill-informed, he has several points of view that can correct and balance each other.

The result is an intensity of information and inspiration that makes the reader's study time exceptionally beneficial. The pass-through effect will enrich the understanding of his students and elevate the level of his teaching.

May God bless you as you seek to know and to teach the Word of God to a world which is hungry to know the Lord.

Wesley C. Reagan, Editor
The Higley Lesson Commentary

Soft Cover ISBN: 1-886763-28-3
Hard Cover ISBN: 1-886763-29-1

Lessons and/or Readings based on International Sunday School Lessons. The International Bible Lessons for Christian Teaching, copyright © 2002 by the Committee on the Uniform Series. Unless otherwise indicated, all Scripture references are taken from the King James Version of the Bible.

Preface

For most of my life I thought Sunday School was for kids only. My only exposure to Bible study was six years of parochial grade school. The lessons consisted of each student reading out loud from the Bible with very little discussion. The Bible used for these studies was difficult to read and even more difficult to understand. Many members of these classes experienced a stifling feeling of boredom.

About eight years ago, a close friend who is a Sunday School Teacher invited me to participate in his class. Each week he would tell me how much I was missing by not attending the class. He was relentless in his interest and concern.

Finally he told me that he would strike a bargain with me. We agreed that if I attended just one class and did not have a desire to return, he would not bring up the subject again. I attended the following Sunday and was instantly hooked.

It was like a new world opening up. Classes were informal and had vigorous participation. Opinions were freely expressed and questions were welcomed. This began a process of growing closer to God in ways that I do not, even now, fully understand. The Bible has become, not just a study guide at church, but a reference book for life. It is as though my eyes have been opened and I have a new understanding of my purpose in life. This has resulted in the developing of new relationships with my fellow men and has given me a peace that I had not known before.

Fred Deats

(*Ed. Note*—Fred Deats is retired from Ford Motor Company where he served as Regional Claims Manager of Insurance Operations. He lives in Richards, Texas, with Joan, his wife of 45 years.)

LESSON CYCLE, 2004–2007

Arrangement of Quarters according to the
Church School Year, September through August

Note: The Committee on the Uniform Series voted to move to a three-year cycle starting in 2004. With that change, gaps in the 2004–2007 cycle may be filled as the Cycle Team works on the 2007–2010 cycle.

	Fall	Winter	Spring	Summer
2004–2005	The God of Continuing Creation (Bible Survey) Theme: Creation (13)	Called to Be God's People (Bible Survey) Theme: Call (13)	God's Project: Effective Christians (Romans & Galatians) Theme: Covenant (13)	Jesus' Life, Teaching, and Ministry (Matthew; Mark; Luke) Theme: Christ (13)
2005–2006	"You Will Be My Witnesses" (Acts) Theme: Community (13)	God's Commitment— Our Response (Isaiah; 1 & 2 Timothy) Theme: Commitment (13)	Living in and as God's Creation (Psalms; Job; Ecclesiastes; Proverbs) Theme: Creation (13)	Called to Be a Christian Community (1 & 2 Corinthians) (Theme: Call (13)
2006–2007	God's Living Covenant (Old Testament Survey) Theme: Covenant (13)	Jesus Christ: A Portrait of God (John; Philippians; Colossians; Hebrews; 1 John) Theme: Christ (13)	Our Community Now and in God's Future (1 John; Revelation) (Theme: Community (13)	Committed to Doing Right (Various prophets; 2 Kings; 2 Chronicles) Theme: Commitment (13)

The cycle is organized around the following six themes that run consecutively, one per quarter:

Creation: God's creative activity in the world.
Call: God's self-disclosure in seeking us as participants in the world's redemption.
Covenant: The relationship created by God's initiative and our response.
Christ: Jesus the Christ, who calls us to community and discipleship.
Community: The coming together of diverse peoples in response to God's love.
Commitment: Living out what it means to be part of the realm of God.

The cycle also follows the church year, to a degree. Specific lessons for Christmas and Easter are offered each year. The seasons of Advent and Lent were also taken into account as much as possible.

iv

FALL QUARTER
You Will Be My Witnesses

In Jerusalem (Lessons 1-4)
In all Judea and Samaria (Lessons 5-9)
To the Ends of the Earth (Lessons 10-13)

WINTER QUARTER
God's Commitment, Our Response

God's Redeeming Love (Lessons 1-4)
God's Gifts of Leadership (Lessons 5-9)
Faithful Followers and Leaders (Lessons 10-13)

SPRING QUARTER
Living in and as God's Creation

The Glory of God's Creation (Lessons 1-4)
Living with Creation's Uncertainty (Lessons 5-9)
Lesson in Living (Lessons 10-13)

SUMMER QUARTER
Called to Be a Christian Community

Servants of God (Lessons 1-4)
Called to Obedience (Lessons 5-9)
The Spirit of Giving (Lessons 10-13)

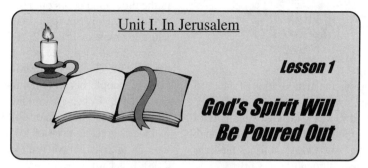

Unit I. In Jerusalem

Lesson 1

God's Spirit Will Be Poured Out

Acts 2:1-8, 38-42

nd when the day of Pente-cost was fully come, they were all with one accord in one place.

2 And suddenly there came a sound from heaven as of a rushing mighty wind, and it filled all the house where they were sitting.

3 And there appeared unto them cloven tongues like as of fire, and it sat upon each of them.

4 And they were all filled with the Holy Ghost, and began to speak with other tongues, as the Spirit gave them utterance.

5 And there were dwelling at Jerusalem Jews, devout men, out of every nation under heaven.

6 Now when this was noised abroad, the multitude came together, and were confounded, because that every man heard them speak in his own language.

7 And they were all amazed and marvelled, saying one to another, Behold, are not all these which speak Galilaeans?

8 And how hear we every man in our own tongue, wherein we were born?

38 Then Peter said unto them, Repent, and be baptized every one of you in the name of Jesus Christ for the remission of sins, and ye shall receive the gift of the Holy Ghost.

39 For the promise is unto you, and to your children, and to all that are afar off, even as many as the Lord our God shall call.

40 And with many other words did he testify and exhort, saying, Save yourselves from this untoward generation.

41 Then they that gladly received his word were baptized: and the same day there were added unto them about three thousand souls.

42 And they continued stedfastly in the apostles' doctrine and fellowship, and in breaking of bread, and in prayers.

Devotional Reading
Psalm 16

Background Scripture
Acts 2:1-42

Memory Selection
Acts 2:38

Acts 2 is a biblical "watershed," recording the inauguration of the third great Covenant between God and man. The first was God's Covenant with Noah, the second His Covenant through Moses. Now God establishes the third Covenant, through Jesus Christ.

In the first two Covenants, God in-teracted with man mainly through *law*. In the third, God pours out His *grace*, through the Holy Spirit, in accordance with the prophecy in Joel 2:23-29.

Acts 2 also marks the beginning of the Church as God's special Family. Previously, people became members of God's Family by being born a Jew. Now all people have the responsibility of making a conscious decision to come to God by faith and obedience (see Acts 2:38). It is hard to over-emphasize the importance of this chapter!

ଃୠଔ

Ask members of your group to imagine how an important message might be delivered instantly to a large group of people who speak many different languages. A natural response might include arrangements like those at sessions of the United Nations. There a variety of translators communicate through headphones with each language group represented.

Note that in this lesson the Holy Spirit communicates even more instantaneously through "speaking in tongues." Diverse people from many parts of the world hear the Word that Jesus is the crucified and resurrected Messiah in their own language. Point out the irony that while modern views of this miracle are diverse, it originally drew people from different nations *together*. It also enabled the Good News to be spread throughout the world.

Teaching Outline	Daily Bible Readings

I. Act of the Spirit—1-8
   A. 'Tongues of Fire,' 1-4
   B. Unity in diversity, 5-8
 II. Response of Faith—38-42
   A. Command, 38
   B. Promise, 39-40
   C. Aftermath, 41-42
	Mon. God's Spirit to Be Poured Out
	       Joel 2:23-29
	 Tue. God Is Always with Us
	       Psalm 16:5-11
	 Wed. The Holy Spirit Comes
	       Acts 2:1-13
	 Thu. Peter Speaks to the Crowd
	       Acts 2:14-21
	 Fri. Jesus Was Crucified
	       Acts 2:22-28
	 Sat. Jesus Was Raised
	       Acts 2:29-36
	 Sun. 3,000 Are Baptized
	       Acts 2:1-8; 37-42

Verse by Verse

I. Act of the Spirit—1-8
A. 'Tongues of Fire,' 1-4

1 And when the day of Pentecost was fully come, they were all with one accord in one place.

2 And suddenly there came a sound from heaven as of a rushing mighty wind, and it filled all the house where they were sitting.

3 And there appeared unto them cloven tongues like as of fire, and it sat upon each of them.

4 And they were all filled with the Holy Ghost, and began to speak with other tongues, as the Spirit gave them utterance.

Pentecost was one of the three most important feast days for the Jews, along with Passover and Tabernacles (or Booths). It took its Greek name (*pentekostes*, "50th") because it came 50 days after Passover began (Lev. 23:15-16). Apparently God chose this feast day for the outpouring of the Spirit and the inauguration of "the Church age" because so many Jews (and proselytes or non-Jewish converts, 2:10) would be in Jerusalem at that time.

The pronoun "they" seems to refer to the 12 apostles, Matthias having been chosen to replace Judas (1:23-26), although some think it refers to the 120 of verse 15. The scene is one of a mighty storm from God,

like that which enveloped the prophet Elijah in 1 Kings 19:11.

As the apostle Peter will explain (vss. 16-21), this astounding event is in direct fulfillment of a prophecy in Joel 2:28-32. In Joel, the outpouring of God's Spirit is portrayed as a part of "the day of the Lord" (Joel 2:1), and the answer to prayers of the faithful in the face of God's judgment against the unfaithful. Although the scene here in Acts 2 is more upbeat, the prophecy in Joel includes doom and destruction for those who oppose the work of the Spirit, whether Jew or Gentile (see Joel 2:1-11). As always, the proclamation of Jesus as the Light is judgment against the darkness.

The miraculous "tongues" or languages poured out by the Spirit is appropriately symbolized by "tongues" (Grk. *glossai*; giving us the modern term "glossalalia") of fire." The fact that they were "cloven" (NIV "fire that separated"), suggests something like an electrical storm that caused forks of lightning to hover over the heads of the apostles.

B. Unity in diversity, 5-8

5 And there were dwelling at Jerusalem Jews, devout men, out of every nation under heaven.

6 Now when this was noised

abroad, the multitude came together, and were confounded, because that every man heard them speak in his own language.

7 And they were all amazed and marvelled, saying one to another, Behold, are not all these which speak Galilaeans?

8 And how hear we every man in our own tongue, wherein we were born?

Luke (the presumed author of Acts) says there were so many Jews in Jerusalem for Pentecost that they represented "every nation under heaven." The great feast days in Jerusalem drew together thousands of Jews from the Diaspora or "scattering" that was the result of numerous defeats by pagan armies. A thorough sampling of the nations represented is given in verses 9-11.

These pilgrims are amazed by the fact that largely untutored Galileans could speak so many languages. We are not told whether each speaker proclaims the Good News in different languages, or whether one spoke the language of the Parthians, another that of the Medes, etc. The important point is that the diverse crowd is drawn together by a common understanding of the momentous news that He who had so recently been crucified had been raised (vss. 31-32), inaugurating the "church phase" of the Kingdom of God (vss. 34-36).

II. Response of Faith—38-42

A. Command, 38

38 Then Peter said unto them, Repent, and be baptized every one of you in the name of Jesus Christ for the remission of sins, and ye shall receive the gift of the Holy Ghost.

The intervening verses have portrayed the apostle Peter preaching (1) that these events fulfill the messianic prophecy in Joel 2, including doom against those who oppose God; (2) the divinity of the One against whom many in the crowd had cried "Crucify Him!"; (3) the resurrection of this same Jesus; and (4) His ascending to the throne of David at the right hand of God. These issues, especially the murder of God's only Son, strike Peter's audience to the heart, and they can but cry out what, if anything, they might do to put the matter right (vs. 37).

Although Peter's answer seems simple, it has prompted widespread arguments: Are people since this scene to be asked to respond to Christ in the same way? Does "repentance" imply that we are saved by the purely human "work" of turning from sin? Does including baptism in the answer of "What shall we do?" imply the doctrine of "baptismal regeneration"—that salvation is in the act itself, whether faith is present or not?

Despite disagreements among many Christians over these issues, there is a general consensus that (1) salvation involves a "turning" (the word for "repentance" literally means having a "change of mind" or heart); (2) baptism should be consid-

4

ered a response of faith, not a work of righteousness (see Rom. 10:9-10); (3) baptism is in some way connected to inviting the presence of the Holy Spirit into the life of converts; and (4) being saved is not in lonely isolation from other believers, but unites converts with other saved people who comprise the Church.

B. Promise, 39-40

39 For the promise is unto you, and to your children, and to all that are afar off, even as many as the Lord our God shall call.

40 And with many other words did he testify and exhort, saying, Save yourselves from this untoward generation.

As huge as the crowds are who hear Peter and the other Spirit-inspired speakers, they are not to think that the promise of salvation is limited to those gathered. The message is also to their children and other people in the lands. "As many as the Lord our God shall call" will become a phrase that works two ways: God calls sinners to Christ, and those who respond show that they are among the called, or elect.

We might well wish we knew more about the content of the "many other words" of Peter and the other apostles at this significant scene. No doubt they drew from prophecies and examples in their Scripture, the Old Testament, as did Jesus, to show how Jesus was the Messiah, Son of David. The additional phrase, "Save yourselves from this untoward generation," speaks of the disciples' rec-

ognition that the world of unbelievers all about them will not ring out this message of salvation and healing. Although many generations have vied for the tag of "Worst Ever," the first century was especially a time of violence and tyranny, political betrayals, wholesale slaughter of innocent people, and widespread ignoring of common decency and respect. Peter's admonition for believers to save themselves from an immoral and godless environment does not imply the ability to lift themselves out of the mire by their own bootstraps, but a responsibility to be loyal to the King who is being preached.

C. Aftermath, 41-42

41 Then they that gladly received his word were baptized: and the same day there were added unto them about three thousand souls.

42 And they continued stedfastly in the apostles' doctrine and fellowship, and in breaking of bread, and in prayers.

Verse 42 gives a brief but remarkably comprehensive list of what the Church is to be about: to learn and apply the teaching the apostles had learned from Jesus, to build each other up by uplifting fellowship, and to continue steadfastly in the rites of prayer and the Lord's Supper. In other words, salvation is not just about *becoming* saved, but also about continuing to meet together to celebrate salvation and perpetuate the message in word and deed.

Evangelistic Emphasis

What kind of trash do you find around your church?

The message of our trash is important in helping us understand what kind of church we are creating. If your trash is basically made up of crumpled bulletins and folded Sunday school lessons, that says you have a church that might be closed to outsiders.

If the trash on your lawn is made up of cigarette butts, beer cans and McDonald's wrappers, it says your church is in an area where there is lots of traffic. It says that your church may be reaching out to those who do not know Jesus Christ.

The radical message of the book of Acts is that Jesus, through the Holy Spirit, creates a church where all are part of the community. Rather than closing our doors to people who smell bad and who have been drinking on Sunday, we are challenged to bring those very people into the doors of the church.

If you are only creating church trash, bulletins, lessons, and such, then maybe you need to think about the kind of garbage you have. Could it be that we are throwing away the wrong things, and that is why evangelism is often not heard? The people whom society has thrown away are the very people that Jesus died for.

&ЭCR

Memory Selection

Then Peter said unto them, Repent, and be baptized every one of you in the name of Jesus Christ for the remission of sins, and ye shall receive the gift of the Holy Ghost."—*Acts 2: 38*

Repentance is a nice church word that is not used on any day except Sunday. When you see your doctor or talk to your minister, rarely will they tell you that what you need is "repentance."

Repentance means walking away from your trash. Actually the word in Hebrew means "to return," and in Greek means to "change your mind." When we repent we change our minds and return to God. In street language we "walk away from our trash." Those cigarettes and beer bottles that I wanted you to look for around your church, should be walked away from when a person repents.

Repentance is literally walking away from our old life so we can join with God in Christ in the new life that He has provided for us. Cleaning the trash out of our souls, allows God to fill those places with the power of His Holy Spirit. Repentance is the doorknob that opens to the power of God. You can't take hold of that doorknob if you are hanging on to your old ways of living.

Weekday Problems

Rusty must have been born with a sin detector. He could find sin in any television show. He could find sin in most magazine articles. It was terrible how the government participated in sin by allowing certain legal unions to happen that Rusty knew were sinful. At church, Rusty always sat near the front, not because he loved to listen to sermons but to be sure he knew it if the preacher made some error of doctrine during the sermon.

Rusty had managed to make almost every member of First Church mad at one time or another. He had criticized the Women's Group for some decisions their national board made. He criticized the Men's Group for their apathy. He thought the missions committee was promoting the social gospel. Rusty knew that without his watchdog eye and his willingness to speak the truth that the whole world was "going to hell."

In all his time at First Church no one ever remembered Rusty doing anything. He was always there on the first row being *right*. He never helped, but he would critique anyone who did.

*How can we talk about the need for repentance and not become judgmental?

*Distinguish between using good judgment and being judgmental.

Speaking of Tongues

As Babel brought as its penalty the confusion of tongues, so the Pentecostal gift of tongues symbolizes the reunion of the scattered nations.—*Fausset's Bible Dictionary*
***

The phenomenon of speaking in tongues described in the New Testament is not some psychological arousal of human emotions that results in strange sounds. This is a genuine work of the Holy Spirit.—*Nelson's Illustrated Bible Dictionary.*
***

When I am in Church I would rather speak five words with my mind (which might teach something to other people) than ten thousand words in a "tongue" which nobody understands.—*1 Corinthians 14:19, The New Testament in Modern English, by J. B. Phillips*

This Lesson in Your Life

At Pentecost, power was given so the Church might preach Jesus Christ boldly. The Holy Spirit came on the disciples in a way that was new. In the Old Testament the Spirit was given and even taken away depending upon the need to the person to be filled with the Spirit. When the Spirit came on the judges and prophets of old, the mighty acts of God were clearly seen.

Jesus promised a new relationship with the Spirit. The Spirit would be the "one called along side" the disciples so that they might know Jesus and be able to remember and apply His words to their situations. The Spirit was the very breath that caused the disciples to live Christ-like lives. Jesus spoke to the disciples about the Spirit as a yet unfulfilled promise. That promise came true at that Pentecost.

The Spirit is that part of the Trinity that dwells within each disciple of Christ. The Spirit begins working with us prior to our knowing Christ, as we are brought under conviction and see our need for repentance. The Spirit then points us to the redeeming grace of Jesus and dwells in us to guide our journey as disciples.

The Holy Spirit was given not for our personal satisfaction, or not to allow us to feel some kind of holy power. The Holy Spirit was given for the sole purpose of pointing all people to Jesus Christ. The true ministry of the Spirit will never point toward the Spirit, but Christ.

All Christian groups can agree on those great truths the Spirit reveals about Jesus. The Spirit points us to the historical person of Jesus Christ. A real man named Jesus, the son of Joseph and Mary walked the earth at a definite point in history. The Spirit reminds us that this real man named Jesus suffered and died for the sins of humanity. His atoning sacrifice on the cross is sufficient for all of us. Three days after He died on the cross, Jesus was physically raised from the dead by the power of God. Jesus lives and is present with us in the person of the Holy Spirit.

God present in our daily lives, that news was so radical and so wonderful that when Peter preached his first sermon about Jesus, 3,000 people joined the church. The Spirit-led preaching of Jesus Christ has the same power in our day. Our world needs to hear powerful preaching. However, more people will be brought to the church when they see you living powerfully, walking daily in the glow of God's Spirit. Pentecost was the birth of the church; Pentecostal power keeps the church relevant in the 21st century.

1. What was the Jewish meaning of the day of Pentecost?
Pentecost was a celebration remembering the day the law was given to Moses. (Leviticus 23: 15-21)

2. On Pentecost the disciples experienced the coming of the Spirit. How is that event described?
There came from heaven the sound of a rushing wind, divided tongues rested on each of them and they were filled with the Holy Spirit.

3. How many disciples were "gathered in one place" when the Spirit came?
One would assume that since the number of disciples had returned to 12, at least 12 were present

4. What are we told about the diversity of people in Jerusalem at this time?
There were devout Jews from many nations in Jerusalem

5. Why will this detail become important later on as the story is told?
These various nationalities will hear the disciples preaching Jesus in their native languages.

6. The "gift of tongues" as described in Acts, appeared to be what kind of gift?
The emphasis in the Acts story was that the gift of tongues was a gift of hearing. The emphasis on the story was in the hearing of the languages, other places it would be on speaking.

7. What different peoples are mentioned in the story of Pentecost?
The peoples listed are Parthians, Medes, Elamites, residents of Mesopotamia, Judea, Cappadocia, Pontus and Asia, Phrygia and Pamphylia, Egypt and Libya, Romans, Cretans, and Arabs.

8. Whose sermon the day of Pentecost was recorded in Acts 2?
The apostle Peter's.

9. How many disciples were standing with Peter, and does that give the answer to question 2?
Peter was standing with the 11. However, we can still only speculate as to how many other disciples were gathered in one place.

10. Why then, does the number 12 become important in this story?
The 12 disciples recall the 12 tribes of Israel.

I really know the Rusty referred to in the Weekday Problem section. I did change his name, but the description of him was not exaggerated. Even if he reads this commentary, he will never see himself. He thinks that his critical stance is right, and that the rest of us are simply wrong. At one level, Rusty has a good heart. He also drives people away from himself and from the church.

Rusty was really upset about the trash around our church. We are at the intersection of a wealthy area and poverty. We are also at the intersection of a commercial area and a residential part of town. There are many different kinds of people who walk into our doors each day. We have such a diverse group of people that we have a team that works on Sunday morning helping all those who come to the church looking for food, a bus ticket, or help with their rent. Sometimes these people stay for church, sometimes they don't.

Rusty is not sure we should be helping them. They leave beer cans and cigarette butts in our landscaping. They smell bad and use foul language. Some of them we lead to faith in Jesus. Some of them just come to the church because they know we are an easy mark. It really doesn't matter why they come; Jesus told us what to do with them while they are here.

The story of Pentecost is about our trash. It is about those trashy people we should be inviting to our pristine churches. I think a good way of determining whether you are doing good ministry is to look at the stains in the carpet at your church. If your carpet is not stained, why not? Don't fold your arms like that, stay with me on this.

The church is not a hotel for saints. We are a hospital for sinners. Some sinners are simply messy and we have to clean up after them. So what kind of trash are you picking up around your church? When your church has the Pentecostal power there is going to be some stuff in the bushes that hasn't been there before. There might be some new stains in the carpet. Believe me, there will be some smelly people, some hearty sinners coming to your door. The Holy Spirit seems to attract riffraff. That is His job: to bring the sinners to a knowledge of Jesus Christ.

Lesson 2

Life Among the Followers

Acts 2:43-47; 4:32-35

A nd fear came upon every soul: and many wonders and signs were done by the apostles.

44 And all that believed were together, and had all things common;

45 And sold their possessions and goods, and parted them to all men, as every man had need.

46 And they, continuing daily with one accord in the temple, and breaking bread from house to house, did eat their meat with gladness and singleness of heart,

47 Praising God, and having favour with all the people. And the Lord added to the church daily such as should be saved.

4:32 And the multitude of them that believed were of one heart and of one soul: neither said any of them that ought of the things which he possessed was his own; but they had all things common.

33 And with great power gave the apostles witness of the resurrection of the Lord Jesus: and great grace was upon them all.

34 Neither was there any among them that lacked: for as many as were possessors of lands or houses sold them, and brought the prices of the things that were sold,

35 And laid them down at the apostles' feet: and distribution was made unto every man according as he had need.

Devotional Reading
Romans 8:9-17

Background Scripture
Acts 2:43-47; 4:32-35

Memory Selection
Acts 2:44

11

Several years ago minister Foy Valentine wrote a book with the interesting title *What Do You Do After You Say Amen?* The same question might be asked after reading of the exciting conversion of the 3,000 people in Acts 2: As new members of Christ's Body, the Church, what happens next? A partial answer was given in Acts 2:47—the new disciples gave themselves to studying apostolic doctrine, having fellowship, praying, and partaking of the Lord's Supper.

This lesson expands on the theme by describing the great generosity in the infant Church, and continuing miracles, along with the proclamation of the Good News about Jesus.

ഇൻൻ

Discuss how your church is involved with helping with the needy. Does it maintain a "benevolent center" or other facility with goods available to the poor? Is there a broader mission to the "have-nots," such as a committee that makes recommendation about such issues as affordable housing? Does the local church contribute to denominational ministries like these?

Note that when such work follows the principles in today's lesson it isn't just "charity," but *community*. The new Christians in Jerusalem followed the Lord of love, so it was natural for them to reach out in love to those in the community with human needs. They were living up to the name "Christian," which means "Christ-like" or "follower of Christ."

Teaching Outline	Daily Bible Readings

I. Active Afterglow—2:43-47
 	
  A. Continuing miracles, 43
 	
  B. Sharing with the needy, 44-45
 	
  C. Glorifying God, 46-47
 	
II. As One Body—4:32-35
 	
  A. Goods in common, 32
 	
  B. Proclamation and grace, 33
 	
  C. Further sharing, 34-35
	Mon. Sharing with the Needy
	       Deut. 15:4-8
	Tue. Come to Life Abundant
	       Isaiah 551-7
	Wed. Parable of the Rich Fool
	       Luke 12:13-21
	Thu. Don't Worry
	       Luke 12:22-34
	Fri. Growing in Faith Together
	       Acts 2:43-47
	Sat. Sharing Possessions
	       Acts 4:32-37
	Sun. Many Are Healed
	       Acts 5:12-16

Verse by Verse

I. Active Afterglow—2:43-47

A. Continuing miracles, 43

2:43 And fear came upon every soul: and many wonders and signs were done by the apostles.

Members of the "New Community"—the 3,000 who responded to Peter's preaching—now set about to follow the Lord they had confessed in their baptism (vs. 38). The "fear" describes not the kind of dread we now associate with the term, but great reverence to the point of obedience. The apostles inspired these efforts with "wonders" and signs," having been endowed not only with the gift of foreign "tongues" but the miracle-working power of Jesus, too. The two words are somewhat synonymous terms for miracles, although the term for "signs" (Grk. *semeia*) points to the supreme Signworker, Jesus Himself.

B. Sharing with the needy, 44-45

44 And all that believed were together, and had all things common;

45 And sold their possessions and goods, and parted them to all men, as every man had need.

It is important to note that the distinctly "religious" activities of signs and wonders appear in the same context as the more "practical" and social ministry activities of relieving human needs, rather than being sepa-

rated as they often are today. Public piety and ministry are part of the same cloth that forms the task of the Church.

Texts such as these were mistakenly taken as the basis of Communism in the early days of the socialist movement founded by Karl Marx and Friedrich Engels. In contrast to such political systems, the sharing described here was a spontaneous movement prompted by special and temporary needs among these early disciples. As noted in the previous lesson, thousands of Jewish pilgrims were in Jerusalem for Passover and Pentecost. The astounding news that a man who had been crucified as a common thief was actually the Messiah convinced many of these pilgrims to extend their stay, over-taxing their ability to feed, clothe, and house themselves. The answer to the problem came in the form of widespread sharing that probably has not been equaled since. It was no doubt a providential situation, since such giving became a means of bonding that the early communities of Christians would need when their allegiance to Jesus would bring persecution.

C. Glorifying God, 46-47

46 And they, continuing daily with one accord in the temple, and breaking bread from house to

house, did eat their meat with gladness and singleness of heart,

47 Praising God, and having favour with all the people. And the Lord added to the church daily such as should be saved.

Again the disciples blend the "religious" and the "secular" in a way that is often ignored among religious people today. Their "breaking bread" or sharing meals in the homes of people who already lived in Jerusalem was as "holy" a part of their lives as their daily worship in the Temple.

This Temple was an ornate structure on the site of the Temple built by King Solomon, and rebuilt by King Herod to endear himself to the Jews. Since most of these converts were Jews, and since Jesus Himself took part in Temple ceremonies, it was natural for members of the New Community to continue to associate with this grand center of Jewish worship. It would be several years before they would consider themselves as anything separate from the larger body of Jews. (In fact the early opponents of Christianity, both pagan and Jewish, considered the earliest Christians to be members of a Jewish sect.)

Verse 47 reminds us of the action of God in receiving people into His Church, the worldwide Body of Christ. Converts did not become a part of that Body merely by making a decision to "join" it. Rather, in their profession of faith and baptism God Himself placed them in the Church. With due respect to differing church policies in receiving new members, this divine action is often ignored today in the rebaptism of Christians who move their church membership.

II. As One Body—4:32-35

A. Goods in common, 32

4:32 And the multitude of them that believed were of one heart and of one soul: neither said any of them that ought of the things which he possessed was his own; but they had all things common.

Again, holding goods together or "in common" is a spontaneous eruption of grace to meet a specific need, rather than a political system designed to prevent people from owning anything. This, however, should not blind us to the vast difference between the fierce, individual ownership of goods so common in society today, and the spirit recorded here that enabled these early Christians to value community over personal property. Community-owned housing, and home-owners who jointly own and share lawn-care equipment are examples of how people today have sometimes emulated the picture here.

B. Proclamation and grace, 33

33 And with great power gave the apostles witness of the resurrection of the Lord Jesus: and great grace was upon them all.

Power and *grace* are two important elements mentioned almost in passing here that actually gave the earliest Christians a foothold in society that would take them through difficult days ahead. The power

(Grk. *dynamis*) no doubt refers to the continuing ability of the apostles to work miracles. This is in direct fulfillment of Christ's promise to them in Mark 16:17-18: "These signs shall follow them that believe; In my name shall they cast out devils; they shall speak with new tongues." T

Equally important is the atmosphere of *grace* or graciousness that seemed to descend on the early Christian community. Apparently they took seriously their Messiah's teaching that "As the Father hath loved me, so have I loved you: continue ye in my love (Jn. 15:9). In this way they fulfilled Christ's prayer "that they all may be one . . . that the world may believe that thou hast sent me" (17:21).

C. Further sharing, 34-35

34 Neither was there any among them that lacked: for as many as were possessors of lands or houses sold them, and brought the prices of the things that were sold,

35 And laid them down at the apostles' feet: and distribution was made unto every man according as he had need.

These early Christians' willingness to share is mentioned yet again, showing how much importance the author Luke placed on this outburst of practical Christian love. Again it is worth noting that late 19th and early 20th century Communism borrowed phrases from this text to establish its policy of "Let each give according to his ability. Let each receive according to his need."

The difference continues, however. The biblical account (Acts 5:1-11) will go on to describe how one Ananias and his wife Sapphira sold a possession, and while pretending to give all the proceeds for distribution to the poor actually withheld part for themselves. In rebuking Ananias, the apostle Peter said that his mistake was not in keeping some of the money for himself, as would be the case under Communist rule, but in the hypocrisy of lying. "Didn't it belong to you before it was sold? And after it was sold, wasn't the money at your disposal?" Peter asked (5:4, NIV). The obvious freedom to own property shows the basic difference between this early incident of Christian "economic policy" and all forced community.

Yet the power of a grace-filled community lifestyle is equally obvious. It created a Spirit-guided atmosphere in which Christ's teaching that "It is better to give than to receive" flourished. Unfortunately this social ambience would not live long past this first outburst of sharing. Most of these Christians would soon return to their homes, form institutionalized churches exert less outreach to the needy, and give more attention to selfish concerns than to sharing. This perhaps partly inevitable cooling of fervor and love gives the sharing described here among the earliest Christians all the more impact as a continuing force and resource for renewal that leads to the rediscovery of the power of sharing.

Evangelistic Emphasis

Denise worked at a McDonald's restaurant in Texas. Every morning a little old man came into that establishment and ordered the same breakfast: coffee and Danish. Denise greeted him with a smile and with kind words.

One day, after sharing in this routine for months, the man put three $100-dollar bills on the counter and told Denise they were for her. Then he added, "You're the only person who talks to me all day long."

Startled, Denise thanked him, but said she couldn't keep the money.

That story would never have happened in the early Church. They would have found room for that man in their fellowship. The Bible teaches that we are all a part of a community. The early Church was so community oriented they didn't have individual possessions. Everything was pooled for the good of all.

Our challenge in bringing good news to our world is to remember many don't feel a part of any community. They are waiting for an invitation to belong. Will you invite them to join your Sunday morning fellowship?

ℰℭ

Memory Selection

And all that believed were together, and had all things common;—Acts 2:44

The definition of church fellowship is found in this verse. Church fellowship has been built around fellowship halls where lots of people gather and drink red Kool-Aid and have conversations about things that have nothing to do with church. It is not a bad thing for Christians to gather and have food and conversation, but it leaves one wanting more.

The kind of church fellowship found in Acts can be recreated in the modern church. Not that we are ever going to pool our financial resources, but there are other ways we can have all things in common.

We can have a common vision for the mission of our church. Our church exists to "make disciples for Jesus Christ." We can work for that common goal. We can share together a common belief in the person of Jesus Christ and in His atoning work on the cross. We can share a of worship and work in the kingdom.

There are many things we can share. It is the essence of Christian fellowship to be able to agree on and share in the work of making disciples for Christ. We can share in the work of making human hurts better. We can share in prayer. We can share in giving for the sake of Christ.

Weekday Problems

After helping the man out of that biblical ditch, the Good Samaritan said to the keeper of the Inn: "Help this man out. I'll take care of any expense." But suppose the injured man said, "You can't leave me. I'm in pretty bad shape here. I need someone to talk to. You're being selfish, leaving me in my time of need."

Feeling guilty, the Good Samaritan stays with the man for three days. On the third day, a messenger tells him that his business contact in Jerusalem waited as long as possible, but he sold the camels to another man. Now the Good Samaritan has lost his business.

Some people manipulate us into giving more that we should. Seldom does the manipulator take responsibility for his or her own life. He makes us responsible for his suffering and pain. Some even want to hold us accountable when their lives do not get better.

Since we as Christians share all things we have a ministry to all people regardless of their suffering or state in life. Jesus gave us this ministry and will judge us on whether we have obeyed Him.

*Discuss how the church can faithfully minister to people who may be spiritually selfish.

*How is sharing all things a problem in a selfish society?

Wondrous Signs

Sign in the window of a travel agency: PLEASE GO AWAY.

In a health food store window: CLOSED DUE TO ILLNESS.

In a veterinarian's office: BACK IN FIVE MINUTE. SIT! STAY!

Sign on a secretary's desk: LACK OF PLANNING ON YOUR PART DOES NOT CONSTITUTE AN EMERGENCY ON MY PART.

Sign in a biology lab: STAPH ONLY.

In another biology lab: DOES THE NAME PAVLOV RING A BELL?

Sign in the elves' workshop at the North Pole: SUBORDINATE CLAUSES.

Sign in a doughnut shop: A WAIST IS A TERRIBLE THING TO MIND.

Sign in an atheists' club: THIS IS A NON-PROPHET ORGANIZATION.

This Lesson in Your Life

A man once came to Jesus and said, "Teacher, tell my brother to divide the family inheritance with me" (Luke 12:13). In response to this man's plea for economic justice, Jesus told the story that has come to be known as the "Rich Fool." It is a story about a farmer who was rich. His fields produced more grain than the farmer could imagine. It was causing a severe storage dilemma. He decided that he would build bigger barns so he could store more stuff. When he finished his self-centered storage campaign, he would enjoy the rest of his life. That night, God said, "Your soul will be required of you, and this stuff, whose will it be?"

The economic system of the early church was so radical and so faithful it will never be replicated. Each member gave all of his stuff to the church and then the church distributed the stuff to the members as they needed it. If your preacher preached that is what you should do as a church, two things would happen. First you would get a new preacher. Second, you would make sure the new preacher never preached from this lesson in Acts. This is one of those passages you just can't get around, so we ignore it. Because sharing all things in common means that we can't lay exclusive claim to our stuff.

I know preachers who preach a gospel of consumption. They teach that God shows His blessings by giving us stuff. If you have stuff you are blessed of God. I even heard one preacher tell his flock they shouldn't share their stuff with the less fortunate, because God would take care of the less fortunate. We have come a long way from the book of Acts.

We have stuff and are called to be good stewards of that stuff. That means we share. We give our tithe to God through the church. We offer our time in service to the kingdom. We do for others. In sharing we become the very body of Christ.

In the early church no one lacked for anything, because the church provided for all of the needs of the members. We can have the material blessings of this world and be faithful to Jesus. That means we must use the blessings he has given us for the benefit of others. I know you are reading this and you will not do it. What is yours is yours after all. You worked hard for it. You earned it. No one gave it to you.

That same kind of thinking caused the economic system of sharing to break down in the early church. By the fifth chapter of Acts, members of the church were becoming selfish. No wonder it is hard to overcome 2,000 years of selfish stewardship theology.

1. Church members sharing everything in common followed what event in the church?

The time when the new Christians shared everything in common follows the outpouring of the Spirit at Pentecost.

2. What activities were the disciples engaged in after Pentecost?

The disciples devoted themselves to the apostles' teaching and fellowship, to the breaking of bread and prayers.

3. Why did the church move toward sharing their financial resources?

They were awed by the signs and wonders being done by the apostles, and had compassion for those in need.

4. How was the economic system in the early church described?

All who believed were together and had all things in common; they would sell their possessions and distribute them as people had need.

5. In what other activities did these early Christians share?

Each day they joyfully spent time together in the Temple and in their homes.

6. How did the surrounding community respond to the Christians?

Because the Christians were filled with glad and generous hearts they had the goodwill of all people.

7. What further description of the stewardship of the early church is made in Acts 4?

The group of believers were of one heart and soul and no one claimed private ownership of any possessions.

8. What was the effect of this radical kind of stewardship?

No one in the community of believers had a physical need.

9. What other significant character in the book of Acts 4 is introduced in chapter 4?

Barnabas, the "son of encouragement," became a part of the Church in this early phase.

10. How did Barnabas introduce himself to the Church?

Barnabas sold a field that belonged to him, and brought the money and laid it at the apostle's feet.

I'll bet some of you think this commentary is in cahoots with your pastor. You will be studying this lesson at a time your church might be doing its annual budget campaign. I want you to know that preachers are as excited about budget campaigns as you are! If we could go back to the way of the early church, we could cancel the fall stewardship program. I can hear you moan from here.

But let me share some numbers that might not qualify as "uplifting," but you need to see them in print. The "Mormons" give the highest per capita for their membership. They average giving 7 percent. The Assemblies of God are close behind with an average of 5 to 6 percent. Nazarenes and Southern Baptists give 3 to 4 percent, on average. Presbyterians and liberal Baptist church groups give 2 to 3 percent. Members of the rest of the Body of Christ average giving 1 to 2 percent of their income to the Church for the work of God.

Before we get our hackles up about this lesson from Acts, we must first ask God's forgiveness for our stinginess. Living in North America we are a part of the most affluent society ever. Yet we give sparingly to causes other than ourselves. There are many reasons for our lack of good stewardship.

For one thing, we do not have a clear picture of *ownership*. I want you to name something you own. Now, here are the guidelines for ownership. You can't owe anyone for it. It has to be something you can take with you when you die. It is that last statement that causes all of us to stumble. In my years as a minister, I have yet to see someone take it with them, although I have seen families argue and fight over "who gets what out of the estate."

Write your name on it as much as you like, hold the deed close to your chest, take a picture of it and put it in your safety deposit box—you are still someone who is called to be a steward over it for your time on earth. I have a biblical responsibility to use the material blessings God has given me in a way that will bring blessing and benefit to others. The only treasure that I will have in heaven is the one that I send up before I get there. When I practice compassion and mercy, when I am generous in my giving and charity, then I will have treasures in heaven.

There are no garage sales in heaven. Garage sales are a living example that we do buy things we don't need. We keep this stuff for a couple of years or more, and when it piles up we have a sale. If only we could learn on the front end that *stuff* will not make us spiritual.

Being rich means that our treasure is being kept safe with God in heaven. Are you storing up treasures in heaven, or is your stuff getting in your way?

Acts 3:1-16

Now Peter and John went up together into the temple at the hour of prayer, being the ninth hour.

2 And a certain man lame from his mother's womb was carried, whom they laid daily at the gate of the temple which is called Beautiful, to ask alms of them that entered into the temple;

3 Who seeing Peter and John about to go into the temple asked an alms.

4 And Peter, fastening his eyes upon him with John, said, Look on us.

5 And he gave heed unto them, expecting to receive something of them.

6 Then Peter said, Silver and gold have I none; but such as I have give I thee: In the name of Jesus Christ of Nazareth rise up and walk.

7 And he took him by the right hand, and lifted him up: and immediately his feet and ankle bones received strength.

8 And he leaping up stood, and walked, and entered with them into the temple, walking, and leaping, and praising God.

9 And all the people saw him walking and praising God:

10 And they knew that it was he which sat for alms at the Beautiful gate of the temple: and they were filled with wonder and amazement at that which had happened unto him.

11 And as the lame man which was healed held Peter and John, all the people ran together unto them in the porch that is called Solomon's, greatly wondering.

12 And when Peter saw it, he answered unto the people, Ye men of Israel, why marvel ye at this? or why look ye so earnestly on us, as though by our own power or holiness we had made this man to walk?

13 The God of Abraham, and of Isaac, and of Jacob, the God of our fathers, hath glorified his Son Jesus; whom ye delivered up, and denied him in the presence of Pilate, when he was determined to let him go.

14 But ye denied the Holy One and the Just, and desired a murderer to be granted unto you;

15 And killed the Prince of life, whom God hath raised from the dead; whereof we are witnesses.

16 And his name through faith in his name hath made this man strong, whom ye see and know: yea, the faith which is by him hath given him this perfect soundness in the presence of you all.

Devotional Reading
Luke 7:18-23
Background Scripture
Acts 3:1-26
Memory Selection
Acts 3:6

We have previously noted that Jesus' ministry of miracles continued after His ascension in the ministry of the apostles. Today's lesson focuses on one of these "signs" or "wonders"—the healing of a man who had been born lame.

Although the healed man's joy is a central part of this lesson, the teacher should be aware that some in the group might not feel so joyful if they have prayed for healing without visible results. Be ready to lift up the sovereignty of God in deciding who is healed (even the apostle Paul was not healed of his "thorn in the flesh" [2 Cor. 12:7-9]). Note also that throughout history, God has used limitations to produce valiant warriors in His service (as in the boy David's victory over Goliath); and that "healing" may come in ways other than physical health.

☜☞

Sharing personal experiences and views on the topic of healing can get this lesson started on the right track. Encourage all views, from skepticism about modern "faith healing" to the experiences of those who believe that they have experienced healing, for themselves or for loved ones, through prayer.

Note that this lesson describes the first healing in the book of Acts. Although some in the group may not have had this experience, or the resulting unbridled joy, remind them of the point made in the "Focus" section of God: God is sovereign, and we may never know why some of our prayers in this arena are not answered. Yet our faith, by definition, must rise above our experience.

Teaching Outline	Daily Bible Readings
I. Encounter with Apostles—vss. 1-10	Mon. Jesus' Healing Power Luke 7:18-23
A. Cripple at the gate, 1-3	Tue. Power to Heal Luke 9:1-6
B. Peter's response, 4-7	Wed. Jesus Rebukes a Demon Luke 4:31-37
1. Expectation, 4-5	
2. Beyond alms, 6-8	Thu. A Beggar Asks for Alms Acts 3:1-5
C. Joy and amazement, 9-11	Fri. A Cripple Is Healed Acts 3:6-10
II. Explanation of Peter—12-16	
A. God set things right!, 12-13a	Sat. Peter's Explanation Acts 3:11-16
B. You committed wrong!, 13b-15	Sun. Call to Repentance Acts 3:17-26
C. The power of Christ, 16	

Verse by Verse

I. Encounter with Apostles—1-10

A. Cripple at the gate, 1-3

1 Now Peter and John went up together into the temple at the hour of prayer, being the ninth hour.

2 And a certain man lame from his mother's womb was carried, whom they laid daily at the gate of the temple which is called Beautiful, to ask alms of them that entered into the temple;

3 Who seeing Peter and John about to go into the temple asked an alms.

We have noticed the "Jewishness" of the earliest Christians, as the first converts after Christ's resurrection and ascension continued to worship in the Temple (Acts 2:46a). The same devotion characterizes the apostles here, as the author focuses on Peter and John making their way to a time of afternoon prayer in the Temple. The noting of "the ninth hour" is one of several remarkably fine details in this narrative, lending credibility to it. Since the Jews reckoned 6 a.m. as the "first hour" of the day, this would have been at 3 p.m. (They seem to have generally observed two other standard times of prayer—one at "the third hour" or 9 a.m. [Acts 2:15], and another at the sixth hour, or noon, [10:9].)

As is still the practice in virtually every major city in the world, a lame man had stationed himself at a place where there was heavy public traffic to beg alms. Unlike the lame man at the Pool of Bethesda in John 5:7, this man had friends who daily carried him to the well-traveled gate called "Beautiful." Although the precise location of this gate has not been identified, some archeologists, guided by the then contemporary Jewish historian Josephus, think it was one with special silver adornment—hence the name "Beautiful." Note the detail that the man had been crippled all his life. The narrative thus tackles a particularly acute problem. The man's disability was not to be blamed on some human cruelty; he had a congenital deformity, which takes the problem of suffering directly to the feet of God.

The man asked alms of Peter and John because it was customary for worshipers to take small sums of money with them to prayer, either to give to beggars like this or to put in the Temple treasury.

B. Peter's response, 4-7

1. Expectation, 4-5

4 And Peter, fastening his eyes upon him with John, said, Look on us.

23

5 And he gave heed unto them, expecting to receive something of them.

Peter commandingly pulls the beggar's attention away from the crowd of worshipers and centers it on himself and John, knowing that they have a gift from Christ not shared by the crowd in general. Of course the lame man immediately, though wrongly, expects this to mean a monetary offering.

2. Beyond alms, 6-8

6 Then Peter said, Silver and gold have I none; but such as I have give I thee: In the name of Jesus Christ of Nazareth rise up and walk.

7 And he took him by the right hand, and lifted him up: and immediately his feet and ankle bones received strength.

8 And he leaping up stood, and walked, and entered with them into the temple, walking, and leaping, and praising God.

Although Peter's famous reply is intended to draw the man's attention from the alms he expected to the healing Peter would give him, it also has a secondary meaning: Even when we do not receive immediate and miraculous healing in answer to our prayers, we can look for some other answer. "Such as I have give I thee" may include the grace to endure suffering, more compassion for others with worse ailments, the forgiveness of sins. The prayer of faith will be open to a broader range of answers than the one we often seek.

The lame man's response could not be more demonstrative. Having suffered all his life, the new strength he feels in his bones causes joy to burst from him in the form not only of praise, but of walking for the first time and even leaping in his new wholeness. Note that he doesn't flee up the street in his enthusiasm, but accompanies Peter and John into the Temple to praise God.

C. Joy and amazement, 9-11

9 And all the people saw him walking and praising God:

10 And they knew that it was he which sat for alms at the Beautiful gate of the temple: and they were filled with wonder and amazement at that which had happened unto him.

11 And as the lame man which was healed held Peter and John, all the people ran together unto them in the porch that is called Solomon's, greatly wondering.

People only observing instead of experiencing the religious fervor of others often scoff at such demonstrations of joy. These bystanders, however, having been accustomed to seeing the healed man begging, now share his excitement upon being able to walk—although they also "greatly wondered" at it. The incident has created a moving celebration, from the gate to the Temple and to Solomon's Porch—a "stoa" or colonnade of pillars forming a porch, thought to be a relic from Solomon's original Temple. It would later become a temporary meeting place for

Jesus' followers (Acts 5:12).

II. Explanation of Peter—12-16
A. God set things right!, 12-13a

12 And when Peter saw it, he answered unto the people, Ye men of Israel, why marvel ye at this? or why look ye so earnestly on us, as though by our own power or holiness we had made this man to walk?

13a The God of Abraham, and of Isaac, and of Jacob, the God of our fathers, hath glorified his Son Jesus;

Peter's first task is to disabuse the people of the notion that he and John had miraculous healing power within themselves. It is essential to attribute the man's healing to the very God these fellow-Jews in the Temple claimed to worship, since the apostles want the observers to follow Him, not them. The God who called the Patriarchs to found a special people had created the world whole, not lame. The man's lameness was not to be attributed to God, but to the sin that first appearing in Eden. Surely this God could restore wholeness in the life of this one man amid an otherwise fallen world.

It was also important to direct the crowd's attention to Jesus. Thus Peter emphatically declares that the healing glorified Him as God's Son. No doubt many of these same people had objected to this claim, since it "made himself equal with God" (John 5:18). Now they must decide whether the miracle that has caused them to rejoice testifies to Jesus' divinity, or was false evidence construed by the apostles.

B. You committed wrong!, 13b-15

13b whom ye delivered up, and denied him in the presence of Pilate, when he was determined to let him go.

14 But ye denied the Holy One and the Just, and desired a murderer to be granted unto you;

15 And killed the Prince of life, whom God hath raised from the dead; whereof we are witnesses.

Knowing the background of the crowd's doubts and their previous assault against Jesus, Peter does not shun the task of indicting them for His death. They cannot have it both ways. If they accept this miracle as evidence of God's power through Jesus, they must repent! Doing so, they can live in the same power of the resurrected Lord that enabled Peter and John to heal the lame man.

C. The power of Christ, 16

16 And his name through faith in his name hath made this man strong, whom ye see and know: yea, the faith which is by him hath given him this perfect soundness in the presence of you all.

Christian preaching must never be content with merely indicting the sinful. If it is to be "good news" or gospel, it must also offer the Yes! of faith—a word that appears twice in this one verse. The soundness the crowd sees in this man can be experienced in their own lives, if they follow "the Name"—turning to the Lord of wholeness who made this remarkable healing possible.

Evangelistic Emphasis

The man looked at Peter and John in a way that invited them to give him a gift. This nameless man was a beggar. He was a beggar because that is all his condition would allow him to do. He may have been a jolly beggar or he might have been a bitter man, but he was a beggar outside of the temple.

Today the church is filled with beggars. Few of us want money. Most of us want God to do something for us. We come praying that God will heal a loved one. We come hoping that God will put a marriage back together. We always seem to have our hand out to God. God always seems to answer us with generosity and grace.

The beggar was looking to Peter and John for something they did not have. He wanted a financial handout. They had no money. Peter would say in our vernacular, "I don't have a nickel to my name." What Peter lacked in financial resources, he made up for in spiritual provision.

He could not offer the man money; he could offer him a new life in Christ. The new life would involve his healing. Now healed, the man no longer needed to be a beggar.

Maybe we are begging God for the wrong things. We should tell the world that Jesus heals what is REALLY broken.

ഏറാ

Then Peter said, Silver and gold have I none; but such as I have give I thee: In the name of Jesus Christ of Nazareth rise up and walk.—Acts 3:6

In Bible times, not being able to walk was a terrible disability. Today, with modern aids, persons who can't walk can still get around. I have found these persons are most adept at driving the shopping carts at Wal-Mart. They are amazing with their spunk and their refusal to give up on life.

The man in Acts, however lacked this kind of technology. He received no disability benefits from the government. He was stuck in and with his physical limitation. It helped some that people gave money to him as one of the poor who received alms. Since Pentecost and the coming of the Spirit, the apostles could offer more than alms. They gave him God's healing power. Now they could now do something about the man's real problem.

This Sunday as you go to church, let God bring healing to what is really broken in your life. Don't ask to have the symptoms removed, let God bring complete healing to your soul, and a positive attitude to your heart

Through Jesus we are given what we really need.

Weekday Problems

Everyone thought that Mary and Jason were happily married. Jason was an attorney. Mary didn't have to work outside the home. They had two children, two dogs, two cars, a nice house, and a membership at the country club. Everyone thought so much of Mary and Jason that Jason was soon on the board of the church.

After Mary started having some mysterious physical problems, she decided to confide in her pastor the truth about her marriage. Mary told her pastor that Jason was not doing things right in his law practice. He was using clients' money for his household expenses. He was not paying his bills at the office, and a few of their bills at home had become late.

Mary was also frustrated because Jason would dip into a trust fund he possessed to get them out of trouble, then blame her because she had not managed "their" money well. Mary was overwhelmed with anger and guilt about their financial situation. Meanwhile, Jason told Mary to stop asking him for money for the household expenses.

*What real issue do Mary and Jason face?

*What was the real problem the beggar faced that needed healing in Acts 3?

Grins from Groucho

(Being some of Groucho Marx's best lines)

I was married by a judge. I should have asked for a jury.

Time flies like an arrow. Fruit flies like a banana.

Hello, room service? Send up a larger room.

I never forget a face, but in your case I'll be glad to make an exception.

You've got the brain of a four-year-old boy, and I'll bet he was glad to get rid of it.

Why, I'd horse-whip you . . . if I had a horse.

I don't care to belong to a club that accepts people like me as members.

One morning I shot an elephant in my pajamas. How he got into my pajamas, I'll never know.

I must say that I find television very educational. The minute somebody turns it on, I go to the library and read a book.

I have had a perfectly wonderful evening, but this wasn't it.

This Lesson in Your Life

In Weekday Problems, Mary and Jason might be persons in your church. Jason needs to learn responsibility, and Mary needs to learn to hold others accountable for their actions. There are people in church every Sunday who don't fully appreciate the desperate shape in which they find themselves. Sometimes, like Mary and Jason, they need a real healing in their marriage. Often people coming to church don't receive the healing they really need, because they are not looking for healing. They are looking for God to make their symptoms better.

Addictions are powerful influences that cause persons to act out of character. There is a 12-step program for every kind of addiction you can name, even for people who are addicted to the Internet. I confess that sometimes I have been driving in bad weather and have called home to ask my wife to look at the weather channel on TV and tell me when the rain will end. I guess I should join an information addiction group.

Healing addictions starts by healing the soul. They are signs of spiritual sickness. We often find it easier to work on the symptoms that we find it to offer healing for the soul.

It has become quaint to talk about sin and salvation. However, many people looking for help from the church need to confess their sins and seek the grace of God. We are almost guilty of reversing the story of Peter and John in this lesson. We act as though we are saying to people, "Here we have the cure for you ailment, but we will not talk to you about Jesus Christ." Our world needs the healing good news of Christ.

Peter healed the man's paralysis and in the process solved his real problem. In healing the paralysis, Peter preached, not only to this man, but to the crowd watching. He preached Jesus Christ. It was the power of Jesus Christ working in those apostles that brought healing to this man. It is the power of Jesus Christ working in the church that will bring healing to our world. It is the power of Jesus Christ, as the savior on the cross and as the Risen Lord that brings transformational healing to our world. Jesus as ONLY a teacher, healer, sage, or rabbi can't transform. Jesus must be seen and accepted by faith as Savior and Lord.

In your life, what do you need to bring to Jesus for healing?

GETTING THE FACTS STRAIGHT

1. Peter and John were going to the Temple at the hour of prayer, what time was the hour of prayer?
The hour of prayer was 3 o'clock in the afternoon.

2. Who would Peter and John meet at the Temple at that hour of prayer?
Peter and John would meet a man who had been lame from birth.

3. How did this lame man arrive at the Temple each day?
He was carried in by people who would lay him at the Beautiful Gate.

4. Why did the lame man come to the Temple every day?
He came to beg alms from those entering the Temple.

5. Why would begging at the Temple be an effective strategy?
Have you ever tried to turn down the Salvation Army at Christmas when you are coming out of Wal-Mart with your buggy full of stuff?

6. What did the man do when he saw Peter and John entering the Temple?
He begged for alms from them.

7. How did Peter respond to the beggar?
Peter told him to look at them. When Peter had his attention he told him they had no money for the beggar. but something better: Jesus Christ.

8. How did the beggar respond to his physical healing?
"Jumping up, he stood and began to walk, and he entered the temple with them, walking and leaping and praising God."

9. What did the crowd think about the man's healing?
The crowd recognized him as the beggar now healed. They were filled with wonder and amazement.

10. What happened when the crowd gathered around Peter and the beggar for a closer look?
Peter began to preach the message of the life, death, and resurrection of Jesus Christ.

Two men were talking. One of them was enormous. He was all with muscles everywhere enormous men should have muscles. The second man was a very small man. He had been sickly as a child and wasn't much better as an adult.

The small man was admiring the monstrous size of the larger man. "Boy if I were as big as you are, I wouldn't be afraid of nothin'. I'd go out into the woods and find the biggest, meanest bear there, and then I'd tear him limb from limb."

The big fellow laughed and said, "There are lots of little bears in the woods. Why don't you go out and tackle one of them?"

This story has a simple yet profound moral. Many people stand on the sidelines loudly proclaiming what they would do if they had the ability or the opportunity of someone else. Can you hear the beggar at the Temple gate telling all of his begging buddies how much better he would do things if only he could walk? Can you hear him dreaming the "if only" big dreams that we all have when we know our limitations will keep us from ever having the "if only" moments in our lives?

This is where this story challenges us. The man was limited by his inability to walk. In a culture where your legs or your donkey were your only transportation options, this man had missed out. He could do very little because of his limitations. His only occupation was dictated by his physical reality. He could beg.

But just like the little guy in the bear story, there is work for all of us. Perhaps we can't take on a "big bear" of responsibility, but that does not mean we should sit idly by and make excuses for doing nothing. Some of us "little fellows" need to get out in the woods and tackle some of those little bears.

The beggar became an evangelist for the new Church. He followed Peter into the Temple praising God. His enthusiasm for God brought others to hear the story. The beggar got to tackle not only some little bears . . . he showed his buddies what he could do now that he could walk.

What could you do if God fixed what was broken in your soul?

Lesson 4

Power to Be Bold

Acts 4:1-4, 23-31

And as they spake unto the people, the priests, and the captain of the temple, and the Sadducees, came upon them,

2 Being grieved that they taught the people, and preached through Jesus the resurrection from the dead.

3 And they laid hands on them, and put them in hold unto the next day: for it was now eventide.

4 Howbeit many of them which heard the word believed; and the number of the men was about five thousand.

23 And being let go, they went to their own company, and reported all that the chief priests and elders had said unto them.

24 And when they heard that, they lifted up their voice to God with one accord, and said, Lord, thou art God, which hast made heaven, and earth, and the sea, and all that in them is:

25 Who by the mouth of thy servant David hast said, Why did the heathen rage, and the people imagine vain things?

26 The kings of the earth stood up, and the rulers were gathered together against the Lord, and against his Christ.

27 For of a truth against thy holy child Jesus, whom thou hast anointed, both Herod, and Pontius Pilate, with the Gentiles, and the people of Israel, were gathered together,

28 For to do whatsoever thy hand and thy counsel determined before to be done.

29 And now, Lord, behold their threatenings: and grant unto thy servants, that with all boldness they may speak thy word,

30 By stretching forth thine hand to heal; and that signs and wonders may be done by the name of thy holy child Jesus.

31 And when they had prayed, the place was shaken where they were assembled together; and they were all filled with the Holy Ghost, and they spake the word of God with boldness.

Devotional Reading
Ephesians 6:10-20

Background Scripture
Acts 4:1-31

Memory Selection
Acts 4:29

In this lesson the disciples face the first of a series of confrontations with both Jewish and Roman officials—a response that will reappear at various times and places throughout the subsequent story of the spread of the Christian faith.

The focus in this lesson, however, is not on the opposition faced by the early Christian teachers, but their boldness and sense of power. Their over-riding strategy of response will be summarized in Acts 5:29: *"We ought to obey God rather than men."* In response, God sends a powerful outpouring of His Spirit in confirmation of the disciples' courage.

Similar protests sometimes meet disciples of Christ today when they boldly communicate the Gospel—among other religious groups, in the workplace, and other settings. What will our response be?

ଈଠଔ

Open this discussion by inviting group members to share instances they have heard or read about, or perhaps even times when they themselves have met resistance when sharing their faith. Be prepared by checking news sources for instances of modern persecution, such as has occurred in Africa, the Philippines, and the Middle East in recent years.

How should Christians respond to such resistance? What about in Islamic countries where it is illegal to proclaim the gospel? Is evangelism inappropriate in the workplace? How can Christian boldness be blended with the spirit of gentleness inherent in our message?

Teaching Outline

I. Blunt Opposition—1-4

    A. Complaint and arrest, 1-3

    B. Success anyway, 4

II. Boldness in Prayer—23-31

    A. Support from the Body, 23

    B. Comfort from Scripture, 24-26

    C. Focus of attack, 27-28

    D. Prayer for boldness, 29-30

    E. Divine demonstration, 31

Daily Bible Readings

Mon.	Be Strong in the Lord Eph. 6:10-20
Tue.	Preaching with Courage 1 Thess. 2:1-8
Wed.	Disciples Arrested Acts 4:1-7
Thu.	Christ Proclaimed Acts 4:8-12
Fri.	Disciples Warned Acts 4:13-17
Sat.	Preaching Anyway Acts 4:18-22
Sun.	Praying for Boldness Acts 4:23-31

Verse by Verse

I. Blunt Opposition—1-4

A. Complaint and arrest, 1-3

1 And as they spake unto the people, the priests, and the captain of the temple, and the Sadducees, came upon them,

2 Being grieved that they taught the people, and preached through Jesus the resurrection from the dead.

3 And they laid hands on them, and put them in hold unto the next day: for it was now eventide.

Acts 3 closed with a reference to the resurrection of Jesus, showing how central that event was to the preaching of the apostles. Suddenly strong opposition arises, led by the Sadducees—a Jewish sect that did not believe in resurrection or an afterlife (see Matt. 22:23). They have also gathered officers or "captains," who were the heads of squads of guards charged with keeping order in the Temple. Although Rome was in overall control of policing Jerusalem, the Empire made a practice of allowing conquered peoples to practice their religion (as long as it did not disturb the State). In keeping with this policy, Rome allowed the Jews their own policing authority—which now comes down on Peter and John as they are jailed in the "hold."

In our day similar opposition is often mounted by members of other religious groups who protest that Christian evangelism violates the rights of others, and is aimed at destroying the predominant culture (such as Judaism, Hinduism, Islam, Buddhism, or even secularism). In some cases, Christians have been imprisoned and even put to death for nothing more than exercising the free speech so highly prized in our own country. The scene here raises the question of how modern Christians can be faithful to their message while respecting the laws and customs of non-Christian cultures.

B. Success anyway, 4

4 Howbeit many of them which heard the word believed; and the number of the men was about five thousand.

As often happens, however, once the Word of the gospel is let out of the bag, it is impossible to keep it from bearing fruit. The Jewish authorities are fighting a defensive battle, with 5,000 men having already responded to the apostolic preaching. (In keeping with the male dominance of the culture, women and youth were often not counted; see Matt. 14:21).

II. Boldness in Prayer—23-31

A. Support from the Body, 23

23 And being let go, they went to their own company, and re-

ported all that the chief priests and elders had said unto them.

Intervening verses (13-21) have described the authorities' dilemma that led to their releasing Peter and John. Peter had boldly asserted that they had an imperative to share the faith (see Matt. 28:18-20).

Set free, at least for a time, Peter and John report to "their own company," or the rest of the apostolic band. Not only is there no Civil Rights board from which to seek recourse; they were theologically committed to stand together as soldiers of Christ. It was important for the other apostles to know the restrictions the Jewish authorities had attempted to impose, and the preachers needed to draw from the larger group the courage to resist efforts to squelch their message.

B. Comfort from Scripture, 24-26

24 And when they heard that, they lifted up their voice to God with one accord, and said, Lord, thou art God, which hast made heaven, and earth, and the sea, and all that in them is:

25 Who by the mouth of thy servant David hast said, Why did the heathen rage, and the people imagine vain things?

26 The kings of the earth stood up, and the rulers were gathered together against the Lord, and against his Christ.

Whatever strategies the apostles may have discussed they do not include appeasement, and we are not told of their hiring attorneys to defend their cause. Their foremost "armor" in the battle they see forming before them is prayer.

Remarkably, they do not pray for protection or for angelic armies to deliver them. Instead, they ask for boldness, on the basis of God's previous aid in the face of "heathen rage" or opposition. They first call on the God of creation: if He has formed "all that is," He has the power to enable those who serve Him to conquer their foes—not with violence, but with the same spiritual power so evident in creation. Then they cite Psalm 2:1, which speaks of God's defending His "anointed"— the Old Testament word for the coming Messiah. Firmly believing that God's Anointed One is none other than the Christ they preach, they appeal to the God who sent Him for boldness.

C. Focus of attack, 27-28

27 For of a truth against thy holy child Jesus, whom thou hast anointed, both Herod, and Pontius Pilate, with the Gentiles, and the people of Israel, were gathered together,

28 For to do whatsoever thy hand and thy counsel determined before to be done.

Now the apostolic prayer for strength to continue to proclaim the Word against opposition is based on faith in the God whose "determinate counsel and foreknowledge" (Acts 2:23) had allowed the Anointed One to be sought out as an infant by King Herod, and finally to be crucified. Surely the One who governed not only at Christ's trials but at His resurrection has the power to give them courage to tell His story!

Verse 27 relates directly to recent and current discussions about who is actually guilty of crucifying Jesus. Although much early Christian preaching is directed at unbelieving Jews, this verse indicts all parties present, Gentiles and Jews alike. The truth is that all sinners are complicit in Christ's death, and that all have equal access to His limitless forgiveness. Ironically, attempts to squelch the message of Jesus' death also shut off the message of grace we all so desperately need.

D. Prayer for boldness, 29-30

29 And now, Lord, behold their threatenings: and grant unto thy servants, that with all boldness they may speak thy word,

30 By stretching forth thine hand to heal; and that signs and wonders may be done by the name of thy holy child Jesus.

The apostles' appeal for boldness, not "rescue," continues. They also call on God to continue the miraculous works of the Spirit that were so prominent in Jesus' ministry. They need not only boldness, but evidence. As verse 16 has said, the Jewish leaders could not deny that in the healing of the lame man at the Temple gate "a notable miracle hath been done." Even today, when reports of such miracles are less prominent, Christian preachers can recount Jesus' miracles as evidence of His claims. Also, modern proclaimers of

the good news can *"live* miraculously" by maintaining a blend of good sense and boldness as they stand for the truth against opposition.

E. Divine demonstration, 31

31 And when they had prayed, the place was shaken where they were assembled together; and they were all filled with the Holy Ghost, and they spake the word of God with boldness.

No sooner do the apostles pray for power than it falls upon them and the place where they assembled! There is significance in the doubling of the concept of *community* in the words "assembled together." This emphasizes that the spiritual resources and courage required to maintain a faithful witness in the face of opposition properly comes from the Body of Christ, not just to the lone warrior praying in private.

God's answer to their impassioned prayer includes another incidence of the outpouring of the Holy Spirit, prompting the disciples to speak out with the very boldness for which they had prayed. The audience listening to this "speaking of the word" is not clear. If the meeting has been open to unbelievers, the Spirit's promptings may have been in the "tongues" or other languages so prominent in Acts 2. If the assembly includes only believers, the Spirit may have moved them to build each other up in the "tongues of angels" that would become both prominent and divisive as the Church grew (see 1 Cor. 14:1-4).

35

Evangelistic Emphasis

It is said that a remarkable layman named Harry Denman remained unmarried throughout his life for Jesus' sake. He had no home and no regular income. He had only one suit and one pair of shoes, which he wore until they were finished and then replaced them. When money came his way, he used what he needed for his very simple wants, and gave the rest away. He traveled widely in the southern states, holding unadvertised camp meetings wherever he went.

People just seemed to show up when Harry Denman was around. He would talk to people on trains and in the streets about the first love of his life, Jesus Christ. In the course of his life, he led many thousands of people to faith in Jesus. He was consumed with a passion to spread the good news. Telling others about the grace available in Jesus Christ was the passion of Harry Denman's life.

We would call it a strange life today. We want to know the name, address, and web address of all who are working for Christ. We need this information so we can "support their ministry." We erect big, beautiful buildings to entice people to hear about Jesus. We pay professional preachers to tell others about Jesus.

The bad news of the good news of Jesus is that YOU are supposed to be telling others about Him. Now put this lesson book down and get to work!

ЄЭСЯ

Memory Selection

And now, Lord, behold their threatenings: and grant unto thy servants, that with all boldness they may speak thy word.—*Acts 4: 29*

How long has it been since you boldly spoke the name of Jesus?

Many Christians work in environments where talking about religion is considered a form of harassment. Still others don't speak the word of Jesus boldly because they are afraid of the reception they might receive. Let me ask you: if that friend or co-worker is that easily offended by the Christian faith, what are you doing hanging around him? Some in the church don't want to be seen as "goody-goody" types. They would be better served to say, "I live for Jesus on Sunday ONLY."

Christians who believe the world is going to hell gather for prayer behind closed doors and hope that something will change the direction things are going. We would be more faithful to the gospel, if we would open our doors, get involved with friends and the culture, and tell them, "Jesus saves."

What do you have to lose? A better question: *"What do you have to gain?"* God can do powerful and miraculous things through those who obey. He can't do anything through those who don't obey.

Weekday Problems

Strange religious things have happened since 9/11.

Prior to that horrible event, my community had a Thanksgiving service shared by all of the downtown churches. All of the Protestant denominations were present. The first year of the service, the Catholic Bishop of the diocese graced us with his presence. It was a great time of worship and celebration of our common faith and American heritage. We even invited the Jewish community to participate. Every year we look forward to the shofar being blown to begin our worship services.

For the Thanksgiving service of 2001, someone suggested that we invited the Islamic community to participate in our service. It was done under the guise of developing "mutual understanding." For three years now the Islamic community has participated at the community Thanksgiving service. This year the service won't be held at a downtown church, we have been invited to the Islamic community center.

Also in I have been invited to preach at this service. I have been struggling with what I should do. So your task in talking about this Weekday Problem is to figure out if I should preach at the service, or if I should politely excuse myself.

The issue for me is that sometimes a Christian can speak boldly for Jesus in what he *doesn't* do. Am I right, or am I being stubborn and narrow-minded?

This is a Test

Q: What is the only thing you can break by saying its name?
A: Silence.

What question can never be answered by "Yes"?
"Are you asleep?"

What is the world's oldest piece of furniture?
The multiplication table.

What driver never gets arrested?
A screwdriver.

What intelligent insects are found in school rooms?
Spelling bees.

What is the hardest thing about learning to ride a bicycle?
The pavement.

This Lesson in Your Life

When Jesus was on earth preaching, His family thought He was crazy. Jesus was preaching at His home synagogue, and they decided to push Him off of a cliff. Jesus was not accepted in His own country. His own people would make sure that He was crucified.

The church began her history in the midst of Jewish people. Peter and John learned that the Jewish people were not enthusiastic about hearing this Gospel. The Jewish people were not thrilled that a couple of their cherished traditions, such as kosher and circumcision would not be a part of the Christian presentation of Jesus. The early Church even co-opted the Old Testament, saying it belonged to Christians, not to Jews.

The Gentiles had all sort of objections to the gospel of Jesus. Cultural practices such as religious prostitution and public drunkenness were condemned by the Church. The Romans were nervous about Christians because they would pledge allegiance only to Jesus, not to Caesar.

The early Church operated in a hostile environment. Some early graffiti found in Rome even includes a cartoon against the Church. Yet in the first 30 years of its history, Christians changed the face of the Roman Empire and the face of Western history.

There are several similarities between the story in Acts and the culture in which we work for Jesus today. The Church often finds herself opposed to cultural norms. We live in a society that seems to be accepting new paradigms for marriage. The family is under attack and the Church, calls herself the "family of God." The world doesn't even like the images we use for ourselves. Sometimes the Church must preach that being a good American and being a Christian are not the same thing. We live in a time in which a simple, warm faith is laughed at by the intellectually elite. As I have mentioned earlier, even talking about Jesus in some settings opens one for a harassment charge. Religious images can't even be shown in public places. We work in a hostile world.

Peter and John give us an example of what to do when faced with a hostile world. They responded to hostility with boldness. We are also called to proclaim the story of Christ with boldness, even though the "deck is stacked against us." Our flimsy excuses for living safely and quietly will not stand on the Day of Judgment. We are not called to be popular; we are called to change the world.

Why are you still reading this lesson? You should be out boldly talking to someone about Jesus! That is what this lesson is all about. Are you worried that someone might be offended or against you? If opposition was good enough for Jesus, it should be good enough for us.

GETTING THE FACTS STRAIGHT

1. Who became annoyed at the preaching of Peter and John?

The priests, the captain of the temple, and the Sadducees.

2. What was the issue that caused the Jews to be upset with Peter and John?

These two apostles were teaching that in Jesus there is the resurrection of the dead.

3. How did the Jewish officials treat Peter and John as a result of their preaching and teaching?

They arrested Peter and John and put them into custody until the next day.

4. What happened to the people who were listening to the teaching of Peter and John?

The people listening were moved by the message. Five thousand people came to believe in Jesus.

5. Who were some of the Jews listed by name in Acts 4?

Annas the High Priest, Caiaphas, John, and Alexander—all of the priestly family.

6. What did the Jewish leaders demand of Peter and John?

The leaders wanted to know "by what power or by what name did you do this?"

7. How did Peter respond to the questioning of the Jewish leaders?

He preached Jesus to them.

8. What image did Peter use for Jesus in this encounter with the Jewish leaders?

Peter said of Jesus, "the stone that was rejected by you, the builders, it has become the cornerstone."

9. What did the Jewish leaders demand of Peter before they released him?

They threatened him and then turned him loose. They could find no way of punishing him, given the popularity of the message of Jesus.

10. When Peter was released and told the other believers what happened, how did they respond to Peter's news?

They were filled with the Spirit and spoke the word of God with boldness.

Have you ever led someone to faith in Christ? You have had a whole lesson to do so. I have asked you a couple of times if you were still reading this lesson, and I'll bet you never got out of your chair! Did you leave your table, put your Bible and your *Higley Commentary* down long enough to talk to someone about Jesus?

In one church in Texas the church does not allow Sunday morning Sunday school classes for adults! The people who would ordinarily be attending Sunday school are put to work in the various ministries of the church. Some of the people teach the children's age class. Other adults are involved with the youth in ministry activities. Still others are helping with the Sunday morning food program. Sunday, for this church, has become a day of work for the Lord. The image of a church gathering to sing and sit on Sunday morning is not an image that will reach the lost person for Jesus Christ.

The central theme of this lesson is *boldness*. In our culture bold action is appreciated. Bold preaching and teaching must be followed up with bold action, for the words to be credible. The challenge I have offered you throughout the lesson to go *do* something for Jesus is an important part of all of this. I know that most of you didn't do anything. You felt as though my words of challenge might have been some editorial oversight. Those words were illustrative.

We have become passive spectators in our faith. For the most part we leave evangelism to the professionals.

Peter and John were not professionals. They were lay persons whose lives had been transformed by the power of the Holy Spirit. They did God's bidding without question and without reservation. They didn't really care what anyone thought as long as God was pleased with their activities.

Boldness is not about being comfortable. It is not about looking good or being politically correct. Boldness, the way the Book of Acts describes it, is life-altering. Boldness in obedience to Jesus Christ, empowered by the Spirit, will turn the world upside down, again.

Now seriously, are you still sitting there reading this lesson? Get to work! Boldly!

Lesson 5

Faithful Servant

Acts 6:8-15; 7:53-60

And Stephen, full of faith and power, did great wonders and miracles among the people.

9 Then there arose certain of the synagogue, which is called the synagogue of the Libertines, and Cyrenians, and Alexandrians, and of them of Cilicia and of Asia, disputing with Stephen.

10 And they were not able to resist the wisdom and the spirit by which he spake.

11 Then they suborned men, which said, We have heard him speak blasphemous words against Moses, and against God.

12 And they stirred up the people, and the elders, and the scribes, and came upon him, and caught him, and brought him to the council,

13 And set up false witnesses, which said, This man ceaseth not to speak blasphemous words against this holy place, and the law:

14 For we have heard him say, that this Jesus of Nazareth shall destroy this place, and shall change the customs which Moses delivered us.

15 And all that sat in the council, looking stedfastly on him, saw his face as it had been the face of an angel.

53 Who have received the law by the disposition of angels, and have not kept it.

54 When they heard these things,

they were cut to the heart, and they gnashed on him with their teeth.

55 But he, being full of the Holy Ghost, looked up stedfastly into heaven, and saw the glory of God, and Jesus standing on the right hand of God,

56 And said, Behold, I see the heavens opened, and the Son of man standing on the right hand of God.

57 Then they cried out with a loud voice, and stopped their ears, and ran upon him with one accord,

58 And cast him out of the city, and stoned him: and the witnesses laid down their clothes at a young man's feet, whose name was Saul.

59 And they stoned Stephen, calling upon God, and saying, Lord Jesus, receive my spirit.

60 And he kneeled down, and cried with a loud voice, Lord, lay not this sin to their charge. And when he had said this, he fell asleep.

Oct. 2

Devotional Reading
Isaiah 6:1-8

Background Scripture
Acts 6:8–7:60

Memory Selection
Acts 6:8

41

The book of Acts is so filled with references to the Holy Spirit that some have suggested that it should be called "The Acts of the Spirit." Today's lesson tells of an heroic "act" of a Christian preacher whose heroism could only be called forth by the Holy Spirit.

The act is the martyrdom of Stephen. It is the first recorded instance of a Christian dying for the faith, and would be followed by uncounted thousands through the centuries. Evidence that Stephen was filled with the Spirit appears not just in his willingness to give his life for the cause, but in his boldness in indicting sinners, then actually praying for their forgiveness!

❧❦

Modern tensions in the Middle East have transformed *martyrdom* from obscure acts of members of little-known groups to a horribly common item in the daily news. Ask group members to describe their feelings about this willingness of so many to give their lives for their cause. Is there anything commend-

able about it? What is in the mind of a person who actually wants to kill himself in a suicide bombing? What result seems to be expected? What is to be said about families and groups who actually train their children to want to become martyrs? What are some similarities and differences between a Muslim militant who kills himself in the act of killing Jews, and the well-known story of Stephen in this lesson? Ordinarily, is it more commendable to live or to die for one's faith?

Teaching Outline

I. Deacon's Ministry—6:8
II. Dispute with Stephen—9-15
   A. Futile challenge, 9-10
   B. False testimony, 11-14
   C. Stephen faces his foes, 15
II. Defense and Martyrdom—7:53-60
   A. (Gist of speech, 7:1-52)
   B. Final indictment, 53
   C. Vision of glory, 54-56
   D. Stephen's death, 57-59
   E. Dying like Jesus, 60

Daily Bible Readings

Verse by Verse

I. Deacon's Ministry—6:8

8 And Stephen, full of faith and power, did great wonders and miracles among the people.

Stephen was one of seven men appointed to help "serve tables" in the feeding of the thousands who had responded to the message that Jesus had died for their sins (Acts 6:1-5). Although the term "deacon" (Grk. *diakonos*) is not explicitly applied to these men, the verb form (*diakonen*) is (6:2); and the seven are therefore almost universally viewed as the first deacons in the early Church. Along with this term, it is common to describe their duties in terms of menial tasks limited to "serving tables." As this account shows, however, this is a gross over-simplification. Stephen is filled with the Spirit, performs miracles, and is an accomplished orator or preacher.

II. Dispute with Stephen—9-15

A. Futile challenge, 9-10

9 Then there arose certain of the synagogue, which is called the synagogue of the Libertines, and Cyrenians, and Alexandrians, and of them of Cilicia and of Asia, disputing with Stephen.

10 And they were not able to resist the wisdom and the spirit by which he spake.

Although "Stephen" is a Greek name, certain Greek-speaking Jews challenge his preaching despite the way he supported it with miracles. Apparently Jerusalem had one or more synagogues for some of these foreign Jews, who were separated at least by language and possibly by doctrine from the main body of Aramaic-speaking Jews in the city. "Libertines" is variously interpreted as referring to Jews who had been liberated from slavery, or people from a now-unknown province or country called "Libertine." The other places mentioned were widely separate in the Mediterranean world, but the Jews in all of them had been "Hellenized" or "contaminated" with Greek influences, in the view of many Jews native to Jerusalem.

B. False testimony, 11-14

11 Then they suborned men, which said, We have heard him speak blasphemous words against Moses, and against God.

12 And they stirred up the people, and the elders, and the scribes, and came upon him, and caught him, and brought him to the council,

13 And set up false witnesses, which said, This man ceaseth not to speak blasphemous words against this holy place, and the law:

14 For we have heard him say, that this Jesus of Nazareth shall

destroy this place, and shall change the customs which Moses delivered us.

Some of the false witnesses "suborned" here may have been among those who gave similar testimony against Jesus—that He had threatened to destroy the Temple (Matt. 26:59-61). It was a charge which, though false, had been used successfully in Jesus' trial; perhaps it would be effective against Stephen, too. The charge that Jesus blasphemed the Law may have grown out of such lessons as those in the Sermon on the Mount, in which He elevated His own teaching over several points of the Law ("You have heard it said . . . but *I* say . . . ."). No doubt Stephen sees immediately that his response to these false charges must include the fact that Jesus' teaching grew out of Moses' Law, rather than undermining it—that He came to "fulfill" the Law, not to destroy it (Matt. 5:17).

C. Stephen faces his foes, 15

15 And all that sat in the council, looking stedfastly on him, saw his face as it had been the face of an angel.

Those who oppose Stephen bring him to "the council" or the Jewish Sanhedrin—the same political/judicial body before Jesus had appeared. Stephen is of such a Christ-like spirit that his face must have given off an angelic glow of thanksgiving for the privilege of standing where his Lord had stood, and defending his faith.

II. Defense and Martyrdom—7:53-60

A. (Gist of speech, 7:1-52)

Stephen's speech against his accusers is the longest in Scripture. It is a sermon based on history—*salvation* history. It holds up the patriarchs and Moses—heroes of the Jews who oppose him—as faithful to the covenants God had made with them, but opposed by disobedient Jews. Stephen refers to these fomenters of rebellion as the true fathers of his accusers, because it was people just like his opponents who wanted to return to Egypt after Moses led them to freedom with accompanying miracles showing God's approval (vs. 39). Stephen is so outspoken and uncompromising that he finally calls his opponents "stiffnecked and uncircumcised in heart and ears," resistors of the Holy Spirit, and murderers of the prophets (vs. 52). He is giving no quarter and taking no prisoners!

B. Final indictment, 53

53 Who have received the law by the disposition of angels, and have not kept it.

Jewish tradition held that the Law of Moses had been administered by, or given through angels (Gal. 3:19). Stephen's final charge is that his opponents have been colossal ingrates by having rejected the very Law they claim Jesus and Stephen had blasphemed. Truly keeping the Law would mean accepting Jesus as the Messiah it foretold.

C. Vision of glory, 54-56

54 When they heard these things, they were cut to the heart, and they gnashed on him with their teeth.

55 But he, being full of the Holy Ghost, looked up stedfastly into heaven, and saw the glory of God, and Jesus standing on the right hand of God,

56 And said, Behold, I see the heavens opened, and the Son of man standing on the right hand of God.

Stephen's barbed words strike to the heart. Unfortunately, however, this doesn't produce proper spiritual "heartburn" leading to repentance, but anger. That they "gnashed on him with their teeth" is figurative, a common way of describing boiling wrath that could spill over into such animalism (Job 16:9).

Like all true martyrs, Stephen is able to endure earthly suffering because he has his eyes fixed on the greater reality of heaven. God graciously gives him a vision of Jesus standing at God's right hand in the throne room of heaven. It is from this source of supreme power, not from some political maneuver, that Stephen expects deliverance—even though it will involve his death.

D. Stephen's death, 57-59

57 Then they cried out with a loud voice, and stopped their ears, and ran upon him with one accord,

58 And cast him out of the city, and stoned him: and the witnesses laid down their clothes at a young man's feet, whose name was Saul.

59 And they stoned Stephen, calling upon God, and saying, Lord Jesus, receive my spirit.

Believing themselves too pure and righteous to hear such visionary claims (despite having brought in false witnesses!), Stephen's accusers stop up their ears, form a mob, and stone him to death—in direct defiance of Roman law, which alone could legally render the death sentence. Stephen, however, prays to a Refuge he knows is able to deliver him *into* eternal life, not merely *from* murder.

Verse 58 testifies to the author Luke's writing skills. He inserts almost casually the name of one Saul of Tarsus who will be described in 8:1 as "consenting" to the death of Stephen. This is like a modern mystery author mentioning the presence of a gun which will only later be seized to commit murder. Not until Acts 9 will Luke return to Saul, on whose adventures, with his name changed to Paul, the rest of Acts will turn.

E. Dying like Jesus, 60

60 And he kneeled down, and cried with a loud voice, Lord, lay not this sin to their charge. And when he had said this, he fell asleep.

Using the common euphemism "falling asleep" for dying, Luke describes one last important way in which Stephen's death resembles Christ's. In both cases, their last words are in behalf of their murderers' souls. In part, it was such "freedom" from the ordinary human impulse to seek revenge that led later Christians to view the date on which a martyr died as a "birthday" to be celebrated, rather than the anniversary of a death to be mourned.

45

Evangelistic Emphasis

Seven year old Mark stole some comic books from the library. His dad discovered the theft and took Mark back to the library to return the comic books. Mark was given a stern lecture by the librarian.

The next year, Mark stole another book from the library and was promptly caught by his father again. This time it was Mark's father who gave the stern lecture. When it happened a third time, Mark's father sat him down, "Son, I've never spanked you before. However, you must learn that stealing is wrong." Dad delivered five swats with his bare hand, said, "I'm going to leave you alone for a while,"—then stepped out of the room and cried like a baby.

Years passed, and as a young man, Mark recalled that evening with his mother. "After that, I never stole again and I never will."

She said, "Was it because your dad spanked you that day?"

Mark said, "Oh no. It was because I heard him crying."

This troubled boy was transformed by the power of love.

Stephen had that kind of love, too. Praying for his murderers transformed the early church. It also must have had a powerful impact on one of the early opponents of the church, whose name was Paul. Following verses make it plain that Paul was at least one who approved the stoning of Stephen and was probably present for this event.

It is in death that we show the greatest love. Jesus said, "No greater love has any person than he lay down his life for his friends."

℘ℂ℞

Memory Selection

And Stephen, full of faith and power, did great wonders and miracles among the people."— *Acts 6:8*

Stephen was one of those lay persons whom God called into ministry. The only qualification for being a servant of God and a minister for God is that you are filled with faith and with power. There is a double parallelism in this passage. The faith and power produces the wonders and miracles.

We wonder why the modern Church seems bereft of miracles. Our answer is found in the description of Stephen: *he had faith and power.* Faith in the New Testament is almost always a verb. We have made faith a noun. Faith to modern Christians is something you have in your heart or in your head. Faith for the first century Christians was a verb. Faith was something one did. Faith was action which required power.

God does not call the equipped, He equips the called.

Weekday Problems

Jeanie Barnett didn't know any better. She came from a church that was teeming with young adults and new Christians. The church she came from grew so rapidly their church directory was in a ring binder so they could add new pictures to it on a monthly basis. The preacher at her former church told the visitors, "Bring your coffee into the sanctuary and join your spills with our spills." It was a powerful experience of what faith and power will do in a church.

When Jeanie and her husband Doug were transferred to a new community, Jeanie immediately threw herself into church work. She sang in the choir, made costumes for the children's fall program, volunteered to teach Sunday school—and suggested that coffee be allowed in the sanctuary to enhance the pre-worship fellowhip time.

The worship guild could not imagine that! They nearly told Jeanie to repent of her sins and be rebaptized, but fortunately refrained...for a while.

*How do we respond when we think people are not honoring the sacred things in our church world?

*Explain why the Jews might have been mad enough to stone Stephen.

Views of Martyrdom

Christianity has made martyrdom sublime, and sorrow triumphant.—*E. H. Chapin*

***

It is admirable to die the victim of one's faith; it is sad to die the dupe of one's ambition.—*Alphonse Lamartine*

***

It is more difficult, and calls for higher energies of soul, to live a martyr than to die one.—*Horace Mann*

***

The blood of the martyrs is the seed of the church.—*Justin Martyr*

***

When we read, we fancy we could be martyrs; when we come to act, we cannot bear a provoking word.—*Nathaniel Howe*

This Lesson in Your Life

Stephen died for his faith.

The idea of martyrdom is strange to our culture. We have watched on the news as people have blown themselves up in an attempt to kill others. They call themselves martyrs for Islam. Others who carry rifles and missiles and fight for their cause also call themselves martyrs. These people are either crazy or mean, or both. They are not martyrs.

A martyr is someone who dies as a witness to his faith. The difference is that we have Islamic persons dying because they hate. The list of things they hate is long. They don't compare favorably with someone like Stephen. Stephen knelt down and prayed for mercy for those who were stoning him. Stephen prayed trusting his spirit to God.

Stephen lived by a rule that was higher than the golden rule. The golden rule is doing unto others as you would have them do unto you. A higher form of that rule is the platinum rule of Jesus who said, "No greater love has any person than he lay down his life for his friends."

In a way you could say that Stephen's martyrdom was laying down his life for his friends in the church. Still we are not sure about this "laying down our life." Jesus has called us to have such love for a person that we would be willing to die for the person.

Yet there is another way to "die." We are called to die to the *self*. This has become a foreign concept. We live in a world which makes tons of money on helping us put and keep ourselves as number one. If you want it, buy it. If you can't afford it, charge it. If you can't pay for your charges, declare bankruptcy and walk away from it. There are no rules; no ethics involved except the ethics of getting what we want.

We might not ever die for our faith, but we can make our relationship with Jesus Christ the top priority in our life. We are good at having Jesus as *a* priority, but he needs to be our *primary* priority. Does that sound too radical?

Perhaps you could live like that if you believed that God would give you the faith and the power to live with Jesus, as Stephen did. The time has arrived for the church to raise up some radical lovers—people who will do anything to show the world the love of God that dwells in them through Christ.

1. What official job did Stephen hold in the church?
Stephen was one of seven men elected by the church to serve the tables at the daily distribution of food.

2. Who were the other men who were elected with Stephen for this task?
The others elected were Philip, Prochhorus, Nicanor, Timon, Parmenas, and Nicolaus, who was a proselyte of Antioch.

3. How were these men set apart for service?
These men stood before the apostles, who prayed and laid their hands on them.

4. How is Stephen described?
Stephen is described as being full of grace and power, a man who did wonders and signs among the people.

5. Who were the men who rose up and argued with Stephen?
Men from the Freedmen synagogue, consisting of Cyrenians, Alexandrians, and others from Cilicia and Asia, argued with Stephen.

6. Were they successful in their argument with Stephen?
No. "They could not withstand the wisdom and Spirit with which he spoke."

7. What did the men from the Freedmen synagogue do next?
They got men to say, "We have heard him speak blasphemous words against Moses and God."

8. What else did these people from the synagogue do?
They stirred up the people, as well as the elders and the scribes.

9. What was the result of their devious plot against Stephen?
Stephen was arrested and brought to stand before "the council"—the Sanhedrin, or ruling Jewish council.

10. What was the charge made against Stephen at the council?
The witnesses claimed that he "never stops saying things against this holy place and the law."

English is a difficult language. Some actual signs posted in various establishments around the world for English-speaking guests betray this fact.

In a Copenhagen Airline ticket office: "We take your bags and send them in all directions."

In a Norwegian Lounge: "Ladies are requested not to have children in the bar."

In a Paris hotel: "Please check your values at the front desk."

In a hotel in Athens: "Visitors are expected to complain at the office between the hours of nine and eleven a.m. each day."

A Hong Kong dentist advertised: "Teeth extracted by the latest Methodists."

A Swiss Menu read: "Our wines leave you nothing to hope for."

And in an Acapulco hotel: "The manager has personally passed all the water here."

It is so easy to miscommunicate. It happens at work and at home. It happens in a marriage and with family. It happens with strangers and friends. We can take all of the educational opportunities presented to help us with our communication but it is still fuzzy when we use only words.

Stephen communicated clearly with his words. He answered his critics not with emotion but with fact. He then communicated clearly with his body language. As he was being stoned, he knelt down to pray. He communicated clearly with the totality of his life. He was willing to serve the tables at the time of the daily distribution of food. He was willing to give his life for his beliefs. He graciously communicated love and mercy in his final words as his life was being taken.

If we are to be heard when we speak, our actions must be consistent with our words. We can't talk about the love of God and "pass by on the other side" when we see human hurts. We can't talk about mercy when we are judging others. Our walk must match our talk. Otherwise we are just talking.

Acts 8:4-17

Therefore they that were scattered abroad went every where preaching the word.

5 Then Philip went down to the city of Samaria, and preached Christ unto them.

6 And the people with one accord gave heed unto those things which Philip spake, hearing and seeing the miracles which he did.

7 For unclean spirits, crying with loud voice, came out of many that were possessed with them: and many taken with palsies, and that were lame, were healed.

8 And there was great joy in that city.

9 But there was a certain man, called Simon, which beforetime in the same city used sorcery, and bewitched the people of Samaria, giving out that himself was some great one:

10 To whom they all gave heed, from the least to the greatest, saying, This man is the great power of God.

11 And to him they had regard, because that of long time he had bewitched them with sorceries.

12 But when they believed Philip preaching the things concerning the kingdom of God, and the name of Jesus Christ, they were baptized, both men and women.

13 Then Simon himself believed also: and when he was baptized, he continued with Philip, and wondered, beholding the miracles and signs which were done.

14 Now when the apostles which were at Jerusalem heard that Samaria had received the word of God, they sent unto them Peter and John:

15 Who, when they were come down, prayed for them, that they might receive the Holy Ghost:

16 (For as yet he was fallen upon none of them: only they were baptized in the name of the Lord Jesus.)

17 Then laid they their hands on them, and they received the Holy Ghost.

Oct. 9

Devotional Reading
Acts 19:1-10

Background Scripture
Acts 8:4-25

Memory Selection
Acts 8:14

51

This lesson emphasizes: (1) how God can use persecution to spread His Word; and (2) the power of the gospel over pagan views of spirituality.

Philip the deacon takes advantage of the expulsion of Christians from Jerusalem to carry the Word to nearby Samaria. This was an area be-tween Judea in the southern part of the holy lands, and Galilee in the north. Centuries earlier, conquerors had imported foreign peoples to in-termarry with Jews here. Religiously, this resulted in a form of Judaism viewed as heresy by orthodox Jews in Jerusalem.

Yet just as Jesus had not shunned Samaria, He had said His disciples would be witnesses "in Judea, and Samaria . . ." (Acts 1:8). Philip's work helps fulfill this prophecy.

ഇന്ദ്ര

Ask what members of your group think about the subject of *magic.* Is all magic composed of tricks and sleight of hand, or do some so-called "tricks," such as Ouija-boards, ac-tually involve occult (hidden) pow-ers? Note that in some cases, it may not matter whether something is real or imagined, if it holds power over a "true believer." For example a pla-cebo "medication" such as sugar water may improve the health of one who thinks it will.

Point out that whatever the truth about magic, today's lesson shows the power of the Good News of Christ over a "sorcerer" or magician in New Testament times. As in the case of Stephen, the message is pro-claimed by one of the seven servants named in Acts 6, who adds preach-ing to his ability to "wait tables."

Teaching Outline

I. Philip Goes to Samaria—4-8
   A. Fruits of "diaspora," 4
   B. Preaching and Signs, 5-8
II. Simon the Sorcerer—9-13
   A. His work, 9
   B. His influence, 10-12
   C. His conversion, 13
III. Spread of the Spirit—14-18
   A. Jerusalem's leadership, 14
   B. Spirit transmitted, 15-17

Daily Bible Readings

Verse by Verse

I. Philip Goes to Samaria—4-8
A. Fruits of "diaspora," 4

4 Therefore they that were scattered abroad went every where preaching the word.

In the original, the word "scattered" is from a Greek word that gives us the term "diaspora," often used to describe the scattering of the Jews when conquerors dispersed them into foreign lands. This time the scattering, or diaspora, was of Christians (vs. 1)—although the Romans and Jews who drove them from the city no doubt thought they were merely a heretical sect of Jews.

This might seem to be an accident of history unless we recall that Jesus had commissioned His followers to be witnesses "in all Judea, and in Samaria, and unto the uttermost part of the earth" (Acts 18). Thus what an outside observer might call an accidental tragedy is used by God to accomplish His will. As the second-century church leader Justin Martyr would say, "the blood of martyrs [in this case, Stephen] is seed" because the Christian who were scattered "went everywhere preaching the word."

B. Preaching and Signs, 5-8

5 Then Philip went down to the city of Samaria, and preached Christ unto them.

6 And the people with one accord gave heed unto those things which Philip spake, hearing and seeing the miracles which he did.

7 For unclean spirits, crying with loud voice, came out of many that were possessed with them: and many taken with palsies, and that were lame, were healed.

8 And there was great joy in that city.

The author of Acts zooms in on one of these early preachers who turned persecution into opportunity. Philip had been named a special servant (perhaps a deacon) when Stephen and the others were appointed in 6:5. He may have been a Greek (as his name, which means "crown," indicates; for Jews and Samaritans [denoting both an area and a city] ordinarily would not associate with each other (John 4:9). Philip faced centuries-old antagonism between southern "orthodox" Jews and the Samaritans, who were descendants of King Jeroboam's rebellion from King David, Judea, and Jerusalem. The estrangement was heightened when King Ahab built a temple to Baal there (1 Kings 16:32-33). Samaritan Jews had intermarried with foreigners brought in by conquerors such as the Assyrians, Greeks, and Romans. Their worship became "syncretistic" or mixed with pagan practices. Yet, through the years, they preserved their own copies of the Pentateuch, some versions of which survive to this day.

Apparently the "leveling" influence of the gospel, which was directed to all without prejudice, had made Philip open to associating with Samaritans. His message was so powerful, and the miracles he worked were so convincing, that racial and religious barriers fall. This is both a remarkable judgment against racial prejudice, and a direct fulfillment of Christ's promise that those of His followers who carried the gospel to other places would be accompanied by signs and wonders (Mark 16:15-18).

II. Simon the Sorcerer—9-13

A. His work, 9

9 But there was a certain man, called Simon, which beforetime in the same city used sorcery, and bewitched the people of Samaria, giving out that himself was some great one:

The author of Acts no doubt includes the following story to distinguish the miracles of the gospel from acts of magic and superstition in general that permeated the ancient world. The "black arts" such as sorcery which "Simon Magus" (or the "magician," the name he would be given in later writings) practiced had long been condemned in the Jewish Scriptures (see Deut. 18:10-12). Later literature would not only describe his dabbling in magic, but attribute to him many of the "Gnostic" doctrines that infiltrated the early Church.

B. His influence, 10-12

10 To whom they all gave heed, from the least to the greatest, saying, This man is the great power of God.

11 And to him they had regard, because that of long time he had bewitched them with sorceries.

12 But when they believed Philip preaching the things concerning the kingdom of God, and the name of Jesus Christ, they were baptized, both men and women.

Working among gullible people who longed for relief from the burdens of oppressive armies and even of everyday life and death, Simon had achieved wide influence. Yet the very needs and longings of the people also made them open to Philip's miracles and message. His words had the advantage of being tied to the Old Testament predictions of a coming Messiah, which had been preserved among many Samaritans. We are not told whether Philip attributed Simon's work to Satan, or claimed they were a hoax; it was enough that he preached that Christ and His Spirit were more powerful.

C. His conversion, 13

13 Then Simon himself believed also: and when he was baptized, he continued with Philip, and wondered, beholding the miracles and signs which were done.

If this verse were all we knew of

Simon's career, it might be taken at face value: a magician is converted to Christ. In verses 18ff., however, we are told that Simon tries to buy from the apostles the ability to work their miracles, leading to the implication that his conversion was less than genuine. The gospel apparently appealed to him not for its power to deliver him from sin, but the promise of doing an even more profitable business in magic. The fact that he "wondered" as he beheld the apostolic miracles Philiip performed indicates that he may have thought that he had discovered a "real" basis for the magic he had performed by sleight of hand.

III. Spread of the Spirit—14-18

A. Jerusalem's leadership, 14

4 Now when the apostles which were at Jerusalem heard that Samaria had received the word of God, they sent unto them Peter and John:

Acts 8:1 had noted that the apostles stayed in Jerusalem when persecution scattered other believers. Here we see that the earliest Christians depended on the apostles for leadership, and looked to the Church at Jerusalem as the "mother church" (see also the important "Jerusalem conference" in Acts 15). This relationship worked both ways, with the apostles wanting to keep the scattered Christians faithful to the true doctrine. Peter and John are sent no doubt both to encourage Philip and those he had converted, and to strengthen them in the faith—pre-cisely against charlatans such as Simon Magus.

B. Spirit transmitted, 15-17

15 Who, when they were come down, prayed for them, that they might receive the Holy Ghost:

16 (For as yet he was fallen upon none of them: only they were baptized in the name of the Lord Jesus.)

17 Then laid they their hands on them, and they received the Holy Ghost.

The Holy Spirit (the KJV "Ghost" comes to us through the German *Geist* or "Spirit") is spoken of as "descending" on or "filling" certain believers to endow them with special gifts (as here), and as dwelling "within" all believers. By this time in the developing Church, the normal way for the Spirit to be transmitted is by the laying on of the apostles' hands. It was this method of transmission that Simon the Magician observed, and tried to buy (vss. 18-23). His attempt to make this wrongful purchase has given the name "simony" to bribery to this day. When rebuked, Simon asks the apostles to pray that he might be spared judgment for this attempt to misuse spiritual gifts (vss. 24); but later history indicates that he allowed his original orientation to magic to cause him to stay separate from mainstream Christianity.

The main point the author makes, however, as that the new movement of Christians is expanding, precisely as Jesus predicted in Acts 1:8.

Evangelistic Emphasis

Maybe Philip didn't know he shouldn't have preached in Samaria. Everyone in that time knew that Jews and Samaritans didn't get along. Since the early Church was made up mostly of Jews, certainly it would retain all the old prejudices of the Jewish people. Yet Philip just preached where the Spirit led him.

Does everyone in your church look like you, or does it reflect the diversity of our world?

We have people in our church who just don't belong anywhere. Several suffer from mental challenges. One individual whispers to me every Sunday, "They are still after me." Another person shares her hallucinations with us when we are sharing joys and concerns. A 20-year-old-boy has the emotional maturity of a 12-year-old. Yet they have all been accepted and loved by our congregation.

Another lady who has muscular dystrophy can barely speak, yet when she shares a prayer concern with the congregation we all seem to understand what she is saying.

I thank God that the people who showed me Jesus Christ were not prejudiced against me. I was not judged , but was loved and accepted as someone whom God loved. Do people who "don't belong" come to your church?

ಐಃಇ

Memory Selection

Now when the apostles at Jerusalem heard that Samaria had accepted the word of God, they sent Peter and John to them. —*Acts 8:14*

A promising young doctor, Julius Hickerson, felt called to be a missionary to Columbia. His friends thought he was crazy, but he felt there was more to life than just making money. Yet, after two years in missions he could point to few results.

Julius died when his plane crashed as he was taking supplies to a remote village. But in the wreckage, some natives found a Bible in their own language. They began to read it. They told others about it, and before long, churches were being formed all over the region.

A few years later, another missionary came to the region and discovered that the area was full of Christians. When the missionary asked how it happened, the Columbians showed him a Bible. On the inside cover of the Bible was a name, Julius Hickerson.

When early disciples from Jerusalem went to Samaria, the Samaritans began to see their words lived out in deeds. Who is watching you live your life? Can they see clearly that your *live* what you say you believe?

Weekday Problems

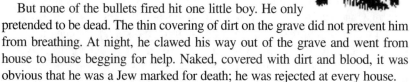

The Nazis rounded up some Jews in Poland and forced them to dig their own graves. They were lined up against a wall and machine-gunned. Their bodies fell into the graves and the Nazis covered them with dirt.

But none of the bullets fired hit one little boy. He only pretended to be dead. The thin covering of dirt on the grave did not prevent him from breathing. At night, he clawed his way out of the grave and went from house to house begging for help. Naked, covered with dirt and blood, it was obvious that he was a Jew marked for death; he was rejected at every house.

Finally, he timidly knocked at the door of one house and said, "Don't you recognize me? I'm Jesus, the one you say you love." After a pause, the woman who stood in the doorway swept him into her arms, kissed him and cared for him as one of her very own.

Many people in our culture feel like they are outcasts, marked as those who don't belong. Our daily problem is that we have a list of people we would easily exclude from the church because of some of our prejudices.

*Make a list of peoples the Church has excluded.

*Whether Nazi against Jew or Jew against Samaritan, how does God challenge our cultural distinctions and prejudices?

Did You Hear About ...

The man who claimed to have seen King Henry the 16th?
Actually, he saw Henry the 8th twice.

The leopard who ate the hot dog?
It really hit the spot!

The tea-sipper who swallowed her teaspoon?
She wasn't able to stir.

The sailor who reported to his captain, "We're surrounded by ships as thick as peas in a pod. What shall we do?"
"Shell them, of course," said the captain.

The young girl who said she'd been especially good at church?
"They offered me a plate of money but I said No thank you," said she.

The kangaroo mama who lost her baby?
She had her pocket picked.

This Lesson in Your Life

We are not told how Philip ended up going to the Samaritans, but his success is an indication that God had called him there. We just don't understand the radical nature of the Samaritan preaching mission. The only way we could understand the religious bigotry directed at them would be to confess our own dislike for some radical elements of the Muslim religion. We don't understand these people and we are not disposed to give them any time in learning about them. The Samaritans were simply outcasts. They were turncoats who were despised for religious and political reasons. Yet Philip preached to them, and they listened! They converted to the faith. They received the Holy Spirit!

Another teachable element in this text is the mission of Peter and John. They were sent by the church at Jerusalem to see what had happened in Samaria. They were so thrilled by the results of Philip's preaching that they preached the power of the Spirit, laid hands on the Samaritans, and they received the Spirit.

Each person has a place in the ministry of the church. Philip was an evangelist. Philip did the tent meeting. Peter and John turned all the converts into functioning Christians. The church needs both evangelists and pastors. The church needs visitors and scholars. We need each other as the Body of Christ. A good discussion could center on how we fit together in our different abilities and callings.

Another element in this lesson is the work of the Holy Spirit. In his Gospel, Luke emphasized the work of prayer in the life of Jesus. In Acts, Luke emphasizes the work of the Holy Spirit in the life of the Church. Simon becomes an interesting character because he receives the Spirit. Yet, Simon will turn around and ask the apostles to sell him the ability to lay hands on people so they might receive the Spirit.

One of the great divisions in the Church universal centers around the working and ministry of the Holy Spirit. If you want to stir up a discussion, ask your class what they think about the working of the Holy Spirit in the 21st-century Church. You will have such a lively discussion that leaders of "the Jerusalem church" will send a Peter and John to your class to see what is going on!

Isn't that the idea of Christianity, to get so excited that people are curious about what is going on?

STRAIGHT

1. Why was Philip preaching to the Samaritans?
The church in Jerusalem had been persecuted, and some members fled to Samaria.

2. Where did Philip go and what did he do?
Philip went to the city of Samaria and he preached Jesus to them.

3. "Signs" accompanied Philip's preaching. What were some of those signs?
Unclean spirits came out of those who were possessed. Many who were paralyzed and lame were cured.

4. How did the city of Samaria respond to the ministry of Philip?
There was great joy in the city.

5. What information is given about Simon?
Simon lived in Samaria, and he had previously practiced magic.

6. Did Simon have a following in Samaria?
Yes, many people listened to Simon because he had amazed them with his magic.

7. What happened when Simon heard the preaching of Philip?
Even Simon himself believed in Jesus, and he was baptized.

8. After Simon believed, what kind of relationship did he have with Philip?
Simon stayed constantly with Philip and was amazed when he saw the signs and great miracles that took place.

9. What did the Jerusalem church do when it heard about the events in Samaria?
The Jerusalem church sent Peter and John to the Samaritans, that they might receive the Holy Spirit.

10. When Simon saw the laying on of hands followed by the receiving of the Spirit, what was his request?
Simon was willing to pay for the ability to have the Holy Spirit come when he laid his hands on someone.

Some 50 years ago, a very sophisticated church was terribly embarrassed because one of their members had a very untidy appearance. But even worse was that every Sunday morning he'd drive to a downtown hotel and give tracts to the soldiers there on weekend leave. Then he'd bring as many as he could in his old car to church. The congregation was mortified that someone from their respectable church would make such a spectacle of himself. But no one had the courage to stop him. A few years passed, and the pastor of that church started getting letters from all over the U.S. that basically said the same thing.

"I was a soldier on leave during the war. One Sunday, a man from your church came to my hotel and told me about Jesus and invited me to church. I'm writing to let you know that that has made all the difference in my life."

Philip was run out of Jerusalem because of the persecution started by people such as Saul of Tarsus. He fled right into an opportunity to share his faith. When our schedule or plans are upset do we find in these interruptions an opportunity to share our faith? We must allow God to readjust our plans to align us with His plans. In our story, those boys in the Army had their plans interrupted by a simple man who was sharing his soul with them.

One day someone might thank you for sharing your time with him. You might be the catalyst for someone to come to faith in the Lord Jesus. Never doubt that God can use even the smallest effort on our part. Asking a visitor his name, remembering his name, and smiling at him when you see him in church are some good ways to help move those persons from visitors to members.

Being willing to mentor others in the faith is a precious gift to share with others. Peter and John came from Jerusalem to work with Philip. They bolstered each other's ministry.

Christ calls today for churches who are unashamed of their members who are leading people to faith in Jesus Christ. Are you are part of building such a church in your community?

Acts 8:26-38

And the angel of the Lord spake unto Philip, saying, Arise, and go toward the south unto the way that goeth down from Jerusalem unto Gaza, which is desert.

27 And he arose and went: and, behold, a man of Ethiopia, an eunuch of great authority under Candace queen of the Ethiopians, who had the charge of all her treasure, and had come to Jerusalem for to worship,

28 Was returning, and sitting in his chariot read Esaias the prophet.

29 Then the Spirit said unto Philip, Go near, and join thyself to this chariot.

30 And Philip ran thither to him, and heard him read the prophet Esaias, and said, Understandest thou what thou readest?

31 And he said, How can I, except some man should guide me? And he desired Philip that he would come up and sit with him.

32 The place of the scripture which he read was this, He was led as a sheep to the slaughter; and like a lamb dumb before his shearer, so opened he not his mouth:

33 In his humiliation his judgment was taken away: and who shall declare his generation? for his life is taken from the earth.

34 And the eunuch answered Philip, and said, I pray thee, of whom speaketh the prophet this? of himself, or of some other man?

35 Then Philip opened his mouth, and began at the same scripture, and preached unto him Jesus.

36 And as they went on their way, they came unto a certain water: and the eunuch said, See, here is water; what doth hinder me to be baptized?

37 And Philip said, If thou believest with all thine heart, thou mayest. And he answered and said, I believe that Jesus Christ is the Son of God.

38 And he commanded the chariot to stand still: and they went down both into the water, both Philip and the eunuch; and he baptized him.

Oct. 16

Devotional Reading
Acts 11:19-26

Background Scripture
Acts 8:26-40

Memory Selection
Acts 8:35

This lesson again finds Philip the deacon helping spread the gospel across racial and ethnic lines. In our preceding lesson he took advantage of the persecution of Christians in Jerusalem to take Christ's message north, to the Samaritans. Now we find him going in the opposite direction to the desert region of Gaza, southwest of Jerusalem, where he becomes, briefly, a kind of private tutor to a an Ethiopan nobleman. The man is converted, then goes on his way to become the first recorded Christian in Africa.

The lesson not only focuses again on the early Christians' cross-cultural zeal in sharing the Good News, but gives us a snapshot of an evangelistic approach commonly used—that is, beginning with an Old Testament reference to the Messiah and applying it to Jesus.

ℰℛℂℛ

Ask group members who they turn to for help in understanding Scripture. Responses may include a minister or other church leadeers, a widely-published Christian author, a particular set of commentaries, and official church publications. Note that our backgrounds, often including our home life, also influence how we understand Bible teaching.

Point out that in this lesson an African man is aided in his own Bible understanding by a person, Philip, who was very close to that first great explosion of the Spirit in Acts 2—probably a man who heard the apostles themselves teach the Word. We will also learn that he used the Bible (the Old Testament) to understand the Bible.

Teaching Outline

I. Mission of the Spirit—26-29
  A. A way in the desert, 26
  B. Ethiopian official, 27-29
II. Message of Isaiah—30-34
  A. Need for guidance, 30-31
  B. Text from Isaiah, 32-33
  C. Question and answer, 34-35
III. Moment of Response—36-38
  A. Jesus and baptism, 36
  B. Obedience of faith, 37-38

Daily Bible Readings

Mon.	Responding to Others Matthew 5:38-42
Tue.	Teaching on Signs Matthew 12:36-42
Wed.	The New Birth John 3:1-15
Thu.	Woe to You Hypocrites! Matthew 151-9
Fri.	Jesus Asks a Question Matthew 22:41-46
Sat.	Philip and the Official Acts 8:26-31
Sun.	Good News from Isaiah Acts 8:32-40

Verse by Verse

I. Mission of the Spirit—26-29

A. A way in the desert, 26

26 And the angel of the Lord spake unto Philip, saying, Arise, and go toward the south unto the way that goeth down from Jerusalem unto Gaza, which is desert.

The author of Acts now moves to the third stage of Jesus' commission in 1:8—the movement of the gospel from Judea to Samaria and "the uttermost part of the earth." The conversion of the Ethiopian eunuch will take the gospel into Africa. "The angel of the Lord" appears more commonly in the Old Testament. Here He is active in a role much like the Spirit, who whisked Christ here and there while He was in the wilderness (Matt. 4:1).

Gaza is one of the few cities in the ancient world that has retained its name and place. In modern times it has been associated with "the Gaza Strip," a desert region southwest of Jerusalem disputed between Israel and the Palestinians. It is also the place where Samson was held captive, then punished his captors (Judg. 16:1-3).

B. Ethiopian official, 27-29

27 And he arose and went: and, behold, a man of Ethiopia, an eunuch of great authority under Candace queen of the Ethiopians, who had the charge of all her treasure, and had come to Jerusalem for to worship,

28 Was returning, and sitting in his chariot read Esaias the prophet.

29 Then the Spirit said unto Philip, Go near, and join thyself to this chariot.

The term "eunuch" referred not only to a castrated man, but (since so many court officials were eunuchs) also simply to an "official" (as in the *Williams Translation*). Although the modern country of Ethiopia often lays claim to this event as occurring within its borders, it can rightly do so only by recalling that in New Testament times the land also included what is now the modern state of Sudan. It is also usually assumed that the official was a black man, as most Ethiopians are today, although ancient monuments depict mixed races. (Moses' marriage to an Ethiopian [Num. 12:1] may be the oldest record of an inter-racial marriage.) The important point is that the Christian message is now becoming international.

This highly-placed Ethiopian official is none other than treasurer of the nation. He served under a queen called "Candace," a term that may be a title like "Pharaoh," rather than a personal name. At any rate, the faith he is about to adopt will have high visibility. He had been to Jerusalem for the Passover and/or Pentecost observances, and was therefore a foreign Jew, a proselyte, or one of the "hangers on at the gate." If he had actually been castrated, he could not have been a full-fledged Jew with the right to enter the Temple, under current rabbinic law. It would have been unusual for a stranger on foot to accost a high official in a chariot, but Philip is under the Spirit's guidance.

II. Message of Isaiah—30-34
A. Need for guidance, 30-31

30 And Philip ran thither to him, and heard him read the prophet Esaias, and said, Understandest thou what thou readest?

31 And he said, How can I, except some man should guide me? And he desired Philip that he would come up and sit with him.

Philip heard the Ethiopian read because few people read silently in ancient times, but aloud. Although he is a high official, the nobleman in the chariot shows great humility in admitting the need for guidance in understanding what he was reading. Although of course much of the Bible can be easily understood by virtually any reader, this particular text was interpreted even by Jewish rabbis in widely different ways. No doubt Philip had heard the correct interpretation either from Jesus or an apostle. It is notable that the early spread of the gospel was facilitated by "laymen" like Philip. The situation is comparable to the days in the American westward expansion, when churches with devout lay spokesman, largely self-taught in the Scriptures, grew much faster than those who required a seminary degree for a person to be recognized as a religious teacher.

B. Text from Isaiah, 32-33

32 The place of the scripture which he read was this, He was led as a sheep to the slaughter; and like a lamb dumb before his shearer, so opened he not his mouth:

33 In his humiliation his judgment was taken away: and who shall declare his generation? for his life is taken from the earth.

Although it is obvious to modern Christians that this text (Isaiah 53:7) is about Jesus of Nazareth, it was only after Christ was "slaughtered" like a lamb that it became clear to the earliest Christians. The passage is imbedded in the "Suffering Servant" texts of Isaiah. Some rabbis held that the texts referred to suffering Israel, others to a Messiah who was yet to come. The scene is an important reminder that accepting apostolic and New Testament teaching is essential for reaching the conclusion that Jesus of Nazareth was in fact the Messiah longed for by ancient Israel.

C. Question and answer, 34-35

34 And the eunuch answered Philip, and said, I pray thee, of whom speaketh the prophet this? of himself, or of some other man?

35 Then Philip opened his mouth, and began at the same scrip-

ture, and preached unto him Jesus.

The Ethiopian apparently was considering the possibility that Isaiah was speaking of himself. Yet, probably with the help of rabbis in Jerusalem, he also knew enough to ask whether the suffering "Coming One" might be the Messiah. Of course that is just the opening Philip needs. He wisely begins where the official is, rather than where he wishes he were—a course that modern evangelistic endeavors wisely follow.

III. Moment of Response—36-38
A. Jesus and baptism, 36

36 And as they went on their way, they came unto a certain water: and the eunuch said, See, here is water; what doth hinder me to be baptized?

How did Philip get from Isaiah 53:7 to baptism? Obviously there is much in his presentation of the gospel that is omitted. Apparently baptism was an integral part of accepting the Messiah predicted in the Isaiah passage. Philip seems to understand that accepting Jesus as the Suffering Servant involves acting out that suffering by being "buried" in baptism—a connection that will be made explicit in Romans 6:4-6, where baptism is described as a symbol of the burial (after the suffering) of Jesus. Philip's presentation also reminds us that even though this event occurs quite apart from any assembled church, even on this lonely road in Gaza baptism incorporated the Ethiopian into the larger Body of believers (see 1 Cor. 12:13, with

Eph. 1:22-23). Already there is a spiritual tie between Jerusalem and Ethiopia, like the one that will eventually provide a basis for unity among Christians all over the world.

B. Obedience of faith, 37-38

37 And Philip said, If thou believest with all thine heart, thou mayest. And he answered and said, I believe that Jesus Christ is the Son of God.

38 And he commanded the chariot to stand still: and they went down both into the water, both Philip and the eunuch; and he baptized him.

Philip has no concept of "baptismal regeneration," or a ritual of water washing away sins apart from faith. He does not offer baptism as an option unless the Ethiopian official believes in the Sonship (and thus the divinity, see John 5:18) of Jesus, the Christ (Messiah).

Knowing of the desert setting of modern Gaza, it is strange that the party comes to a body of water large enough for both to go down into. Apparently they come upon an oasis with a spring-fed pool with sufficient water.

The remaining two verses of the chapter are important: baptism by faith in Christ normally results in joy. In this spirit of having found a Person, not just a new doctrine, on his visit to Jerusalem, the Ethiopian official returns to his homeland. This sets the stage for another incursion of the Good News among Gentiles, to be described in our next lesson.

Evangelistic Emphasis

After a week of hard selling, the boy still had the floppy-eared dog. A salesman had passed by each day, admiring the boy's patience but pitying him because he knew the frustration of not making a sale. One day he stopped and said, "Young man, if you want to sell this dog, you've got to see it BIG! You've got to take him home, clean him up and raise your price. If people believe they are getting a great deal, you'll sell him."

Later, the salesman passed by and the boy had his well groomed puppy with a big sign: "Great puppy for sale: $5,000." The salesman realized he'd forgotten to tell the boy to "keep it simple." But as the salesman passed the stand an hour later, the word "SOLD" was on the sign. Curious, he rang the boy's doorbell and said, "You sold that dog for $5,000?"

"Yes sir I did, and I want to thank you for your help"

"How'd you do it?"

"Easy—I took two $2,500 worth of cats in exchange."

One man's junk is another man's treasure. When it comes to the people of the world, all people are God's treasure. In this lesson we again travel with Philip as he leads another "outsider" to faith in Jesus Christ. Philip reminds us that God treasures all of humanity, and calls us to love them the way He does

&)G?

Memory Selection

Then Philip opened his mouth, and began at the same scripture, and preached unto him Jesus.—*Acts 8: 35*

A good hint about how to win souls is found in the words, "Philip opened his mouth." I have found that the easiest way to tell someone about Jesus Christ is to tell your own faith story. People love a good story. I can argue biblical interpretation with you all day. But I can't argue with you when you share your faith story. It really happened to you, and that makes it worth hearing to me.

Another effective way of leading persons to faith in Christ is to tell the story of Christ. Philip started with the scripture the Ethiopian was reading, and used that frame of reference to tell the story of Jesus. Not debating scripture with him, but in his own style telling the Ethiopian about Jesus' life, death, and resurrection. The story of salvation is really a wonderful story and is an attention getter.

Either way, you have to open your mouth and tell people about Jesus. Philip was willing to be used in such a way by God. God blessed Philip with many opportunities to share his faith.

Weekday Problems

Rosie lived next door to the parsonage. She was thrilled to have all her preachers close by. When Rosie had a problem, slight though it was, a preacher could come running. Rosie was particularly happy to have the new preacher next door to her. Dave was a bachelor minister. Rosie's proximity to his house would give her an inside track on his social life.

Rosie loved to talk to Dave about everything. She told the new preacher all about her neighbors. Since Rosie stayed home all day, she knew who was "stepping out" on whom, who was sick, and who was not keeping up their car payments. Rosie liked it when someone in the neighborhood got a repossession. She was the neighborhood information system and clearing house.

One Sunday, Dave was teaching Rosie's Sunday school class. Dave had a passion for leading souls to Christ. He was talking about the example of Philip. Philip engaged people where they were, without compromise and without condemning people. Philip opened his mouth and spoke the words that God gave him. Those powerful words brought salvation.

Rosie listened politely. She raised her hand, "Preacher, I don't think that my neighbor's spiritual life is any of my business."

*Is it true that we will talk with anyone about anything other than our faith?

Definitions: Off the Wall but on the Ball

Adult—A person who has stopped growing at both ends and is now growing in the middle.

Beauty parlor—A place where women curl up and dye.

Cannibal—Someone who is fed up with people.

Chickens—The only animals you eat before they are born and after they are dead.

Committee—A group who keeps minutes but wastes hours.

Dust—Mud with the juice squeezed out.

Egotist—A person who is usually me-deep in conversation.

Handkerchief—Cold storage.

Myth—A female moth.

Mosquito—An insect that improves your opinion of flies.

Raisin—A grape with a sunburn.

Skeleton—A bunch of bones with the person scraped off.

This Lesson in Your Life

Do you know what a eunuch did? There are not many job openings in our country for eunuchs. The eunuch's job was to guard the harem. Some Eastern rulers had a gaggle of girls who made up his harem. The Bible mentions them, but not by name. The Old Testament says that Solomon had about a thousand wives and concubines. If Solomon was so wise, why did he have so many women?

Eunuchs wer castrated so they could be trusted with this noble task. In many cultures, eunuchs were celebrities. They were as famous as our entertainers. There are also stories about eunuchs who lied about having the surgery. They became celebrities for other reasons.

In our lesson, the Ethiopian eunuch was reading Scripture while traveling back home from Jerusalem. He was so trusted that he had graduated from the harem to the queen's money. He guarded the treasury. Perhaps a proselyte to Judaism, he had been on a religious pilgrimage. Not only was this eunuch trusted, he was a spiritual man.

Philip met him on the road and began the wonderful conversation we have recorded in Acts. Philip started where the man was in his spiritual journey and through listening and story telling, invited this man to travel to the next level of faith. Philip told the eunuch about Jesus. The eunuch was so enthusiastic that when they came to a body of water, the eunuch asked for baptism.

So, we have a eunuch accepting Christ and being baptized. I'm not sure about this lesson in your life, because I have never met a eunuch, and I don't want to apply for the job, ever. I have met some very interesting people who have really great jobs. I have found these very interesting people are often ready to listen to the gospel if those sharing the gospel are ready to listen to their stories. I have known some spiritual people, who needed to be guided in the right direction. The eunuch was coming home from Jerusalem. He was spiritual, but needed guidance.

He was a person who was curious about God. It was that curiosity that caused him to read the Scriptures. It was that "wanting to know" that was honored by God, as the Spirit directed Philip to the eunuch.

STRAIGHT

1. Where did the angel of the Lord tell Philip to go?
Philip was told to get up and go toward the south to the road that goes down from Jerusalem to Gaza.

2. Who did Philip meet on the road from Jerusalem to Gaza?
He met a eunuch from Ethiopia. He was a court official of Candace, the queen of the Ethiopians.

3. What was the responsibility of the eunuch?
He was in charge of her entire treasury.

4. Why was the eunuch on this road?
He had come to Jerusalem to worship and was returning home.

5. What was he doing when Philip met him?
He was riding in his chariot and reading from the prophet Isaiah.

6. What interesting information was shared about how the eunuch was reading Isaiah?
He was reading the passage of Scripture aloud, for "Philip heard him reading."

7. How did Philip engage the eunuch in a spiritual conversation?
Philip asked the eunuch if he understood what he was reading.

8. What passage from Scripture was the eunuch reading?
"Like a sheep he was led to the slaughter and like a lamb silent before his shearer, so he does not open his mouth."

9. Where was this section of Scripture found?
The eunuch was reading from Isaiah 53.

10. How did Philip move the conversation along?
Philip started with the scripture the eunuch was reading, then proclaimed to him the good news of Jesus.

In West Texas there is a sign that boasts, "Horses for Everyone."
In small print it reads:

> For skinny people, we have skinny horses.
>
> For fat people, we have fat horses.
>
> For disabled people, we have disabled horses.
>
> For people who have never ridden horses, we have horses
> that have never been ridden.

That sums up the spiritual world in which we live. Church-related books have become best sellers. The "Left Behind" series has made the New York Times Bestseller list. Rick Warren's *Forty Days of Purpose* has taken the Church world by storm. Books by Marianne Williamson and Deepak Chopa are part Christian and part Eastern Mysticism. Some of the preachers on television, in an attempt to raise mega money, have gone over to the dark side called Gnosticism. The problem with the world today is not a lack of religion. There is a religion for everyone. There are some religions in which you decide what you want to believe, and that becomes the religion. (I know, it is strange, isn't it?)

The Ethiopian eunuch was religious. His religion was a curiosity. He was seeking, but he wasn't exactly sure what he was seeking. He needed someone who could guide him from where he was to where he needed to be in Jesus Christ.

The default setting of most church people when they hear a "strange" theology is to say to the speaker, "You are so wrong. Jesus is the way, the truth, and the life." That person may get points in heaven for quoting Scripture, but he has just turned off a potential convert to Christianity.

Philip heard the eunuch quoting Scripture and asked about how the eunuch interpreted the verse. Philip listened to the eunuch where he was and then moved him on the journey of faith.

The first step in being a good faith mentor is to use your ears. Listen. and once you understand where a person is, take him by the hand and lead him gently to the Savior.

Breaking the Gospel Barriers

Acts 10:1-20

There was a certain man in Caesarea called Cornelius, a centurion of the band called the Italian band,

2 A devout man, and one that feared God with all his house, which gave much alms to the people, and prayed to God alway.

3 He saw in a vision evidently about the ninth hour of the day an angel of God coming in to him, and saying unto him, Cornelius.

4 And when he looked on him, he was afraid, and said, What is it, Lord? And he said unto him, Thy prayers and thine alms are come up for a memorial before God.

5 And now send men to Joppa, and call for one Simon, whose surname is Peter:

6 He lodgeth with one Simon a tanner, whose house is by the sea side: he shall tell thee what thou oughtest to do.

7 And when the angel which spake unto Cornelius was departed, he called two of his household servants, and a devout soldier of them that waited on him continually;

8 And when he had declared all these things unto them, he sent them to Joppa.

9 On the morrow, as they went on their journey, and drew nigh unto the city, Peter went up upon the housetop to pray about the sixth hour:

10 And he became very hungry, and would have eaten: but while they made ready, he fell into a trance,

11 And saw heaven opened, and a certain vessel descending unto him, as it had been a great sheet knit at the four corners, and let down to the earth:

12 Wherein were all manner of fourfooted beasts of the earth, and wild beasts, and creeping things, and fowls of the air.

13 And there came a voice to him, Rise, Peter; kill, and eat.

14 But Peter said, Not so, Lord; for I have never eaten any thing that is common or unclean.

15 And the voice spake unto him again the second time, What God hath cleansed, that call not thou common.

16 This was done thrice: and the vessel was received up again into heaven.

17 Now while Peter doubted in himself what this vision which he had seen should mean, behold, the men which were sent from Cornelius had made inquiry for Simon's house, and stood before the gate,

18 And called, and asked whether Simon, which was surnamed Peter, were lodged there.

19 While Peter thought on the vision, the Spirit said unto him, Behold, three men seek thee.

20 Arise therefore, and get thee down, and go with them, doubting nothing: for I have sent them.

Oct. 23

Devotional Reading
Acts 13:44-49
Background Scripture
Acts 10:1-48
Memory Selection
Acts 10:19-20

Step by step, the Good News that Jesus is the Christ is being taken to those whom the Jewish establishment in Jerusalem often disdained. First there were the "half-breed" Samaritans, then an official from Africa. In today's lesson, the Holy Spirit shows the apostle Peter and his companions that Gentiles in general are to be included in the New Community God is establishing.

The Gentile chosen for this significant step is named Cornelius. He is said to be a devout man, and one who gave alms to the poor. Although he worshiped the God of the Jews, he would not have been permitted into the Temple. He was apparently a "God-fearer," or a "hanger-on," as some Jews called this class of people.

Are we today any better at creating a "classless" Church?

≈≈≈

Ask group members what "classes" or walls of prejudice exist in our world. Some may think of the "castes" which still exist in India, although officially outlawed. Others, in our own country, may have experienced racism. Do we also see prejudice against the poor, the elderly, the handicapped, or women?

Ask the group, *Which of these groups does God love most?* Of course most will respond that God loves all the same. Then how should we apply this lesson, which challenges Jewish-Christians to accept Gentiles? Are some divisions an inevitable condition in society, or should we be doing more to demonstrate that "God is no respecter of persons" (Acts 10:34)?

Teaching Outline

I. A Gentile's Vision—1-8
   A. The man Cornelius, 1-2
   B. A vision and a message, 3-6
   C. Obeying the angel, 7-8
II. A Jew's Response—9-20
   A. Peter at Joppa, 9-10
   B. Inclusive vision, 11-16
      1. Clear command, 11-13
      2. Peter's hesitance, 14-16
   C. Cornelius and Peter, 17-18
   D. The angel's command, 19-20

Daily Bible Readings

Mon. Cornelius' Vision
     Acts 10:1-8
Tue. Peter's Vision
     Acts 10:9-16
Wed. Calling on Peter
     Acts 10:17-22
Thu. Peter Visits Cornelius
     Acts 10:23-33
Fri. An Inclusive Gospel
     Acts 10:34-43
Sat. Gentiles Receive the Spirit
     Acts 10:44-48
Sun. Peter's Report
     Acts 11:1-15

Verse by Verse

I. A Gentile's Vision—1-8

A. The man Cornelius, 1-2

1 There was a certain man in Caesarea called Cornelius, a centurion of the band called the Italian band,

2 A devout man, and one that feared God with all his house, which gave much alms to the people, and prayed to God alway.

Centurions were Roman officers who commanded a cohort of 100 troops. Scripture consistently portrays them as men of good character—and Cornelius, who headed a band from Italy, is an exceptional man among exceptional men, serving the God of the Jews instead of Mithra, whom most Roman soldiers worshiped. In fact, Cornelius may have been officially classed as a "God-fearer"—a Gentile who was respected as nearer to the Kingdom than the general run of people, but was uncircumcised, and thus excluded from Temple services.

B. A vision and a message, 3-6

3 He saw in a vision evidently about the ninth hour of the day an angel of God coming in to him, and saying unto him, Cornelius.

4 And when he looked on him, he was afraid, and said, What is it, Lord? And he said unto him, Thy prayers and thine alms are come up for a memorial before God.

5 And now send men to Joppa, and call for one Simon, whose surname is Peter:

6 He lodgeth with one Simon a tanner, whose house is by the sea side: he shall tell thee what thou oughtest to do.

God chooses an angel (lit. "messenger") to give the landmark message to Cornelius that would start the transformation of Christianity from a Jewish sect to a worldwide body of believers open to all races. The KJV "evidently" means "distinctly" (NIV): the author wants us to understand that this was no apparition half-hidden in some divine mist, so the impact of the vision will not be clear. The angel appears while Cornelius, although a gentile, is observing the customary Jewish 3 p.m. prayer time. To say that Cornelius' "prayers and alms" are being memorialized does not mean they have earned his salvation, but that they will always be remembered as characteristic of him.

As in so many instances among the earliest Christians, Peter's leadership is seen in God's selecting him for this remarkable event. It will also be important when Peter is chosen to go to the Jews with the gospel (Gal. 2:8), so he will not be misled into thinking that they were the *only* people to be included in the Kingdom. (Even with the aid of this vision, Peter will be slow to put racial inclusiveness into practice—see Gal. 2:11-14.) To be living temporarily with a tanner at the city of Joppa, some 30 miles away, may indicate that Peter was already moving toward a more relaxed interpretation of the Law of "clean and unclean" designations, since the rabbis had classified hide tanning as an unclean trade.

C. Obeying the angel, 7-8

7 And when the angel which spake unto Cornelius was departed, he called two of his household servants, and a devout soldier of them that waited on him continually;

8 And when he had declared all these things unto them, he sent them to Joppa.

Cornelius apparently waits until the next day to dispatch three of the men assigned to him as a centurion ("on the morrow," vs. 9). We can only wonder at how filled with expectation and not a little anxiety he was while awaiting word from their journey to Joppa and back.

II. A Jew's Response—9-20

A. Peter at Joppa, 9-10

9 On the morrow, as they went on their journey, and drew nigh unto the city, Peter went up upon the housetop to pray about the sixth hour:

10 And he became very hungry, and would have eaten: but while they made ready, he fell into a trance,

In his own noon prayer time, Peter falls into a trance to equip him to

see his own vision and prepare him to accept the angel's announcement to Cornelius. Middle eastern houses are still often constructed with flat roofs and stairs leading to them, as a kind of porch residents can resort to in the cool of the evening.

B. Inclusive vision, 11-16

1. Clear command, 11-13

11 And saw heaven opened, and a certain vessel descending unto him, as it had been a great sheet knit at the four corners, and let down to the earth:

12 Wherein were all manner of fourfooted beasts of the earth, and wild beasts, and creeping things, and fowls of the air.

13 And there came a voice to him, Rise, Peter; kill, and eat.

Peter's own trance or vision will have far-reaching implications. The author of Acts understands this, and gives most of two chapters to the incident, repeating both Cornelius' and Peter's visions in 10:30ff. and 11:4ff. "A certain vessel turns out to be a "great sheet," no doubt something like a side of a tent such as the apostle Paul would have made, since it is strong enough to hold animals. As Peter will respond in verse 14, none of the "four-footed beasts" or fowls of the air in the sheet are of the sort designated by Jewish Law as "clean." That is, they were animals that did not chew the cud, or have cloven hooves, or, in the case of birds, abstain from eating carrion (see Lev. 11:1).

2. Peter's hesitance, 14-16

14 But Peter said, Not so, Lord; for I have never eaten any thing that is common or unclean.

15 And the voice spake unto him again the second time, What God hath cleansed, that call not thou common.

16 This was done thrice: and the vessel was received up again into heaven.

It is almost impossible to expect Gentile Christians to imagine how difficult it would have been for Peter, a faithful Jew, to obey this command. It is so foreign to both his doctrine and his life-style that in addressing the voice as "Lord" he may only mean "Sir" (the Grk. *kyrios* can mean either). He cannot imagine a divine being telling him to go against centuries of Jewish tradition by killing and eating "unclean" meat. Yet so emphatic is the command that the sheet-full of animals descends and ascends three times, to make the picture all the more vivid. To reinforce the command, the voice from heaven issues the unheard-of command that God has *made clean* the very animals He had made *unclean* under the Jewish system.

An alternate reading of Mark 7:19 does say that Jesus "declared all foods 'clean,'" (NIV). This surely is a later addition to Mark, inserted after the vision Peter gazes on here had taken root in the Christian tradition. Also, only later will Peter realize that this reversal in God's will is an allegory of the fact that not only do Jewish dietary restrictions no longer ap-

ply. All *people*, not just animals, are now to be viewed as clean.

C. Cornelius and Peter, 17-18

17 Now while Peter doubted in himself what this vision which he had seen should mean, behold, the men which were sent from Cornelius had made inquiry for Simon's house, and stood before the gate,

18 And called, and asked whether Simon, which was surnamed Peter, were lodged there.

In His providence, God arranges for the messengers from Cornelius to arrive just at the time Peter was contemplating what the vision might mean. ("Simon" is Peter's Jewish name.)

D. The angel's command, 19-20

19 While Peter thought on the vision, the Spirit said unto him, Behold, three men seek thee.

20 Arise therefore, and get thee down, and go with them, doubting nothing: for I have sent them.

Peter is told to come down off the rooftop and speak with the delegation from Cornelius. The "voice" is now identified as "the Spirit," which would have surely helped Peter understand that his vision is from God. As the rest of the chapter records, he goes with the messengers, preaches to Cornelius and his household, and sees, by the fact that the Spirit falls on these Gentiles, that they too are fit subjects of the Kingdom. Peter has learned what so many have yet to learn: that "God is no respecter of persons" (10:34).

Evangelistic Emphasis

The story of Peter and Cornelius is the story of food.

As an adult, no one liked a good meal better than Jesus. In the Gospels you will find that Jesus did much teaching with his "feet under someone's table." From forgiving sinners to arguing with the religious leaders, Jesus used a meal as a time for sacred fellowship. He told the church to remember His death each time we gather at the Lord's Table.

It is not surprising then, that as the Spirit led the church to preach to the Gentiles it was a meal that started the whole Gentile movement. The lesson about Peter and Cornelius is a pivotal chapter in the life of the Church. After Acts 10, the church is firmly set in a direction which will take it to the ends of the earth. God uses the image of food to expand Peter's understanding of what is clean and unclean. If God has called anything clean, then it is.

You may be sitting right now at a life-changing station. Your table could become a place where you change the world. I know that church people are the best cooks in all of creation. Have you ever considered it a ministry opportunity to invite some people over to your house and break bread with them in the name of Jesus? He will be present there, too.

ℰ☞ℭℜ

Memory Selection

While Peter was still thinking about the vision, the Spirit said to him, "Look, three men are searching for you. Now get up, go down, and go with them without hesitation; for I have sent them.—*Acts 10: 19-20*

After years of recruiting people for various tasks in the church I finally understand what the words, "I'll pray about it" mean. They mean, "No."

"Will you serve on the food committee?"

"I'll pray about it."

That phrase means that "I want to get home and come up with an excuse not to do what you asked me to do."

When someone calls you to serve on a committee, why don't you do what God wants you to do? I have learned a new recruiting technique; don't let a person go until he says, "Yes." You might think you are being asked by a church to serve, but perhaps you are hearing the call of God on your life.

Peter had a vision that called him to a new level of service. Before he could "pray about it," God sent three men to get Peter. God's technique involves getting people working before they have a chance to use the time-honored excuses.

Weekday Problems

Martha was the church organist and a long time member of First Church. Her parents had given much of the money for the construction of the sanctuary. She and Jerry were committed to Jesus Christ. Jerry owned his own business and was ethical in all of his dealings. Both Martha and Jerry had served as leaders of the official board of the church.

Martha and Jerry invited their new minister over for supper one night, along with some other couples from First Church. Everyone enjoyed the conversation and the appetizers. At supper, Martha offered her guest the choice of water, tea, or wine. Several chose to drink a glass of wine with their meal. No one had more than one glass. No one got drunk. The new minister and his wife chose water. The evening was a pleasant one with good conversation ranging for the weather to the excitement of the new minister's ministry.

The next Sunday the minister began a tirade on the evils of drinking.

*Discuss what the Bible says about drinking alcohol and what your faith tradition says about it.

*Is the use of alcohol a parallel to the issue of kosher food in Peter's day?

The Dream Continues . . .

I have a dream that one day every valley shall be exalted, and every hill and mountain shall be made low, the rough places will be made plain, and the crooked places will be made straight, and the glory of the Lord shall be revealed and all flesh shall see it together. This is our hope . . . With this faith we will be able to transform the jangling discords of our nation into a beautiful symphony of brotherhood. With this faith we will be able to work together, to pray together, to struggle together, to go to jail together, to stand up for freedom together, knowing that we will be free one day . . . .

And when this happens . . . when we [let] freedom ring from every village and every hamlet, from every state and every city, we will be able to speed up that day when all of God's children—black men and white men, Jews and Gentiles, Protestants and Catholics—will be able to join hands and sing in the words of the old Negro spiritual: "Free at last! Free at last! Thank God Almighty, we are free at last!"—*Excerpted from "I Have a Dream," by Martin Luther King*

This Lesson in Your Life

Cornelius was a Roman centurion. He was stationed far from his native Rome. No doubt Cornelius had a positive experience with the Jewish people with whom he had contact. He and all his household feared God. This fear did not mean they were afraid of God, but that they held Him in awe and respect. Cornelius gave his hard-earned money to the poor Jews he met. The Bible calls it giving alms. Cornelius was also a man of prayer. Luke describes him as a man who "prayed constantly" to God.

So Cornelius was a godly man. He was a Roman citizen. For Cornelius to convert to Judaism he would have to obey the kosher food laws. Some of the early Christians even thought one needed to convert to Judaism before becoming a Christian. Cornelius would also need to be circumcised. It was an ordeal for a Gentile to convert to the Jewish movement.

Peter was a good Jew before becoming a good Christian. He believed that there were foods that were kosher or clean and other foods that should be avoided, even by Christians. As Cornelius prayed, he was shown a vision of people who would talk to him about a relationship with the Lord. Cornelius found some of his soldiers who were also righteous men, and sent them to get Peter.

While Cornelius had these visions, Peter was having visions of his own. He saw all kinds of food on a floating table cloth. He was invited to eat something he felt was unclean. God was correcting Peter's perspective on the nature of clean and unclean foods. God was also using food as the illustration of a larger truth. Peter's conception that certain people were unclean also needed to be corrected. Despite this revelation, Peter becomes the apostle to the Jewish people. It will be the apostle Paul who becomes known as the apostle to the Gentiles.

However, Peter is remembered for his ministry with Cornelius. This was a turning point in the life of the Church, when the Spirit threw open the doors of the church and invited "whosoever" to come to faith in Jesus Christ.

You can apply this lesson by discussing with your class the cultural differences that keep the Church from presenting a unified message to the world today. You can also talk about how some of our cultural norms might be keeping people from coming to the church for ministry.

If you are a really brave teacher, find some people who do not go to church and ask them, lovingly, of course, why they don't attend church. You might find, in their perspective that the church has put up barriers that keep people out.

GETTING THE FACTS STRAIGHT

1. What information did Luke share about Cornelius?

Cornelius was a centurion stationed at Caesarea. He was a member of the Roman Cohort.

2. What do we know about Cornelius' spiritual life?

He was a devout man who feared God. He gave alms generously, and prayed constantly.

3. What happened to Cornelius at 3 o'clock one afternoon?

He had a vision in which he saw an angel of God coming down and addressing him.

4. What did the angel of the Lord tell Cornelius?

"Your prayers and your alms have ascended as a memorial to God."

5. What did the angel tell Cornelius about the location of Peter?

Peter was staying in Joppa at the home of Simon the Tanner.

6. Where was Simon the Tanner's house located?

Simon's house was by the seaside.

7. About noon the next day, what happened to Simon Peter?

Peter went up to the roof to pray. He got hungry and fell into a trance.

8. What did Peter see in his trance?

He saw a large sheet coming down, being lowered from heaven by its four corners.

9. What was on the large sheet?

Peter saw all kinds of four-legged animals, birds, and reptiles. Some were considered "unclean," but Peter was told that God had made them clean.

10. What was this incident intended to illustrate to Peter?

That just as God had removed the differences between clean and unclean food, so He accepts all people, Jew and Gentile alike.

We swapped prayers!

I am writing these lessons from home, where I grew up. My mother is very ill, and I have just come from the hospital where I watched her sleep. While I was watching her, I was praying for her. It was a prayer for healing, but it was also a prayer that God's will be done mercifully.

I know there was a time in my life when my mother did the same thing for me. I was a puny baby with an attitude. Nothing they fed me stayed down long. (You should see how far I have come.) I am not supposed to be here, according to the doctors. Because my mother watched me sleep and prayed for me as in infant, here I am.

So now we swap prayers, the son praying one of those "God's will" prayers over his mother. The son asking God for the same thing his mother once asked for him. It is truly a wonderful circle of life!

When you read the story of Peter and Cornelius, you understand the notion of swapping prayers. Cornelius prayed for a way into the people of God. Peter promised Jesus he would tend lost sheep and I know he prayed for the power to do so. Their prayers were swapped. Cornelius became the answer to Peter's prayer and Peter became the answer to Cornelius' prayer.

Swapping prayers has an appeal as we seek to minister in our day. People are hurting and lonely; they need a community of faith. Many of you pray for your own community of faith, because you need new people to keep your church alive and vital. It is time to look for those people with whom we can swap prayers.

Rather than pray that the the church will be filled with YOUR people, we need to change our prayer a little and pray, "Fill the church house with those who don't know they are your people." In this way we would join the long line of apostles and disciples who have invited new generations and different kinds of people to participate in this family of God called the Church.

Have you swapped any prayers recently?

Acts 12:1-16

Now about that time Herod the king stretched forth his hands to vex certain of the church.

2 And he killed James the brother of John with the sword.

3 And because he saw it pleased the Jews, he proceeded further to take Peter also. (Then were the days of unleavened bread.)

4 And when he had apprehended him, he put him in prison, and delivered him to four quaternions of soldiers to keep him; intending after Easter to bring him forth to the people.

5 Peter therefore was kept in prison: but prayer was made without ceasing of the church unto God for him.

6 And when Herod would have brought him forth, the same night Peter was sleeping between two soldiers, bound with two chains: and the keepers before the door kept the prison.

7 And, behold, the angel of the Lord came upon him, and a light shined in the prison: and he smote Peter on the side, and raised him up, saying, Arise up quickly. And his chains fell off from his hands.

8 And the angel said unto him, Gird thyself, and bind on thy sandals. And so he did. And he saith unto him, Cast thy garment about thee, and follow me.

9 And he went out, and followed him; and wist not that it was true which was done by the angel; but thought he saw a vision.

10 When they were past the first and the second ward, they came unto the iron gate that leadeth unto the city; which opened to them of his own accord: and they went out, and passed on through one street; and forthwith the angel departed from him.

11 And when Peter was come to himself, he said, Now I know of a surety, that the Lord hath sent his angel, and hath delivered me out of the hand of Herod, and from all the expectation of the people of the Jews.

12 And when he had considered the thing, he came to the house of Mary the mother of John, whose surname was Mark; where many were gathered together praying.

13 And as Peter knocked at the door of the gate, a damsel came to hearken, named Rhoda.

14 And when she knew Peter's voice, she opened not the gate for gladness, but ran in, and told how Peter stood before the gate.

15 And they said unto her, Thou art mad. But she constantly affirmed that it was even so. Then said they, It is his angel.

16 But Peter continued knocking: and when they had opened the door, and saw him, they were astonished.

Devotional Reading
Psalm 46
Background Scripture
Acts 12:1-17
Memory Selection
Acts 12:7

This account recalls for the believer the fact that God's Son was called "Immanuel," which means "God with us" (Matt. 1:23). It is apparently included in the Acts narrative as a reminder that regardless of opposition, persecution, and imprisonment, God was with the followers of Jesus—even to the point of, at times, using miraculous means of delivering them frm persecution.

A secondary theme here is the importance of corporate prayer. Peter is not alone in prison; his brothers and sisters in Christ are with him in spirit, as they lift up his plight to God in prayer. At first they find it incredible that God has answered their prayer—a subtle rebuke to a frequent attitude among believers today!

ℰℛ

In Jesus' own ministry, He healed some people, but not all. At times Paul healed people, but God declined to remove Paul's own "thorn in the flesh. In our own times of stress, God often seems to be "a very present help in times of trial," but absent in other cases.

Ask group members how they deal with the fact that God sometimes seems to answer our prayers, while at other times He seems to be silent. In this lesson, James dies at the hands of King Herod (12:2), while Peter is released from prison as his brethren pray for him. Did they neglect to pray for James?

Lead group members to recognize that God's sovereignty rules in all such cases. We are not asked to understand His ways. We *are* called to remain steadfast in prayer.

Teaching Outline

I. Government Oppression—1-4
  A. James' execution, 1-2
  B. Peter's imprisonment, 3-4
II. Miraculous Release—5-11
  A. Unceasing prayer, 5
  B. Fetters fall, 6-7
  C. Guidance, 8-11
III. Surprising Appearance—12-16
  A. Finding refuge, 12
  B. Astonished reception, 13-16

Daily Bible Readings

Mon. Peter's Healing Ministry
     Acts 9:32-42
Tue. Jesus Is Tempted
     Luke 4:1-13
Wed. Jesus Prays in Gethsemane
     Matt. 26:36-46
Thu. Jesus Dies on the Cross
     Mark 15:33-37
Fri. Government Oppression
     Acts 12:1-5
Sat. Peter Freed from Prison
     Acts 12:6-11
Sun. Telling Others the News
     Acts 12:12-17

Verse by Verse

I. Government Oppression—1-4
A. James' execution, 1-2

1 Now about that time Herod the king stretched forth his hands to vex certain of the church.

2 And he killed James the brother of John with the sword.

The Herod who had James killed was Herod Agrippa, the grandson of Herod the Great, who had ruled Palestine when Jesus was born. We have no information on why he chose to execute James, brother of John and son of Zebedee. James could have easily been the victim of Herod's angry whim after causing a disturbance by his preaching. After all, he and John were nicknamed "Sons of Thunder" (Mark 3:17).

B. Peter's imprisonment, 3-4

3 And because he saw it pleased the Jews, he proceeded further to take Peter also. (Then were the days of unleavened bread.)

4 And when he had apprehended him, he put him in prison, and delivered him to four quaternions of soldiers to keep him; intending after Easter to bring him forth to the people.

Although he was king, Herod also had to keep an eye on what pleased the people. Like a modern politician who looks over a crowd to gauge reaction to what he said, then says

more along that line if the response is positive, Herod sees that James' death pleases the Jewish establishment. These opponents of the early Christians were likely Sadducees, since they were the wealthy and politically-minded elements of Jewish leadership who often had the ear of the current Roman ruler.

Four "quaternions" of soldiers were four squads of four men each, or 16 in all. Two were chained to their prisoner (vs. 7)—all in all quite a strong guard, indicating the threat the authorities assumed Peter posed. Ironically, after this point in Acts, Peter' prominence will recede while Luke's focus shifts to the ministry of Paul.

"Easter" is a mistranslation picked up by the KJV translators from the ancient Anglo-Saxon version. In the original the word is *pascha*, or Passover (as in other translations); the Anglo-Saxon translators wrongly supposing that the Jewish Passover coincided with Easter.

II. Miraculous Release—5-11
A. Unceasing prayer, 5

5 Peter therefore was kept in prison: but prayer was made without ceasing of the church unto God for him.

Although we are not told the specific content of the church's prayer, some have supposed that they were praying not for Peter's release but that he would not recant his beliefs, as he had denied Jesus more than a decade earlier. Later Christians would in fact pray that captives would be "released" to death instead of denying the faith.

B. Fetters fall, 6-7

6 And when Herod would have brought him forth, the same night Peter was sleeping between two soldiers, bound with two chains: and the keepers before the door kept the prison.

7 And, behold, the angel of the Lord came upon him, and a light shined in the prison: and he smote Peter on the side, and raised him up, saying, Arise up quickly. And his chains fell off from his hands.

Although many modern commentators are skeptical about the miraculous element introduced here, the author seems to go out of his way to emphasize that Peter could not have escaped without divine intervention. Surely a God who can raise His Son from the grave could cause chains to fall and open a few prison doors! Obviously Peter himself is not expecting to be released—the angel has to "smite" him sharply to awaken him.

C. Guidance, 8-11

8 And the angel said unto him, Gird thyself, and bind on thy sandals. And so he did. And he saith unto him, Cast thy garment about thee, and follow me.

9 And he went out, and followed him; and wist not that it was true which was done by the angel; but thought he saw a vision.

10 When they were past the first and the second ward, they came unto the iron gate that leadeth unto the city; which opened to them of his own accord: and they went out, and passed on through one street; and forthwith the angel departed from him.

11 And when Peter was come to himself, he said, Now I know of a surety, that the Lord hath sent his angel, and hath delivered me out of the hand of Herod, and from all the expectation of the people of the Jews.

Anyone who has dreamed something that seems real, or experiences an event that is like a dream, can identify with Peter's confusion here. Some archeologists believe that Jerusalem at this time was surrounded by three walls, accounting for the maze of gates that open at the mere approach of the angel with his ward in tow. Only when Peter is a safe distance from possible pursuers does the angel leave him on his own. Then the apostle "comes to himself," and realizes that he has not been dreaming, but that his release was accomplished by a messenger from God. What a faith-building experience this must have been!

III. Surprising Appearance—12-16

A. Finding refuge, 12

12 And when he had considered the thing, he came to the house of Mary the mother of John, whose

surname was Mark; where many were gathered together praying.

This Mary was the mother of John Mark, the author of the Gospel that bears his name, and the missionary companion of Paul and Silas (vs. 25). Since "many were gathered" at her home, Mary must have been a woman of means and the owner of a large house. Peter seems to know that brethren would be gathered there, since he goes there directly.

B. Astonished reception, 13-16

13 And as Peter knocked at the door of the gate, a damsel came to hearken, named Rhoda.

14 And when she knew Peter's voice, she opened not the gate for gladness, but ran in, and told how Peter stood before the gate.

15 And they said unto her, Thou art mad. But she constantly affirmed that it was even so. Then said they, It is his angel.

16 But Peter continued knocking: and when they had opened the door, and saw him, they were astonished.

Although we are not specifically told that Rhoda is a servant, the term translated "damsel" is often translated "maidservant"—another indication that Mary was well off. Yet Rhoda is also probably a part of the congregation, because she recognizes Peter's voice and is glad to hear it—although she is so shocked that she runs back to tell the group instead of opening the door.

At first they think that Rhoda is out of her mind, then that she must have heard "his angel." Many Jews of this period believed that every person had a "shadow-image" or guardian angel (a possibility that seems strengthened by Matthew 18:10). It was thought that this personage could take on the appearance of the person to whom they were assigned; and at times appear as a ghost (see Luke 24:37-38). At any rate, only Peter's persistent knocking finally persuades someone to come and open the door.

The band of disciples have been roundly criticized for being surprised that God would answer their prayer. Yet their astonishment might be explained because they were praying not for Peter's release but for his faithfulness under persecution. In the next verse, Peter calms the crowd and tells them that he has not been released because he renounced the faith but because the angel miraculously intervened.

As a footnote to this story, the contemporary Jewish historian Josephus elaborates on the manner of Herod Agrippa's death (vss. 21-23). He says that the king appeared in an arena at dawn, dressed in a robe spun entirely of pure silver. "Illumined by the touch of the first rays of the sun [he] was wondrously radiant and by its glitter inspired fear and awe," Josephus writes. Those who wanted to flatter him accorded him divine status, and for his arrogance in accepting their flattery God struck him with the attack recorded in verse 23.

Evangelistic Emphasis

Do you believe in miracles? Maybe not those big ones, but would you settle for "miracle moments?"

What's a miracle moment? Some wit has suggested that men need classes on miracles like these:

Refrigerator Forensics: Identifying and removing the dead.

Accepting Loss: If it's empty, you can throw it away.

Romance: More than a cable channel.

"I Don't Know": Be the first man to say it.

Directions: It's OK to ask for them.

Accepting Your Limitations: Just because you have power tools doesn't mean you can fix it.

Miracle moments are more than these. A miracle is a God-moment in our human environment. I believe you have to look quick to see them, but that God works them every day if we learn to look for them.

Peter had been set free from prison by an angel. I believe it happened just the way that Acts describes it. I believe that God can walk a man out of prison just as much as I believe He could raise His son from the dead. I believe in these miracles as much as I believe God can forgive my sins and change my life.

The greatest miracle moment is when a sinner realizes his sin, asks for God's forgiveness, and then accepts Jesus as his Savior and Lord. That is the miracle moment that begins a life of faith.

ଛୋଋ

And, behold, the angel of the Lord came upon him, and a light shined in the prison: and he smote Peter on the side, and raised him up, saying, Arise up quickly. And his chains fell off from his hands.—*Acts 12: 7*

Sometimes God has to slap you silly to get your attention. The positive part of this story is that Peter's faith in Jesus allowed him to sleep even though his life was hanging in the balance, there in Herod's prison. Yet Peter was sleeping like a baby. The negative part of the story is that the angel for of the Lord had to slap him to wake him up.

Does God have to slap you to get your attention? Has there been any divine "smiting" going on in your life? Are things not working out the way you had planned? Are you tossing and turning over what and why things are happening to you? We put God on the last page of our calendar with the promise, "We's get back to you, Lord." When we do that, He takes action.

Or are you sleepwalking through life, with God having to "smite" you to wake you up?

Weekday Problems

A man was concerned about his wife's lack of sparkle, energy, and zest in life. Finally, he took her to a doctor who really took an interest in her. He listened to her talk. He listened to all of her problems both real and imagined. Then suddenly he got out of his chair and went over and kissed her on both cheeks. The results were amazing. She was transformed. The old sparkle was back in her eyes and color in her cheeks. She was radiant again. The doctor said, "Well, I think that ought to do it!"

But her husband said, "I don't understand! What do you mean?"

"Well, it's really simple." the doctor explained. "Your wife just needs to be kissed twice a week. That's all she needs."

The man scratched his head and said, "I really don't understand it, Doc, but if that's what she needs, then I'll bring her in every Tuesday and Thursday."

There are some things that only you should be doing for others. Are you doing them? Or are you delegating your responsibility?

"Miracle moments" in life create additional responsibility for us. Talk about the role of miracles and responsibility. You know you can't pray for a weight-loss miracle while eating ice cream. You can't pray for a financial miracle while charging all your purchases.

*How do miracles create opportunities for us to live with a responsible faith?

Brain(less) Teasers

Sam Patch always takes off his boots, goes up to the tallest trees, and jumps over them. How can this be?
He jumps over his boots, not the trees.

***

Down south, they say the mosquitoes are so large that a good many of them weigh a pound, and that they sit on logs and bark. How can this be?
A good many of them <u>together</u> weigh a pound, and they sit on the bark of the trees.

***

A carpenter made a cabinet door that proved too big. He cut it, but unfortunately he cut it too little. So he cut it again and it fit just right. How can this be?
He but cut it "too little"—not enough—the first time.

This Lesson in Your Life

Do you remember Dayna Curry and Heather Mercer? If not let me remind you that God still sets people free.

Dayna Curry, age 30, and Heather Mercer, 24, were American missionaries who were captured by Afghan terrorists. These Christians, charged with attempting to convert Muslims to Christianity, spent months in prison. The evidence against them was a copy of a children's book about Jesus, and a couple of CD ROMs about the life of Jesus.

Eventually the Afghans released the women, and they held a news conference. They used the opportunity to express thanks to the many people who were praying for them. Though it wasn't widely reported in the secular media, they also thanked their Lord Jesus. They described the ordeal as a roller coaster of emotions.

One day up and full of hope, the next, full of despair, fearing for their lives. Heather and Dayna also thanked their Lord for his deliverance. They said, "He was faithful to his promises." Curry and Mercer believed God fulfilled his promise to ransom them and deliver them from their enemies.

The faithfulness of these Christians is amazing. After their arrest their situation changed with the attacks on the World Trade Center in September. War broke out, and the danger increased. They did not know if a bomb from the United States might destroy their jail and kill them. Curry said, "There were times when we didn't know if we'd make it out alive." Throughout the ordeal, they held on to their faith and trusted God completely. He delivered them, and strengthened them through their trial.

Their faith was a witness to their Muslim captors.

God works "miracle moments" around us so that we can be witnesses to His power. When Peter was released from jail miraculously, it gave encouragement to the Christians. Peter's miraculous release also allowed him to continue the work the Lord gave him to do.

With each moment our faith is deepened, our responsibility increases. Miracles don't happen just for our benefit. They happen so that we might reflect the love and power of Jesus Christ in our lives. A "miracle moment" gives us the opportunity to point to Jesus.

Remember that miracles are "a God-moment in our human environment." Remember that they are *God* moments, not ours.

1. What was the historical context for the twelfth chapter of Acts?
Herod laid violent hands on some who belonged to the Church.

2. Whose martyrdom is recorded in this chapter?
James, the brother of John was killed with the sword.

3. What impact did Herod's persecution have on the Jewish community opposed to the church?
It pleased the Jews that the Church was being persecuted.

4. When was Peter arrested?
He was arrested during the festival of Unleavened Bread.

5. What were his fellow-Christians doing while Peter was in jail?
They prayed fervently to God for him.

6. How was Peter kept secure in the jail that night?
He was bound with two chains and was sleeping between two soldiers.

7. What happened when the angel told Peter to get up?
The two chains that were holding Peter fell off his wrists.

8. What other instructions did the angel give Peter before he fled?
"Fasten your belt, put on your sandals, wrap your cloak around you and follow me."

9. What did Peter think was happening?
Peter thought he was having some kind of vision. He was not sure his release was real.

10. Where did Peter go when he realized he had been freed from jail?
Peter went to the house of Mary, the mother of John Mark, where many had gathered to pray for him.

Years ago, a young teen had to work because his father became ill. The meager money the boy brought in was the only money the family had.

At nine each evening, Tony bought bread from a company for a nickel a loaf and delivered it to restaurants for a quarter a loaf. He made quite a sight delivering these loaves of bread on bicycle, but it was his only means of transportation. One cold, rainy night he hit a pothole that blew out his tire.

Shivering and discouraged, he railed at God.

"You're mean! Everyone says your kind, but I know you're mean!" Sobbing, he pushed his bike down the street and came to a closed service station. In a daze he tried to pump air into the tire. It was futile, but he persisted. Suddenly the tire was hard. He looked up into the rainy night and said, "Thank you!"

Two deliveries later and just before 1 a.m., Tony placed his bike on the front porch. As he opened the front door, he heard a hissing sound. The miracle was over and the tire went flat.

We don't depend on miracles to get us through the day. But each time a miracle does happen in our lives we are reminded of God and the power He has to help us. Praying for a miracle does not release us from the responsibility to live before God a life that "becomes the gospel." Part of our "responsibility" as Christians is to know when we are in over our heads and when it will take a miracle of God to get us where we need to be.

In an age of technology wizardry and gadgetry, we need to learn to trust in the power of God. God is still in the miracle-working business. He is still releasing people from prison. He continues to help the lame to walk, the blind to see, and the deaf to hear. God still brings about the miracle of all miracles called salvation.

If you doubt the miracle-working power of God just wait until tomorrow morning when the sun comes up. Just as the sun drives the dark of night away, we know that God brings resurrection after death. God has saved the best miracle for last. We will be resurrected just as Jesus was resurrected!

To quote the announcer at the 1980 Olympics, when the U. S. men's hockey team won the Gold medal: "Do you believe in miracles?"

Unit III. To the Ends of the Earth

Lesson 10
Encountering Truth

Acts 9:3-18

And as he journeyed, he came near Damascus: and suddenly there shined round about him a light from heaven:

4 And he fell to the earth, and heard a voice saying unto him, Saul, Saul, why persecutest thou me?

5 And he said, Who art thou, Lord? And the Lord said, I am Jesus whom thou persecutest: it is hard for thee to kick against the pricks.

6 And he trembling and astonished said, Lord, what wilt thou have me to do? And the Lord said unto him, Arise, and go into the city, and it shall be told thee what thou must do.

7 And the men which journeyed with him stood speechless, hearing a voice, but seeing no man.

8 And Saul arose from the earth; and when his eyes were opened, he saw no man: but they led him by the hand, and brought him into Damascus.

9 And he was three days without sight, and neither did eat nor drink.

10 And there was a certain disciple at Damascus, named Ananias; and to him said the Lord in a vision, Ananias. And he said, Behold, I am here, Lord.

11 And the Lord said unto him, Arise, and go into the street which is called Straight, and inquire in the house of Judas for one called Saul, of Tarsus: for, behold, he prayeth,

12 And hath seen in a vision a man named Ananias coming in, and putting his hand on him, that he might receive his sight.

13 Then Ananias answered, Lord, I have heard by many of this man, how much evil he hath done to thy saints at Jerusalem:

14 And here he hath authority from the chief priests to bind all that call on thy name.

15 But the Lord said unto him, Go thy way: for he is a chosen vessel unto me, to bear my name before the Gentiles, and kings, and the children of Israel:

16 For I will shew him how great things he must suffer for my name's sake.

17 And Ananias went his way, and entered into the house; and putting his hands on him said, Brother Saul, the Lord, even Jesus, that appeared unto thee in the way as thou camest, hath sent me, that thou mightest receive thy sight, and be filled with the Holy Ghost.

18 And immediately there fell from his eyes as it had been scales: and he received sight forthwith, and arose, and was baptized.

Nov. 6

Devotional Reading
Acts 9:23-31

Background Scripture
Acts9:1-31

Memory Selection
Acts 9:18

It would be hard to over-emphasize the importance of the conversion of Saul of Tarsus, the rabbinically-trained Jew, to Paul, the Christian apostle to the Gentiles. Most readers of this commentary have inherited their allegiance to such doctrine as justification by faith from Paul, who wrote more about this fundamental principle that any other New Testament writer.

Prepare for this lesson, by reading the parallel accounts of Paul's conversion in Acts 22 and 26. Since these two secondary accounts show Paul recounting his conversion experience as the basis of his ministry, a secondary focus arises: the extent to which our own personal experience is rightly used in explaining to others why we believe.

ഇറ

To start this lesson, ask group members to share their own conversion experience. Although the apostle's conversion was to some extent unique, everyone's story contributes to their spiritual formation.

Perhaps most of members of your group will have been raised in the faith, and lack the dramatic style of conversion that occurred in Paul's life. Others will credit their faith to the guidance of a family member, friend, or minister. Yet others, like Saul, may have had an identifiable and even sudden or surprising event that led to their conversion. Note that the point of all these stories is to compare and contrast them with the way God confronts Saul, and all believers, with the truth . . . and awaits our response.

Teaching Outline	*Daily Bible Readings*

I. Encounter with the Light—3-5
 	
II. Obeying God's Voice—6-9
  A. Instructions from God, 6-7
  B. Waiting for God, 8-9
 	
III. Ananias' Involvement—10-18
  A. Messenger prepared, 10-12
  B. Hesitation overcome, 13-16
  C. Saul's conversion, 17-18
	Mon. Jesus Calls Disciples
	        Luke 5:4-11
	Tue. Peter Responds to Criticism
	        Acts 11:1-10
	Wed. Believers Praise God
	        Acts 11:11-18
	Thu. Saul's Vision of Jesus
	        Acts 9:1-9
	Fri. Instructions to Ananias
	        Acts 9:10-16
	Sat. Saul Proclaims Christ
	        Acts 9:17-22
	Sun. Believers Accept Saul
	        Acts 9:23-31

Verse by Verse

I. Encounter with the Light—3-5

3 And as he journeyed, he came near Damascus: and suddenly there shined round about him a light from heaven:

4 And he fell to the earth, and heard a voice saying unto him, Saul, Saul, why persecutest thou me?

5 And he said, Who art thou, Lord? And the Lord said, I am Jesus whom thou persecutest: it is hard for thee to kick against the pricks.

As verses 1-2 have explained, the journey of Saul ("who also is called Paul," 13:9) to Damascus is in behalf of official Jewry's persecution of Christians. Saul has been introduced in 7:58 and 8:1; and from this point he will be the dominant figure in Acts, except for the encounter of Peter with the Gentile Cornelius in chapter 10. It is generally supposed that Saul was a Jewish name and Paul is Greek (from *paulus*, "little"). He was a highly educated Pharisee (Acts 23:6), and since he was "freeborn" in the Roman-controlled city of Tarsus, in Cilicia (in what is now southeastern Turkey), he was a Roman citizen (22:25-28). God has obvious considered this cosmopolitan man's credentials seriously for a cross-cultural mission.

Paul's cry to the "Lord" (Grk.

kyrios, "sir," or "master") only indicates that he has been "mastered," for he clearly asks for further clarification ("Who art thou?"). The answer is equally clear, and comes quickly: the power that struck Saul to the ground, the light that he sees, and the voice he hears are all from Jesus, the very One Saul is so zealously persecuting. (Note that to persecute members of Christ's Body, the Church, is to persecute Jesus.)

The latter part of verse 5 is not found in any Greek manuscript, so most translations other than the KJV omit it. "Pricks" or "goads" were barbs on the harness or traces on both sides of an oxen pulling a cart, to keep the animal in line. God obviously had a plan for Saul that he was not following, and being struck to the ground is a "goad" he should heed.

II. Obeying God's Voice—6-9

A. Instructions from God, 6-7

6 And he trembling and astonished said, Lord, what wilt thou have me to do? And the Lord said unto him, Arise, and go into the city, and it shall be told thee what thou must do.

7 And the men which journeyed with him stood speechless, hearing a voice, but seeing no man.

This time, "Lord" must surely be

taking on its religious meaning. Paul is unable to attribute the astonishing blow, the blinding light, and the voice from heaven to anyone else. His question shows an immediate willingness to follow the Lord's will. In fact, he had been convinced that he was following Yahweh's will in persecuting Christians, the very ones who claimed that Jesus was Yahweh's Son.

When Paul recounts this event in 22:9, he says that those who were with him did not hear a voice, apparently meaning that they did not understand the noise, as indicated here. In the third account of his conversion experience, he adds that the voice from heaven went on to outline the commission to the Gentiles which God has in mind for him (26:16-18).

B. Waiting for God, 8-9

8 And Saul arose from the earth; and when his eyes were opened, he saw no man: but they led him by the hand, and brought him into Damascus.

9 And he was three days without sight, and neither did eat nor drink.

"Obeying the vision" (26:19), Paul allows himself to be led into Damascus, still blinded by the brilliant light. There he "waits on the Lord," blind and fasting, for three days. Obviously this is a man who earnestly desires to please God, and cannot yet understand why his persecution of Christians is not being considered God's will. As is often

observed, this indicates that we can be sincere, but sincerely "wrong," and argues for a lifelong willingness to reconsider our actions in the light of God's true will for us. Yet sincerity is not to be disparaged, only guided and informed by the true Light.

III. Ananias' Involvement—10-18
A. Messenger Prepared, 10-12

10 And there was a certain disciple at Damascus, named Ananias; and to him said the Lord in a vision, Ananias. And he said, Behold, I am here, Lord.

11 And the Lord said unto him, Arise, and go into the street which is called Straight, and inquire in the house of Judas for one called Saul, of Tarsus: for, behold, he prayeth,

12 And hath seen in a vision a man named Ananias coming in, and putting his hand on him, that he might receive his sight.

The Eastern Church has a tradition that Ananias was one of the 70 (or 72) sent out on the "Limited Commission" of Luke 10:1, 17. All we actually know about him is recorded here and in Acts 22:17, where Paul adds that he "was a devout man according to the law," with a good reputation among the Jews. This latter would be important as a stepping stone for Saul to use in making the transition from Judaism to Christianity. Some think that "Straight Street" can still be identified in the Old City of Damascus. Perhaps the house on that street was one where Paul usually stayed while in the city.

B. Hesitation overcome, 13-16

13 Then Ananias answered, Lord, I have heard by many of this man, how much evil he hath done to thy saints at Jerusalem:

14 And here he hath authority from the chief priests to bind all that call on thy name.

15 But the Lord said unto him, Go thy way: for he is a chosen vessel unto me, to bear my name before the Gentiles, and kings, and the children of Israel:

16 For I will shew him how great things he must suffer for my name's sake.

Ananias understandably asks whether he has correctly heard the Lord, since he knew well of Saul's reputation as a prosecutor of Christians. He has even heard that Saul carries with him the authority to imprison Ananias himself. God repeats His commission to Ananias, with the brief explanation that He has a far different plan for Saul. It is not only one that will take him before kings, Jews, and Gentiles; it will involve suffering in ways similar to what Saul has been inflicting upon Christians. Perhaps it is this dimension of God's plan that convinces Ananias to go to Saul.

C. Saul's conversion, 17-18

17 And Ananias went his way, and entered into the house; and putting his hands on him said, Brother Saul, the Lord, even Jesus, that appeared unto thee in the way as thou camest, hath sent me, that thou mightest receive thy sight, and be filled with the Holy Ghost.

18 And immediately there fell from his eyes as it had been scales: and he received sight forthwith, and arose, and was baptized.

Saul is both a "brother" to Ananias in their common Jewish heritage, and as a potential brother in Christ. We can only imagine the tension that must have first existed between the two men; but it is overcome in their common obedience to the separate visions that have brought them together.

Ananias comes with the miraculous ability to heal Paul's blindness, which must have been an important factor in convincing the future apostle that his experience is indeed from God, and not just his imagination. Paul's recollection of this crucial event in chapter 22 includes a commissioning statement by Ananias: "The God of our fathers hath chosen thee [Saul], that thou shouldest know his will, and see that Just One [an important qualification for an apostle], and shouldest hear the voice of his mouth. For thou shalt be his witness unto all men of what thou hast seen and heard" (22:14-15).

Upon receiving his sight, and hearing the words of Ananias, Saul wastes no time in being baptized. The fact that this event is a part of having his sins "washed away" does not infer that the waters of baptism in themselves have forgiving power. As the Great Commission has said (Matt. 28:18-20), baptism is not a work of human merit, but is effective as a response of faith.

Evangelistic Emphasis

Years ago, a Johns Hopkins professor had some graduate students the assignment to take 200 boys from the slums, ages 12 to 16, investigate their background and environment, then predict what would become of them.

The students talked to the boys, consulted social statistics, and compiled their data. They concluded that 90 percent of the boys would spend some time in jail.

Another group of graduate students 25 years later were assigned to test the prediction. They went back to the same area, and were able to get in touch with 180 of the original 200.

They found that only four of the group had ever been sent to jail.

Why did these men, raised in a breeding place of crime, have such a surprisingly good record? The researchers were continually told: *"Well, there was a teacher . . . ."*

They further found that in 75 percent of the cases it was the same woman. They found her, now living in a home for retired teachers. How had she exerted this remarkable influence over those children? Could she give them any reason why these boys should have remembered her?

"No," she said, "no, I really couldn't." And then, thinking back over the years, she said musingly, more to herself than to her questioners: "I loved those boys. . . ."

That kind of dramatic love is what saved Paul on the Damascus Road. all.

ഇൗറ

And immediately there fell from his eyes as it had been scales: and he received sight forthwith, and arose, and was baptized.—*Acts 9:18*

Simon Tugwell retells an old story of two Japanese monks traveling a muddy road in the rain. Around a bend in the road, they met a lovely girl in a flowing silk kimono, unable to cross the muddy road. One monk, Tanzan, took the girl in his arms and carried her through the mud and onto more secure ground.

The other monk, Ekido, spoke not a word until they reached their lodging that night. Then he could restrained himself no longer: "We monks never go near females," he challenged Tanzan, "most particularly not young and pretty ones. "It is dangerous, it is tempting fate. Why did you do it?"

"I left the girl there," replied Tanzan quietly. "Are you still carrying her?"

Meeting Jesus on the Damascus road changed Saul's life. After Ananias came and prayed for him, the scales fell from his eyes. He got up and was baptized. Saul's old life was over. His sins were forgiven. Neither Paul nor we need to keep carrying around our sins after Jesus relieves us of the burden.

Weekday Problems

Mike was excited about sharing his testimony with the congregation at the Wednesday night testimony time. "Before I met Jesus I was a sinner I was a heavy drinker," he said. "I could tell you when happy hour was at every in go from one bar to another for six hours if I made all the lights. I used to go out with women who had few morals, and what scruples they had I talked them out of. I used to curse like a sailor. I had dirty magazines all over the house. I never read the Bible and I didn't care about Jesus. On Sunday morning, if I wasn't too hung-over I was on the golf course." Mike said it with so much enthusiasm the preacher wondered if he were confessing or bragging.

Then Mike took a deep breath, almost a heavy sigh. And said with very methodical tones, "Then I repented and I met Jesus, and I don't do those things any more. If you meet Jesus you can be just like me."

Then one church member spoke up. "Who would want to?" he asked. You were having more fun before you repented."

*Discuss your testimony. Is it positive?

*Compare the way modern testimonies are shared with Paul' own "witness" of his conversion experience.

Encounters with Baptism

A Methodist and a Baptist were arguing the virtues of springkling vs. immersion as baptism. "All right," said the Methodist, "if I take a man and lead him into water up to his ankles, is he baptized?"

"No," the Baptist answered firmly.

"Well, what about if I bring him on in until the top of his head is showing above the water. Is he baptized?"

"No," was the answer.

"Well," said the Methodist. "That's where we baptize them."

***

It really happened: The minister had just immersed a very heavy woman, and helped her climb up the steps to the ladies' dressing room. The audience was getting impatient, so instead of parading back across the baptistry to the men's dressing room, he took a deep breath, bobbed underwater, and began to breast-stroke his way. Halfway across, he looked sideways— and realized that since the baptistry had a glass front he had reduced his audience to laughter.

This Lesson in Your Life

How does the church call "hardened sinners" to faith in Jesus Christ? The conversion of Paul on the Damascus Road gives us a workable pattern for evangelizing the "hardened hearts" of the world.

There was an appeal to conscience. Jesus said, "Saul, Saul, why do you persecute me?" This was the question that Paul could not dodge. We might speculate that since the stoning of Stephen, Paul's conscience was bothering him. He knew at a deep level that what he had done was not right. He knew what the law said. When a sinner comes face to face with the holiness and righteousness of Jesus Christ, that person is going to feel is going to feel guilty. What the Church should understand is that when the Holy Spirit is convicting someone of a guilty conscience, we don't need to let them off of the hook. Jesus made the persecution of the church personal.

Second, *the conversion of Paul reached his mind.* The Greek word for repentance means to "change your mind." When a person is on his way to an experience with Jesus Christ, he starts thinking differently. The world order tends to break down when the Holy Spirit starts working on a person's mind. Power doesn't matter in a kingdom where a condemned, crucified peasant is the leader of the movement.

Before we worry about having the new convert memorize all of our pet doctrinal positions, we should agree that the basic idea of theology is "Jesus is Lord." As a matter of fact, that is really all the doctrine a person has to keep in their mind for conversion to happen. It is the basic truth of the Christian faith. We need to start using our minds and confronting the bad thinking of other current world views.

Paul's conversion was of the will. Jesus did not break his spirit, but he did tell Paul what steps to take next. Paul was obedient to the direction that Jesus gave him.

Jesus changed Paul's life. We can't have a life-changing experience with Jesus until we are willing to let the Lord serve us. We have to open our lives and let others minister to us in Jesus' name. Paul waited in Damascus helpless until God's people representing Jesus, came to his aid. This new man could then go toe to toe not only with the Jewish community who opposed him; he would face down the awesome power of the Roman Empire.

A man who was murdering Christians became the leader of the new Church. He always remained humble and awed by the grace Jesus Christ had shown him. If Jesus can do that with Paul, he can do it with the sinners you know, too.

1. Why was Saul of Tarsus on his way to Damascus?

Saul, had obtained permission from the high priest to rid Damascus of Christians.

2. What can you infer from Saul seeking letters to enter the Jewish synagogues?

At this time in early church history, the Christians were still closely associated with the Jewish synagogues.

3. What happened to Saul on the road to Damascus?

There was a bright light which flashed from heaven. He fell down and heard a voice.

4. What did the voice say to Saul?

"Saul, Saul, why do you persecute me?

5. What was the experience of those who were traveling with Saul?

Saul's companions heard the voice, but didn't see anyone speaking. The text does not say they saw the light.

6. What happened after the voice spoke to Saul?

Saul got up and, although his eyes were opened, he could not see. His companions led him into Damascus.

7. Describe Saul's condition in Damascus.

For three days he was without sight, and he neither ate nor drank.

8. What did the Lord do to minister to Saul?

The Lord gave a vision to a disciple named Ananias, telling him where to go and who to see.

9. What was Ananias' first response to Jesus command?

Ananias argued with the Lord. He told Jesus that Saul was a danger to the Christian community.

10. How did Saul respond to the laying on of hands and the words of Ananias?

Immediately something like scales fell from his eyes. His sight was restored. Then he got up and was baptized.

Does anyone remember "The Masked Bolo"? He was a wrestler who had his start in the late '50s and early '60s. The reason he was so popular was because of his mask. His opponents were always trying to pull it off. We were all sure that when they finally succeeded, the Masked Bolo would turn out to be somebody we all knew, like Bob Hope or Ed Sullivan or somebody like that.

"Who is that masked man?" In this lesson, Paul is sure he knows the true identity of the false messiah worshiped and proclaimed by the disciples and those so-called Christians.

Paul thought Jesus was someone other than who He purported to be. He saw Jesus as a threat to the stability of Judaism and to the faith of Israel. Paul believed that the title "messiah" merely masked a man with a destructive, hurtful motive.

Of course, Paul wasn't the first to be confused about Jesus' identity and purpose. Jesus' own family even found His behavior mystifying. After all, Jesus left the security of home and a profitable business to become an itinerant preacher. He took up with a rough crowd of people: smelly fishermen, a white-collar crook, and a political revolutionary. He started alienating the religious establishment. Observing all this, Jesus' own family asked, "Who is this man? He's not the Jesus we know!"

Jesus' family could only conclude: He's lost His mind. He's gone over the edge. He's out of control. He's gone crazy.

Paul didn't think Jesus was crazy. Paul thought Jesus was evil — in cahoots with the devil himself. Paul couldn't deny the reality of the healings and exorcisms, but he could deny their source, viewing them as simply the work of Satan. In his blindness, Paul saw Jesus as one who was in league with Satan.

Why couldn't Paul see the real Jesus? Not because His personality was masked, but because the real masked man in this lesson was Paul himself. Jesus wasn't wearing a mask. Paul was wearing a blindfold.

Wasn't it Jesus who said that it's awfully hard to see a speck in someone else's eye if you have a log in your eye? It is fittingly ironic that when Paul at last hears and recognizes Jesus as the risen Christ, he is struck blind.

Do you see what I'm saying? Or are you blindfolded too?

Lesson 11

Offering of Oneself

Acts 16:6-15

Now when they had gone throughout Phrygia and the region of Galatia, and were forbidden of the Holy Ghost to preach the word in Asia,

7 After they were come to Mysia, they assayed to go into Bithynia: but the Spirit suffered them not.

8 And they passing by Mysia came down to Troas.

9 And a vision appeared to Paul in the night; There stood a man of Macedonia, and prayed him, saying, Come over into Macedonia, and help us.

10 And after he had seen the vision, immediately we endeavored to go into Macedonia, assuredly gathering that the Lord had called us for to preach the gospel unto them.

11 Therefore loosing from Troas, we came with a straight course to Samothracia, and the next day to Neapolis;

12 And from thence to Philippi, which is the chief city of that part of Macedonia, and a colony: and we were in that city abiding certain days.

13 And on the sabbath we went out of the city by a river side, where prayer was wont to be made; and we sat down, and spake unto the women which resorted thither.

14 And a certain woman named Lydia, a seller of purple, of the city of Thyatira, which worshipped God, heard us: whose heart the Lord opened, that she attended unto the things which were spoken of Paul.

15 And when she was baptized, and her household, she besought us, saying, If ye have judged me to be faithful to the Lord, come into my house, and abide there. And she constrained us.

Nov. 13

Devotional Reading
Acts 16:25-35

Background Scripture
Acts 16

Memory Selection
Acts 16:15

This lesson takes the fourth step in the missionary plan Jesus proposed to the disciples in Acts 1:8: "unto to the uttermost part of the earth." Here Luke records for the first time the proclamation of the Good News on the continent of Europe (although others had previously taken the message to major European cities such as Rome and Corinth). A classroom-size map of Paul's second missionary journey will aid the presentation

The shows strong dependence on the Holy Spirit, as He directs the missionaries' steps. God seems to have a specific plan that involves closing some doors and opening others. We are also treated to the story of the conversion of Lydia, who becomes a model of how Christian hospitality aided the spread of the gospel.

℘℧

"Whatever happened to old-fashioned, open-door hospitality?" Asking this question is a good way into the story of Lydia. In this lesson she opens the doors of her household to wandering missionaries.

Ask how times have changed since people sat out on their front porch in the evenings, invited strangers they just met at church to come home with them for Sunday dinner, and otherwise visited freely in each other's homes. Discuss how increased crime may have contributed to some of these changes, and what cost in fellowship and community we have had to pay, in reaction. Ask also whether some of this "retreat" mentality might be safely loosened so Christians can once again exercise the gift of hospitality (see Heb. 13:2).

Teaching Outline	**Daily Bible Readings**

I. Confrontation with the Spirit—6-8
    A. Work in Asia Minor, 6a
    B. The Spirit's 'No,' 7b-8
II. Call from Macedonia—9-13
    A. Call from Europe, 9-10
    B. Working toward Philippi, 11-12
    C. Riverside prayer meeting, 13
III. Conversion of Lydia—14-15
    A. Open heart, 14
    B. Open home, 15
	Mon. Show Hospitality
	         Heb.13:1-6
	Tue. Welcoming Jesus
	         Luke 10:38-42
	Wed. Serving One Another
	         1 Pet. 4:7-11
	Thu. Conversion of Lydia
	         Acts 16:11-15
	Fri. Paul and Silas Imprisoned
	         Acts 16:16-24
	Sat. A Jailer Converted
	         Acts 16:25-34
	Sun. Paul and Silas Freed
	         Acts 16:35-40

Verse by Verse

I. Confrontation with the Spirit—6-8

A. Work in Asia Minor, 6a

6a Now when they had gone throughout Phrygia and the region of Galatia,

Acts 16 is prefaced by an introduction to Paul's second missionary journey, on which he chose Silas to accompany him (15:40-41). Starting out from Antioch of Syria, they pass through Paul's home town of Tarsus, in southeastern Asia Minor (now Turkey), then move west to the cities of Derbe and Lystra, where they add a promising young man named Timothy to join their missionary team (16:1-3).

B. The Spirit's 'No,' 6b-8

6b and were forbidden of the Holy Ghost to preach the word in Asia,

7 After they were come to Mysia, they assayed to go into Bithynia: but the Spirit suffered them not.

8 And they passing by Mysia came down to Troas.

Twice in only two verses we are told of the Holy Spirit's careful direction in this missionary enterprise. Apparently God has a distinct plan that points Paul and his company away from northern and eastern destinations in Asia Minor, and westward to Europe instead. "Asia" re-

fers not to the continent east of India, but to a Roman province in western Asia Minor (see Acts 6:9), of which Ephesus was the capital. Going north to the province of Mysia, the missionaries started to turn eastward toward Bithynia, along the southwestern shore of the Black Sea; but again the Spirit says No. We will soon learn the way the Spirit gives positive directions in this case. For now, the group waits in the port city of Troas, thought by most historians to be the site of the legendary Troy of Homer's epics.

II. Call from Macedonia—9-13

A. Call from Europe, 9-10

9 And a vision appeared to Paul in the night; There stood a man of Macedonia, and prayed him, saying, Come over into Macedonia, and help us.

10 And after he had seen the vision, immediately we endeavored to go into Macedonia, assuredly gathering that the Lord had called us for to preach the gospel unto them.

Finally, after receiving several negative nudges from the Spirit, Paul has a positive sense of direction. It comes in the form of a now-famous vision in which the need for the Good News is expressed poignantly by a man in the

Roman province of Macedonia, north of Greece. Surely few visions have led to such worldwide consequences—the "Macedonian call" means that the Christian faith will not remain a Middle-Eastern sect. Once on European soil, it will be on its way to spreading to "all nations" (Matt. 28:19; Acts 8:1).

The phrase "assuredly gathering" has interesting inferences for modern believers who seek the Spirit's guidance. Even after at least two directly negative messages and one positive vision, the missionaries have to use their own wits to discern the Spirit's will. The two words "assuredly gathering" (NIV "concluding") translate one word that infers the quite human mental process of "putting it all together." It is as though God refrains from giving a Word of guidance that is so obvious and clearly-discerned that it robs these Christians of the necessity of using their own good sense.

B. Working toward Philippi, 11-12

11 Therefore loosing from Troas, we came with a straight course to Samothracia, and the next day to Neapolis;

12 And from thence to Philippi, which is the chief city of that part of Macedonia, and a colony: and we were in that city abiding certain days.

Paul and his companions take a direct rout across the narrow stretch of ocean in the northeast Aegean Sea, island-hopping to Samothrace, then, finally, to the port city of Neapolis. The apostle to the Gentiles is now on European soil for the first time.

Philippi was named after one of the namesakes of the great Philip of Macedon, father of Alexander the Great. Its importance lay in its location on the great "Egnatian Way," a primary trade route uniting Europe and Asia. It was also one of the capitals of the province of Macedonia, and had won status as a "colony" under Roman rule.

C. Riverside prayer meeting, 13

13 And on the sabbath we went out of the city by a river side, where prayer was wont to be made; and we sat down, and spake unto the women which resorted thither.

The fact that the missionaries seek out a place of prayer by a river probably indicates that there was no synagogue in Philippi, since Pau's usual practice was to go first to a local synagogue when entering a new city. It was his commission to go "to the Jew first," and only then to the Greeks (Rom. 1:16, etc.). He no doubt asked about the city seeking some place where Jews met. The fact that he found only women there is a clue to why there was no synagogue. The rabbis required a minimum of 10 heads of household (males) for the establishment of an officially recognized synagogue.

III. Conversion of Lydia—14-15
A. Open heart, 14

14 And a certain woman named Lydia, a seller of purple, of the city of Thyatira, which worshipped

God, heard us: whose heart the Lord opened, that she attended unto the things which were spoken of Paul.

Lydia would probably have been a prominent woman in the commerce of Philippi, since "purple" designated the cloth commonly sought by rulers. Coincidentally, her home city of Thyatira was the capital of the province also named Lydia, in western Asia Minor, the origin of the purple dye used in the textiles in which she traded.

The fact that the Lord opened Lydia's heart does not indicate that He closed the hearts of others, but that He discerned that Lydia herself was a person who would be open to the gospel. This "pre-readiness" for the Good News was, according to some translations, a part of the very first announcement of Jesus' birth: it was a message for people "of good will" (Luke 2:14). The fact that God requires a heart for truth and good will in order to receive His message of good will is also emphasized by Paul, who promises God's wrath on those who "received not the love of the truth" (2 Thess. 2:10).

B. Open home, 15

15 And when she was baptized, and her household, she besought us, saying, If ye have judged me to be faithful to the Lord, come into my house, and abide there. And she constrained us.

Once again, baptism is included as a part of the initiation into the Christian faith, although it did not originate with Christian preaching. We recall that John the Baptist also baptized the penitent (John 1:26-28), and ceremonial washings were also a part of some forms of Judaism by Paul's day. Advocates of infant baptism note the fact that Lydia's "household" was baptized as authorization for baptizing children, while their opponents point out that since no mention is made of Lydia's being married, her "household" probably consisted of her servants.

Lydia's statement, "If ye have judged me to be faithful" probably was designed to assure the missionary team that she had in mind no ulterior motives or improprieties by inviting them to stay in her own home. It must have been large, to accommodate all of them—another indication that she must have been a woman of means. Beyond that, she exhibits a surprising amount of trust by inviting these strangers into her home. Because early Christianity was spread by itinerant missionaries, this kind of hospitality quickly became a hallmark of the faith. It would be related to the teaching that those who preach the Word were to be financially compensated (Gal. 6:6; 1 Cor. 9:14).

Unfortunately, some itinerant preachers would take unfair advantage of Lydia's kind of hospitality. In a second-century writing called *The Didache,* the faithful were warned that an itinerant missionary who stayed more than three days was a false prophet!

Evangelistic Emphasis

How you prepare for a trip reveals a lot about your personal character and your life circumstances. Cautious travelers contact AAA and get stacks of details to guide them.

Spontaneous, travel-as-adventure types like to hop in the car and head out of town before they even begin thinking about what route they might take. Seat-of-the-pants travelers don't worry about what may be around the next corner because they enjoy not knowing what lies ahead.

Of course, traveling with small children can be a survival test. Instead of AAA, parents may head for "Toys R Us." And with children along, running out of snack food and Oreos is a disaster second only to running out of gas.

When we think of the apostle Paul, we may envision someone spiritually on fire, making daring escapes from the authorities, or boldly witnessing even from the confines of jail. Today's lesson begins by depicting an almost stalled-out Paul, one who knows he must get moving, but isn't at all sure which way to go. He had to rely on the Holy Spirit for direction, and went at a moment's notice.

On whom do you rely for directions? In bringing the good news to our world, we need to go where the Spirit blows us.

৪০০৪

Memory Selection

And when she was baptized, and her household, she besought us, saying, If ye have judged me to be faithful to the Lord, come into my house, and abide there. And she constrained us.—*Acts 16:15*

Lydia was an important person in the New Testament. She was in ministry with Paul. Lydia became important because she was a lady who prayed. That was how Paul found her, at a "place of prayer." You can touch lives for Jesus Christ as you engage in the spiritual discipline of prayer.

In Guttenberg, Iowa, United Methodist minister Rev. Dr. Karl Goodfellow discovered that when children prayed over a tray of germinated seeds for two weeks but ignored an identical tray, the prayed-for plants grew four inches, while the neglected ones grew only two.

Some doctors are now prescribing prayer for their patients. Isn't it ironic that the medical world sometimes seems to believe in the healing power of prayer more than the church?

Because Lydia believed in and practiced the power of prayer, she joined Paul in changing her world and ours. Are you praying?

Weekday Problems

Lacy was confused. She had clearly heard the call to ministry. She believed that God wanted her to surrender her life to full-time Christian service. She had already completed her undergraduate degree. Lacy had preached many times in her home church and was an excellent preacher. Lacy loved to visit in the hospitals and nursing homes. The elderly of the church loved her, and she was effective with the youth group as well. Lacy had a deeply spiritual walk with Jesus Christ. She prayed before every big decision and had the confidence that the Lord was directing her steps.

What caused her confusion was Lacy's uncle who was a minister in another faith tradition. Lacy had gone home for Thanksgiving, and her uncle spent the whole holiday showing Lacy passages in the Bible he felt forbade female ministers. In front of her whole family he quoted Paul that women should keep silent in the church.

Lacy wanted to know how to harmonize the leadership role of women in the Bible, with Paul telling women to be silent.

*Discuss the role of women in your faith tradition. Is it biblical?

Memos on Missions

We are the children of the converts of foreign missionaries; and fairness means that I must do to others as men once did to me . . . . Your love has a broken wing if it cannot fly across the sea.—*Maltbie D. Babcock*

***

The measure of the Church's successful missionary effort reveals the moral biography of her individual membership.—*Anonymous*

***

For God so loved the world, not just a few,
The wise, the great, the noble and the true,
Or those of favoured class or race or hue.
God loved the world. Do you?

—*Grace E. Uhler*

***

I have but one candle to burn, and would rather burn it out where people are dying in darkness than in a land which is flooded with lights.—*Anonymous missionary*

This Lesson in Your Life

The book of Acts gives a high priority to the home. It was the focal point for the Christian church advancing into the Roman Empire. For example, early Christians met in the home of Jason (17:5), Justus (18:7), and Philip (21:8). They met for prayer (12:12), fellowship meetings (20:7), Holy Communion (2:46), and study (28:17ff). Occasionally they found a house full of seekers who were just waiting to hear the good news of Jesus Christ (10:22) Lydia's house became a hub of ministry for the apostle Paul in his work.

We often forget that for the first 300 years of church history there were no church buildings. The early church met mostly in the homes of members. There were very few public gatherings of the infant church.

The very table in your home has such an appeal to many people. At the table there is good food. I have said elsewhere that church folk know how to cook. At your table there is warmth and love. I would challenge you to make this lesson of Lydia your very own.

At a time when Paul was struggling over which way to go and Lydia was struggling with her own spirituality, the Spirit put them together under Lydia's roof. Imagine the exciting ministry you could have at your home. You could start by asking two or three couples to come to a meal.

Once you have them there, turn the discussion to Jesus Christ and your experience of His life, death, and resurrection. Most of the people you have invited will hear you because you are their friend. Don't ask for a decision, or what they think. Let the Spirit guide the conversation.

There are opportunities for you to open your home for Bible study. Home Bible studies are times when we are close to the way the New Testament Church acted. Small groups in intimate settings are prime grounds for the Spirit of God to work.

There are even programs such as *Alpha*, which work well in a small setting. This basic course in Christianity is built around a meal and the showing of a video presentation. The video is great. After the video presentation, there is an opportunity for small group discussion on the topic for the evening.

If we want to go back to the New Testament Church, we must take the Church back into the home. This is more than a family praying together. It involves inviting other persons to join us in our quest to know Jesus Christ better.

Perhaps if you want to make "This lesson in your life" real, you will suggest that your class meet on Monday night, at your house!

1. Where were Paul and Timothy prior to meeting Lydia?
They were going through the region of Phrygia and Galatia, having been forbidden by the Spirit from entering Asia.

2. Where else did the Spirit keep them from going?
When they were opposite Mysia, they attempted to go to Bithynia, but the Spirit did not allow them.

3. What happened to Paul as they were staying in Troas?
Paul had a dream of a man from Macedonia asking Paul to come to Macedonia and "help us."

4. What happened as a result of Paul's dream?
He immediately began to cross over to Macedonia, convinced that God had called him to that region.

5. Who was now traveling with Paul and Timothy?
From this point on the book of Acts uses first-person pronouns. Scholars believe that Luke joined Paul and Timothy for the Macedonian trip.

6. Where did "we" set sail for after Macedonia?
From Troas they set a straight course to Samothrace, then to Neapolis, and then to Philippi.

7. Who was the "we" making the journey?
Paul, Timothy, and Luke were at least three of the "we's" making the journey.

8. What did the missionaries do on the Sabbath?
They went outside the gate to the river where they found a place of prayer.

9. Who did they meet at this place of prayer?
They met Lydia, a worshiper of God, who was from Thyatira and a merchant in fine purple cloth.

10. What did Lydia do when she met Paul, Timothy, and Luke?
She invited them to stay at her house. The text says that she "prevailed on us" which is Greek for "wouldn't take No for an answer."

It is a particularly male fault that we don't and won't ask for directions. No matter how lost we are, we know that just around the next corner is a landmark that will help us find our way to our destination. We even make jokes about guys who do ask for directions.

There is a story of a Swiss man, looking for directions, who pulls up at a bus stop where two Americans are waiting. *"Entschuldigung, koennen Sie Deutsch sprechen?"* he asks.

The two Americans just stare at him.

"Excusez-moi, parlez vous François?" he tries. The two continue to stare.

"Parlare Italiano?" No response.

"Hablan ustedes Espanol?" Still nothing.

The Swiss guy drives off, extremely disgusted. The first American turns to the second and says, "Y'know, maybe we should learn a foreign language."

Why?" says the other. "That guy knew four languages, and it didn't do him any good."

The story of Paul and Lydia intersects on a couple of fronts. First both of them were really ships sailing without a rudder. Paul had been forbidden by the Spirit from going a couple of places he wanted to go. When the vision of the man of Macedonia occurred, Paul was on the ship before the other two with him could pack. He was being blown by the winds of the Spirit

Lydia was a little different in her life in her journey. She wasn't lost; she was more like a ship without a rudder.

Lydia, a dealer in rich, expensive purple cloth, was herself also without direction. Her life was well-ordered. She was successful and independent. Her "boat" was well-equipped. However even her exquisite purple cloth couldn't fashion a sail capable of moving her heart and soul out of the spiritual doldrums that kept her from moving with divinely directed purpose and perspective.

Only when she heard Paul's preaching did Lydia finally see that there was a different way, a God-informed way, to direct her life. Her own starved soul listened eagerly to Paul. She responded with faith, having herself and her whole household baptized.

Acts 18:1-4, 18-21, 24-28

fter these things Paul departed from Athens, and came to Corinth;

2 And found a certain Jew named Aquila, born in Pontus, lately come from Italy, with his wife Priscilla; (because that Claudius had commanded all Jews to depart from Rome:) and came unto them.

3 And because he was of the same craft, he abode with them, and wrought: for by their occupation they were tentmakers.

4 And he reasoned in the synagogue every sabbath, and persuaded the Jews and the Greeks.

18 And Paul after this tarried there yet a good while, and then took his leave of the brethren, and sailed thence into Syria, and with him Priscilla and Aquila; having shorn his head in Cenchrea: for he had a vow.

19 And he came to Ephesus, and left them there: but he himself entered into the synagogue, and reasoned with the Jews.

20 When they desired him to tarry longer time with them, he consented not;

21 But bade them farewell, saying, I must by all means keep this feast that cometh in Jerusalem: but I will return again unto you, if God will. And he sailed from Ephesus.

24 And a certain Jew named Apollos, born at Alexandria, an eloquent man, and mighty in the scriptures, came to Ephesus.

25 This man was instructed in the way of the Lord; and being fervent in the spirit, he spake and taught diligently the things of the Lord, knowing only the baptism of John.

26 And he began to speak boldly in the synagogue: whom when Aquila and Priscilla had heard, they took him unto them, and expounded unto him the way of God more perfectly.

27 And when he was disposed to pass into Achaia, the brethren wrote, exhorting the disciples to receive him: who, when he was come, helped them much which had believed through grace:

28 For he mightily convinced the Jews, and that publickly, shewing by the scriptures that Jesus was Christ.

Nov. 20

Devotional Reading
Luke 10:1-11

Background Scripture
Acts 18:1–19:10

Memory Selection
Acts 18:3

111

The passages in our lesson today provide rare glimpses into how the apostle Paul interacted with other believers. They picture him as a "team player," not arrogantly protecting his own "turf" as *the* apostle to the Gentiles, but joining hands with others engaged in the task of proclaiming the Good News about Jesus.

This spirit of cooperation was not universal. Competition and jealousy occasionally marred the Church of the first century, just as it does today. Diotrophes, "who loves to have the preeminence" (3 John 9), has had his spiritual relatives. Yet we can take the picture Luke paints of Paul's relationships as the ideal pattern—working together, being willing to teach and to be taught in order to fulfill the Great Commission.

ೞେ

This lesson raises the subject of "Who's in charge here, anyway?" Some traditions have a highly developed "pastor" and clergy-ordination system, while others insist that "We are all ministers," and seek a higher degree of "lay" participation.

Explain to your group that although Paul was "ordained" as an apostle, this lesson shows him working side-by-side with unordained or "lay" persons. What does it take for this kind of cooperation in the modern church? Why is it important to have someone specific "in charge"? Should appointing or ordaining someone specific include the exclusive right to administer ordinances such as baptism and the Lord's Supper? Call the group's attention to the advantages of cooperation of the kind described here.

Teaching Outline	*Daily Bible Readings*
I. Tent-making missionaries—1-4	Mon. 'Limited Commission' Luke 10:1-11
A. Refugees from Rome, 1-2	Tue. Preparing for a Parade Luke 19:28-34
B. Tent-making and preaching, 3-4	Wed. Paul Preaches in Corinth Acts 18:1-8
II. Tour to Jerusalem—18-21	Thu. Preaching and Controversy Acts 18:9-17
A. Companions in mission, 18-19	Fri. Traveling Together Acts 18:18-23
B. Determined journey, 20-21	Sat. Team Ministry Acts 18:24-28
III. Teaching corrected, 24-28	Sun. Appreciation for Co-ministers Rom. 16:3-16
A. Work of Apollos, 24-26	
B. Reference for mission, 27-28	

I. Tent-making missionaries—1-4

A. Refugees from Rome, 1-2

1 After these things Paul departed from Athens, and came to Corinth;

2 And found a certain Jew named Aquila, born in Pontus, lately come from Italy, with his wife Priscilla; (because that Claudius had commanded all Jews to depart from Rome:) and came unto them.

"After these things" refers to some very interesting "things" indeed, including Paul's famous sermon on Mar's Hill, in Athens, the center of Greek culture, philosophy, and the arts (17:22ff.). The apostle is still on his second missionary journey, although he is now beginning to loop back toward Jerusalem for an important feast, and to Antioch of Syria, his home base for this tour.

His tour through Greece would not be complete without visiting the worldly and bustling city of Corinth, the busiest commercial city in the land and the capital of the Roman-ruled province of Achaia. Paul's work here will result in two of the most valuable epistles in the New Testament. He seeks out a colony of Jews, some of whom had fled there during the occasional "pogroms" or waves of persecution against Jews (which often included Christians as well, since Rome often failed to see the distinction early on).

Among these ex-patriot Jews Paul meets Aquila and Priscilla, who had been driven from Rome during persecution instigated by the emperor Claudius—which is independently corroborated in the writings of the Roman historian Suetonius. These Jews, with Greek names, were apparently already Christians, indicating that Christianity had previously been introduced to Rome.

B. Tent-making and preaching, 3-4

3 And because he was of the same craft, he abode with them, and wrought: for by their occupation they were tentmakers.

4 And he reasoned in the synagogue every sabbath, and persuaded the Jews and the Greeks.

Even though he is an apostle, Paul does not seem to consider himself "above" this couple. He joins them both in preaching and in their common trade of tent-making. Tents, made either of goat-hair or leather, were in high demand because of far-flung campaigns by Roman soldiers, and the work of nomadic sheep-herders in the ancient Near East. (Paul's rabbinic training would have included learning a trade, since rabbis were expected to be able to be self-supporting.)

As was his practice, Paul immediately seeks out a synagogue as a base for his preaching, going "to the Jew first" (Rom. 1:16), the people through whom Messiah had come. His message centered on the fact that their Messiah (Grk. *christos,* "anointed") was none other than Jesus of Nazareth. Although some would oppose him (vs. 6), the apostle was encouraged by the response of others (vs. 8), and stayed there a year and a half (vs. 11).

II. Tour to Jerusalem—18-21
A. Companions in mission, 18-19

18 And Paul after this tarried there yet a good while, and then took his leave of the brethren, and sailed thence into Syria, and with him Priscilla and Aquila; having shorn his head in Cenchrea: for he had a vow.

19 And he came to Ephesus, and left them there: but he himself entered into the synagogue, and reasoned with the Jews.

When Jewish opposition reached the point of bringing down the secular authorities upon them, Paul sees that is time to point back toward Antioch of Syria, where he had started (15:35:-41). He takes with him his fellow-tent-makers, showing that by now the three have proved to be a compatible missionary team. (Note that Priscilla [the diminutive form of "Prisca"] is mentioned first here, as in Rom. 16:3. The order in which names were listed often indicated their relative importance, suggesting that by now Priscilla has proved to be the lead evangelist be-

tween the two.)

Why did Paul the Christian take a Jewish vow? Perhaps because of his roots in Judaism, or to show other Jews that his new faith did not call for him to deny those roots. This may have been a "Nazirite" vow of special consecration to God, which included not cutting one's hair for a period of time, then shaving the head and presenting God the hair, a symbol of strength (see Num. 6 for details; note the difference between *Nazirite,* "separate," and *Nazarite,* "from Nazareth"). Cenchrea, where Paul has his hair cut, was Corinth's nearby port city.

When Paul and his companions reach Ephesus, he leaves them to once again preach in the local synagogue. This suggests again that Priscilla and Aquila are Greeks, who may not have been welcome in the synagogue.

B. Determined journey, 20-21

20 When they desired him to tarry longer time with them, he consented not;

21 But bade them farewell, saying, I must by all means keep this feast that cometh in Jerusalem: but I will return again unto you, if God will. And he sailed from Ephesus.

The Jews of the Ephesian synagogue prove to be much more open to Paul's message than many have been, so much so that they beg Paul to stay longer. In an unusual decision, given their interest, the apostle insists that he must go on to Jerusalem. Although this was possibly a Passover, we do not know with certainty. Nor are we told why attending the feast was so important that Paul would leave a Jewish audience actually wanting to know more about Christianity. As it turns out, Paul is able to fulfill his hope to return to Ephesus, on his third missionary journey (19:1).

III. Teaching corrected, 24-28

A. Work of Apollos, 24-26

24 And a certain Jew named Apollos, born at Alexandria, an eloquent man, and mighty in the scriptures, came to Ephesus.

25 This man was instructed in the way of the Lord; and being fervent in the spirit, he spake and taught diligently the things of the Lord, knowing only the baptism of John.

26 And he began to speak boldly in the synagogue: whom when Aquila and Priscilla had heard, they took him unto them, and expounded unto him the way of God more perfectly.

Yet another "layman" who proved important for the spread of the gospel is introduced here. Apollos' home city, Alexandria (Egypt) included an entire section filled with Jews, and had for centuries been an important center of education. Its famous library once included nearly a million books and papyrus rolls, but was later destroyed by fire. As in the case of Rome, the scattering of Christians from Jerusalem had apparently brought the gospel to Alexandria

(traditionally by John Mark). Apollos had taken advantage of the opportunity to study the Scriptures—including no doubt the "Septuagint," the famous Greek version of the Old Testament thought to have been produced in Alexandria in the third- to second-century B.C.

Apollos was already a convert to at least a form of Christianity. He knew "the baptism of John" which was for the repentance of sin (Luke 3:3), but had not heard that baptism into the saving death of Christ had succeeded John's baptism (Rom. 6:3-4), and that this was now the rule of faith. Aquila and Priscilla take him aside with only the authority of "ordinary" Christians, teach him the full gospel, and Apollos gracefully accepts their important correctives.

B. Reference for mission, 27-28

27 And when he was disposed to pass into Achaia, the brethren wrote, exhorting the disciples to receive him: who, when he was come, helped them much which had believed through grace:

28 For he mightily convinced the Jews, and that publickly, shewing by the scriptures that Jesus was Christ.

The eloquent Apollos, now equipped with the full version of Christian initiation as baptism in the name of Christ, now goes to Achaia to build on the foundation Paul had laid in Corinth (19:1). His introduction from the Christians in Ephesus paves the way for his "mighty" and effective preaching there.

Evangelistic Emphasis

For most people the word "evangelism" conjures up a negavite image. I learned the four spiritual laws and know all the evangelistic campaign "tricks." I can answer every objection to accepting Jesus. I have all the pertinent verses highlighted in my "sword." Strangely, however, I never have lead a soul to Christ using those "methods."

The story of Aquila, Priscilla and Paul teaches us more positive lessons about sharing Christ with others. I'll bet those two men had some deep, wonderful conversations about the faith while making tents together.

The good news of Jesus Christ is more effectively shared over a cup of coffee than over an opened religious tract. When we enter into a person's life, we are able to communicate with them as friends. I believe that you can't share the good news of Jesus with a person until you are willing to become a friend to that person. If we don't care enough about a sinner to drink coffee with him, then it is doubtful we care much about his eternal destiny.

Evangelism means finding something in common and building a communication bridge from that. In tent-making Paul and Aquila had something in common. They became friends who shared the adventure of faith.

ଓଇ

And because he was of the same craft, he abode with them, and wrought: for by their occupation they were tentmakers.—*Acts 18:3*

Memory Selection

Carla, invited to attend an important function with her husband, reluctantly asked a wealthy friend if she could borrow a necklace. She borrowed it and then, somehow, lost it. You can imagine her feelings. Carla and her husband took out a loan and bought a very expensive duplicate. It took them years to repay the loan.

Some time later, Carla happened to bump into the woman and she confessed to her what had happened to the original necklace. The lady said, "On no, I wish you had told me. That piece of jewelry was an imitation made of paste."

It is sad that often we find ourselves working, even as a team, for things that do not matter. Paul and Aquila were tent-makers. I am sure they swapped tent-making hints with each other. I am also sure that as they made tents they talked about their experience with Jesus Christ.

Teams are the best way to get the work of the Kingdom done. Jesus sent His disciples out two by two, and it appears as though the Spirit called the early apostles, two by two. Who can you pair up with in order to do the good work of the kingdom of God?

Weekday Problems

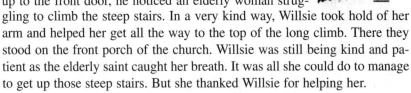

Willsie Martin was a pastor in Los Angeles. His was a large and prominent church at that time. While there, he once had a very humbling experience.

He arrived an hour before the services. As he walked up to the front door, he noticed an elderly woman struggling to climb the steep stairs. In a very kind way, Willsie took hold of her arm and helped her get all the way to the top of the long climb. There they stood on the front porch of the church. Willsie was still being kind and patient as the elderly saint caught her breath. It was all she could do to manage to get up those steep stairs. But she thanked Willsie for helping her.

Then she asked, "Sonny boy, can you tell me who is preaching this morning? Willsie Martin swelled with pride and said, "Willsie Martin is preaching this morning."

She stood there for a moment then said, "Sonny boy, would you mind helping me back down these stairs?"

Some of our weekday problems are reminders that life has a way of bringing us back down the stairs. The trick is never to become too high or too low, but always to keep our Jesus perspective.

*Share a time when a friend kept you from getting too high. Share also a time when someone lifted you up when you were too low.

Speaking of Eloquence

Only one man applauded during the speech. He was slapping his face to stay awake.

***

Ah yes, I remember when this speech began. I was just a teenager.

***

He: He is such a great speaker. I'd rather hear him talk than eat.

She: Me, too. I sat at the head table with him, and I've heard him eat.

***

Student: You heard my speech, professor. Do you think my delivery would improve by putting pebbles in my mouth, like the Greek orator Demosthenes?

Professor: Actually, I would recommend quick-dry cement.

This Lesson in Your Life

The story is old and all too familiar to preachers and church people alike. Mr. and Mrs. Jones have a crisis in their family and they want a preacher with them at that moment. Never mind that the Joneses haven't darkened the door of the church for decades. Overlook the fact that the reason for their absence was the preacher's wife didn't fawn over Mrs. Jones' peach cobbler at a pot-luck back in the '50s. Ignore all the visits, time, and effort that were given to wooing the Joneses back to church. They want a preacher to drop everything and make them the center of his life. At least they want that much ministerial attention until the crisis has past and things are "normal" again.

The aggravation for us professional clergy is that this happens almost every week. The reason we can live with it, and sometimes through it, is that there are others in the church that are faithful. Aquila and Priscilla would have made wonderful additions to any church. These two people were obviously well-traveled. They were well versed in their faith. They were open to the ministry of Paul.

In Romans, Paul told the church that these two "risked their necks for him." They welcomed him, first into their home and lives. Paul and Aquila went into business together for a while. Wouldn't you have like to have been a fly on the tent canvas as those two worked?

Aquila and Priscilla "pulled up stakes" and took a trip with the Paul. They had to have known how dangerous it would be to travel with him. He had this ability to anger the Jews in any city.

Aquila and Priscilla were right in the middle of the explosive growth of the Church. We learn from their encounter with Apollos that they were also involved in sharing the faith. Some adults are willing to be adventurous in the faith, without thinking through their decisions or faith positions. From the encounter with Apollos, you might assume Aquila and Priscilla had a faith that was well reasoned and logical. The scholar Apollos from Alexandria learned more about the faith from a tent-maker and his wife.

Reading the story of Aquila and Priscilla makes one wish for a church full of people with adventurous faith. They wouldn't spend all of their time "chatting across the fence" about the hymns the preacher was picking. The flowers in the sanctuary wouldn't matter to them. They wouldn't be interested in the report of the committee on committees. People with adventurous faith have only one thing on their minds. People with adventurous faith want to talk about Jesus.

GETTING THE FACTS STRAIGHT

1. What information does the 18th chapter of Acts give about the travels of Paul?
After preaching in Athens, Paul traveled to Corinth.

2. What did the same chapter of Acts tell about the travels of Aquila?
He was born in Pontus, and later moved to Rome. When Claudius ordered the Jews out of Rome, Aquila traveled to Corinth.

3. What did Paul and Aquila share in common?
They were both tent-makers. Since tents in the 1st century were made of leather, they could also have been tanners. (The word "tent-makers" is vague in Greek.)

4. While Paul was working with Aquila, what else was he doing?
Paul was going to the synagogue and arguing with the Jews and the Greeks about Jesus.

5. How long was Paul in Corinth?
Verse 18 states that Paul stayed in Corinth for "a considerable time."

6. Where did Paul travel from Corinth?
Paul went to Syria. Aquila and Priscilla accompanied him on this trip.

7. Putting the information from the 18th chapter together, construct the travel itinerary of Aquila and Priscilla.
From Rome they traveled to Corinth. They then left with Paul for Syria. By the end of the chapter they had arrived in Ephesus.

8. What preacher did Aquila and Priscilla encounter in Ephesus?
Apollos was in Ephesus preaching "the way of the Lord."

9. What happened between Apollos and Aquila and Priscilla?
Apollos had an inadequate understanding of some matters of faith. Priscilla and Aquila explained things to him "more accurately."

10. What does Romans 16:3 indicate about Aquila and Priscilla?
Apparently they had returned to Rome after Claudius' ban was lifted, and a church was meeting in their house.

Two brothers owned a threshing floor on Mt. Moriah. Tradition held that in exchange for the use of the threshing floor, the brothers got to keep all the grain that wasn't collected in a day. When several people came to thresh out grain on a daily basis there was an abundant supply left over. According to the rabbis, several sacks would be left over.

The two brothers were quite different. One brother had a wife and 12 children. He lived in an area on one side of the threshing floor. The other brother had no wife and had no children. He lived on the other side of the threshing floor.

The business the brothers shared thrived so that each of them had a room where their share of the grain could be stored. Each afternoon they would gather the grain into sacks, and store it in their respective bins.

Each night, neither of the brothers would sleep well. One brother would lie on his pallet and thinking. "It is not right that I have so much grain. I am all alone. I have no wife. I have no children. And my brother has all those hungry mouths of feed." So this brother would rise and, hidden by the darkness, would take one of his sacks of grain across the threshing floor and place the bag in his brother's storage room.

Later, the other brother would lie awake thinking to himself, "It is not right that I have all this grain. My brother is all alone in the world. When I am an old man I will have 12 sons to take care of me. Who will take care of my brother in his old age? So this brother would rise, take one of *his* sacks of grain, and take it to his brother's storage bin.

This went on for years. Each night the brothers took a sack from their supply and gave it to the other brother. Until one night, for whatever reason—the rabbis never really said—the brothers were awake at the same time, each one worrying about the other. They both arose at the same time, and both went to their supply of grain. Sure enough, they met in the middle of the threshing floor. When they looked at one another and saw the sacks, they fell together in an embrace.

God looked down from heaven and decided to honor the place and the brothers by having a temple built on their threshing floor.

Paul, Priscilla, and Aquila are also examples of what powerful results are realized when we work together for God's cause.

Lesson 13

Saying Goodbye

Acts 20:17-28, 36-38

And from Miletus he sent to Ephesus, and called the elders of the church.

18 And when they were come to him, he said unto them, Ye know, from the first day that I came into Asia, after what manner I have been with you at all seasons,

19 Serving the Lord with all humility of mind, and with many tears, and temptations, which befell me by the lying in wait of the Jews:

20 And how I kept back nothing that was profitable unto you, but have shewed you, and have taught you publickly, and from house to house,

21 Testifying both to the Jews, and also to the Greeks, repentance toward God, and faith toward our Lord Jesus Christ.

22 And now, behold, I go bound in the spirit unto Jerusalem, not knowing the things that shall befall me there:

23 Save that the Holy Ghost witnesseth in every city, saying that bonds and afflictions abide me.

24 But none of these things move me, neither count I my life dear unto myself, so that I might finish my course with joy, and the ministry, which I have received of the Lord Jesus, to testify the gospel of the grace of God.

25 And now, behold, I know that ye all, among whom I have gone preaching the kingdom of God, shall see my face no more.

26 Wherefore I take you to record this day, that I am pure from the blood of all men.

27 For I have not shunned to declare unto you all the counsel of God.

28 Take heed therefore unto yourselves, and to all the flock, over the which the Holy Ghost hath made you overseers, to feed the church of God, which he hath purchased with his own blood.

36 And when he had thus spoken, he kneeled down, and prayed with them all.

37 And they all wept sore, and fell on Paul's neck, and kissed him,

38 Sorrowing most of all for the words which he spake, that they should see his face no more. And they accompanied him unto the ship.

Devotional Reading
Acts 20:31-35
Background Scripture
Acts 20:17-38
Memory Selection
Acts 20:38

Nov. 27

121

The setting of this lesson is toward the end of Paul's third missionary journey, and the last recorded in the book of Acts. His next and final trip in Luke's account will be when he is taken to Rome as a prisoner.

The selected passages focus on one of the most poignant scenes in Paul's life—his farewell to the elders of the church at Ephesus. We have seen the openness of some in the synagogue at Ephesus where Paul first preached. Perhaps some of those very hearers were converted then, and became the leaders to whom Paul bids a tearful good-bye here. We are treated to a glimpse of both the over-riding purpose of Paul's life, and the depths of some of his relationships.

What significant "Good-byes" have members of your group experienced? We say Good-bye to parents when we leave home to begin life on our own. We part from friends when work takes us to other cities. Many have special memories of saying Good-bye to when military service calls. The teacher will need to be careful not to probe tender feelings that are too sad to share.

Alternatively, you can review other farewells in Scripture, such as those referred to in two of the Daily Bible Readings. Naomi said good-bye to Ruth and Orpah (Ruth 1:6-14). There is David's farewell to his close friend Jonathan (1 Sam. 20:32-42). Note that Paul's farewell to the Ephesian elders also offers some practical insights into this common if sometimes painful experience.

<table>
<tr><td colspan="2">

Teaching Outline

I. Faithful Service—17-21
  A. Tears and temptations, 17-19
  B. Testifying to all, 20-21
II. Future Expectations—22-24
  A. Uncertain road, 22-23
  B. Central issue, 24
III. Fulfilling the Ministry—25-28
  A. Responsibility discharged, 25-27
  B. Charge to the elders, 28
IV. Final Farewell—36-38

</td></tr>
</table>

Daily Bible Readings

Mon.	Parting from Orpah Ruth 1:6-14
Tue.	David and Jonathan 1 Samuel 20:32-42
Wed.	Returning to Jerusalem Acts 20:1-6
Thu.	Last Visit to Troas Acts 20:7-12
Fri.	Farewell at Ephesus Acts 20:17-24
Sat.	Charge to the Elders Acts 20:25-31
Sun.	Sorrowful Farewell Acts 20:32-38

Verse by Verse

I. Faithful Service—17-21

A. Tears and temptations, 17-19

17 And from Miletus he sent to Ephesus, and called the elders of the church.

18 And when they were come to him, he said unto them, Ye know, from the first day that I came into Asia, after what manner I have been with you at all seasons,

19 Serving the Lord with all humility of mind, and with many tears, and temptations, which befell me by the lying in wait of the Jews:

Paul is on the last leg of his third missionary journey. He is heading once more back to Jerusalem for a Jewish feast day (vs. 16b), and revisiting congregations he had established on his second missionary tour. It is not clear why he wants to bypass the city of Ephesus (vss. 16-17). Perhaps it is because he knows that going there would plunge him into visits with so many friends from his previous visit that his stay would extend too long for him to reach Jerusalem in time for the Passover feast. Or, in view of the civil disturbance Paul's earlier visit had precipitated (Acts 19), he may want to avoid a similar time-consuming scene. At any rate, he sends word to the elders of the church at Ephesus to come to nearby Miletus for a farwell visit.

"Elders" were basic and natural in the polity or organization of the early church, since the earliest Christians were Jews, and their synagogues had elders. (The word for elders is *presbyteroi*, which would become the basis for "Presbyterian" church organization.)

Because Paul is making a somewhat formal "hand-off" of responsibility to the elders from Ephesus, he is careful first to recount, as a pattern, his own responsible behavior when he had been among them. He had beem like a general who will not command his troops to enter a battle he himself will not fight. He has been a *servant* who is *constant* and *steadfast* (faithful "at all seasons"); *humble*; concerned to the point of *tears;* and resistant against *temptations.* Since this term is followed by a reference to Jewish persecution, Paul perhaps refers to his lack of enmity and retaliation in response to Jewish attacks (see 19:9).

B. Testifying to all, 20-21

20 And how I kept back nothing that was profitable unto you, but have shewed you, and have taught you publickly, and from house to house,

21 Testifying both to the Jews, and also to the Greeks, repentance toward God, and faith toward our Lord Jesus Christ.

Paul had withheld no useful teaching from the Ephesian church, whether from his in-depth training in Jewish studies or from his more recent acquaintance with Christian truth received directly from Christ, himself (see Gal. 1:11-12). No one could accuse Paul of being secretive or selective in sharing this teaching, for he had delivered it in both public places and in private homes. The core of his teaching, both to Jews and Greeks, was that Jesus is the Christ, and that He calls all people to him through repentance and faith. Implied in this statement is Paul's typical insistence that this means of coming to salvation is apart from keeping the Law of Moses.

II. Future Expectations—22-24

A. Uncertain road, 22-23

22 And now, behold, I go bound in the spirit unto Jerusalem, not knowing the things that shall befall me there:

23 Save that the Holy Ghost witnesseth in every city, saying that bonds and afflictions abide me.

Paul feels a certain amount of coercion from the Holy Spirit in his intent to go to Jerusalem, no doubt because He is sensitive to God's overall plan to use him in reaching as many people as possible. Apparently the apostle also had some personal desire to make this trip, as well as to "see Rome" (19:21b). This is no pleasure trip or political junket at the brethren's expense: the Spirit is not only urging him to go, but promising more persecution. Of course this only increases Paul's opportunities to preach the Word, as Luke will faithfully record in the rest of Acts.

B. Central issue, 24

24 But none of these things move me, neither count I my life dear unto myself, so that I might finish my course with joy, and the ministry, which I have received of the Lord Jesus, to testify the gospel of the grace of God.

We are not surprised that the promised trouble that awaited Paul does not keep him from wanting to press on. His ambition is set on a higher goal than safe passage: that of fulfilling the ministry of telling the Good News of God's grace, to which he had been called by none other than the Lord Jesus. Even the prospect of losing his life in this cause did not disturb him, for "to depart and be with Christ is far better" (Philip. 1:23) than merely clinging, without a higher purpose, to the extension of life on earth. He has a "course" to finish, as a runner determines to finish a race. Not long before his death, he will tell his younger co-worker Timothy that he has finished this course (2 Tim. 4:7).

III. Fulfilling the Ministry—25-28

A. Responsibility discharged, 25-27

25 And now, behold, I know that ye all, among whom I have gone preaching the kingdom of God, shall see my face no more.

26 Wherefore I take you to record this day, that I am pure from the blood of all men.

27 For I have not shunned to declare unto you all the counsel of God.

Whether from a premonition based on the developing religious and political opposition he sees forming, or from direct revelation, Paul is certain that he and the Ephesian elders will not meet again. Thus he repeats in summary form his assertion that no one at Ephesus can rightly accuse him if they are lost, because he has given them all the message God gave him.

B. Charge to the elders, 28

28 Take heed therefore unto yourselves, and to all the flock, over the which the Holy Ghost hath made you overseers, to feed the church of God, which he hath purchased with his own blood.

Now it is the Ephesian elders' turn to take responsibility for sharing the whole counsel of God. In a somewhat formal charge or commission, Paul describes the elders' work as *overseeing* (from Grk. *episcopos*) and *feeding* or "pasturing" the church as a shepherd pastures his sheep. Along with the word *elder*, previously used, we learn here that helping the early churches function and protecting them from heresy was basically the responsibility of (1) *older* persons, with the authority and responsibility of (2) *overseeing* (lit. "bishoping") and (3) *nurturing* (lit. "pasturing," thence "pastoring") the people of God.

With the terms "elders," "bishops" and "pastors" interchangeably describing local church leadership, we may also note here that bishops would only later come to have authority over local elders. They were first given such roles over churches in a particular city ("metropolitan bishops"). Beyond that, a hierarchical pattern gradually developed, probably influenced by the organization of the Roman Empire.

IV. Final Farewell—36-38

36 And when he had thus spoken, he kneeled down, and prayed with them all.

37 And they all wept sore, and fell on Paul's neck, and kissed him,

38 Sorrowing most of all for the words which he spake, that they should see his face no more. And they accompanied him unto the ship.

The most common position in prayer among Jews was standing, and we are not told when kneeling became the norm among early Christians. More striking than the posture here is the emotion and feelings of kinship that had developed between these elders and the man who had first come to them with the gospel. The thought of never seeing his friends again was itself enough to drive him to his knees. With such an emotional farewell, the elders see Paul off to a future that was uncertain only to human eyes. The Spirit seems to know very well the significance of what lies ahead for the great apostle to the Gentiles.

Evangelistic Emphasis

It can be tough to say "Good-bye." Watch people at the airport. Hugs. Tears. Emotions. Like the train station was in a bygone era. A place of great emotion as people who love each other say good-bye.

Some "good-byes" have become famous. In *Romeo and Juliet*, the heroine says, "Good-night, Good-night, / parting is such sweet sorrow. / That I shall say, good-night, till it be morrow . . . ."

Romeo floated home after hearing those sweet words.

What about the farewell that Rhett Butler made famous as he stood in the Georgia fog? Scarlett asked him, "Where shall I go? What shall I do?" Rhett famously replied that frankly he didn't give a . . . . Well, the answer almost got censored in 1939.

General Douglas MacArthur didn't say Good bye, but "I shall return." He kept his word. Richard Nixon told reporters in 1962, "You won't have Dick Nixon to kick around any more." He was wrong.

The phrase "good-bye" combines the Old and Middle English words "God be with you." They can be the hardest words of all to say.

Paul said Good-bye very well. He reminded those he was leaving that their duty was to keep working to tell the world about Jesus Christ.

ೞೞಐ

Memory Selection

Take heed therefore unto yourselves, and to all the flock, over which the Holy Ghost hath made you overseers, to feed the church of God, which he hath purchased with His own blood.—*Acts 20:28*

In saying good bye to his fellow workers for Christ, Paul left some instructions that still are helpful as we work in the Church. His first words were "take heed unto yourselves." You have a responsibility to take care of yourself spiritually. No one is going to stand over you and make sure you pray. No one is going to keep track of the number of verses you read each day. Only you will know how much time you give to the service of God. These are wise words that advise us to stay away from those places and situations that are not conducive to our soulful growth. We need to care for our soul because we have a responsibility.

As teachers, preachers, and leaders Jesus is looking to us as examples of Christ-likeness. Are you growing each day into a person who looks more and more like Jesus Christ? Paul's farewell words challenge us to be and do our best for the work of the Church and the kingdom. They say that the torch has been passed to you. Live faithfully, and pass it on to the next generation.

Weekday Problems

Dorothy was a saint of the church. At age 95, she was still going strong. Dorothy would pick the preacher up every Thursday afternoon and together they would visit the shut-ins of the congregation. Dorothy insisted that she drive. The preacher discovered that riding with a 95-year-old enabled him to feel closer to God. As she ran a red light, Dorothy would giggle that she had had a driver's license for 75 years. She explained that she would have had one longer, but they didn't issue them until the 1920s.

One day Dorothy checked into the hospital for surgery. The surgeon discovered she had an advanced cancer. He did what he could. As a result of his efforts, Dorothy was on a breathing machine and she would have to take IV food for the rest of her life. One afternoon the pastor was called and told that Dorothy wanted to be removed from the machine.

When the pastor arrived in the room, Dorothy was awake but still on the machine. When the pastor said, "Dorothy don't you want to stay on these machines and get better?" She shook her head, "No." When he asked, "Are you ready to go to heaven and see Jesus?" She shook her head, "Yes." The machine was removed, and four hours later Dorothy went to see Jesus.

*Discuss how final good-byes have changed your life.

Church Bulletins' Hmms *and* Oops

The sermon this morning is "Jesus Walks on the Water." The sermon tonight will be "Searching for Jesus."
***
Come to the recreation hall Wednesday at 8 pm. and watch our youth basketball team kill Christ the King.
***
Ladies, don't forget the rummage sale. It's a good chance to get rid of those things not worth keeping around the house. Don't forget your husbands.
***
The peace-making meeting scheduled for today has been cancelled due to a conflict.
***
Don't let worry kill you off. Let the church help.
***
For those of you who have children and don't know it, we have a nursery downstairs.

This Lesson in Your Life

You might enjoy studying with your class all of the farewells of the apostle Paul. You would simply need to read the last three or four verses of every New Testament book he wrote. You have heard his words used often in church as benedictions. Benedictions are also final words.

A Methodist minister was once holding a revival service. It was Sunday at lunch time. After a wonderful morning service, the Methodist evangelist was invited to lunch at the home of the local Methodist pastor. The tea was on the table, poured. The visiting evangelist asked for the sugar which he was promptly given. Like most of us ministers do after preaching, he gulped it down. Then he asked for more, which the hostess was glad to serve. They had the prayer.

After the "Amen" the food started around. The Methodist evangelist was holding up the mashed potatoes. He was looking for the sugar for his new glass of tea. He spied the sugar beside the wife of the local Methodist pastor, and asked, "Would you please pass me the sugar?" Looking at the contents in the bottom of his glass, the hostess replied, *"Why don't you stir up what you've already got."* They were the last words of that particular conversation.

Paul wanted his final words to stir up the faith that was already in the leaders of the church at Ephesus. It was more than a half-time pep talk. He knew he was speaking words that the people were waiting to hear. His words were meant to last them a lifetime as they worked for the sake of Jesus Christ.

We never know when we might be speaking our last words. I hope that you will make all of your words count. I hope that your lesson this Sunday is the best lesson that you have ever given. We never know when a member of our church will be sitting in God's house for the last time. We never know when it is our time to sit in the church for the last time.

Make your words count as people listen to you talk about the life of Jesus Christ. Make your words meaningful as you tell how the resurrected Lord has changed your life. People want to hear your words of challenge as they seek to live in a Christ-like way in the coming week.

In the Church's theology, our last words are only final on earth. When we are finished speaking here, we will see Jesus face to face and we can hear His words of welcome, "Well done good and faithful servant." Until you hear those words of Jesus, let your words be loving—because one day you will speak your last words.

1. Paul's farewell speech was spoken where, and to whom?
Paul was in Miletus when he sent messengers to Ephesus asking the elders of the church to meet him.

2. How did Paul sum up his ministry in Asia?
He said he had endured the trials and the plots of the Jews, and that he had proclaimed the message of Christ publicly and from house to house.

3. What was the message Paul preached?
He preached a message of repentance toward God and faith toward Jesus Christ.

4. To whom did Paul preach his message of repentance and faith?
Paul preached to both Greeks and Jews.

5. Where was Paul going when he said Good-bye to the Ephesian elders?
Paul was on his way to Jerusalem, not knowing what would happen there.

6. What testimony did the Holy Spirit make to Paul in each city?
The Spirit testified to Paul that imprisonment and persecution was awaiting him in Jerusalem.

7. What was Paul's ultimate goal in life, despite what lay ahead?
Paul wanted to finish his course and ministry that he received from the Lord Jesus.

8. What did Paul confidently tell the Ephesian elders about their relationship?
He was sure that none of them would ever see his face again.

9. What happened when Paul finished speaking to these elders?
He knelt with all of the elders and they prayed.

10. Describe the final scene here as Paul said Good bye.
There was much weeping. The elders embraced Paul and kissed him, grieving especially because of what he had said.

This story is told of Moses Mendelssohn, grandfather of the celebrated composer, who lived in the 18th century. When the time came for him to marry, his father arranged for the warm and compassionate young man to marry Fromet Guggenheim, a wealthy and beautiful young woman.

What made this union unique was not only the humble origins of Mendelssohn, but the fact that although he had a brilliant mind, he was a small, ugly hunchback. As was the custom of the day, the marriage was arranged and a celebration was held for the young couple to meet. When the bride-to-be arrived, Mendelssohn was deep in conversation. Seeing him across the room she was repulsed, and emphatically informed her father that the engagement was not to be.

On hearing that the woman did not wish to marry him, Mendelssohn requested and was granted a conversation with her. After they had talked awhile, he said "I wish to tell you a story. As you know, all marriages are arranged in heaven. Before I was born an angel was escorting me to earth, and I asked if it was possible to see the woman God had selected for me. The angel answered that although this was somewhat unusual, he did not think it impossible. I was granted one look, and to my astonishment the woman had an ugly hump on her back. I pleaded with God, 'It is not fair that a beautiful young woman have a hump on her back. She will be the object of scorn and derision. Give *me* the hump, and let her be beautiful.'" Mendelssohn was silent for a moment before he said, "God heard my prayer."

Fromet Guggenheim is said to have been astounded at the warmth and compassion of this young man, whom she later married.

God took our deformities and our sins, making them His own. He conquered forever the power of sin and death in our lives. Through the grace of Jesus we experience the love of God. Those are really beautiful final words, don't you think?

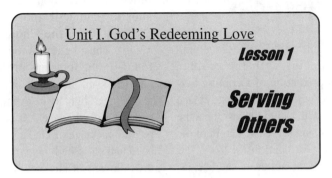

Unit I. God's Redeeming Love

Lesson 1

Serving Others

Isaiah 42:1-8

Behold my servant, whom I uphold; mine elect, in whom my soul delighteth; I have put my spirit upon him: he shall bring forth judgment to the Gentiles.

2 He shall not cry, nor lift up, nor cause his voice to be heard in the street.

3 A bruised reed shall he not break, and the smoking flax shall he not quench: he shall bring forth judgment unto truth.

4 He shall not fail nor be discouraged, till he have set judgment in the earth: and the isles shall wait for his law.

5 Thus saith God the LORD, he that created the heavens, and stretched them out; he that spread forth the earth, and that which cometh out of it; he that giveth breath unto the people upon it, and spirit to them that walk therein:

6 I the LORD have called thee in righteousness, and will hold thine hand, and will keep thee, and give thee for a covenant of the people, for a light of the Gentiles;

7 To open the blind eyes, to bring out the prisoners from the prison, and them that sit in darkness out of the prison house.

8 I am the LORD: that is my name: and my glory will I not give to another, neither my praise to graven images.

Devotional Reading
Isaiah 41:8-13

Background Scripture
Isaiah 41–42

Memory Selection
Isaiah 42:6

This unit on "God's Redeeming Love" begins with the prophet Isaiah's prediction of a coming Servant who will right wrongs, replace injustice with righteousness, heal the suffering, and serve as "a light of the Gentiles" (or "nations").

Some eight centuries later, Jesus, the Messiah, will prove to be the fulfillment of such prophecies. Then the apostle Paul will apply them to Christ's Body, the Church (Acts 13:47). Thus, believers today are to follow in the footsteps of the "Servant Messiah," meeting human needs, and being a "light to the nations." This is not a "social gospel"; it is *the* gospel, the message of God's love enlivened and enfleshed—*incarnated*—by the followers of His only Son.

෬෬

Ask group members to name particular examples of *injustice* in today's world. They may think of countries in which a dictator such as Saddam Hussein kills thousands of innocent people, court systems in which the wealthy have vastly more opportunity than the poor to get "the best justice money can buy," areas at home or abroad where the poor are denied adequate housing and/or health care, etc.

Point out that historically, while mostly Christian nations do not have a spotless record, individual Christians have made a difference. One example was Lord Wilberforce, a Christian member of Parliament in England, who influenced anti-slavery legislation. The Old Testament included justice as one element of the rule of the Messiah. How can the Church promote that cause today?

Teaching Outline	*Daily Bible Readings*	
I. Judgment and Grace—1-5	Mon.	Victor from the East Isaiah 41:1-7
A. Gentle servant, 1-2	Tue.	God Will Strengthen Israel Isaiah 41:8-13
B. Judgment and truth, 3-4	Wed.	God Will Care for His Own Isaiah 41:14-20
II. Justice and Healing—5-8	Thu.	Greater than Babylon Isaiah 41:21-29
A. Creator's Covenant, 5-6	Fri.	My Servant Brings Justice Isaiah 42:1-9
B. Healing and justice, 7-8	Sat.	Sing Praise to God! Isaiah 42:10-17
	Sun.	Blind and Deaf to God Isaiah 42:18-25

Verse by Verse

I. Judgment and Grace—1-5
A. Gentle servant, 1-2

1 Behold my servant, whom I uphold; mine elect, in whom my soul delighteth; I have put my spirit upon him: he shall bring forth judgment to the Gentiles.

2 He shall not cry, nor lift up, nor cause his voice to be heard in the street.

The prophet Isaiah preached in the courts of the kings of the southern kingdom of Judah some 800 years before Christ. Most of his ministry was during a period of moral and spiritual decline in the land. It seemed as though the people were ignoring the fact that they, in God's love and grace, had been separated from "the nations" to be His special people. He had delivered their forefathers from Egypt, and granted them the land of Canaan. Yet they had followed after other gods, ignored the needs of the poor and the sick, and set up courts that defended the greed of the wealthy. Isaiah was one of several prophets during these dreary days who called for spiritual and moral renewal.

The section of Isaiah that begins with chapter 40 envisions a divine Servant of God who would both judge people for their unfaithfulness and lead a movement of reform. At first, Israel itself is said to be this servant (41:8, 44:1). Then Isaiah predicts that God will have to resort to using Cyrus, king of Persia, as God's "anointed" who will bring about justice even at the expense of allowing him to conquer God's own people (45:1). Even though Israel abandoned their status as God's "elect" people, He would choose a Remnant and elect a Servant in their stead.

Although both Israel and Cyrus brought partial fulfillment of Isaiah's prophecies, their reforms were sadly flawed and short-lived. Furthermore, neither Cyrus nor Israel had a vision of spreading God's justice to the Gentiles. Eventually it became clear to the early Christians that Jesus of Nazareth was the ultimate fulfillment of the Servant of whom Isaiah prophesied.

Thus Matthew 12:14-21 applies these opening verses of Isaiah 42 to Jesus. It is in the light of the New Testament's treatment of Isaiah that we see Christ as the suffering Servant in whom God put His Spirit. It is Jesus whose teaching brought the foundations of justice that would become "a light to the Gentiles." Matthew applies Isaiah 42:2-3 to the gentle way the Messiah began His work, without fanfare or loud street-preaching, and even, at first, the admonition to keep His identity secret until it is time to make it known (as in Mark 3:10-12).

B. Judgment and truth, 3-4

3 A bruised reed shall he not break, and the smoking flax shall he not quench: he shall bring forth judgment unto truth.

4 He shall not fail nor be discouraged, till he have set judgment in the earth: and the isles shall wait for his law.

Verse 3 seems to imply that Isaiah knows that in some people, both Jew and Gentile, concepts of justice will survive even during general times of immorality and injustice. When Messiah comes, He will not quench these remnants of God's justice and righteousness, but will "blow on the coals" He finds glowing, however faintly, until they are revived into a flame of truth.

One of Isaiah's distinctive concepts is that the Coming One will administer His will universally, not just to the Jews. Thus "the earth," and not just Israel, will benefit from His judgment. "The isles" was a phrase commonly used referring to the islands in the nearby Mediterranean Sea as standing for "the ends of the earth."

Nothing could be more obvious than that the rule of the Messiah has not been accepted universally. However, in the triumph of the resurrection of the Suffering Servant we see the seeds of the just and universal reign of Christ at the end of the ages. It is only by the longer view that includes the Second Coming of Christ that this vision of universal justice will be seen to be fact. Until then, God's people are to practice justice in His name as a sign of the reality of what the Old Testament refers to as "He who comes."

II. Justice and Healing—5-8

A. Creator's Covenant, 5-6

5 Thus saith God the LORD, he that created the heavens, and stretched them out; he that spread forth the earth, and that which cometh out of it; he that giveth breath unto the people upon it, and spirit to them that walk therein:

6 I the LORD have called thee in righteousness, and will hold thine hand, and will keep thee, and give thee for a covenant of the people, for a light of the Gentiles;

Verse 5 again reveals Isaiah's concept of a God who created not just the Jewish nation but the entire heavens and earth, with all their peoples. This universal vision is remarkable for the eighth-century B.C. It grounds justice not in the laws of local regimes but in the Creator of all regimes.

Although the rabbis would struggle to understand it, verse 6 addresses the Servant himself, the Messiah. It promises that throughout His struggles God's hand will keep Him, offering Him as a "covenant" not just to the Jews but as "a light to the Gentiles." It is this passage that old Simeon will recall when he realizes that God had allowed him to live long enough to see the infant Jesus, the Messiah Himself (Luke 2:32). It is also this "light to the Gentiles" (or "nations") concept that the apostle Paul will apply to the Church in Acts 13:47. Although the Jews declined to accept the Messiah God sent to them, the Church and its missionaries took on themselves, as "the Body of Christ," the commission to be the Light to the world, as God intended. They did this by proclaiming the New Covenant, which Isaiah foresees will be for all people instead of, as in the case of the Old Covenant, being limited to the Jews.

B. Healing and justice, 7-8

7 To open the blind eyes, to bring out the prisoners from the prison, and them that sit in darkness out of the prison house.

8 I am the LORD: that is my name: and my glory will I not give to another, neither my praise to graven images.

A part of this New Covenant that God will extend, through His Servant, Christ, includes healing and justice. This is why the healing miracles of Jesus are so important. They not only blessed the people who received healing; they were a sign that Jesus came in the power of fulfilled prophecy. The reference to bringing out prisoners is prompted by the wide injustices so prominent in the ancient world—and in some parts of the world today. It does not

envision criminals not being punished, but the eventual freedom of "political" prisoners and others who are unjustly imprisoned.

Why does verse 8 bring up the subject of "graven images" in the context of justice? Because Israel's tendency to substitute idol worship for the true God shows that humans tend to behave like the being they worship. In ancient Canaan, for example, some idols were thought to demand child sacrifice. Thus, why should their worshippers consider children, indeed human life in general, to be sacred? We have only to recall that revivals in Christianity have often been accompanied by social reforms to see how this principle has been evident in history. Although "Christian" societies have been guilty of slavery and the forced labor of children, when they have been true to the worship of the true God, the violation of human rights has been corrected.

Isaiah is famous for preserving this relationship between human justice and the worship of the true God. One of the finest pieces of irony or satire is Isaiah 44:9ff. There, the prophet ridicules anyone who goes to the artistic trouble to carve a "god" out of one end of a log, and stick the other end in the fire by which to warm himself! The concept of treating other human beings with respect is grounded in the idea of respecting God, and understanding that as a loving Creator He also respects His handiwork.

Evangelistic Emphasis

We are much more comfortable with evangelism that happens in a crowd. When we go to mass rallies or join with an arena full of people in worship, that takes the responsibility of evangelism off of our shoulders. We leave the personal approach to the preachers and the televangelists. To this extent, evangelism has joined step with mass marketing schemes and strategies.

Isaiah, however, presents a Suffering Servant who is a meek person. Meekness is not a good word for our culture and maybe not the word you would think about when thinking about evangelism. Meekness, in the Biblical usage, means "power under control." The servant has all the power of God yet is very careful in how he uses that power.

I wonder what it means when we say someone has a "powerful witness" for Jesus Christ? Does it mean the "witness" overwhelms the message of Jesus? Can someone with a "powerful witness" really point to Christ, or do they end up pointing to themselves? The meek and gentle witness of the servant pointed beyond the personality of the servant to the essence of God.

A meek witness is a personal witness. It is not the powerful witness of mass appeal, but the gentle witness of a personal contact with another soul.

ॐ

I, the Lord, have called thee in righteousness, and will hold thine hand, and will keep thee, and give thee for a covenant to the people, for a light of the nations.—*Isaiah 42: 6*

We live in a scary world. Since 9/11, the world is less secure than it was 10 years ago. We have solved the arms race and now deal with the faceless threat of terrorism. We are learning that the usual ways of fighting wars don't work with terrorists. So, what can we do?

The verse from Isaiah has two images that offer us comfort and hope. The first image is that *God will hold our hand.* When we are walking "through the valley of the shadow of death," it is comforting to know that the hand we hold belongs to Almighty God.

The second image that brings hope is that *we are called to be a light to the nations.* Even in uncertain times we can be confident that we are God's people and that He is with us. The confidence we have in Christ is a witness to "the nations." As people see Jesus in us, they may come to know His saving love and power for their lives. Our hope is that we so let the light of Christ shine in our lives that our whole world is transformed.

Weekday Problems

Steve was too good for his own good. He didn't believe in saying "No" to anyone. He had a good job as custodian of First Church. He loved his job, because as custodian he could help anyone. If someone needed a room readied for a meeting, Steve would do it. If a group needed a room and a small meal, Steve would be in the kitchen cooking. If one of the widows of the church needed a light fixture changed or some plumbing fixed, Steve was at her house before she knew it. He was always saying Yes to invitations to help others. Sometimes he said Yes to several people at once, and found himself calling to apologize for being late, because he was busy helping another person.

Steve's wife and family were not thrilled with Steve's helpfulness. Steve missed family outings and important family events because he was helping others around the church. His marriage and family sufffered from it.

Steve's helpfulness caused other men in the church to feel their skills weren't needed. When the men's group volunteered to paint a couple of rooms for a widow, they found that Steve had already done their work for them.

*How can we balance our priorities and still be servants of the Lord?

*How could you help Steve's wife and family?

*Why do you think Steve might be working so hard "for the Lord?"

Fresh from the Farm

What do you get when you cross a sheep with a porcupine?
An animal that can knit its own sweaters.
***

What is a twip?
A twip is what a wabbit takes when he wides a twain.
***

What happens if you sit on a grape?
It gives out a little wine.
***

How can you start a self-service dairy?
You cross a cow with an octopus.
***

If I have seven apples and you ask me for two, how many would I have left?
Seven. I'm a little selfish.

This Lesson in Your Life

We don't hear the term "servant leader" around the church much." We have moved to committees and structures and staff-members, and down-played the critical role of servant leadership in guiding the Church into the twenty first century. Servant leadership can come from either a layperson or a clergy person. No matter the source of the leadership, it is where Christ is calling His Church.

A servant leader is one who has a sense of God's calling in his or her life. There is a natural attraction toward people who have this overarching sense that God has called them and gifted them for leadership in the church. We are attracted to the spirit of spiritual adventure we see in these people. Because God calls them, they can often see beyond the horizon to the possibilities of service open to those faithfully following God's leadership. This leader must be able to clearly communicate his vision to the people. A leader who can't communicate the vision that God has given him is only a dreamer. A servant leader is also willing to be held accountable for the vision he has and the direction he leads. A leader who refuses to be held accountable by the community of faith is simply a demagogue.

Servant leaders have a clear understanding that their power and vision is not their own but comes through the power of the Holy Spirit. A spirit-filled leader draws people to a faith in Jesus Christ. The Holy Spirit guides the leader in accomplishing the steps necessary to follow the vision given by God. The Spirit allows the leader to be a servant. He gives him the power to lead people in the direction that God is calling him. Those who lack the Spirit may have a vision, but they are usually not very patient and not gentle in their leadership of others.

The Church has a twofold purpose. The first is to make disciples for Jesus Christ. We are not called to maintain the organizational structure of the Church, but to organize the Church to fulfill that calling of making disciples. So a servant leader might find himself without a committee. The Church might have to learn to empower leaders who don't need a committee structure to follow the vision God has given them. At the same time, committees can serve to hold leaders accountable for their ministry.

Our second purpose is to call out from our midst new "servant leaders." We call out leaders by giving people an opportunity to take leadership roles in the Church. How long has it been since someone "new" was in a leadership role in your church? Are you raising up servant leaders?

1. Why did the Lord rejoice in His servant?
The servant was God's elect and His Spirit dwelt within the servant.

2. What do you think it means for the servant not to "cry nor lift up, nor cause his voice to be heard in the street"?
The words of the servant will be gentle and softly spoken, calling attention to God, not the speaker.

3. What two images of brokenness indicate the gentleness of the preaching and work of the servant?
He would not harm a bruised reed nor extinguish a dimly burning wick.

4. How long would the ministry of the servant last?
The servant would minister until he established justice in the earth and until the coastlands wait for His law.

5. How was the image of judgment in verse 4 reflected in the ministry of Jesus?
He preached judgment on those who perverted justice (as in Matt. 23).

6. Verse 5 pictures God as One who did what?
God was the creator God. He formed the earth and all life upon the earth.

7. What image is used to describe God in the verse 6?
God is described as nurturing and protecting His people because of His righteousness.

8. How are those two images, creator and protector, related?
God would not allow His creation to be destroyed. The ultimate act of nurture and protection was sending His son to us.

9. What familiar theme is sounded again in verse 7?
The Lord would bring light to the nations, open the eyes of the blind, and set the prisoners free.

10. According to verse nine, when did God make declarations to His people?
God declared things to His people before they happened. If the future is good, we were promised it would happen. If bad, we were warned.

Remember when you were a kid and you wanted to ask your mom and dad for permission to do something really special? The more outlandish the request, the more unlikely the prospect of approval, the more you knew that *timing* was everything.

You knew you had to catch them in just the right mood and at just the right time of day. It always helped to do a few unexpected good deeds as well—make your bed, take out the trash, pick up your room, and just generally be around and be good company. Only when all these signs were favorable would you dare broach the subject of the desired event or item. If something went wrong—dinner got burned or a bad day at work—forget it! You knew the answer ahead of time: Permission denied!

Children may complain about having to follow house rules, but the truth is that it is reassuring to know just who is in charge. But besides needing a powerful image of someone in charge, we all count on that intangible, unpredictable quality of compassion. There are always good excuses, extenuating circumstances, and forces beyond our control that merit special consideration. Even when we fall far outside the rules of the house, we hope for the tempering gentleness of compassion.

Isaiah's first servant song praises the qualities both of justice and of mercy that are part of the divine temperament. Justice and mercy are God's expression of power and compassion. Yet these two qualities have often forced men and women of faith into awkward corners.

If God is the God of justice, then we may rest assured that the wicked are punished and the good are rewarded. On the other hand, the knowledge that all of us fall far short of the divine mandates for for practicing justice (Heb. *mishpat*) in all our relationships with others should make us a little nervous about this God of justice. We all have "bad days" when we snipe and snap at family and friends for no reason; when we practice deceit; when we are unfair, cruel, even abusive.

Still it is easy for us to call for a God of justice when we are incensed by the crimes of others, horrified by the evil that stalks our world. But if any of us were to die tonight, which would we want to prevail—God's mercy or God's justice?

Lesson 2

Strength from God

Isaiah 49:1-6; 50:4-9

L isten, O isles, unto me; and hearken, ye people, from far; The LORD called me from the womb; from the bowels of my mother hath he made mention of my name.

2 And he hath made my mouth like a sharp sword; in the shadow of his hand hath he hid me, and made me a polished shaft; in his quiver hath he hid me;

3 And said unto me, Thou art my servant, O Israel, in whom I will be glorified.

4 Then I said, I have laboured in vain, I have spent my strength for nought, and in vain: yet surely my judgment is with the LORD, and my work with my God.

5 And now, saith the LORD that formed me from the womb to be his servant, to bring Jacob again to him, Though Israel be not gathered, yet shall I be glorious in the eyes of the LORD, and my God shall be my strength.

6 And he said, It is a light thing that thou shouldest be my servant to raise up the tribes of Jacob, and to restore the preserved of Israel: I will also give thee for a light to the Gentiles, that thou mayest be my salvation unto the end of the earth.

50:4 The Lord GOD hath given me the tongue of the learned, that I should

know how to speak a word in season to him that is weary: he wakeneth morning by morning, he wakeneth mine ear to hear as the learned.

5 The Lord GOD hath opened mine ear, and I was not rebellious, neither turned away back.

6 I gave my back to the smiters, and my cheeks to them that plucked off the hair: I hid not my face from shame and spitting.

7 For the Lord GOD will help me; therefore shall I not be confounded: therefore have I set my face like a flint, and I know that I shall not be ashamed.

8 He is near that justifieth me; who will contend with me? let us stand together: who is mine adversary? let him come near to me.

9 Behold, the Lord GOD will help me; who is he that shall condemn me? lo, they all shall wax old as a garment; the moth shall eat them up.

Devotional Reading
Isaiah 49:7-13

Background Scripture
Isaiah 49–50

Memory Selection
Isaiah 50:7

141

We have noticed that Isaiah's "suffering Servant" passages may refer to Israel, to the king of Persia, or to the coming Messiah. The passages in today's lesson indicate that both Israel *and* the Messiah, as Israel's representative, are spoken of as God's Servant. The Servant speaks poignantly of the way most people will not listen to

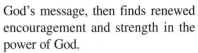

God's message, then finds renewed encouragement and strength in the power of God.

One instance of the fulfillment of this prophecy is the agony of Jesus in the Garden, and on the Cross. Although He cried to God, "Why hast thou forsaken me?," His sacrifice was vindicated in the resurrection. Today, when we too feel abandoned, we can recall both Christ's own victory and His promise never to leave us (Heb. 13:5-6).

ଚ୦ଔ

You may want to start this lesson at "the end," rather than the beginning. That is, you can describe the agony of Jesus when He prayed in the Garden that if it were God's will, the cup of suffering might be taken from Him . . . and when He cried on the Cross, "Why hast thou forsaken me?" Ask what enabled Jesus, in the face of such

suffering, to persevere to the end and to accomplish God's will.

Responses might include the fact that in the Garden, an angel came to strengthen Jesus (Luke 22:43) . . . and that He had a strong sense of who He was, and of His need to fulfill God's plan (Matt. 26:53-54). Note that the passages today from Isaiah both predict this sense of need, and affirm that the same strength and comfort that empowered the Servant are available to us in our points of need today.

Teaching Outline

I. Call to Serve—49:1-3
  A. From the womb, 1
  B. A weapon of victory, 2
  C. For God's glory, 3
II. Call for Reassurance—4-6
  A. Discouragement, 4a
  B. Affirming trust, 4b
  C. Sticking to the plan, 5-6
III. Confidence in God's Help—50:4-9
  A. In speaking and suffering, 4-6
  B. 'God will help me!,'7-9

Daily Bible Readings

Mon.	'Comfort Ye My People' Isa. 40:1-5
Tue.	The Powerless Strengthened Isa. 40:27-31
Wed.	God, My Strength Isa. 49:1-7
Thu.	The Lord Comforts His People Isa. 49:8-13
Fri.	'I Will Not Forget You' Isa. 49:14-18
Sat.	'I Am the Lord, Your Savior' Isa. 49:22-26
Sun.	'The Lord God Helps Me' Isa. 50:4-11

Verse by Verse

I. Call to Serve—49:1-3
A. From the womb, 1

1 Listen, O isles, unto me; and hearken, ye people, from far; The Lord called me from the womb; from the bowels of my mother hath he made mention of my name.

Moving to verse 3 helps us understand that the speaker here is not Isaiah, as we might think at first, but "the Servant" who, as we have seen, is so prominent in this section of the Isaiah. The Servant here seems to be Israel herself, or more specifically, the faithful Remnant among Israel who take seriously God's call to be an example to "the isles," or the Gentiles. This call was a part of God's plan long before Israel was "born" from the seed of the patriarchs. Actually, because God's Servant is often identified now as Israel, then as the coming Messiah, what is said can often apply both to the nation and to Christ.

B. A weapon of victory, 2

2 And he hath made my mouth like a sharp sword; in the shadow of his hand hath he hid me, and made me a polished shaft; in his quiver hath he hid me;

"The weapons of our warfare," the apostle Paul will write later, "are not carnal," but spiritual (2 Cor.

10:4). The "sharp sword" is therefore the Servant's mouth, or Word, "the sword of the Spirit" (Eph. 6:17). Then, slightly shifting the imagery, like an ancient warrior polishing the shaft of his arrow, God has carefully prepared Israel for being His "Word" to the nations, just as He is preparing the nation to bring forth the Messiah, His ultimate spokesman.

C. For God's glory, 3

3 And said unto me, Thou art my servant, O Israel, in whom I will be glorified.

Clearly specifying the identity of the Servant as Israel, God affirms that the role He has planned for this Servant is not for the Servant's glory, but for God's. This truth was sometimes neglected by Israel, who boasted in its having been elected to be God's special Servant/Son, forgetting that election is for *service,* and for glorifying Him who calls, not those who are called.

II. Call for Reassurance—4-6
A. Discouragement, 4a

4a Then I said, I have laboured in vain, I have spent my strength for nought, and in vain:

We can well imagine both Israel and Jesus raising this complaint. Israel's efforts at lifting up the one God in a land of idolatry were not widely rewarded with success. Switching to Jesus as the Suffering Servant, the words in verse 4 are echoed in Gethsemane, and again from the Cross where Christ temporarily felt abandoned by the One who sent Him. A footnote to this scene is that if the divine Son was susceptible to feelings of discouragement, we should be gentle and supportive toward brothers and sisters who also find themselves walking through dark valleys.

B. Affirming trust, 4b

4b yet surely my judgment is with the LORD, and my work with my God.

Even in the midst of discouragement, the Servant recalls that just as He is not serving for His own glory, but for God's, so God will supply whatever is needed for the Servant's mission to be completed. Even in our day, many ministers find encouragement amid set-backs by recalling that they are not serving for personal glory, but for God's, and that "where God guides, He provides."

C. Sticking to the plan, 5-6

5 And now, saith the LORD that formed me from the womb to be his servant, to bring Jacob again to him, Though Israel be not gathered, yet shall I be glorious in the eyes of the LORD, and my God shall be my strength.

6 And he said, It is a light thing that thou shouldest be my servant to raise up the tribes of Jacob, and to restore the preserved of Israel: I will also give thee for a light to the Gentiles, that thou mayest be my salvation unto the end of the earth.

Now the identity of the Servant seems to switch to the Messiah, for a voice speaks *about* "Jacob" (or Israel), instead of *as* Israel. Isaiah writes after the nation of Israel had split into the 10 tribes to the north and two tribes in the south. Israel is far from "gathered" or united, and her influence as a Servant is therefore diluted. Still, the Messiah sees hope for being "glorious"—if not in the eyes of the nations He came to serve, then "in the eyes of the Lord." This can occur if He remains *faithful*, instead of insisting on being *successful*.

Verse 6a can be translated as a question: "Is it too light a thing . . . ?" The KJV rendering portrays the role of the Servant as progressing from the "light" duty of being a light only to "the tribes of Jacob" (Israel) to the more challenging role of being also a light to the Gentiles (or "the nations"). It is this role that the apostle Paul applies to himself, and therefore to the early Church who sent him to the Gentiles, when the Jews to whom he was to preach first rejected his message (Acts 13:47). Because they interpreted the Servant passages as applying to Christ, early Christians also applied them to the Body of Christ, the Church, after His ascension.

In light of all this emphasis upon Israel, then Israel's Messiah, being the Servant sent to be a "light to the nations," it is strange that Israel failed to develop much of a missions program. The New Testament has a single reference to Jewish missions, and it is negative: "Woe unto you, scribes and Pharisees, hypocrites! for ye compass sea and land to make one proselyte, and when he is made, ye make him twofold more the child of hell than yourselves" (Matt. 23:15).

III. Confidence in God's Help—50:4-9

A. In speaking and suffering, 4-6

4 The Lord GOD hath given me the tongue of the learned, that I should know how to speak a word in season to him that is weary: he wakeneth morning by morning, he wakeneth mine ear to hear as the learned.

5 The Lord GOD hath opened mine ear, and I was not rebellious, neither turned away back.

6 I gave my back to the smiters, and my cheeks to them that plucked off the hair: I hid not my face from shame and spitting.

Because God was with Him, it is foreseen that the Servant will recover from His brief discouragement and let the Word become the Light it was intended to be. It is a Word informed by God's wisdom, so it is intelligible to "the learned" who are attuned to it, instead of to worldly wisdom. The "voice" here is in the "prophetic past," foreseeing the work of the Servant Messiah as though it had already occurred.

Furthermore, this sustaining power and grace from God equipped the Servant to respond with love to maltreatment. Because He had an obedient ear, He was able to turn a submissive back and cheek to those who abused Him—a forecast both of the way Jesus would respond to opposition, and the way He counseled His followers to respond.

B. 'God will help me!,'7-9

7 For the Lord GOD will help me; therefore shall I not be confounded: therefore have I set my face like a flint, and I know that I shall not be ashamed.

8 He is near that justifieth me; who will contend with me? let us stand together: who is mine adversary? let him come near to me.

9 Behold, the Lord GOD will help me; who is he that shall condemn me? lo, they all shall wax old as a garment; the moth shall eat them up.

At one point in Jesus' earthly ministry, He "set his face" to go to Jerusalem, even though death awaited Him there (see Luke 9:51). This determined willingness to suffer and die is forecast here in verse 7. How could Jesus, as the Servant *par excellence,* persist in such a mission? Because of His confidence that "the Lord God will help me." His opponents will soon wear out like an old piece of clothing, while the Living God will sustain Him. Following Paul in applying the Servant passages to the Church, this becomes an invitation to modern Christians to partake of this courage and confidence as well.

Evangelistic Emphasis

It was winter, and an especially cold and bitter night. Very few people were on the New York subway at that hour. At each station, the train would screech to a halt, open its doors, and allow a few people to come and go. At one station, a peculiar woman got on. Her clothes were ragged and dirty. She was either extremely tired or drunk. As the train lurched forward, she stumbled and fell into a seat and went fast asleep. Through the screeching and swaying of the train, she slept, her hands nestled inside two tattered worn-out gloves. How could she go anywhere in that bitter cold without freezing her hands? Few people in the train could take their eyes off this homeless person, asleep on the subway, her useless gloves on her hands.

Then a young Puerto Rican boy got up to get off the train as it slowed to a stop. Instead of leaving by the closest exit, he went by the sleeping woman. He paused for a few moments, then removed his gloves, laid them on her lap, and got off the train.

As we prepare for another Christmas we are reminded how one small child changed the world. Our calling as Christians is to take on the ministry of Jesus, as the servant of God, and do our part to change the world around us. As you think about the gifts you will give this Christmas, is one of them your love?

ℰℭℛ

For the Lord God will help me; therefore I shall not be confounded; therefore I have set my face like a flint, and I know that I shall not be ashamed.—*Isaiah 50:7*

Manuel Garcia, who lives in Milwaukee, had cancer, and the chemotherapy treatments caused his hair to fall out in patches. The patterns of fall-out were so strange and eccentric that he decided just to shave his entire head. But he began worrying and brooding about how he would appear to his friends.

When his brother Julio learned how upset Manuel was about his appearance, Julio shaved his own head. Then he enlisted some 50 neighbors and relatives who did the same thing. Soon Manuel's hospital room looked like a convention suite for baldheaded men. Manuel was ecstatic and encouraged.

Very often we get confounded in life, but because God has called others along side to walk the journey of faith, they become encouragement for us. As I face the problems of life, I can turn my face like flint into those problems because I know that I have friends who are standing with me and who are praying for me. They become Immanuel, God with us, for me, reminding me that I have Jesus who walks with me through all the troubles of life.

Weekday Problems

Becky found herself in a horrible predicament, especially since she should have been feeling the Christmas spirit. Becky was in charge of the open house at the church rectory. Since the preacher wasn't married, the ladies thought Becky should help plan the event for him.

She was also the church organist. The choir was working very hard on the Christmas music and Becky had to practice extra to be ready. On top of all of this, Becky's two grown children announced that they were planning to spend Christmas at home with Becky and her husband. Each of Becky's children had children. Then, Becky's mom and her older brother and his family announced that they too would be spending Christmas at Becky's house. Becky had a long list of things she had to get done before all of this family descended on her house for a Christmas celebration.

The rub came when the preacher asked Becky if she would give a "word of witness" during the Christmas Eve service. He wanted Becky to speak about the "importance of family during the holiday season." Becky gave him a "If you value your life you will ask someone else to do that" look. She bit her tongue and graciously turned down the invitation—but felt guilty..

*Do your Christmas celebrations cause you to be "confounded" each year?
*How can we return to the simplicity of the first Christmas?

Caddies Call the Shots

Golfer: I'd move heaven and earth if I could break my 110 score.
Caddie: Try heaven. You've already moved enough earth today.

***

"Look!" screamed the golfer. "If you don't keep you big mouth shut you're going to drive me out of my mind!"
"That's no drive, mister," the caddy replied. "That's a short putt."

***

Golfer: My doctor says I can't play golf.
Caddy: Ah. He's played with you, too, huh?

***

Golfer: Caddy, why didn't you see where that ball went?
Caddy: Sorry, sir, I was caught off guard. It usually doesn't go anywhere.

***

Golfer to new caddy: Well, what do you think of my game?
Caddy: It's all right, sir, but I still like golf better.

This Lesson in Your Life

We've all seen it. That too-cute poster of a clinging kitten, hind feet dangling in the air, only its front paws, claws dug in frantically, keeping it chin-upping somewhere above the ground. Underneath the picture of this panicked pussycat is the admonition, "Hang In There!"

We are told that this is the kind of visual message we need at 7 a.m. Friday morning to encourage us to make it through the day and stick it out to the almost-arrived weekend.

Why does this picture evoke a grin or a chuckle when we look at it? Surely, we aren't all abusive cat-haters, pleased at the distresses of any and all frantic felines. No, we smile for the same reason we laugh at slapstick comedy. Our laughter is a burst of relief that, at least this time, the one falling flat isn't us. We sympathize. We even empathize. But we also heave a great sigh of thanks for our own safety.

I think we also assume that some rescue awaits that kitten . . . if only it can just "hang in there" long enough. But in all the versions of this portrait I have seen, the viewer can't see beyond a few inches below the kitten's toes. We can't tell if she is afraid to let go and drop three inches to a grassy lawn, or if she is dangling above the open jaws of a snarling pit bull or the whizzing traffic of a four-lane highway. We assume a happy ending or a safe landing. Otherwise, the encouragement to "hang in there" wouldn't make any sense.

Most of us tend to manufacture little crises in our lives that can be weathered by just "hanging in there." A frustrating week of work is followed by a weekend. A sniping, snarling car trip with the kids eventually comes to an end. Head colds do eventually loosen their grip and go away. Even tedious, do-nothing meetings finally adjourn. Sometimes "hanging in there" is all that is required.

But there are other situations in our lives that call us to do much, much more than simply dangle our way through disasters. When your ship is sinking, you can't just "hang in there." You've got to get moving, break out the life rafts, and start rowing for all you are worth.

Think about the differences between "hang in there" times and "get moving times" in your own life. Regardless of the situation, Jesus has promised us help. He has promised to be with us when we are confounded, so we can "hang in there." His promise allows us "to set our face like flint" when we need to get moving. No matter which situation you face, Jesus Christ is with you.

1. Isaiah 49 contains a description of the servant of the Lord. When was the servant "formed"?
The servant of God was formed by God in the womb.

2. What Christmas image does this bring to mind?
Jesus was conceived in the womb of Mary by the power of the Holy Spirit.

3. What ministry was given to the servant of the Lord?
He was to bring Jacob (Israel) back to God.

4. What promise would God fulfill through His servant?
The servant of God would be a light to the nations and he would bring God's salvation to the end of the earth.

5. Who do you think is being described in Isaiah 49?
The description of the servant of the Lord is like that of Jesus Christ.

6. Isaiah 50 continues the description of the servant of God. How is the servant described in this chapter?
The servant is given the tongue of a teacher so that his words might sustain the weary.

7. As a Christian, what does this description remind you of?
This reminds us of the teaching ministry of Jesus. His use of parables confounded the wise and sustained the weak.

8. How is the servant of God sustained in his ministry?
The servant is sustained by listening to what God was telling him.

9. What other details are given about the life and ministry of the servant of the Lord?
This servant gave his back to those who struck him and his cheeks to those who pulled out his beard. He did not hide his face from insult and spitting.

10. What event in the life Jesus is called to mind as you read Isaiah 6?
It is an appropriate description of the suffering of Jesus during His Passion.

How does servanthood translate into a way of living? How can we continue to embody the spirit that made Jesus a servant for others before He claimed his lordship over all?

In 1983 United Press International released a poignant story of a young leukemia patient and the special friendship that he enjoyed during the course of his illness. P. J. Dragan was only 5 years old when he was diagnosed with leukemia. Soon thereafter the boy began to receive a series of cheery notes and cards, little gifts and goodies to brighten his spirits. Each was adorned with a large green bow. These presents all came from an anonymous friend who signed each card simply: "Magic Dragon." One of P. J.'s favorite gifts was a large green plush toy dragon, which quickly became the embodiment of the gift-giver and P. J.'s constant companion.

As P.J. grew sicker, "Magic Dragon's" attentions never waned; notes of encouragement and support arrived continuously. The treasured toy dragon accompanied P. J. to the hospital, sympathetically sporting the same bandages and sharing all the painful, unpleasant treatments with this little boy. Tragically, despite all efforts, P. J. lost his battle with leukemia. At his funeral the largest bouquet was a huge spray of daisies, all tied up with an enormous green bow—"Magic Dragon's" final gift.

No one ever discovered "Magic Dragon's" identity. After some initial inquiries, P. J.'s parents wisely realized that it was more appropriate to honor "Dragon's" chosen anonymity, allowing both P. J. and "Magic Dragon" the joy of a friendship based solely on love, dedication, and service. "Magic Dragon" saw an opportunity to reach out in love, to risk serving another with no thought for reward, no concern for self. Thank you, "Magic Dragon."

Among the most difficult challenges confounding our own attempts at servanthood is the battle with selfishness. Our egos crave recognition. We want to be patted on the back and told "well done" for our sacrifices. Too often our own need for affirmation and approval overshadow our attempts at servanthood and undermine even the best-intended motivations.

Hope for Those Who Suffer

Isaiah 53:1-6; Luke 1:46-55

Who hath believed our report? and to whom is the arm of the LORD revealed?

2 For he shall grow up before him as a tender plant, and as a root out of a dry ground: he hath no form nor comeliness; and when we shall see him, there is no beauty that we should desire him.

3 He is despised and rejected of men; a man of sorrows, and acquainted with grief: and we hid as it were our faces from him; he was despised, and we esteemed him not.

4 Surely he hath borne our griefs, and carried our sorrows: yet we did esteem him stricken, smitten of God, and afflicted.

5 But he was wounded for our transgressions, he was bruised for our iniquities: the chastisement of our peace was upon him; and with his stripes we are healed.

6 All we like sheep have gone astray; we have turned every one to his own way; and the LORD hath laid on him the iniquity of us all.

Luke 1:46 And Mary said, My soul doth magnify the Lord,

47 And my spirit hath rejoiced in God my Saviour.

48 For he hath regarded the low estate of his handmaiden: for, behold, from henceforth all generations shall call me blessed.

49 For he that is mighty hath done to me great things; and holy is his name.

50 And his mercy is on them that fear him from generation to generation.

51 He hath shewed strength with his arm; he hath scattered the proud in the imagination of their hearts.

52 He hath put down the mighty from their seats, and exalted them of low degree.

53 He hath filled the hungry with good things; and the rich he hath sent empty away.

54 He hath holpen his servant Israel, in remembrance of his mercy;

55 As he spake to our fathers, to Abraham, and to his seed for ever.

Devotional Reading
Rom. 12:9-16

Background Scripture
Isaiah 53; Luke 1

Memory Selection
Luke 1:50

FOCUS

This lesson combines two of the best-known texts in Scripture, in preparation for next week's observance of Christmas. In the first passage we continue to examine Isaiah's "Servant Songs," although the tone here is more somber than those previously noted. It is from chapter 53, the famous prediction of the Messiah's redemptive suffering for the sins of the world.

Then we move to the opposite end of the emotional scale—to the , celebratory tones of the "Magnificat" —the outburst of praise from Mary, when she learns that she will bear the Christ-child. The lesson therefore exposes us to both the lows and highs of the Christ-story . . . very much like the emotional texture of life itself.

℘⊙℥

FOR A LIVELY START...

Remind your group that the approaching season of joy also includes one of the saddest scenes in Scripture—the "slaughter of the innocents," as King Herod went on his killing spree in an attempt to rid the land of any competition for the throne. Ask group members to share some of the highs and lows some people feel at this time of year. For example, some who have outlived other family members look with sadness as other families have joyous celebrations. Others find "going home for Christmas" reopens old relational wounds. At the other extreme is the unbounded joy of remembering the Good News that the Christ-child has been born.

Point out that despite the emotional extremes of the season, the story of the Birth ultimtately overpowers the picture of the "man of sorrows."

Teaching Outline	*Daily Bible Readings*	
I. 'He Has Borne Our Sorrows'—Isa. 53:1-6	Mon.	Man of Suffering Isa. 52:13–53:3
A. Despised sufferer, 1-3	Tue.	He Bore Our Sins Isa. 53:4-12
B. He bore our sins, 4-6	Wed.	John the Baptist Luke 1:5-17
II. 'My Soul Rejoices!'—Luke 1:46-55	Thu.	Jesus' Birth Foretold Luke 1:26-38
A. He has done great things, 46-49	Fri.	Mary Visits Elizabeth Luke 1:39-45
B. He is mighty and merciful, 50-51	Sat.	Mary's Song of Praise Luke 1:46-55
C. The high and the low, 52-55	Sun.	Home Through Suffering Romans 5:1-11

Verse by Verse

I. 'He Has Borne Our Sorrows'—Isa. 53:1-6

A. Despised sufferer, 1-3

1 Who hath believed our report? and to whom is the arm of the LORD revealed?

2 For he shall grow up before him as a tender plant, and as a root out of a dry ground: he hath no form nor comeliness; and when we shall see him, there is no beauty that we should desire him.

3 He is despised and rejected of men; a man of sorrows, and acquainted with grief: and we hid as it were our faces from him; he was despised, and we esteemed him not.

This passage is the crown of Isaiah's "Servant Songs," although it is not easy to discern what it meant to its first hearers. Some scholars believe it describes the way God used Cyrus, king of Persia (see Isa. 45:1), and Darius, a successor, Ezra, or Zerubbabel to deliver the Jews from Babylonian captivity, despite the way their leadership was "despised" by some (see Ezra 6 for Darius' work as a "servant" of God, though a non-Jew, in behalf of the Jews).

Ultimately, however, we look in vain for any historical figure who fully reaches the heights of service described in these verses. What is said about the Servant strains the language past merely human capacities. Thus, the early Church saw the ultimate fulfillment of this suffering Servant in one who was both God and man, Jesus, the Messiah.

It is easy to see how being born as a helpless infant to an unlettered and unknown Jewish family fits the description of having no comeliness or beauty—no impressive human credentials to be "the arm of the Lord." The Gospel of Luke (22:37) finds the crucial role of sin-bearer described especially in Isaiah 53:12, filled by Jesus (compare also Mark 10:45 with Isa. 53:10). Yet the masses at Golgotha "esteemed" (or "accounted"—the word is a bookkeeping term) this work as nothing! Thus the sorrowful tone of the passage lies not only in the Servant's suffering, but in His rejection by those for whom he suffered: "we hid as it were our faces from him," recalling the way even Christ's own disciples turned their backs on Him at His crucifixion.

The doctrine that Messiah could

have been "despised" (vs. 3) was widely rejected by the Jews. By the end of the second century A.D., a Jewish commentary rewrote this passage thus: "Then shall the glory of all kingdoms [not the Messiah's glory] be despised . . . they [not the Messiah] shall be infirm and sick, even as a man of sorrows."

B. He bore our sins, 4-6

4 Surely he hath borne our griefs, and carried our sorrows: yet we did esteem him stricken, smitten of God, and afflicted.

5 But he was wounded for our transgressions, he was bruised for our iniquities: the chastisement of our peace was upon him; and with his stripes we are healed.

6 All we like sheep have gone astray; we have turned every one to his own way; and the LORD hath laid on him the iniquity of us all.

It is tempting to explain the Messiah's suffering as the result of Satan's work in the human heart, and of sinful humanity. While that is certainly a factor, a monotheistic faith cannot dodge the fact that ultimate God had to be involved also. It is "the Lord" who smote the Servant, and laid on the Him the iniquity of us all. Yet because, in the New Testament interpretation of this awe-inspiring event, the Father is one with the Son, the role of God and the Servant blend on the Cross. Since sinful humanity cannot bridge the gap between itself and God, He bridges it with the gift of Himself. This self-giving aspect of God saves the doctrine of "sub-stitutionary atonement" from being reduced to the caricature we sometimes see of Jesus pleading with a reluctant Father in behalf of a sinful people. The fact is that the Father, through giving His Son, took the first step toward us.

II. 'My Soul Rejoices!—Luke 1:46-55

A. He has done great things, 46-49

46 And Mary said, My soul doth magnify the Lord,

47 And my spirit hath rejoiced in God my Saviour.

48 For he hath regarded the low estate of his handmaiden: for, behold, from henceforth all generations shall call me blessed.

49 For he that is mighty hath done to me great things; and holy is his name.

Our lesson text moves abruptly from Isaiah's painfully magnificent picture of a Suffering Messiah who would bear the sins of the world, despite widespread rejection, to the joyous praise of the young Jewish woman chosen to bear the Christ-child. The divine Being who alone is able to bear the sins of the world begins life as a pure infant born not of man but of the seed of the Holy Spirit (Luke 1:35). Mary's first impulse (after her earlier hesitancy about how it could happen) is pure praise, or "magnifying" the Lord— giving these verses, from early Latin translations, the title "The Magnificat."

B. He is mighty and merciful, 50-51

50 And his mercy is on them

that fear him from generation to generation.

51 He hath shewed strength with his arm; he hath scattered the proud in the imagination of their hearts.

Although Mary is a simple Jewish girl, we wonder if her inspired vision of the role her Child will play—"from generation to generation" seems to push past narrow nationalist Jewish concepts and to conceive of a Messiah for "the nations" (although see the comment on verse 54, below). She must have been steeped in the Scriptures, since she picks up the word "arm" which Isaiah often used to described the saving work of God and/or His Servant (see 51:9; 52:10, 53:1, etc.).

C. The high and the low, 52-55

52 He hath put down the mighty from their seats, and exalted them of low degree.

53 He hath filled the hungry with good things; and the rich he hath sent empty away.

54 He hath holpen his servant Israel, in remembrance of his mercy;

55 As he spake to our fathers, to Abraham, and to his seed for ever.

One of the distinctive roles of the Messiah was that He would lower the status of the status-seekers while elevating the standing of the poor and the humble. This reversal of status is prominent in the "Beatitudes," at the beginning of Jesus' most famous sermon, the Sermon on the Mount. What worldly prominent philosopher would put the poor in spirit, the mournful, and the meek at the top of the list of those God "blesses"?

The concept of role reversal is also closely connected to the previous discussion of "substitutionary atonement" from Isaiah 53. The story of Naaman the leper from 2 Kings 5 is a good example of how difficult it is for the "great" to accept that the business of getting right with God is done *for* them, instead of being something that they can do for themselves. (Of course the hesitance to accept the free gift of forgiveness is not limited to those in high position.)

In verse 55, Mary does prove to be a Jewish girl, knowing that through sending the Messiah God "hath holpen" (KJV for "has helped") first of all the chosen race. Yet she may envision Israel as God's instrument to reach the rest of the human race, since that was the true aim of the election of Father Abraham in the first place (see Gen. 12:3).

Evangelistic Emphasis

The good news. The bad news.

Truth is, we want to hear the good news, but only if there is bad news to go with it. And given a choice between good news and bad news, we'll take the bad news every time.

People often say to veteran broadcaster Paul Harvey, "Paul, why don't journalists and broadcasters emphasize more good news instead of tragedy, destruction, discord and dissent?" Harvey's own network once tried broadcasting a program devoted solely to good news. The program survived 13 weeks. In Sacramento, California, a tabloid called *Good News Paper* lasted 36 months before it went bankrupt, and the publisher of a similar tabloid in Indiana had to *give it away*. Evidently, the good news people say they want is news they just won't buy.

Listen to any broadcast, or pick up any newspaper. You'll learn about the worst car crash or the worst storm or fire or flood or earthquake or whatever—because *noise* makes news.

The good news of the Christmas story is that Jesus has come into our noisy world. He is as a shepherd silently searching for lost sheep. In a world that thrives on bad news, Jesus is the good news that has come to all us. Have you been quiet enough in this Christmas season to hear his "still small voice"?

෨෮෬

And his mercy is on them that fear him from generation to generation.—*Luke 1: 50*

That is a strange combination of words, fear and mercy. We are told that the "fear of the Lord is the beginning of wisdom." This fear is not being terrified or afraid. It might be better translated the awe of the Lord. When my kids are describing doing something that is really meaningful they often say that it was "awesome." God's mercy falls on those that are in awe of Him.

It also happens in reverse order: the awe of the Lord falls on those who experience His mercy. God's love and mercy are two concepts that are beyond human words to explain.

Mercy and fear (awe) can travel hand in hand in our world. Living with both mercy and awe in your life is a sign that God has made a difference in your world. Most of us before Christmas live in a sense of befuddlement. We wonder why we have scheduled so many events on our calendars, why we are buying presents for so many who have so much. We need to pray, "Lord forgive us our Christmases as we forgive those who Christmas against us."

Like the shepherds in the first Christmas story, we need to recapture that sense of the fear of the Lord which grows out of experiencing His mercy.

Weekday Problems

Christmas or not, Catherine was not in a festive mood. She had come to the church as the new choir director, having moved her family hundreds of miles away from their ancestral home. She was following her heart in what she believed God had called her to do, but she was having adjustment problems. Actually her husband, Ed, was having the problems. He kept going back to their former home. He refused to make friends in the new community. He really didn't like going to the new church, and would not have gone, had his wife not been on staff.

Catherine was a wonderful musician and loved sharing her gifts through music. She especially loved the Christmas season and the songs of that holiday time. Yet this Christmas there was no song in her heart. The choir had received Catherine with open arms, but after only a couple of rehearsals, it was obvious that she and the choir were not a match. The senior minister had talked to her about her musical style, and was taking the choir's side. Her parents missed her. She was feeling like she had made this *huge* mistake.

"Silent Night" and "Joy to the World" were not stirring her heart. She told one of her few friends at church, "I just don't feel like Christmas."

*If you were the friend Catherine confided in, how would you respond?

*What can we learn from Mary's song of praise about facing our problems with feeling joyous about our faith?

Affirming the Atonement

I must die or get somebody to die for me. If the Bible doesn't teach that, it doesn't teach anything. And that is where the atonement of Jesus Christ comes in.—*Dwight L. Moody*
***

In the Cross, God descends to bear in his own heart the sins of the world. In Jesus, He atones at unimaginable cost to Himself.—*Woodrow A. Geier*
***

When we think of the atonement we are apt to think only of what man gains. We must remember what it cost God and what it costs Him now when men refuse His love.—*Frank Fitt*
***

By Thine agony and bloody sweat; by thy Cross and passion; by Thy precious death and burial; by thy glorious resurrection and ascension; and by the coming of the Holy Ghost, good Lord, deliver us.—*The Book of Common Prayer*

This Lesson in Your Life

We have, in turn, both trivialized Mary and have given her too much credit in the Christmas account. Have you noticed that in the Christmas plays, Mary doesn't get any lines? Joseph gets to lead the donkey and argue with the innkeeper. Mary remains silent throughout most of these reenactments.

Yet Mary stands out as a strong witness to a woman's unflinching faith in God. We have glossed over all the social stigmas that the birth of Christ placed on her. Throughout her life, she probably heard the whispers of the people as they labeled her immoral and her son illegitimate. Perhaps that is why she convinced Jesus that it was important to do something about the couple who had run out of wedding wine. She remembered the pain of not being able to carry out her wedding plans. She was not about to let this couple feel any regrets about their day. She endured the whispers. She lived with the fear that something dreadful would happen to Jesus. She can even be seen as joining the rest of the family in misunderstanding the Master.

Mary probably had a good sense of humor. We overlook that in God's people. We take the Almighty so seriously that we deny Him and us the ability to laugh. I remind you that God created the giraffe and the ostrich. He even put you together in a unique way. He has a holy sense of humor. Mary had to have shared God's sense of humor. God had placed her in an indefensible position. Can you hear her having to explain to Joseph her condition?

Mary was a visionary. Now think about that for a moment. She was given the promise of God, and nothing else. She risked it all, because in that promise, she could see into the future. How could a child born to peasants in a cave in Bethlehem, raised in a carpenters shop in Nazareth, ever amount to anything? His critics would echo those very same questions. Yet, even with her son dying on the cross, Mary could see with God's vision. She knew what had been spoken about this child. She knew that He was God's Messiah. She knew, at least in part, what that would mean for the human race. She was more than willing to do what needed to be done, because she could see into the future what God was going to do.

Our Christmas celebrations might be different if we could strip away all the hype and really look at the characters involved in the story. There are no heroes in this Christmas portrait gallery. There are simply people who listened to God and did what they were commanded to do.

1. According to Luke 1, the angel Gabriel appeared to Mary in the sixth month. To what did the sixth month refer?

The reference was to the sixth month after the conception of John the Baptizer.

2. What did both Mary and Elizabeth share?

The birth of both of the children was announced to the mothers by the angel Gabriel.

3. What was Mary's marital state when the angel Gabriel visited her?

Mary was a virgin, engaged to Joseph. They had not consummated the marriage.

4. What was Mary's reaction to the angel Gabriel's salutation?

She was perplexed, and she pondered on what kind of greeting this might be.

5. What did the angel Gabriel tell Mary?

He told her not to be afraid because she had found favor with God. She would conceive and bear a son, and He would be named Jesus.

6. What did Mary learn about Elizabeth from her visit with Gabriel?

Mary was told that Elizabeth had conceived a son. Elizabeth was in the sixth month of her pregnancy.

7. What did Mary do as a result of the message of the angel?

She went to Elizabeth and Zechariah's home. She did this before any mention is made of her telling Joseph what had happened.

8. What happened when Mary and Elizabeth saw each other?

The baby inside of Elizabeth jumped for joy, and Elizabeth was filled with the Holy Spirit.

9. What is interesting about the pregnancies of Mary and Elizabeth?

Neither one should be with child. Elizabeth is "too old," and Mary is a virgin.

10. What title has been given to Mary's outburst of praise in Luke 1:46-55?

Many call Mary's hymn of praise the "Magnificat."

If life were a restaurant, it would be divided into the proud and powerful on the customer side of the tray, and humble and harassed people on the waitress side.

One waitress recalls the time when she was waiting tables and had a tray full of drinks, and then had the misfortune of crashing into her manager, causing them both to tumble to the floor.

She, however, while falling, managed to keep the drink tray she was carrying horizontal, so that even as she lay on the floor, not a drop was spilled, not a glass was broken.

It was such a spectacular performance that the customers, far from chuckling at her clumsiness, instead gave her a rousing cheer and round of applause!

Unfortunately, such responses are rare.

Waitresses. They're hauling heavy trays. Crashing into co-workers. Being poked and grabbed and yelled at. Having to smile and be nice to rude customers. Receiving lousy tips.

It can be a brutal way to make a buck.

An honorable profession to be sure, and some wait staff make good money. But most work hard for their money with not much more than bruises and bunions to show for the effort.

Suzy Hansen, who has studied the restaurant business, agrees that the world seems divided beetween those on the customer side of the tray, and those on the waitress side.

On the customer side are the proud and the powerful; on the waitress side are the humble and the harassed. Far too many customers assume that waitresses are low-class women without skills, beneath conversation and consideration. Too often, they are snubbed, underpaid, and ignored

Welcome to life on the other side of the tray.

It's the other side with which Mary, the mother of Jesus, was all too familiar. Along with other women of first-century Galilee, Mary was a second-class citizen, deemed not worthy of conversation or consideration. She had little or no authority, virtually no rank or status in her culture.

Yet it is to this humble woman that Jesus was born. The Son of God would invite us all to sit on God's side of the table!

Lesson 4

Be Joyful!

Isaiah 61:1-2; Luke 2:8-20

The Spirit of the Lord GOD is upon me; because the LORD hath anointed me to preach good tidings unto the meek; he hath sent me to bind up the brokenhearted, to proclaim liberty to the captives, and the opening of the prison to them that are bound;

2 To proclaim the acceptable year of the LORD, and the day of vengeance of our God; to comfort all that mourn;

Luke 2:8 And there were in the same country shepherds abiding in the field, keeping watch over their flock by night.

9 And, lo, the angel of the Lord came upon them, and the glory of the Lord shone round about them: and they were sore afraid.

10 And the angel said unto them, Fear not: for, behold, I bring you good tidings of great joy, which shall be to all people.

11 For unto you is born this day in the city of David a Saviour, which is Christ the Lord.

12 And this shall be a sign unto you; Ye shall find the babe wrapped in swaddling clothes, lying in a manger.

13 And suddenly there was with the angel a multitude of the heavenly host praising God, and saying,

14 Glory to God in the highest, and on earth peace, good will toward men.

15 And it came to pass, as the angels were gone away from them into heaven, the shepherds said one to another, Let us now go even unto Bethlehem, and see this thing which is come to pass, which the Lord hath made known unto us.

16 And they came with haste, and found Mary, and Joseph, and the babe lying in a manger.

17 And when they had seen it, they made known abroad the saying which was told them concerning this child.

18 And all they that heard it wondered at those things which were told them by the shepherds.

19 But Mary kept all these things, and pondered them in her heart.

20 And the shepherds returned, glorifying and praising God for all the things that they had heard and seen, as it was told unto them.

Devotional Reading
Isaiah 52:7-12

Background Scripture
Isaiah 61:1-3; Luke 2:8-20

Memory Selection
Luke 2:11

161

This lesson begins with the theme of "Joy to the Jews!," whose situation after returning from Babylonia is about to improve, and progresses to "Joy to the world!" because of the birth of Jesus.

As we have already seen, many of the Servant Songs of Isaiah 40ff. seem to have double or even triple

meanings. They often refer first to a "deliverer" who is contemporary with the Jews and who will facilitate their return from Babylonian captivity in the sixth-century B.C. The language, however, is so lofty that New Testament authors find that it also applies to Jesus, the Messiah.

Combining the story of the shepherds to whom the angels announce the birth of Christ with Israel's experience some 600 years earlier can help put a fresh face on the familiar Christmas story.

ଛଠଓଃ

Ask group members to describe how they might feel if they were ancient Jews, six centuries before Christ, who had been captured and taken to Babylonian captivity. Reflect on how we get attached to our homeland . . . to our native language . . . to a local church . . . to the "American" way in general. Then contrast

these familiar feelings with the inevitable feelings of displacement, loneliness, and, in the case of the Jews, being held against their will.

Then imagine receiving the "good news" that you can return home! How would you go about rebuilding the life you feared you had lost forever? All these feelings arise from today's Isaiah passage, and the story of the shepherds who first heard the Good News about Jesus' birth.

Teaching Outline	*Daily Bible Readings*

I. Joy to the Jews!—Isa. 61:1-2
  A. The anointed prophet, 1a
  B. Delivery and vengeance!, 1b-2
II. Joy to the World!—Luke 2:8-20
  A. Shepherds in the field, 8-9
  B. The angel's message, 10-12
  C. Angelic chorus, 13-14
III. Journey to Bethlehem, 15-20
  A. Infant Messiah, 15-16
  B. Telling the news, 17-18
  C. Reflecting on the event, 19-20
	Mon. Justice and Deliverance
	    Isa. 51:1-6
	Tue. He Bore the Sins of Many
	    Isa. 52:7-12
	Wed. God Will Be Your Glory
	    Isa. 60:17-22
	Thu. Good News for the Oppressed
	    Isa. 61:1-7
	Fri. Salvation and Righteousness
	    Isa. 61:8–62:3
	Sat. Mary Has a Baby
	    Luke 2:1-7
	Sun. Good News from Angels
	    Luke 2:8-21

Verse by Verse

I. Joy to the Jews!—Isa. 61:1-2
A. The anointed prophet, 1a
1a The Spirit of the Lord GOD is upon me;

A basic question of Bible interpretation is, Who is speaking? Because of the first person "me," the answer here seems at first to be the prophet Isaiah. If this is so, he is either predicting something that will happen nearly 200 years after he lived (since he lived in the eighth-century B.C., and the good news he predicts for the Jews occurred in the sixth century); or another, later writer, is writing in the spirit and style of Isaiah.

Another possibility, however, is that the author is writing in the "voice" of the Coming Messiah. This possibility arises from the next verse, from the word "anointed" (Heb. *meshiach,* messiah). Perhaps the prophet foresees not only relief for home-coming Jews, and those being mistreated in their homeland, but also how this is a picture of the ultimate relief to accompany the Messiah who is to come.

B. Delivery and vengeance!, 1b-2
1b because the LORD hath anointed me to preach good tidings unto the meek; he hath sent me to bind up the brokenhearted, to proclaim liberty to the captives, and the opening of the prison to them that are bound;

2 To proclaim the acceptable year of the LORD, and the day of vengeance of our God; to comfort all that mourn;

The "good tidings" of the "anointed" messenger are directed to the *meek,* the *brokenhearted,* and those who are *captives* and *imprisoned* or *bound.* If we seek an immediate application of the prophet's good news, he must be speaking of political prisoners left in Jerusalem and Judea after Nebuchadnezzar conquered the land, or those imprisoned there after having been part of one of the early returns such as that led by Ezra and Nehemiah. Although the Bible never teaches against imprisoning actual criminals, here is a call for political oppressors to release those unjustly imprisoned.

Whatever immediate application this text had for its first readers is overwhelmed for Christians by the fact that the Messiah saw Himself as the bearer of these stirring words of freedom. According to Luke 4:18-21, Jesus applied this passage in Isaiah to Himself and His mission the very first time He preached. Although the historical situation had changed, there were still political prisoners and widespread injustice. Thus, Christians who are, in any age, concerned for justice and humaneness have been motivated to reach out to the poor and the mistreated in the name of Christ. Additionally, there is the spiritual dimension: Christ was anointed to free those in the ultimate "bondage" of sin.

In addition to the Good News in this prophecy we should not fail to note also its judgment or "vengeance" against those who perpetrate injustice—then, now, or in the future when Christ returns in final judgment against those who oppose the love and justice of Christ.

II. Joy to the World!—Luke 2:8-20
A. Shepherds in the field, 8-9

8 And there were in the same country shepherds abiding in the field, keeping watch over their flock by night.

9 And, lo, the angel of the Lord came upon them, and the glory of the Lord shone round about them: and they were sore afraid.

Although the scene seems to change abruptly from Old Testament to New, since Isaiah's prophecy was fulfilled in Jesus, the Messiah, it is appropriate to focus now on His arrival. The "same country" is the region around Bethlehem of Judea (see vss. 1-7). It was far enough away from Jerusalem, with its holy Temple, that sheep could be herded freely—their odor and the disdain the rabbis had for people who care for them, had prompted a rule that except for sacrificial lambs sheep had to be kept away from Jerusalem.

Thus the earliest announcement of the birth of the long-awaited Messiah comes not to the Herods or oth-ers in the privileged classes, but to shepherds, the "meek" in society (just as Isaiah had predicted). God turns the social order upside-down and graces these humbly-employed men with the Good News.

B. The angel's message, 10-12

10 And the angel said unto them, Fear not: for, behold, I bring you good tidings of great joy, which shall be to all people.

11 For unto you is born this day in the city of David a Saviour, which is Christ the Lord.

12 And this shall be a sign unto you; Ye shall find the babe wrapped in swaddling clothes, lying in a manger.

Naturally, the first reaction to seeing a heavenly being in the dark of night would have been fear, so the angel quickly reassures the shepherds of his divinely friendly intention. The KJV "good tidings" will become the familiar term "gospel" ("God-spell"), the Good News of the arrival and saving power of "Christ the Lord." This term must have struck the shepherd with awe, for *Christ* was the Greek way of saying *Messiah,* and *Lord* was associated with *Yahweh,* the personal name of God.

The angel anticipates that the shepherds will want to go to Bethlehem to greet the Christ-child. His birth there in the hometown of King David, the Jewish hero, fulfills God's promise that Messiah would come as David's heir (see Matt. 2:6). The angel tells the shepherds how to identify the divine Child. Although several other babies may have been born in the town that night, no other would have had a stable for a birthing-room or a manger for a cradle.

C. Angelic chorus, 13-14

13 And suddenly there was with the angel a multitude of the heavenly host praising God, and saying,

14 Glory to God in the highest, and on earth peace, good will toward men.

The news of the Messiah's arrival is so astonishingly welcome that the heavens burst with an angelic "host" or army—the word comes from the same term that gives us the word "strategy" for a master military plan. In this case, however, the army's strategy is to sing! The song is not first about how great it is for *mankind* that the Messiah has arrived, but how the event glorifies *God*; and then how it should result in peace on earth, good will to men. (The latter phrase is variously translated "men of good will" or, NIV, "men on whom his [God's] favor rests.")

III. Journey to Bethlehem, 15-20
A. Infant Messiah, 15-16

15 And it came to pass, as the angels were gone away from them into heaven, the shepherds said one to another, Let us now go even unto Bethlehem, and see this thing which is come to pass, which the Lord hath made known unto us.

16 And they came with haste, and found Mary, and Joseph, and the babe lying in a manger.

Recognizing that they have been especially favored with this rare piece of Good News, the shepherds must hurry to Bethlehem. Perhaps they wanted some visible evidence that the heavenly display they have witnessed is true, but they also no doubt wanted to pay homage to this Messiah-Child.

B. Telling the news, 17-18

17 And when they had seen it, they made known abroad the saying which was told them concerning this child.

18 And all they that heard it wondered at those things which were told them by the shepherds.

Seeing with their own eyes proof of the angel's announcement, what could the shepherds do but disperse and tell everyone they knew? Only the weariness, failures, and disillusionment of intervening years keep believers today from doing the same thing when they consider how momentous this event is.

C. Reflecting on the event, 19-20

19 But Mary kept all these things, and pondered them in her heart.

20 And the shepherds returned, glorifying and praising God for all the things that they had heard and seen, as it was told unto them.

In contrast with the shepherds, the mother of the Babe of Bethlehem keeps her own counsel. After all, she is a teenage Jewish mother who has borne a Child whose father is actually God; it is a wonder that bears not only telling others about, but simply, and deeply, pondering.

Bible Quiz

Evangelistic Emphasis

Christmas Day 2005 is here. It is a unique time when Christmas Day actually falls on Sunday. Churches all over America have "adjusted" their regular times of worship to make attendance on this Sunday more "convenient."

I'll bet you that you have a very sparse crowd on this morning. The people who are at church are the ones who are always there. You won't get any of the C and E people on Christmas. C and E people show up around Christmas and Easter to get their faith ticket validated.

Ironic isn't it? One of our two biggest days and we can't stir up a crowd. We have to change the times of worship just to get a quorum. Most congregations this week won't have Sunday school either, because they have modified their time of worship, and Sunday school is out of luck.

I guess the gift for you from the **Higley Commentary** people is that we will go ahead and publish this full lesson and you can enjoy it. I will fill up the usual places with Weekday Problems and Lesson in Your Life, but I might have a little fun. It can be my Christmas present to you.

Still, doesn't it bother you just a little that the elf in the red suit seems to draw more attention on this day than the Savior in the manger?

ഇറ

Memory Selection

For unto you is born this day in the city of David a Savior, who is Christ the Lord.—*Luke 2: 11*

Jesus wants to get personal with you. That is what Christmas is about—God coming in a way in which we would have to get personal with Him. We all have this part of our souls that causes us to be attracted to a baby. None of us are afraid of babies. So God came to earth in a way that we would not fear and that would be attractive for us.

He came to earth to call us by name. We have that kind of personal relationship with Jesus. We are on a first name basis with him. We call Him what His mother and His friends called Him. Part of being called by name is to know the name of the other. Friends don't call each other by their titles.

He calls us by name. He knows the name your parents gave you. He knows the nicknames your friends call you. He even has heard those names you have been called that have hurt your soul. He whispered your name when you were born. He laughed and said your name when you came to into a saving relationship with Him. He will gently speak your name when you close your eyes in this life and awaken in eternity.

So, read the passage again, and this time put your name into it.

Weekday Problems

How in the world can I get someone into trouble during Christmas week? I could tell you about the lie that department stores print on those special presents you purchase for your kids. You know the lie, it is in bold letters: "*Some Assembly Required*." You open the box and find out that this gizmo has about a billion parts. You also discover the instructions were written by a person for whom English was not his primary language.

The other horrible phrase that is heard, especially on Christmas morning, is when the kids and adults want to play with a new toy and discover that "batteries are not included." I have taken batteries out of essential appliances to make sure my kids had batteries on Christmas morning.

Then there are the dangerous initials QVC found on the outside of a package. Yes, your friend or your in-laws have purchased your gift over the television. At 3 a.m. I was sure that my brother wants a combination pop up toaster and CD player. QVC or the Home Shopping Channel will do it all: wrap it, mail it, and bill you for it. You don't have to leave your recliner.

These are some problems that can arise even on Christmas morning. That is the point; Jesus came to save people who can't always put things together, who forget batteries, and who buy a gift that wasn't well thought out. He came to save us. He came to help with our Weekday Problems.

Q: What simple affliction brought on the death of Samson?
A: Fallen arches.

***

Q: Who was the best financier in the Bible?
A: Noah. He floated his stock while the whole world was being liquidated.

***

Q: Who was the straightest man in the Bible?
A: Joseph. Pharaoh made a ruler out of him.

***

Q: Where is tennis mentioned in the Bible?
A: In Genesis, when Joseph served in Pharaoh's court.

***

Q: What animal took the most baggage into the ark?
A: The elephant. He took his whole trunk, while the rooster only took his comb.

—Thanks to Bob Phillips, in *The World's Greatest Collection of Clean Jokes*

This Lesson in Your Life

Anita Wheatcroft tells of a Christmas not too long ago.

"It happened in a large church in New York City where I grew up. During an annual Nativity pageant, the church was especially full. Hushed in darkness, the congregation watched the lighting of the candles. Toward the back, I sat, one timid little girl, with my family. Newly moved to the city after a family separation and trauma, my life had settled down, but I was still overwhelmed and homesick for my grandparents and familiar friends. That night, however, caught up in awe as organ music rolled out from balcony to rafters, I heard a familiar story I loved, and was transported to another time and place. Down the aisle swept a colorful procession as the lights went up, revealing the magnificent manger scene. Travelers, bearded shepherds, and finally the three kings bearing gifts advanced majestically. Before anyone knew it, I found myself following them.

"The journey down that long aisle was an early spiritual pilgrimage for me, yet it felt like a kind of homecoming. When I reached the manger scene, there were a sleepy donkey, real sheep, and Mary and Joseph beneath an angel with outstretched wings. Above all, there was a light in the manger, enfolding us in its glow. Kneeling in front of it, I had a sense of exaltation, of self-offering as real as any I have ever known since. This was real to me, and I was there. Of course, it didn't last long. I was lifted to my feet by an usher and carried down the aisle, back to my embarrassed family, and the pageant swept on. I was vaguely aware of subdued smiles, and my parents' whispered scolding didn't matter. My discovery was my own, and I had something now that no one could ever take from me. I had been to Bethlehem. I had seen it all for the first time and I would never forget it."

Is that what you have experienced this Christmas morning, the wonderment of traveling again to Bethlehem. The story is and old one, but each time we tell we are reliving the real story of the birth of the Son of God. Jesus Christ is born to today!

How did you feel this morning about priorities? Were yours wrapped up in unwrapping? Did you have a burning desire to get to church and worship Jesus on this very special day? Christmas morning on Sunday morning tells us a lot about ourselves. What lessons has this day taught in your life?

STRAIGHT

1. Jesus was born at a specific time in world history. What historical figures did Luke list?
Caesar Augustus was emperor of Rome. Quirinius was governor of Syria.

2. What was the essence of the decree that was issued?
The decree was a call for a census of the Roman Empire. Each citizen of the empire had to register.

3. What was the purpose of the trip that Joseph and Mary made from Nazareth to Bethlehem?
Joseph was going to Bethlehem to be enrolled for the tax rolls.

4. What was the significance of Bethlehem?
Bethlehem was the ancestral home of David, and the predicted birthplace of the Messiah.

5. When comparing Matthew with Luke, what do you notice about the family tree of Jesus?
Matthew traces the family tree back to Abraham. Luke traces the family tree back to God.

6. What other differences exist between the way Luke and Matthew trace the ancestry of Jesus?
Matthew traces the family tree through Joseph. Luke gives Mary's genealogy.

7. According to Luke, were Joseph and Mary married to each other when they traveled to Bethlehem?
No, they were only engaged.

8. Which verse of the Gospels mentions the Innkeeper?
The innkeeper is never mentioned in any scripture. This character is not in the Christmas story.

9. To whom was the birth of Jesus first announced?
The announcement of Jesus' birth was made first to the night shift shepherds who were watching the sheep sleep.

10. What is the significance of shepherds being the first to hear the news?
Jesus came for all people. No one was excluded from His love, even lowly shepherds.

Clark Kimberly Oler tells this story:

"There he was again. He was barely six years old and wearing his red stocking hat. His face was pressed against the iron fence that surrounds the church garden. I had seen this little boy before, always wearing the same ragged red hat pulled over his ears, the same old sneakers, and the same tattered jacket.

"Several times I had spoken to him, trying to find out who he was. But each time he just looked at me in distrust, with large solemn eyes and, without a word, ran off down the street.

"It was Christmas Eve. The snow had been falling all day, and I was looking out the rectory window. The street was dark and deserted. The only bright spot shone from a huge nativity scene erected in the church garden. Life-sized figures attended the figure of the baby Jesus. And on the ground, surrounding the manger was a thick covering of real straw. The figure of Mary knelt by the manger, tenderly contemplating the holy child.

"Then it was that I saw him again, wearing that unmistakable red hat, peering through the fence at the crèche. As I watched, he ventured timidly into the garden. For a long time he stood before the crèche. Then, suddenly, he climbed inside and curled up in the straw, under the gaze of the Virgin Mary.

"For half an hour I watched, not daring to go outside, because I knew that the moment I opened the door he would scurry away.

"Now and again, when there as no one passing by, I could see a little arm reach up and small fingers would touch Mary's cheek. Then something startled the boy, and in a flash, he was up, out the gate, and down the street. He disappeared into the night.

"I felt as though I had been granted a momentary look into a child's heart. I grieved for him, I felt utterly helpless. All I could do was breathe a prayer that, somehow, he had been comforted by Mary's unchanging expression of love.

"Aren't we all like that little boy in one way or another?

"Do we not reach out in our imagination, to touch, with aching fingers, the loving cheek of God?"

Merry Christmas

Unit II. God's Gifts of Leadership

Lesson 5

Finding Strength to Serve

1 Timothy 1:12-20

And I thank Christ Jesus our Lord, who hath enabled me, for that he counted me faithful, putting me into the ministry;

13 Who was before a blasphemer, and a persecutor, and injurious: but I obtained mercy, because I did it ignorantly in unbelief.

14 And the grace of our Lord was exceeding abundant with faith and love which is in Christ Jesus.

15 This is a faithful saying, and worthy of all acceptation, that Christ Jesus came into the world to save sinners; of whom I am chief.

16 Howbeit for this cause I obtained mercy, that in me first Jesus Christ might shew forth all longsuffering, for a pattern to them which should hereafter believe on him to life everlasting.

17 Now unto the King eternal, immortal, invisible, the only wise God, be honour and glory for ever and ever. Amen.

18 This charge I commit unto thee, son Timothy, according to the prophecies which went before on thee, that thou by them mightest war a good warfare;

19 Holding faith, and a good conscience; which some having put away concerning faith have made shipwreck:

20 Of whom is Hymenaeus and Alexander; whom I have delivered unto Satan, that they may learn not to blaspheme.

Devotional Reading
Romans 16:17-27

Background Scripture
1 Timothy 1

Memory Selection
1 Timothy 1:12

171

FOCUS

From the profound doctrine of the Incarnation we take up a series of lessons from the "Pastoral Epistles" (1 and 2 Timothy, Titus) that deal with the very practical issue of our response to God's gift of salvation through Christ. They deal with church order, organizational duties, and similar practical matters.

In this first lesson the apostle Paul writes to the younger minister Timothy, reflecting on his (Paul's) own call. He is overwhelmed with his unworthiness to be chosen a leader of God's people, but he knows that leadership is vital, and that with God's grace he can rise to the challenge. He is also concerned that Timothy (and Christian leaders today) possess this sense of commitment.

ഇറ

Ask group members to say the first word or phrase that comes to mind when you say the word *minister.* (If the teacher is a minister, or if one is in the group, he or she should be prepared for some good-natured ribbing, as some members predictably come up with responses like "only works on Sundays.")

Focus especially on responses such as "servant" and "servanthood," since the New Testament word minister also meant *servant.* Note that the spread of the faith has depended on *missionary servants,* and the continued establishment of the practice of faith depends on *local ministers.* Point out that, like Paul, many ministers feel unworthy of their calling, but that this makes it no less essential.

Teaching Outline	*Daily Bible Readings*
I. Merciful Ministry—12-17	Mon. 'Strengthen Me, O God' Psalm 119:25-32
A. 'Put' into ministry, 12	Tue. God Can Give Strength Romans 16:17-27
B. Grace for ministry, 13-14	
C. Patience for ministry, 15-16	Wed. Timothy Sent to Strengthen 1 Thess. 3:1-5
D. Ministering for God's glory, 17	Thu. 'May God Strengthen You' 1 Thess. 3:6-13
II. Charge to Minister—18-20	Fri. Strengthening the Churches Acts 16:1-5
A. Fight the good fight, 18	
B. Hold on to the faith, 19	Sat. Paul Writes to Timothy 1 Tim. 1:1-11
C. Warning re. blasphemy, 20	Sun. Strengthened by Christ 1 Tim. 1:12-20

Verse by Verse

I. Merciful Ministry—12-17
A. 'Put' into ministry, 12

12 And I thank Christ Jesus our Lord, who hath enabled me, for that he counted me faithful, putting me into the ministry;

This letter is the first of three "Pastoral Epistles"—letters attributed to the apostle Paul, designed to stabilize leadership in the early Church. Although written specifically to guide the ministries of Timothy and Titus, these letters provide valuable guidance to the modern Church because of their insights into the ways and means of organizing and guiding Christian ministry.

Here Paul is writing to the younger minister Timothy, whom the apostle has mentored since his second missionary journey (Acts 16:1-3). Paul had been rather abruptly "put" into the ministry in his sudden conversion experience on the Damascus Road. In turn he feels responsible for guiding Timothy's ministry, partly because of the ever-present danger of slipping into doctrinal error. Thus Paul not only offers positive guidance, but warns against "any other thing that is contrary to sound doctrine" (vs. 10). When we read of the immoral acts Paul lists there, we see that "sound doctrine" isn't just orthodox but abstract teaching. The word translated "sound" also gives us the word "hygienic"; so the Pastoral Epistles point us to life-related principles that have to do with keeping the Church "healthy." Paul expresses gratitude for God's having trusted him enough—especially in view of his having persecuted Christians as Saul of Tarsus—to place him in such a ministry (the word for which is *diakonon*, or service [as in the NIV]). From the start, we realize that Paul does not consider ministry an "office" that enables a dominant personality to "lord it over the flock," but an opportunity to serve others.

B. Grace for ministry, 13-14

13 Who was before a blasphemer, and a persecutor, and injurious: but I obtained mercy, because I did it ignorantly in unbelief.

14 And the grace of our Lord was exceeding abundant with faith and love which is in Christ Jesus.

Now Paul refers specifically to his previous misguided ways when he persecuted Christians in behalf of the official Jewish establishment. As Jesus taught, "he who has been forgiven little loves little" (Luke 7:47, NIV). By the same token, Paul's attitude reveals that he who has been forgiven much loves much; and he now grateful and zealous for the opportunity for ministry. His "ignorance" and "unbelief" shows that at least he was genuine and sincere in his former ways—traits that no doubt played a central role in God's extending mercy toward him.

C. Patience for ministry, 15-16

15 This is a faithful saying, and worthy of all acceptation, that Christ Jesus came into the world to save sinners; of whom I am chief.

16 Howbeit for this cause I obtained mercy, that in me first Jesus Christ might shew forth all longsuffering, for a pattern to them which should hereafter believe on him to life everlasting.

An interesting feature of the Pastoral Epistles is the recurring phrase "this is a faithful saying" (see also 4:9; 2 Tim. 2:11; Titus 3:8). This was like putting an English sentence in italics—the writer's special way of drawing attention to the importance of what follows. In this first instance (vs. 15), what follows is the foundation "mission statement" of the Incarnation: *to save sinners.* Paul is saying that it is typical of Christ to choose him, "the chief of sinners," since saving sinners, not those who think they have no need for salvation, was why God sent His only-begotten Son into the world.

Verse 16 serves as a "good news" verse for all who think they aren't "worth" saving. Paul's genuineness, not his prior righteousness, was the reason he was selected to be a minister. In His divine "longsuffering" (NIV "patience"), Christ selected Paul in an instance of the amazing grace that now is a "pattern" for all other sinners. It says to us, that, despite our unworthiness, in the title of a sermon by the late theologian Paul Tillich, *"You are accepted."*

"Live everlasting" (NIV "eternal life") refers not just to life unending, but to the eternal *quality* of life that defines God, and that amazingly is given to those who follow Him. This is why Paul and so many other ministers in the early Church could give their lives for the faith: they had been given a heavenly life that made giving up their earthly life more than worth it.

D. Ministering for God's glory, 17

17 Now unto the King eternal, immortal, invisible, the only wise God, be honour and glory for ever and ever. Amen.

Paul seems to be unable to contain himself in light of God's grace. He bursts out in a brief hymn of praise ascribing glory to the God who loves sinners enough to entrust them with the ministry. The adjectives Paul uses to describe God are a short course in His nature: He is without beginning or end ("eternal, immortal"), invisible, one, and uniquely wise (see also 6:15-16). The sentence is significant in the way it gives glory to the God who ordains ministers, not to the ministers themselves.

II. Charge to Minister—18-20

A. Fight the good fight, 18

18 This charge I commit unto

thee, son Timothy, according to the prophecies which went before on thee, that thou by them mightest war a good warfare;

Now Paul gets to the kernel of his reason for writing to the younger minister. The word for "charge" was used for an authoritative message delivered to a soldier. Timothy therefore "is solemnly reminded that the ministry is not a matter to be trifled with, but an order from the commander-in-chief" (Donald Guthrie, *The Pastoral Epistles,* Tyndale New Testament Commenties, p. 77). The language of spiritual warfare confirms this observation.

We do not know what prophecies pointed Timothy to the ministry. No doubt they were based in part on the good foundation he had inherited from his mother Eunice and his grandmother Lois (2 Tim. 2:5), which created not merely a message from heaven about the young man's future ability as a minister, but a "trajectory" that provided a relatively predictable estimate of his calling.

B. Hold on to the faith, 19

19 Holding faith, and a good conscience; which some having put away concerning faith have made shipwreck:

Although faith and a good conscience are essential equipment for all Christians, they are especially important traits for ministers because their work is so visible. These two elements are also linked in 1:5 and 3:9, showing that faith and morals are inseparably related. All genuine Christians cringe when the news media turn up cases when ministers have claimed to be "full of faith," but are in fact "unfaithful," in their handling of finances or their personal moral conduct. Paul is not over-stating the case when he says that such lapses "shipwreck" Christ's cause on earth.

C. Warning of blasphemy, 20

20 Of whom is Hymenaeus and Alexander; whom I have delivered unto Satan, that they may learn not to blaspheme.

Hymenaeus is also mentioned in a negative reference in 2 Tim. 2:17, and Alexander may be the person mentioned in 2 Tim. 4:14, who did "much evil" to Paul. We do not know specifically how they made "shipwreck" of the faith. Whatever the case, they had become precisely what Paul is warning against: ministers who claimed to have faith but whose works denied the claim. This amounted to "blasphemy," which means literally to "speak against" or defame God. Paul had admitted the same sin in verse 13; but unlike Paul, these two ministers had apparently lacked Paul's genuineness of heart; their blasphemy was deliberate.

Apparently their sin was so serious that the apostle had administered some kind of church discipline, probably excommunication—indicating the need to make their discipline as public as their blasphemy. Note that the purpose was not just to punish them but "that they may *learn* . . . ." Paul had in mind rehabilitation, not just retaliation.

Evangelistic Emphasis

Let's get something out of the way from the start. I am a sinner. I woke up this morning and before I had gotten much out of bed I committed a sin. It had something to do with my dog tripping me. It was the dog's fault after all that she sleeps at the foot of my bed and I can't see her in the early morning dawn.

I am an expert sinner. I have had years of practice. I know how to sin in public and in private. I also know how to have my sins forgiven! So before you refuse to read any further because of the sin of this author, let's admit something else. You are a sinner too! I know you are a sinner. I know this because the Bible has turned you in. "For all have sinned," it says. I know that you don't mean to be a sinner. And I hope you know that the blood of Jesus cleanses your sins.

Now I have been tongue and cheek with this, but there is also "serious good news." Since we are all sinners, we have common ground to talk to people about a faith relationship with Jesus Christ and being saved by His amazing grace.

So, sinners let's unite, and tell the world there is a cure for our common sin problem. Our sins can be forgiven in the name of Jesus.

&)(&

And I thank Christ Jesus, our Lord, who hath enabled me, in that he counted me faithful, putting me into the ministry.—*1 Timothy 1: 12*

Today is the first day of 2005! Have you made your New Year's resolutions yet? Sunday morning, January 1, 2006, would be a good day to make a couple of resolutions that would change you life. Let me help you. In 2006, why not claim the ministry to which God called you? The moment you were baptized you were called into the service (ministry) of the Church. You don't have to be ordained to do ministry. You don't have to possess a seminary degree to do ministry. Your baptism was your authorization in the name of Jesus Christ to serve Him through His church.

Paul was clear with Timothy that it was the power of Jesus Christ that enabled him to do his ministry. That is the key to working faithfully for Christ. Do you serve Him in your own power? Do you serve Him using His power?

It is His grace that brings us into relationship with Him. It is His Holy Spirit that gives us the ability we need to live for Him. It is His continuing presence with us that allows us to engage in the mystery we call "ministry."

Weekday Problems

Mavis Martin was not in a good mood. She had been a member of the Triple L Sunday school class for only six months. She had found that Triple L meant, "love, life, and loyalty." Mrs. Webster had asked Mavis if she would teach the class on New Year's Day, 2006.

Mavis had worked very hard on the lesson from 1 Timothy. She had read the lesson in many translations. She had consulted her *Higley Lesson Commentary* for information about how to teach the class. She felt confident that she had grip on the lesson and how she would share insights with the class. She knew that she might have a small turnout on New Year's Day, but she was confident that she would have a class. After all the ladies of Triple L were not known for their "nightlife." They were the pillars of the pillars of the church.

The hour for Sunday school arrived. The lesson was ready. The coffee was hot. The Bible was opened. The room was the right temperature. Everything was in place. Mavis had prayed that God would use her words to touch lives in this lesson.

Thirty minutes later, Mr. Tom, the Sunday school superintendent opened the door. He noted on his attendance sheet for the Triple L Sunday school class: One teacher. Zero students.

*In 2006 how can you help increase the size of *your* Sunday school class?

Spotlight on Ministry

After the funeral, the minister posted this notice on the church bulletin board: "Brother Poure departed for heaven at 3:30 a.m."

The next day he found the following "telegram" written below his announcement: "Heaven, 8 a.m.—Mr. Poure has not arrive yet. Great anxiety."

***

Minister: Mrs. Janelli, what did you think of the sermon?

Mrs. Janelli: It was so very instructive, Pastor. You know, we didn't really know what sin is until you came.

***

Joe Jones had a bad heart, but the minister decided to call on him and inform him that he had just inherited $1 million. He decided to ease into the subject gently.

"Joe," he asked, "what would you do if you inherited a million dollars?

"Why, I'd give half of it to the church," Joe replied.

The minister fell over dead with a heart attack.

This Lesson in Your Life

Guilt.

It's pervasive. It's persistent. Worse than a summer cold, more annoying than seasonal allergies, and completely resistant to the Paxils and Prozacs provided by modern medicine. The condition grips you like a free-floating sense of worthlessness or an existential dread. It burrows deep down inside you, an agonizing writhing of conscience permanently lodged in the soul.

Modern secular guilt squats inside us constantly, unrelieved and unarticulated, growing ever more rancid. Millions of seemingly innocent people feel guilty. Yet they have committed no crimes, done nothing truly shameful. "Nonetheless their guilt persists, at least in their own eyes," one writer observed, "and often neatly folded away, though it cannot help but inject their other emotions and acts with unmentioned pain."

Where does this guilt come from? And what does it mean?

First, there are the lawn-watering laws and their ilk. We feel hemmed in by all kinds of new laws that regulate every aspect of life: littering laws, seat-belt laws, drink and drug laws, gambling laws, parking laws. Cross any of these lines and you immediately feel a twinge of guilt.

Second, there's our day-to-day respectability. There is another kind of guilt that arises out of mediocrity, conformity, and unfulfilled potential. We believe that we could do more with our lives, be truer to ourselves, take more risks and have more fun, and we feel guilty when we compromise our potential by following the safe road of quiet respectability.

Third, we feel guilty about rejecting guilt. We think that a clear conscience is the sign of a bad memory. We feel guilty about our modern abandonment of genuine morality, nagged by our rejection of traditional guilt. When everything was black and white, we knew precisely why we felt guilty, and we knew what to do about it. Now we live in a world of grayness and confusion and moral relativity; we have no widely accepted moral truths to give shape to our guilt. We need a strong morality to make sense of our suffering conscience, or else our guilt festers and consumes.

The modern world gives us a deep and disturbing sense that there is something terribly wrong with our lives. We're facing a guilt glut, and it feels absolutely awful.

So, what are we going to do about it?

Paul claimed to be the greatest of sinners. He confessed his sin and was forgiven and restored by Jesus Christ.

What do you do with your guilt?

Give it to Jesus.

1. How did Paul describe his relationship with Timothy?

Timothy was addressed as Paul's "loyal child in the faith."

2. Timothy was in Ephesus and was dealing with what problems in the church?

Timothy was dealing with those who "occupy themselves with myths and endless genealogies and promote speculations."

3. The speculations mentioned in verse 4 were a poor substitute for what?

They were a poor substitute for "divine training that is known by faith."

4. What is the aim of "divine training that is known by faith"?

The aim of that instruction is "love that comes from a pure heart, a good conscience, and a sincere faith."

5. How did Paul describe his life before meeting Jesus Christ?

Paul was a blasphemer, persecutor, and a man of violence.

6. What had been Paul's motivation for his actions?

He was acting "ignorantly in unbelief" when he was a blasphemer, persecutor, and a man of violence.

7. What saying, apparently prevalent in the church of that day, does Paul quote several times in the Pastoral Epistles?

"This is a faithful saying, and worthy of all acceptation . . . ."

8. What level of sinner had Paul sunk to in his pre Christian days?

Paul had achieved the dubious distinction of being, in his mind, "the chief of sinners."

9. What doxology did Paul place in the middle of this letter?

"To the King of the ages, immortal, invisible, the only God, be honor and glory forever and ever. Amen."

10. What two people in Ephesus were causing trouble for Paul?

Hymenaeus and Alexander were two people whom Paul had turned over to Satan so that "they may learn not to blaspheme."

Dogs are great at guilt. The moment you walk into the house, a dog will telegraph to you with its whole body the sin it has committed. The eyes squint and dart this way and that. The ears are flattened. The head is lowered. The tail trails. Pathetically ingratiating behavior usually accompanies all this—desperate little hand licks, half-hearted tail wags, general obeisance.

When you discover the actual crime—a mistake on the rug, a broken whatnot, a chewed shoe—it only takes one phrase to crush your dog's faint optimism and fawning spirit. In a low, I'm-the-master-voice, you intone: "Shame on you! Oh, how could you? Shame!" Complete canine collapse ensues. Guilt overwhelms the creature. It throws itself on your mercy or slinks away in abject misery. This is probably one of the main reasons people like to have dogs as pets—it allows us to wield the power of punishment and forgiveness with such clear-cut, unambiguous results.

Unfortunately for God, human beings are not nearly as reliable or repentant. Indeed, we seem to possess an uncanny ability to shift blame, ignore consequences, and shirk responsibility. After one particularly corrupt boondoggle during the infamous administration of Chicago's Mayor Richard J. Daley, he was confronted by a young reporter. "Aren't you concerned and embarrassed by these activities, Mayor?"

Daley said imperiously, "Son, nothing embarrasses us!"

That sentiment appears to be guiding our behavior today. Outlandishly corrupt, overtly immoral, banally violent, and shocking evil are paraded before us, invited on talk shows, made rich and famous, and given control of our streets. It seems there is no longer any sense of shame or guilt or embarrassment operating in our culture.

To live without a sense of shame or embarrassment suggests that we can go through our entire lifetime without ever being ashamed of our behavior, no matter what transpires. Are we really so calloused that we can routinely compromise our integrity, betray the trust of others, hurt those we claim to love, and dishonor God, without ever feeling a twinge of guilt or a flicker of conscience?

Actually, there does seem to be an intensified tendency to register all these feelings—but then to successfully pass final blame onto someone else. We acknowledge our sins, but point the finger at someone else to take responsibility. Of course, such behavior is a time-honored human trait (see Genesis 3:12-13 for Adam and Eve's original rendition).

What will you do about guilt and shame in your life?

Jesus is the answer.

Lesson 6

Everyone Needs Prayer

1 Timothy 2:1-8

I exhort therefore, that, first of all, supplications, prayers, intercessions, and giving of thanks, be made for all men;

2 For kings, and for all that are in authority; that we may lead a quiet and peaceable life in all godliness and honesty.

3 For this is good and acceptable in the sight of God our Saviour;

4 Who will have all men to be saved, and to come unto the knowledge of the truth.

5 For there is one God, and one mediator between God and men, the man Christ Jesus;

6 Who gave himself a ransom for all, to be testified in due time.

7 Whereunto I am ordained a preacher, and an apostle, (I speak the truth in Christ, and lie not;) a teacher of the Gentiles in faith and verity.

8 I will therefore that men pray every where, lifting up holy hands, without wrath and doubting.

Devotional Reading
1 Thessalonians 5:16-22

Background Scripture
1 Timothy 2

Memory Selection
1 Timothy 2:1

Jan. 8

We have noted that the Pastoral Epistles were written in part to define how to respond to the grace of salvation. This includes living together as the Church; and this lesson focuses on a divine dimension of this togetherness—the importance of corporate *prayer* as a link between God and His gathered people.

Paul's teaching on this topic reflects the teachings of Jesus, who emphasized prayer. He brought a fresh, personal perspective, urging us to take the smallest details of our lives to God in prayer, with the faith that "whatsoever ye shall ask in my name, that will I do" (John 14:13). The "model prayer" or "Lord's Prayer" He taught remains a central part of much Christian worship to this day. Regardless of any questions we might have about unanswered prayer, God's people are challenged here to be a people of prayer.

To begin this lesson, invite group members to share their experience with prayer. Some may have testimonies of answered prayer, but be sure also to encourage others to share any questions they may have about times when their prayers have apparently gone unanswered.

Note what the fact that Scripture urges us to pray says about God. Unlike most pagan gods, the God of the Bible dares to open Himself up to hearing the needs of His people. He wants to establish intimate communication with us. Many Christians are accustomed to praying for a miracle. The fact that God has even provided this means of communicating with Him is itself a miraculous thing.

Teaching Outline	*Daily Bible Readings*

I. How to Pray—1
 	
II. The Who and What of Prayer—2
  A. Civic authorities, 2a
  B. A life of peace, 2b
 	
III. Foundations for Prayer—3-7
  A. The willing God, 3-4
  B. The One and giving God, 5-6
  C. Paul's commission, 7
 	
IV. Plea for Prayer—8
	Mon. Praying for the Philippians
	       Philip. 1:3-11
	Tue. Pray Without Ceasing
	       1 Thess. 5:16-22
	Wed. God Hears Our Prayers
	       1 Pet. 3:8-12a
	Thu. Parable About Prayer
	       Luke 18:1-8
	Fri. Praying for Enemies
	       Matt. 5:43-48
	Sat. Praying for All
	       1 Tim. 2:1-7
	Sun. Power of Prayer
	       James 5:13-18

Verse by Verse

I. How to Pray—1

1 I exhort therefore, that, first of all, supplications, prayers, intercessions, and giving of thanks, be made for all men;

The word for "exhort" means literally to "call alongside," as a private tutor takes a favorite pupil under his wing to give an especially important lesson. This expresses Paul's passion about what he considers to be of "first" importance in ordering a faithful congregation. It is not having elders or deacons, or getting the liturgy just right, or even ensuring orthodox doctrine, as important as that was for Paul. Of *first* importance, he says, is that a church be a praying church. He uses four terms to describe this activity.

1. Supplications. This strong word means an urgent petition or request. It is possibly related to the Greek *dei*, meaning "it is necessary." When we bring a supplication to God we feel deeply emotional about the need for an answer to our request, whether it is in our own behalf or that of another. Words such as "plead" or "beg" come to mind to describe the pressing need we feel in a supplication. In Ephesians 6:18 Paul uses the term twice as he literally piles word upon word to indi-

cate urgency in prayer: "Praying always with all prayer and supplication in the Spirit . . . with all perseverance and supplication for all saints." From all this we can gather that strongly and emotionally felt needs are properly expressed even in public prayer.

2. Prayer is the more general and common word for communicating with God. It most often appears in the context of public prayers, as here, and can even mean a *place* of prayer, as a chapel. Yet it can also cover a wide range of sub-meanings, including the three other terms Paul uses here.

3. Intercessions are the prayers we pray in behalf of others. In these, we express our willingness to stand between those in need and the loving God who can supply that need. One of the many mysteries of prayer arises here: Why does God want to hear us express a need of which, as an all-knowing and loving Father, He already knows? Perhaps a partial answer is that God wants those who pray to clarify the need in their own minds, and to share the issue with those assembled about them.

4. Giving of thanks translates a single word in the original. It is the same term from which we get the word "Eucharist" for the Lord's Supper, reminding us that Jesus "gave thanks" when He instituted it.

The closing words of verse 1 remind the Church that all four of these aspects of prayer are to be made in behalf "of all men," anticipating the *whom-we-should-pray-for* element in verse 2. "Men" here is the general Greek term for "people" (cp. "everyone" in the *New Revised Standard Version*), not "males"—a distinction Paul will also make later in verse 8.)

II. The Who and What of Prayer—2
A. Civic authorities, 2a

2a For kings, and for all that are in authority;

In addition to "everyone," Paul elevates governmental authorities for the Church to pray for. Why would he single out this group, when he may well have mentioned the sick, church leaders, or any number of others who need our prayers? Because, as the rest of verse 2 shows, the rulings of kings and the heads of local government are crucial for the very existence of the congregation in the community.

B. A life of peace, 2b

2b that we may lead a quiet and peaceable life in all godliness and honesty.

Governmental authorities were those who were so often responsible, in the early Church, for bans against Christians even meeting together; so Paul counsels urgent prayer for them because the life of the congregation was in their hands.

It was possible even for a pagan ruler to reign "in all godliness," since the term can mean "piety" or "reverence" without regard to the god worshiped. This seems virtually equivalent for praying that an official would pay allegiance even to "the rule of law," as opposed to playing favorites or ruling for purely self-serving motives. Even in free societies it is still important to pray for governmental leaders to lead honestly and wisely, "paying allegiance" to justice whether or not they are believers.

III. Foundations for Prayer—3-7
A. The willing God, 3-4

3 For this is good and acceptable in the sight of God our Saviour;

4 Who will have all men to be saved, and to come unto the knowledge of the truth.

Here Paul affirms that prayer is appropriate even though the good we seek in prayer is already known by a good God. In fact, one of the fundamental bases for praying in the first place is that God is willing to answer prayer. Affirming this truth at this point in Paul's teaching may imply that some early believers wondered whether it was appropriate for Christians to pray for non-Christians.

More generally, Paul affirms that prayer is not trying to convince a grumpy, divine despot to come over to our side and tend to human needs, when He would really rather do them harm. While this raises again the question of prayer's purpose, Paul does not go into this issue. He only affirms that the good for which we ask is already in the mind of the God who wants and knows the good for all, including their salvation.

B. The One and giving God, 5-6

5 For there is one God, and one mediator between God and men, the man Christ Jesus;

6 Who gave himself a ransom for all, to be testified in due time.

Again, Christians are to ask God to bless even non-Christians because of the solidarity that exists between God and all creation. The doctrine of monotheism means, among many other things, that believers do not have their own Creator who is willing to answer their prayers, while there is another creator-god for non-believers. Also, Paul affirms that there is ultimately only one mediator or go-between. Believers and unbelievers alike have only one High Priest through whom they go to present their needs to God.

While Christian prayer is in a sense a "mediation" between God and man, Paul insists that the ultimate mediation lies with "the man Christ Jesus." Although He is also divine, as God's Son, the human aspect is emphasized here because the subject under discussion is prayer for human needs. The obscure phrase "to be testified in due time" probably refers to the missionary work Paul envisions which was even then going on—taking "into all the world" the testimony that Jesus is our

Mediator with God.

C. Paul's commission, 7

7 Whereunto I am ordained a preacher, and an apostle, (I speak the truth in Christ, and lie not;) a teacher of the Gentiles in faith and verity.

"Whereunto" connects what was just said about spreading the testimony about Jesus as Christ and Mediator with Paul's own missionary charge. As God told Ananias, Paul was a chosen vessel to take the Good News to the Gentiles (Acts 9:15).

IV. Plea for Prayer—8

8 I will therefore that men pray every where, lifting up holy hands, without wrath and doubting.

Now the word for "men" means "males," (from Grk. *aner*), as opposed to the more general word for "people" (from *anthropos*). This counsel seems to follow the practice in the Jewish synagogue, where men were allowed to be more demonstrative than women (see the more modest instructions for women in vss. 9-10). Paul assumes that Christian men would carry this posture over into Christian worship.

Uplifted hands are an appropriate gesture to accompany the sense of pleading which prayer often involves, as well as a kind of "salute" when our prayers express praise and exaltation. Paul adds that raised hands should be accompanied by a peaceable mind, not one that is preoccupied either with congregational strife or anger toward officials for whom we are praying.

Evangelistic Emphasis

A little boy went to the fair with his dad and saw one of those inflatable clowns that you try to knock down. Of course, the harder you hit it, the quicker it comes back up. The father watched as the little boy continued to punch the clown, only for it to bounce back up again. Finally his dad interrupted him and asked, "How is it possible for the clown to keep standing back up, no matter how hard you hit it?"

The little boy scratched his head and said, "Dad, I think this clown is standing up on the inside."

Have you known people that no matter what hit them seemed to be "standing up on the inside?" They had an appealing sense of peace and calm in the midst of calamity. More often than not, their source of strength is a vital prayer life and a relationship with Christ that grew out of that prayer life.

Paul urged the church, through Timothy that "supplications, prayers, intercessions and thanksgivings be made for everyone." The good news today is that there are people in your community who are praying for you.

৪০০৪

Memory Selection

I exhort, therefore, that first of all, supplications, prayers, intercessions, and giving of thanks, be made for all.—*1 Timothy 2:1*

News stories, morning talk shows, and celebrity figures such as Deepak Chopra claim that prayer can improve health. Biologists, pundits, and others scoff at the same assertion. As is typical of so many debates regarding faith, people often see what they want to see: believers see proof of prayer, while skeptics see disproof. This raises the question: What does the research really show?

Dr. Harold Koenig, an associate professor of medicine at Duke University and the country's leading authority on faith-and-medicine studies, says that academic research does show that prayer has beneficial health effects, although mainly for the person who does the praying. Studies of "intercessory" prayer—Person A prays for the health of Person B—find scant if any effect.

However, studies of "petitionary" prayer, in which a person prays for his or her own health or peace of mind, show tangible statistical results. When you pray for your own health—especially your own mental health, in cases of clinical depression—science suggests you may be on solid ground.

Paul called us toward balance. We are challenged to pray for the needs of others, to give thanks for good things that happen, then to pray for ourselves.

Our prayer life can sometimes get out of balance. How is yours?

Weekday Problems

The Bible study had broken off into two camps. The poor pastor, new to the congregation, felt the sudden desire to call the bishop and recant his acceptance of this church.

The fight for the evening was on the nature of salvation. One side of the room was firmly convinced that the Church could do nothing to help or hinder God's plan of salvation for humanity. Their view was that God would save those persons who were "predestined" for salvation. They further believed that an individual held little responsibility when it came to matter of salvation. If you were part of God's elect, you were going to heaven no matter what you did.

Sitting next to the coffee pot on the other side of the room were the "free will" people. They believed that a person could decide to accept salvation or reject it. They also believed that the Church was a partner with God in bringing a person to faith in Christ. The pastor was caught in the middle of this furious, centuries old, and usually poorly understood debate.

*Divide your class along similar lines and discuss whether "free will" or "predestination" is implied in Paul's words, "This is right and is acceptable in the sight of God our Savior, who desires everyone to be saved and come to the knowledge of the truth."

Let Us Pray

Little Jimmy slipped and started to fall from the tree he was climbing. He had just cried out, "Help, Lord!" when he stopped and added, "Never mind, Lord, my pants just caught on a branch."

***

Beth told her mother that brother Billy had set some traps to catch birds. "What did you do about it?" her mother asked.

"I prayed that the traps might not work," said Beth. "And then I prayed that the poor little birds wouldn't go in them." Then, after a pause, she admitted, "And then I went and kicked the traps to pieces."

***

A tourist in Jerusalem saw a faithful Jew praying at the famous "Prayer Wall" in the Old City. When he was finished the tourist asked, "How did you feel, praying at such a historic place?"

"To tell the truth," said the devout man, "I was praying for peace with the Palestinians, and I felt like I was talking to a stone wall."

This Lesson in Your Life

"If no one has linked you to a prayer chain, count your blessings."

So ran the headline of a *Wall Street Journal* article. The story sounded rather strange, if not sacrilegious. It invites us to consider the case of a certain Church of Christ missionary from Dallas named David Allen.

Allen picked up a parasitic infection while stationed in Thailand in 1997. For about a year, he couldn't eat much except soda crackers, and his weight dropped from 172 pounds to 139. "I am in constant pain," he told four colleagues in a lengthy e-mail.

His message, with details of messy symptoms and frank admissions of despair, was meant to be private. But it was forwarded to several Internet sites that solicit prayer on behalf of those in need. Some people posting the messages embellished the facts, and added a diagnosis that Allen would "apparently die within two months" without divine intervention.

Allen was deluged with 10,000 e-mails and 2,000 letters in the first six months alone. And now, even though he has recovered, he continues to get responses. He's also being confused with an "Ezekial David Allen," a Southern Baptist working in Africa.

There seems to be a point at which prayer chains become a problem. If not a complete pain. Unless, of course, you happen to enjoy sorting through 55 e-mails a day while doubled over with a parasitic infection.

This is not to prattle against prayer. But Allen's experience does give one pause. An online site called Beliefnet.com has over 1,000 prayer chains which invite people to pray for women with breast cancer, folks with financial concerns, people living with chronic disease, adolescents with developmental handicaps, divorced moms, families with sick children, the mentally ill and their families, and bereaved parents who have lost a child. "These are real relationships that form on our message boards," claims Beliefnet's editor-in-chief. "Real consolation is offered, real compassion expressed, real prayers traded." (Real stuff in cyberspace?)

But is all this really necessary? Is this what the Bible means when it talks about praying for one another? Will the sheer number or volume of prayers offered somehow spur God into action? This smacks of a Washington lobby's approach to prayer. The prayer-chain assumption seems to be that you've got more clout with God when 10,000 people pray for you. If there's only one poor person praying over your sorry state of affairs, you might as well forget it.

Still, "the prayer of a righteous person avails much." Keep praying for those you know, and don't worry about the volume of prayer. Offer up the prayer of your heart and God will look with favor on your need.

1. List the different kinds of prayer that Paul urged the church to pray.

Paul urged that supplications, prayers, intercessions, and thanksgivings be made.

2. For whom did Paul urge prayers to be made?

Paul urged Christians to pray for kings and all who are in high positions.

3. What advantage could the Church realize by praying for kings and all in high positions?

The church would be able to lead a quiet and peaceable life in all godliness.

4. How did Paul describe the ministry of Jesus in the area of prayer?

Jesus is the one mediator between God and man because, while human himself, He gave himself as a ransom for all.

5. What was Paul's desire for the men as they prayed?

Paul urged that men should pray, lifting up holy hands without anger or arguments.

6. What was Paul's desire for the women in the church?

Paul wanted the women to dress modestly and decently.

7. If Paul's fashion advice were still followed today, what would women wear?

Women would only wear modest clothing. Their hair would not be styled. They would not wear jewelry.

8. How were women to behave in the church, according to Paul?

Women were to learn in silence with full submission.

9. What did Ephesus and Corinth have in common, and do you know how that commonality affects what Paul told the women in these communities?

They both had temples to Aphrodite in which pagan women were leading services. Paul didn't want Christian women compared to these priestesses.

10. What do you believe to be the role of women in the church today?

(I'm glad I won't be in your class to hear this discussion!)

189

Have you recovered from that last "seed thought" question? It was a tough one, wasn't it? Either we believe Paul literally or we find a reason why he said what he did to people in Corinth and Ephesus. It would help to do some research on the subject before diving in, especially if you have outspoken women in your class. I will be praying for you. You can relax now, because the rest of this Uplift page will be about prayer.

A bee flew into the car one day while the family was stopped at a traffic light. Try as they might to get it out through an open window, it insisted on buzzing blindly into the windshield. When the family got home, they tried again to get it to leave, but this only made the bee buzz angrily against the rear window. Again and again the family tried to direct the bee outside through the open windows and doors. Yet each time it evaded them. Afraid of injuring the bee by trying any further, the family left the car with the windows open and parked it next to a flowering bougainvillea vine, hoping this would entice the bee to freedom.

Alas, the next morning they found the little creature dead on the back dash under the rear window, mortally exhausted from its desperate efforts. This poor bee was sure it had the answer to its dilemma, so it buzzed with greater and greater intensity into the window. It stubbornly maintained that it could solve its own problem, when the truth was that the bee's way got it nowhere. All the bee had to do to reach the flowers outside the car was to admit personal powerlessness. Then the family could have taken it gently from the midst of its prison and released it to the sweetness of freedom.

How often do we humans try to solve a problem on our own, trying harder and harder to overcome some perceived difficulty? It is rather sobering to realize that whatever predicament we are now facing, it was our best thinking that got us there and our best thinking that is keeping us there—just like that little bee.

We need to change the way we approach life's problems. Pray first; work very hard only after you have prayed. This will put you in the proper position for God to help you with what you are facing.

Lesson 7

Leading God's People

1 Timothy 3:2-15

A bishop then must be blameless, the husband of one wife, vigilant, sober, of good behaviour, given to hospitality, apt to teach;

3 Not given to wine, no striker, not greedy of filthy lucre; but patient, not a brawler, not covetous;

4 One that ruleth well his own house, having his children in subjection with all gravity;

5(For if a man know not how to rule his own house, how shall he take care of the church of God?)

6 Not a novice, lest being lifted up with pride he fall into the condemnation of the devil.

7 Moreover he must have a good report of them which are without; lest he fall into reproach and the snare of the devil.

8 Likewise must the deacons be grave, not doubletongued, not given to much wine, not greedy of filthy lucre;

9 Holding the mystery of the faith in a pure conscience.

10 And let these also first be proved; then let them use the office

of a deacon, being found blameless.

11 Even so must their wives be grave, not slanderers, sober, faithful in all things.

12 Let the deacons be the husbands of one wife, ruling their children and their own houses well.

13 For they that have used the office of a deacon well purchase to themselves a good degree, and great boldness in the faith which is in Christ Jesus.

14 These things write I unto thee, hoping to come unto thee shortly:

15 But if I tarry long, that thou mayest know how thou oughtest to behave thyself in the house of God, which is the church of the living God, the pillar and ground of the truth.

Jan. 15

Devotional Reading
Mark 9:33-37

Background Scripture
1 Timothy 3

Memory Selection
1 Timothy 3:9

FOCUS

This lesson on the qualifications of bishops and deacons in the early Church may not fit the pattern of church leadership in your own congregation. The great reformer Martin Luther said that church leadership and organization should follow the *essence* of such teachings as these, but that the titles of church offices need not be considered an essential pattern to follow for all time.

Yet it should be a matter of concern to your class that even the essence the apostle Paul outlines here is too often neglected by Christians. Every believer is hurt when the morals or financial practices of church leaders come to light. Yes, the Church has the right to expect above-average standards from those who dare to be leaders in Christ' name.

৪০০৪

Some members of your group will likely have been exposed to training on the topic of leadership, or perhaps are presently leaders of business or civic organizations. Everyone has had experience in *following* a leader. Thus this lesson can be started by inviting general comments on the qualities of a good leader.

Be sure common traits such as these are mentioned: Good leaders inspire others to follow. They have the ability to lead by example. They have training and/or experience in the areas in which the people they lead are expected to produce, so they know good work when they see it.

Note that in this lesson group members can compare these traits with the qualifications Paul discusses for *church* leaders in this lesson.

Teaching Outline

I. Qualification of Elders—1-7
   A. Character, 1-3
   B. Leadership ability, 4-5
   C. Experience and reputation, 6-7
II. Qualities for Deacons—8-13
   A. Personal, 8-10
   B. Family and influence, 11-13
III. Concluding Comments—14-15

Daily Bible Readings

Mon.   Tribal Leaders Appointed
       Deut. 1:9-18
Tue.   Paul the New Leader
       Gal. 2:1-10
Wed.   Respect Your Leaders
       1 Thess. 5:6-15
Thu.   Qualities of a Leader
       Titus 1:5-9
Fri.   Leadership as Service
       Mark 9:33-37
Sat.   Qualifications of Overseers
       1 Tim. 3:1-7
Sun.   Qualifications of Helpers
       1 Tim. 3:8-15

Verse by Verse

I. Qualification of Elders—1-7
A. Character, 1-3

1 This is a true saying, If a man desire the office of a bishop, he desireth a good work.

2 A bishop then must be blameless, the husband of one wife, vigilant, sober, of good behaviour, given to hospitality, apt to teach;

3 Not given to wine, no striker, not greedy of filthy lucre; but patient, not a brawler, not covetous;

It has been said that no idea has ever lasted long without a supporting institution. Although the "institutional church" has been criticized for bureaucratic tendencies, Paul is concerned here that the faith not die for lack of structure. One reason for this was the danger of heresy. Another was the need for collective action. There needed to be an effective answer to the question, "Who's in charge here, anyway?" Paul finds that answer in a model that had proved workable in the Jewish synagogues— one based first on the work of the *elder* or, here, *bishop* (Grk. *episkopos*, NIV "overseer"). Other passages (such as 1 Pet. 5:1-2) show that the terms *presbyter* (elder), *pastor*, and *bishop* seem to have been used interchangeably in the earliest churches.

Although "a man" is not in the original, the qualifications to follow indicate that Paul assumes that the rule of men in the synagogue is to be followed in the Church. Whether this is to be retained in differing times and cultures, and whether bishops or elders were local, and always a plurality, (as was true in the synagogue) are issues that are widely debated.

The first qualification Paul lists is that elders should be *above reproach* (NIV "blameless") or of "good behavior." Ideally every Christian seeks this standard of life, but it is especially important for those whom nonbelievers see as examples of the faith *live* the faith. Paul also says that a bishop or elder must be *married to only one woman,* in effect "baptizing" the monogamy in Jewish and Roman marriage customs. The church would have a poor image if it tolerated in its leaders a practice that many Jews and pagans had already come to view as immoral.

A church overseer must also be *able to teach,* keeping the congregation doctrinally straight. The earliest divisions in the church were over doctrine, particularly as it differed from Jewish teaching (see the first "general church council" in Acts 15).

In the area of character, an elder must not be a *drunkard* or a *striker.* The original term here also gives us our word "plectrum," for a pick with which to strike a stringed instrument, so the NIV says "not violent" (see also *"not a brawler"*). Because full-time bishops were sometimes paid (see 5:17-18), they must not be *greedy* or *covetous,* with the salary as their primary motivation. They should also be *patient,* especially since they will have to deal with untaught people with pagan backgrounds.

B. Leadership ability, 4-5

4 One that ruleth well his own house, having his children in subjection with all gravity;

5 (For if a man know not how to rule his own house, how shall he take care of the church of God?)

We have only to recall the reproach the old priest Eli brought on Israel because his sons were not "in subjection," to remember how important it is that a person who presumes to lead a congregation prove first that he can lead his own family. Of course "children" do not stay children forever, and Paul stops short of requiring a bishop to resign if his grown children go astray.

C. Experience and reputation, 6-7

6 Not a novice, lest being lifted up with pride he fall into the condemnation of the devil.

7 Moreover he must have a good report of them which are without; lest he fall into reproach and the snare of the devil.

The Pastoral Epistles were written late in the New Testament era, providing time enough for the early churches to develop leaders who were not new to the faith. Some, who had been elders in their synagogues, would already have much of the leadership ability Paul seeks here. Novices, he notes, are too vulnerable to the pride that can rule a young person who is called on to rule others.

The matter of reputation has already been hinted at in previous qualifications. Paul makes it explicit here: some of Satan's deadliest work has been in the form of church leaders whose lack of character has seeped out into public view, damaging not only victims, as in case of sexual abuse, but the perpetrator's reputation and, inevitably, the reputation of the entire Church. In our own day, almost every major denomination has found it necessary to formulate in written form the moral standards it expects from its leaders.

II. Qualities for Deacons—8-13

A. Personal, 8-10

8 Likewise must the deacons be grave, not doubletongued, not given to much wine, not greedy of filthy lucre;

9 Holding the mystery of the faith in a pure conscience.

10 And let these also first be proved; then let them use the office of a deacon, being found blameless.

The word for "deacon" (*diakonos*) simply means "servant" or "minister." It was used informally in the earliest Christian circles, since all were expected to be servants (see Matt. 25:21). By the time of the Pastoral Epistles this work had developed into an "office" with qualifications similar to those of an elder.

Their first qualifications are to be "grave," not over-imbibers, and truth-tellers. These particular traits were especially important for those male deacons who dealt with the needs of widows and other women in the church (see 5:9-11). Again like elders, those who are paid must not be in the work "for the money."

Previous lessons have shown that the preaching and evangelizing of the early deacons Philip and Stephen indicate that their work was not confined to mechanical tasks." So in verse 9 Paul speaks of their need to be able to reflect on the truths of the faith, and to keep their consciences pure. Only in this way could they be "found blameless" (vs. 10)—not perfect, but at least the sort of person who, when realizing an error in himself, tries immediately to correct it.

B. Family and influence, 11-13

11 Even so must their wives be grave, not slanderers, sober, faithful in all things.

12 Let the deacons be the husbands of one wife, ruling their children and their own houses well.

13 For they that have used the office of a deacon well purchase to themselves a good degree, and great boldness in the faith which is in Christ Jesus.

The KJV "wives" can also simply mean "women"; and because it seems odd to have qualifications for deacons' wives that are more stringent in some cases than for deacons themselves, many interpreters believe these verses apply to women who were deacons. This would also avoid verse 11 being an interruption in the list of qualifications for deacons. Like elders, deacons are to be monogamous and good home-managers—all in all, serving in a way that gives them a "good degree" or standing in the community, bringing boldness, not embarrassment, to the church.

III. Concluding Comments—14-15

14 These things write I unto thee, hoping to come unto thee shortly:

15 But if I tarry long, that thou mayest know how thou oughtest to behave thyself in the house of God, which is the church of the living God, the pillar and ground of the truth.

Whether Paul is delayed in coming to Ephesus (1:3) to visit Timothy or not, he hopes that what he is writing, especially about church leadership, will contribute to the younger minister's knowledge of how life in the "house of God," or the church, should be managed. Already we see that God's "house" or dwelling place is no longer in the Temple in Jerusalem (which by now had probably been destroyed by the Romans), but amid His *people.*

Paul expects that faithful churchmanship will show that the Church is the very "pillar and ground of the truth," not a take-or-leave option for Christians. This requires faithful "pastoring"; which is why these "Pastoral Epistles" are so valuable.

Evangelistic Emphasis

What it all boils down to is that people don't really care what you say. We live in a world of words. The television bombards us with words about all the stuff we need to buy to make us happy. If you are feeling bad, there are more words on what pill you should ask your doctor to give you. Words abound that will sway you on whom to vote for.

There are words in print. In this volume there are many words about Christ and your relationship with Him.

These are important words. But how do you know if you can trust them?

We share a common belief that the Word of God is powerful and the Bible is the source of most of these words. But what about "my" words about His Word?

I hope you see where I am headed. In winning souls for Christ your words are not very important! What is more powerful is your "style." How are you living your life? Is your life-style backing up your words about God, or contradicting them? The answer is as important as a lost soul who is looking at the way you are practicing your faith before he is willing to trust the words you speak to him about God.

ഇരുന്ന

Holding the mystery of the faith in a pure conscience.—*1 Timothy 3:9*

There have been times when I was ashamed to say I was a minister of the gospel. When someone would ask what I did, I would say, "I work for J.C. and the boys." They would respond, "You work for J.C. Penny's?" It was really tough being a minister in the late '80s. In an 18-month span of time, Oral Roberts saw a 600-foot Jesus who threatened Oral unless he raised $20 million for a medical school. Jim and Tammy Baker were selling time-shares. Jimmy Swaggart was confessing his sins before God and the nation.

Oral is still around, although the ministry belongs to Richard. Jim Baker repented and wrote a book. His wife Tammy remarried and is struggling with cancer. Jimmy Swaggart repented and is still preaching. But they all contributed to harming the cause of Christ.

What about you? You are a "spiritual super-star" to someone. I know you didn't ask for that responsibility, but someone is watching the way you are living out your faith claims about Jesus. My prayer for you is that your actions will always match your affirmations of faith. I know that as a minister people are watching to see how I live my life. I'm encouraging you as a teacher to know, people are watching you too.

Weekday Problems

Hugh had just moved to the dream church in the big city. It was his desire to pastor this church. Hugh was a great preacher, an able administrator, and a wonderful pastor. His first year in the church was a honeymoon period for both Hugh and the congregation.

As Hugh and the church prepared to do a building campaign, strange things started happening. The treasurer seemed to be oblivious to checks bouncing. He was vague when asked about account balances. When the electric company sent a disconnect notice, Hugh called a Trustee meeting.

Through weeks of investigation, it was determined that the church treasurer had been embezzling church funds. Everyone was in shock. This man was the son of one of the patriarchs of the church. Although Hugh tried to calm the strong emotions and opinions expressed, it was determined that the best course of action would be to turn the matter over to legal authorities. The patriarch of the family asked Hugh to please reconsider, and that he was willing to pay back everything taken from the church.

*If you were Hugh, what would you do?

*Discuss forgiveness and restoration in the context of this situation.

Leading Thoughts on Church Leaders

The Lord opened unto me that being bred at Oxford or Cambridge was not enough to fit and qualify men to be ministers of Christ.—*From the* Journal *of George Fox, founder of the Quaker movement.*

***

The life of a pious minister is visible rhetoric.—*Herman Hooker*

***

One of the tragedies of our time is that the minister is both overworked and unemployed; overworked in a multitude of tasks that do not have the slightest connection with religion, and unemployed in the serious concerns and exacting labors of maintaining a disciplined spiritual life among mature men and women.—*Samuel H. Miller*

***

The preacher is not an artist but a prophet. It is possible to sacrifice the prophet for the artist. Not how beautiful but how essential is the quality of the ministry.—*G. Campbell Morgan*

This Lesson in Your Life

The passage from 1 Timothy is about leadership. It is unfortunate that we have kept the older translations of the Greek for bishop and deacon. It leaves us out of the discussion about leadership unless we are a bishop or a deacon. If Paul's language is meant as an official description of ordination, then there are three classes of ordained leaders in the church; bishops, deacons, and women. Or this passage could be implying that women could be ordained to the office of bishop.

We need to understand that the passage is more about leadership than formal titles. Paul was giving the qualifications for leaders in the church. Leaders in the church are to live Godly lives. They should understand that people are watching them.

Leaders in the church set the example in terms of their church attendance. It is hard to follow the leadership of someone who is rarely in church. We have all experienced that in some form. Leaders need to be present when the church is gathered for worship. Leaders need to be seen in church.

Leaders set the example in terms of attitude. I know a church right now that is dying, not because of the minister but because of the lay leadership. Some of the leaders of that church are more interested in holding on to their "power" than they are in seeing the church grow. Let me ask: Just how important is the job of trustee chairperson? People who think their job in the church makes them somebody are sorely mistaken about the nature of Christian leadership. Leaders ought to be the visionaries who are helping the church claim a bright future for Jesus Christ. Some leaders are more interested in maintaining the status quo than they are in mission.

Leaders set the example with their giving. If you are a leader in the church and you are not tithing, then step down! You can't lead if you are miserly in your giving. That is hypocrisy. Your stewardship reflects how you really feel about Jesus Christ and His Church. If your giving is not what it should be, then you should work it out with God.

Leaders set the example in terms of spiritual support. One of the greatest joys is to be able to support your minister as he (or she) is doing the work of God in your congregation. You have an opportunity to grow in your faith. You have a chance to pray for the spiritual leader of your congregation. Set an example of support by praying for your pastor and the other leaders of your church.

GETTING THE FACTS STRAIGHT

1. In today's text Paul told Timothy of another "saying" that could be depended on. What was it?
"Whoever aspires to the office of bishop desires a noble task."

2. What personal characteristics should a bishop possess?
A bishop must be above reproach. He must be temperate, sensible, respectable, and hospitable.

3. What kind of home life should a bishop have?
A bishop should be the husband of one wife. He should manage his household. His children should be submissive and respectful in every way.

4. What inference would be drawn if a bishop's home was in disarray?
It could be assumed that he would not be able to run a church.

5. What one characteristic of a bishop would be directly related to working in the church?
A bishop should be an apt teacher.

6. What are some other traits a bishop should *not* possess?
He should not be a drunkard, not violent, not quarrelsome, and not a lover of money.

7. Why should a recent convert not be a bishop?
Paul wrote that such a person might be "puffed up with conceit."

8. How should a bishop be viewed by the community?
The bishop should be well thought of by outsiders, so that he might not fall into disgrace personally, or disgrace the church.

9. What other office in the church is listed in this chapter?
Paul also talked about deacons.

10. How much wine can deacons drink?
They must not indulge in much wine. The Greek says, "a little bit drunk." This would make a lively discussion for your class about leadership and the use of alcohol.

So you have been reading my words about leadership. You still don't know what kind of person I am. If you paid attention to the last question of "Getting the Facts Straight" you will discover a bit of my sense of humor. I hope you can appreciate leadership that challenges, "the way we have always thought" or the "way we have always done it." I believe that a leader's words are very important, but I believe that actions are *more* important. You can't be pious on Sunday and then live in sin the other six days of the week. That is not being Christ-like. Watch your words, but make very sure your actions are Christian. Your deeds will change lives for Christ quicker than your words.

I read this story recently.

Administrators of the school district in New Haven, Connecticut, are doing something about the childhood obesity problem. They are moving to make their schools "junk-food free," by removing vending machines with snack foods like cookies, candy, and soda. They are offering after-school exercise classes and nutrition education for the families of their students.

They know that the kind of change they are trying to effect in their students begins with them. Reginald Mayo, the district's superintendent, is leading by example, trying to shed 30 pounds by living a healthier life-style. "It won't be easy," he said. Unfortunately, he put on two pounds during the first three weeks! But he is serious about the change he wants to see in his students and himself. "I'm going to look pretty hypocritical if I'm talking about healthy eating to kids and parents, and I'm walking around at 217 pounds," he said.

That school administrator has the right idea. We lead by example. We preach with our lives. The qualifications of leadership found in 1 Timothy 3 are not states of being. They are specifically related to how bishops and deacons acted around others. It isn't said that bishops and deacons should be smart, saintly, or sinless. There are more basic qualifications such as being sober and respectable, and mangaging one's home life in a way that shows he or she can also help manage a church.

Leadership as described by Paul means consistency of behavior.

Lesson 8
Set an Example

1 Timothy 4

Now the Spirit speaketh expressly, that in the latter times some shall depart from the faith, giving heed to seducing spirits, and doctrines of devils;

2 Speaking lies in hypocrisy; having their conscience seared with a hot iron;

3 Forbidding to marry, and commanding to abstain from meats, which God hath created to be received with thanksgiving of them which believe and know the truth.

4 For every creature of God is good, and nothing to be refused, if it be received with thanksgiving:

5 For it is sanctified by the word of God and prayer.

6 If thou put the brethren in remembrance of these things, thou shalt be a good minister of Jesus Christ, nourished up in the words of faith and of good doctrine, whereunto thou hast attained.

7 But refuse profane and old wives' fables, and exercise thyself rather unto godliness.

8 For bodily exercise profiteth little: but godliness is profitable unto all things, having promise of the life that now is, and of that which is to come.

9 This is a faithful saying and worthy of all acceptation.

10 For therefore we both labour and suffer reproach, because we trust in the living God, who is the Saviour of all men, specially of those that believe.

11 These things command and teach.

12 Let no man despise thy youth; but be thou an example of the believers, in word, in conversation, in charity, in spirit, in faith, in purity.

13 Till I come, give attendance to reading, to exhortation, to doctrine.

14 Neglect not the gift that is in thee, which was given thee by prophecy, with the laying on of the hands of the presbytery.

15 Meditate upon these things; give thyself wholly to them; that thy profiting may appear to all.

16 Take heed unto thyself, and unto the doctrine; continue in them: for in doing this thou shalt both save thyself, and them that hear thee.

Jan. 22

Devotional Reading
1 Cor. 3:6-11

Background Scripture
1 Tim. 4

Memory Selection
1 Timothy 4:6

Almost from its beginning, Christianity has ricocheted off the walls of two extremes. One extreme is being too "doctrinaire"—supposing that being faithful requires the minute study of countless doctrines and separating from everyone who disagrees over any jot or tittle. The other extreme is supposing that faith is only a warm, fuzzy feeling, and that doctrine doesn't matter.

This lesson seeks to find balance between these extremes. It urges the young minister Timothy (and us through him) to find and stick to the core of the faith by faithful teaching. As we shall see, this requires more than mere knowledge. It requires "living the faith" in the form of being a good example. The Church can never have too many such teachers.

≈≈≈

Ask group members to recall the best teacher they've ever had. Perhaps it was a junior high math teacher, a high school coach, or an outstanding Bible teacher who grounded them in the faith.

Ask what makes these teachers memorable. Was it their grasp of the *content of the subject matter?* Was it the *personal concern* they showed individual students? Was it the fact that the teachers themselves were *personally excited* about what they taught, or that they *lived what they taught?* Were they *rigid* or *permissive* in discipline?

Point out that the root of the word *discipline* means "teaching," and that it can include both *learning* and *behavior.* In this lesson, the apostle Paul is concerned about maintaining, both aspects of the Christian faith.

Teaching Outline	Daily Bible Readings
I. False Teaching Ahead—1-6 　A. Demonic departures, 1-2 　B. False asceticism, 3-5 　C. A good servant, 6 II. Faithful Teachers Needed—7-11 　A. Godly discipline, 7-8 　B. A worthy cause, 9-11 III. Personal Qualifications—12-16 　A. Good, though young, 12 　B. Specific practices, 13 　C. 'Take heed to yourself,' 14-16	Mon. Moses Teaches Israel 　　　Deut. 4:1-8 Tue. 'Give Ear to My Teaching' 　　　Ps. 78:1-8 Wed. Rules for the New Life 　　　Eph. 4:25–5:2 Thu. Teaching Is a Gift 　　　Rom. 12:3-8 Fri. Warning: False Teaching 　　　1 Tim. 4:1-5 Sat. Training in Godliness 　　　1 Tim. 4:6-10 Sun. Practice These Things 　　　1 Tim. 4:11-16

Verse by Verse

I. False Teaching Ahead—1-6
A. Demonic departures, 1-2

1 Now the Spirit speaketh expressly, that in the latter times some shall depart from the faith, giving heed to seducing spirits, and doctrines of devils;

2 Speaking lies in hypocrisy; having their conscience seared with a hot iron;

Many people in the early Church seem to have thought that the term referred to the Second Coming of Christ, and expected it within their lifetimes. However, the Pastoral Epistles themselves were written late in the New Testament era, during a time period that was relatively "later" than "earlier"; and since we know from other letters that the doctrines warned of here were actually taught, the "latter times" seems to refer to any time later than Christ's resurrection.

We may wonder why Paul condemns as "doctrines of devils" the false teachings that will be listed in verse 3. At first glance they seem to be mere dietary issues. Why is this topic so dangerous? Probably because these matters were raindrops from a larger cloud of heresy that held that *all flesh is evil.* Paul, guided by the Spirit, saw that if this were true, then the body of Christ was either evil or unreal, as some heretics, called "Gnostics," would later teach.

Not only did such teaching stem from a false "world view"; it denied that the bodily resurrection of Jesus was an essential and wholesome event that was a part of salvation. Furthermore, as we shall see below, it even invited the teaching that there was a plurality of gods.

B. False asceticism, 3-5

3 Forbidding to marry, and commanding to abstain from meats, which God hath created to be received with thanksgiving of them which believe and know the truth.

4 For every creature of God is good, and nothing to be refused, if it be received with thanksgiving:

5 For it is sanctified by the word of God and prayer.

At first the two main false teachings Paul warns against seem to be unrelated. A closer look, however, shows that both marriage, which includes sex, and eating meat have in common *the flesh.* Some false teachers would forbid both marriage and eating meat because they believed that only *spirit* is good, and all flesh evil. Later, full-grown Gnosticism would hold that the true God whom Christians should worship created only the spiritual realm, and that another "evil" god created the material world, including the human body. This of course not only threatened the saving effect of the death, burial, and resurrection of Christ but the entire Judeo-Christian doctrine of monotheism.

True teaching, Paul says, affirms the goodness of the material world. After all, at Creation, God had pronounced it "very good" (Gen. 1:9-12), and it was both a Jewish and Christian custom to "give thanks" at meals for the good things God has given us to eat. Even meats considered "unclean" by the Jews were "sanctified by the word" in the vision God gave Peter in Acts 10. And regarding the "fleshly" aspect of marriage, other New Covenant writings specifically hold that "marriage is good, and the bed undefiled" (Heb. 13:4).

C. A good servant, 6

6 If thou put the brethren in remembrance of these things, thou shalt be a good minister of Jesus Christ, nourished up in the words of faith and of good doctrine, whereunto thou hast attained.

Resisting such false teaching and teaching the truth to his brothers and sisters in Christ was a part of what would make Timothy a "good minister" (Grk. *diakonos,* "servant"). Notice that Paul is upholding the "good doctrine" (Grk. "fine teaching") that *God's world is essentially "good"*—not the finer and finer points of doctrine that would divide the church over and over again in the ages to come.

II. Faithful Teachers Needed—7-11
A. Godly discipline, 7-8
7 But refuse profane and old

wives' fables, and exercise thyself rather unto godliness.

8 For bodily exercise profiteth little: but godliness is profitable unto all things, having promise of the life that now is, and of that which is to come.

"Gnostic-type" teaching about the flesh's being evil would lead, in some extreme circles, to bodily abuse. This might take the form of self-flagellation (like that which still occurs in the "Penitentes" movement of northern New Mexico), or simply in severely restricted "starvation diets." Although Paul dismisses this teaching as "fables," he affirms that while *some* bodily discipline is healthy in "the life that now is," the discipline of the *spirit* that is healthy both now and in the world to come.

B. A worthy cause, 9-11
9 This is a faithful saying and worthy of all acceptation.

10 For therefore we both labour and suffer reproach, because we trust in the living God, who is the Saviour of all men, specially of those that believe.

11 These things command and teach.

Verse 9 is another of the four "faithful sayings" in the Pastoral Epistles. It is not clear whether Paul means for it to be a statement of approval for what he has just stated, or for what follows; but most interpreters choose the latter view. Verses 10-11 do seem to provide justification for the "worthiness" of viewing the flesh as good instead of evil (though not being ruled by it). It was for preaching the worth of the bodily resurrection of Christ that Paul had labored and suffered reproach, and he earnestly expects the younger man he is mentoring to "command and teach" the same thing.

III. Personal Qualifications—12-16
A. Good, though young, 12

12 Let no man despise thy youth; but be thou an example of the believers, in word, in conversation, in charity, in spirit, in faith, in purity.

Wisdom is not always the exclusive province of those with grey hair. All teachers, young or old, are to remember that they will teach as much or more by the way they conduct their lives as they will in formal instruction. As the saying goes, "Preach the Word; when necessary, use words." (As the NIV reminds us, the KJV word "conversation" meant "life" or "behavior.")

B. Specific practices, 13

13 Till I come, give attendance to reading, to exhortation, to doctrine.

Paul had left Timothy to strengthen the church at Ephesus (1:3) while the apostle went on into Macedonia. Now we see that he plans to return; and in the interim the younger minister is to give special attention to three items at the public gatherings of the church: *reading* (of Scripture, since both those who could read and copies of the Scriptures were not plentiful); *exhortation,* or preaching; and *doctrine,* or

teaching—of the sort Paul has been teaching Timothy. The first practice, reading, was something of a carryover from synagogue worship. At this time in the life of the Church this probably consisted mainly of the Old Testament, although some of Paul's epistles were beginning also to be considered "Scripture" (lit. "holy writing," see 2 Pet. 3:15-16).

C. 'Take heed to yourself,' 14-16

14 Neglect not the gift that is in thee, which was given thee by prophecy, with the laying on of the hands of the presbytery.

15 Meditate upon these things; give thyself wholly to them; that thy profiting may appear to all.

16 Take heed unto thyself, and unto the doctrine; continue in them: for in doing this thou shalt both save thyself, and them that hear thee.

Paul himself had conferred a spiritual gift (Grk. *charisma*) on Timothy. The mention here of elders doing the same thing may mean that Paul was simply an "older" person (since he was unmarried, and see 1 Tim. 3:2); that his being an apostle made him considered an elder also; or that these are two different incidents of the laying on of hands. This was the common way spiritual gifts were transmitted (see Acts 8:14-17).

It is important to note the human dimension of using this gift. Although it was from God, Timothy was to be careful not to *neglect* it, but to *meditate* on it, and to *give himself wholly* to it.

Evangelistic Emphasis

In a survey, of the ten moral behaviors evaluated, a majority of Americans said they believed that each of these activities were "morally acceptable": gambling (61%), co-habitation (60%), and sexual fantasies (59%). Nearly half of the adult population felt that two other behaviors were morally acceptable: having an abortion (45%) and having a sexual relationship with someone of the opposite sex other than their spouse (42%). About one-third of the population approved of pornography (38%), profanity (36%), drunkenness (35%) and homosexual sex (30%). The activity that garnered the least support was using non-prescription drugs (17%).

On the other hand, fewer than one out of every 10 evangelical Christians said that "adultery, gay sex, pornography, profanity, drunkenness and abortion are morally acceptable."

We are working in a world that has a different belief system than the church has. As witnesses for Jesus Christ we had better know what we believe. Not only should we know what we believe, we need to be able to clearly articulate why we believe what we do. The quickest way to make that articulate witness is to share your faith story. Someone is looking to you for hope.

℘ℭ

Take heed unto thyself and unto the doctrine; continue in them; for in doing this thou shalt both save thyself and them that hear thee.—*1 Timothy 4: 16*

Let's say you are walking along the edge of a cliff and you see a sign that reads, "Don't stand close to the edge." You have to get a look at what the bottom of the canyon looks like. So you step closer to the edge of the cliff. You know just how close to get. You have been at the edge of a cliff many times and you have not fallen yet. So with confidence you edge even closer to get this "once in a lifetime view."

Suddenly there is a tremor and the ground beneath your feet gives way and your find yourself falling toward the floor of the valley. You have not broken the law of gravity; you have just proven that the law of gravity is true.

Paying close attention to doctrine is vital for our lives as Christians. We have so many safety nets built around our lives as we live out true doctrine. When we get bold and try to "live on the edge" we very often find the words of warning that Paul gave Timothy are so true.

Watch your step. You may think you have everything under control as you "live on the edge," but things can happen that are out of your control and will affect your life. There are tremors that can come along and cause us to fall.

Weekday Problems

Heather had become an "apostle" to everyone who would listen to her. Actually Heather was one of those people you couldn't ignore. She was a know-it-all. She would help the choir director direct. She helped the preacher after the service by telling him everything he got wrong. She even helped the janitor by pointing out crumbs on the carpet.

Now Heather was into dieting. She heard a sermon about the dangerous diet that Americans were consuming. He had studied Scripture and come up with the diet that Jesus ate. He tried the diet, had lost 30 pounds, and said he now felt closer to Jesus. Heather wasn't really fat, just vertically challenged. But she converted to this diet, and inflicted it onto the youth group when it was her month to prepare snacks suppers for them. They hated the Jesus diet, preferring foods that sinners might eat, like hamburgers and fries.

Heather was in the pastor's study demanding that he stand with her and make these kids eat the Jesus diet rather than the usual junk foods.

*What would you tell Heather?

*Paul warned against following "profane myths and old wives' tales." Do you see some of these being followed in today's church?

For Goodness' Sake

Those who say they are just as good as half the folks in the church seldom specify which half.

***

Two boys were trying to outdo each other. "My dad's a doctor," said the first, "and I can be sick for nothing!"

"Yeah?" the second younger shot back. "Well my dad's a preacher and I can be *good* for nothing."

***

Five-year-old Johnny was ill, and Mom was trying to convince him to take some medicine. "It's good for you," she said, "and God wants you to take it."

"I can't believe that!" replied Johnny. "I'll ask Him." Whereupon he stuck his head under the blanket, and sure enough, from deep within the bed covers came a deep voice, saying, "Certainly not!"

***

Sin writes histories; goodness is silent.—*Goethe*

This Lesson in Your Life

Godliness, Paul wrote, is of value in every way. So are you living a godly life? The lessons from Timothy keep hitting this theme. How is your living?

Have you been passed by one of those big trucks on the road and there is a sticker on the back that says, "How's my driving?" There is a toll free number for you to call if the driving isn't up to snuff. Knowing that someone is watching their driving has improved the driving habits of many truckers. How is you "driving," in life?

In his world, some saw the apostle Paul as a loser. The Jews didn't like him. Some gentiles didn't like him. But he never changed the way he lived to please people. Paul was always living for God. He plugged along with his plan to spread the gospel throughout the Roman Empire anyway, caring only what God thought about him.

What about us? Do we care what everyone is saying about us? Do we spend great effort collecting letters of recommendation? Positive reviews? The affection of those who can give us something in return?

We have forgotten how to ignore criticism and stay the course we believe God has laid before us. As we vie to perfect our resumes, as we ambitiously generate and collect sparkling references, as we set up lives that appear to be "just fine, thank you very much," Paul at his finest would be the first to remind us that there are some complaints which actually do warrant our attention. For while the world at large may see what we want to be seen, God spots the unseen sinfulness that simmers in our souls. Paul reminds us that God monitors us . . . and his is the only monitoring that matters.

"How's my living?" What if we transferred this question inward to be inscribed on our hearts? What if we directed this question solely to God? What if the answer led us to a deeper awareness that God watches us very closely in our daily travels, checks our actions, and notices our attitudes, lest we emulate the average cranky trucker with a late shipment—or an opponent of Paul with a checklist?

As our world becomes increasingly obsessed with all that glitters and impresses, Paul reminds us that God is not impressed with anything other than a change of heart, then a change of life. "How's my Living? How's Yours? God knows exactly how we are living. And while it may seem burdensome to be monitored constantly by the living God who never sleeps, Paul also reminds us that this same God rules with grace and reconciliation.

GETTING THE FACTS STRAIGHT

1. What vision of life in "the latter times" did the Spirit give Paul?

Some would renounce the faith by paying attention to deceitful spirits and teachings of demons.

2. In your opinion, how is that prophecy being fulfilled in the world today?

(Discuss some of the "strange theology" especially prevalent among the televangelists.

3. What other strange teachings were predicted for the latter times?

People would be discouraged from marriage. Abstinence from certain foods would be demanded.

4. How did Paul counter this kind of teaching?

"Everything created by God is good and nothing is to be rejected."

5. If everything is good, how do we set limits on some of our world's activities?

Everything is good if it is received with thanksgiving and is sanctified by God's Word and by prayer.

6. What did Paul warn Timothy to avoid?

He was to avoid profane myths and old wives' tales.

7. How was Timothy to show himself as an example to others?

He was to be an example in speech, conversation, in love, loyalty and purity.

8. What was to be the focus of Timothy's ministry?

He was to give attention to public reading of Scripture, to exhorting, and to teaching.

9. Paul was giving advice to the young preacher Timothy. What advice would you give to your preacher?

You might write positive words of encouragement and support for your minister.

10. As a layperson, what tasks in the church are you qualified to do?

Your baptism qualified you to do any task in the church. Your church polity may set limits on serving communion and baptizing.

Are you growing in your faith relationship with Jesus Christ, or are you satisfied with where you are now? Growth is essential in our day; we need to stay "one step ahead" of the game. There is an old joke that illustrates this for me.

The Pope met with his cardinals to discuss a proposal from the Prime Minister of Israel. "Your Holiness," said one of the Cardinals, "The Prime Minister wants to challenge you to a game of golf to show the friendship and ecumenical spirit shared by the Jewish and Catholic faiths."

The Pope thought it was a good idea, but he had never touched a golf club. "Have we not," he asked, "a cardinal who can represent me against the leader of Israel?"

"None that plays golf very well," a cardinal said. "But," he added, "there is a man named Jack Nicklaus, an American golfer who is a devout Catholic. We can offer to make him a cardinal; then ask him to play the Prime Minister as your personal representative. In addition to showing our spirit of cooperation, we'll also win the match."

Everyone agreed it was a good idea. The call was made. Of course, Nicklaus was honored and agreed to play. The day after the match, Nicklaus reported to the Vatican to inform the Pope of the result. "I have some good news and some bad news, Your Holiness," Nicklaus said.

"Tell me the good news first, Cardinal Nicklaus," said the Pope.

"Well, your Holiness, I don't like to brag, but even though I've played some pretty terrific rounds of golf in my life, this was the best I have ever played, by far. I must have been inspired from above. My drives were long and true, my iron shots were accurate, and my putting was perfect. With all due respect, my play was truly miraculous."

"There's bad news?" the Pope asked.

Nicklaus sighed. "I lost to Rabbi Tiger Woods by three strokes."

We have to keep growing in our faith because we will constantly be facing new challenges as individual Christians and as the body of Christ.

Lesson 9

Practicing Justice and Mercy

1 Timothy 5:1-8, 17-25

Rebuke not an elder, but intreat him as a father; and the younger men as brethren;

2 The elder women as mothers; the younger as sisters, with all purity.

3 Honour widows that are widows indeed.

4 But if any widow have children or nephews, let them learn first to shew piety at home, and to requite their parents: for that is good and acceptable before God.

5 Now she that is a widow indeed, and desolate, trusteth in God, and continueth in supplications and prayers night and day.

6 But she that liveth in pleasure is dead while she liveth.

7 And these things give in charge, that they may be blameless.

8 But if any provide not for his own, and specially for those of his own house, he hath denied the faith, and is worse than an infidel.

17 Let the elders that rule well be counted worthy of double honour, especially they who labour in the word and doctrine.

18 For the scripture saith, Thou shalt not muzzle the ox that treadeth out the corn. And, The labourer is worthy of his reward.

19 Against an elder receive not an accusation, but before two or three witnesses.

20 Them that sin rebuke before all, that others also may fear.

21 I charge thee before God, and the Lord Jesus Christ, and the elect angels, that thou observe these things without preferring one before another, doing nothing by partiality.

22 Lay hands suddenly on no man, neither be partaker of other men's sins: keep thyself pure.

23 Drink no longer water, but use a little wine for thy stomach's sake and thine often infirmities.

24 Some men's sins are open beforehand, going before to judgment; and some men they follow after.

25 Likewise also the good works of some are manifest beforehand; and they that are otherwise cannot be hid.

Jan. 29

Devotional Reading
Matt. 23:23-28

Background Scripture
1 Tim. 5

Memory Selection
1 Tim. 5:1-2

Consistent with the practical purpose of the Pastoral Epistles, this passage of Scripture deals with ordered and respectful relationships among members of the Body of Christ, the Church. It focuses especially on the attitude between the young and he old—an arena that can easily become a battleground. Feuds between these two age groups have been recorded from the time of ancient Greek philosophers.

Of special concern to Paul is a fair and just system of caring for the needy. In his day, this concern dealt especially with poor widows, since there were few opportunities other than prostitution for unmarried women to support themselves. The principles of justice and mercy Paul lays down for caring for widows are to be broadened to include other disadvantaged groups today.

&)CR

Systems for caring for the needy are far different in our society than in Paul's day. Government retirement systems such as Medicare, and social service programs such as Medicaid and child welfare agencies were unknown. The early Church became a leader in establishing such systems, especially in the case of hospitals; and this lesson shows the practice of caring for indigent widows.

Ask your group what government services are available for the needy, and which disadvantaged groups in the community need more help. Should government be more involved? Or should the Church take over some of these services? Ask what your own church is doing to help care for such needs, and whether and how it could do more.

Teaching Outline

I. Older People's Needs—1-8
  A. Young-old relationships, 1
  B. The case of needy widows, 2-8
    1. Home or church?, 2-4
    2. Qualifications for help, 5-7
    3. Personal responsibility, 8
II. Organizing Principles—17-25
  A. Supporting elders, 17-18
  B. Relating to elders, 19-22
  C. Proof of the pudding, 23-25

Daily Bible Readings

Mon. Righteousness and Justice
    Ps. 33:1-5
Tue. Integrity and Mercy
    Prov. 28:4-13
Wed. Weightier Matters
    Matt. 23:23-28
Thu. Mercy Trumps Judgment
    James 2:8-13
Fri. Mercy for All
    1 Tim. 5:1-8
Sat. Justice for Widows
    1 Tim. 5:9-16
Sun. Justice for Elders
    1 Tim. 5:17-25

Verse by Verse

I. Older People's Needs—1-8
A. Young-old relationships, 1

1 Rebuke not an elder, but intreat him as a father; and the younger men as brethren;

Timothy's age was obviously somewhere between the older and the younger members of the congregation at Ephesus. Paul's instruction first tends to his relationship with those who are older. Although the term for elder (*presbyteros*) is the same here as in verse 17, the context here seems to refer to those who are simply older in years, and in verse 17 to those who hold the *office* of elder. Although showing respect for older people has historically been more common in the East than in the West, it is elevated here to the level of a biblical norm, wherever God's people gather. In fact, since Timothy is also told to show brotherly respect to those who are younger, respect for others in general can be said to be a fundamental Christian relational principle.

B. The case of needy widows, 2-8
1. Home or church?, 2-4

2 The elder women as mothers; the younger as sisters, with all purity.

3 Honour widows that are widows indeed.

4 But if any widow have children or nephews, let them learn first to shew piety at home, and to requite their parents: for that is good and acceptable before God.

Paul continues by telling us that men in the church should honor older women as their own mother, and younger women as sisters—adding "purely" to underline the importance of keeping that relationship above reproach morally.

The word "honor" moves us from respect to "putting our money where our mouth is" (see Matt. 15:5-6). As mentioned in the "Focus" section, unmarried women in Paul's day sometimes turned to prostitution; so the early Church undertook to provide for widows "indeed" —that is who were "really in need" (NIV), having no other means of support. Note how helping to support them is said to be "honoring" them, taking away some of the stigma of poverty; and that true "piety" involves good works such as this, not just a holy feeling toward God.

Before adding such women to the congregation's benevolent list, Timothy is instructed to see if their immediate family can care for them, "requiting" or repaying them for the care they had given their children. Today, in a time when medicines are able to keep ill persons alive longer, and with the accompanying need for medical care in nursing homes, applying this principle today may take a different form. Yet the principle of *tending* to the elderly is still an important part of being a faithful family member, and a faithful church.

2. Qualifications for help, 5-7

5 Now she that is a widow indeed, and desolate, trusteth in God, and continueth in supplications and prayers night and day.

6 But she that liveth in pleasure is dead while she liveth.

7 And these things give in charge, that they may be blameless.

Naturally any organized program for assistance is subject to abuse; so Paul lays down some qualifications for enrolling a truly destitute widow in a church assistance program. Primarily he intends that they be faithful to the church's moral and spiritual principles instead of succumbing to the temptation, especially common in his day, of "living in pleasure," or becoming a prostitute. They must not be earning money in that way while "running a scam" and getting church support as well. Note that Paul's main intent is not to condemn them, but, as it were, to "raise" them from their dead life and instill in them a "blameless" character.

3. Personal responsibility, 8

8 But if any provide not for his own, and specially for those of his own house, he hath denied the faith, and is worse than an infidel.

Paul now uses particularly strong language to insist on the personal responsibility of family members to care for their own elderly relations. To refuse to do so is worse than not believing in the first place. This is apparently because it is goes beyond merely professing unbelief, and involves one who already believes then abandoning the faith once enjoyed, cutting one off from the means of grace (see 2 Pet. 2:20-22).

II. Organizing Principles—17-25

A. Supporting elders, 17-18

17 Let the elders that rule well be counted worthy of double honour, especially they who labour in the word and doctrine.

18 For the scripture saith, Thou shalt not muzzle the ox that treadeth out the corn. And, The labourer is worthy of his reward.

Now the context suggests that Paul moves from the general principle of honoring the elderly to the specific matter of "honoring," or financially caring for, those who hold the *office* of the elder by working full-time at it, especially in the areas of preaching and teaching. It is often noted that Paul himself declined to accept church support for ministry. Actually this was true only part of the time, when for special reasons he was self-supporting. At other times he did accept support from the Church (see 1 Cor. 9:6; 2 Cor. 11:8). This follows the Old Testament teaching about feeding working animals (Deut. 25:4), that is summed up with the maxim, "The laborer is worthy of his reward." The expression about elders who "rule well" is not a judgment about the quality of their ministry so much as the equivalent of "widows indeed," above.

B. Relating to elders, 19-22

19 Against an elder receive not an accusation, but before two or three witnesses.

20 Them that sin rebuke before all, that others also may fear.

21 I charge thee before God, and the Lord Jesus Christ, and the elect angels, that thou observe these things without preferring one before another, doing nothing by partiality.

22 Lay hands suddenly on no man, neither be partaker of other men's sins: keep thyself pure.

Here Paul lays down principles for dealing with disputes among, and with, the "ruling elders" or bishops of a congregation. Adequate witnesses must be present when a charge was made against an elder. As the founding minister of the church in Ephesus, Timothy is given the right to "rebuke" elders found guilty of misdeeds.

This rather delicate and public matter of "church polity" was to be administered even-handedly, without prejudice or bias. Many squabbles could even be avoided if Timothy would be careful about those he selected to "lay hands on" (or "ordain")—the sign not only of imparting spiritual gifts but of installing into offices such as that of the elder.

C. Proof of the pudding, 23-25

23 Drink no longer water, but use a little wine for thy stomach's sake and thine often infirmities.

24 Some men's sins are open beforehand, going before to judgment; and some men they follow after.

25 Likewise also the good works of some are manifest beforehand; and they that are otherwise cannot be hid.

It is not immediately clear how this fits into the context. Possibly it is related to the warning against being hasty about church appointments, lest a deliberately sinful church officer infect the Body with his corruptness. Perhaps in verse 23 Paul advises Timothy to fortify himself with a little wine so he will be up to the task of making good selections. Then he acknowledges that even that won't prevent some unqualified candidates from being appointed, since the sin of some is invisible, defying the best efforts of those who to try to weed out unfit church officials. Others' weaknesses are apparent, and may be dealt with openly and overcome in the maturing process.

It can be observed that the counsel to take a little wine must be applied today in the light of local custom. While it was no doubt necessary in parts of the ancient world where water was impure, it may not be wise in some social contexts, such as in societies with a high incidence of alcoholism.

215

Evangelistic Emphasis

We have all kinds of labels for people in the church.

The "blue hairs" are the little old ladies who are in church every Sunday. Their hair may be blue, but their passions for the Lord run white hot.

The "cemetery roll" are members who are on the church roll but who never come. They don't even bother coming on Christmas and Easter.

The "C and E" people show up on Christmas and Easter. They really appear to love these special services, but you can't get them back.

The "saints" are those servants of the Lord that we all look up to. They teach Sunday School, usher, sing in the choir, and serve on the committees of the church. They are there any time the doors of the church are opened. We depend on them.

Then there are "sinners." You know, I have never met a sinner. Not someone I wanted to label a sinner. They have all had names. I talk to them using their names. I tell them about Jesus, using their name.

I think we should hear anew what Paul was teaching Timothy. We lead people to faith in Christ not by calling them names but by calling *their* name. We lead them to Christ by helping particular, named persons understand that He has called them.

ഇന്ദ

Memory Selection

Rebuke not an elder, but exhort him as a father, and the younger men as brethren; the elder woman, as mothers, the younger, as sisters, with all purity.—*1 Timothy 5: 1-2*

A man called a church and asked if he could speak to the "head hog at the trough." The secretary was shocked by his language so she said, "Sir, I'm sorry, but I don't understand whom you're referring to."

The man said again, "I want to speak with the head hog at the trough." Then it dawned on the secretary that he wanted to talk with the Pastor.

Admonishing him, she said, "Sir, if you mean you'd like to talk with our pastor, you must have more respect. You will want to ask for 'The Reverend' or 'The Pastor.' But certainly, you don't call him 'The head hog at the trough.'"

The man shot back, "Well, I was thinking about giving $100,000 to the building fund."

There was a slight pause and the secretary said, "Wait a minute sir, I believe the 'big pig' just walked in the door."

The Church as the Body of Christ is reflective of His love and character. Jesus saved His harshest barbs for the religious who were always talking down to the outcasts of society.

With your words, do you build people up or do you tear them down?

Weekday Problems

Consider Paul's words to Timothy: "The sins of some people are conspicuous and precede them to judgment." What do you think he means?

Could it be like this? You can take a pig out of the pig pen, bring her into the house, give her a bath, tie a ribbon on her tail, and even put some "Victoria's Secret" fragrance on her. But when you open the door, she heads right back out to the pigpen only to roll in the mud. A pig doesn't respect how you have tried to improve her life. We won't and don't blame her, because that is her nature.

So, it is with us. We can fix ourselves up on the outside with our "Sunday finest," but until we change on the inside it's like giving a pig a bath. It only lasts for a moment. That is why people go from diet to diet, fad to fad, and church to church. They are looking for something that fixing the exterior can't resolve. Their sins are "conspicuous and precede them to judgment."

*How can we confront this type of superficial approach to living, while maintaining respect for the person?

*What did Jesus mean by saying, "Don't throw your pearls before swine?"

Signs of Aging

You can tell you're getting old when . . .

You would rather go to work than stay home sick.

You enjoy hearing about other people's operations, and telling about yours.

Your dreams about good things to eat include prunes.

People who call at 9 p.m. say, "Oh, did I wake you?"

You have a party and the neighbors don't even realize it.

You refer to the refrigerator as the ice box.

Your back goes out more often than you do.

You remember when the St. Louis Browns won the pennant, and that the Washington Senators were a baseball team.

Your best friends are dating someone half your age . . . and they aren't breaking any laws.

You think of speed limits as a good law, not just a challenge.

217

This Lesson in Your Life

An 80-year-old golfer was losing his vision. He learned of a golf course that had caddies who would mark a golfer's ball after it was hit. When he arrived at the course, he was told to go to the first tee box. When his caddy appeared, the golfer was shocked. The caddy was 90 years old. He asked, "Can you see well enough to do this?

The caddy said, "I have the eyes of a 20-year old."

So the golfer teed off. The caddy confidently said, "I saw exactly where it went."

They went to where the ball should be, but they couldn't find it. They looked and looked. Finally, the golfer said, "I thought you said you could see. Where is it?

The 90-year-old caddy said, "I saw where it went. But I guess I just plain forgot."

We all have a tendency to forget.

Paul's words to Timothy are refreshing in that they remind us to respect our elders. The fastest growing age group in America consists of people who are more than 100 of age.

The church I pastor has a delightful lady named Duvergne Roberts. Mrs. Roberts is 106 years old. She rarely misses a Sunday. When she was 104 she had hip replacement surgery. She was slow to recover. It took her three months to get back to church.

I remember the first Sunday I met her. She came to the back door of the church, shook my hand and said, "I'm Duvergne Roberts and I'm 100 old and last week they took my driver's license away from me and I'm not happy." I sure was happy that she was not driving! Our elders have lessons to teach us. They have the wisdom that comes with long years of living. They know what matters and what is not important in life's journey.

Likewise, Paul would admonish us not to despise youth. There are vital lessons to be learned from young people. They are so full of life and energy. They want a personal relationship with Jesus Christ, one that is free from some of the religious trappings we try to place on them. They may not dress like us. They may not sing "Amazing Grace" in the key of G. They may dress funny and listen to rock and roll tunes and sing "our" songs of faith to "their" music. They are in church. We as "elders" need to keep them coming.

Discuss in your class how you can really be the family of God, with all sorts of ages from infants to grandparents.

GETTING THE FACTS STRAIGHT

1. How are we to address older men in the church?
We are not to speak harshly to older men but address them as we would our fathers.

2. How are we to speak to the younger men in the church?
We are to address them as brothers.

3. How are we to treat older women in the church?
We are to treat them as mothers.

4. How are we to address younger women?
We are to address them as sisters and relate to them in purity.

5. What is the exception for the church supporting its widows?
The church would support a true widow, but if a widow had children they should support their mother.

6. How would the real widow be cared for?
In addition to the church providing for her, she would set her hope on God and continue to trust Him for provision.

7. What are the implications for Christians who don't provide for their family?
If we fail to provide for our family we deny the faith and are worse than unbelievers.

8. How are elders to be considered?
They are worthy of "double honor" if they teach and preach—that is, they are to be honored personally, and financially supported in their work.

9. If charges are brought against an elder, what evidence should be received?
There should be two or three witnesses before any accusation should be heard.

10. Did Timothy drink wine?
Yes. Paul told him, "No longer drink only water, but take a little wine for the sake of your stomach."

Do you remember what it was like to drive a car before they had power steering? Do you remember when you had to turn the key and then press the starter button? How about shifting gears? Do you remember three on the column or four on the floor? What about cars before air conditioning?

Do you remember cars before seat belts?

Let's stop there for a moment. Before seat belts, parents could pack eight kids into a family car, ages one week to 18 years, with no restraining thoughts or devices.

Automobile safety is much more regulated than it used to be. Today we have laws requiring children less than 4 years and 40 pounds to be buckled into some sort of child car seat. You can't even bring your newborn home from the hospital until they make sure a child car seat is in your car. For slightly older kids there are booster seats. With the mandatory installation of airbags, no kids under the age of 12 are supposed to be allowed in the front seat at all—for fear that the an exploding air bag might cause them more injury than any crash.

Before all these mechanical safety devices, however, some of us no doubt grew up with a different kind of child-restraint system. My mother would take us in the car for our Sunday afternoon outing. Remember when you used to go on an afternoon drive? This was before Driver's Ed. Part of the fun was conning Mom into letting you drive the car.

My mother and we three kids would pile in the Chevy Nova, with not a seat belt in the car. No AC, so our little heads were hanging out the windows. There was a very formidable restraint system in Mom's car. It was quicker than any air bag, safer than any belt. When something happened and Mom had to slam on the brakes, her arm came over automatically to the child that was in the front seat. My mother was the original seatbelt.

We honor those members of our church who have acted as spiritual seat belts for us, who have protected us and guided us as we were children in the faith. God bless you for caring for us.

Lesson 10

A Heritage of Faith

2 Timothy 1:3-14

I thank God, whom I serve from my forefathers with pure conscience, that without ceasing I have remembrance of thee in my prayers night and day;

4 Greatly desiring to see thee, being mindful of thy tears, that I may be filled with joy;

5 When I call to remembrance the unfeigned faith that is in thee, which dwelt first in thy grandmother Lois, and thy mother Eunice; and I am persuaded that in thee also.

6 Wherefore I put thee in remembrance that thou stir up the gift of God, which is in thee by the putting on of my hands.

7 For God hath not given us the spirit of fear; but of power, and of love, and of a sound mind.

8 Be not thou therefore ashamed of the testimony of our Lord, nor of me his prisoner: but be thou partaker of the afflictions of the gospel according to the power of God;

9 Who hath saved us, and called us with an holy calling, not according to our works, but according to his own purpose and grace, which was given us in Christ Jesus before the world began,

10 But is now made manifest by the appearing of our Saviour Jesus Christ, who hath abolished death, and hath brought life and immortality to light through the gospel:

11 Whereunto I am appointed a preacher, and an apostle, and a teacher of the Gentiles.

12 For the which cause I also suffer these things: nevertheless I am not ashamed: for I know whom I have believed, and am persuaded that he is able to keep that which I have committed unto him against that day.

13 Hold fast the form of sound words, which thou hast heard of me, in faith and love which is in Christ Jesus.

14 That good thing which was committed unto thee keep by the Holy Ghost which dwelleth in us.

Feb. 5

Devotional Reading
2 Thess. 2:13-17

Background Scripture
2 Tim. 1

Memory Selection
2 Tim. 1:5

Nearing the end of his ministry, the apostle Paul seeks to ensure that his work will go forward after he dies. As one step, he writes a final letter to Timothy, the young minister Paul has mentored through the years.

To stress the importance of carrying on his work, Paul emphasizes the theme of *continuing a faithful heritage*. He establishes for Timothy the hope that there can be a "trajectory of faith," one that began in Timothy's having been grounded in faith by his mother and grandmother, then complemented and deepened by the younger minister's association with the apostle.

Since not everyone has this kind of faith-full background, the thoughtful teacher should keep in mind how we can motivate ourselves and others even when we lack a heritage like Timothy's.

଼ଠଓ

This lesson can be opened by inviting group members to recall family members or friends who pointed them to the Lord.

Encourage group members who have a long lineage in the faith to tell briefly how far back they can trace it. Some may surprise you by knowing, for example, that their great-grandfather was a minister.

Ask how this kind of heritage can be passed on to children in today's culture, with its many distractions. Note that in this lesson Paul calls Timothy to recall his heritage of faith—not to boast, but to draw strength as he presses on into a future that may be hostile to faith.

Teaching Outline	Daily Bible Readings
I. Faithful Family—3-5	Mon. God Gives the Heritage Ps. 111
A. Personal note, 3-4	Tue. We Can Lose Our Heritage Jer. 17:1-8
B. Heritage of faith, 5	
II. Fanning the Flames—6-8	Wed. Stand Firm, Hold Fast 2 Thess. 2:13-17
A. Gift from God, 6	Thu. Faithful Mother Acts 16:1-5
B. Courage to serve, 7-8	
III. Foundation for Ministry—9-12	Fri. Passing on the Faith 2 Tim. 1:1-5
A. Called by Christ, 2-10	Sat. Proud Heritage 2 Tim. 1:6-10
B. Confidence & courage, 11-12	
IV. Firm Commitment—13-14	Sun. Guard the Treasure 2 Tim. 1:11-18

Verse by Verse

I. Faithful Family—3-5

A. Personal note, 3-4

3 I thank God, whom I serve from my forefathers with pure conscience, that without ceasing I have remembrance of thee in my prayers night and day;

4 Greatly desiring to see thee, being mindful of thy tears, that I may be filled with joy;

Through the years, Paul has grown especially close to the young man Timothy since inviting him to join the missions team on his second tour (Acts 16:1-3). Having had a Jewish mother and a Greek father (16:3), Timothy's family heritage had no doubt enabled him to ask just the right questions about Paul's conversion from Judaism to what was fast becoming a Gentile-dominated faith. Although Paul has repented of his having persecuted Christians, he insists that even while pursuing all possible means to put a stop to the Christian "heresy," he did it with a "pure conscience." No doubt he is laying the groundwork for encouraging the younger minister to be sure his own motives are pure.

Yet this is no purely "ministerial" relationship. Paul is personally fond of Timothy, and remembers his "tears," apparently shed at some point when he and Paul had parted (as in Acts 17:14). In fact, Paul told

the Philippian brethren that "I have no one else like him" (Philip. 2:20). It is only those who are that close that we remember in our prayers "night and day," and look forward with keen anticipation to being with them again. Although in 4:9 he asks Timothy to come visit him in prison in Rome, we do not know whether this hope was fulfilled.

B. Heritage of faith, 5

5 When I call to remembrance the unfeigned faith that is in thee, which dwelt first in thy grandmother Lois, and thy mother Eunice; and I am persuaded that in thee also.

Paul had been able to see that Timothy's faith was "unfeigned" (the original word also gives us the term "unhypocritical"). His mother was a Jew, and his father a Greek (16:3); and this blended family must have posed just the right questions to Timothy as he came to know Paul, who had formerly persecuted Christians as faithfully as he now served Christ. As is so often the case, it has been strong women in the family who have handed down the faith to Timothy. Although we cannot be absolutely sure, Timothy's grandmother, and perhaps his mother, would have been faithful Jews when Paul first met them. In those days, before the modern distinction between "observant" and "secular" Jews, most Jewish homes took seriously the responsibility of teaching the children the faith (see Exod. 13:14-15; Deut. 4:9).

II. Fanning the Flames—6-8
A. Gift from God, 6

6 Wherefore I put thee in remembrance that thou stir up the gift of God, which is in thee by the putting on of my hands.

Some New Testament references suggest that Timothy was either shy or had a tendency to become discouraged and faint-hearted. Paul had urged him to "neglect not the gift that is in thee" (1 Tim. 4:14), no doubt referring to the same "gift (Grk. *charisma*) of God" mentioned here. We are not told what this gift was, but it was apparently transmitted to Timothy by the laying on of Paul's hands, as well as the hands of "presbyters" or elders (1 Tim. 4:14b; see also Acts 8:14-17). It is significant that as "miraculous" as this gift might be, it could still be squelched or under-employed—hence Paul's encouragement that Timothy keep it "stirred up."

B. Courage to serve, 7-8

7 For God hath not given us the spirit of fear; but of power, and of love, and of a sound mind.

8 Be not thou therefore ashamed of the testimony of our Lord, nor of me his prisoner: but be thou partaker of the afflictions of the gospel according to the power of God;

Verse 7 is one of the strongest passages in Scripture for giving heart to the discouraged. Paul uses powerful language to counter Timothy's tendency to depression or timidity. Those traits did not come from God, for He sends courage instead of fear, power instead of weakness, aggressive love instead of indifference, and a sound mind instead of indecisiveness. Countless ministers have been able to press on in the face of discouragement by reflecting on these traits, which are themselves gifts from God.

III. Foundation for Ministry—9-12
A. Called by Christ, 9-10

9 Who hath saved us, and called us with an holy calling, not according to our works, but according to his own purpose and grace, which was given us in Christ Jesus before the world began,

10 But is now made manifest by the appearing of our Saviour Jesus Christ, who hath abolished death, and hath brought life and immortality to light through the gospel:

Another way in which Paul urges courage in Timothy is by reminding him that their calling is from God. Neither Paul nor Timothy had done, or could do, enough good works to "deserve" or earn the commission God had given them to go into all the world with the Good News of Christ. That these gifts were in the mind of God "before the world began" should also have been an encouragement during times when Timothy felt like giving up in the face of persecution or false brethren.

The former "secret" of Paul and Timothy's calling has now been revealed openly. In Paul's case, he had only to recall the public nature of his conversion, when he was struck down on the Damascus Road. That this calling was from Jesus, whose own resurrection promised the abolishment of death, provides the strength to continue proclaiming His message even in the face of death.

Saying that "life and immortality" have been brought to light by the gospel has raised speculation about the nature and destiny of man. Is he *by nature* "immortal," as the Greeks taught? If so, the soul is an unquenchable spark that survives even death, inviting visions of both heaven and hell in virtually every religion. On the other hand, if immortality is not "inborn" but a "gift" endowed on those who respond to the call of God, then hell is, as some teach today, the extinguishing of the soul instead of an eternal burning of that which is imperishable.

B. Confidence and courage, 11-12

11 Whereunto I am appointed a preacher, and an apostle, and a teacher of the Gentiles.

12 For the which cause I also suffer these things: nevertheless I am not ashamed: for I know whom I have believed, and am persuaded that he is able to keep that which I have committed unto him against that day.

Paul reaffirms that his appointment or call is based on what he has referred to in verse 10: the revelation of eternal life through the Good News about Jesus. It is this, not a self-appointed ego-trip, that made him a preacher (Grk. *kerux,* "herald"), an apostle ("one sent" on a special mission), and a teacher sent to the Gentiles.

Throughout his career, Paul battled accusations that he was a false apostle. Here he recalls the hardships and suffering in which he had been involved, tacitly asking why anyone would take on such afflictions out of a merely self-serving sense of call. He is ashamed neither of false accusations nor the hardships themselves, because of the rock-solid confidence that the same God who called him would also reward him on the final Day of reckoning.

IV. Firm Commitment—13-14

13 Hold fast the form of sound words, which thou hast heard of me, in faith and love which is in Christ Jesus.

14 That good thing which was committed unto thee keep by the Holy Ghost which dwelleth in us.

Now Paul turns toward Timothy, hoping that the words of conviction and firmness of purpose he had used for himself would also be "caught" by the younger minister. He challenges Timothy not only to keep the faith Paul has taught him, but to keep active the *charisma* or gift he has referred to earlier. It was a gift given by the Spirit who manifests Himself not only by such miraculous measures; He is also a "real presence" within the heart of every Christian.

Evangelistic Emphasis

There is nothing like the enthusiasm of a beginner. Watch the antics of a young kitten or puppy rolling and rollicking around its stretched-out parent. They can't wait to explore every nook and cranny, investigate every piece of lint, or tussle with every squeaky toy.

The one who has already "seen it all" would rather take a nap. That's why the rampant exuberance of youth can exhaust the rest of us. We tend to roll our eyes and moan about these "red hots," even while we secretly admire their dedication and envy their energy.

The problem with being "red hot"

is that it takes a lot of time and effort to maintain that degree of enthusiasm for any length of time. That is the reason not many New Year's resolutions make it past March. The joy of exercising gradually becomes just another chore on your long list of "things to do." Getting away to that perfect fishing hole never seems possible on your schedule. Sunday morning services and Wednesday night praise group and Friday lunchtime Bible study seem to be consuming your week, and you feel the need for some "time off."

Paul recognized the need for Timothy, and all Christians, periodically to "rekindle the gift of God" (vs. 6). How long has it been since you felt passionate about winning a soul to Christ? Is there something you need to rekindle?

ഇ൬൧

Memory Selection

When I call to remembrance the unfeigned faith that is in thee, which dwelt first in thy grandmother, Louis, and they mother, Eunice, and I am persuaded that in thee also.—*2 Timothy 1:5*

Just a month ago, I buried my mother. Her death was quite sudden. Mom had three adult kids who were not ready to plan a funeral. After planning the funeral, another normal question arose. Where will we bury her? Mom raised us three alone, so there is no dad to ask questions like that. We made a bold decision. We buried mom with her parents and grandparents.

When I walked away from the cemetery that morning I knew that two ladies who influenced my faith journey were in that hallowed ground. I am a product of my grandmother's faith and my mother's tenacity. I would not be a minister of the gospel if not for those two very special ladies.

Timothy had a similar experience. His faith was planted in the faith of his grandmother and nurtured in the faith of his mother. We are a product of our parents. We are also a spiritual product of our parents.

Weekday Problems

Frank was waxing poetic about all the failures of the younger generation in the church. He was complaining that they were always busy doing something other than serving on committees. Frank had been the chairman of the committee on committees for years and he was having a terrible time finding other people to serve on the committee with him.

He complained most about Thad, who would never make any Monday night commitments. Frank failed to consider the fact that Thad was the Scout Master, and the Troop met on Monday nights. When Thad was not with the Scouts he was helping his daughter's soccer coach and team.

Thad sang in the choir and he was a generous contributor. He and his wife raised two children who were always in church. Thad was proud of their young family's active witness to the faith. But Frank was not satisfied; Thad wasn't doing his duty as a Christian until he volunteered to serve on a committee.

*Do you think Frank's chagrin over Thad's failure to serve on a committee is a valid criticism?

*How do we confuse church work with the work of the church? Is there a difference? (Hint: a BIG difference.)

*Why are young people afraid to take roles of leadership in the church? Is it their problem, or is it that we don't let them?

Wisdom from Kids

No matter how hard you try, it's really hard to baptize a cat.

When your mom is mad at your dad, don't let her brush your hair.

The reason why you should never hit back when someone hits you is because they always catch the second person.

You can't trust your dog to watch your food while you go to the bathroom.

Never sneeze while someone is cutting your hair.

You can't hide a stalk of broccoli in a glass of milk.

Don't war polka-dot underwear under white shorts.

The best place to be when you're sad is in a grandma's lap.

You can learn a lot by reading what people write on their desks, but you can't always repeat it.

This Lesson in Your Life

Paul and Timothy got along from the very beginning. The book of Acts tells us that Paul didn't have that kind of relationship with everyone. He "fell out" with several people during his ministry. Paul stayed close to Timothy his whole ministry.

Timothy's faith grew out of how he was raised. Whether we like it or not, the saying that "the nut doesn't fall far from the tree" is very true in matters of the spiritual realm. If you attend church, chances are better than average that your children will also attend church. If other things claim your attention on Sunday when you are growing up then you learn you can miss a Sunday or two each month.

A Christian mother and grandmother raised Timothy. They influenced him to become a Christian. Paul recalled this relationship to encourage Timothy in his faith walk. Paul told Timothy to "live up" or "live into" the faith of his mother and grandmother. That is a challenge that we could offer to our classes—to "live up" to the faith of our spiritual mentors.

The other issue is a bit bothersome. It involves allowing the next generation to take leadership in the church. You know the universal complaints against young people: their music is too loud, the clothes are too crazy-looking, and they don't respect the traditions of their elders. If you're honest, you will have to say that those same criticisms were leveled against you and your generation when you were younger.

When we were younger, another generation built a church for us. Now it is time for us to build a church for the next generation. That means spiritually, and it also means financially. Young couples are struggling as never before. Both parents often work outside the home, not because they want to, but because they must. Are we building a church that supports and loves them through the struggles of raising children?

Are we mentoring the next generation in the faith?

Paul gave Timothy responsibility and authority. He kept his eye on young Timothy, but he didn't tell him every step to take. Are you ready to share church leadership? Are you ready for one of those young people to plan the church worship service? The fact that they don't respect the worship traditions of my generation is a good thing! It means that they are building a church for the next generation

So smile! One day these young people will be old, too, and think just as you do.

1. According to the book of Acts, were did Paul meet Timothy?

Paul was traveling from Syria and Cilicia to Derbe and Lystra. He met Timothy in Lystra (Acts 15:40–16:1).

2. What Biblical information can you discover about Timothy's parents?

Timothy's mother was a Jewess who professed faith in Jesus. Timothy's father was a Greek. The implication was that his father was not a believer.

3. How did Paul describe his relationship with Timothy?

In most cases, Paul referred to Timothy as a son. He wrote to the Philippians, "How like a son with a father he has served with me."

4. What was the genealogy of Timothy's faith?

His faith lived first is his grandmother Lois, then in his mother, Eunice.

5. What church relationship did Paul and Timothy share?

Timothy had been "ordained" by Paul. "For this reason I remind you to rekindle the gift of God that is within you through the laying on of my hands" (2 Tim. 1:6).

6. Paul was in prison when he wrote to Timothy. What was Paul's word of encouragement?

Paul told Timothy not to be ashamed of the testimony of Paul's suffering for Christ (vs. 8).

7. What did Paul rely on in his suffering?

On the power of God, who saved him and called him to a holy purpose (vs. 9).

8. Why was Paul suffering?

He was being persecuted by both Jews and gentiles because he was a herald, an apostle, and a teacher of the gospel.

9. Why did Paul have confidence even in his suffering?

Because he was sure that God would keep that which he entrusted to Him.

10. What admonition about teaching did Paul give to Timothy?

"Hold to the standard of sound teaching you have heard from me, and to the faith and love of Jesus, and guard the good treasure given by the Holy Spirit" (vs. 13).

There are three ways we fan the flames and keep the Spirit burning brightly in our lives.

We need Pentecost power. On our own, we are totally incapable of remaining faithful to anyone or anything—not even ourselves. The greatest gift each of us receives as new children in Christ is that special presence Christ sent to be among us: the Holy Spirit. Two images always seem to accompany the Holy Spirit—fire and wind.

Just as all fire needs oxygen, so the flames of faithfulness that are kindled within us cannot be kept going without the breath of the Holy Spirit. The Holy Spirit's continued presence with us acts like a bellows to the flames we tend in our hearts. If we ignore the presence of this "spirit of power," cut ourselves off from the possibility of a living spirit within us, we shut down our own air supply.

We need to live exemplary lives. It is not enough simply to fan the flames of faithfulness within ourselves. Until we open ourselves up to others and let the warmth of this fire spread though our family, our friends, our church, our community, it is bound to gradually die out.

Paul never shirked from citing his own life as an example to the Christian communities he addressed. Sometimes he pointed to his previous life as a persecutor of the church, but more often he used his life after his conversion as a template for believers. But Paul himself followed only one example—the love-life lived by Jesus.

We need a self-disciplined life-style. Even those who acknowledge the power of the Holy Spirit and who encounter others with a loving attitude may gradually lose their spark. The famous preacher G. Campbell Morgan said that it was possible to be "homiletically brilliant, verbally fluent, theologically profound, biblically orthodox, and spiritually useless"

To avoid becoming "spiritually useless," we must all practice a self-disciplined lifestyle. Paul, in his letter to Timothy, testified to the comfort daily prayer brought him. He practiced this discipline whether among friends or shut up in a lonely prison. Prayer is not always easy. But when our own tongues cannot express the needs and longings of our hearts, the Spirit voices those needs for us.

2 Timothy 2:14-26

Of these things put them in remembrance, charging them before the Lord that they strive not about words to no profit, but to the subverting of the hearers.

15 Study to shew thyself approved unto God, a workman that needeth not to be ashamed, rightly dividing the word of truth.

16 But shun profane and vain babblings: for they will increase unto more ungodliness.

17 And their word will eat as doth a canker: of whom is Hymenaeus and Philetus;

18 Who concerning the truth have erred, saying that the resurrection is past already; and overthrow the faith of some.

19 Nevertheless the foundation of God standeth sure, having this seal, The Lord knoweth them that are his. And, Let every one that nameth the name of Christ depart from iniquity.

20 But in a great house there are not only vessels of gold and of silver, but also of wood and of earth; and some to honour, and some to dishonour.

21 If a man therefore purge himself from these, he shall be a vessel unto honour, sanctified, and meet for the master's use, and prepared unto every good work.

22 Flee also youthful lusts: but follow righteousness, faith, charity, peace, with them that call on the Lord out of a pure heart.

23 But foolish and unlearned questions avoid, knowing that they do gender strifes.

24 And the servant of the Lord must not strive; but be gentle unto all men, apt to teach, patient,

25 In meekness instructing those that oppose themselves; if God peradventure will give them repentance to the acknowledging of the truth;

26 And that they may recover themselves out of the snare of the devil, who are taken captive by him at his will.

Devotional Reading
1 Pet. 2:1-10

Background Scripture
2 Tim. 2

Memory Selection
2 Tim. 2:22

Feb. 12

This lesson is a virtual "catchechism" for Christ's followers—a summary of Paul' basic teaching. In this case, Paul's catechism is couched not in questions but commands, and it deals more with practice than abstract doctrine. Like a standard catechism, however, he moves from topic to topic.

Previously the apostle has laid down principles for church *leadership* and qualities of good leaders. But leaders are effective only if they have willing and capable *followers*. So some of Paul's strongest teaching as his ministry drew to a close dealt with what might be called "the average Christian life." They are standards by which Christians can walk in the footsteps of their Lord.

You can begin this lesson by leading a discussion of *followership*. Just as Paul has set down qualifications for church leaders, what qualifications can rightly be expected of members? Followin are points to be suggested if they aren't brought up by the group:

• *Being familiar with the purpose of the group* (in the case of the Church, this means a good working knowledge of the Bible, and of the congregation's mission).

• *Supporting group leaders* as they try reach these goals.

• *Being consistent in attendance and participation.*

• *Maintaining an attitude of co-operation and good will.*

• *Volunteering for specific tasks* and *utilizing your abilities.*

• *Living in a way that reflects positively on the group.*

Teaching Outline	Daily Bible Readings

I. Staying On-Center—14-18
  A. Core values, 14-15
  B. Eroding arguments, 16-18
    1. Living illustrations, 16-17
    2. False teaching, 18
II. Sure Foundation—19-22
  A. God knows!, 19
  B. Vessels for God's use, 20-21
  C. Foundation stones, 22
III. Strife Is Unproductive—23-26
  A. Be able but gentle, 23-24
  B. Rescuing the trapped, 25-26
	Mon. Faith in God's Promise
	       Rom. 4:13-25
	Tue. Growing into Salvation
	       1 Pet. 2:1-10
	Wed. Growing in Knowledge
	       Col. 1:3-10
	Thu. A Good Soldier of Christ
	       2 Tim. 2:1-7
	Fri. Remember the Model
	       2 Tim. 2:8-13
	Sat. An Approved Worker
	       2 Tim. 2:14-19
	Sun. What to Pursue
	       2 Tim. 2:20-26

Verse by Verse

I. Staying On-Center—14-18
A. Core values, 14-15

14 Of these things put them in remembrance, charging them before the Lord that they strive not about words to no profit, but to the subverting of the hearers.

15 Study to shew thyself approved unto God, a workman that needeth not to be ashamed, rightly dividing the word of truth.

From a modern viewpoint it may be disturbing to know that false doctrine plagued Paul everywhere he went, and the early Church at large. On second thought, however, we can understand that the Christian message was so startlingly new that adherents to other views were naturally upset. In a way these early disputes served for the good of the Church, since they prompted an outpouring of Scripture giving succeeding generations a guide to true doctrine.

Many in the early Church (and today?) had difficulty realizing that not every issue is worth an argument, much less a church split. Here Paul warns against striving with each other over inconsequential details. A good example was the eating of meats offered to idols, which the apostle deals with in 1 Corinthians 8. He shows that when members center on the core value that there is only one God, dietary rules should not divide them. Continuing to argue over such issues "subverts" instead of building up. (The word translated "subverting" gives us the word "catastrophe," meaning literally "turning things upside down.")

Instead of becoming bogged down in such trivialities, faithful followers should "do [their] best" (NIV) to focus on more essential issues. (Although this of course *requires* Bible study, the word translated "study" in the KJV means "try hard" or "pay attention to," rather than to pore intensely over a book.) The word for "rightly dividing" means "to guide along a straight path." When applied to "the word of truth," it means applying Scripture appropriately and in context, rather than "proof-texting" or otherwise mishandling the Bible to support already established views and preconceptions.

B. Eroding arguments, 16-18
1. Living illustrations, 16-17

16 But shun profane and vain babblings: for they will increase unto more ungodliness.

17 And their word will eat as doth a canker: of whom is Hymenaeus and Philetus;

The damage that wrangling does within the Body is illustrated here

233

with a medical term: it spreads like a "canker" or a cancerous sore. Although all such dissension does damage, it can be over *central* doctrines, not just trivialities; and Paul uses as an example some false teaching about the resurrection being propagated in Ephesus (vs. 18). Hymanaeus was introduced in 1 Timothy 1:20. Here he is joined by another false teacher, Philetus, whose heresy will now be explained.

2. False teaching, 18

18 Who concerning the truth have erred, saying that the resurrection is past already; and overthrow the faith of some.

Two influences in the surrounding culture may have led to the false teaching that the resurrection had already occurred. Some church members may have been Sadducees, who denied the bodily resurrection (Matt. 22:23). Others may have held to the teaching of the "pre-Gnostics" mentioned in previous lessons who taught that the body is evil. Some of these people "spiritualized" the resurrection by saying that it actually referred to salvation, or a kind of "Aha! experience" of sudden awareness—anything but the reappearance of a body that they considered evil in the first place. Although Paul does not go into the importance of believing in a literal, bodily resurrection, he does so extensively in 1 Corinthians 15, affirming that if Jesus and His followers were not to be raised at the last Day, "we are of all men most miserable" (1

Cor. 15:19).

II. Sure Foundation—19-22
A. God knows!, 19

19 Nevertheless the foundation of God standeth sure, having this seal, The Lord knoweth them that are his. And, Let every one that nameth the name of Christ depart from iniquity.

Against the possibility that the faith of some Ephesian believers had been shaken by those who taught that their hope in a future bodily resurrection was misplaced, Paul emphatically affirms the opposite. Those who believe the apostolic teaching about the resurrection need not fear that God cannot tell the difference between them and the false teachers.

To illustrate, he cites the Old Testament incident when Korah, Dathan, and Abiram rebelled against Moses and were destroyed. Of course this illustration cuts two ways: it offers comfort to those who might have been troubled by the false teachers at Ephesus, and it promises judgment against the false teachers. The bottom line is that we should avoid false teaching, which is "iniquity."

B. Vessels for God's use, 20-21

20 But in a great house there are not only vessels of gold and of silver, but also of wood and of earth; and some to honour, and some to dishonour.

21 If a man therefore purge himself from these, he shall be a vessel unto honour, sanctified, and

meet for the master's use, and pre-pared unto every good work.

Having used the metaphor of the "foundation" of a fine house, Paul elaborates on the theme with an illustration about the furnishings in such a palace. He speaks, of course of the Church, which he often compares to "God's building," or "the house of God."

It would be natural to suppose that in the mansion of a wealthy family not all the "vessels" or utensils would be as fine as the house itself. An ornate urn standing near the entrance would be a "vessel of honor," while a broken bucket at the cistern would not. Hymenaeus and Philetus are examples of the broken bucket; but they need not be allowed to set the standard for other "utensils" or members of the Body. Those who oppose their false teaching will be put to good use in the Church.

C. Foundation stones, 22

22 Flee also youthful lusts: but follow righteousness, faith, charity, peace, with them that call on the Lord out of a pure heart.

Turning to other issues, more related to personality than to doctrine, Paul urges Timothy (and other younger persons as they "read over Timothy's shoulder") to flee the passions and resist the raging hormones that too often characterize youth. Instead, youth are to be an example to others in the Christian graces (as Paul had also emphasized in 1 Tim. 4:12).

III. Strife Is Unproductive—23-26

A. Be able but gentle, 23-24

23 But foolish and unlearned questions avoid, knowing that they do gender strifes.

24 And the servant of the Lord must not strive; but be gentle unto all men, apt to teach, patient,

Returning to the damage that internal dissension can do to any group, but especially the Church, Paul inserts the very practical fact that one's attitude and personality, not just doctrinal issues, affect the harmony and health of the Body. In almost any argument, observers can spot those for whom doctrinal correctness is not the only matter that divides believers, but who consider an "irenic" or peace-seeking spirit of equal importance.

B. Rescuing the trapped, 25-26

25 In meekness instructing those that oppose themselves; if God peradventure will give them repentance to the acknowledging of the truth;

26 And that they may recover themselves out of the snare of the devil, who are taken captive by him at his will.

Those who do exhibit the traits of peacefulness, gentleness, and meekness have a special ministry in the Church: recovering false and argumentative teachers from the trap that Satan sets for them in an attempt to nullify the Church's overall ministry. The fact that they are taken captive at Satan's will does not mean that the teachers themselves are not willing to be taken captive as well.

Evangelistic Emphasis

We have all kinds of fads in our country. Right now, everyone is counting carbs. Sylvester Graham, C.W. Post, and J.H. Kellogg all responded to such fads. "Graham Crackers" were a "natural food" answer to fears about the bad effects of factory work for the urban masses. White-collar workers, fearful that they might be "feminized" by the shift from manual to non-manual labor, were reassured that their masculinity could be preserved by eating natural foods. "Grape Nuts" were originally sold as "brain food" for middle class people.

J.H. Kellogg's breakfast products were "good for you," especially Corn Flakes, because they reduced your sexual drive: "Eat enough Corn Flakes and you would be freed from sin!" If breakfast food could free us from sin, then you and I would be out of business on Sunday morning. We know that it was a fad.

We also have theological fads. They come and go as swiftly as food fads. One thing that is not a fad is our call to "make disciples for Jesus Christ." While the church argues over the minutiae of theological points that no one cares about, people are dying without a personal knowledge of Jesus Christ.

ഇറ

Flee also youthful lusts, but follow righteousness, faith, love, peace, with them that call on the Lord out of a pure heart.—*2 Timothy 2: 22*

A young man saw and attractive girl on the road and followed her for a mile. Finally, she turned around and demanded, "Why are you following me?"

He answered, "Because you are the most beautiful woman I have ever seen in my life. I have fallen madly in love with you. Will you be mine?"

She replied, "You only have to look behind you to see my younger sister. She is far more beautiful than I am."

He immediately whirled around only to see the homeliest girl that he'd ever seen.

"What mockery is this?" he demanded. "You lied!"

"So did you," she replied. "If you were so madly in love with me, why did you turn around?"

Youthful lusts cause us to profess our commitment to a task or our love for another person until something better comes along. Paul's cure for that kind of capricious behavior: follow righteousness, faith, love and peace.

Weekday Problems

Ben was in his pastor's office with his head in his hands, weeping. He said, "I don't know what came over me. I am ruined. My life is ruined." Ben Bradford had been a leader at First Church since before anyone could remember. He had headed up every board, committee, and task group ever held in that church. He sang in the choir. He gave generously of his time and his talents. His two grown children who were active in their churches.

Ben had purchased a computer for his grandkids and they had shown him how to use it. Before long Ben was navigating the Internet like a teenager. That is what got him into trouble. Before long Ben found himself in the strange world of chat rooms. He found himself chatting with total strangers. One of his new friends was named "*rightplacewrongtime*," and it turned out she was a divorcee about half Ben's age. They struck up one of those anonymous Internet relationships. While things started innocently enough, "*rightplacewrongtime*" made it clear that she might be interested in more than just chat. She wanted to meet, and even though Ben told her he was happily married, she still wanted to meet her new "friend."

Ben's face was red from weeping. "I don't know what came over me, Pastor. I don't know why I agreed to meet her."

*What other "youthful passions" sometimes tempt mature adults?

Theme Songs of Bible Characters

Noah: "Raindrops Keep Fallin' on My Head"
Adam and Eve: "Strangers in Paradise"
Job: "I've Got a Right to Sing the Blues"
Salome: "I Could Have Danced All Night"
The Magi: "When You Wish Upon a Star"
Lazarus: "The Second Time Around"
Daniel: "The Lion Sleeps Tonight"
Jezebel: "The Lady Is a Tramp"
Jonah: "Got a Whale of a Tale"
Moses: "The Wanderer"
Elijah: "Up, Up, and Away"
Methuseleh: "Stayin' Alive"
Nebuchadnezzar: "Crazy"
Esau: "Born to Be Wild"
Peter: "I'm Sorry"
Samson: "Hair"

"

This Lesson in Your Life

We think Paul's warning about youthful passions is quaint. Some of us are so old that we would honored if someone described us as youthful. I had a preacher friend once who complained about ageism in the ministry. He said, "For the first 20 years of my ministry I was too young. In the last 20 years of ministry, I was too old. There was a two-week span when I was just the right age. Unfortunately for me I was on vacation then." We think youthful passions can't happen to anyone over 25. They can. However, the emphasis of this verse is not on the behavior to avoid, rather it is on the behavior to acquire. The encouragement is to pursue righteousness, faith, love, and peace.

Righteousness is a big "church word," but with a simple meaning. Righteousness means that we are in a right relationship with God. We honor God with our lives when we strive for right relationships with our fellow human beings. This means that we honor their dignity as people created in the image of God. It means we practice forgiveness and grace in our relationships with them when that is necessary. It means we hold them accountable for their growth in godliness.

We practice faith. In most places in the New Testament, faith is verbal in form. People of faith act in the assurance that God is with us. We have a confidence that allows us to see beyond "what we have always done" and claim the bright future to which God has called us. Living in faith means we have no ruts.

We practice love. Love is a word that is thrown around too easily. Love is a deep, sacrificial commitment of one person to another or to the causes of Christ. Love is not just a feeling; it is also a set of very distinct actions and behaviors. Paul defined love for us. "Love is patient. Love is kind. It is not envious or boastful. Love does not insist on its own way. It is not rude or arrogant. Love bears all things, believes all things, hopes all things, and endures all things. Love never ends."

We are to seek peace. Peace is not just the absence of conflict. We cover up too many things in the church under the guise of "trying to keep things peaceful." Jesus never called us to this perverse kind of peace. It is dishonest! Peace as biblically illustrated is the ability to move through a problem knowing that God is with us and we will complete our journey. That opens the door for all kinds of healthy discussions in the church. It means that we can agree to disagree.

Righteousness, faith, love, and peace. Seeking these things with passion will keep us from "youthful passions." It will also give us something practical and helpful to do in our "mature years."

GETTING THE FACTS STRAIGHT

1. About what was Timothy to remind the church?

He was to remind them and warn them that they were to avoid "wrangling over words."

2. What do you think it means to wrangle over words?

Many discussions of words such as "charismatic," "baptism," or the "role of women" illustrate what it means!

3. How was Timothy to present himself to God?

Timothy was to be a worker approved of God, one who rightly explained the word of truth.

4. What was Paul's warning about profane chatter?

Profane chatter would lead people into impiety and it would spread like gangrene.

5. What do you think profane chatter is?

The best example of profane chatter is not so much gossip but the sharing of incorrect information about the church.

6. Who were the two heretics that are listed in this chapter.

The two that had swerved from the truth were Hymenaeus and Philetus.

7. How had Hymenaeus and Philetus swerved from the truth?

They were claiming that the resurrection had already taken place.

8. What was the result of their false teaching?

They "are upsetting the faith of some."

9. What is the meaning of the "utensils" in the house?

This refers not to cooking, but to people of faith who purify themselves for usefulness to God.

10. Who is the house's owner, and what is its nature?

The house is the kingdom of God, and the owner would be the Lord Himself.

I wonder how many Christians have read the second chapter of 2 Timothy. Seems that had we been more familiar with these words we would have avoided much of the heartache of church history. Paul warns the Church to avoid "wrangling over words" and to "have nothing to do with stupid and senseless controversies." The warnings are the same; yet we have fallen into these traps repeatedly.

The illustrations are too numerous to mention, but in your class you can discuss some of the "wrangling over words" that has taken place in your particular faith tradition. If you are brave, you might talk about how language has divided the family of God. For instance, would you agree that the Eucharist, the Lord's Supper, and Holy Communion are all the same act of worship? Our traditions give us words by which to understand our faith, and then we battle over the words.

"Stupid and senseless controversies" are those moments when the Church is caught protesting something it ought not protest or doesn't really know enough about to protest. Several years ago there was a movie about the "The Last Temptation of Christ" and many Christians protested up a storm. Had they left the matter alone, few people would have seen the movie. But because so many Christians warned against it, many decided that the very bad movie was worth seeing. Of course, I'm sure that some felt they were doing what Jesus wanted them to do.

Then a few years ago we had the hubbub over the Ten Commandments being taken out of the Alabama Supreme Court Building. Everyone was outraged about the removal; they were taking God's law out of the courts of law. You know, I thought that God told us to "write his law on our hearts." If we were doing what we ought to be doing as His children, we would be "up in arms" about fewer issues and would be wrapping our arms around the people who need Jesus.

2 Timothy 3:10–4:8

But thou hast fully known my doctrine, manner of life, purpose, faith, longsuffering, charity, patience,

11 Persecutions, afflictions, which came unto me at Antioch, at Iconium, at Lystra; what persecutions I endured: but out of them all the Lord delivered me.

12 Yea, and all that will live godly in Christ Jesus shall suffer persecution.

13 But evil men and seducers shall wax worse and worse, deceiving, and being deceived.

14 But continue thou in the things which thou hast learned and hast been assured of, knowing of whom thou hast learned them;

15 And that from a child thou hast known the holy scriptures, which are able to make thee wise unto salvation through faith which is in Christ Jesus.

16 All scripture is given by inspiration of God, and is profitable for doctrine, for reproof, for correction, for instruction in righteousness:

17 That the man of God may be perfect, throughly furnished unto all good works.

4:1 I charge thee therefore before God, and the Lord Jesus Christ, who shall judge the quick and the dead at his appearing and his kingdom;

2 Preach the word; be instant in season, out of season; reprove, rebuke, exhort with all longsuffering and doctrine.

3 For the time will come when they will not endure sound doctrine; but after their own lusts shall they heap to themselves teachers, having itching ears;

4 And they shall turn away their ears from the truth, and shall be turned unto fables.

5 But watch thou in all things, endure afflictions, do the work of an evangelist, make full proof of thy ministry.

6 For I am now ready to be offered, and the time of my departure is at hand.

7 I have fought a good fight, I have finished my course, I have kept the faith:

8 Henceforth there is laid up for me a crown of righteousness, which the Lord, the righteous judge, shall give me at that day: and not to me only, but unto all them also that love his appearing.

Devotional Reading
Ps. 119:9-16

Background Scripture
2 Tim. 3–4

Memory Selection
2 Tim. 3:14

Feb. 19

"Famous last words" have universal appeal. The closing portion of 2 Timothy contains some of Paul's last words, and are therefore some of the most poignant passages in Scripture. Although Paul, Timothy's mentor, has expressed the desire to see the younger minister again, we do not have a record that he did so. The present lesson capsules some of the departing thoughts we can well imagine Paul wanted Timothy to remember. The lesson can be summarized with the line, *Ministry isn't a bed of roses; but if you stay grounded in the Scriptures and what I've taught you, you can share a crown of righteousness like the one I'm confident of receiving!*

Second Timothy may be Paul's last recorded epistle. We do well to give its closing portion special attention.

Invite your group to imagine that they are, all together, the apostle Paul, writing his last words to the younger minister Timothy. They will need to pare down all that *might* be said to the bare bones of what *can* be said, in a brief conclusion to a letter such as 2 Timothy.

Ask such questions as: *What feelings would be in your heart if you were Paul? . . . What issues would you consider most important to write about? . . . Would there be challenges you would want to warn Timothy about—road blocks he would have to face in the years ahead? . . . What resources could you point him to that would equip him to successfully encounter any difficulties?*

Note that in today's lesson group members can compare their ideas with the apostle Paul's.

Teaching Outline	*Daily Bible Readings*

I. Roadblocks—10-13
  A. Paul's experience, 10-11
  B. Realistic warning, 12-13
II. Resources—14-17
  A. Faithful mentors, 14
  B. Scriptural grounding, 15-17
III. The Road Ahead—4:1-8
  A. Charge to Timothy, 1-2
  B. Enduring the future, 3-5
  C. Paul's expectations, 6-8
	Mon. The Word in the Heart
	      Ps. 119:9-16
	Tue. Teach Me Thy Statutes
	      Ps. 119:33-40
	Wed. An Example to Imitate
	      2 Thess. 3:6-13
	Thu. Avoid Godless People
	      2 Tim. 3:1-9
	Fri. Stay Faithful!
	      2 Tim. 3:10-17
	Sat. Fulfill Your Ministry
	      2 Tim. 4:1-8
	Sun. Final Instructions
	      2 Tim. 4:9-22

Verse by Verse

I. Roadblocks—10-13

A. Paul's experience, 10-11

10 But thou hast fully known my doctrine, manner of life, purpose, faith, longsuffering, charity, patience,

11 Persecutions, afflictions, which came unto me at Antioch, at Iconium, at Lystra; what persecutions I endured: but out of them all the Lord delivered me.

Paul and Timothy shared a long history, and in this, perhaps the apostle's last letter, he calls on the younger minister to recall the experiences they have had together in which Paul served as a mentor in ministry. Who else could know more "fully" the doctrine Paul taught, his purpose and faith, the patience and love with which he met "persecutions and afflictions"?

Antioch, Iconium, and Lystra were all cities in Asia Minor which Paul, Silas, and Timothy visited on Paul's first missionary tour. What could Timothy have learned from the accounts in Acts 13–14 of Paul's experience there? First, he knew how Paul first preached positively the Good News that the Messiah had come in Jesus of Nazareth. Then he followed his Lord's teaching about not returning evil for evil when he was attacked for his message. He had

a great capacity to invite his attackers as calmly as possibly to examine their own presuppositions, and in the case of Jews their own Scriptures, instead of simply wrangling over opinions.

B. Realistic warning, 12-13

12 Yea, and all that will live godly in Christ Jesus shall suffer persecution.

13 But evil men and seducers shall wax worse and worse, deceiving, and being deceived.

Paul seems to be the ultimate realist, predicting both that believers will be persecuted and that the world will go from bad to worse. No one can rightly accuse him of wanting Timothy to have a Polyanna complex. Even the godly who live where there is religious freedom often suffer the "persecution" of being ignored and opposed in word if not in violent deed.

Verse 13 presents a sobering picture of an unbelieving world building increasingly bad structures on evil foundations. Presumably Paul has a philosophy of history that assumes that this spiritually downhill course will eventually lead to some sort of Armageddon like that described at the end of the Gospels and in the book of Revelation.

II. Resources—14-17

A. Faithful mentors, 14

14 But continue thou in the things which thou hast learned and hast been assured of, knowing of whom thou hast learned them;

It would be a mistake to gather that Paul's gloomy prediction in verse 13 leaves him and those he mentored with a pessimistic world view. As St. Augustine would later outline in his famous work *City of God,* believers and evil "seducers" are on different roads. The first resource for Timothy's staying on the "straight and narrow" road is to continue in the teachings he had learned from Paul. To remind Timothy "of whom thou hast learned them" indicates that Paul had a remarkably settled confidence that his manner of life was open, Christ-like, and worth emulating. From the presumably Old Testament foundation Timothy had received as a child (see vs. 15), he had built an understanding of the New Covenant as he traveled and lived with Paul, then was given responsibility for grounding the church at Ephesus.

B. Scriptural grounding, 15-17

15 And that from a child thou hast known the holy scriptures, which are able to make thee wise unto salvation through faith which is in Christ Jesus.

16 All scripture is given by inspiration of God, and is profitable for doctrine, for reproof, for correction, for instruction in righteousness:

17 That the man of God may be perfect, throughly furnished unto all good works.

The younger minister's theological education began with his grandmother Lois and mother Eunice (1:6). After acknowledging this solid foundation, Paul moves in verses 16-17 to a comprehensive and foundational statement on the nature and inspiration of Scripture.

We may assume that the term "all scripture" refers first to the Jewish Scriptures. However, even while this letter was being produced, it and other of Paul's writings, along with the earliest Gospels, were quickly coming to be considered equally holy writings (see 2 Pet. 3:15-16). The fact that these writings were "God-breathed" or inspired gives them the qualities necessary for basing doctrine, reproof, correction, and instruction in righteousness.

Recent claims that early "Gnostic" writings and "gospels" should have also been included in the "canon" or list of inspired writings (as in the book *The Da Vinci Code*) have produced no hard evidence not already considered, and rejected, by early Church councils. As verse 17 affirms, the traditional collection of Old and New Covenant Scriptures are "throughly" (thoroughly or completely) able to supply believers with a saving knowledge of Christ and the good works He expects of them.

III. The Road Ahead—4:1-8

A. Charge to Timothy, 1-2

1 I charge thee therefore before

God, and the Lord Jesus Christ, who shall judge the quick and the dead at his appearing and his kingdom;

2 Preach the word; be instant in season, out of season; reprove, rebuke, exhort with all longsuffering and doctrine.

After giving Timothy fair warning of the road ahead, Paul issues a stirring challenge that has become the "mission statement" championed by generations of ministers as they are ordained to follow in Paul's footsteps. They are to preach a message that will be found to approve of the "quick," or spiritually alive who follow Christ, and to oppose the "dead," or those previously described as "waxing worse and worse." They are to be faithful to the message whether history proves favorable or unfavorable to propagating the faith. While they will mainly have a positive message, they will also be faithful when the Word rebukes wrong-doers. To do so will take both patience or longsuffering, and commitment to true doctrine (see also 1 Tim. 4:13).

B. Enduring the future, 3-5

3 For the time will come when they will not endure sound doctrine; but after their own lusts shall they heap to themselves teachers, having itching ears;

4 And they shall turn away their ears from the truth, and shall be turned unto fables.

5 But watch thou in all things, endure afflictions, do the work of an evangelist, make full proof of thy ministry.

One reason Paul's insisted on being faithful in the preaching ministry is the view God gave him of periods of declining faithfulness. He knew well that human nature often drives the best of us to believe what we wish, or what "tickles our ears," when the truth is painful. Note from verse 5 that the antidote for this mentality is not just countering it with preaching, but with a consistent life on the part of the minister. Teaching by example is a good way of making "full proof" (NIV "discharg[ing] all the duties") of ministry.

C. Paul's expectations, 6-8

6 For I am now ready to be offered, and the time of my departure is at hand.

7 I have fought a good fight, I have finished my course, I have kept the faith:

8 Henceforth there is laid up for me a crown of righteousness, which the Lord, the righteous judge, shall give me at that day: and not to me only, but unto all them also that love his appearing.

This famous and poignant passage may be considered Paul's own epitaph or benediction on having kept the commission God gave him on the Damascus Road. His moving words make it actually seem possible that those who try to follow in his footsteps will, at the Day of Christ's "appearing," also receive "a crown of righteousness." As the apostle himself might add, this would not be based on one's own works of righteousness, but on God's grace.

Evangelistic Emphasis

When anyone asks Billy Graham who is going to take his place when he is gone, he always gives the same response: "You are." You are called by God to win souls to Jesus Christ. Are you ready to take your place in this great task of making disciples for Jesus Christ?

The time is coming, we are warned, that people will not put up with sound doctrine, but will want their ears tickled. One of the ways we tickle those ears is to tell them they have no responsibilities in the church. We make the faith too easy. When we take responsibility from the life of the disciple, we remove the joy of living the Christian life. There is joy in heaven when a soul is led to Christ. Have you experienced that joy in your faith walk?

In evangelism training, we learned the **ABCD**s of bringing people to Christ. **A** is Admit your need of God and Acknowledge your waywardness. **B** is Believe in the Lord Jesus Christ and that he died for you. **C** is Confess your sins and Come to Christ. **D** is Decide to follow Jesus and become a Disciple.

But what about **E**? Now that you've learned your ABCDs of faith, get to **E**, for Enjoy! Enjoy God! Enjoy reaching out to others!

෧෧෬

Memory Selection

But continue thou in the things which thou hast learned and has been assured of, knowing of whom thou hast learned them.—*2 Timothy 3:14*

Dwight L. Moody, in his Edinburgh crusade, spoke to a large congregation of very young boys and girls. Moody began his sermon with a question: "What is prayer?"

He wasn't expecting an answer, but the words were no sooner out of his mouth than hands were raised all over the hall. Stunned, Moody asked one boy for his answer. The young child immediately said: "Prayer is an offering up of our desires unto God, for things agreeable to his will, in the name of Christ, with confession of our sins and thankful acknowledgment of his mercies." Moody, recognizing that the words were from the Shorter Catechism, declared: "Thank God, my boy, that you were born in Scotland."

Can anyone imagine such a thing occurring in morning worship today? How many of us have "continued in the things which thou hast learned," as Paul said? If asked a question such as "What is prayer?," how many of us would have an answer? Paul was confident that Timothy would remember the lessons he had been taught, because he had seen them lived out in Paul's life.

Can Christ be this confident that you are living what you have learned?

Weekday Problems

First Church was growing rapidly. The church had added a new worship service, and that had filled up. There was no more space for a new Sunday school class. The youth had outgrown their space. The church was bursting at the seams.

The pastor called together some of the leaders of the church and set before them the church's need. He explained that a church has only two options. It can grow or it can die. He hoped and prayed that this church would choose to keep growing. For that growth to continue, a building program was going to be necessary. The church needed to raise more money than had ever been raised in its history.

The new pastor began talking about conducting a capital stewardship campaign. This campaign would call the church to prayer about the project and how God would have them give to the church to meet the needs.

Michael Reeves sat in the back listening patiently. He was also writing furiously on his notepad. After listening to the preacher set the vision and explain the stewardship program, Michael made a suggestion. "Pastor, I have figured that if we get each family to commit to buying 10 chicken dinners a year and we charge $8 each, in five years we can raise most of the money." Michael was serious too!

*Discuss ways in which we "don't think things through" as Christians.

Other 'Famous Last Words'

"You can make that crossing easy—that train's not coming fast."

***

"Gimme a match. I can't see, but I think we have a gas leak."

***

"Just lean the gun there against the fence. It's not loaded."

***

"Wanta see me dive into that pond from the bridge?"

***

"If you had any sense, you wouldn't be a traffic cop."

***

"Wife, these biscuits are shore tough."

***

"*What?* Your mother-in-law is going to stay how long?"

***

"Wait a minute! Who's boss of this joint, anyhow?"

This Lesson in Your Life

Not so long ago, if we wanted to impress the faith upon the hearts and souls of our children we required them to memorize an entire catechism of theological questions and answers before confirmation. Most of us today would cringe at the prospect of such an exercise, expecting it to be as dull as dirt and dry as dust. Traditions like the catechism were assumed to be little more than theological jabbering and have lost favor in all but the most rigorous Sunday schools. But there is something important about memorizing such truths. In many cases, it is also the only way to "rightly handle the word of truth."

Does anyone remember the "sword drills" from Sunday school days so long ago we're embarrassed to admit when? For those of you who missed out on this particular tradition, a "sword drill" was kind of the scriptural equivalent of a spelling bee. Two teams faced off, their champions confronting one another. The teacher would then call out the chapter and verse of a biblical text, and the young combatants would see who could "draw their sword" first—that is, accurately quote the biblical text in its entirety before anyone else.

Squelched as "rote memorization" and purposeless grand-standing, sword drills are no longer played out in Sunday schools these days. But what has stepped in to replace these scriptural learning games?

We've all been stunned by stories about 12-year-old church attenders who have no idea what "manna" is; or watched as a class of teenagers desperately flipped through their Bibles on a retreat searching in vain for the location of Ephesians; or heard some highly creative but completely wrong recitations of the "Lord's Prayer" at a youth gathering.

It is time we took seriously our faith community's responsibility to "learn the ABCs"—to learn "About the Bible in Church." Unless we read it, study it, learn what's in it, and feel comfortable with it in our hands and on our tongues, we cannot truly love the Word of God. Instead, we are intimidated by it, afraid of it, shocked by it or simply remain ignorant of it.

Every one of our churches is one generation away from extinction. The church must communicate itself, its essence, so completely to each new generation that its future is ensured in the hearts of each member. Each one of us shares with Timothy Paul's charge to "do the work of an evangelist" and "carry out [our] ministry fully" (2 Tim. 4:5).

1. What had Timothy witnessed in the life of Paul?
Timothy had witnessed Paul's teaching, conduct, aim in life, steadfastness, persecutions, and sufferings.

2. How had Timothy witnessed these things?
By accompanying Paul on his missions, especially in Antioch, Iconium, and Lystra.

3. How did Paul respond to the persecution he experienced?
He had endured them in the strength of God, who sustained him.

4. What did Paul say would be the fate of wicked people?
These wicked people and impostors would go from bad to worse deceiving others and being deceived.

5. What did Paul say about Scripture?
Paul said all Scripture is inspired and is useful for teaching, reproof, correction, and for training in righteousness.

6. What did Paul warn about the time that is coming?
There would be a time when people would not endure sound doctrine.

7. What would these people desire rather than sound doctrine?
The people would want to have their ears tickled.

8. How do you think this kind of theology is showing up in the church?
This kind of theology is found in the prosperity gospel that is being preached by so many televangelists.

9. What was Paul preparing for as he wrote 2 Timothy?
Paul was preparing for his death.

10. What did Paul say about his approaching death?
"I have fought the good fight, I have finished the course, I have kept the faith."

 Meet Mairead Corrigan.

Mairead is a shorthand typist and secretary in Belfast, Northern Ireland. But she wasn't typing on the afternoon of August 10, 1976. Instead, she and her sister and her three children, hopped on bicycles and went for an outing. That same afternoon, the Irish Republican Army sent snipers to open fire on a British army patrol. Missing their targets, they fled, pursued by the same patrol. The chase led the parties inexorably closer to the women and children enjoying their bicycle ride. Then the British troops fired on the fleeing IRA car. The IRA terrorist lost control of the car and it careened directly into the innocent bystanders on their bikes. The three children were killed, snuffed out as so much collateral damage.

In the aftermath, Mairead Corrigan and colleagues Betty Williams and Ciaran McKeown began to organize some of the largest peace demonstrations in their region's history. The rallies throughout London, Belfast, Derry/Londonderry, and Dublin spurred Corrigan and her compatriots to found an organization which they named "Women for Peace." Now it continues to exist under the title, "The Peace People Organization," a movement of Catholics and Protestants dedicated to ending sectarian fighting in Northern Ireland.

Within only one month of its birth, Corrigan's organization had united over 30,000 women under a common cause, and by its third planned march, the demonstrators included both Protestants and Catholics, marching side by side.

For their fight for peace and justice, the two women were awarded the 1976 Nobel Peace Prize.

In winning the prize they achieved a sort of immortality. They joined a pantheon of modern giants, an exclusive club of luminaries such as Albert Schweitzer, Marie Curie, William Faulkner, T.S. Eliot, Martin Luther King Jr., Albert Einstein, and Mother Teresa. The Nobel Prize is given for human achievement, grit, and determination.

For the Christian, grit and determination allow us to finish the race. Then we receive the "Crown of Righteousness."

Lesson 13

Live the Truth, Teach the Truth

Titus 2

But speak thou the things which become sound doctrine:

2 That the aged men be sober, grave, temperate, sound in faith, in charity, in patience.

3 The aged women likewise, that they be in behaviour as becometh holiness, not false accusers, not given to much wine, teachers of good things;

4 That they may teach the young women to be sober, to love their husbands, to love their children,

5 To be discreet, chaste, keepers at home, good, obedient to their own husbands, that the word of God be not blasphemed.

6 Young men likewise exhort to be sober minded.

7 In all things shewing thyself a pattern of good works: in doctrine shewing uncorruptness, gravity, sincerity,

8 Sound speech, that cannot be condemned; that he that is of the contrary part may be ashamed, having no evil thing to say of you.

9 Exhort servants to be obedient unto their own masters, and to please them well in all things; not answering again;

10 Not purloining, but shewing all good fidelity; that they may adorn the doctrine of God our Saviour in all things.

11 For the grace of God that bringeth salvation hath appeared to all men,

12 Teaching us that, denying ungodliness and worldly lusts, we should live soberly, righteously, and godly, in this present world;

13 Looking for that blessed hope, and the glorious appearing of the great God and our Saviour Jesus Christ;

14 Who gave himself for us, that he might redeem us from all iniquity, and purify unto himself a peculiar people, zealous of good works.

15 These things speak, and exhort, and rebuke with all authority. Let no man despise thee.

Devotional Reading
Ephesians 4:11-16
Background Scripture
Titus 2
Memory Selection
Titus 2:7a

Feb. 26

A book titled *Faith Works* was a part of the ongoing Christian conversation about the relationship between faith and works. While upholding the classic Reformation doctrine of salvation by faith, the book endeavored to show that works are the inevitable *fruit* of saving faith.

Ask group members to recall some of the best examples of faith they can recall, from both genders and all age groups. For example:

Young men—**Eric Liddell**, a main figure in the movie "Chariots of Fire," who stuck by his religious convictions and won an Olympic race.

Older men—**Winston Churchill**, who, after several failed political at-

The apostle Paul's opposition to salvation by keeping the works of the Mosaic Law places him at the center of the doctrine of justification by faith. Today's lesson, however, asks *So what?* At every age and every stage, believers are to demonstrate by their works that they have been saved by faith. They are called to be an example not only to unbelievers, but to the power of faith to motivate them to live pure lives.

tempts, was finally named Prime Minister of England, and motivated Allied Troops in World War II with his famous message, *"Never give up!"*

Young women—**Ruth**, of the Old Testament, who forsook her own homeland to be with her mother-in-law, Naomi.

Older women—The late **Mother Teresa**, who gave her life helping the poor and outcast of India.

Note that this lesson calls believers to be good examples of the faith regardless of their status, age, or gender.

Teaching Outline	Daily Bible Readings	
I. Good Examples—1-10	Mon.	Speak Truth in Love Eph. 4:11-16
A. Adorning the doctrine, 1	Tue.	Be Grounded on Truth 2 Pet. 1:3-12
B. Aged men, 2		
C. Older women, 3-5	Wed.	Walk in the Light of Truth 1 John 1:5-10
D. Young men, 6-8	Thu.	Support Believers in Truth 3 John 2-8
E. Servants, 9-10		
II. Grace Works—11-15	Fri.	To Older Men and Women Titus 2:1-5
A. Impact of grace, 11-12	Sat.	To Younger Men and Slaves Titus 2:6-10
B. Resulting hope, 13-14		
C. An authoritative word, 15	Sun.	What God Expects Titus 2:11-15

Verse by Verse

I. Good Examples—1-10
A. Adorning the doctrine, 1

1 But speak thou the things which become sound doctrine:

Like Timothy, Titus was one of the Paul's close protégés (see 1:4). The apostle had left him in Crete to firm up existing churches with elders (or bishops; see 1:5-7). Paul had just spoken of those who profess God, but deny Him by their works (1:16). Beginning chapter 2 with the word "But" shows that he is moving to a discussion of the opposite—the importance of aligning works with faith. This was not only important for personal integrity. As we shall see, Paul is also oncerned that Christians do right in order to influence outsiders.

We have already encountered the phrase "sound doctrine" in 1 Tim. 1:10 (Lesson 5). There it was noted that we get the term "hygienic" from the word translated "sound," indicating that Paul is writing about how *good works* show that *good doctrine* makes for *wholesome churches*. He will specify how comprehensive this teaching is by speaking of several classes and age groups.

B. Aged men, 2

2 That the aged men be sober, grave, temperate, sound in faith, in charity, in patience.

"Aged men" is from the same root as "elders" in 1:5. There Paul gives the qualifications for those in the office of elder; here he is speaking of older men in general. They are to be *sober* and *grave* in the sense of using good sense (not in the sense of never having fun!); *temperate* not just in their use of wine but in all things; *sound in the faith* (as in vs. 1); and full of love and patience. Few faithful churches cannot point to several older men who could be described in just these terms.

C. Older women, 3-5

3 The aged women likewise, that they be in behaviour as becometh holiness, not false accusers, not given to much wine, teachers of good things;

4 That they may teach the young women to be sober, to love their husbands, to love their children,

5 To be discreet, chaste, keepers at home, good, obedient to their own husbands, that the word of God be not blasphemed.

Perhaps more space is devoted to how older women are to behave because, as in most modern churches, there are more of them than older men. Paul asserts that since they worship a holy God, their behavior must reflect that holiness. They are not to spend their time passing on false gossip about others, or being too much "in their cups." Instead, they are to be good teachers of good things.

Especially in the male-dominated society in which Paul wrote, the older women were to teach good family skills to the younger women. They also are to be *sober* or wise, and of course to love their families. This is in remarkable contrast to the modern notion that love can't be taught, but is a "feeling" that "just happens." Paul, along with any good marriage counselor today, believes that the *feeling* of love often follows *behaving* in loving ways.

The word for *discreet* speaks of being in firm possession of one's mind (hence the NIV "self-controlled"; the idea that young women are given to giddiness isn't a Bible idea!). Note that they are to be pure, keepers at home, and obedient to their husbands *so that "the word of God be not blasphemed."* Outsiders in the culture of Crete (and in the ancient world at large) would have disdained a system in which women in general went into the work force. Even now, in societies where it has become an economic necessity for some women to work outside the home, studies show that children in general do better when Mom tries to be a "keeper at home" during their youngest and most formative years.

D. Young men, 6-8

6 Young men likewise exhort to be sober minded.

7 In all things shewing thyself a pattern of good works: in doctrine shewing uncorruptness, gravity, sincerity,

8 Sound speech, that cannot be condemned; that he that is of the contrary part may be ashamed, having no evil thing to say of you.

Paul had not heard that teen-age boys were supposed to rebellious! Here he challenges them with much the same standards of conduct as in the case of older men and women. Once again, the conduct of young men is not all that is at stake. Paul was concerned that unruliness and rebelliousness among Christian young men would place the Church in a bad light. Instead, he hopes that obedient youth would "put to shame" the Church's critics, removing excuses for them to speak evil of it.

E. Servants, 9-10

9 Exhort servants to be obedient unto their own masters, and to please them well in all things; not answering again;

10 Not purloining, but shewing all good fidelity; that they may adorn the doctrine of God our Saviour in all things.

The word for "servants" here is from *doulos,* "slave," not *diakonos,* a "minister" or servant. Throughout the ancient world, and no less in the Mediterranean world of Crete, slavery was a given. Instead of tackling this social injustice on a society-wide scale, early Church leaders sought to make the master-slave relationship wholesome on the level of personal morality. Only centuries later would it be possible for Christians to grow in enough numbers and influence to help abolish slavery. For the time being, Christian slaves, who were often given the run of the household, were taught not to take advantage of their masters by being thieves. Nor were they to use their freedom in Christ to "talk back." Instead, they were to "adorn" their faith so it reflects well on the God they served, and whose long-range plan was human freedom.

II. Grace Works—11-15

A. Impact of grace, 11-12

11 For the grace of God that bringeth salvation hath appeared to all men,

12 Teaching us that, denying ungodliness and worldly lusts, we should live soberly, righteously, and godly, in this present world;

Although Paul has just touched on the duty of *slaves* to be honest, he now shows that the doctrine of grace that should motivate believers to good works has actually appeared to *everyone*—not in the sense that everyone throughout the world had (or even now has) heard it, but that it has been publicly announced as the universal path of salvation. The essence of the moral standards he is teaching is not only in order to give the Church good standing in the eyes of unbelievers; they are also universally true in themselves. Also, living righteously is not just a way to influence God to let us into heaven; it is the proper way to live in this life.

B. Resulting hope, 13-14

13 Looking for that blessed hope, and the glorious appearing of the great God and our Saviour Jesus Christ;

14 Who gave himself for us, that he might redeem us from all iniquity, and purify unto himself a peculiar people, zealous of good works.

Now the apostle moves from emphasizing righteous living for its own sake to the way it gives us ground to hope for a heavenly reward. Even so, it is not human works of righteousness but "the grace of God that brings salvation" (vs. 11). Yet that grace was for the purpose not just of salvation but to prompt the saved to do good works. It was through grace that Christ's blood bought believers to be Christ's "own." (The KJV translates this word "peculiar" in the sense of "special," as we would say "America has a level of freedom that is *peculiar* among the nations of the world.")

C. An authoritative word, 15

15 These things speak, and exhort, and rebuke with all authority. Let no man despise thee.

Just as Paul had urged Timothy to let no one despise his youth (1 Tim. 4:12), so the apostle encourages Titus to assume the authority of saying, in effect, "These moral standards I am delivering are the authoritative Word of God, from one of His duly appointed apostles." Even today, an evangelist's "authority" lies more in the biblical basis of his teaching rather than in any "official" power.

Evangelistic Emphasis

Three years ago God called farmer Ken Holladay, who lives an hour and a half away from downtown Los Angeles, to minister to the down and out in the inner city. Now, Holladay travels there each week to pass out New Testaments and get acquainted with street people.

"At first I thought I was going to win every drug addict and homeless person on those streets to Christ instantly," Holladay says. It didn't work that way. He says he doesn't know exactly how many lives have been changed.

When he first ventured in the new outreach, Holladay targeted a hotel that's home to more than 500 people who share common bathrooms, and are not allowed to have cooking appliances. At first, the management would only let Holladay in for five minutes every Friday. After a few months of constantly showing up, Holladay was allowed to stay longer.

Today, Holladay holds church services in the hotel lobby every week. He says, "One day I told God that I would tag along with him and that's when he led me to people who were open to the Gospel. I call it a tag-along ministry."

Jesus commanded us to go out and win the world for Him. Have you been diligently sharing the good news?

&)CR

Memory Selection

In all things showing thyself a pattern of good works.—*Titus 2:7a*

They sure don't make things like they used to.

The North Fort Worth Historical Society recently celebrated the birthday of a light bulb that has burned continuously since September 21, 1908. Though the 40-watt bulb has burned for 96 years, it sold for only a few cents. The bulb is made of thick glass and sturdy carbon filament.

Though the bulb has lasted 96 years, it doesn't hold the record for the longest continuously burning bulb in the world. The Guinness Book of World Records says the official record belongs to a 4-watt bulb that has been burning at a firehouse in California since 1901. Sarah Biles, the administrator of the museum where the Texas bulb now burns says, "We have no idea why it has lasted so long. That is the wonderful mystery of it." Biles adds, "Our bulb has a unique past and can hold its own, even if it's number two."

The good works of Christians are to be a light that continually shines for Christ. There is no on-off switch. There is never a time we can let down our guard or let our good works be diminished by sin. There is no such thing as a Christian on Sunday and a "normal" person the rest of the week. Keep your good works burning brightly for Him.

Weekday Problems

When the church staff saw Rosie turn the corner into the office, they wished they could vanish. No one wanted to deal with Rosie. She was born in the objective case and it just seemed to get worse the older she got.

This day Rosie was on a "mission." The church newsletter had failed to emphasize the ladies mission conference. Only three ladies from First Church attended the mission conference. It was not a piece of thrilling news. How many mission conferences ever are? The preacher had decided to edit the newsletter down to a simple thank you to the ladies for so ably representing the church at the conference, listing Rosie's name last. Rosie had submitted a 1,000-word article, with perfect grammar. It was long and boring, in contrast with other items about coming events.

Rosie saw the secretary and said, "I want to speak to the preacher." Before the secretary responded, Rosie was in the pastor's office. "I'm going to let you have a piece of my mind, young man," she said.

The pastor smiled and said, "Be careful giving out pieces of your mind Rosie. That's how people lose their minds."

*Does reaching a certain age in life give you the right to say what you please?

*What would Titus say about Rosie?

The Prodigal Son —in the Key of F

Feeling footloose and frisky, a feather-brained fellow forced his fond father to fork over the farthings. He flew afar to foreign fields and frittered away his fortune with faithless friends. Fleeced by his fellows and facing famine, he found himself in fellowship with pigs in a filthy farmyard. Fairly famishing, he fain would have filled his frame with foraged food from fodder fragments.

"Fooey!" said the foolish fellow one day. "My father's flunkies fare better than this." So, frankly facing the facts, he fled forthwith to fix things with his family. Falling at his father's feet, he cried, "Father, I've flunked as a faithful son. Forgive me, for I've been a fool!"

The far-sighted father told his flunkies to fetch a fatted calf and fix a feast. But the fugitive's fault-finding brother figured, "Why all this fervent festivity? So much for my filial fidelity!"

But his father said, "What forbids feasting and fun-making? Let fanfares flair, let flags unfurl, for the lost has been found!" Furthermore, how faithful is our heavenly Father's forgiveness!

This Lesson in Your Life

One stormy night many years ago, an elderly couple entered the lobby of a small hotel and asked for a room. The clerk explained that because there were three conventions in town, the hotel was filled. "But I can't send a nice couple like you out in the rain at 1 o'clock in the morning," he said. "Would you be willing to sleep in my room?"

The couple hesitated, but the clerk insisted. The next morning when the man paid his bill, he said, "You're the kind of manager who should be the boss of the best hotel in the United States. Maybe someday I'll build one for you."

The clerk smiled, amused by the older man's little joke. A few years passed. Then one day, the clerk received a letter from the elderly man, recalling that difficult night and asking him to come to New York for a visit. A round-trip ticket was enclosed. When the clerk arrived, his host took him to the corner of 5th Avenue and 34th Street, where stood a magnificent new building. "That," explained the man, "is the hotel I have just built for you to manage."

"You must be joking," said the clerk.

"I most assuredly am not," came the reply.

"Who—who are you?" stammered the other.

"My name is William Waldorf Astor." That hotel was the original Waldorf-Astoria, and the young clerk who became its first manager was George C. Boldt.

The story illustrates the truth of the second chapter of Titus. We are to live as faithful Christians no matter what our age or station in life.

You might discuss with your class what challenges face each age group as they seek to be faithful to Jesus Christ. The elderly have a certain set of challenges, as do the young adults. In listing these challenges, you might discover ways that you could be a mentor for younger Christians. Or if you are a young adult, you might adopt an older couple so you can help them with their spiritual challenges.

We never can retire or take a break from our Christian witness. Being a follower of Jesus Christ is something that we do all the time. Titus is also very forceful in showing us that people are watching how we are living for Christ.

Neither do circumstances give us an excuse to be anything less than Christ-like. The reference to slaves in the text was not an endorsement of the hideous act. Titus recognized the reality of his world. Yet even slaves were called to live Christ-like lives. You have no excuse for not being on your Christian best behavior—all the time.

GETTING THE FACTS STRAIGHT

1. What instruction did Paul gave to Titus?
He was to teach what was consistent with sound doctrine.

2. What advice was he to share with older men?
He was to tell the older men to be temperate, serious, prudent, and sound in faith, in love, and in endurance.

3. How were the older women to act?
They were to be reverent in behavior, and not be slanderers, or slaves to drink.

4. By being taught what was good, what would the younger women learn from the older women?
The younger women would learn to love their husbands and children.

5. What kind of behavior would the younger women learn from the older women?
They would learn to be self-controlled, chaste, good managers of their households, and submissive to their husbands.

6. How do you think women can be submissive to their husbands in the 21st century?
Enjoy this class discussion, especially if there are many different age groups in your class.

7. How are younger men to act?
Younger men are to be self-controlled, and in all respects models of good works.

8. As the young men teach, what should their teaching show?
Their teaching should show integrity, gravity, and sound speech that cannot be censured.

9. How were slaves to act?
They were to be submissive to their masters.

10. Do you think the Bible condones slavery?
No the Bible does not condone slavery. Paul wrote about an economic system that was in place at the time.

 Missionary Milton Cunningham told a story several years ago that was certainly convicting. He said he had just settled in for a flight from Atlanta to Dallas when a little girl who obviously had Downs Syndrome took the window seat next to his. She turned to Milton, and in all her innocence, said, "Mister, did you brush your teeth this morning?"

With a smile, Milton said, "Yes, I brushed my teeth this morning."

"Good," she said, "'cause that's what you're supposed to do."

Her next question was, "Mister, do you smoke?"

Milton assured her that he didn't, and she responded, "Good, 'cause smoking can make you dead."

Her third question was even easier to answer: "Mister, do you love Jesus?"

He answered with confidence, "Yes, I love Jesus."

"Good," she said again, "'cause we're all supposed to love Jesus."

About that time, a man settled into the aisle seat on Milton's other side. Immediately, the little girl nudged him: "Ask him if he brushed his teeth this morning."

He wasn't about to disturb the stranger, but the little girl was persistent, so Milton turned to the man and said, "Excuse me, Sir, but my little friend here wants to know if you brushed your teeth this morning."

The man smiled at the little girl and assured them both that he had brushed his teeth. With a sinking feeling, Milton realized where this was going. As if on cue, she urged him to ask the man if he smoked. Reluctantly, he asked, and fortunately, the man didn't. Then, sure enough, the little girl wanted him to ask the man her third question: Did he love Jesus?

Milton protested that the question was too personal, that he wouldn't be comfortable asking, but she was persistent, so he finally turned to the man and said awkwardly, "Now she wants to know if you love Jesus."

At this, the man's face darkened: He began to talk about his desire to know God. He had been searching for God, for meaning and purpose, but he didn't know where to turn. Milton Cunningham picked up from there and shared the good new of Jesus Christ. But the conversation never would've started without the help and persistence of a little girl with a big heart.

There is no excuse for not living a fully Christian life. Whether young or old, regardless of our circumstances, we are called to glorify Jesus Christ with our lives.

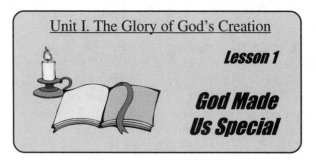

Unit I. The Glory of God's Creation

Lesson 1

God Made Us Special

Psalm 8

O LORD our Lord, how excellent is thy name in all the earth! who hast set thy glory above the heavens.

2 Out of the mouth of babes and sucklings hast thou ordained strength because of thine enemies, that thou mightest still the enemy and the avenger.

3 When I consider thy heavens, the work of thy fingers, the moon and the stars, which thou hast ordained;

4 What is man, that thou art mindful of him? and the son of man, that thou visitest him?

5 For thou hast made him a little lower than the angels, and hast crowned him with glory and honour.

6 Thou madest him to have dominion over the works of thy hands; thou hast put all things under his feet:

7 All sheep and oxen, yea, and the beasts of the field;

8 The fowl of the air, and the fish of the sea, and whatsoever passeth through the paths of the seas.

9 O LORD our Lord, how excellent is thy name in all the earth!

Devotional Reading
Gen. 1:26-31

Background Scripture
Ps. 8

Memory Selection
Ps. 8:4-5

Psalm 8 sets the theme for this entire quarter. It is a poem consisting of an outburst of praise to God as the magnificent Creator of a magnificent creation.

Second only to the theme of praise for the entire creation is the psalmist's gratitude for the role of human beings as the crown of the creative process. With amazing deftness, the author is able both to exalt the place of persons in creation, and to remind us that we are *only* persons—that is, we are not God, and are even lower than the angels. Although a commentary by definition "takes apart" a text to comment on it verse-by-verse, be sure to read the entire psalm as a whole, also, to get before the group the total piece as a work of art.

Arrange for hymnbooks in advance if you choose to introduce this lesson as follows.

Have a song leader lead your group in singing the hymn, "For the Beauty of the Earth." Its recurring theme and last line of each verse is also the theme of Psalm 8: "*Lord of all, to thee we raise / this our hymn of grateful praise.*"

This classic hymn was written by the young Englishman Folliot Sanford Pierpoint (1835-1917), after being abroad and then returning to Bath, England, the city of his birth. He was so overwhelmed by the beauty of the countryside in the late spring that he penned the words to this hymn. They were later set to music by composer Conrad Kocher. The idea of raising a song to God as an offering or sacrifice is based on Hebrews 13:15.

Teaching Outline	*Daily Bible Readings*
I. Creative Power—1-2 　A. God's name, 1 　B. Silencing enemies, 2 II. Crowning Glory—3-4 　A. Heavens are great, 3 　B. Man is greater, 4-5 III. Sweeping Rule—6-7 　A. Dominion, 6 　B. Comprehensiveness, 7-8 IV. Closing Praise—9	Mon.　Humankind Created 　　　Gen. 1:26-31 Tue.　Man and Woman 　　　Gen. 2:7, 15-25 Wed.　Covenant with Noah 　　　Gen. 9:8-17 Thu.　Our Help and Strength 　　　Ps. 63:1-8 Fri.　Our Guide and Refuge 　　　Ps. 73:21-28 Sat.　All in Subjection 　　　Heb. 2:5-10 Sun.　A Little Lower than Angels 　　　Ps. 8

Verse by Verse

I. Creative Power—1-2

A. God's name, 1

1 O LORD our Lord, how excellent is thy name in all the earth! who hast set thy glory above the heavens.

The book of Psalms has been called "The Hymnbook of the Second Temple." This is because many scholars believe that they were a collection of songs which, while written by King David, were not compiled until the days of the Babylonian captivity, for use in worship after the Jews returned from Babylon and rebuilt the Temple destroyed by the Babylonian King Nebuchadnezzar.

It is instructive to note how many of the psalms in this section have the term "LORD" in the very first verse. When spelled with a capital followed by small capitals, this translates "Yahweh" (or "Jehovah"), the personal name for God. It was important for the Jews, surrounded by pagans, to show that their worship was directed not to "gods" in general but to *the* God, whose personal name "Yahweh" (whose letters can also spell "I AM") had been revealed to Moses (see Exod. 3:14-15; 6:3). Only this God was *Lord* (Heb. *adonai,* "sovereign" or "master")— so the "phrase-name" *Yahweh Adonai* became a common way to praise the only true Creator-God.

Long after the Psalms were composed, when an ancient Jewish copyist or reader would come to the Name "Yahweh" he would substitute the term *adonai* (Lord), because the Name was thought to be too holy to be heard from sinful human lips.

B. Silencing enemies, 2

2 Out of the mouth of babes and sucklings hast thou ordained strength because of thine enemies, that thou mightest still the enemy and the avenger.

Perhaps the psalmist had in mind the way the infant Moses grew to confound and defeat the wisdom of Egypt because God was with him. God's glory is so beyond human wisdom that even infants who can barely lisp the name of God are evidence that He is greater than all His enemies who boast of their superior knowledge and strength.

In Matthew, Jesus applies this theme to grown persons who are "mere babes" in the sense of the largely unschooled associates of Jesus (Matt. 11:25). The fact that God's strength and glory are beyond human learning is implied even in the section of Scripture in which the Psalms have been placed—the "Wisdom Literature," so called because "the fear of the Lord [not human scholarship] is the beginning of wisdom" (Ps. 111:10. The other Wisdom books in Protestant Bibles are Job, Proverbs, Ecclesiastes, and Song of Solomon).

II. Crowning Glory—3-4

A. The Heavens are great, 3

3 When I consider thy heavens, the work of thy fingers, the moon and the stars, which thou hast ordained;

Genesis 1 affirms in prose what the psalmist sings of in poetry: the heavens were the creative work of God's hand. No merely human artisan (not even "Nature" as an impersonal force) could do this. The heavens, with their awesome stars, planets, and moons, speak of a realm "above" even the glories of the earth. We are often told that modern science shrank our view of mankind when it discovered the vastness of space. Actually, as this verse shows, even primitive man had only to gaze at the starlit heavens to be humbled by their vastness.

B. Man is greater, 4-5

4 What is man, that thou art mindful of him? and the son of man, that thou visitest him?

5 For thou hast made him a little lower than the angels, and hast crowned him with glory and honour.

The opening question of verse 4, "What is man?," is often quoted as a precedent for raising the philosophical issue of the nature and destiny of persons. (The question is also asked elsewhere in Scripture [Ps. 144:3, Job 7:17 and 25:6]). The tone here, however, is not philosophical, but religious. It is a rhetorical question without an answer, but is raised in worship and awe of the Creator. Who has not gazed at the vastness of the skies at night and wondered how man, who is so small in comparison, could come to be "visited" or graced with God's presence in a way far greater than the heavens? For as glorious as are the sun, moon, stars, planets, galaxies, comets, etc., they cannot *know* or *realize* or *contemplate* their own greatness. Only humankind, beings with *minds*, can be "visited" with the awareness of God's greatness.

Being uniquely crowned with the honor of knowing God makes people only a little lower than the divine order of angels. The Hebrew term for "angels" here introduces a third term for God in this one brief psalm. It is *elohim*, which is a generic term for God or "divine beings" in general. Some translations therefore have "a little lower than God." However, when the Hebrew writer quotes this verse, he uses "angels," since he is applying the whole passage to Jesus, who was made human (or "below angels") in order to die for our sins (Heb. 2:9).

III. Sweeping Rule—6-8

A. Dominion, 6

6 Thou madest him to have dominion over the works of thy hands; thou hast put all things under his feet:

The main example the psalmist gives of the "glory and honor" with which persons are crowned is that they have been given dominion or rule over the rest of creation, just as God had said at the beginning (Gen. 1:26). Unfortunately, this teaching has been misused by some who think that this implies that man can exploit other elements of creation (natural resources, wildlife, etc.). They forget that "dominion" can also mean "care"; and that man, as Adam, was placed in creation to "tend" it or see to its well-being. Still, when the welfare of *things* or *animals* conflicts with that of *persons,* both Genesis and the Psalms insist that humankind should come first.

B. Comprehensiveness, 7-8

7 All sheep and oxen, yea, and the beasts of the field;

8 The fowl of the air, and the fish of the sea, and whatsoever passeth through the paths of the seas.

The psalmist, after all, is writing poetry, so he does not bother to conform to the order of creation in Genesis 1 in being specific about the glory God gave humans as ruler or "tender" of creation. First he lists mammals, beginning with those that God has given man the power to domesticate. Then he also includes wild animals, which provided food for hunter-gatherer cultures of his day.

Verse 8 focuses on fowl and sealife. Man exercises rule over some examples—eagles and giant squid, for example—with less frequency than he does over food fish. The point, however, is not just man's ability to tame wildlife, or to subdue it for food. The psalmist is celebrating the qualitative difference between man and animals—the spirit that gives humankind self-consciousness, and the spirit of conquest that keeps in its sights not just the subjection of wildlife but climbing the highest mountain peaks, peering into the most minute forms of microscopic life, and visiting the farthest planets as well.

So fiercely has this spirit been employed by moderns that we have now been forced to ask whether we should voluntarily place limits to our God-given inquisitiveness and technical know-how. Dwindling natural resources and environmental damage must now be factored into the relationship between man and creation. New technology that extends and all but creates life raises the question not whether man *can*, but whether we *should.* The psalmis suggests that whatever man does with creation should glorify the Creator.

IV. Closing Praise—9

9 O LORD our Lord, how excellent is thy name in all the earth!

Just as in some modern poetry, the line that opened the psalm is repeated to give it symmetrical closure. From beginning to end, therefore, the inspired poet shows not only that mankind is blessed by God, but that man's position is forever subservient to God. Creation, including its human element, does not exist for its own sake, but to give greater glory to the Creator.

Evangelistic Emphasis

When we think of God and His determination to redeem humankind, we often ask *Why*. Why does He love us so much? Why did He send His Son to die for us? Are we actually that important to Him? The answer is an unqualified "Yes!" Even God's Creation speaks of His love for us. Everything in the universe is made in perfection for humanity.

If the only thing God did for us was to create this magnificent world, He would still be worthy of our worship. However, He did far more than create. He gave Jesus to redeem us. The Bible speaks of angels and their unending hymns of praise for God. Certainly when we consider His acts of love for us through Creation and the atonement, our praise should be unending as well.

The psalmist shows his humanity as well as his complete dependence on God. He also makes clear that God will never abandon us. The mystery of God's love will never be completely understood. However, we can bathe in His love and accept His offer of salvation. Complete understanding is not required.

꧁꧂

What is man, that thou art mindful of him? And the son of man, that thou visitest him? For thou hast made him a little lower than the angels, and hast crowned him with glory and honor.—*Psalm 8: 4-5*

Sometimes when we think about God we can often feel insignificant and unimportant in the realm of creation. However, of all God's creation, we are the one entity that He treasures most of all. Jesus said that when a sparrow falls to the ground, God knows about it. How much more is He aware of persons, the crown of His creation! It is this God who paid so much attention to every detail of creation who still loves and cares for each one of us.

God not only created man but He "crowned him with glory and honor." God did not abandon us at creation but continues to be active in our lives. He truly cares what happens to us. It is a marvel that such a marvelous Creator could be so loving and understanding of His creatures.

I have always believed that a mother sparrow feels emotions of fear and sadness as she pushes her young hatchlings out for their first flight. Can you imagine how much more God is concerned about us as we walk in this magnificent world? God walks with us and carries us when we cannot walk under our own strength. Sometimes He enlists His servants to do this work; but it is still God, forever leading us "beside the still waters."

Weekday Problems

Lisa and Sam met while attending church youth meetings. Sam moved with his family to the small rural community only a year before being promoted into the youth department of the church. Lisa was a lifelong member of the church. After college, they began their careers, Lisa as an administrative assistant at a small community college, and Sam as a coach and teacher. They married, bought a small house, and became even more active in their church. There was one thing that Lisa and Sam wanted more than anything, and that was a baby. Years went by, and finally Lisa discovered that she was infertile. It was like a death. They grieved for the baby that was not meant to be.

Then Sam read an article about little girl babies in China who had been given to orphanages by their birth parents. Sam and Lisa prayed, asking God if this was the answer to their prayers. After almost two years of red tape and constant correspondence, they flew to China and met little Sue. She was only three months old and they fell in love immediately.

When they got home there were many adjustments. Sue's body clock was set for "China Time"—daylight in the U.S. meant darkness in China. But Sam and Lisa's love for their new daughter didn't need adjusting. They wanted to keep her Chinese heritage by giving her a name in her native tongue. That name means "flower" in English. Lisa had often bitter that God had not made her body "perfect" in order to have a child. Now, she and Sam realize that their adopted daughter Sue represented God and His perfect creation.

Nature Is Supernatural

Art is man's nature: nature is God's art.—*Philip James Bailey*

***

Nature is God's tongue. He speaks by summer and by winter. He can manifest himself by the wind, by the storm, by the calm. Whatever is sublime and potent, whatever is sweet and gentle, whatever is fear-inspiring, whatever is soothing, whatever is beautiful to the eye or repugnant to the taste, God may employ. The heavens above, and the procession of the seasons as they month by month walk among the stars, are various manifestations of God.—*Henry Ward Beecher*

***

God made man a little lower than the angels, and he has been getting a little lower ever since.—*Will Rogers*

***

Man is too noble to serve anyone but God.—*Cardinal Wyszynski*

This Lesson in Your Life

Can you think of a chapter in the Bible that makes a case for the existence of God? Actually, there is only one half of one verse that talks about God being real. The Psalmist says, "The fool hath said in his heart, 'There is no God'" (Ps. 14:1a.).

We own some property in the Blue Ridge Mountains of North Carolina just a few miles from the Blue Ridge Parkway. The elevation is about 3,500 feet, and you can see Mt. Mitchell in the distance. It is one of the most elegant and breathtaking places on earth. My favorite activity is to go for a walk in the early morning and see the wildlife as the mountains wake up to a new day. It is easy to see God anywhere and everywhere.

The thing that is truly amazing is that God created this for humankind. Our purpose is to enjoy this creation and not to abuse it. How many times have you witnessed someone throw a bag of trash out of the car window? It is so easy to take advantage of our wondrous world and not to treasure it as God's perfect creation. People pour used motor oil down sewer drains and it winds up in the water table only to be consumed by the person who disposed of the oil.

In contrast, nature works in perfect harmony. The trap-door spider digs a hole about one inch in diameter and about 12 inches long. Above this nest rests a "trap door" that is often covered with dirt or gravel. This not only disguises the "trap" but adds weight. An unsuspecting insect will come along and the door will spring shut on top of it. Then the trap-door spider will have a meal. Who taught the spider how to build such an elaborate "meal-maker"?

Our God is "excellent" in name and actions. It is up to us not only to proclaim it but to recognize it when we look at the wonders of nature. Within every human being is an inner voice that tells us not only of the existence of God, but points us to God's hand.

Furthermore, God did not end creation in history, but is constantly in the act of creating. Every time a baby cries its first breathless blast in a deliver room, we are reminded that God is continuing to make life and a world for that life to live in. The fresh greenery that sprouts from the devastation of a forest fire is yet another reminder of new creation. Look around you and see where God has created and is creating.

GETTING THE FACTS STRAIGHT

1. How does the Psalmist describe God?
God is more excellent than anything in the universe. He even has the ability to bring praise from the helpless (babies).

2. In awe of creation, what strikes the writer the most?
That in view of creation's magnificence, God would even notice humans.

3. What position does humanity have in relation to the heavenly beings?
We are created a little lower than the heavenly beings.

4. What recognition did God give us as His creation?
He has crowned humanity with glory and honor.

5. What position do humans have in relation to creation?
We have dominion over all God's creation. This would include the universe (space) and all living creatures.

6. How does the writer of this Psalm view himself?
He sees himself as inferior to God, but at the same time important to Him. God has regard for all humanity.

7. Is there an order to God's creation?
Yes. The heavenly beings are superior to humans. Humans come second in creation, followed by animals, birds, and sea creatures.

8. What attitude should we have toward God for our existence?
We should honor God because He thought to create us and to give us the world as our domain.

9. What has God done to show us that we are precious to Him?
He has "visited us" and walked among us.

10. What significance is it that this Psalm begins and ends with the same declaration?
That it is a poem that exalts God's name above all other names on earth.

The editors of the King James Bible attribute this Psalm to David. This is the same David we see as a young boy willing to face the giant in battle. This is the same David who feared for his life when King Saul was angry with him. David knew about enemies, but he also knew about the divine providence of God. He knew he could trust the God of creation to sustain him during his darkest moments.

David was also a good shepherd. The nature of the work of a shepherd is to live and work outdoors. There is little doubt that the seeds for this Psalm were sown in the wind-swept plains of Palestine in the days of his youth. Many nights David, the shepherd, sat alone with his sheep, gazing at the heavens and thinking about God and His creation. He also thought about his place in this world and in the mind of God. Later, as he writes Psalm 8, his mind goes not only to the splendor of this world and the heavens, but also to the greatness of God Himself. Without the modern instruments of science, David can clearly see that his God is worthy of all the adjectives and metaphors of praise that can possibly describe a God with the power to create the universe, yet also the love of a nurturing parent.

When our children are young we make sure that their every need is met. As they grow older they begin to meet many of their needs themselves. However, we are constantly ready to step in if they ever need us. The difference between human parents and God is that He parents perfectly.

Love can be shown in many ways. God has decided to show His love to us through the splendor and beauty of all things made just for us. It is our responsibility not only to recognize creation as a gift of love but also to treat the universe with the respect that a precious gift deserves.

Lesson 2

God Created Wonderful Things

Psalm 104:1-13

Bless the LORD, O my soul. O LORD my God, thou art very great; thou art clothed with honour and majesty.

2 Who coverest thyself with light as with a garment: who stretchest out the heavens like a curtain:

3 Who layeth the beams of his chambers in the waters: who maketh the clouds his chariot: who walketh upon the wings of the wind:

4 Who maketh his angels spirits; his ministers a flaming fire:

5 Who laid the foundations of the earth, that it should not be removed for ever.

6 Thou coveredst it with the deep as with a garment: the waters stood above the mountains.

7 At thy rebuke they fled; at the voice of thy thunder they hasted away.

8 They go up by the mountains; they go down by the valleys unto the place which thou hast founded for them.

9 Thou hast set a bound that they may not pass over; that they turn not again to cover the earth.

10 He sendeth the springs into the valleys, which run among the hills.

11 They give drink to every beast of the field: the wild asses quench their thirst.

12 By them shall the fowls of the heaven have their habitation, which sing among the branches.

13 He watereth the hills from his chambers: the earth is satisfied with the fruit of thy works.

Devotional Reading
Ps. 104:31-35

Background Scripture
Ps. 104

Memory Selection
Ps. 104:1

Psalm 104 is an invitation for everyone, but especially city-dwellers, to take time-out to exult in the majesty of God. In the selected verses, the psalmist reflects first on the glory of God, then on the way He employs angels as His ministerial agents, and finally on the glory of earth's oceans and other waters—which we often need to leave the high-tech city environment to appreciate.

The teacher should read the entire Psalm before focusing on today's text. The author moves from the waters to the earth to the skies, then returns to the seas to explore the totality of God's creation. Throughout, God's handiwork evokes the awe and reverence that should characterize all believers even today.

Invite members of your group to reflect on a part of creation that has at some time impressed them with the majesty of the Creator. They may have stood at the rim of the Grand Canyon, breathless at the sweeping vistas that lie below. Perhaps the thunderous waterfalls at Yellowstone National Park or Niagara Falls have humbled them with their roaring display of power. The beach or the ocean, mountains or desert, flying above the clouds in a modern airliner—any such marvel on a grand scale may have inspired awe.

Tiny marvels of God's handiwork should not be overlooked—the intricate patterns in a rose, the social instinct of a colony of ants, the delicate patterns of cellular tissue that can be seen only with a microscope. Lead from these personal experiences into this Psalm's own vision of God that results in a hymn of praise.

Teaching Outline

I. God and His Dwelling—1-3
  A. Garments of glory, 1-2
  B. Earth as God's home, 3
II. God and His Messengers—4
III. Glories of the Waters—5-13
  A. The flood, 5-7
  B. Its boundaries, 8-9
  C. Life-giving waters, 10-13
    1. Land animals, 10-11
    2. Fowls of the air, 12-13

Daily Bible Readings

Mon. The Sky, God's Handiwork
   Ps. 19:1-6
Tue. Make a Joyful Noise!
   Ps. 66:1-9
Wed. God's Love Endures Forever
   Ps. 136:1-9
Thu. God, the Great Creator
   Ps. 104:1-13
Fri. An Orderly Universe
   Ps. 104:14-23
Sat. Manifold Works of God
   Ps. 104:24-30
Sun. Rejoice in the Lord!
   Ps. 104:31-35

Verse by Verse

I. God and His Dwelling—1-3

A. Garments of glory, 1-2

1 Bless the LORD, O my soul. O LORD my God, thou art very great; thou art clothed with honour and majesty.

2 Who coverest thyself with light as with a garment: who stretchest out the heavens like a curtain:

The Psalms are never dull or prosaic. In this passage the author (presumably King David) uses all the skills of a wordsmith who knows how to create vivid imagery. Bursting with a sense of gratitude for the grandeur of creation, he stretches the language to provide unusual turns of phrases that express his deep emotions.

His first impulse is to give figurative "garments" for the invisible God. Since he is describing an extraordinary Being, the garments he describes are extraordinary, too. It is not enough to use abstractions such as "honor" and "majesty" to describe them. The psalmist dares to say that God clothes Himself with light. The metaphor hints of the way God reveals Himself openly, giving the light of revelation to those who want to know Him. It fits the brilliance often perceived by people who have been given special visions of God or His angels—such as the apostle Paul

who was, for a time, blinded by the brilliance of the light that clothed the God who called him to a change of life (Acts 9:3-9). Darkness, the opposite of light, is in turn often used to describe God's opponents, the forces of evil (Job 12:22-25; John 8:12).

B. Earth as God's home, 3

3 Who layeth the beams of his chambers in the waters: who maketh the clouds his chariot: who walketh upon the wings of the wind:

Now the poet lays the foundation for speaking, through verse 13, of the wonders of the earth's waters, which comprise two-thirds of the earth's surface. We usually think of God's home as in "heaven"; but the psalmist reminds us that He is God of heaven *and earth.* The very "beams" or floor joists of God's "house" can therefore be said to lie in the deepest crevices of the earth's oceans. Then, showing His universal Presence, the focus suddenly shifts from the depths to the heights: if God's "house" can be said to be founded in the deeps, He also "travels by cloud," and His daily "constitutional" might by said to be on the winds (note the carefully-constructed alliteration in the KJV: "he *w*alks on the *w*ings of the *w*ind").

The whole point is to show the uniquely sweeping Presence of God, from the depths of the ocean to the farthest reach of the universe.

Despite this close association of God with His creation, the Psalm differs from religions of the day (and with some "New Age" thought today) in identifying God *with* creation. The biblical God may *visit* nature, but He is distinct from it. This distances biblical faith from "pantheism," the view that God *permeates* creation; and from "panentheism," the view that the world exists as a part of, and within, God.

II. God and His Messengers—4

4 Who maketh his angels spirits; his ministers a flaming fire:

The psalmist is also in awe of God's unique ability to use divine beings or angels (lit. "messengers") as his servants or ministers. As God is clothed with "light," His messengers are frequently described as having garments of fire. The mysterious cherubim, and seraphim, which are a kind of angel, are associated with fire (Gen. 3:24; Isa. 6:6-8). If God is not only *clothed* in light, but is Light itself (1 John 1:5), then it is little wonder that angels, who are constantly at His side to do His bidding, "catch fire" from the heat of the divine light (see this imagery especially in Ezek. 1:4-6).

The word for "spirits" can also mean "winds"; and it is in this sense that this verse is quoted in the New Testament. The writer to the Hebrews joins the psalmist in seeing the grandeur of God in being able to use wind and fire as his angels or servants. Then he remarkably indicates that this is faint praise for the angels themselves when compared with God's own Son, who is actually addressed as God! (See Heb. 1:7-8.)

III. Glories of the Waters—5-13

A. The flood, 5-7

5 Who laid the foundations of the earth, that it should not be removed for ever.

6 Thou coveredst it with the deep as with a garment: the waters stood above the mountains.

7 At thy rebuke they fled; at the voice of thy thunder they hasted away.

The psalmist now turns to mankind's eternal preoccupation with the relationship between earth and the seas. His first word is one of reassurance: God has given us the earth as a solid foundation on which to live. The waters that cover so much of it, and the Great Flood that God sent in the time of Noah, are an added but controlled element. Ancient people of the desert, as were the Jews, often deeply feared the ocean, from what little contact they had with it. (Even in the book of Revelation the evil "beast" rises from the sea, Rev. 13:1ff.)

Here, however, the psalmist seeks to reassure such "landlubbers" that even in Noah's flood God only "clothed" the earth with waters for a time. Then He rebuked them and required them to return to their depths, reestablishing safe boundaries for man to dwell on the security of dry land.

B. Its boundaries, 8-9

8 They go up by the mountains; they go down by the valleys unto the place which thou hast founded for them.

9 Thou hast set a bound that they may not pass over; that they turn not again to cover the earth.

To further reassure man, the psalmist emphasizes the boundaries God has set for earth's waters. The mountains and lakes of Switzerland make a good illustration of this description. The waters seek the lowest level of every crevice, as though obediently remaining within the boundaries God has set for them. He is so concerned that we be released from our fear of unbounded waters that he repeats God's promise to Noah after the flood: "Neither shall there any more be a flood to destroy the earth" (Gen. 9:11). Based on this Covenant, we can join the psalmist in finding in the great oceans of earth reasons for praising and loving God, rather than being terrified of Him.

C. Life-giving waters, 10-13

1. Land animals, 10-11

10 He sendeth the springs into the valleys, which run among the hills.

11 They give drink to every beast of the field: the wild asses quench their thirst.

Lest his people focus only on how "the waters" can be destructive, the psalmist moves into praise for their life-giving capacity. Only once did

God destroy all living things with a flood; His usual way of using water is to slake the thirst of the beasts of the field (tamed animals, as in Gen. 2:20) and wild animals. He does this from underground springs (which at some time were charged by a "flood"). Earth would have no wildlife were it not for the water God supplies.

2. Fowls of the air, 12-13

12 By them shall the fowls of the heaven have their habitation, which sing among the branches.

13 He watereth the hills from his chambers: the earth is satisfied with the fruit of thy works.

"By them" probably refers again to the springs mentioned in verse 10, indicating the psalmist's move from the way God uses water to nourish land animals to the fact that even the birds of the air depend on water for their existence as well. We would do well not to so fear the waters that we cannot appreciate the songbird's music from the trees! (God's care for even the birds is mentioned by Jesus in Matt. 6:26.)

In short, God, from His "chambers" or Presence both on the earth, in the Deep, and in the skies, waters the earth so it will be fruitful. We recall that He originally sent man into the earth to be "fruitful"; but man did not go forth without the accompanying fruit-giving rains and springs. So the psalmist, in the last phrase, turns to God, speaking in the second person of "the fruit of thy works."

Evangelistic Emphasis

The psalmist reminds us that God's creation is a perfect circle. For example, rain waters the grass so that animals can graze and life can be sustained. I can remember helping my father on our farm as a child. He took such pride in watching his crops grow to maturity. I cared very little about the subject, only wanting to harvest the crops so I could rest before planting time came again. However, for my father, to grow something was the greatest joy of his life. My father had many faults, but he always thanked God for the bless-ing of the miracle of the harvest. No matter how much my father learned about farming, he knew that it was God's hands that made everything work in perfect harmony.

Christians should never fail to thank God for our world, and acknowledge that He is worthy of our praise and thanksgiving for giving us such an astounding planet as Earth. Others are watching us, and Christians should be keenly aware that we should set the example for appreciation and honor to our world.

God is worthy to be praised, not only for the harvest, but also for the means to make the harvest. By acknowledging God as the One who is still creating, we become a testimony to others.

ഇൗരുൽ

Bless the Lord, O my soul. O Lord my God, you are very great. You are clothed with honor and majesty."—*Psalm 104:1*

Psalm 104 is not about creation but about the greatness of the Creator. Why do we worship God? The answer lies in who God is. He is not creation but Creator. The psalmist tells us that God's very clothing consists of "honor and majesty." When you meet someone on the street, perhaps the first thing you notice is what they are wearing. God is wearing honor and majesty.

In God we do not find our fear but our joy. We love to commune with God because He is the center of our joy, and of our peace. This Psalm encourages us to "bless the Lord." The result of this blessing is that it will leave us with the peace we all desire for ourselves and the ones we love.

I can remember being required to attend a silent retreat at an old abbey. I thought I was much too busy to "waste" a week of my time. The monks would walk around in their long robes in silence going about their tasks. I thought about how peaceful they looked and how tense I must have looked. After a week of prayer and worship, I could feel that peace within me, too.

Do you experience the peace of God, or does it elude you?

Weekday Problems

When my oldest daughter was little, her mother bought her some chalk that was made to use on sidewalks and driveways. She had drawn a beautiful rainbow, a pond with a fish jumping in the air and a deep blue sky complete with horizon. When she went into the house for a little while, her little brother destroyed her creation. The way she cried told me that she was extremely hurt. It was the kind of cry that would normally tell me that she had fallen off her bike and was bleeding from a hurtful scrape. When I ran to her aid and saw what she was crying about, I was amazed that such hurt could come from such a small incident. However, it was an honest cry that radiated from the depth of her soul.

Can you imagine how God must hurt when we do not take His Creation seriously and watch it being destroyed? Our environment is a reflection of God, in that it tells us how He pictures beauty. The sunset, the blue sky, the mountains, animals, insects, and our entire world tell us about God. It tells us what He thinks is beautiful and what we need. The Bible tells us that the entire universe is God's handiwork. It is hurtful to God when it is misused.

*Have you ever thanked God for His creation? Have you ever thought about the creation as you worshiped? Are you careful not to destroy God's creation?

Rumors of Angels

A person who is always up in the air and harping on something isn't necessarily an angel.

***

A conscientious minister decided to get acquainted with a new family in his congregation, and he called at their home one evening about the time the woman of the house was expecting her daughter home from school. After his knock on the door, a lilting voice from within called out, "Is that you, angel?"

"No," replied the minister, "but I'm from the same department."

***

A little girl whose father was a photographer was out fishing with her parents one afternoon when a sudden storm came up. After a brilliant flash of lightning the girl said, "Look, Daddy! The angels are taking our picture!"

***

Did you know that angels can die? Sure, if they have harp failure.

This Lesson in Your Life

Our lesson gives us a rare peek at the throne of God. The view is not exact, but filled with metaphors. Perhaps the psalmist didn't exactly know what God was like and examples from this world were all he could think about. Perhaps he could not find words to describe what he saw.

I was in my 50s when I saw the Grand Canyon for the first time. If I had to describe it, I would be at a loss for words. I had seen pictures, I had heard stories, but I never imagined such superb splendor. The deep, rich colors of the clay and layers of soil were breath-taking. The trees blended in like decorations on a Christmas tree. Can you imagine what it would be like to describe God and His throne?

We are also reminded that God has made provisions for His creation to be sustained. Sometimes when we despair about a problem, we question whether God can continue to make a way for us. Doesn't it seem logical that, if God can order nature to thrive, He can do it for humans? P.A. Sorokin said, "Life, even the hardest life, is the most beautiful, wonderful and miraculous treasure in the world." Life is wonderful because God gave us everything to make it wonderful.

There are many endangered species in the world. Most of them are endangered not because God didn't provide for their survival but because humans have encroached on them. Left alone, they have everything they need to thrive. Is a God who creates so beautifully and perfectly worthy of our praise? Are you aware that God has provided for you? He loves us and wants us not just to survive, but to thrive.

STRAIGHT

1. According to the psalmist, with what does God clothe Himself?
Verses 1 and 2 tell us that God is clothed with honor, majesty, and light.

2. When God laid the foundations of the earth, how long would they last?
The foundations of the earth would last forever.

3. How deep were the waters of the earth when God began His creation?
The waters covered the mountains.

4. During creation, what caused the waters to recede?
The voice of God, which was like thunder.

5. What provision did God make to keep the waters from returning to cover the earth?
He made a boundary that the waters could not pass over.

6. How does God take care of the needs of the animals?
He provides springs that run down from the hills to allow the animals to drink freely.

7. What attribute does God give to angels?
He makes angels to become spirits.

8. What attribute does God give the angelic ministers?
He makes them into flaming fire.

9. Where does the psalmist say the birds live?
In the trees by the springs of water created by God.

10. What does God think about His creation?
He is pleased with the fruit of His works.

Sometimes we cannot see God's provision in our lives. Sometimes we lament the fact that we don't have as many possessions as other people, or perhaps we have not achieved as much as someone else we admire. The truth for all of us is that God has given us everything we need to be happy. Often happiness eludes us because we can't see that God provides everything we need to be happy.

Jesus used several illustrations to point this valuable truth out to us. Perhaps the one we remember best is the "lilies of the field." He says that these flowers did absolutely nothing themselves to create their beauty. Yet He questions whether anyone has ever seen anything more beautiful.

In the movie "Shenandoah," Jimmy Stewart plays the part of the patriarch of a large family during the Civil War. He always prays the same prayer before the meal: "Lord, I planted the seeds, I plowed the ground, I gathered in the harvest. If I hadn't of put the food on the table it wouldn't be here. But we thank you anyway."

Unlike this fictional character, we can look around us and see God's bounty of the earth. We take comfort in knowing He created all of this to sustain His most precious creation: humankind. What a joy!

Lesson 3

God Created and Knows Us

Mar. 19

Psalm 139:1-3, 7-14, 23-24

O LORD, thou hast searched me, and known me.

2 Thou knowest my downsitting and mine uprising, thou understandest my thought afar off.

3 Thou compassest my path and my lying down, and art acquainted with all my ways.

7 Whither shall I go from thy spirit? or whither shall I flee from thy presence?

8 If I ascend up into heaven, thou art there: if I make my bed in hell, behold, thou art there.

9 If I take the wings of the morning, and dwell in the uttermost parts of the sea;

10 Even there shall thy hand lead me, and thy right hand shall hold me.

11 If I say, Surely the darkness shall cover me; even the night shall be light about me.

12 Yea, the darkness hideth not from thee; but the night shineth as the day: the darkness and the light are both alike to thee.

13 For thou hast possessed my reins: thou hast covered me in my mother's womb.

14 I will praise thee; for I am fearfully and wonderfully made: marvelous are thy works; and that my soul knoweth right well.

23 Search me, O God, and know my heart: try me, and know my thoughts:

24 And see if there be any wicked way in me, and lead me in the way everlasting.

Devotional Reading
Ps. 100

Background Scripture
Ps. 139

Memory Selection
Ps. 139:14

281

This lesson cuts to the heart of one of the most crucial questions of the ages: *Is the Being who set creation in motion actually aware of me, on a personal basis?* It is relatively easy to believe that a distant God or an impersonal Force created the universe. Existence itself seems to most people to point to such a Being.

This, however, is a far cry from believing that whatever Force is behind creation is *personal,* and that He also knows and cares for *me* as a person. In this lesson, the psalmist makes precisely that claim.

How can he know that God knows us personally, even our deepest thoughts? God *tells* him, both that He made us, and that He knows and loves each one of us. That may be a greater miracle than existence itself.

ഇⓒⓡ

Tell group members that you are going to state the main theme of today's lesson, from Psalm 139, to see whether they can respond to the sentence both *positively* and *negatively.* The sentence is: *Where could I go to get away from God?*

Note that positive responses show relief and even joy that God is *ev-* *erywhere.* Negative responses might include "getting in a space ship and going to the farthest reaches of the universe," to escape the hounding of an ever-present God. Of course all will soon recognize the point of the psalm: *God is everywhere, but for our good,* not to "hound" us.

Explain that Psalm 139 is famous for describing God's "omnipresence"—a somewhat scholarly term that is made very personal in this lesson.

Teaching Outline

I. Omniscience of God—1-3
   A. God knows our thoughts, 1-2
   B. God knows our whereabouts, 3
II. Omnipresence of God—7-14
   A. From heaven to Sheol, 7-8
   B. Universal guidance, 9-10
   C. In darkness or light, 11-12
   D. Marvelously made, 13-14
III. Openness of the Heart—23-24

Daily Bible Readings

Mon. We Belong to God
    Ps. 100
Tue. Our Help Is from God
    Ps. 121
Wed. God Watches Over All
    Ps. 146
Thu. God Knows All My Ways
    Ps. 139:1-6
Fri. God Is Always with Me
    Ps. 139:7-12
Sat. Fearfully and Wonderfully Made
    Ps. 139:13-18
Sun. 'Search Me, O God!'
    Ps. 139:19-24

Verse by Verse

I. Omniscience of God—1-3
A. God knows our thoughts, 1-2
1 LORD, thou hast searched me, and known me.

2 Thou knowest my downsitting and mine uprising, thou understandest my thought afar off.

In recent years a good deal of theological discussion has centered on whether God knows everything— the future as well as the past, scientific truth which man has yet to discover as well as theological or "revealed" truth. Psalm 139 seems to support the position that there is nothing that God does not know. At least in the human realm, the psalmist affirms that God not only knows our individual whereabouts, from sitting down to arising, but that He knows our inner being, our thought-world, as well.

This sense that the Being we worship knows us personally is universally sought, but not always appreciated. On the one hand we want the comfort and security of God's being always at our side, "even through the valley of the shadow of death" (Ps. 23:4). Yet there are times when even the best Christians have stray thoughts that they would rather keep from God, if it were only possible. The psalmist expresses both these feelings, but logically concludes that we cannot have it both ways. In the

final analysis, this is a psalm of praise; so God's knowing all (his "omniscience") must be taken as a trait at which we stand in awe, and for which we give thanks.

B. God knows our whereabouts, 3
3 Thou compassest my path and my lying down, and art acquainted with all my ways.

The word translated "compassest" (NIV "discern") literally means "to winnow"—to beat grass crops such as wheat to separate the kernel from the chaff and debris. The picture is well known to any parents who have gone ahead of a child as they make their way through high grass to drive away any snakes or to point out a thorn bush for the child to avoid. The psalmist praises God for being so aware and attentive as to clear the path before us. Although that path may still be rocky and difficult, God the Winnower has promised that He will clear it of any temptation that would be too much for us to bear (1 Cor. 10:13).

II. Omnipresence of God—7-14
A. From heaven to Sheol, 7-8
7 Whither shall I go from thy spirit? or whither shall I flee from thy presence?

8 If I ascend up into heaven, thou art there: if I make my bed in hell, behold, thou art there.

This statement is well-known for providing the theme for Francis Thompson's famous poem, "The Hound of Heaven." As a young man, Thompson tried his best to flee God, and his duty to Him. He wrote:

I fled Him down the nights and down the days;
I fled Him down the arches of the years;
I fled Him down the labyrinthine ways
Of my own mind . . . .

Yet "The Hound of Heaven," the God who is everywhere, awaited Thompson at every turn, wanting only for His all-pervading presence to bless, not inhibit.

As Thompson learned, the psalmist knew that the divine motive for being omnipresent was pure. Yet, in his words here, there is something of the wish to escape God's heavy tread. Still, though he were to fly to the heavens on wings like the Greek hero Icarus attempted to do, God would be there. If he fled the other direction to the grave (NIV "hidden place," from Heb. *sheol,* not the place of eternal torment), God would await him there as well. The point, of course, is not that God lives in the grave but that, being Spirit, He is not confined to any physical location.

B. Universal guidance, 9-10

9 If I take the wings of the morning, and dwell in the uttermost parts of the sea;

10 Even there shall thy hand lead me, and thy right hand shall hold me.

With skillful poetic development

of thought, the psalmist begins to move past his feeling of God "hounding" him. That He is everywhere-present provides divine guidance, not smothering control. The exquisite phrase "wings of the morning" conjures up the vision of arising early to leave on a journey; but even if it takes the poet to the uttermost parts of the world, God's omnipresence is there for protection and guidance. We may apply this comforting truth to the dizzying "journey" the world is on as science plunges into issues that were the stuff of science fiction only a few years ago. Even in the sometimes frightening world of cloning, genetic manipulation, and atom-splitting warfare, God's will lead us—if societies will but allow it.

C. In darkness or light, 11-12

11 If I say, Surely the darkness shall cover me; even the night shall be light about me.

12 Yea, the darkness hideth not from thee; but the night shineth as the day: the darkness and the light are both alike to thee.

Again the poet seems ambivalent about whether he wants God to be so present in his life. Seeking "darkness" is a common biblical reference to trying to hide misdeeds from God—"Men loved darkness instead of light because their deeds were evil" (John 3:19). If it were not so universally true, it would be laughable for us to think we could hide wrongdoing from God, because of His very omnipresent nature being praised here. Ananias and Sapphira learned the hard way that pretending to give all proceeds of their land sale for the ministry of the early Church, but withholding part for themselves, was not done in darkness but in the light of divine discernment (Acts 5:1-11).

D. Marvelously made, 13-14

13 For thou hast possessed my reins: thou hast covered me in my mother's womb.

14 I will praise thee; for I am fearfully and wonderfully made: marvelous are thy works; and that my soul knoweth right well.

Although the Hebrew word for "reins" literally refers to the kidneys, it is used figuratively for one's inner, driving force (hence "inmost being," in the NIV). The psalmist stands in awe at how God superintends the shaping of this life-force from the womb. The discovery in modern times of the presence of the entire complex genetic make-up of the human being in the embryo from its earliest stages only makes this reference more awesome.

The KJV "covered" and the NIV "knit together" are not as far apart as they may seem. The word was used to describe the tightly-knit branches used to make primitive shelters or "coverings." The psalmist is praising God for the protection afforded him from the womb. This passage has been at the center of modern debates over abortion, although it must be noted that it provides no indisputable answer as to precisely when life begins.

Long treatises have been written on the complex workings of the human body by believing scientists who, with the psalmist, stand in awe at the human body's apparently divine composition. The complexities and function of the human eye alone are a lesson in divine anatomy. An outstanding testimony to being "fearfully and wonderfully made" is the book by that title by the late Paul Brand, M.D. It should also be noted that the Bible additionally honors the body by calling it the "temple of the Holy Spirit," and on that basis exhorting us to give it the care and respect due its Creator (1 Cor. 6:19-20).

III. Openness of the Heart—23-24

23 Search me, O God, and know my heart: try me, and know my thoughts:

24 And see if there be any wicked way in me, and lead me in the way everlasting.

Moving to this great poem's last lines, we can see that the author finally leaves behind all hesitance and fear at the omniscience and omnipresence of God. In light of this inevitable part of God's nature, he submits to the astonishing ability of God to look within the heart, and pleads for that divinely searing gaze to burn out all impurities. In the New Testament, it is this attitude that is involved in the necessity of "repentance," or the decision to turn one's heart and mind around upon learning of their sinfulness in God's eyes.

Evangelistic Emphasis

Do you like to "people watch"? I do. I love to sit on a bench in a large mall corridor and watch people walk by. There are tall people, short people, large people, slim people, and people of different colors. However, despite this diversity, they are all God's children. The one thing that all humans have in common is that God created all of us.

Many of us do not feel that God created us perfectly. What we must realize is that He created us uniquely ourselves. There is not one other person exactly like us. Even identical twins have something about them that is different from their sibling. This is important to know. It's important to know because that is what makes us special to God. If humans were not so cherished by God, He would have made us more alike.

Just as God knows our bodies, He also knows our hearts. God can look inside us and see what makes us behave the way we do. He accepts us although our bodies are imperfect and our hearts are not all they should be. In other words, this God loves us from the inside out. If we are not aware of this love ourselves, how can we share this love with others?

ഇറ

I will praise thee; for I am fearfully and wonderfully made: marvelous are thy works; and that my soul knoweth right well.—*Psalm 139:14*

The Psalmist tells us that God has made our bodies with great precision. When we criticize the way we and others look, we are reflecting this criticism on God. How would you feel if you built something and someone came behind you and talked about how ugly it was?

It's true that many of us have not taken good care of our bodies, and it shows. However, it's never too late to bring our bodies back into shape. The body is amazing in its capacity to heal itself even from our neglect. We need to take care of our bodies. In this, we honor God and His creation.

It is also interesting to note how God made us. Everything in our bodies works with marvelous precision. Some organs eliminate waste; others create waste by removing impurities from our bloodstream. Every fiber of our bodies moves and works in exact coordination to allow us to move and work. The human body is a testament to the brilliance and perfection of God. It is up to us to be good stewards of His creation in our bodies.

Weekday Problems

A friend told me recently that she did not like for her two young daughters to play with their older cousin. It seems that her niece was in her pre-teen years and did not have a healthy self-image. The niece was always saying that she was fat, when in fact she was ideal in height and weight ratio. This mother wanted her girls to have a healthy self-image. How we see ourselves is often distorted by a cloudy mind. In order to have a healthy body, our minds must be healthy as well.

People often have true disabilities. Sometimes we are born with bodies that have limitations. Sometimes disease or accidents afflict us, leaving our bodies less than perfect. In these circumstances it is important to realize that God is aware of our limitations. After all, He made us and therefore knows more about us than we will ever know ourselves.

God also has the power to enable us to overcome our handicaps. He has the ability to enable us to cope with them and continue on with our lives. God did not place us in the world to fend for ourselves. He made us in His image to return our gifts to Him. When we refuse to accept ourselves for what we are, it makes it difficult for us to give Him the praise He deserves.

*Name someone such as a local or national sports figure, who has overcome handicaps and exhibited good self-esteem as a result.

Another Bible Quiz

Q: When was baseball mentioned in the Bible?
A: In Genesis, when Rebecca went to the well with her pitcher.

***

Q: Who is the first man mentioned in the Bible?
A: Chap 1.

***

Q: When is money first mentioned in the Bible?
A: In Genesis, where the dove brought the green back to the ark.

***

Q: Was there any more money on the ark?
A: Yes, the duck had a bill, the frog had a green back, and the skunk gave away a scent.

***

Q: What instructions about fishing did Noah give his sons?
A: "Go easy on the bait, boys, we only brought two worms."

This Lesson in Your Life

Most of us either adopt a healthy life-style or wish we had one. How can we honor God if we do not take care of our bodies, which He made? On the other hand, those who worry about the shape of their bodies make things worse by worrying. Stress from concern about our appearance and self-image causes us to deteriorate even more.

We are a nation that is obsessed with healthy bodies. We see them on magazine covers and on TV. Sometimes it seems that everyone has a good body but us. Thousands of dollars are spent at gyms and spas. Even more is spent at clinics and hospitals. Oliver Wendell Holmes said this: "There is nothing people will not do, there is nothing people have not done to recover their health and save their lives. They have submitted to be half drowned in water, half cooked with gasses, to be buried up to their chins in earth, to be seared with hot irons, to be crimped with knives, like cod-fish, to have needles thrust into their flesh and bonfires kindled on their skin, to swallow all sorts of abominations, and to pay for all this as if to be seared and scalded were a costly privilege, as if blisters were blessings and leeches were a luxury." What is the Christian's responsibility to his body?

Our church has a large family life center. In this center we have a state-of-the-art exercise room. This room is equipped with all the machines that are suppose to help you get into shape. In the kitchen of this building we also have a soft-serve ice cream machine. Guess which area is most popular? If you guessed the kitchen you are correct. I cannot help but laugh when I see people leave the exercise room huffing and puffing and head straight for the ice cream machine.

There is something else that is interesting about the exercise facilities. Our gym is absolutely free. However, many members choose to pay a membership fee in a gym to use the same equipment that is free at church. Do you suppose they think if they have to pay that it is better? We work hard and spend our money because we think our bodies are important.

The Bible tells us that the body is the temple of the Holy Spirit where God chooses to live inside of us. That dwelling place is known as the heart. Many times we give all of our attention to the "outer" self rather than the "inner" self. However, God is more concerned about our hearts. The Psalmist speaks to God: "Search me, O God, and know my heart: try me and know my thoughts . . . ." Many of us were taught to practice good physical hygiene as children. We should adopt good "heart hygiene" as well. After all, that's where God lives.

STRAIGHT

1. According to the psalmist, what does God know about us?
God knows whether we are resting or working, what we are thinking, and even our values.

2. In what realm does God exist?
God exists from heaven to the grave and to the utter most parts of the earth.

3. What promise does the psalmist give us that is made by God?
God will lead us by His right hand (the strong hand).

4. What two elements of nature that seem opposites are alike to God?
Night and day are alike to God.

5. What reason does the psalmist give to praise God?
God deserves our praise because we are "fearfully and wonderfully made."

6. What attribute of God do we know about naturally, within our souls?
We know that all of God's works are marvelous.

7. What does the psalmist desire for God to search?
The Psalmist asks God to search his heart.

8. Why does the psalmist challenge God to "try" or test him?
He asks for God to try him in order to know his thoughts.

9. Why does the psalmist ask God to look into his thoughts?
To see if there is a wicked tendency within him.

10: Where does the psalmist want God to lead him?
He desires that God should lead him into life everlasting.

289

One of the best preachers I know was born with a terrible birth defect of the mouth. The doctors told his mother that he would never be able to speak. They said that if he did speak, the impediment would be so severe that he would be hard to understand. If you were to meet this man today you would never guess that he had a handicap.

One of the best pianists I have ever heard was disabled in the hands and fingers. When he was young he fell on a furnace and his hand were severely burned and scarred. If you were to watch him play the piano now, you would swear that he played all the black and white keys, never leaving out a single one. He is fast and he is good.

We serve a perfect God who made us. However, sometimes we look at our bodies and we can't see much perfection. It is in fact, the things we *can't* see that would amaze us. The tiny cells in our body are dying and replicating themselves so fast that we never even know it. They are part of a miraculous process that keeps us going. That is only one illustration of how our bodies operate in perfect synchronization as we go about our lives.

No wonder that the author of Psalm 139 was in awe of God's creation! It is not only God's creation but God Himself that amazes the writer. Perhaps he is thinking of the prophet Jonah and how he tried to run from God. We look at Jonah and think how foolish it was to try to hide from God. God created our world and He certainly inhabits every corner of it.

It is also important to notice that the psalmist saved the best for last. God is a God who looks at our hearts. God has great respect for a pure and clean heart. Have you checked your heart lately? Would you be as brave as the psalmist, and ask God to put your heart to the test? What would He find?

Lesson 4

A Hymn of Praise to the Creator

Psalm 145:1-13

I will extol thee, my God, O king; and I will bless thy name for ever and ever.

2 Every day will I bless thee; and I will praise thy name for ever and ever.

3 Great is the LORD, and greatly to be praised; and his greatness is unsearchable.

4 One generation shall praise thy works to another, and shall declare thy mighty acts.

5 I will speak of the glorious honour of thy majesty, and of thy wondrous works.

6 And men shall speak of the might of thy terrible acts: and I will declare thy greatness.

7 They shall abundantly utter the memory of thy great goodness, and shall sing of thy righteousness.

8 The LORD is gracious, and full of compassion; slow to anger, and of great mercy.

9 The LORD is good to all: and his tender mercies are over all his works.

10 All thy works shall praise thee, O LORD; and thy saints shall bless thee.

11 They shall speak of the glory of thy kingdom, and talk of thy power;

12 To make known to the sons of men his mighty acts, and the glorious majesty of his kingdom.

13 Thy kingdom is an everlasting kingdom, and thy dominion endureth throughout all generations.

Devotional Reading
Ps. 150

Background Reading
Ps. 145

Memory Selection
Ps. 145:8

The book of Psalms rise to a crescendo of pure praise toward the end. There have been frequent complaints; but now, all questions give way to outbursts of praise for God's greatness that overwhelm questions about His ways.

The theme here is therefore seen in the repetition of terms such as *great* and *greatness, bless* and *praise, glory* and *majesty,* and various words describing the *benevolence* and *lovingkindness* of God.

Although it is a surprise to some, leaving complaints behind in favor of praise actually serves to reduce our complaints, since, as one famous confession has it, "The chief end of man is to glorify God and enjoy Him forever."

ഇൻ

Ask group members to recall titles of all the songs and hymns they can think of that express praise to God. Turning through a songbook, or browsing in its Index, will yield such titles as "Great Is Thy Faithfulness," "Praise Him, Praise Him!," "The Doxology," "Praise God from Whom All Blessings Flow," and

"Hallelujah! Thine the Glory!"

Point out that praise is the theme of this lesson, and of most of the latter part of the book of Psalms. Ask *What effect does such praise have on the worshiper?* Note that it enlarges our hearts to ascribe to God the glory that is His due, and also draws our attention upward, away from our difficulties and complaints.

Alternatively, consider reading Psalm 150 responsively (see p. 297).

Teaching Outline	Daily Bible Readings	
I. Object of Praise—1-3	Mon.	God's Holy Name Ps. 105:1-11
A. The Name, 1-2	Tue.	I Sing Your Praise Ps. 138
B. The Greatness, 3	Wed.	Sing to God a New Song Ps. 149
II. Those Who Give Praise—4-5	Thu.	Praise the Lord! Ps. 150
A. Chain of praise, 4		
B. God's wondrous works, 5	Fri.	Extolling the Lord Ps. 145:1-7
III. Reasons for Praise—6-9	Sat.	An Everlasting Kingdom Ps. 145:8-13a
A. Greatness and goodness, 6-7		
B. Compassion and mercy, 8-9	Sun.	God Is Faithful Ps. 145:13b-21
IV. Praiseworthy Kingdom—10-13		

Verse by Verse

I. Object of Praise—1-3
A. The Name, 1-2

1 I will extol thee, my God, O king; and I will bless thy name for ever and ever.

2 Every day will I bless thee; and I will praise thy name for ever and ever.

Psalm 145 is the last of eight "acrostic" psalms—hymns that begin each verse with successive letters of the Hebrew alphabet. In English it would be like writing:

1 **A** ll praise be to thee
2 **B** ecause of the great works
3 **C** oming from thy hands (etc.).

Such a method of writing offers God a special artistic device. Another way to see the artistry of the author is to look closely at the verbs the poet uses here. To *extol* God is to "lift Him up"—that is, to raise His name in public and private estimation and esteem. Sometimes the Hebrew word means literally to "raise up" a stone of remembrance to God; but here it is an act of the heart or mind. God does not suffer from low self-esteem, and in one sense He does not need us to pay Him what philosopher A. N. Whitehead called "excessive metaphysical compliments." It is *our* heart, not God's, that needs to be lifted up or enlarged by the practice of praise. Something miraculous happens when we allow the spirit of the psalms to permeate our thoughts of God, especially in worship. By focusing on His greatness we not only see ourselves in our proper relative lowness, but paradoxically become "larger" persons ourselves.

The other two important verbs of worship in verses 1-2 are *bless* and *praise*. Again, as creatures we can hardly "bless" God in the sense of doing Him any favors. In its purest sense, however, the word for "bless" means *to kneel before,* then *to honor.* As noted above, to *praise* God is to sing of His greatness. The Hebrew root appears in English in the word *Hallelujah,* which means literally "Praise to Yah!" (God). The preposition "to" is significant: When we offer praise and thanksgiving to God, we shift our attention from ourselves and our problems to God's glory.

B. The Greatness, 3

3 Great is the LORD and greatly to be praised; and his greatness is unsearchable.

The psalmist is overwhelmed, as we should be, by God's *greatness,* especially in comparison with the lowliness of the worshiper. To proclaim that God is great is to admit that He is our divine King, and we are His subjects (see also verses 10-13). We should not take this confession as permission to take flights of fancy, trying to say precisely *how* God is great in flowery words; for the psalmist quickly adds that His greatness is "unsearchable" (NIV "no one can fathom"). God's greatness is therefore not measured by the length of our prayers. Here it is good to remember the words of the wise man: "God is in heaven, and thou upon earth: therefore let thy words be few" (Eccles. 5:2).

II. Those Who Give Praise—4-5
A. Chain of praise, 4

4 One generation shall praise thy works to another, and shall declare thy mighty acts.

One of the fundamental truths of the Old Covenant Scriptures (and one reason Christians should study them) is the great sense of "traditioning" younger generations in the faith. Trust in God was something that was to be taught "diligently unto thy children," and spoken of in the home and while walking along life's pathway (Deut. 6:7). Faith is like passing the baton in a relay race. When times are hard in our own "generation," we are to be able to draw faith from Noah, and such "mighty acts" as those by which God delivered him, along with Abraham, Isaac, and Jacob. In turn, our own children see us enduring hardships with faith and hopefully "inherit" a similar capacity for praise in the midst of problems.

B. God's wondrous works, 5

5 I will speak of the glorious honour of thy majesty, and of thy wondrous works.

For the first-person "I" here, some versions have "They," tying this with the "generations" of verse 4. The point is that the "honor" or "glory" of God's majesty (or, "splendor") is so great that it should well up virtually unbidden from the depths of the believer's heart. It is of course important to praise and give thanksgiving in personal meditation; but the "wondrous works" of God are those done in public, such as the deliverance or exodus from Egypt through the Red Sea, the feeding of the people with manna in the wilderness, and the conquest of Canaan. Our praise is to be equally public as we speak of it to each other and lift our voices in praise in the assembly.

III. Reasons for Praise—6-9
A. Greatness and goodness, 6-7

6 And men shall speak of the might of thy terrible acts: and I will declare thy greatness.

7 They shall abundantly utter the memory of thy great goodness, and shall sing of thy righteousness.

How can some of the acts of God be called "terrible," when He is the epitome of goodness? The answer is that we are to understand "terrible" as meaning "awesome" (as in the NIV). Bringing the waters of the Red Sea crashing together and killing the Egyptians who pursued Moses and the children of Israel was such an awesome or "terrible" deed. God also sometimes allows His own people to suffer under His "terrible" hand. At such times we are to consider it to be the "chastening" of God, as of a Father who loves His children (see Heb. 12:5-11). Even then, being able to lift up our heads and sing God's praise is often a good antidote for feeling "chastened."

B. Compassion and mercy, 8-9

8 The LORD is gracious, and full of compassion; slow to anger, and of great mercy.

9 The LORD is good to all: and his tender mercies are over all his works.

Anticipating that the reader or hearer might protest that not all of our dealings with God are pleasant, the psalmist again affirms God's essential goodness. Even hard times may be viewed as strengthening measures taken by a God "full of compassion" and slow to anger. In verse 9, the goodness of God is proclaimed "to all," not just to the children of Israel (or as we read the psalm, to Christians). Here is an example of how much more inclusive the Bible is than believers often are. God consistently affirms His willingness to accept the unbeliever, even over the protests of those who want to make Him their own private or national god. It was difficult even for Peter to learn that "God is no respecter of persons: but in every nation he that feareth him and worketh righteousness, is accepted with him" (Acts 10:35).

IV. Praiseworthy Kingdom—10-13

10 All thy works shall praise thee, O LORD; and thy saints shall bless thee.

11 They shall speak of the glory of thy kingdom, and talk of thy power;

12 To make known to the sons of men his mighty acts, and the glorious majesty of his kingdom.

13 Thy kingdom is an everlasting kingdom, and thy dominion endureth throughout all generations.

The psalmist's awareness and appreciation of the mighty works of God lead him to the familiar biblical theme of God's Kingdom. He has spoken of God's goodness toward *all;* but here he affirms that the matrix from which God's blessings pour is His "everlasting kingdom."

Here again, the reasons for praising God are expanded from personal gratitude (as essential as this is) to the public realm. God's blessings are not just inner feelings. They also take the shape of outer, concrete blessings showered on flesh and blood people who comprise the community of faith. The psalmist no doubt looked forward to the restoration of the Kingdom promised to David, or through the Messiah. With the coming of the Jesus, the Messiah, the blessings of the Kingdom became more manifest for all peoples, and the spread of His Good News became yet another source of blessings for which we lift our voices in praise.

Evangelistic Emphasis

Many people take worship for granted. We often attend worship services at our churches out of mere habit. We never think about all the people in our lives who are silently watching us. Our neighbors watch as the family loads the car and hurriedly leave to be on time for worship. Our extended family will know not to call or visit at worship time on Sunday. It is often difficult to see our acts of worship as a witness, but they are vivid testimony of our faith.

Many Christians feel that they never share a testimony to others about their faith. The reason is often because many of us find it difficult to verbalize our faith. We know we have faith, but finding the courage to express it in words is almost impossible for some. However, when we worship God, we are indeed expressing our faith. When we make worship a priority in our lives we send a strong signal to all those who know us that our faith is important. There are many ways to praise God. We do so in words, songs, actions, and prayer. There are also many ways that this praise can be a witness of our faith. In how many ways are you a witness to your faith?

ഔര

The Lord is gracious, and full of compassion; slow to anger, and of great mercy. — *Psalm 145:8*

For centuries many students of the Bible saw God in two very different ways. The God of the Old Testament was portrayed as harsh and cruel, while the God of the New Testament was seen as compassionate and quick to forgive. How can the same God be seen in two very different ways? The problem does not exist with God but with human beings. God does not change, nor has He ever changed. It's all in the way we see Him.

The patience of God celebrated in this passage is clearly seen throughout the Old Testament. Over and over God gives His people another chance as He forgives their sins. Poor Jonah would still be in the belly of the fish if God were not compassionate. Look at the former slaves wandering in the wilderness, complaining about their God who was constantly providing for their needs.

Of all the reasons to praise God, certainly the greatest is to praise Him for His love. Have you experienced the love of God? Do you think about this experience when you worship? Do you believe that God is worthy of our praise because He loves us so much?

Weekday Problems

It is a natural response to God's blessings for believers to praise Him. Pausing in our lives to praise is not limited to church. We can praise God wherever we are. Some people want to praise Him when they look at a beautiful flower. Others might want to praise Him when they observe ants scurrying about building their kingdom in perfect precision. How can we look at a beautiful sunset or sunrise and not instinctively want to praise God?

People also praise God for other reasons. An event or surprise might cause us spontaneously to break into silent or public praise to God. Some seemingly have more reason to praise God than others. However, there is no human being alive today that does not have a reason to lift his adoration to our loving, compassionate God.

Praise of God may be in prayer or song, individually or as a group. We can worship as the Scripture is read. We worship when we give our offerings as the plate is passed. Praise can originate from our deepest emotions in complete spontaneity. It can also be a matter of will as we purposefully gather in corporate worship at our churches.

We should express our joy to God not only for what He has done but also just for who He is. This psalm reminds us that God is gracious, full of compassion, and slow to anger. There are not better reasons to praise Him!

*What blessings can you name right now as reasons to praise God?

Praise Ye the Lord!

(Psalm 150, to be read responsively)

Leader: Praise ye the Lord! Praise God in his sanctuary:
People: Praise him for his mighty acts: Praise him according to his excellent greatness.
Praise him with the sound of the trumpet:
Praise him with the psaltery and harp.
Praise him with the timbrel and dance:
Praise him with stringed instruments and organs.
Praise him upon the loud cymbals:
Praise him upon the loud cymbals: praise him upon the high sounding cymbals.
(Together): **Let every thing that hath breath praise the Lord. Praise ye the Lord.**

This Lesson in Your Life

How do we get feelings that are inside of us to come out so others can see them? This is the challenge of praise. To praise God in worship means that we express what we feel. Worship is also expressing our thanks and awe for God's actions both personally and as a group. What is the best way to do this? There is no perfect answer to this question.

Sometimes we forget that the ways we worship are varied by conditioning, culture, and regional bias. Most worship is derived from our faith tradition. It is handed down through the generations through oral and written tradition. Even churches that do not think of themselves as being "traditional" use worship methods that are very traditional.

My wife and I make a pilgrimage each year to worship in a very untraditional church. For us it is a welcome change in our worship. We enjoy the worship of our church very much but we also enjoy the radical difference in our "vacation church." In both experiences, we leave refreshed, with a feeling that we have truly experienced the presence of God.

In most churches we sing songs that are referred to as hymns. Other songs are called "gospel songs." The difference between a hymn and a gospel song is in the words. A hymn is God speaking directly to us. A good example of a hymn is a Scripture passage in which God is speaking to us, and the words are set to music. Another example of a hymn is when we speak directly to God. A prayer to God set to music is an ideal hymn. A gospel song, however, is our witness of God's acts to others. A gospel song is a testimony of God's love shown to us or others.

What is the best music to use in our worship to God? The answer is that all of it honors God. Certainly God wants us to share His love to us with others. God also wants to hear our praise to Him. To repeat the words of God from the Scripture reminds us of God's eternal providence toward human-kind. All of this honors God and is a fitting form of worship.

Many people do not participate in the music portion of worship because they feel they are inadequate in singing. However, they are missing out on one of the oldest forms of worship. The children of Israel in Exodus broke out in song to God when they saw His miracle at the parting of the water. They simply could not help but sing. Music is only one of many ways to worship and praise God. Do you pay attention to the words of the songs you sing in church? Do you allow those words to express your personal feelings during worship?

1. How often does the psalmist plan to engage in praise and worship of God?
He will bless God's name in praise for ever and ever and will worship Him every day.

2. How will future generations know about God and His mighty acts?
The current generation will teach the next generation about God.

3. What attributes of God teach us about His love?
The Lord is gracious, full of compassion, slow to anger. He has great mercy, and is good to all. His tender mercies are seen in creation.

4. How will we praise our God, according to the psalmist?
We will praise God through remembering God's acts, in our speech and in music.

5. To whom does God show His goodness ?
The Lord is good to all.

6. Who is singled out to bless the Lord?
All the saints will bless the Lord.

7. To whom will the saints give testimony about the mighty acts of God?
The sons of men.

8. How long will God's Kingdom last?
His Kingdom is an everlasting kingdom.

9. How long will the dominion of God last?
His dominion will endure throughout all generations.

10. To whom does the Lord draw near?
All who call upon Him.

I have been a minister for over 35 years. Like all ministers, I have preached sermons that I was extremely proud of and at other times I have been rather ashamed and wished that I had studied more. On one particular Sunday, I can remember not doing so well. I remember saying to myself that I had to find more time to study in the coming weeks.

As I was standing at the door of the church following service, a woman came up to me with tears in her eyes. Her face literally glowed with the love of God. She was smiling and crying all at the same time. She went on and on about how the worship touched her. I'm sure that my sermon was not the focal point of her experience. Instead, I think the opportunity to pour her heart out in worship had almost overwhelmed her. I'll never forget that Sunday.

Worship is extremely private yet equally as public. The setting makes some difference but not all of the difference. The psalmist pledges to "bless God's name" each day. Worship should never be limited to Sundays only. Worship is done each time we think about God and His greatness.

Of course, God's greatness is so large that we can never fully comprehend it. In this Psalm, we see where God is to be worshiped for His mighty acts of creation. When Jonah was bemoaning the fact that God is gracious and forgiving, he quotes to God verse 9 of our text. When God mentions that He has compassion on Nineveh, He mentions the animals as well as the humans. It's as though God is quoting verse 10 of our text right back to Jonah. God is worthy of our praise because of His acts seen in human-kind and nature. All of God's creation is good and we need to praise Him for it.

There is a book entitled *The Worship Wars*. It's about how people today worship differently. Strange that we even debate how to worship. One way Psalm 145 would bring us together is that it is actually a poem in which each verse starts with a different letter of the Hebrew alphabet. Clearly, the Psalmist is giving his readers an aid to worship and praise. They could remember the psalm by knowing what letter the first word would begin with. Apparently it was extremely important to the Psalmist to worship. In song, in spoken word, and in the communication of the human heart, God is to be praised, always.

Unit II. Living with Creation's Uncertainty

Lesson 5

When Tragedy Takes Place

Job 1:14-15, 18-19, 22; 3:1-3, 11

And there came a messenger unto Job, and said, The oxen were plowing, and the asses feeding beside them:

15 And the Sabeans fell upon them, and took them away; yea, they have slain the servants with the edge of the sword; and I only am escaped alone to tell thee.

18 While he was yet speaking, there came also another, and said, Thy sons and thy daughters were eating and drinking wine in their eldest brother's house:

19 And, behold, there came a great wind from the wilderness, and smote the four corners of the house, and it fell upon the young men, and they are dead; and I only am escaped alone to tell thee.

22 In all this Job sinned not, nor charged God foolishly.

3:1 After this opened Job his mouth, and cursed his day.

2 And Job spake, and said,

3 Let the day perish wherein I was born, and the night in which it was said, There is a man child conceived.

11 Why died I not from the womb? why did I not give up the ghost when I came out of the belly?

Devotional Reading
Psalm 22:1-11

Background Scripture
Job 1–3

Memory Selection
Job 2:10

The previous unit focused on the glories of God's creation. Yet we learn early in life that all is not perfect. Along with man, creation "fell." Thus, while we marvel that we are "fearfully and wonderfully made," we are also painfully aware that cancer is a part of our fallen creation. The present unit therefore deals with the reality that creation, for all its beauties and joys, can be uncertain, and even a source of suffering.

Three lessons focus on the most famous of sufferers, Job. It is for good reason that the epistle of James says, "Ye have heard of the patience of Job" (Jas. 5:11). Yet before we rush to the end of the story, when Job showed such patience, we do well to focus realistically on his anguish, seeking a basis for hope in times when tragedy enters our own lives.

❧❧

Since this treatment of Job is limited to three lessons, start this session by asking group members to "fill in the blanks" by recalling what they can about his story.

The discussion should recall James' reference to *the patience of Job* (Jas. 5:11) . . . the fact that *God allowed Satan to test Job by taking away all he had, both animals and family . . . he refused to curse God despite his difficulties . . . well-meaning friends refused really to hear his complaint . . . in the end he was blessed with even more than he had in the beginning.*

The thoughtful teacher might also add that the book's purpose was not to answer the question of why the innocent suffer, but to call believers to live faithfully even in the midst of unexplained tragedy.

Teaching Outline	Daily Bible Readings
I. Introduction	Mon. Job: Blameless and Upright Job 1:1-5
II. Tragedy Strikes—1:14-15, 18-19	Tue. Satan Plots Against Job Job 1:6-12
A. Beasts and servants lost, 14-15	Wed. Faithful Amid Loss Job 1:13-22
B. Children die, 18-19	Thu. Praise Amid Illness Job 2:1-10
III. Hanging Tough—22	Fri. Cursing His Birth Job 3:1-10
IV. Despairing of Life—3:1-3, 22	Sat. Wishing for Death Job 3:11-19
A. 'Why was I born?,' 3:1-3	Sun. Questioning God Job 3:20-26
B. 'Why was I not stillborn?,' 22	

I. Introduction

The book of Job, which may be the oldest book in the Bible, also deals with one of the world's oldest questions: *Why do the innocent suffer?* Some therefore call the book as a "theodicy"—a justification of the ways of a good God in an evil world. Dealing with that question, however, would require a philosophical treatise; and the book of Job pointedly does not meet the requirements for a satisfying philosophical answer. Instead, the book asserts that we can trust God and live in faith even *without* "the answer to suffering." It calls us to faith and worship, not to philosophical speculation.

The book is therefore more accurately read as an example of a kind of ancient literature called "the test." Several examples of such writings have been discovered from various parts of the Middle East, including Mesopotamia and Egypt; but none seem to have had significant influence on this book, or to have dealt with the issue of suffering in the depth Job does. Job's "test" is whether he will remain a person of faith even amid his questions.

II. Tragedy Strikes—1:14-15, 18-19
A. Beasts and servants lost, 14-15

14 And there came a messenger unto Job, and said, The oxen were plowing, and the asses feeding beside them:

15 And the Sabeans fell upon them, and took them away; yea, they have slain the servants with the edge of the sword; and I only am escaped alone to tell thee.

Although we are told in 1:1-3 that Job was a God-fearing and wealthy man in the land of Uz, we are told only that the land was in "the east." The lack of Job's explicit dependence on the Covenant God made with Abraham probably means the story preceded the beginnings of the Jewish race. Yet, as is true in virtually all religions, Job and the other figures in the book assume that God will bless His worshipers.

In fact, it may be pressing the book beyond its intent to examine Job's views of God in too much detail, since it is possible that the book is not based on actual historical events, but was intended to be a word-picture, much like the NT's parable of Lazarus going to "Abraham's bosom" after his death. Job has a similar other-worldly description of a heavenly council attended by Satan himself (1:6-12). There, Satan is actually described as one of "the sons of God," seemingly placing him on a par with the angels who come regularly to "report" to God as to a cosmic CEO. However, it should be noted that the author of Job does know the personal name of God, Yahweh, which was revealed to the Jews, instead of just referring to Him as "El" or "Eloah," as pagans may have done (see "LORD," or Yahweh, in 1:6, etc.).

Of course a parable can be even "truer" than a historical event; and the truths in the book of Job are some of the most valuable in all of Scripture. Nothing could be more true than the fact that God, in His sovereign but often opaque will, often allows suffering. In Job's case, the suffering results from Satan's conviction that Job served God only because God so richly blessed him. He therefore secures permission to test Job by removing his blessings (1:9-12).

The first front in this battle or test dealt with Job's material blessings. The "Sabaeans" were apparently well-known lawless raiders, possibly from the land of Sheba. They descend on Job's oxen and asses, take the animals away, and slay all but the servant who escapes to tell about the loss. In verses 16-18, Job also loses the rest of his possessions. The end of verse 19, "I only am escaped alone to tell thee," is identical to the report received here in verse 15b. This "duplication" of a literary device is another reason some scholars view the story as a parable (although the repetition could simply occur because the book is written in poetry, which often relies on such stylistic designs).

B. Children die, 18-19

18 While he was yet speaking, there came also another, and said, Thy sons and thy daughters were eating and drinking wine in their eldest brother's house:

19 And, behold, there came a great wind from the wilderness, and smote the four corners of the house, and it fell upon the young men, and they are dead; and I only am escaped alone to tell thee.

With pre-planned steps, the story progresses to a more personal level of tragedy. Job's (presumably grown) children were partying in the eldest son's house when a storm struck, destroying both the building and the people within. Of course there are plenty of wholesome parties at which nothing untoward happens; but we have had a hint that some of their feasting may have been in excess, or possibly in honor of false gods; for part of the author's commendation of Job as a good man was that after some of their banquets he offered burnt offerings to the Lord lest "my sons have sinned, and cursed God in their hearts" (1:5).

Any believer who has suffered even a semblance of such tragedy can identify with Job in verses 20-21. He practices the customs of his culture by shaving his head and tearing his garments to show the depths of his sorrow and grief. Yet he does so philosophically, trying to dismiss the tragedy with the "trade-off" of accepting the fact that since we enter the world with nothing, there is nothing unfair about leaving with nothing. This is an admirable and rational sentiment; but those who have suffered deeply know that there are feelings of grief that pierce deeper than such a consumer-oriented dismissal of tragedy.

III. Hanging Tough—22

22 In all this Job sinned not, nor charged God foolishly.

True to the requirements of a story

about a successful "test," the author affirms that despite all these material and personal losses, Job does not sin against God, or blame Him for the unjust suffering he has experienced. He "did not sin by charging God with wrongdoing" (NIV). Apparently he sees that Satan, not God, has been at work and is the primary source of his suffering.

Again, however, this is only a partial answer. Job apparently believes in only one all-powerful God, who *could* have prevented his losses. A "monotheist" does not enjoy the luxury of crediting a "good god" for blessings and blaming a "bad god" for misfortunes. With God, like Harry Truman, "the buck stops here." Although Satan is the immediate cause of Job's sufferings, if God is God He is in control of Satan. At this stage, Job is able to leave this difficulty in God's hands.

IV. Despairing of Life—3:1-3, 22

A. 'Why was I born?," 3:1-3

1 After this opened Job his mouth, and cursed his day.

2 And Job spake, and said,

3 Let the day perish wherein I was born, and the night in which it was said, There is a man child conceived.

"After this" includes a preceding third stage of suffering, when God agreed to allow Satan to go beyond attacking Job's possessions and family and attack his person. The cruelty came in the form of horrible boils (2:7). Job's wife's advised him to "curse God and die," but he refused. Intervening verses have also told of the well-meaning efforts of three friends, who sit with Job in sympathy for the customary seven days and nights (2:11-13).

Our lesson text takes up the story at the point when Job's anguish has grown to the point of cursing "the day," referring to the day of his birth (vs. 3). Most people feel that they have been born for a purpose, and when suffering or other obstacles defeat that purpose, it is natural to wonder why they were born at all. Suffering is so all-consuming that it can overwhelm all logic ("Others have suffered more") and inspiration ("Some find purpose in suffering, as an example to others"). Such attempts to comfort those in such suffering are usually futile at best and minimize the feelings of the sufferer at worst.

B. 'Why was I not stillborn?,' 22

11 Why died I not from the womb? why did I not give up the ghost when I came out of the belly?

This agonizing question is only a step removed from "Why was I born?" If life hurts this much, why did God not snuff it out immediately after birth? Inevitably, such passages as this have found their way into modern discussions of abortion, and whether life begins in the womb. The general sense in the Hebrew Bible is that life is associated with breath or "separate viability," the ability to breathe independently. Yet it seems to strain the intent and context of such passages as this to to use them as a basis for a biological theory of when life begins, when a suffering person is simply crying out in deep grief.

However, there *is* a reason Job was born. Possibly it was to show others that even without final answers we can pass the test. How this unfolds in Job's test will be the subject of the next two

Evangelistic Emphasis

Of all the people in the Bible, Job is the most illogical candidate for this tragedy. The Bible says that he has given himself in selfless service to God and that he was "blameless." Why do we always assume that righteous people are immune to tragedy? The reader of the book of Job has a vantage point that Job does not have. As we read the account of what happens, we can clearly see Satan as the initiator of the whole affair. Job is clueless as to the cause of his trouble.

Job lost his entire family except his wife. How does one deal with that? We would probably react just like Job. We would question God and try to reason everything out in our minds. It is interesting how human nature has not changed since this ancient story. We still raise an anguished *Why?* when tragedy strikes.

Job is not the only figure in the story who is patient (see Jas. 5:11). God is infinitely patient as we blame Him for everything that goes wrong in our lives. We should also keep in mind that God and Christ are also hurt by unjust suffering. Jesus wept at the gave of His friend Lazarus. Isn't it logical to assume that when we suffer, God suffers, too? He loves us beyond all His creation. When we hurt and suffer, whether physically or emotionally, God is there with us holding us and defending us, just as He did Job.

೭ಂೞ

Shall we receive good at the hand of God, and shall we not receive evil? In all this did not Job sin with his lips.—*Job 2:10*

Job did not have very much help in his struggle. His wife encouraged him to curse God and die. His three friends came quickly to his aid, but only tried to convince him that he was guilty of some forgotten sin against God.

Job understood that both good and evil are in our world, but he didn't understand that the evil did not come from God. We can see that thinking in our memory verse. However, Job reminds his wife that with all the blessings we receive, we also receive things that we really don't want or need.

As a pastor, I feel it is my duty to help people with their faith when tragedy strikes. Often people will say that God will not put more on them than they can bear. I want to say to them, "Look, God did not put this on you." The book of Job does not give us all the answers, but it certainly answers many important questions. Is God on our side? Yes, most certainly so. Is God aware when we are hurting? Yes, God knew every pain Job experienced. God does not walk ahead of us or behind us, but *with* us, even in suffering.

Weekday Problems

The church secretary called to tell me that a family was in crisis at the hospital. They were expecting their second child and the mother went into labor early. The baby had been born, but was in critical condition. When I arrived at the hospital a nurse was waiting for me at the elevator. She whisked me up to the delivery floor and into this young mother's room. On the way up the nurse told me the child was not going to live. Only a ventilator was keeping him alive.

I can remember trying to minister to that family. I have never felt so hopeless in my entire life. I never expected what would happen during the coming days. This family actually ministered to me by their faith. They refused to blame God. They said that God had blessed both them and the baby because he would have lived a painful life full of suffering had he not died. They took the view that the baby came from the arms of God and returned to the arms of God. According to the family, the infant stayed here long enough to bless them by showing them firsthand the love of God. It takes great faith to look into the eyes of tragedy and see the hand of God.

*Have you ever experienced good in the midst of apparent evil?

*How would you comfort this young mother in her sorrow?

Problems and Blessings

It's easy to give large doses of advice to some who is hurting, but sometimes it's difficult to swallow.

***

An alarm clock is certainly a great blessing in that it helps many people rise and shine. The problem is that it makes some people rise and whine.

***

Alimony is a blessing for a single parent. The problem is that it's the billing without the cooing.

***

Boss to wife: The good news is that we've installed a system that requires all employees to take an aptitude test. The bad news is that I flunked it.

***

Fortunately, the last word in an argument is what a wife has. Unfortunately, anything a husband says after that is the beginning of another argument.

This Lesson in Your Life

Job was a good man who was stripped of his wealth, his children, and his health. He does not know why this has happened to him, but the reader is fully aware it is the work of the devil. Satan assumes that the only reason Job serves God is so that God will bless him with wealth. Job is an extremely wealthy man for his time. This was in the days where wealth was measured in the size of your herds and your family.

My father was a farmer and also a man of faith. He trusted God, read his Bible each night, and never missed church or a day's work. However, one thing that disturbed my dad very much was how his neighbors who never went to church seemed to have more than he did in the way of possessions. My father's favorite song was "Farther Along." His favorite verse went: "While there are others living about us, never molested though in the wrong." My dad had a keen sense of right and wrong. To him, everything was black and white. The good should prosper and the wrong should suffer. Sometimes I wish the world were that simple.

Job clearly rejects his friends' theory that he suffered because he had committed a grave sin. He also rejects their advice to repent and make peace with God. Instead, he insists on his own innocence and questions the justice of God. Scholars tell us that the story of Job is one of the oldest stories in the Bible, although when it was actually written down is a matter of debate.

It is interesting that people today still react as Job did to tragedy. Often when we suffer, friends gather and offer their explanation of why it happened. I have often wondered how much the presence of Job's friends comforted him. I know that in my life, the support of family and friends is irreplaceable. Like Job's friends, they have good motives of love and devotion. However, they move us no closer to answering the "why" question than did Job's friends. Our faith may falter, and we have unanswered questions, just as in Job's case. We wonder why God did not prevent the tragedy.

Grief and loss are universal in our world. Sooner or later we will all know what it is like to lose someone close to us. If we live long enough, we will experience the sorrow of disease and sickness. Perhaps we can prepare ourselves to some extent by nailing down our faith and concentrating on the things we do know. God loves us. We can no more explain the mystery of tragedy than we can explain the mysteries of the universe. But we know that if God is great enough to create such a magical universe, He can see us through our most difficult moments.

STRAIGHT

1. How many children did Job have?
Job had seven sons and three daughters.

2. How did Job make provision for the sins of his children?

He offered sacrifices to God for all of his children in case they had sinned in some way.

3. What was Satan doing with his time on the earth?
He was going from one end of the earth to the other.

4. What happened to Job's children in the story?
They were killed when the roof of the house of Job's oldest son collapsed during a storm.

5. What happened to Job's servants and animals?
The Sabeans stole the oxen and asses. Lightning struck and killed his sheep and the servants watching them. The Chaldeans stole the camels.

6. What did Job do when he learned of the death of his children?
He rent his mantle, shaved his head, and fell down upon the ground and worshiped God.

7. After Satan took Job's children and possessions and he did not curse God, what did Satan do to him?
He caused him to break out in boils from his head to his feet.

8. What did Job's three friends do when they saw Job?
They wept and rent their mantles, and threw dust upon their heads—all as signs of mourning.

9. When Job finally spoke to his friends, what did he say?
He cursed the day he was born.

10. What was Job's wish?
He wished that he had not been born.

There is an old saying that misery loves company. This is certainly true. No one wants to be hurting alone. I grew up as an only child. I think I appreciated my friends much more than my playmates who had siblings at home. I would have given anything to have had a brother or sister to comfort me when I was hurting. Nothing is said about Job's siblings. He had his wife and his three friends, but they were certainly poor comforters.

We are told today by social experts that people do not have the need, as we once did, for organized religion. People today are reluctant to join a church. It seems commitment is a problem for some. However, the comfort and love of a church family is invaluable to someone who is hurting.

There is one good thing you can say about Job's friends. They were faithful. The Bible tells us that they sat with him for seven days before they could say a word. They were aware of Job's great hurt, and they were afraid they would say the wrong thing. They also grieved themselves because they were watching their friend hurt. None of us like to see our friends hurt. I cannot imagine how people survive a tragedy without the warmth and attention of fellow Christians. The church offers something that money cannot buy: help in time of need. This is not superficial help but the strength of genuineness and compassion. I have seen it more times than I can count. Does your church do a good job of comforting those who are suffering from sickness and grief?

Loss can come in many ways. I heard a story once of a woman who had stopped attending church. When someone asked her what happened, she said that she had lost her husband. After some discussion about the circumstances she echoed the thoughts of her heart. Through tears she said, "If my husband had died, the ladies of the church would have been here with covered dishes and words of comfort. Instead he has left me and wants a divorce. I haven't seen anyone from the church."

We grieve in different ways and our churches must be ready to respond to different kinds of grief. Everyone hurts. Everyone must be willing to comfort.

Job 14:1-2, 11-17; 32:6-8; 34:12, 37:14-19

Man that is born of a woman is of few days, and full of trouble.

2 He cometh forth like a flower, and is cut down: he fleeth also as a shadow, and continueth not.

11 As the waters fail from the sea, and the flood decayeth and drieth up:

12 So man lieth down, and riseth not: till the heavens be no more, they shall not awake, nor be raised out of their sleep.

13 O that thou wouldest hide me in the grave, that thou wouldest keep me secret, until thy wrath be past, that thou wouldest appoint me a set time, and remember me!

14 If a man die, shall he live again? all the days of my appointed time will I wait, till my change come.

15 Thou shalt call, and I will answer thee: thou wilt have a desire to the work of thine hands.

16 For now thou numberest my steps: dost thou not watch over my sin?

17 My transgression is sealed up in a bag, and thou sewest up mine iniquity.

32:6 And Elihu the son of Barachel the Buzite answered and said, I am young, and ye are very old; wherefore I was afraid, and durst not shew you mine opinion.

7 I said days should speak, and mul-titude of years should teach wisdom.

8 But there is a spirit in man: and the inspiration of the Almighty giveth them understanding.

34:12 Yea, surely God will not do wickedly, neither will the Almighty pervert judgment.

37:14 Hearken unto this, O Job: stand still, and consider the wondrous works of God.

15 Dost thou know when God disposed them, and caused the light of his cloud to shine?

16 Dost thou know the balancings of the clouds, the wondrous works of him which is perfect in knowledge?

17 How thy garments are warm, when he quieteth the earth by the south wind?

18 Hast thou with him spread out the sky, which is strong, and as a molten looking glass?

19 Teach us what we shall say unto him; for we cannot order our speech by reason of darkness.

Devotional Reading
Job 36:24-33
Background Scripture
Job 14:32:1-8; 34:10-15; 37:14-24
Memory Selection
Job 14:14

April 9

311

Since our last lesson, three men have sat with Job seven days and nights in silent support of their friend. Then, unable to keep their counsel any longer, they pour out the conventional wisdom that Job is suffering because he is sinful. Job protested that he has done the best he can. Now, in this lesson, he reflects on the brevity and uncertainty of a person's life, and his inability to see his faults clearly.

Then a new voice enters the dialogue. Elihu, a younger man claims to hesitate to speak in the presence of his elders; but then proceeds to rebuke them with what he feels is his superior wisdom. His main contribution to the discussion is that Job should not complain because he, as other mortals, lacks the wisdom to see God's plan for our lives.

೮೦೦೩

Invite group members to put themselves in the shoes of the four friends who offer Job counsel in his suffering. Ask for "one-liners" often handed out to those who suffer, whether they're adequate or not. Contributions may run like this:

Job, we suffer when we don't do God's will . . . Examine your life, Job, and confess your wrongs . . . Job, *we aren't meant to understand why we suffer. Relax! . . . We may not know why we suffer, Job, but God is in control . . . I understand exactly how you feel, Job.*

Point out that while such counsel is well-meaning, the book of Job shows that there are no "pat" answers to why the innocent suffer; and that sometimes the best we can do is to sit with a suffering friend in a "ministry of silence," as three of Job's friends did—for a week!

Teaching Outline	Daily Bible Readings

I. Helpless in the Dark—14:1-2, 11-17
 A. Life is fleeting, 14:1-2
 B. The eternal yearning, 11-17
 1. Hiding in the grave, 11-13
 2. Hoping for life, 14-15
 3. Hidden transgression, 16-17
II. Hope in God's Hands—32:6-8; 34:12; 37:14-19
 A. A young man speaks, 32:6-8
 B. God is just, 34:12
 C. We lack knowledge, 37:14-19
 1. Only God rules the heavens, 14-18
 2. We live in darkness, 19
	Mon. Pleading for Relief
	    Job 14:1-6
	Tue. The Grave as Refuge
	    Job 14:7-17
	Wed. No Hope Apart from God
	    Job 14:18-22
	Thu. Wise Men Lack Answers
	    Job 32:1-10
	Fri. God Will Do Right
	    Job 34:11-15
	Sat. Great Beyond Knowing
	    Job 36:24-33
	Sun. Just Beyond Understanding
	    Job 37:14-24

Verse by Verse

I. Helpless in the Dark–14:1-2, 11-17
A. Life is fleeting, 14:1-2
   1 Man that is born of a woman is of few days, and full of trouble.
   2 He cometh forth like a flower, and is cut down: he fleeth also as a shadow, and continueth not.

At this point in the book of Job, the world's most famous sufferer is in dialogue with three friends. Although they are well-meaning, their main "answer" to Job's problems is that he suffers because of some sin he committed. Job answers that while he isn't perfect, his suffering is worse than he deserves.

"Man that is born of woman" means "everyone." When we are suffering, as Job was, all our days seem only to contain trouble. Although Job's words here are bleak, verse 1 joins many other passages in this book that are so profound that they have become a part of the accepted wisdom of the ages. We hear its wisdom at funerals, and the older we get the more we understand its truth: life is fleeting, and brief. As children, the years can seem to drag on as we long to be older. As older persons, we wonder where the years went.
B. The eternal yearning, 11-17
1. Hiding in the grave, 11-13
   11 As the waters fail from the sea, and the flood decayeth and drieth up:
   12 So man lieth down, and riseth not: till the heavens be no more, they shall not awake, nor be raised out of their sleep.
   13 O that thou wouldest hide me in the grave, that thou wouldest keep me secret, until thy wrath be past, that thou wouldest appoint me a set time, and remember me!

Job's suffering is so acute that he cites the universal fact of death as his only hope! At least in the grave (Heb. *sheol*, vs. 13) he would not be conscious of his physical and psychic pain (remember that he has lost his family and possessions, and is covered with painful sores). Job's vision of life after death is typical of the Old Covenant. Not surprisingly, it is less hopeful than those who accept the revelation of a resurrection by the power of Christ. Yet even in the Old Testament life after death is expressed as a hope, as in the next verse.
2. Hoping for life, 14-15
   14 If a man die, shall he live again? all the days of my appointed time will I wait, till my change come.
   15 Thou shalt call, and I will answer thee: thou wilt have a desire to the work of thine hands.

Verse 14 is another classic line that has become a part of the collective memory of virtually all English-speaking people because it voices the universal hope of life after death. Although it is in the form of a question, the context indicates that Job wants to answer, Yes! This hope appears even in non-biblical religions; but without the resurrection of Christ as a "guarantee" that the hope will come true, it can only be voiced as a question. Job yearns for it so strongly that he "leans into the future" and ventures at least limited confidence that a "change" will come, from death to life.

Job's view of God leads him to the conclusion that He will not abandon the ones He created to the grave, but will issue a "resurrection call" that Job looks forward to answering. He expresses an even more famously optimistic view in 19:25-26, a remarkably prophetic statement of the resurrection hope.

3. Hidden transgression, 16-17

16 For now thou numberest my steps: dost thou not watch over my sin?

17 My transgression is sealed up in a bag, and thou sewest up mine iniquity.

Hope for life after death aside, Job hurts in this life. He feels hounded by a God who never grows weary of testing him. God seems to have put a "tracking device" on him like the electronic surveillance devices in a modern detective tale, looking "narrowly unto all my paths" (13:27).

There can be a positive sense to "numbering our days" (Ps. 90:12); but to Job God seems to be counting each of his steps as part of a plot to punish him—looking for some sin that He will not reveal, but keeps sewn up in a bag. This is a universal frustration for all who think suffering is punishment for specific sins.

II. Hope in God's Hands—32:6-8; 34:12; 37:14-19

A. A young man speaks, 32:6-8

6 And Elihu the son of Barachel the Buzite answered and said, I am young, and ye are very old; wherefore I was afraid, and durst not shew you mine opinion.

7 I said days should speak, and multitude of years should teach wisdom.

8 But there is a spirit in man: and the inspiration of the Almighty giveth them understanding.

Up to now, the dialogue in the book of Job has been among Job and three friends—Eliphaz, Bildad, and Zophar (2:11). After sitting with Job for seven days and nights, they took turns unleashing bitter streams of verbiage which they pretend is for Job's comfort, but which actually repeat in tiresome detail the theme that God is punishing Job for some sin. This sense seems to be built into the human psyche: even people who do not pretend to be believers often look to the skies and mutter "What did I do to deserve this?"

Now a new voice enters the dialogue, that of a younger man, Elihu. He pretends to be humble, having de-

314

layed entering the debate out of deference for his elders. Now, however, the "spirit in man" bursts forth; he can no longer be silent. Unfortunately, while he will give Job some of the same counsel as God will later, Elihu does so with something of the arrogance of youth, and indicates that in some way he is the epitome of the "angry young man."

B. God is just, 34:12

12 Yea, surely God will not do wickedly, neither will the Almighty pervert judgment.

Actually, Job has not accused God of "doing wickedly," although that inference might be drawn from the simple fact that Job has protested that he has not sinned in proportion to his suffering, with the implicit accusation that God has not dealt justly with him. However we may resent Elihu's arrogance, what he says here should be taken seriously. Even when we suffer, it may be evidence of God's paternal care and concern, as a loving father disciplines his children (Heb. 12:5-13). To attribute evil to God is not only to falsely impugn His character. It is also to cast doubt on the way good and evil are defined. In a sense, God *is* goodness personified. An example is in the arena of truth-telling, in which "It is impossible for God to lie" (Heb. 6:18). For "the Good" to do the evil of lying is a contradiction in terms.

C. We lack knowledge, 37:14-19
1. Only God rules the heavens, 14-18

14 Hearken unto this, O Job: stand still, and consider the wondrous works of God.

15 Dost thou know when God disposed them, and caused the light of his cloud to shine?

16 Dost thou know the balancings of the clouds, the wondrous works of him which is perfect in knowledge?

17 How thy garments are warm, when he quieteth the earth by the south wind?

18 Hast thou with him spread out the sky, which is strong, and as a molten looking glass?

Now Elihu launches into a spiel along the lines by which God will correct Job's understanding later in the book, but since it is based only on the limited experience of youth it lacks the same convincing authority. Elihu does not answer the question of why the innocent suffer, but insists that God is so great, and man is so small, that it is presumptuous to "haul God into court." When Job can control the weather and order the heavenly bodies, *then* let him presume to argue on an equal with God.

2. We live in darkness, 19

19 Teach us what we shall say unto him; for we cannot order our speech by reason of darkness.

Elihu's last word here is almost a taunt to Job, inviting him to instruct us in what to say, as a prosecuting attorney might shed light on God's "errors." The fact is that the merely human plane on which we dwell is too dark to see even how God orders the heavens, much less how He balances good and evil on the earth.

Evangelistic Emphasis

I have a friend who owns a large department store. Every time something new comes in that he thinks would interest me, he has to show me. The other day he took me to the men's toiletry counter. He had a new spray that was labeled "Rose Water." I wasn't sure I wanted any "rose water" because it sounded like something a woman would like. He told me to take off my glasses and close my eyes. When I did he sprayed my face with a cool mist. I was pleasantly surprised. It was late in the day and the cool, slightly scented mist felt good on my face. I had just walked across the parking lot and the temperature was 95 degrees. Needless to say, he made a quick sale. I love the stuff! I keep it at my desk for a quick refresher in the afternoon.

This is something like what God does when the cruelty of the world weighs down upon us. We are tired of the struggle and we need His cool, refreshing voice to comfort us. Yet to depend on God only when trouble comes speaks of a lack of faith. To have real faith, one must depend on God in the good times and the bad. Still, it is good to serve a God who can provide us with that refreshment of the soul only He can give.

৪০৫৪

Memory Selection

If a man die, shall he live again? All the days of my appointed time will I wait, till my change come.—*Job 14:14*

As long as humanity has existed, people have been asking Job's question. In Jesus' day, it was in hot debate. The Pharisees believed in life after death, the Sadducees did not. Jesus entered the debate when the Sadducees approached Him about a woman who had lost her husband and married his brother. The question to Jesus was not asked to make Him choose sides, but to trap Him into the sin of violating the law of Moses. Jesus not only believed in life after death; He demonstrated it by His resurrection. Perhaps that's what the Bible means when it calls Jesus "the pioneer and perfecter of our faith" (Heb. 12:2 RSV). He was the first to come back from the grave and not die again. Now that's what I call a true pioneer!

The comfort that will sustain us over time is the comfort in knowing that we will see our loved ones again. Jesus promised that we would, and this is the hope of every Christian.

My mother gave birth to a little girl 11 months before I was born. The baby died after living only three days. To this day I wish that I could have known her. I wish that I could have grown up with her and that she was in my life today. My hope and comfort is that I will see her one day. I can answer the question that Job posed thousands of years ago. Yes, Job. We will live again!

Weekday Problems

When tragedy strikes, everyone has a choice. We can blame God or we can ask God to help us through the trial. If we choose to blame God, we will be like Job and his friends: without answers. If we choose to seek God's help, we still will not have all the answers but we will have the greatest power in the universe at our disposal. Which would you rather do?

David Brainerd is not a name you probably would recognize. His father died when he was 7, and by the age of 14 his mother had passed away as well. He was depressed until his conversion at age 21. After that, he was sick most of his life until he died at age 29.

However, during the eight years of his Christian life, David Brainerd kept a diary of his walk with God. In 1749, Jonathan Edwards published his diary under the title, "An Account of the Life of the late Reverend Mr. David Brainerd." This book influenced Baptist William Carey, Methodist Thomas Coke, Anglican Henry Martyn, and countless other religious leaders. Other than Jesus Christ, few have had more positive influence than David Brainerd in such a short life.

When tragedy comes we cannot see anything but the tragedy itself. God has a way of miraculously turning tragedy into triumph. Our job is not to understand but to trust. Trust in God.

Obesity Alert!

It's not the minutes you spend at the table that make you fat. It's the seconds.

***

I fell asleep on the beach and burned my stomach. You should see my pot roast!

***

Wife: I've lost quite a bit of weight.
Husband: Well, I sure don't see it.
Wife: Of course you don't. I *lost* it.

***

Wife, measuring her husband's waist: It's amazing when you think that it takes an oak tree 200 years to get that big around!

***

The public health service reports that there are at least 20 million overweight people in the United States. Of course those are round figures . . . really round.

This Lesson in Your Life

Perhaps if Job lived today we might say he was having a mid-life crisis. Psychologists say that some of us, mostly men, go through a time when we contemplate life and its brevity. When we look back at our lives we are indeed reminded that life is short, at best. Job is not only grieving for the loss of his family. He is also suffering from physical pain. He wishes that his life would end.

Then Job makes an about turn. He boldly states that even if God kills him, he will still serve him. What a triumphal statement of faith! I wonder sometimes if, when confronted with problems such as Job's, we would be able to make such a statement.

Have you ever wondered why God always chooses to deal with human-kind on the basis of faith? It is obvious that trust is a big issue with God. When God called Abram out of Ur of the Chaldeas, he had no idea where God was leading him. He asked, but all God would tell him was that He would show him the place. When he came to Haran, Abram must have been tempted to stay. Surely he could have said that he had gone far enough, and God would just have to make do. Sometimes when we face trouble we would be happy to only go half-way with God. Grief is a process. It is also a balm that God gives us to heal after a loss. Some people want to bury their grief because it is too hurtful to go on. That is where trust in God comes in. We must trust Him to carry us when we can't walk any more.

I can remember teaching my oldest daughter how to ride her bike. I have never run so many miles in all my life. The entire time I was holding on to the back seat of that little pink bicycle, I was praying that she would not fall and that this would be the time she finally learned to balance. Years later, when her younger sister began to ride, I encouraged training wheels. I didn't have much confidence in them, but I was buying time. I was older and not confident that I could run as far as I did with her sister. One day I came home and my son had just taken the training wheels off and my little girl was about to ride down the driveway. Before I could yell "Stop!" she pushed off. She never fell. She rode that bike from the beginning and I never had to run along behind her. I had absolutely no faith in her ability.

I know that is the way we appear to God sometimes. We have experience with God. He has never let us down. Only when we do not fully understand does it appear that He has failed us. The real truth is that He will never fail us. He is on our side. He loves us.

1. To what does Job compare a man's life?
Job says that a man is like a flower, a shadow, and a tree.

2. What is Job's question to God about eternal life?
Job asks, "If a man dies, will he live again?"

3. Who was the young man who counseled Job when his three friends had given up?
Elihu the Buzite.

4. How did Elihu defend God?
He said that God's intention for humankind is good and not wicked.

5. How does Job describe life in 14:1?
Man is of few days and full of trouble.

6. How did Elihu encourage Job to look at God?
He encouraged Job to look on the majesty of God.

7. What motivated Elihu to speak with Job?
He was angered because Job justified himself rather than God.

8. What others made Elihu angry, and why?
Job's three friends angered him because they didn't have answers and only condemned Job.

9. Why did Elihu wait until last to speak?
He waited until last out of respect because the others were older.

10. Where did Elihu claim to get his inspiration?
From the Spirit of God.

The problem with the book of Job is that you have to read the entire book to get a feeling of redemption. Job and his friends go on and on about their troubles until the reader begins to wonder if God will ever speak. Elihu is a refreshing change, and he comes just in time. It's interesting that he is young, and yet seems so wise.

I sometimes think that we rob ourselves in the church of leadership because we overlook our youth. I sat recently in a committee meeting that was charged with hiring a new staff member. There was a young lady on the committee that had just graduated high school. I marveled at her wisdom and depth. In fact, the committee asked her to go to the front of the room and write down all the qualifications for a new minister we were looking for. As the crowd began to shout out suggestions, she would quickly evaluate the merit and would often challenge the person making the suggestion to defend it. It was amazing to watch, and was a lesson to us all.

I once asked a psychologist why some people always insisted on control. He explained that often when a person is insecure he demands control because he knows what the result will be and he can control the process. In that way, he will not be put on the spot. If he can control the questions and the answers, he will never be embarrassed. It made sense to me.

I do wonder, however, if that is the case with God. Do we not turn control over to God because we are not sure of the outcome? Are we afraid that God will ask us to do something that we can't do or that we do not want to do? I'm sure that Job thought he had lost complete control over his life and his world. However, we know that God was still acting in His power to control the end result.

It is unsettling to turn our lives over to God. However, when we think about the fact that God knows the outcome, it becomes a little easier.

Job 38:1,4, 16-17; 42:1-2, 5; Mark 16:1-7, 9-14

When the LORD answered Job out of the whirlwind, and said, Where wast thou when I laid the foundations of the earth? declare, if thou hast understanding.

16 Hast thou entered into the springs of the sea? or hast thou walked in the search of the depth?

17 Have the gates of death been opened unto thee? or hast thou seen the doors of the shadow of death?

42:1 Then Job answered the LORD, and said,

2 I know that thou canst do every thing, and that no thought can be withholden from thee.

5 I have heard of thee by the hearing of the ear: but now mine eye seeth thee.

Mark 16:1 And when the Sabbath was past, Mary Magdalene, and Mary the mother of James, and Salome, had bought sweet spices, that they might come and anoint him.

2 And very early in the morning the first day of the week, they came unto the sepulchre at the rising of the sun.

3 And they said among themselves, Who shall roll us away the stone from the door of the sepulchre?

4 And when they looked, they saw that the stone was rolled away: for it was very great.

5 And entering into the sepulchre, they saw a young man sitting on the right side, clothed in a long white garment; and they were affrighted.

6 And he saith unto them, Be not affrighted: Ye seek Jesus of Nazareth, which was crucified: he is risen; he is not here: behold the place where they laid him.

7 But go your way, tell his disciples and Peter that he goeth before you into Galilee: there shall ye see him, as he said unto you.

9 Now when Jesus was risen early the first day of the week, he appeared first to Mary Magdalene, out of whom he had cast seven devils.

10 And she went and told them that had been with him, as they mourned and wept.

11 And they, when they had heard that he was alive, and had been seen of her, believed not.

12 After that he appeared in another form unto two of them, as they walked, and went into the country.

13 And they went and told it unto the residue: neither believed they them.

14 Afterward he appeared unto the eleven as they sat at meat, and upbraided them with their unbelief and hardness of heart, because they believed not them which had seen him after he was risen.

April 16

Devotional Reading
Luke 24:1-9

Background Scripture
Job 38:1-4, 16-17; 42:1-6; Mark 16

Memory Selection
Mark 16:6

At first glance, it may seem quite a leap from the brooding pessimism of the book of Job to the Easter story. A second look at these texts, however, reveals the underlying theme that *the resurrection of Jesus is the ultimate answer to Job's anguished quest to find meaning in suffering.*

For all his distress, Job is not the worst case of the innocent sufferer. After all, Job admitted that he was a sinner. The ultimate example of innocent suffering is Jesus, God's Son. Although having lived a sinless life, He was unjustly condemned, cruelly tortured, and finally executed. Somehow, while we may never fathom the details of why *we* suffer, believers find in the resurrection of Jesus, the Messiah, that *life,* not suffering and death, is the last word in the human story.

A vivid introduction to this lesson is to ask one group member to read a part of God's challenge to Job's previous complaints, and another to respond with Job's statement of hope, and his final confession of inadequacy.

Although God does not give a final answer to why the innocent suffer, He charges that until Job could function as a "Creator," he could never have the depth of knowledge he seeks. A reader might summarize this charge by reading **Job 40:6-14.**

In reply, ask another reader to read how Job anticipates "Easter" in **19:25,** and his final confession in **Job 42:1-6.** Then note that the lesson will move to Mark's account of Christ's resurrection, which shows that God's final word on the story of life is *new life,* not *death.*

Teaching Outline	*Daily Bible Readings*

I. God's Challenge—Job 38:1, 4, 16-17
  A. 'Where were you?,' 1, 4
  B. 'Do you know the depths?,' 16-17
II. Job's Reply—42:1-2, 5
III. 'He Is Risen!'—Mark 16:1-7
  A. Solemn duty, 1-2
  B. Astonishing discovery, 3-5
  C. A 'great commission,' 6-7
IV. Testimony and Appearances—9-14, 20
  A. Too good to be true, 9-11
  B. Other appearances, 12-14
	Mon. Where Were You?
	    Job 38:1-7
	Tue. Do You Understand Creation?
	    Job 38:8-18
	Wed. I Know You, and I Repent
	    Job 42:1-6
	Thu. Job's Fortunes Restored
	    Job 42:10-17
	Fri. 'He Is Not Here!'
	    Mark 16:1-8
	Sat. Jesus Appears
	    Mark 16:9-14
	Sun. 'Go Tell the Good News!'
	    Mark 16:15-20

Verse by Verse

I. God's Challenge–Job 38:1, 4, 16-17

A. 'Where were you?,' 1, 4

1 Then the LORD answered Job out of the whirlwind, and said,

4 Where wast thou when I laid the foundations of the earth? declare, if thou hast understanding.

God asserts here that to answer such a universal question as why the innocent suffer we would have to have universal and divine knowledge, not only of human life but of creation itself. Obviously, Job cannot know this, so God rebukes him for the sin of presumptuousness.

B. 'Do you know the depths?,' 16-17

16 Hast thou entered into the springs of the sea? or hast thou walked in the search of the depth?

17 Have the gates of death been opened unto thee? or hast thou seen the doors of the shadow of death?

To His question about where Job was at creation, God now adds more specific areas of man's ignorance. How could someone who demands to know why a loved is lost at sea, for example, possibly expect to discover an answer if he has not "entered into the springs of the sea"— in other worlds, knows nothing of its origins and mechanism?

Furthermore, in verse 17, God asks how we could expect to explain why and how people die without hav-

ing had "the gates of death" opened to us, as though we could learn all about it in a book. (The second line of verse 17 repeats the thought of the first, reminding us that virtually all of the book of Job is written in poetry, and that Hebrew poetry "rhymes" in thought, not sound.)

II. Job's Reply—42:1-2, 5

1 Then Job answered the LORD, and said,

2 I know that thou canst do every thing, and that no thought can be withholden from thee.

5 I have heard of thee by the hearing of the ear: but now mine eye seeth thee.

To Job's credit, his previous defenses melt before God's rhetorical questions and the other ways He has reminded Job that mere humanity cannot fathom the ways of God. Note that in verse 2 Job rightly credits God with knowing both the outer ways in which the world works, and the inner thought world of man. It is no accident that both realms are involved in the unanswerable question of why the innocent suffer: outer events (such as floods, earthquakes, and the events that destroyed Job's wealth and family) are interpreted by inner thoughts, resulting in the questions that have plagued Job (and that his friends have wrongly supposed they can answer).

Of course Job has not actually "seen" God with the *eye*, but with the *understanding* (as we say "I see," when we are given an answer to a question). What Job "sees" is that he *cannot* see, at least into all the workings of the world and the ways of its Creator. Even what he is "seeing" now, however, is a great blessing. God has condescended to speak personally with Job, and to deal with, if not answer, his questions about suffering. This rare appearance should reassure even modern sufferers that our questions are not an affront to God. He rebukes Job and his friends for being presumptuous, not for being honest in saying "This seems wrong, and I don't understand it!"

III. 'He Is Risen!'—Mark 16:1-7
A. Solemn duty, 1-2

1 And when the Sabbath was past, Mary Magdalene, and Mary the mother of James, and Salome, had bought sweet spices, that they might come and anoint him.

2 And very early in the morning the first day of the week, they came unto the sepulchre at the rising of the sun.

To coincide with the celebration of Easter, the lesson text now moves thousands of years forward, to a scene that at first may seem unrelated to the questions of Job. Yet there is a a very close one relationship; for ultimately our hope in dealing with the problem of innocent suffering lies in the story of the empty tomb.

The suffering of Jesus surpasses every story of human suffering. Although, as the book of Job shows, not every incident of suffering is due to immediate sin on the part of the sufferer, much of it is. As the Hebrew writer reminds us, God *may* allow us to suffer as a means of discipline and a sign of His fatherly love (Heb. 12:6). Jesus, however, lived a sinless life. Instead of our question, "What did I do to deserve this?," Scripture poses a larger question: *What did Christ do to deserve the Cross?* Nothing, of course; His suffering was His free choice, overwhelming our own unanswered questions by His own death, atonement for our sins, and the triumph of the resurrection.

The women here are doing on Sunday what laws against working on the Sabbath prohibited—embalming the body of their Lord. Historic Christianity would soon elevate this "first day of the week" into the universally accepted day of worship, replacing the Sabbath with Sunday, "the Lord's Day."

B. Astonishing discovery, 3-5

3 And they said among themselves, Who shall roll us away the stone from the door of the sepulchre?

4 And when they looked, they saw that the stone was rolled away: for it was very great.

5 And entering into the sepulchre, they saw a young man sitting on the right side, clothed in a long white garment; and they were affrighted.

The stone before the tomb presented a problem to the women not only because of its great weight and size, but because it had been sealed (Matt. 27:66). Although the seals may have only been wax, the women could not legally break them. Imagine their surprise, however, to discover that all such problems are banished by divine intervention. Matthew calls the "young man" an angel (282), while Luke speaks of "two men in dazzling apparel" (24:4).

C. A 'great commission,' 6-7

6 And he saith unto them, Be not affrighted: Ye seek Jesus of Nazareth, which was crucified: he is risen; he is not here: behold the place where they laid him.

7 But go your way, tell his disciples and Peter that he goeth before you into Galilee: there shall ye see him, as he said unto you.

The angel seeks to banish the natural fright of the women in words designed to remind them that Jesus himself had said he would rise after three days (Matt. 12:40; 26:61). The women become the first "evangelists" as they disperse to tell Christ's closest followers of the miracle of the empty tomb. (The wording "The disciples and Peter" indicates that Peter's leadership is already appearing.) The Galilean appearance is recorded in Matthew 28:16-17.

IV. Testimony and Appearances— 9-14, 20

A. Too good to be true, 9-11

9 Now when Jesus was risen early the first day of the week, he appeared first to Mary Magdalene, out of whom he had cast seven devils.

10 And she went and told them that had been with him, as they mourned and wept.

11 And they, when they had heard that he was alive, and had been seen of her, believed not.

The narrative seems to repeat vs. 1 because, as the notes in many Bibles indicate, the earliest manuscripts of Mark end with verse 8. Yet the incidents recorded here agree in broad outline with the accounts of Jesus' resurrection and appearances in the other Gospels.

B. Other appearances, 12-14

12 After that he appeared in another form unto two of them, as they walked, and went into the country.

13 And they went and told it unto the residue: neither believed they them.

14 Afterward he appeared unto the eleven as they sat at meat, and upbraided them with their unbelief and hardness of heart, because they believed not them which had seen him after he was risen.

Verse 12 likely refers to the Lord's appearance to the disciples on the road to Emmaus (Luke 24:13-35). The appearance to the 11 apostles (Judas has hanged himself) is back in Jerusalem, as described in Luke 24:36-49. Christ's rebuke for their "hardness of heart" was based on the fact that they should have accepted the prophecies and His own promise that He would rise again.

325

Evangelistic Emphasis

The Bible is filled with metaphors and examples of the resurrection. Genesis begins with the story of hope as God creates light from darkness. Hope of life beyond death is a common theme in Job. The metaphor that Job uses of a sprout growing from a stump is only one example.

Also in Job is the hope of restoration after disaster. God doesn't tell Job all he wants to know, but he does reassure him that He (God) has been in control of our world since the beginning. Job was so focused on his condition that he could not see God's rule.

Job, like so many today, did not recognize the source of his trouble. He assumed it was God. It is interesting to note that God does not attempt to defend himself. Neither does he condemn Job for his lack of faith. This same loving, patient God is seen throughout the Scriptures.

God prepared a new life for Job. He restored his fortune and his family. Job went from brokenness to blessing. In much the same way, God restored Christ. Just as Jesus' body was broken, He arose to reveal a new body that was fully restored. Just as Job bore the scars of his experience, so Jesus bore the scars of the crucifixion. Job was a forerunner of Jesus.

ॐ◌ॐ

Memory Selection

And he saith unto them, Be not affrighted: Ye seek Jesus of Nazareth, which was crucified: he is risen; he is not here: behold the place where they laid him.—*Mark 16:6*

To the early Church, the resurrection was not simply an event in the life of Christ. It was everything. So important was the resurrection that the early Christians broke with tradition and moved their worship from the Sabbath to the first day of the week. The resurrection story was certainly an earth-shattering moment for those first disciples, and their excitement over that event has carried on through the centuries.

The baptismal pools in the earliest churches were carved out of the floor. They looked exactly like a grave. When someone wanted to be marked as a Christian, he would submit himself for baptism. As he was lowered into the water, it was an exact mirror image of a burial. When he was raised, it was a sign that he would follow Christ in the resurrection of the dead. In Mark's account of the resurrection, the sign of the risen Savior was in the emptiness of the tomb. Perhaps the reason the other disciples did not believe was because they did not experience the empty tomb. It wasn't until Jesus actually met with them that they believed.

What is the evidence of the resurrection in your life?

Weekday Problems

A co-worker was talking to me about faith. He said that he thought he had enough faith that he could argue with God. Then he asked me if I had ever argued with God. I told him that indeed I have, but that I never associated it with faith.

When it comes to contending with God, Job wrote the book. Most of the poem records Job's constant challenge to God to tell him *why*. Why did this happen to him? Why did God allow it to happen? Was not God aware of his sinless life? Perhaps you have asked many of the same questions in one form or another.

The conclusion to the book of Job doesn't answer his questions. In fact, God's response simply gives us more questions. So what are we to conclude from Job? God makes it crystal clear to Job that as a mere human he could not understand the spiritual world. We also know by reading God's response that if God is anything, He is patient. He certainly had the power to do anything He wanted to punish Job, but that is not God's nature. His nature is to listen to our arguments and love us anyway.

This lesson combines the conclusion of Job with the resurrection of Christ. We see from both stories a pattern. The God who exercised almost unlimited patience with Job was the same God Incarnate who, day after day, continues to have patience with His disciples.

*What events and attitudes in our own times indicate God's patience?

Easter Chorus from Faust

Johann Wolfgang von Goethe

Christ is arisen,
    Joy to thee, mortal,
Out of His prison,
    Forth from its portal!
Christ is not sleeping,
    Seek Him no longer.
Strong was His keeping,
    Jesus was stronger.

Christ is arisen.
    Seek Him not here;
Lonely His prison,
    Empty His bier;

Vain His entombing,
    Spices and lawn,
Vain the perfuming,
    Jesus is gone.

Christ is arisen,
    Joy to thee, mortal!
Empty His prison,
    Broken its portal!
Rising, He giveth
    His shroud to the sod.
Risen, He liveth,
    And liveth to God.

This Lesson in Your Life

Have you ever been hurt? Someone said that emotional hurt is far greater than physical pain. The disciples' excitement as they entered the tomb is best seen when we look at their tremendous hurt just moments before. It is in this contrast that we see the rollercoaster of emotions that began to overwhelm them. They witnessed the agony of Christ in the Garden of Gethsemane. They saw Him beaten and nailed to a cross in shame. They saw the cruelty of the Romans toward their Lord. Such hurt! Such pain! On Friday, they were despondent and disillusioned. They were also afraid for their own lives. However, the following Sunday, their minds were mixed with confusion and excitement. Where was He? Is this person real, and is His message reliable? The words of the Savior began to make sense.

Job's journey was similar except for the time element. First, he experienced the shock of losing everything . . . home, family, possessions. Then, there was the long season of questioning God and refusing to admit fault. Friends came and offered their best counsel, but nothing could give Job the relief he needed. When God appeared on the scene, Job was confused and bewildered. However, God's word brought repentance and acceptance to Job. This eventually led him to restoration by the hand of God.

It is also interesting to note that God did not restore Job's fortunes until he had prayed for his friends. When we look at the Bible in its entirety, we can see how important others are in relationship to ourselves. The challenge of God to Abram was that his people should be a blessing to the world. Jesus' story of the Good Samaritan is a poignant example of our responsibility to others. What if the disciples had decided to keep this good news of the resurrection to themselves? Surely God would have found some way to share it with the world, but the disciples would have missed out on the greatest news ever told.

In Job we see the clear promise of the resurrection. In Mark we actually see the resurrection. One is a prophecy written in poetry. Another is a prose account of the events before and after the resurrection. Together, these narratives give us the assurance that every living thing is renewable. God did not end His creation with Genesis. He is always creating new life, both in our world and within our hearts. God, the Creator, never stops creating. Life is eternal.

STRAIGHT

1. Out of what medium did God speak to Job?
God spoke to Job from a whirlwind.

2. What did God tell Job to do?
He told him to gird up his loins like a man. God challenged Job's manhood perhaps because of his lack of faith.

3. Who came to the tomb on resurrection morning?
Mary Magdalene, Mary mother of James, and Salome.

4. What was their concern as they came to the sepulcher?
They wondered who would roll the stone away. They came to anoint His body, as was the custom.

5. What did they see when they entered the tomb?
They saw a young man sitting to the side, clothed in white garments.

6. What did this stranger tell them to do?
He told them to tell the disciples that Jesus was going to Galilee and would see them there.

7. When Mary reported to the disciples what she had seen at the sepulcher, what was their reaction?
At first they did not believe, despite the fact that Jesus on more than one occasion had told them what to expect.

8. What was Jesus' reaction when He met with the 11 disciples at a meal?
He upbraided them because they refused to believe the witness of the women.

9. What instructions did Jesus give the 11 disciples?
He told them to go into all the world and preach the gospel to everyone.

10. After Jesus ascended into heaven, what did the disciples do?
They preached everywhere, with signs confirming their words. The book of Acts records many of their experiences.

Sue and Cathy are sisters. They live in the same town and attend the same church. Both sisters lost their husbands within six months of each other, with Sue's husband dying first. When Sue's husband died, she told her pastor that she would never be able to recover from his death. The pastor did his best to help her in her grief, to explain the hope of the resurrection, and to assure her that life must go on. He explained that the church and her family would be valuable tools in overcoming her grief. Cathy was by her side and supportive, but Sue refused to believe that she would ever live a productive life.

When Cathy's husband died, she said the same things as Sue. Life was over as far as she was concerned. This was a hurt that would never go away. Then, almost a year after Sue's husband was buried, she met someone. This man became a companion for her. They were both in their 70s and enjoyed dancing and dining out. They shared many of the same friends. Sue continued to attend grief support classes, but her life definitely changed for the better.

Cathy, on the other hand, retreated into a cave of silence and isolation. She never allowed herself to meet anyone new. Her family and friends continued to worry about her, and did everything in their power to bring her out of her shell.

What was the difference in these sisters? In Sue's case, she experienced a new life. She was living her new life every day. In Cathy's case, she refused to look beyond her personal anguish.

The faith that, as Christ arose from the dead, we can also experience new life, was the primary difference.

When the disciples encountered the risen Christ, it made all the difference in the world. They saw and believed. However, for centuries believers have gathered in worship and praise to One whom they have not seen or touched. This universal Church is much larger than the small gatherings of those earliest bands of believers. No wonder Jesus said, "Blessed are those who believe and yet have not seen."

Ecclesiastes 1:1-9; John 20:19-23

The words of the Preacher, the son of David, king in Jerusalem.

2 Vanity of vanities, saith the Preacher, vanity of vanities; all is vanity.

3 What profit hath a man of all his labour which he taketh under the sun?

4 One generation passeth away, and another generation cometh: but the earth abideth for ever.

5 The sun also ariseth, and the sun goeth down, and hasteth to his place where he arose.

6 The wind goeth toward the south, and turneth about unto the north; it whirleth about continually, and the wind returneth again according to his circuits.

7 All the rivers run into the sea; yet the sea is not full; unto the place from whence the rivers come, thither they return again.

8 All things are full of labour; man cannot utter it: the eye is not satisfied with seeing, nor the ear filled with hearing.

9 The thing that hath been, it is that which shall be; and that which is done is that which shall be done: and there is no new thing under the sun.

10 Is there any thing whereof it may be said, See, this is new? it hath been already of old time, which was before us.

11 There is no remembrance of former things; neither shall there be any remembrance of things that are to come with those that shall come after.

John 20:19 Then the same day at evening, being the first day of the week, when the doors were shut where the disciples were assembled for fear of the Jews, came Jesus and stood in the midst, and saith unto them, Peace be unto you.

20 And when he had so said, he shewed unto them his hands and his side. Then were the disciples glad, when they saw the Lord.

21 Then said Jesus to them again, Peace be unto you: as my Father hath sent me, even so send I you.

22 And when he had said this, he breathed on them, and saith unto them, Receive ye the Holy Ghost:

23 Whose soever sins ye remit, they are remitted unto them; and whose soever sins ye retain, they are retained.

Devotional Reading
Luke 24:36-48
Background Reading
Eccles. 1:1-11; John 20:19-23
Memory Selection
John 20:19

331

The current unit theme, "Living with Creation's Uncertainty," is illustrated in this lesson and the next from the book of Ecclesiastes. This book is famous for its pessimistic outlook on life. In this lesson, however, the quest for meaning of which Ecclesiastes despairs is shown to be fulfilled in the resurrected Christ.

Including the text from John allows you to show how faith has the power to change our outlook from pessimism to optimism. It should also be admitted that the Old Covenant is not as bleak as the picture painted in Ecclesiastes. Jewish believers could look forward to the future, especially in light of Messianic prophecies. Yet Christ's appearances provide the fulfillment of that hope, along with a new purpose in life.

Recreate with your group how Jesus' disciples must have felt after His crucifixion. They had believed Him to be the long-awaited Messiah who would free them from the heavy hand of Rome. Then suddenly He was taken from them by the very power they detested.

Note that the despair the disciples must have felt can be compared with the general tone of the book of Ecclesiastes, which declares that "all is vanity." Then point out that the second part of today's lesson, which portrays Jesus in one of His post-resurrection appearances, cancels this pessimistic view, promising us a brighter future and new meaning for our lives. Reading Ecclesiastes without recalling Christ's resurrectiion yields an incomplete view of life and the renewed sense of meaning and purpose He gives.

Teaching Outline	Daily Bible Readings

I. 'All Is Vanity'—Eccles. 1:1-11
  A. Solomon's experiment, 1-2
  B. Nature's repetitive cycle, 3-7
    1. Day and night, 3-5
    2. Wind and water, 6-7
  C. 'No new thing,' 8-10
  D. No memories, 11
II. Vanity Is Vanquished—John 20:19-23
  A. Resurrection's proof, 19-20
  B. New Meaning and Mission, 21-23
	Mon. Nothing New Under the Sun
	    Eccles. 1:1-11
	Tue. Futility of Human Wisdom
	    Eccles 1:12-18
	Wed.Futility of Self-Indulgence
	    Eccles 2:1-11
	Thu. 'All Is Vanity'
	    Eccles. 2:12-17
	Fri. Of What Good Is Toil?
	    Eccles 2:18-26
	Sat. New Meaning and Mission
	    Luke 24:36-48
	Sun. 'Receive the Spirit'
	    John 20:19-23

Verse by Verse

I. 'All Is Vanity'—Eccles. 1:1-11
A. Solomon's experiment, 1-2

1 The words of the Preacher, the son of David, king in Jerusalem.

2 Vanity of vanities, saith the Preacher, vanity of vanities; all is vanity.

Translators have added the subtitle "The Preacher" to the book of Ecclesiastes, since that is the meaning of the Hebrew word *koheleth,* which comes out "Ecclesiastes" after being strained through the Latin. The book is attributed to Solomon, since he was the only one of David's sons who was "king in Jerusalem."

How does a man who claims to believe in God reach the bleak conclusion that "all is vanity," or "life is meaningless"? Solomon came to this view (temporarily; see 5:1-7, and the entire book of Proverbs) by amassing great wealth and worldly wisdom, then standing back and asking himself what impact his efforts would have on the future (see 1:13-14). Without the hope, future, and sense of purpose revealed by the New Covenant, Solomon's conclusion is understandable. Christians therefore read "All is vanity" in this book, then add, as it were, under their breath, "without Jesus."

B. Nature's repetitive cycle, 3-7
1. Day and night, 3-5

3 What profit hath a man of all his labour which he taketh under the sun?

4 One generation passeth away, and another generation cometh: but the earth abideth for ever.

5 The sun also ariseth, and the sun goeth down, and hasteth to his place where he arose.

An old folk song goes: *The sun comes up and the sun goes down / The hands of the clock keep goin' around / Life gits tejious* [tedious]*, don't it?* This is as eloquent as the view of more sophisticated philosophers such as King Solomon, whose similar views are based on the idea that *nature* is the only reality. With a world view limited to life *"under the sun,"* nature can seem to be a meaningless repetition of night following day and death following life. The king did not have the advantage of the New Covenant revelation that there is more to life than that which is "under the sun."

To the question, "What profit hath a man of all his labor?" Solomon answers in 6:2, "Very little!" He sees that although a person can work and save his money, or inherit a fortune, he still must die; and all the material wealth he gained may go to a foolish son or a stranger. Again we see that the view that "All is vanity" is the result of not having a vision of life that extends beyond death.

2. Wind and water, 6-7

6 The wind goeth toward the south, and turneth about unto the north; it whirleth about continually, and the wind returneth again according to his circuits.

7 All the rivers run into the sea; yet the sea is not full; unto the place from whence the rivers come, thither they return again.

Most people feel better about themselves, others, and life in general if they feel that "life is going somewhere." Again, however, Solomon asserts that this sense is not gained by looking only at nature—in this case the endless circuits of wind and water. A "low pressure" cell draws wind to fill it, only to have those air currents move on. The water of the rivers that run into the sea evaporates, rises to the heavens, then condenses and falls as rain, which again runs into the rivers, which run into the sea . . . and "the beat goes on." To the question, "Where is peace to be found?," the winds and the waters can only answer, "Not here!"

C. 'No new thing,' 8-10

8 All things are full of labour; man cannot utter it: the eye is not satisfied with seeing, nor the ear filled with hearing.

9 The thing that hath been, it is that which shall be; and that which is done is that which shall be done: and there is no new thing under the sun.

10 Is there any thing whereof it may be said, See, this is new? it hath been already of old time, which was before us.

Solomon turns from the endless cycles of nature to the restless nature of human beings. He himself labored extensively in building the Temple in Jerusalem, a fabled stable full of the finest horses in the world, and great houses, without finding peace of mind and a sense of purpose. He planted vineyards, groves, and gardens, but failed to find in his own heart the sense of robust life that grew out of the earth (see 2:4-11). If one were to claim that a shoot growing from the earth was "new," another can always point out that it actually came from a seed, which was produced by a previous "new" plant that wasn't really new—and the unending cycle goes on without relief to the heart whose vision is limited to things "under the sun."

Even human history can take on this sense of tired repetition. In verse 10 we can see the roots of the familiar phrase "history repeats itself." Even in one generation, older people look at the excitement youth have over some "new" thing, and inevitably point out that its roots are in the past. The "new" inventions of today are the fruits of that which "hath been already of old time."

D. No memories, 11

11 There is no remembrance of former things; neither shall there be any remembrance of things that are to come with those that shall

334

come after.

Now Solomon voices the view that "the dead know not any thing" (9:5). Again we see the limitations of revelation under the Old Covenant. This view was prevalent enough in the time of Christ that the entire party of the Sadducees is said to have denied the concept of a resurrection after death (Mark 12:18).

II. Vanity Is Vanquished—John 20:19-23

A. Resurrection's proof, 19-20

19 Then the same day at evening, being the first day of the week, when the doors were shut where the disciples were assembled for fear of the Jews, came Jesus and stood in the midst, and saith unto them, Peace be unto you.

20 And when he had so said, he shewed unto them his hands and his side. Then were the disciples glad, when they saw the Lord.

The Sunday after Easter is an especially appropriate time to balance the pessimistic world view of Ecclesiastes with the new viewpoint brought by the resurrection of Christ. In this passage, John records one of the several times when Jesus appeared to His disciples after His crucifixion and resurrection. It is hard for Christians, who have believed all along in life after death, to imagine the impact this tangible evidence of that view must have had on those who may have been influenced by Solomon's viewpoint. We recall that some, notably Thomas (vss. 24-29), were slow to accept the reality of this appearance; but most welcomed their resurrected Lord gladly. Suddenly everything is different, both in the way they view their purpose in life now, and in their hope for life after death.

B. New meaning and mission, 21-23

21 Then said Jesus to them again, Peace be unto you: as my Father hath sent me, even so send I you.

22 And when he had said this, he breathed on them, and saith unto them, Receive ye the Holy Ghost:

23 Whose soever sins ye remit, they are remitted unto them; and whose soever sins ye retain, they are retained.

For the second time Jesus urges "peace" on the hearts of His disciples, possibly because some were fearful that He was only a ghost. John adds that they were also assembled in hiding out of fear of persecution from the Jews (vs. 19). Jesus' resurrection has the power to banish all such fears.

Almost as though in direct counterpoint to Ecclesiastes' provisional view that "there is nothing new under the sun," Jesus breathes "new life" into His disciples in the form of the Holy Spirit. Just as God breathed the breath of life into Adam at creation, so Jesus is building the "new" creation, the era of the Spirit. The gift of the Spirit is followed by the commission of preaching and offering forgiveness to those who respond (cp. Matt. 28:18-20).

Evangelistic Emphasis

The Gospel of John tells us that when Jesus was present with the disciples they were glad. When the Spirit of Christ is present in our worship, we should be glad, too. Our attitude about the presence of Christ should play an important role in our attitude about worship.

When I was a boy growing up in rural America, church was the place to catch up on the news. Sometimes when my mom was not feeling well she would stay home, but my father never missed church. When he returned she would always ask my father the same question: what news did you learn at church? For my mother, going to church was the same as catching up on the events of the community. My father attended church for his Sunday school class. He loved that class more than anything in his life. He stayed after class for worship but it was just icing on the cake as far as he was concerned.

I think of all the reasons to attend church, to come into contact with the living, risen Christ is the noblest of all reasons. This experience alone is enough to make us happy. Some come into contact with Christ through the music, others through prayers, and others through Scripture or the spoken word. It really doesn't matter how we find Him, just as long as we do not leave without an encounter with the risen Lord. Why do you go to church? When you go, does it make you glad?

෨ාঞ

Then the same day at evening, being the first day of the week, when the doors were shut where the disciples were assembled for fear of the Jews, came Jesus and stood in the midst, and saith unto them, peace be unto you.—*John 20:19*

In the entire history of the world, peace has been the one thing that the world has wanted the most. However, this same history records that peace has successfully eluded world leaders since the beginning of time.

Jesus offers His disciples His peace. The peace that Jesus gives is different from any peace offered by a treaty drawn up by diplomats. Jesus offers a lasting peace. This is what He was offering the Samaritan woman at the well. The metaphor was water, but it was water that would quench the thirst forever. The thirst for peace in our world is great today. People are literally starving for peace, but we rarely find it, for long.

In John 14:27, Jesus says, "Peace I leave with you, my peace I give unto you: not as the world giveth, give I unto you." How can we have peace in our homes, schools, nations, and in the world if it doesn't abide in our hearts?

Weekday Problems

The word "new" appears prominently in the media. We have "new" pictures of a news event. We have "new" episodes of our favorite TV shows. Somehow, new is always better. The writer of Ecclesiastes tells us there is nothing new in our world. This rather negative view of his world sounds strangely like our world.

Someone once suggested to me that God could not see the future. God was an excellent forecaster of the future because He had lived the past; but He lacked the ability to actually see into the future. Whether you believe this or not, we must admit to ourselves that as for history, it always comes back to us. The names of the people involved are different, the places are often different, but the basic event is much the same.

That view is why Ecclesiastes is such negative reading. However, the writer leaves us with a positive truth: *God does not change.* In a changing world, it is refreshing to know that we can always count on God. As we live our lives, we know that God's character will never change. Just as He showed His love for Israel in the Old Testament, so He shows His love for us today.

*Why is it a comfort to know that God doesn't change like people do?

The Pity Party Pessimist

Money doesn't go as far as it used to, but at least it goes faster.

***

The owner of a service station decided to get married. He invited all his friends and neighbors to the wedding, in a large room over the station. So many showed up that their combined weight caused the building to collapse.
The moral to the story? Never marry above your station.

***

My mother-in-law gave me two sweaters for Christmas. I put one of them on first thing, but she said, "What's the matter? Don't you like the other one?"

***

The only advantage to growing old is that you can make a fool of yourself in a more dignified way.

***

I loved the play. It had a happy ending. Everyone was glad when it was over.

This Lesson in Your Life

This lesson compares the new and the old. In the new, Jesus breathes into His disciples the Holy Spirit. This is new. Jesus promised the Holy Spirit would come upon them and teach them all things. In Ecclesiastes, we are told that there is nothing new. This passage represents the old.

In the Bible, a person's breath was a symbol of life. In days before modern equipment could monitor the lungs and heart, the only way a person could be determined to be alive was through the breath. To be without breath meant death. Certainly everyone that Jesus breathed upon was living. However, this symbolized the old life. Here, Jesus breathes upon them new life. Life was now going to be with them in a new way, a way promised in John 14. When we read the Gospel account of Jesus and His disciples, we wonder how in the world a small band of common men could ever get the gospel out to the entire world. The answer is found in this one New Testament story of Jesus preparing His disciples to do just that. It was the power of the Holy Spirit that enabled ordinary men to do extraordinary things. When we look at the disciples, we see nothing great enough about them to wind up being the great men that each of them turned out to be. We can read Peter's discourse at Pentecost and wonder if it is the same bumbling, clumsy Peter of the Gospels. The Holy Spirit made all the difference in the world to Peter.

The Holy Spirit has always been the mysterious part of the Trinity for many believers. Jesus adds to this mystery when he compares the Spirit to the wind. He notes that we cannot know where the wind is coming from or where it is going. So it is, He says, with the Spirit of God. However, the same word for "spirit" in the original language is our word for breath. Since breath equals life, so must the Spirit of God equal life. It was spiritual life that Jesus was breathing into His disciples. The Spirit of God brings life, real life, to us. We do not merely exist as Christians, we live life to its fullest in the Spirit. When we live this life, it draws others to the life that God offers, just as a piece of metal is drawn to a magnet. It made all the difference in the world to the disciples. It will make all the difference in the world to us, too.

GETTING THE FACTS STRAIGHT

1. Who wrote the book of Ecclesiastes?

The writer is identified as the son of David, who was a king in Jerusalem. Since Solomon was the only son of David to succeed him as king, the writer must be Solomon.

2. In 1:9, how does the writer of Ecclesiastes describe the world?

Everything in the world simply repeats the past. There is "nothing new under the sun." This is the way it has always been and always will be.

3. What do we tend to forget according to the Preacher?

We forget the past, and he predicts that future generations will also forget the past. We could learn by remembering the past, but we refuse.

4. What was the atmosphere among the disciples when Jesus appeared to them?

They were afraid and in hiding. They thought that the Jews were going to kill them as they had Jesus.

5. When did Jesus choose to appear to the disciples?

It was on resurrection Sunday, to fulfill the angel's promise that Jesus would appear to His disciples if they would gather and wait.

6. What was Jesus' greeting to them?

He offered them peace, knowing that they were terrified and confused.

7. How did Jesus prove to them that He was real?

He showed them His hands and feet that demonstrated the cross and His suffering.

8. What was the disciples' reaction to Jesus' appearance?

They were very happy that He appeared and that He was so willing to calm their fears and erase their doubts.

9. What commission did Jesus give to His disciples?

He commissioned them to go in His name. He told them that their calling was just like His calling. They were all called by God.

10. What ability did Jesus give to His disciples?

He gave them the right to forgive others' sins. Perhaps this was reminiscent of the phrase in the Lord's Prayer, "Forgive us our trespasses as we forgive those who trespass against us."

 Have you ever wished that you could have been one of the disciples? It is exciting indeed to think about talking to the Savior in person. It makes my heart race to think about eating with Him and having a chance to know Him as a person. What would it have been like to have received His breath upon me and to have received the Holy Sprit directly from our Lord?

I can remember growing up listening to George Beverly Shea sing in the Billy Graham crusades on TV. He was my hero. I loved to sing and I always wanted to sing like Shea. I spent many hours practicing in order to sound just like him. However, with my tenor voice I could never achieve that rich baritone that only Bev Shea could produce.

Later in life, I became a music minister. I was scheduled to attend a conference for church music directors in Georgia. My friend, Jim, was always playing practical jokes on me. We knew that George Beverly Shea was the guest for a banquet that night. Jim came to me and said that he had arranged for me to sit next to the famous singer at the banquet. I had been stung too many times by his tricks, and never believed it for a single moment. When we arrived at the banquet I was looking at the huge crowd gathered trying to find their table. I heard a voice behind me call my name. I turned around to see George Beverly Shea and my friend smiling at me. I sat next to this great man and thought that I had died and gone to heaven. What a wonderful evening. I told him how much he had meant to me over the years. He was the most humble man I have ever known. He didn't want to talk about himself but he only wanted to encourage me in my ministry. Somehow, I think this might be somewhat like meeting the Savior.

When Jesus appeared to His disciples, His first concern was for their feelings. They were feeling fear and were extremely anxious. His words were, "Peace be unto you." I imagine that is what He is telling us today. "Be at peace. I have given you the Holy Spirit. Now take this assurance and power and go into the world."

Lesson 9

In God's Own Time

Ecclesiastes 3:1-15

To every thing there is a season, and a time to every purpose under the heaven:

2 A time to be born, and a time to die; a time to plant, and a time to pluck up that which is planted;

3 A time to kill, and a time to heal; a time to break down, and a time to build up;

4 A time to weep, and a time to laugh; a time to mourn, and a time to dance;

5 A time to cast away stones, and a time to gather stones together; a time to embrace, and a time to refrain from embracing;

6 A time to get, and a time to lose; a time to keep, and a time to cast away;

7 A time to rend, and a time to sew; a time to keep silence, and a time to speak;

8 A time to love, and a time to hate; a time of war, and a time of peace.

9 What profit hath he that worketh in that wherein he laboureth?

10 I have seen the travail, which God hath given to the sons of men to be exercised in it.

11 He hath made every thing beautiful in his time: also he hath set the world in their heart, so that no man can find out the work that God maketh from the beginning to the end.

12 I know that there is no good in them, but for a man to rejoice, and to do good in his life.

13 And also that every man should eat and drink, and enjoy the good of all his labour, it is the gift of God.

14 I know that, whatsoever God doeth, it shall be for ever: nothing can be put to it, nor any thing taken from it: and God doeth it, that men should fear before him.

15 That which hath been is now; and that which is to be hath already been; and God requireth that which is past.

Devotional Reading
Ps. 34:1-8

Background Scripture
Eccles. 3

Memory Selection
Eccles. 3:1

April 30

As we have seen, the book of Ecclesiastes often descends into pessimism, since the author lacks the full revelation Christ will one day bring. Yet this does not mean that life "under the sun" is useless. In this famous section, the author holds that

every human endeavor has its place. If an eternal perspective is lacking, at least we can gain a sense of "living in the moment" from such texts.

Ecclesiastes is a good antidote for the disease of "futurism," which can afflict those who are dissatisfied with the present and say "Tomorrow I'll be happy." Here the wise man, Solomon, affirms that the present has its own happiness and rewards. *Now* is the time to accept life and to live in the joy of the Lord.

Ask group members if they have a "mission statement" for life. As starting points, reflect on such statements as the Westminster Shorter Catechism, which holds that life's purpose is to *"love God and enjoy Him forever."* Augustine sought to simplify the moral life by saying, *"Love God, and do as you please."*

On the other hand, a non-biblical, pessimistic view of life has it that *"Life is hard, and then you die."*

A mission statement of King Solomon that might be drawn from today's lesson is *Life is now. Enjoy it while you can.* Obviously this can be taken to the extreme if we ignore the future, when we must live with the consequences of our actions. Still, there is much to learn from those who find that right now, where they are, is "the right time."

Teaching Outline	*Daily Bible Readings*

I. Observing Life's Seasons—1-8
  A. A time for opposites, 1
  B. Laughter vs. tears, 2-4
  C. Gathering vs. scattering, 5-6
  D. Loving vs. hating, 7-8
II. Obeying Eternity's Call—9-15
  A. Amid unseen purpose, 9-10
  B. Eternity in our hearts, 11
  C. Accepting life with joy, 12-13
  D. God's sovereignty, 14-15
	Mon. The Lord Is Good
	    Ps. 34:1-8
	Tue. Moderation and Respect
	    Eccles. 7:15-22
	Wed. A Time for Everything
	    Eccles. 8:2-8a
	Thu. Life Is in God's Hands
	    Eccles. 9:1-12
	Fri. A Season for Everything
	    Eccles. 3:1-8
	Sat. God's Work Endures
	    Eccles. 3:9-15
	Sun. The Future Belongs to God
	    Eccles. 3:16-22

Verse by Verse

I. Observing Life's Seasons—1-8
A. A time for opposites, 1

1 To every thing there is a season, and a time to every purpose under the heaven:

Up to this point, the theme of "the Preacher" (1:1) has been generally that "all is vanity" or meaninglessness (1:2). As we have seen, this bleak view is based on "life under the sun" (1:3b), without the advantage of the vision of purpose and of an after-life which the Messiah would bring.

It can seem especially hard to perceive meaning in life when we consider it as juggling sets of opposites. Yet in 3:1-8, the author bravely maintains that each of these seeming opposites has a place in God's plan, even if we cannot see it. To continue to live *as though* we see God's plan is one aspect of faith (see Heb. 11:1).

B. Laughter vs. tears, 2-4

2a A time to be born, and a time to die;

The author boldly plunges into life's extremities—birth and death—in his affirmation that all events have their propriety. As highly valued as individual freedom is to moderns, we have nothing to say about why or when or where we are born, and usually the time of our death. It is remarkable that this confession giving

to God the beginning and end of life should appear in a book that otherwise struggles to gain a sense of meaning in life apart from faith.

2b A time to plant, and a time to pluck up that which is planted;

God ordered the agricultural cycles to occur regularly, instead of allowing nature to be capricious and unpredictable. However, as in the rest of these opposites, the author seems also to hint that they may have a figurative meaning as well. In the course of human affairs, God at times "plants" or establishes persons and nations, too, while also seeing to their downfall if they prove unfruitful (see also vss. 7-8, and John 15:5-6).

3a A time to kill, and a time to heal; a time to break down, and a time to build up;

This surely expresses a uniquely Old Covenant view, based on the times when God occasionally told His people to destroy their enemies (e.g., Deut. 7:2). At other times, peace treaties and the healing of relationships between people and nations are more appropriate. Since the fulfilling of the Land Promise to the Jews, as recorded in 2 Kings and 2 Chronicles, it has been impossible to justify killing others in God's name. This saying may also simply describe what *is* rather than what ought to be. Often God uses even evil deeds for good purposes (see Rom. 8:28).

4 A time to weep, and a time to laugh; a time to mourn, and a time to dance;

As the apostle Paul will write much later, we are to weep with those who weep and rejoice with those who rejoice (Rom. 12:15). Believers surely have a strong basis for genuine joy, but equal sensitivity to the sorrows of others. The Preacher's observation here is especially pertinent at times of bereavement. Instead of advising mourners "You ought not to grieve so," the author reminds us that "grief-work" is an essential part of recovery from loss.

C. Gathering vs. scattering, 5-6

5 A time to cast away stones, and a time to gather stones together; a time to embrace, and a time to refrain from embracing;

This statement continues the theme of warfare against God's enemies, referring to the tearing down of enemy buildings vs. the time when it is appropriate for opposing kings to make a treaty and rebuild the ruins. The author also has the integrity to advise embracing in genuine friendship, vs. refraining from it when we are actually at enmity with each other.

6 A time to get, and a time to lose; a time to keep, and a time to cast away;

This counsel is especially helpful at times of loss. "It is appointed unto man once to die" (Heb. 9:27), and they are wise who can both mourn their loss while bearing it with a sense of acceptance. As for 6b, "a time to keep . . . ," many a business person knows the value of knowing when to press forward in a new venture and when to cut one's losses.

D. Loving vs. hating, 7-8

7 A time to rend, and a time to sew; a time to keep silence, and a time to speak;

8 A time to love, and a time to hate; a time of war, and a time of peace.

Again, this advice seems aimed at times such as Israel's covenant-making with other nations, and other similar relationships. Rending one's garments was a sign of grief or rage. Speaking out clearly against injustice obviously has its appropriate times. In other instances, when peace is possible, keeping one's silence about past offenses is more appropriate. Even when war seems necessary, Christians are obliged not to hate their enemy (Matt. 5:43-44). How precious is the gift of discernment in distinguishing between these times!

II. Obeying Eternity's Call—9-15
A. Amid unseen purpose, 9-10

9 What profit hath he that worketh in that wherein he laboureth?

10 I have seen the travail, which God hath given to the sons of men to be exercised in it.

With his balanced list of opposites concluded, the author returns to reflecting on the purpose of man's

344

sometimes tortured existence "under the sun." Chapter 2 was given over to a record of his experiments in the laboratory of life, in which he tried to find happiness and fulfillment in work and pleasure. Within the confines of this life, it often seems no better to be wise than foolish (see also 2:15). With the pop song of a generation ago, we are often left asking "Is that all there is?"—unless we have a "heavenly" view of doing our duty, or doing good for its own sake.

B. Eternity in our hearts, 11

11 He hath made every thing beautiful in his time: also he hath set the world in their heart, so that no man can find out the work that God maketh from the beginning to the end.

The first part of this verse is better understood in versions that translate the word for "world" as "eternity" (as in the NIV). God has placed in man a natural yearning to live forever. Yet "special revelation" is required for realizing that this desire is fulfilled through Christ; otherwise, God's ways are "past finding out" (see Job 36:26).

C. Accepting life with joy, 12-13

12 I know that there is no good in them, but for a man to rejoice, and to do good in his life.

13 And also that every man should eat and drink, and enjoy the good of all his labour, it is the gift of God.

"No good" is better translated "nothing better," as in the NIV. The author is not saying that there is no good to be found in creation, but that, with his limited view of life "under the sun," there is nothing better than to enjoy what we can in this life. The NIV reading gives a healthy emphasis even for believers in an after-life. The general rule is that God has given even this life to be enjoyed; and the believer who postpones joy until "pie in the sky by and by" misses out on many of the good things God gives in the present for our enjoyment.

D. God's sovereignty, 14-15

14 I know that, whatsoever God doeth, it shall be for ever: nothing can be put to it, nor any thing taken from it: and God doeth it, that men should fear before him.

15 That which hath been is now; and that which is to be hath already been; and God requireth that which is past.

These verses can be read in a fatalistic way, as though God has predetermined everything and nothing we do makes any difference. Indeed, given "the Preacher's" pessimistic view, this may be what he means. The fuller revelation of the New Covenant will reveal that God has only predetermined the future in large strokes. The faithful will be rewarded and the unfaithful punished. Yet God leaves us the freedom to choose in what group we wish to be included. Even in this life we often have the freedom to make wise or foolish choices; but we often find that living with the consequences is one of God's fixed rules.

345

Evangelistic Emphasis

No other book has sold as many copies as the Bible. Truly, the Scriptures have withstood the test of time. Because of the Bible's popularity, many people know Bible facts and stories while not being real students of Scripture. Like many passages, parts of today's text have become a part of our culture.

As Solomon reminds us, most people reach a time in their lives when they are inclined to make their peace with God. Some take advantage of this, some say No, and others choose to put it off.

However, in all of life there are certain times to do certain things and times when we should refrain from doing those same things. I guess you could say that it just depends. The writer of our text takes a snapshot of life from the cradle to the grave. Much of life is about knowing what to do and when to do it. The real difference is allowing God to guide us and to walk with us through life. The best way is God's way. Only then can we be assured that we will know when the right time has come.

ജ്ഞ

Memory Selection

To every thing there is a season, and a time to every purpose under the heaven.—*Ecclesiastes 3:1*

One experience that all humans share is that at one time or another, all of us have been embarrassed. Often the source of our embarrassment is that we will do or say something that is inappropriate. It's just not the time or place for our action or words. The writer of Ecclesiastes is not trying to lecture us on embarrassment but to make us see that life and living go in cycles. As we live, we go through the circle of life. We experience what it is like to be young, middle aged, and old. We have joys and sorrows, disappointments and successes. It is only when we attempt to do things out of season, out of the realm of appropriateness, that we have difficulty.

I was raised in the country. Hunting and fishing were a way of life for me. My father taught me how to set a line to catch fish and how to use a gun safely and effectively. One of the first things he taught me was to observe the hunting and fishing seasons. Every year the conservation department would issue a sportsman's calendar. This was like gold to me. I wanted to know when I could hunt and when I could fish. I wanted to know the rules so that I would not get into trouble.

God has given us, through His Word, all the instructions necessary to live our lives according to His seasons. To ignore Ecclesiastes' admonition to observe the "seasons" of life is to invite a life that is not fruitful and blessed.

Weekday Problems

Adolescence is undoubtedly one of the most difficult times of life. A teenager doesn't feel like a child any more, but also is keenly aware that he is not an adult. He is caught in the middle, part adult and part child. It is also a time of change. The body, voice, mind, and psyche are all going through radical change. When an adolescent acts like a child, there is tremendous pressure exerted by his peers. He often feels ashamed, embarrassed, and angry at himself for behaving like a child. In contrast, when he takes on the responsibilities of an adult, he often gets into serious trouble. He then realizes that he is not ready to make adult decisions. When his parents tell him to be patient and his day will come, it seems like forever.

The writer of Ecclesiastes is apparently taking a chapter out of his younger days. He looks back and sees times when he did not wait for the right time to do some things. He realizes the pain and confusion that acting out of season caused him. He also realizes that God created the seasons of life for a reason. He proclaims that God created everything perfect in His (God's) time. In all we do, we must remember that timing is important. We must learn to wait on the seasons of life and wait on God. His will is perfect.

*Recall a time in your life when your timing was not appropriate.

Wisdom(?) in Bumper Stickers

He who laughs last, thinks slowest.
***
Ever stop to think, and forget to start again?
***
As long as there are tests, we'll have prayer in public schools.
***
The more people I meet, the more I like my dog.
***
WARNING: I took an IQ test, and the results were negative.
***
Where there's a will, I want to be in it.
***
Few women admit their age. Few men act it.
***
I don't suffer from insanity. I enjoy every minute of it.

This Lesson in Your Life

Recently, my wife and I were traveling on vacation. We attended a church in the center of the business district of a large city. We sat with some of the city's brightest and best business professionals. We also sat with people who were homeless. I looked around that worship area and saw the world. It must have been like God sees the world when He looks at everyone at once. The amazing thing was how every one made us feel at home. I felt as if I had known every person in that room all my life. When I left, I felt as if I had really worshiped. The skies were threatening rain, but it seemed to be the brightest day of my life. It was Sunday and it was the time to worship God. People from everywhere came for a single purpose. We even found some people from our home state who knew many of the people we know. The most common thing that we shared was that we all felt it was the right time in the week and in our lives to worship. It is a wonder that having only a few basic things in common can bring us together in such an intimate way. I know God was there because everything was perfect. When we see perfection, we can always look for God.

Many see the words in Ecclesiastes as negative. Actually, in our text the writer challenges us to live life to its fullest. He encourages us to enjoy the fruits of our labor. He wants us to enjoy God's creation as a gift from Him. We certainly don't have to stand at the banks of the Grand Canyon to enjoy God's world. One of my favorite things to do is to fire up the grill on our tiny patio in the evenings. I can sit and wait for the food to cook and look out over my back yard. I have worked hard all day and I'm ready to enjoy my home and life in general. It is amazing how many things I notice in my yard that I have never seen before. I see a new plant or flower. I notice the grass is greener or is beginning to turn the color of fall. My wife is an excellent cook, but the food always tastes better if it comes off the grill. I always say to myself at those times that life is truly worth living.

Some people need a reason to enjoy life. On an average day, they find little to enjoy. The text gives us an excellent reason to make life a big party. God made it for us to enjoy, and His creation is perfect.

I think this is the message of the Preacher in Ecclesiastes. Life is worth living, especially if we realize that there is a time and place for everything. It is when we forget this and get things out of the natural order that we tend to lose the joy of life and living.

1. What does the writer of Ecclesiastes tell us about time?

There is a time for everything. Nothing in God's creation is without a purpose.

2. What does the writer think of God's creation?

Everything that God has made is appropriate, because God has perfect timing.

3. What is the mystery surrounding this passage?

The mystery is that no one can understand God's creation. We cannot understand God's timing nor can we duplicate it.

4. What does the author identify as a gift from God?

He wants us to enjoy the fruit of our labor. We should enjoy God's bounty because He gave it to us as a gift.

5. How does God guard His creation?

Human beings cannot change God's work. His work will endure forever. He makes it so in order that we might have the proper respect for Him.

6. What is the last "season" that is mentioned in the text?

It is when all humans must give an accounting of their lives to God. This involves both the good and the bad that we do.

7. Why does God test us?

He tests us so that we can fully see our mortality. In this way, we can fully trust and depend on Him.

8. What do humans have in common with animals?

Both humans and animals go back to the dust of the earth. The writer raises the question of humans having a soul and challenges the reader to think about it.

9. What is the best thing that a person can enjoy, according to the Preacher?

We are to enjoy our work. It is God's will that all of us should be productive in order to help others and provide for ourselves and our families.

10. What reminder does the author give us about life and death?

We are reminded that after we die we cannot come back and do the things that are left unfinished.

As I write this lesson, it is an unusual day. It is the middle of August and a cold front has pushed through the Deep South. All of the weather forecasters on TV are talking about how different this weather pattern is from the norm. Many have said that they cannot remember when it has been so cool in August.

I cannot help but think about my childhood and what happened every year when the weather turned cool. My father and our hired hands on the farm would prepare the hogs for slaughter. We would fire up the large tank that would scald the hogs and remove the hair from the carcass. It would be an all-day affair. In fact, the sausage making would go on for several days. We would hang those long, lanky ropes of sausage in the smoke house until they turned dark brown. You could smell that hickory smoke for miles. All the neighbors would gather and take home plenty of fresh pork and sausage. It was not just a time on the calendar. It was a time to do something, a time of purpose.

God has a purpose for every one of us, too. His purpose is clear in many cases. It is clear that He wants to have fellowship with all of humanity. It is clear that He wants us to be His disciple and to serve Him. The text from Ecclesiastes reminds us that we have many things to do on this earth. Some of our activities are pleasant. To love, to plant, to dance, are all activities we all enjoy. To bury someone we love, to weep, to tear something beautiful down are all unpleasant things. However, all of these things are life. When placed together in a full lifetime, we look back and most of us see a life that has been beautiful and productive. It is when we follow God's natural order that we achieve our greatest success in living. The degree to which we live a fulfilled life will be in direct proportion to our willingness to do God's will.

How close are you to doing what God wants, when He wants it?

Lesson 10

A Treasure Worth Seeking

Proverbs 2:1-5; 3:1-6, 13-18

My son, if thou wilt receive my words, and hide my commandments with thee;

2 So that thou incline thine ear unto wisdom, and apply thine heart to understanding;

3 Yea, if thou criest after knowledge, and liftest up thy voice for understanding;

4 If thou seekest her as silver, and searchest for her as for hid treasures;

5 Then shalt thou understand the fear of the LORD, and find the knowledge of God.

3:1 My son, forget not my law; but let thine heart keep my commandments:

2 For length of days, and long life, and peace, shall they add to thee.

3 Let not mercy and truth forsake thee: bind them about thy neck; write them upon the table of thine heart:

4 So shalt thou find favour and good understanding in the sight of God and man.

5 Trust in the LORD with all thine heart; and lean not unto thine own understanding.

6 In all thy ways acknowledge him, and he shall direct thy paths.

13 Happy is the man that findeth wisdom, and the man that getteth understanding.

14 For the merchandise of it is better than the merchandise of silver, and the gain thereof than fine gold.

15 She is more precious than rubies: and all the things thou canst desire are not to be compared unto her.

16 Length of days is in her right hand; and in her left hand riches and honour.

17 Her ways are ways of pleasantness, and all her paths are peace.

18 She is a tree of life to them that lay hold upon her: and happy is every one that retaineth her.

May 7

Devotional Reading
Proverbs 2:6-15

Background Scripture
Proverbs 2–3

Memory Selection
Proverbs 3:13

351

This lesson introduces a four-lesson unit on the book of Proverbs. The lesson will be more meaningful if you define from the start that a "proverb" is literally a "fore-word," a word that "goes before." In the sense it is used in the Bible, a proverb is a word from God that arms us in advance for life situations that come our way. Those who accept the guidance are deemed wise, and those who ignore it are foolish.

This first lesson in the series deals not so much with specific "forewords," but with the general value of, and rewards for, depending on true wisdom. Wisdom is spoken of as a personal entity, not just a vague force in the world. Although wisdom does not promise to tell us everything there is to be learned, she is viewed as an essential guide to "fearing the Lord."

ဆာယ

You can introduce this lesson with a "devil's advocate." Although our text emphasizes the message that true wisdom is to be found in faithfulness and obedience to God, ask group members to think first of some common *alternatives* to this view.

Ask, *Where do many people in our day turn for wisdom?* Lead responses so that they include the effect of *mass media* (TV, movies, newspaper, books, and magazines) . . . of *popularity polls . . . the public acts of prominent people,* and, more and more, by *formal education.*

Point out that while we are richer in many ways because of these and other influences, the book of Proverbs insists that "the fear of the Lord is the beginning of wisdom."

Teaching Outline

I. Road to Understanding—2:1-5
  A. An inclined heart, 1-2
  B. As buried treasure, 3-4
  C. The 'fear of the Lord,' 5
II. Rewards of Obedience—3:1-6
  A. Length of days, 1-2
  B. Mercy and truth, 3-4
  C. Direction to God, 5-6
III. Riches of Wisdom—13-18
  A. True happiness, 13
  B. True wisdom, 14-15
  C. True life, 16-18

Daily Bible Readings

Mon. Seek Wisdom
      Prov. 2:1-5
Tue. What Wisdom Brings
      Prov. 2:6-15
Wed. Follow God's Way
      Prov. 2:16-22
Thu. Trust and Honor God
      Prov. 3:1-12
Fri. Wisdom Is Precious
      Prov. 3:13-20
Sat. Wisdom Brings Security
      Prov. 3:21-30
Sun. Do What Is Right
      Prov. 3:31-35

Verse by Verse

I. Road to Understanding—2:1-5

A. An inclined heart, 1-2

1 My son, if thou wilt receive my words, and hide my commandments with thee;

2 So that thou incline thine ear unto wisdom, and apply thine heart to understanding;

As mentioned in the "Focus" section, a "proverb" is literally a "foreword," a saying designed to equip us to act wisely *before* we are faced with the need to act. This definition fits neatly with the position of the book of Proverbs in the "Wisdom Literature" of ancient Israel (which also includes Job, Psalms, Ecclesiastes, Song of Solomon; and in Catholic Bibles, the Wisdom of Solomon and Ecclesiasticus). The "If" that begins our text underlines an important condition for being a wise person: being *receptive* and *inclined* toward obeying God's commandments. This stands on its head some secular views that hold that great knowledge and learning are the paths to wisdom. This is not to deplore the advantage of having a good education; but Proverbs tells us to place more confidence on "the fear of the Lord" than on knowledge as "the beginning of wisdom" (Prov. 1:7, etc.). Thus, here in 2:1-2, those who want to be wise must start with obedience to God's

commandments, rather than with philosophy or science.

B. As buried treasure, 3-4

3 Yea, if thou criest after knowledge, and liftest up thy voice for understanding;

4 If thou seekest her as silver, and searchest for her as for hid treasures;

It takes an urgency of spirit to be wise in the biblical sense. We must "cry out" after knowledge and understanding. They must be valuable to us, just as silver and hidden treasure are valuable. Hundreds of years later, Jesus would endorse this view, teaching that the Kingdom of heaven, like wisdom here, is to be considered as valuable as treasure hidden in a field or a pearl of great price (Matt. 13:44-46).

C. The 'fear of the Lord,' 5

5 Then shalt thou understand the fear of the Lord, and find the knowledge of God.

The preceding *"if's"* are now to be seen to point to the chief goal of Proverbs: *fearing the Lord.* The phrase does not mean to be "terrified" of God, but to respect Him so much that we are reverently obedient to His will. Again, this is the opposite from much worldly wisdom. From Proverbs, we learn of God by doing His will, rather than obeying Him because we know about Him intellectually.

II. Rewards of Obedience—3:1-5

A. Length of days, 1-2

1 My son, forget not my law; but let thine heart keep my commandments:

2 For length of days, and long life, and peace, shall they add to thee.

Conventional wisdom is that good health care and a nourishing diet enable us to live to "a ripe old age." In the Proverbs, it is more important to have a heart that is inclined to keep God's commandments than one that is aerobically healthy. This, of course, is to be understood as the general rule. Sometimes "the good die young." Yet those who make a practice of obeying God will have His blessing in their lives however long they live.

B. Mercy and truth, 3-4

3 Let not mercy and truth forsake thee: bind them about thy neck; write them upon the table of thine heart:

4 So shalt thou find favour and good understanding in the sight of God and man.

Now the author moves from wisdom as revealed in our attitude toward God and His commandments to our attitude and actions toward other people. This "horizontal" dimension of Wisdom is an important outgrowth of our "vertical" relationship with God. The wise person is to "wear" truth-telling and mercy or compassion toward others as they would wear an article of clothing, or as a commandment written not on a "To do" list for the day, but on the heart. God's people were to tie God's commandments as symbols on their hands and bind them on their foreheads (Deut. 6:8)—which led, in Christ's day, to wearing the "phylactery" or leather box carrying bits of Scripture (Matt. 3:5).

C. Direction to God, 5-6

5 Trust in the Lord with all thine heart; and lean not unto thine own understanding.

6 In all thy ways acknowledge him, and he shall direct thy paths.

Whether we are able to make Wisdom the focus of our life depends on whether we accept God's ways or our own. The Proverbs continually take us back to the simplicity of "two ways," or two roads—God's way or our own. This fundamental theme was embedded in the Covenant through Moses: "I have set before you life and death, blessing and cursing: therefore choose life" (Deut. 29:19). This does not mean that decisions may not be complex, but that we approach them with the *willingness* to choose God's way insofar as we can see it. The promise is that God will direct the steps of those whose hearts are so inclined, and will even *misdirect* those who are otherwise inclined (see 2 Thess. 2:8-12).

III. Riches of Wisdom—13-18

A. True happiness, 13

3 Happy is the man that findeth wisdom, and the man that getteth understanding.

Another reward offered by the pursuit of wisdom is true *happiness.* The root of the Hebrew word here does not mean superficially giddy or pleased, but *straight, honest,* or *proper.* Pursuing wisdom brings a joy that is deeper than being momentarily happy. The argument here is circular logic: those who are wise are happy, and those who choose God's definition of happiness are wise. In a sense, therefore, wisdom is its own reward, and is important to pursue for the joy of being wise. Wisdom and understanding are used here as synonyms, as often in Proverbs.

B. True wisdom, 14-15

14 For the merchandise of it is better than the merchandise of silver, and the gain thereof than fine gold.

15 She is more precious than rubies: and all the things thou canst desire are not to be compared unto her.

The healthy Old Testament attitude toward this-worldly material goods comes through in this comment on wisdom. The author places the pursuit of wisdom on a profit-and-loss basis. The word for "merchandise" means profit (cp. the NIV, "She [wisdom] is more profitable than silver, and yields better return than gold"). Yet there surely is no license for unbridled materialism here. In fact, verse 15 shows the opposite emphasis: wisdom is more precious than the gems that make people materially wealthy. Earlier, youth who would be wise are actually warned

against those who say "We shall find all precious substance" (1:13).

Verse 15 accurately translates as feminine ("She") the Hebrew pronoun referring to Wisdom. In fact, in the Greek translation of the Old Testament the word for wisdom is *sophia,* which we recognize as a fairly common name for women. This may be the result of the personification of wisdom as virtually the "mother" of all creation, having been present from the beginning, before the rest of the earth was made (see Prov. 8). In the New Testament, wisdom is virtually identical to the *logos,* the Word or rationality of God, the "sperm" of creation (see John 1:1).

C. True life, 16-18

16 Length of days is in her right hand; and in her left hand riches and honour.

17 Her ways are ways of pleasantness, and all her paths are peace.

18 She is a tree of life to them that lay hold upon her: and happy is every one that retaineth her.

Verse 18 introduces a new element, referring to wisdom, remarkably, as a "tree of life." We immediately recognize this imagery as being from the creation account (Gen. 2:7; 3:22). The implication is that while man, through sin, lost the right to partake of the tree of life in the Garden, this source of eternal nourishment is restored to those who "lay hold" or seek wisdom, as God defines it.

Evangelistic Emphasis

We owe our faith to the art of oral tradition. For centuries the people of God would pass down the rudiments of the faith by word of mouth to the younger generation. Finally, it was written down and then later printed. We have that faith before us today in written form.

Today we have books and multimedia that we depend on to teach our children. However, the interaction of people and the example of an older person has diminished our modern ways. This is a pity. Many young people are raised by only one parent today. In days past, the members of the community of faith would help to fill the gap as role models.

My daughter lives in the community that I grew up in. She calls occasionally to tell me of someone who taught me in Sunday school or Bible school who has passed away. These are the people who passed the wisdom they received on to me. When I learn of another passing, it is a challenge to me to be a mentor and a teacher of wisdom to others. I sometimes doubt that I have the wisdom that my elders had but the challenge is still before me. Are you a teacher of wisdom to someone?

We are never too old to learn from others. The more we learn, the more wisdom we have.

§ × ×

Happy is the man that findeth wisdom and the man that getteth understanding.—*Proverbs 3:13*

In counseling couples who are contemplating marriage, I often hear them say, "He/she makes me happy." The truth is that no one can make us happy unless we are happy in ourselves. If we are not happy before we meet that special someone, it is doubtful that he or she can make us happy for very long.

In our text, the writer tells us that wisdom will make us happy. Wisdom helps us to make the right choices. Much of the source of unhappiness is because we make the wrong choices over and over. Being happy is a two-part project. First, we must seek wisdom and find it; and second, after wisdom comes understanding.

Wisdom is not knowledge. Someone can be extremely intelligent and not have much wisdom. In fact, sometimes it seems those who are the most intelligent of all have little in the way of wisdom. Understanding is not knowledge. To know how something works requires raw intelligence. To understand why it works requires wisdom. God gave us wisdom as a gift. It is not obtained through education or even experience. Many people make the same mistakes over and over. The best wisdom comes from God.

Weekday Problems

How do you know whom you can trust? This is a question we ask ourselves each day. We shop the internet and we must give our credit card number to some stranger thousands of miles away. Can we trust him? We see someone on the street who is begging for money for food. We want to help him, but how do we know he will not take our hard-earned money and buy drugs? The offering plate is passed in church and we struggle to get our check written before it arrives. In a split second a doubt comes to us; Can we trust the church to spend our money wisely?

The writer of Proverbs is assuring us that we can trust God. He is trustworthy to give us not just wisdom, but the wisdom that we need and seek. We can also trust Him to direct us in life. We are given a warning that if we go it alone, we will risk taking the wrong path.

It is often frightening to trust someone else. We must be willing and have an open heart and mind to receive the right words. When we pray to God to teach us and lead us, He will respond and answer our prayer. However, we must have a receptive ear to hear and be willing to apply His teaching.

*How can you tell if someone is really open to God's Word?

Wise Answers to Good Questions

Q: What is more clever than speaking in several languages?
A: Knowing when to keep your mouth shut in *one.*
***

Q: When rain "falls," does it ever get up again?
A: Yes, in dew time.
***

Q: How do they take a census of all the monkeys in Africa?
A: They use ape recorders.
***

Q: What do you get when you cross an elephant and a chicken?
A: I don't know, but Col. Sanders would have a tough time dipping it in batter.
***

Q: Why does the ocean roar?
A: You would too if you had lobsters in your bed.

This Lesson in Your Life

The most pivotal event in my life happened one Sunday morning when I was 15 years old. This one event set my life on a course that would push me into my life's work of ministry. It was homecoming at our church. They invited an elderly preacher, who was known by all the older members, to be the guest speaker. He was tall and had snow-white hair. He walked with a cane and he wore a navy blue suit with all the buttons fastened. He had the thickest lenses on his glasses that I had ever seen. When he stood to preach he announced his text as Isaiah 53.

I didn't realize it before the service, but I could finally see that he was blind. He stood erect at the pulpit and with the most confidence I had ever heard he recited the entire chapter from memory. His message captivated me as no message ever had. I was mesmerized. To my delight, he came to our house for Sunday dinner that day. I can remember sitting at his feet all afternoon as he related his experiences in the ministry. He challenged me to do my best for God and I committed myself to do just that. He was a mentor to me until he died a few years later. I shall never forget him.

The writer of the Proverbs challenges us to listen to our elders. We are to seek out mentors to teach us the ways of God. Those who have had experience are also challenged to be mentors and to teach those who are young. This is an age-old tradition with the Hebrews. It is not the one who *possesses* wisdom who is held in esteem but the one who *seeks* wisdom. The Scripture implies that if we are truly wise, we will be careful where we seek wisdom. Clearly it is divine wisdom that is the best and most sustaining.

Everyone wants to be a success in life. What better way than to seek God's wisdom? For millennia, novices have sought out the wise who are known for success. Unfortunately, today we measure success in dollars and cents and possessions. Our sense of success is skewed. We need to look for those who have been successful in God's eyes. There are many who have been productive in their professions and have not placed all their faith in what they have gained in material things. These have also maintained a spiritual life and have achieved a balance between the spiritual and material. They have received their wisdom from God, and He has blessed them. These are the mentors we want for our children and ourselves.

1. What does the writer of Proverbs challenge the reader to do?
We are to heed his words and remember them so that we can be open to receive wisdom and understanding.

2. What prerequisite is there to receiving wisdom and understanding (Prov. 2:2-3)?
We are to earnestly cry out for knowledge and understanding.

3. If we seek wisdom diligently, what can we expect to receive?
We will understand what it means to fear the Lord and we will find the knowledge of God.

4. If we remember God's laws and keep His commandments, what can we expect from Him?
We will live a long and productive life.

5. How can we find favor with both God and man?
By practicing mercy and truth not as a ritual but out of our hearts

6. What can we do to insure that God will lead us in our daily walk?
We can always trust Him with our whole hearts. We can give Him praise for His leadership in our lives.

7. What is Proverbs' prescription for a happy life?
We must learn that happiness is not in material things. Those who seek wisdom will acquire things more precious than anything money can buy.

8. What value does the writer of Proverbs place on wisdom?
It is the most valuable thing a person could have.

9. What metaphor does the writer use to describe wisdom?
Wisdom is compared to the tree of life. This relates back to the Garden of Eden, which is associated with contentment and peace.

10. What do the two hands of wisdom hold?
A long life is in her right hand and riches and honor are in her left hand. These riches, as explained earlier, are much more precious than anything one could buy.

A professor in the psychology department of the seminary I attended gave us a phrase and a principle that I have used over and over. He said that everyone should practice good mental hygiene. What he meant was that we should think in a healthy way and to make a practice of it just like we have good body hygiene. For example, we must practice thinking positive thoughts and avoid negative thoughts. He saw this as a matter of will. One of the exercises I use to practice good mental hygiene is to count all the blessings I have that were not purchased. I literally take an inventory of all the things in my life that are most valuable to me. I try to avoid all the things that have been acquired with money. I sometimes compare material things with God's gifts to make sure that I am focused on what is important. William Shakespeare once said, "Blow, blow, thou winter wind, thou art not so unkind as man's ingratitude."

The writer of Proverbs reminds us that wisdom is one of the most valuable commodities that one can attain. Of course, wisdom cannot be purchased or traded. We cannot go to Wal-Mart and buy wisdom. Wisdom is a gift from God. The text challenges us to be grateful for wisdom and to value it like a valuable possession. All of us have known people who we thought were intelligent but were not wise. Perhaps the world sees intelligence and wisdom as the same thing, but not Proverbs. It makes a clear distinction between the two.

Wisdom is also not common sense. Common sense can be a valuable tool as we work our way through life. However, one can have much common sense and not have wisdom.

Wisdom teaches us about God. Wisdom helps us to understand the ways of God. We can know God's works by reading the Bible. However, His ways are different. His ways are reflected in His character traits—attributes that He wants us to possess, too. His love and compassion are example of His ways. Anyone can know God's works, but to know His ways is special indeed. We know his ways by receiving the gift of wisdom.

The writer of Proverbs also tells us that to acquire wisdom we must have an open heart and mind. We must be like a sponge, ready to soak up God's offering of wisdom. We must be receptive and open in order to receive wisdom. Once God has given it to us, we must always understand and acknowledge its high value. We should thank and praise God for this precious gift.

Proverbs 8:1-5, 22-31

Doth not wisdom cry? and understanding put forth her voice?

2 She standeth in the top of high places, by the way in the places of the paths.

3 She crieth at the gates, at the entry of the city, at the coming in at the doors.

4 Unto you, O men, I call; and my voice is to the sons of man.

5 O ye simple, understand wisdom: and, ye fools, be ye of an understanding heart.

22 The LORD possessed me in the beginning of his way, before his works of old.

23 I was set up from everlasting, from the beginning, or ever the earth was.

24 When there were no depths, I was brought forth; when there were no fountains abounding with water.

25 Before the mountains were settled, before the hills was I brought forth:

26 While as yet he had not made the earth, nor the fields, nor the highest part of the dust of the world.

27 When he prepared the heavens, I was there: when he set a compass upon the face of the depth:

28 When he established the clouds above: when he strengthened the fountains of the deep:

29 When he gave to the sea his decree, that the waters should not pass his commandment: when he appointed the foundations of the earth:

30 Then I was by him, as one brought up with him: and I was daily his delight, rejoicing always before him;

31 Rejoicing in the habitable part of his earth; and my delights were with the sons of men.

Devotional Reading
Proverbs 8:10-21

Background Scripture
Proverbs 8–9

Memory Selection
Proverbs 8:1

May 14

The depth and significance of the claims for "Wisdom" in Proverbs 8 is hard to over-state. They make the astounding assertion that "the fear of the Lord," or Wisdom in the way that God defines it, is the very basis of creation. Among other things, this means that creation is *rational.* The human mind can access it. It is not capricious, but sensible. For all its mysteries, it is there for the human mind to analyze, meaning that it is accessible to science.

Yet all this is affirmed not just for philosophers, but for Everyman. Wisdom is available in the market-place and on the farm. It can make this claim because it has existed with God from the beginning. Anyone who fears the Lord can therefore live in tune with the universe, and pleasing to its Creator.

$\mathcal{EO)Q}$

Try a word definition exercise to introduce this lesson. Ask your group to define these four words: *Knowledge, intelligence, understanding,* and *wisdom.* (Because their definitions often overlap, give all four words at once; then return to the first word and define them one by one.)

Point out both the similarities and differences in the way we use these words. The object of the lesson is to lift out the term *wisdom* from the list, since this is this term that Proverbs 8 focuses on. Explain that in this lesson the author claims that *wisdom* is the foundation both of creation and of the perceptive life. Challenge group members to be open, as the lesson progresses, to the implications of this remarkable claim.

Teaching Outline	*Daily Bible Readings*

I. Call to All—1-5
 	
  A. Where to find wisdom, 1-3
 	
  B. Who can be wise, 4-5
 	
II. Creation's Attendant—22-31
 	
  A. Blueprint for creation, 22-23
 	
  B. Before heights and depths, 24-26
 	
  C. Before sky and earth, 27-29
 	
  D. Delighting in humankind, 30-31
	Mon. Acquire Wisdom
	    Prov. 8:1-9
	Tue. Receive My Advice
	    Prov. 8:10-21
	Wed.Wisdom at Creation
	    Prov. 8:22-31
	Thu. Listen to Wisdom!
	    Prov. 8:32-36
	Fri. Wisdom's Invitation
	    Prov. 9:1-6
	Sat. Wisdom Extends Our Days
	    Prov. 9:7-12
	Sun. An Inferior Invitation
	    Prov. 9:13-18

Verse by Verse

I. Call to All—1-5

A. Where to find wisdom, 1-3

1 Doth not wisdom cry? and understanding put forth her voice?

2 She standeth in the top of high places, by the way in the places of the paths.

3 She crieth at the gates, at the entry of the city, at the coming in at the doors.

Many people consider "wisdom" to be a word that only philosophers and other scholars use. Also, we must keep in mind that, from the beginning, Proverbs has defined "wisdom" as being available only to those who have "the fear of the Lord" (1:7; 9:10). Thus, many will not respond to wisdom's call because they decline to subject themselves to the rule of God in their lives.

Little wonder, therefore, that this profound and poignant chapter opens with Wisdom seeming from the start to be distressed: although she cries out from the mountain tops to the city gates, she knows that she will not be overwhelmed with response. This insight anticipates Jesus' admission that "small is the gate and narrow the road that leads to life, and only a few find it" (Matt. 7:14, NIV).

B. Who can be wise, 4-5

4 Unto you, O men, I call; and my voice is to the sons of man.

5 O ye simple, understand wisdom: and, ye fools, be ye of an understanding heart.

In the previous lesson we noticed that the author of Proverbs often "personifies" wisdom, speaking of it as a female person. In verse 4, the "voice" or "person" of wisdom changes from third ("she") to first ("I, me, my"), making her appeal to us even more direct and personal. No longer is "wisdom" as a common noun something that would be nice to have. Now "Wisdom" is the proper name of the foundational principle of the universe (to be explained in detail below).

Note again that Wisdom does not wait for us to seek her out, but takes the initiative to speak directly to us with a personal appeal. Here is advance notice of a God who does not wait for His prodigal children to discover Him by returning home or seeking Him in books about religion and philosophy. Instead, through Wisdom, God seeks us out, revealing Himself to us instead of depending on our wisdom revealing Him.

Who will respond? As above, it will not be the philosophers or those wise in the ways of the world. It will be those who fear the Lord. Therefore even "simple" and unlettered people can be wise in the ways of God. Here we recall that Jesus warned that His teachings must be received "As a little child" (Mark 10:15), and that the crowds about Him marveled that His closest lieutenants were not highly-educated men (Acts 4:13). It was quite enough that "they had been with Jesus," for, as we shall see, Jesus Himself will be identified with Wisdom.

II. Creation's Attendant—22-31
A. Blueprint for creation, 22-23

22 The Lord possessed me in the beginning of his way, before his works of old.

23 I was set up from everlasting, from the beginning, or ever the earth was.

From earliest times, Christians have heard in this passage an echo of John 1, where Jesus, as "the Word," the One made flesh and dwelling among men, is said also to have been with God at Creation (John 1:1, 14). Jesus of Nazareth is therefore identified with "Wisdom." With the help of Greek views of the *logos* or "word" being the energizing spark running through, and responsible for, creation, Jesus can somehow be viewed as the "blueprint" of creation (see also Heb. 1:1-3; Col. 1:16-17).

The implications of this claim are profound, and not just on a philosophical or metaphysical level. On a very practical level they mean that those who follow Jesus are in tune with the way the world works. Loving one's neighbor, forgiving one's enemy, and even Jesus' self-giving for others on the Cross can now be viewed not as aberrant or naïve behavior, but as the way persons were created to behave. No wonder Paul will say that (1) Christ is "the wisdom of God," but that (2) many who are wise in the ways of the world will think Jesus' teaching is "foolishness" (see 1 Cor. 1:20-25).

B. Before heights and depths, 24-26

24 When there were no depths, I was brought forth; when there were no fountains abounding with water.

25 Before the mountains were settled, before the hills was I brought forth:

26 While as yet he had not made the earth, nor the fields, nor the highest part of the dust of the world.

Wisdom, the Word or rationality of God, preceded both the depths of the oceans from which the waters spring forth and the heights of creation—the mountain tops on which pagan gods are often said to dwell. There is a not-too-subtle slap here at the paganism surrounding God's people in Palestine during Solomon's day. Pagan gods were often associated with trees (or "groves") atop certain mountains. Centuries later, "Bathos" or "the

Deep" would be identified as a semi-god by the Gnostics, whose predecessors the apostles opposed so strongly. No matter what pagans claim, the wise man says here that the Wisdom of the One God preceded all false gods, having existed before any depths or mountain tops could become their "throne."

C. Before sky and earth, 27-29

27 When he prepared the heavens, I was there: when he set a compass upon the face of the depth:

28 When he established the clouds above: when he strengthened the fountains of the deep:

29 When he gave to the sea his decree, that the waters should not pass his commandment: when he appointed the foundations of the earth:

Wisdom also preceded all the so-called earth-gods (such as Baal) and sky gods, having been present when their realms were created. In this claim there is even a hint that so-called gods of the earth and sky are actually uninvited tenants of these realms. They are "squatters" on what is rightfully the property of God, and of Wisdom as His supervisor of the task of world-building.

Against many ancients' innate fear of the sea, and against any Israelite's fear of another Flood, Wisdom was present when God set the boundaries or limits of the oceans (see also Job 38:8-11). Whatever, if any, reality, is to be given to half-gods such as Bathos, from the mythic depths of the sea, God has set limits on their actions by virtue of being their divine Landlord. How foolish, as Isaiah would say, for anyone to worship the created instead of the Creator! (See Isa. 44:9-20.)

D. Delighting in humankind, 30-31

30 Then I was by him, as one brought up with him: and I was daily his delight, rejoicing always before him;

31 Rejoicing in the habitable part of his earth; and my delights were with the sons of men.

Now another remarkable insight emerges from the fact that Wisdom existed before Creation, at God's right hand. Wisdom found delight and joy not in the material world, but in *persons,* as the crowning act of creation. Here again, idolatry and pantheism receive a punishing blow. "God so loved the world" is seen to refer first and foremost not to the earth, and thus to any supposed gods within it, but to humankind. Here the foundation for treating persons with respect is found to be a part of the foundation of creation. Wisdom loved persons; we should make the rule of Wisdom the guiding principle of our lives; therefore we should also love persons.

Because, as we have seen, Jesus would later be identified with Wisdom, His teaching that we must "love others as I have loved you" becomes a principle of wise behavior. It is grounded, not in the whims of just any religious teacher, but in the way God constructed the world.

Evangelistic Emphasis

Before God created the world, two things were present in the universe. The first was darkness. Genesis tells us that out of darkness, God began His creation. We know by this that darkness had to have existed before creation.

According to Proverbs, the other thing that existed before time was wisdom. Wisdom preceded creation.

Many think that wisdom comes with age. As we learn from our mistakes, certainly we receive wisdom from those experiences. However, the wisdom mentioned in the text is wisdom that does not come from ex-perience, but from God. God gives us more and more wisdom as we grow older. However, it is our desire for wisdom that causes God to give it to us. It does not automatically come with age.

Wisdom does many things and helps us in many ways. Wisdom helps us to determine God's will for us. Wisdom helps us to see that God has shown us His will in many different places. Wisdom helps us to recognize that many times we cannot see God's will even though it is right in front of us.

The good news of God's wisdom must be shared with others. Would we be good neighbors if we kept such a valuable treasure to ourselves? God's wisdom, just like His love, is available to all who seek it.

℅℃℞

Doth not wisdom cry? And understanding put forth her voice?—*Proverbs 8:1*

In everything spiritual there is a secular counterpart. Wisdom is no exception. The world offers its version of wisdom, and many have flocked to it. The secular world has many awards to recognize those whom it values as wise. However, God's wisdom is entirely different. The world does not know the wisdom of God. This is not because God does not offering it to everyone who desires it, but because to obtain it we must desire it will all our hearts. This godly wisdom is the wisdom that is crying out in the text.

Recently, a member of my church came to see me in tears. This man had just completed a 34-week Bible study class. He did not clearly state exactly what he wanted; he only said that he wanted to give some things a chance that he had opposed in the past. When I asked him why he had this change of heart, he struggled for words. Finally he said, "You know I have been taking this Bible class. Well, the Bible works on you."

God's Word indeed works on us; and it cries out for us to seek and respect God's wisdom.

Weekday Problems

When bottled water first became popular, it was a slow seller, to say the least. Most people did not see the benefit of paying a dollar for something you could get free at any water fountain. Many people told me that the water at home tasted better than what they could get in a bottle. As we all know, that has certainly changed. Recently, I stopped at a convenience store to get a bottle of spring water. Several people ahead of me were buying the same thing; the store was doing a brisk business in bottled water that day.

I had always bought the cheapest water in the cooler. To me, water was water. One day my wife read on a label that the water she was drinking was simply filtered tap water. Imagine, paying over a dollar for tap water! On this hot day, however, I bought the best. It was imported from France. No tap water for me, no sir. It was twice as much as the cheap stuff, but I thought I deserved it. After almost draining the bottle, I was shocked. The bottom of the bottle was full of sand. That's right, sand! The gourmet water was dirty.

Wisdom is important because it helps us make right choices. We must decide what to eat and drink, what kind of car to buy, whether we should change careers, etc. God and His wisdom help us make the right choices.

*Tell of a time when you needed "supernatural" wisdom to make a good decision.

Wisdom from the Wise

Wisdom is not finally tested in the schools,
Wisdom cannot be passed from one having it to another not having it,
Wisdom is of the soul, is not susceptible of proof, is its own proof.—*Walt Whitman,* "Song of the Open Road"
***

There are but two classes of the wise: [those] who serve God because they have found Him, and [those] who seek Him because they have not found Him.—*Richard Cecil*
***

To know that which before us lies in daily life is the prime wisdom.—*John Milton*
***

In seeking wisdom, thou art wise; in imagining that thou hast attained it, thou art a fool.—*Rabbi Ben-Asia*

This Lesson in Your Life

As we have pointed out, wisdom and intelligence are not the same. However, if a person has wisdom, he will know exactly how and when to use his intelligence. To know when to do the right thing is wisdom. To know the right thing to do is often intelligence.

To show the love of God to others doesn't necessarily take intelligence. It is wisdom given from God that would tell us that there is value in helping others. A really intelligent person might not logically understand how helping someone could possibly benefit himself. A very wise person would automatically offer help, if needed, and not worry about any benefit to himself.

Jesus' story of the Good Samaritan is a perfect example. The church leaders that passed the man who had been robbed were intelligent men. They could not have attained their status in the Temple if they were not intelligent. We have no indication about the intelligence of the Samaritan. He was obviously successful in life because he had money to pay the inn keeper. The inn keeper must have recognized that the man had the resources to reimburse him for extra expenses when he returned. However, we know for certain that the Samaritan was *wise,* because Jesus used him for an example of goodness and virtue.

When I was in seminary, I flew onto campus every Monday and returned to my home and church for the weekends. I usually took a cab to campus from the airport, but as is true of most preacher/ students, money was tight. After a Friday seminar, I saw some of the people in my class gathered outside the chapel talking. I walked up and saw that the conversation wasn't about anything very important. I asked if one of them could drop me off at the airport, about three miles from campus. They all looked embarrassed and looked at the ground. Finally, one of them said that they were very busy and the rest took the cue and walked away. I have no doubt in my mind that they were all extremely intelligent. They were my classmates, and I marveled at their intellect every day. However, I think a wise person, who received his wisdom from God, would have seen the value of helping a colleague.

The difference between worldly wisdom and Godly wisdom can be seen all around us. True wisdom comes from God. Is the person you are observing for wisdom acting like God?

1. What does wisdom do to get our attention to let us know we should desire her?
Wisdom cries out at all the popular places. These are places where crowds gather. Wisdom does everything in her power to attract people to her.

2. What intelligence requirement does the writer of Proverbs give for receiving wisdom?
There is no intelligence requirement. Even fools are invited to partake of God's wisdom.

3. What traits are present when wisdom speaks?
Wisdom always speaks with truth, righteousness, and understanding.

4. What characteristics are never parts of wisdom?
Wisdom is never part of wickedness, perversion, and behavior or thinking that are not right.

5. What is described as the "fear of the Lord"?
The fear of the Lord is to hate evil, pride, arrogance, evil ways, and perverse speech.

6. What positive things does wisdom possess?
Counsel, sound wisdom, understanding, and strength are all attributes of wisdom.

7. Who does wisdom love?
Wisdom loves those who love wisdom.

8. When should we seek wisdom?
Those who would desire wisdom must seek her early in their lives. Wisdom does not wait for old age, as many believe.

9. How old is wisdom?
Wisdom pre-existed God's creation. She was here before the earth was formed, created by God to be everlasting.

10. How much is wisdom worth?
Wisdom is worth more than gold or choice silver.

I have a friend whose son is a young doctor. Recently my friend told me that his son was considering the ministry. I was in total shock. I wanted to blurt out, "Please stop him! He doesn't know what he's saying. The ministry is hard and he will never make as much money as he would in medicine." I should have seen it coming. For years he has told me about his son's interest in God, the Bible, and other spiritual matters. It always seemed odd to me that he would take hours discussing theology if he was studying to be a physician. After my initial reaction, I was ashamed that I would question what God was leading the young man to do. How do we know we are doing what God wants us to do? Can we ever be sure we are in God's will?

Discerning the will of God is not always difficult. The Bible is full of things that God wants us to do. For example, we know that God wants us to help those who can't help themselves. There is an abundance of Scripture written about that subject. We know that God wants us to give gifts to His work. This also, is very clear. It is God's will that we all seek wisdom. Our text makes that abundantly clear. It even tells us when we are to seek wisdom. We are to find wisdom early in our walk. The reason for the urgency is that we don't get all the wisdom we will ever get or need in one dose. Wisdom comes to us as we are able to absorb it. God knows how much we can process at one time.

Also, God gives us wisdom in many different ways. Our experience as we serve God is a route to wisdom. Studying God's Word is another way we can get wisdom. God has so many ways to teach us that we can't begin to name them all. The important things are that we should understand how valuable and precious wisdom is and that it only comes from God. The first step is understanding. After that, comes wisdom.

Lesson 12

The Path of Integrity

Proverbs 11:1-14

A false balance is abomination to the LORD: but a just weight is his delight.

2 When pride cometh, then cometh shame: but with the lowly is wisdom.

3 The integrity of the upright shall guide them: but the perverseness of transgressors shall destroy them.

4 Riches profit not in the day of wrath: but righteousness delivereth from death.

5 The righteousness of the perfect shall direct his way: but the wicked shall fall by his own wickedness.

6 The righteousness of the upright shall deliver them: but transgressors shall be taken in their own naughtiness.

7 When a wicked man dieth, his expectation shall perish: and the hope of unjust men perisheth.

8 The righteous is delivered out of trouble, and the wicked cometh in his stead.

9 An hypocrite with his mouth destroyeth his neighbour: but through knowledge shall the just be delivered.

10 When it goeth well with the righteous, the city rejoiceth: and when the wicked perish, there is shouting.

11 By the blessing of the upright the city is exalted: but it is overthrown by the mouth of the wicked.

12 He that is void of wisdom despiseth his neighbour: but a man of understanding holdeth his peace.

13 A talebearer revealeth secrets: but he that is of a faithful spirit concealeth the matter.

14 Where no counsel is, the people fall: but in the multitude of counselors there is safety.

Devotional Reading
Prov. 10:27-32

Background Scripture
Prov. 11

Memory Selection
Prov. 11:3

May 21

We have noted the *practical* nature of Proverbs. This lesson, for example, focuses on the day-to-day values of *integrity, righteousness,* and *uprightness in social relationships.*

However, this does not mean that Proverbs has no "theology." The right living or "righteousness" referred to in Proverbs 11 is to be preferred over wickedness because it is in fact based on the theological principle that *God* is righteous. The wise man knows that people become like the gods they worship. It works the other way, too: it is a poor reflection on God when worshipers behave in a way unlike Him.

The material here is for the street and the office, at home, and at work. Yet it is not just about behavior. It is about what Wes Reagan, the editor of the *Higley Commentary,* calls "blue jeans theology."

ഇന്ദ്ര

Admit at the start that the principles of right living taught in this lesson are often considered "prosaic." Then proceed to define the term as that which is *dull, uninspiring, predictable,* and *unimaginative.* Originally, "prosaic" meant "like prose," as opposed to poetry. Somehow it's easy to assume that lessons on right living are dull.

Note, however, how this changes when we apply principles of morality to our public officials. We insist that they act with honesty and integrity. Suddenly morality becomes more like "poetic justice"—important, maybe even "beautiful," and certainly not dull! The moral principles this lesson teaches us to value become "prosaic" only when we lack the imagination and creativity to apply them to everyday life.

Teaching Outline	Daily Bible Readings

I. Integrity—1-3
  A. Just practices, 1
  B. Integrity and pride, 2-3
II. Right-ness—4-8
  A. Wickedness is self-defeating, 4-6
  B. Wickedness is hopeless, 7-8
III. Social Values—9-14
  A. Hypocrisy is destructive, 9
  B. How to build up a city, 10-11
  C. Don't tell all you know, 12-13
  D. Get good input, 14
	Mon. God's Way Is a Stronghold
	      Prov. 10:27-32
	Tue. Wisdom, not Pride
	      Prov. 11:1-5
	Wed. Righteousness, not Treachery
	      Prov. 11:6-10
	Thu. Guidance and Counsel
	      Prov. 11:11-15
	Fri. Blameless, not Wicked
	      Prov. 11:16-21
	Sat. Generous, not Stingy
	      Prov. 11:22-26
	Sun. Goodness, not Evil
	      Prov. 11:27-31

Verse by Verse

I. Integrity—1-3

A. Just practices, 1

1 A false balance is abomination to the LORD: but a just weight is his delight.

Note the *structure* of most of these statements on moral principles in this lesson. First the author states the positive value of the principle, then he states the negative value of the opposite behavior, or restates the positive in another form. This style reminds us that much of Wisdom literature, including the Proverbs, was originally written in poetic style (as indicated in the print style in versions such as the NIV, which give a second line to the parallel phrase). In Hebrew, *ideas* rather than words are made to rhyme, with a second line either repeating or stating the opposite of the first.

In verse 1 the positive element is the just or honest business practice of, say, a butcher refraining from weighing the customer's purchase with his finger on the scale. Why is this practice wrong? Not just because it cheats the customer, or will cause him to go to another butcher next time, but because *"The LORD abhors dishonest scales"* (NIV). Throughout, the very *practical* nature of the moral principles discussed will be based on the *theological* nature of how God views our

actions, and how they reflect on Him. If an unbelieving customer knows that a dishonest butcher is a "believer," presumably committed to behavior of which God approves, then his dishonesty reflects badly on both the believer and on God.

B. Integrity and pride, 2-3

2 When pride cometh, then cometh shame: but with the lowly is wisdom.

3 The integrity of the upright shall guide them: but the perverseness of transgressors shall destroy them.

Why are being "lowly" or humble, and having "integrity," factors in being just or honest? Because the proud person refuses to subject himself to God's rules. The word "integrity" comes from the same root as the term "integer," meaning a whole number. This leads to the truth that a person of integrity is a "whole person"—integrity is not a "face" or trait a true believer puts on when it seems convenient or self-beneficial, but is a natural expression of his entire values system.

Another indication of the "this-worldly" nature of Proverbs is that defying practical moral principles is self-destructive. Integrity is its own reward because it guides us into right pathways, while "perverseness" or going our own way is not only displeasing to God but will prove to be our own downfall. Of course everyone is aware that some who lack integrity seem to "get away with it." Although the wise man's view generally assumes that they won't, really, he also has an idea of future punishment, as the next verse shows.

II. Right-ness—4-8

A. Wickedness is self-defeating, 4-6

4 Riches profit not in the day of wrath: but righteousness delivereth from death.

5 The righteousness of the perfect shall direct his way: but the wicked shall fall by his own wickedness.

6 The righteousness of the upright shall deliver them: but transgressors shall be taken in their own naughtiness.

Our outline substitutes "rightness" for "righteousness" here to avoid the common association of righteousness with *self*-righteousness. This was the mistake of the Pharisees in the time of Christ, for whom "righteousness" had become a badge of reward proving that they had earned God's approval (Matt. 6:5). Although this view is not approved even under the Law, the apostle Paul would be the leading biblical theologian to clarify that while believers are to live righteously, it is God's grace that empowers them to do so, and His mercy that covers their unrighteousness. The idea here is that only right living will equip us to stand before the judgment bar of God. Ill-gotten gain is too unlike His character to vindicate us. In verse 5, "perfect" in Hebrew, as in the Greek *telos* of the New Testament, hints of being "whole" or "complete," rather than absolute moral sinlessness.

Again, both righteousness and wickedness have within them the seeds of their own reward or destruction. Living with integrity is its own reward, and being "naughty" commonly has negative pay-offs quite apart from future judgment.

B. Wickedness is hopeless, 7-8

7 When a wicked man dieth, his expectation shall perish: and the hope of unjust men perisheth.

8 The righteous is delivered out of trouble, and the wicked cometh in his stead.

Again we are given a glimpse of both the similarity and difference of expectations of future reward and punishment between the Old Covenant and the New. The Old Testament emphasis is on being delivered from trouble in this life, as in verse 8. The future expectation is not so much of a personal resurrection for judgment and an after-life as it is the continuation of human expectations for the righteous, versus destruction of all hope for the wicked.

It is not easy to understand how verse 8 fits, in the KJV. The NIV translators suggest reversing some words, resulting in the "trouble" coming upon the wicked instead of the righteous.

III. Social Values—9-14

A. Hypocrisy is destructive, 9

9 An hypocrite with his mouth destroyeth his neighbour: but through knowledge shall the just be delivered.

It has been well said that "character" refers to what we really are, while "reputation" is what others perceive us to be. For the wise man, however, private morals should be inseparable from public and social living. Being a hypocrite (literally "wearing a mask") is self-destructive, but it also hurts others. Note how the second line balances the "hypocrite" with a person of "knowledge." This speaks of knowing one's "best self," and living in accordance with that instead of living below the person God wants us to be.

B. How to build up a city, 10-11

10 When it goeth well with the righteous, the city rejoiceth: and when the wicked perish, there is shouting.

11 By the blessing of the upright the city is exalted: but it is overthrown by the mouth of the wicked.

In context, when it "goeth well with the righteous" probably means when they *do* well, or act according to the moral precepts being taught here. Again presuming that God rewards right behavior in this world, we can see why a city would be "exalted" (vs. 11) at such times, and why people in general shout with joy when the wicked are overthrown. Just as a righteous soul brings a blessing to the body in which it resides, so conscientious believers bring blessings to the body politic.

C. Don't tell all you know, 12-13

12 He that is void of wisdom despiseth his neighbour: but a man of understanding holdeth his peace.

13 A talebearer revealeth secrets: but he that is of a faithful spirit concealeth the matter.

Now the wise man brings moral precepts to bear on relationships "across the back fence." The man of wisdom (which, we recall, begins with "the fear of the Lord," 1:7, etc.) knows to "love his neighbor as himself," and when to "hold his peace" or decline to let differences escalate to a fight between neighbors. This counsel of silence especially applies to "tale-bearing" or gossip. The person of virtue does not reveal secrets that would damage a neighbor.

D. Get good input, 14

14 Where no counsel is, the people fall: but in the multitude of counselors there is safety.

This famous proverb affirms the wisdom of seeking advice from others in making crucial decisions. Despite our culture's traditional valuing of the "rugged individual," it is foolish to plunge recklessly into a course of action without advice from those who are in touch with broader sources of information than one person could ever cultivate. The classic illustration of this in Scripture is King Rehoboam, who, after hearing from wise counselors, went his own course after all, forever dividing the nation of Israel (1 Kings 12).

Evangelistic Emphasis

Amos was one of the bravest men in the entire Bible. He was from the southern kingdom, Judah. He lived in the small town of Tekoa and was a shepherd and a farm worker. He was brave because, as an uneducated farmer, he ventured to the northern kingdom, Israel, and spoke to the king about the injustice shown to God's people. For example, the poor would come to market with their meager resources and attempt to buy food and clothing. The merchants would hollow out the weights of their scale so that only a small portion of the purchase would balance them. Because God has always loved the poor and downtrodden, Amos preached against such dishonesty.

There is little doubt that the leaders and merchants of Israel in Amos' time knew of the emphasis on justice as "wisdom" in Proverbs. Since God never changes, do you think He still demands this of business today? Of course He does. God will also bless those of us who demand that all of God's children be treated fairly in the market place. It is easy for us to look the other way and say that it is none of our business. However, God's disciples cannot sit still and watch the poor be trampled.

ഇൗരു

Memory Selection

The integrity of the upright shall guide them: but the perverseness of transgressors shall destroy them.—*Proverbs 11:3*

I can remember when I first realized that a man I had looked up to all my life was a crook. It was one of the most traumatic moments in my life. I had been told that his business practices were not above board, but I refused to believe it. Later, I saw with my own eyes that he was not ethical in his business. It was a hard truth to accept.

Some people see God as a vengeful God. I see Him as a God of love and forgiveness. I know that he has forgiven me, loves me, and accepts me. I cannot imagine His doing anything less for anyone else. This text talks about people with integrity in a positive way. However, it mentions those who do not walk with integrity being destroyed. Is it God who destroys them, or the things that they are doing? If someone engages in destructive behavior and those actions cause him harm in some way, is it fair to blame God?

The person I mentioned who delved into unfair business practices is now a broken man. He is bitter, sad, and lonely. God did not make him this way. It was a life-style choice this man made for himself. God wants and expects more out of him. He tells us this in our text.

Weekday Problems

Our text talks about the righteous being delivered while the wicked will suffer. Sometimes we can't see this happening. Too many people seem to get away with wrongdoing. We need to understand that the pride in doing what is right and always acting out of love can be a reward in itself. Those who do the wrong things will never know what it feels like to live as a person of integrity.

In front of the courthouse in my hometown is a monument to the fallen heroes of World War I. It commemorates the efforts of the men from my home community and their bravery fighting for freedom. They were remembered because they did something great. Have you noticed that all monuments like this commemorate something good and noble? Do we erect monuments for evil deeds? Are there statues of any politicians or leaders in your area who are honored because they were crooked? Not likely.

Our text reminds us that some people will experience the pleasure of knowing that they have done their best. The ones who do the wrong things will be punished, not necessarily by anything or anyone other than the deeds themselves. The crushing weight of evil acts will cause those who commit them to implode under the weight of wrong itself.

*Recall an incident when someone reaped the fruits of wrong-doing.

The Attraction of Opposites

How many "oxymorons"—self-contradictory phrases—can you add to this list?

exact estimate	working vacation
definite maybe	diet ice cream
extinct life	tight slacks
clearly misunderstood	plastic glasses
acting naturally	passive aggression
taped live	synthetic natural gas
new classic	sweet sorrow
12-ounce pound cake	child-proof
terribly pleased	pretty ugly
temporary tax	soft rock
small crowd	legally drunk
sanitary garbage dump	alone together
good grief	almost exactly
genuine imitation	airline food

This Lesson in Your Life

I live in a state that has a reputation for public corruption. We are not alone in this distinction because many officials in many different states have been caught in varying forms of misconduct. Does this mean that all public officials are corrupt? The truth is that a large majority of our governmental officials are extremely moral and would never breach the public's trust. We depend on the good men and women who serve in the public sector to bless us with their energy and efforts. It is the small minority who get the headlines.

I can remember my first experience at discovering that someone I had known and trusted all my life had taken the public's money and used it for his personal use. He had diverted tax money for personal expenses. The amount of money that was taken had grown each year. No doubt he gained confidence that he would never be prosecuted. I was serving a church in a small town, and one day the mayor shared with me a state auditor's report about a public official that I knew well. He told me that the public had turned its back on this problem because everyone liked this person. The auditors had turned up corruption leading back many years, but because of his influence and authority, he was never prosecuted.

Being young and naive, I began a crusade to oust the official. Many people told me that they did not care what he had done, they still supported him. After a year of work getting the information to the people, I gave up. People that I cared for and respected lectured me that I shouldn't be trying to get this person in trouble. I was discouraged and defeated. I questioned whether I should have ever gotten involved. However, my efforts and the efforts of the few who helped me got the attention of the prosecutors in the state capitol. Eventually the man was tried in state court, and convicted. One condition of his sentencing was that he never run for office again.

On the other hand, the public fails if it does not express appreciation for the good and honest public officials who serve them. In many areas of public work, the pay is small for the work performed. Policemen and firemen, for example, are poorly compensated for the risk involved.

Proverbs makes it clear that God is not pleased when the public is cheated. It also teaches us that those who take advantage of others will fall under the weight of their sin. However, the text also praises those who are wise enough to recognize the delight one feels when always being fair and honest. It is the best feeling a person can experience.

STRAIGHT

1. How does God feel about honesty in the market place?

God thinks of cheating in trade as an abomination. However, He looks with delight upon those who strive to be honest.

2. What is the difference between pride and humility?

Pride only offers shame while humility comes from wisdom.

3. What is the judgment of those who strive to do wrong?

The weight of their transgressions shall destroy them.

4. What is the benefit of integrity to the righteous?

Integrity will save a person from the destruction of evil doing and give a person clear direction in life.

5. What responsibility do we have to others?

We should not slander our neighbor. In the truth of wisdom, we will be delivered from those who would choose to destroy us.

6. How can the public help keep their officials honest?

We should praise those who do good and also recognize their accomplishments. However, we should not tolerate corruption in the public arena.

7. What is often a source of conflict with our neighbors?

A lack of God's wisdom in "holding our peace" can cause trouble for others.

8. What is said in this text about loyalty to others?

If we consider ourselves a loyal friend then we will not gossip about them. A loyal friend knows how to keep a secret.

9. How are we to look at our mentors?

We must seek those that are wise and call on them for advice, for there is strength in persons of wisdom.

10. How does Proverbs measure wickedness and righteousness in time?

Wickedness does not carry over beyond this world, but is destroyed. Righteousness lives forever.

The Bible gives us many descriptions of God. It is only when we put all of these together that we can get a clear picture of who God is. Certainly Proverbs tells us that he is a moral God who does not tolerate corruption. God cannot stand for humans to cheat other humans. We have a responsibility to do the right thing every time. God challenges not only our actions, but also our consistency. We see in today's text a description of a lifetime of steady, honest dealings toward others.

I was eating lunch with some friends in a cafeteria recently. When it was my turn to pay my check, the teenager at the register was extremely nervous. I have a feeling it was because the line was so long. No doubt she felt it was her job to move the line along quickly. However, for every person she checked out, two more took his place.

I gave her enough change so that she only had to give me one dollar back to clear my bill. However, she kept insisting on giving me a dollar plus change. I tried to explain to her that she was giving me too much money, but I just couldn't make her understand. Finally, I saw a cup next to the register for those who lacked a small amount of change paying their checks. I simply dropped the extra change she gave me into the cup and went on my way.

Sometimes it seems easier to compromise our principles. However, God demands consistency throughout our lives to do what is right. God wants not only accuracy but also longevity of right actions. We should be like the bunny in the battery commercial, who just keeps going and going . . . . We too should just keep on keeping on, reaping the reward of knowing we are pleasing in God's eyes.

Proverbs 31:10-16, 25-31

Who can find a virtuous woman? for her price is far above rubies.

11 The heart of her husband doth safely trust in her, so that he shall have no need of spoil.

12 She will do him good and not evil all the days of her life.

13 She seeketh wool, and flax, and worketh willingly with her hands.

14 She is like the merchants' ships; she bringeth her food from afar.

15 She riseth also while it is yet night, and giveth meat to her household, and a portion to her maidens.

16 She considereth a field, and buyeth it: with the fruit of her hands she planteth a vineyard.

25 Strength and honour are her clothing; and she shall rejoice in time to come.

26 She openeth her mouth with wisdom; and in her tongue is the law of kindness.

27 She looketh well to the ways of her household, and eateth not the bread of idleness.

28 Her children arise up, and call her blessed; her husband also, and he praiseth her.

29 Many daughters have done virtuously, but thou excellest them all.

30 Favour is deceitful, and beauty is vain: but a woman that feareth the LORD, she shall be praised.

31 Give her of the fruit of her hands; and let her own works praise her in the gates.

Devotional Reading
Prov. 4:10-15

Background Scripture
Prov. 31

Memory Selection
Prov. 31:30

May 28

This description of an ideal wife in ancient times will be applied in various ways today, depending on the reader—especially females. Critics often say it unfairly confines women to the home. Ironically, those who see the ideal "homebody" here ignore this woman's efficiency beyond the home. Actually, the psalm does not claim to define or limit the role of women. It does not even pretend that every woman is like the one described here (she has unusual wealth, for example). Instead it takes womanly traits valued most by men and God in those times, and presents them in a single ideal portrait.

Plunge right into this lesson, which might be called "The Worthy Woman," by inviting members of your study group to give brief (even one-word) definitions of "The World's Finest Wife." Traits you may want to supply, if they are not forthcoming in the discussion, include: *faithful to her husband . . . a nurturer* *of her children . . . one who sets an example in kindness . . . sensitive to the needs of others . . . able to transmit godly values to her children . . . .* Challenge group members to move beyond these more conventional traits by asking how they would rate other qualities such as *independent thinker . . . one who is interested in developing job skills outside the home . . . a good leader.* Note that today's lesson will both uphold ideal womanhood and prompt questions about what this means.

Teaching Outline

I. Ideal Wife—10-12
   A. Virtue as nobility, 10
   B. Trustworthiness, 11-12
II. Industrious Woman—13-16
   A. Homemaking skills, 13
   B. Business sense, 14
   C. Efficient manager, 15
   D. Agri-business person, 16
III. Honored by All—25-31
   A. Joy, wisdom, kindness, 25-26
   B. Kudos from the family, 27-28
   C. 'Enjoy your reward!' 29-31

Daily Bible Readings

Mon. Advice for Children
      Prov. 4:1-9
Tue. Keep on the Right Path
      Prov. 4:10-15
Wed. Valuing Wise Conduct
      Prov. 10:18-23
Thu. Advice from a Mother
      Prov. 31:1-9
Fri.   Portrait of a Capable Wife
      Prov. 31:10-15
Sat.   The Ideal Wife
      Prov. 31:16-23
Sun. Honor to a Wife and Mom
      Prov. 31:24-31

Verse by Verse

I. Ideal Wife—10-12
A. Virtue as nobility, 10

10 Who can find a virtuous woman? for her price is far above rubies.

This description of an ideal wife and mother is, like Psalms 25, 34, and 119, an "acrostic poem"—one in which each verse, in the Hebrew, begins with successive letters of the alphabet. Its author is the otherwise unknown "King Lemuel" (31:1), or his mother (vs. 2).

The word translated "virtuous" in the KJV comes from the same word as that translated "valor" in the phrase "men of valor" (Josh. 6:2, etc.). The NIV uses the more exalted phrase "wife of noble character," while the NRSV uses the verses that follow to scale the phrase down to the more practical and mundane "a capable wife."

Putting various translations together, we may say that the description is about a woman whose capability in many areas makes her exceptionally admirable in the eyes of all she influences, especially her husband and children. As noted in the "Focus" section, the picture is of no one woman, but a compilation of the traits of the women considered in the ancient world to be the finest and best.

Like all models of perfection, it is an ideal, not a picture painted to make women who can't sew feel guilty!

B. Trustworthiness, 11-12

11 The heart of her husband doth safely trust in her, so that he shall have no need of spoil.

12 She will do him good and not evil all the days of her life.

At the top of the list of ideal womanly virtues is the fact that her husband can trust her. This not only means that he can count on her being faithful to him, but to their children as well. She is such a good manager that her husband need not turn to robbery to bring home "spoils" to support the family. If his own values are in the right priority, he also feels no need to turn aside to other women for temporary pleasure; for his wife's capabilities in so many areas do him long-term good.

It is obvious from such a passage that this portrait of an ideal woman is influenced by the needs of a husband. The woman described here not only satisfied his needs and those of his family; she makes him "look good" and feel comfortable—his supportive wife enables him to be "known in the gates," or serve as one of the city's ruling elders (vs. 23).

II. Industrious Woman—13-16
A. Homemaking skills, 13

13 She seeketh wool, and flax, and worketh willingly with her hands.

Since the ancient world had no textile mills or clothing factories, clothes were usually the product of individual homes. Hence there was a premium on women who knew how to make cloth from wool and other materials. (The word "distaff" in verse 19, the staff or spindle used to hold wool for spinning, survives to this day as meaning also "womanly" or "home-side.")

B. Business sense, 14

14 She is like the merchants' ships; she bringeth her food from afar.

This ideal woman was not always a "stay-at-home mom." The "Proverbs 31 woman" could range far and wide in her quest to supplement her husband's income. Food for the family is *"her* food"—implying that she considers herself responsible for providing household needs, while her husband's income is presumably designated for investments or for expanding his business. The reference to "merchant ships," along with some differences in the Hebrew of this chapter, prompt some scholars to suppose that the proverb comes from outside Israel, which (except for a time during Solomon's reign) was not known for its merchant fleet. Against this argument is the the use of "Yahweh" (LORD) for God in verse 30, since this special name for God

was revealed specifically to the Jews (Exod. 6:3).

C. Efficient manager, 15

15 She riseth also while it is yet night, and giveth meat to her household, and a portion to her maidens.

This ideal "composite" woman is not lazy. She arises even before her hired help (although she is hardly typical in being able to afford them), to be sure her whole household is provided for. She is apparently a good manager, to be able to maintain such a household.

D. Agri-business person, 16

16 She considereth a field, and buyeth it: with the fruit of her hands she planteth a vineyard.

Again we see an ancient exposure of the myth that the ideal woman could not "work outside the home." The woman envisioned by the author to be the "noblest" is free to engage in real estate transactions—although again this is for the purpose of bringing food and income to her household. (Her apparent independence from even consulting with her husband about the finances of this transaction is not suggested as a model for today!)

III. Honored by All—25-31
A. Joy, wisdom, kindness, 25-26

25 Strength and honour are her clothing; and she shall rejoice in time to come.

26 She openeth her mouth with wisdom; and in her tongue is the law of kindness.

This noblest of women is

"clothed" with garments of praise and honor because of her efficiency and caring attitude. The "time to come" refers to the uncertainty of the future. The ideal woman has enough provisions stored up so that her family will not suffer during future wars, droughts, or other hard times. Verse 26 shows that she is not given to empty or silly talk or malicious gossip; her words are filled with wisdom and kindness.

B. Kudos from the family, 27-28

27 She looketh well to the ways of her household, and eateth not the bread of idleness.

28 Her children arise up, and call her blessed; her husband also, and he praiseth her.

Verse 27 is a summary of the preceding qualities that are so highly praised. This woman is able to focus on the needs of her family. She is willing and eager (see also vs. 13) to provide for them, rather than being a slacker. (In modern terms, would the author have said "She doesn't watch the soaps all day"?) As a result, this mother is appreciated and honored by her children. Here is another indication that the passage is not meant to be a legalistic "pattern" for all women. Whether children appreciate Mom depends in part on their own attitude and ability to be grateful, not just on her dedication and homemaking skills and dedication.

C. 'Enjoy your reward!' 29-31

29 Many daughters have done virtuously, but thou excellest them all.

30 Favour is deceitful, and beauty is vain: but a woman that feareth the LORD, she shall be praised.

31 Give her of the fruit of her hands; and let her own works praise her in the gates.

The word translated "daughters" here can refer to any woman (see the NIV, "Many women"); and the word for "virtuously" is from the same root as "virtuous" in verse 10, which, as noted above, refers not just to a chaste wife but to one who is strong, noble, or capable. The idea is that while there are women in many fields who are more widely honored (as the queen of Sheba), the "Proverbs 31 woman" with this "ideal composite's" energy, efficiency, and loving dedication to her family is at the top of the list.

As verse 30 indicates, queens and other women in places of more visibility and authority often receive more praise than homemakers—especially if they happen to be beautiful in appearance. Such accolades are fleeting, however, especially when compared with a God-fearing woman who takes seriously, though eagerly, the responsibilities of being an outstanding wife, mother, and homemaker.

"The fruit of her hands," in verse 31, refers to the visible results of this godly woman's extraordinary efforts. It is assumed, as in verse 28, that these "results" will include grateful children, an appreciative husband, and a smooth-running household.

Evangelistic Emphasis

In the popular television show called "Extreme Makeover," participants volunteer to have their faces and bodies made completely over. The producers scour the nation looking for people who are unhappy with their looks and are willing to submit to plastic surgery, new hair-dos, body shaping, and other beauty techniques designed to make them look different.

Why do we place so much importance on the body? Proverbs 31 tells us that the woman who is to be prized concentrates on noble behavior. We are told that her husband and her children will be well thought of because of her wisdom.

Some of the traits in this portrait may not be practical in today's society. However, I'm sure that you can name a woman like the one described in this passage. We all know women who work hard and accomplish much. For a woman to rise to the top of her field with a heart of compassion for others is not impossible. Have you expressed your admiration for that "special" woman you know who is described in our text?

❧❦

Memory Selection

Favor is deceitful, and beauty is vain: but a woman that feareth the Lord, she shall be praised.—*Proverbs 31:30*

I am convinced that the job of being a parent is more difficult than ever. Modern youth have more temptations than ever. One of the best tools for raising a sound, functional child is a good mother. This would be a mother who is filled with God's wisdom and realizes the importance of passing that wisdom to her children. Many will use the excuse of a lack of time to teach her children by words and example. However, it is not the amount of time as much as it is the quality of time.

Several weeks ago, my wife and I were watching a beauty pageant on TV. We had picked out the girl that we thought should win. She had it all. She was pretty, graceful, and extremely talented. However, when they asked her a question and she was given the chance to respond, we could not believe what came out of her mouth. I suppose she was nervous and she certainly didn't have much time to think, but she gave the most ridiculous, trivial answer possible. We quickly changed our minds about who should win. Apparently, so did the judges. Beauty can be a blessing but only when combined with wisdom. If there is a choice, the text tells us that the "fear of the Lord" is the most important quality of all.

Weekday Problems

In my younger days I worked as a youth director in several churches. It always amazed me how parents would insist their youngsters keep good grades, participate in sports, and never miss school, but never insisted they commit to church activities. Invariably I would have to minister in some way to these teens who were given little spiritual direction from their families. Of course, we would occasionally have active youth who would get into some sort of trouble but those episodes were rare.

Everything we did with our youth was free. We offered spiritual groups, religious education, recreation, fellowship, and mentoring without cost or obligation to the parents.

A wise mother will set the example for her children by being successful in her spiritual life. She will insist that her children live a well-rounded life complete with spiritual nourishment that will sustain them for their entire lives. It will be no coincidence that this same woman will be successful in all her endeavors.

*Do you think all of the traits of the ideal woman of Proverbs 31 should apply today?

*What traits might the modern world require that are omitted from this picture?

From Not-So-Ideal Marriages

Wife: Sometimes I think you only married me because my daddy left me a lot of money.
Husband: That's not true. I don't care who left you the money.

***

Husband to artist: Do you think you can paint a good portrait of my wife?"
Artist: I can make it so lifelike you'll jump every time you see it.

***

Wife: Last night I dreamed you gave me $200 for a new wardrobe. You wouldn't spoil that dream, would you?
Husband: Of course not, darling. You may keep the $200.

***

Wife (in tears): Darling, you know that cake you asked me to bake for you? I'm sorry, but the dog ate it!
Husband: That's okay, dear, don't cry. I'll buy you another dog.

This Lesson in Your Life

I have used Proverbs 31 as a text at the funerals of several women over the years. It is impossible to find a passage that will specifically speak to a person's life in every circumstance. However, I remember on one occasion this passage fit exactly. The woman's name was Betty. She was industrious, wise, and a perfect wife and mother.

Conducting funerals is the least favorite thing that I do. I often spend hours trying to come up with a eulogy that is appropriate to the person's life. However, with Betty it was not a problem. I immediately turned to this passage and I saw her in every verse. It was a message that preached itself. I looked out at the family and friends as I spoke and saw their heads nodding almost in unison in complete agreement. Her sister-in-law wrote me after the funeral and said that I really knew her well. Someone once said that all of us preach our own funeral by the way we live. This truth is so clear in our text.

Some people are extremely purposeful in the way they live. They have principles that guide them, and rarely allow themselves to deviate from their goals. Others seem to make decisions on a whim and will cross any boundary when pressed. What makes the difference? The answer lies in God's wisdom. A woman who is aware of what is important and imparts that to her children is a woman who possesses God's wisdom. The point of our lesson is that these same principles will carry over in every aspect of a woman's life. If she is a business woman, we can see God's wisdom. If she is a mother, her children will be raised with a healthy respect for the faith she has handed down to them. If she is a wife, her husband will be respected for his association with her.

Another term to describe the woman in our text is the word *responsibility*. We are often called upon to take on certain responsibilities for a period of time. What the writer of Proverbs describes is a woman who takes her role as a responsibility forever. She lives with her position in society, the church, and at home and it is a part of her life. She knows the proper balance between these roles and maintains that balance throughout the seasons of life. When people observe such a person, they admire her and have a tendency to emulate her. We paint a picture of our world by the way we live.

How many women can you name who fit this image? Are you one of them?

GETTING THE FACTS STRAIGHT

1. How important is it to be a woman of virtue?
It is priceless. We cannot place a price on righteousness because it can't be bought.

2. How does her husband view this virtuous woman?
He sees her as one who can be trusted. This is such a precious commodity that he considers himself to be wealthy, needing no additional fortune.

3. What are the work ethics of this ideal woman?
She uses her time wisely. She is also a generous woman who shares her good fortune with others.

4. What is her responsibility to the poor?
She makes sure that the needs of the poor are met. She is compassionate toward those who are less fortunate.

5. How are we to go about being responsible for others?
We are to be their spokespersons, speaking up for those who can't speak for themselves.

6. What is our responsibility for those less fortunate than we are?
We are to take their cause on as our own. We are to make sure that they are treated fairly.

7. How will the godly wisdom of the ideal woman affect her husband?
Her husband will be respected by his peers.

8. How will her children view their mother?
They will have respect for her, and will tell her so.

9. What are the lasting benefits of God's wisdom in a woman?
Charm can be copied and beauty does not last. However, a woman who fears the Lord has a lasting quality that everyone will admire all her life.

10. How will the world remember a victorious woman?
Her deeds will live on.

Compassion is a wonder____. Many struggle with having compassion for others. Often the lack of compassion is caused by a great hurt earlier in life. Sometimes it is caused by being raised in a home that is extremely rigid, where everything is black or white. No matter the cause, if we struggle with compassion we have a difficult time becoming like Christ. The goal of every Christian is to emulate Christ in all that he does. In everything, Christ was compassionate.

As a child growing up, I can remember the hands of those women who were our neighbors. They seemed to always be kind hands ready to soothe whatever hurt I was feeling at the time. Often my mother's hands would double as comforter and tormentor. She would correct me with harsh hands and those same hands would also comfort me. Our neighbor's hands, along with the hands of my grandmother, were strictly for comforting. I liked those hands. Hands that work hard are often rough hands. They bear the evidence of hard labor. However, hands do not have to be soft in order to comfort. A wise woman will often have the marks of hard work on her face and hands. Since she is wise, she knows that this face, worn with work, can give a comforting smile. She knows that these hands, well worn with hard work, can also soothe any hurt that comes our way.

Have you ever wondered how much money our society spends on face and hand cosmetics? What if we could channel this money to the needy? Think about how many more hungry people we could feed if we were not so preoccupied with beauty. A wise and virtuous woman will somehow set her priorities to include others in her life. She will never forget those who are in need. When she prepares a meal, or produces something that her family needs, she will always share that with others who are in need. This is the mark of a woman who possesses God's wisdom. The Scripture asks the question, "Who can find a virtuous woman?" It then goes on to describe what a virtuous woman is. We all know some. Let us now thank God for them.

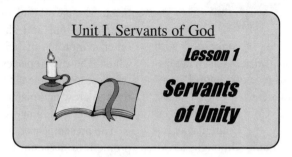

Unit I. Servants of God

Lesson 1

Servants of Unity

1 Corinthians 1:10-17, 30-31

Now I beseech you, brethren, by the name of our Lord Jesus Christ, that ye all speak the same thing, and that there be no divisions among you; but that ye be perfectly joined together in the same mind and in the same judgment.

11 For it hath been declared unto me of you, my brethren, by them which are of the house of Chloe, that there are contentions among you.

12 Now this I say, that every one of you saith, I am of Paul; and I of Apollos; and I of Cephas; and I of Christ.

13 Is Christ divided? was Paul crucified for you? or were ye baptized in the name of Paul?

14 I thank God that I baptized none of you, but Crispus and Gaius;

15 Lest any should say that I had baptized in mine own name.

16 And I baptized also the household of Stephanas: besides, I know not whether I baptized any other.

17 For Christ sent me not to baptize, but to preach the gospel: not with wisdom of words, lest the cross of Christ should be made of none effect.

30 But of him are ye in Christ Jesus, who of God is made unto us wisdom, and righteousness, and sanctification, and redemption:

31 That, according as it is written, He that glorieth, let him glory in the Lord.

Devotional Reading
1 Cor. 1:2-9

Background Scripture
1 Cor. 10

Memory Selection
1 Cor. 1:10

This quarter is concerned with *how to be the Church*—drawing lessons from the apostle Paul's immensely practical letters of 1 and 2 Corinthians. Contrary to popular opinion today, the Church was not optional for Paul. Although, as we often hear, the Church does not save anyone, God places the saved in the Church (Acts 1:47b, KJV).

Some members of your study group may have a background in a church different from yours. While emphasizing church unity, the teacher will need to be sensitive to diversity in the group, and to the strong feelings many people have about the roots of their faith.

After an initial rush of excitement, however, this new Body of people began to quarrel and divide, argue over doctrine, and show various other symptoms of being babes in Christ. These two epistles were Paul's response to this urgent need for Christians to grow and mature in their life together as a community of faith.

The present lesson focuses on the problem of division. It lays a foundation for the unity of the Church that is perhaps even more critically needed now than it was in Paul's day.

ಆರ

Ask what denominational backgrounds are represented, what that heritage has meant to each member's faith, and what brought them together here. (Avoid negative comments!) Ask whether it is possible to have *division* without *divisiveness*—the fact, but not the spirit. Note that Paul calls believers to resist attempts to divide the Church, which is Christ's own Body (Eph. 1:22-23).

Teaching Outline	*Daily Bible Readings*
I. Appeal for unity—10	Mon. God Is Lord of All Rom. 10:9-13
A. 'No divisions,' 10a	Tue. Reconciled in Christ Col. 1:15-20
B. One mind, 10b	Wed. One Body, One Spirit Eph. 4:1-6
C. Reports of division, 11	Thu. Called Together in Christ 1 Cor. 1:1-9
II. Hyphenated Christians—12-16	Fri. Be United in Christ 1 Cor. 1:10-17
A. Following men, 12	Sat. Christ Crucified 1 Cor. 1:18-25
B. No competition, 13-16	Sun. Salvation in Christ, not Men 1 Cor. 1:26-31
III. Core of the matter, 17, 30-31	
A. Paul's mission, 17	
B. Blessings in Christ, 30-31	

Verse by Verse

I. Appeal for unity—10
A. 'No divisions,' 10a
10 Now I beseech you, brethren, by the name of our Lord Jesus Christ, that ye all speak the same thing, and that there be no divisions among you;

Such an appeal to "speak the same thing" sounds radical in a setting such as ours, when the Church of God manifestly speaks so many different things. Depending on how far to follow divisions that continue to subdivide, estimates on the number of denominations in the U. S. alone range from 300 to more than 1,000. Although the history that brought us to this point includes sincere and dearly held differences, few modern Church leaders would argue against trying to work our way back to a point where we can take Paul as seriously as we have taken our differences.

The original word for *divisions* here also gives us the term *schism*, reminding us of the seriousness of thinking "schismatically," or in a *spirit* of divisiveness. While it is unrealistic that one generation can cancel more than 2,000 years of Church history and its divisions, perhaps we can work toward an unsectarian spirit with the help of such teachings as Paul's.
B. One mind, 10b
10b but that ye be perfectly joined together in the same mind and in the same judgment.

A single Greek word translated "perfectly joined together" implies not perfection but a willingness to *repair* that which has been broken. Again we see the importance of a spirit of unity, quite apart from genuine differences. When two believers share the willingness of mind and judgment to be "joined together," they can often co-exist despite differences, and allow diversity to enrich their relationship instead of dividing them.
C. Reports of division, 11
11 For it hath been declared unto me of you, my brethren, by them which are of the house of Chloe, that there are contentions among you.

"Chloe" is an otherwise unidentified woman who apparently traveled widely, including in her journeys both Corinth and Ephesus, from which Paul wrote this letter (16:8). Her report from the Corinthian church which Paul had established on his second missionary tour included unfortunate divisions. ("Contentions" is from the Greek *eris*, which not surprisingly was also the name of the Greek goddess of discord.) The report of division which Chloe brought to Paul was only one of several problems among Corinthian Christians which the apostle will deal with in this letter. Division is serious enough that Paul sees no element of gossip in Chloe's report.

II. Hyphenated Christians—12-16
A. Following men, 12

12 Now this I say, that every one of you saith, I am of Paul; and I of Apollos; and I of Cephas; and I of Christ.

Specific roots of the division in Corinth are traced to three prominent Christian teachers. Apollos had followed Paul to Corinth (Acts 18:24–19:1). While there is no record of Cephas (Peter) having been to Corinth, his teaching would have been spread far and wide because of his prominence among the 12 apostles. As verses to follow will imply, apparently the divisions were in part among those who had been baptized by one or another of these teachers. Note, however, that Paul does not attack any of the teachers, or their doctrine. What is wrong at Corinth is giving undue and divisive allegiance to these teachers under the mistaken notion that they wanted to propagate their own following, not the content of their teaching. Apparently even the Corinthians who said "I follow Christ" were guilty of divisiveness, since they positioned themselves against those who followed others.

B. No competition, 13-16

13 Is Christ divided? was Paul crucified for you? or were ye baptized in the name of Paul?

14 I thank God that I baptized none of you, but Crispus and Gaius;

15 Lest any should say that I had baptized in mine own name.

16 And I baptized also the house-hold of Stephanas: besides, I know not whether I baptized any other.

To ask "Is Christ divided?" is to remind the Corinthians that they had been converted to Him, not to His messengers, and that He only had "one body" (see Eph. 4:4). This is one of three rhetorical question designed to show the foolishness of division. Christ is not divided, Paul was not crucified for anyone, nor did he say to converts, "I baptized you in the name of Paul." Then the expansion on this last theme strengthens the supposition that converts were clustering around the teaching of the one who baptized them. Hence Paul stops to reflect on how few he had baptized, even though he had been first to preach the gospel in Corinth. He can think only of Crispus and Gaius, then, after further reflection, of one Stephanas and his household. Obviously the apostle is not keeping a "score card" or cutting notches on a gospel gun to boast about how many he had converted.

III. Core of the matter, 17, 30-31
A. Paul's mission, 17

17 For Christ sent me not to baptize, but to preach the gospel: not with wisdom of words, lest the cross of Christ should be made of none effect.

Paul's "mission statement" was to preach the gospel, not to baptize—which should settle the issue of whether he was interested in a separate church composed of his own converts. Although preaching would hopefully result in baptisms, bringing people to the water was secondary, not primary, to Paul's work.

The second part of this verse will

send Paul off on a tangent that is basic to the problem of division. There was a danger in couching the Good News in philosophical terms or any other special language that might make Christ's cross of "none effect." Although virtually the rest of the chapter will be given over to the importance of preaching the gospel in all its simplicity, as opposed to "the wisdom of men," Paul does not accuse Apollos, Peter, or anyone else of doing so.

Later eras would prove Paul's point. Often preachers would make well-meaning attempts to make the gospel "relevant" to every culture on earth. The result was that the simplicity of the Good News was often clothed in the complexity of Greek or Jewish thought-categories. Generations would argue, for example, about precisely how Jesus was at once God and man, with resulting splits. In fact every "victory" of one culturally-based "gospel" would result in a split from believers who spoke a different language or were of a different culture. Such cultural differences became the basis, for example, for one of the earliest divisions—the Eastern Orthodox split from the Roman Catholic tradition. In each case, as in the many church splits following, did non-believers in effect decide that "the cross of Christ is of none effect," when those who proclaimed the cross not only disagreed among themselves, but were quite ready to go to war over their differences?

B. Blessings in Christ, 30-31

30 But of him are ye in Christ Jesus, who of God is made unto us wisdom, and righteousness, and sanctification, and redemption:

31 That, according as it is written, He that glorieth, let him glory in the Lord.

Paul's closing argument for church unity in this chapter has to do with precisely where the blessings of salvation are found. He insists that we find four basic elements of salvation in Christ, rather than in the proclaimers.

We find in Christ true *wisdom*. Although Christian preachers have the responsibility to preach in their own tongues how this is so, it is not their teaching but *Christ* who is *the* wisdom. He implies the question, *Why settle for anything less?*

It is also in Christ that we find true *righteousness*. His teachers may call us to righteousness, but only Jesus can impute to us His own righteousness.

In Christ, not men, we find *sanctification*—the quality of being set apart for holy living. How often have Christians been disappointed when they find that the men they have made "models" of holiness have feet of clay! They learn, sometimes tragically late, that true sanctification lies in Christ, not men.

Finally, *redemption* is found only in Christ. Only He is God Incarnate, having taken on the flesh of humanity to share our own, then transforming us into persons who want to grow into His image.

With this "four-fold functional foundation" of why we should follow Christ, not men, Paul quotes loosely from Jeremiah 9:23-24. It is unseemly for a preacher, whether an Apollos, a Peter, or a modern proclaimer of the Good News, to glory in anything but the Lord.

Evangelistic Emphasis

Not long ago I visited some friends in our church unannounced. When they opened the door it was obvious to me something was wrong. Apparently the couple had just had some kind of disagreement with each other. It was terribly uncomfortable the whole time I was there. They were very nice to me, but their hospitality was forced. I excused myself and left as quickly as I could.

Reflecting on the visit, I wondered if folks can sense division and discord in our churches the way I felt the conflict in that home. I suspect people can feel the cold, prickly atmosphere in a divided church, and that this may be why some churches are not growing.

We cannot be effective in sharing the gospel if we are immersed in conflict with each other. We must resolve our differences and join together in unity beneath the Cross of Jesus if we plan to have any success in bringing others into the Kingdom of God through our local churches.

ഇൻൽ

Memory Selection

Now I beseech you, brethren, by the name of our Lord Jesus Christ, that ye all speak the same thing, and that there be no divisions among you; but that ye be perfectly joined together in the same mind and in the same judgment.—*1 Corinthians 1:10*

There is tremendous power in unity. I have witnessed the impotence of disunity just recently in my community. There is about to be a new interstate highway constructed through our area. We were invited by the state and federal highway departments to offer input on the proposed route. Our people met often and discussed the proposed routes at great length.

When it came time to make a recommendation to the highway authorities, we were no closer to an agreement than when we first started our discussions. Each group and faction was convinced the opinion of their particular group was the only valid one. We basically turned in four proposals, none of which was supported by a consensus of our people. The highway authorities met and chose routes for the new interstate that almost bypasses our area completely. Because we could not speak with one voice or agree on one route, we will practically miss out on all the routes.

The same principle is at work in our spiritual lives. If we do not speak with one voice, no voice is heard. When we join together as one, unified in the cause of Christ, the Church begins to move ahead with great power and effectiveness.

Weekday Problems

The atmosphere in the meeting was tense. Pastor Dan, senior pastor of First Church, said "Now, folks, I've been trying to lead you in this matter for a long time. It's time for us to put it to a vote. So, are you for me or against me? Let's see a show of hands."

"Wait just a minute, pastor," Ralph said. "I've heard that John Roberts is against your idea, and that others agree with him. John gives over $5,000 a year to our church. We certainly don't want to offend him."

"Come on! You know John is against anything the preacher is for," Bob shot back. "You're just tagging along with him! I think we ought to go a different direction altogether. Several of us have formed a coalition that has decided we are going to stick together against the preacher and John's group. What do you think about that?"

Then the choir director spoke up. "Friends, why are we arguing about this?" she said. "The point is not to do what John wants or what the coalition wants or even what the pastor wants. What we must do is seek to do what Jesus wants. If we do that, there will be no arguments."

*Is this a good time to ask, "What would Jesus do?"

*What are some of the ways we can effectively seek the mind of Christ?

Kids and Church

The little girl became restless as the preacher's sermon went on and on. Finally she leaned over to her mother and whispered, "Mommy, if we give him the money now, will he let us go?"

***

"Please, Lord," prayed the little girl breathlessly as she dressed for church. "Don't let me be late. Don't let me be late. Don't let me be late." Finally she was out the door on time, but she tripped at the curb and fell, tearing her dress. "Thanks, Lord, for helping me be on time . . . but next time please don't shove me, either!"

***

A little boy was overheard praying, "Dear Lord, if You can't make me a better boy, don't worry about it. I'm having a real good time like I am."

This Lesson in Your Life

Our church has just recently finished a 40-day intensive study of Rick Warren's book, *The Purpose Driven Life.* I pray I shall never forget the book's first line: *"It's not about you."* I think it would be healthy for each individual Christian in every church to remember that "It's not about me."

Most of the conflict I have experienced within the church in my days as pastor has been because someone forgot or ignored the fact that, "It's not about me." We get into trouble or cause trouble when we begin to think that the Kingdom of God revolves around me: my needs, my dreams, my comfort, my ambitions, my agenda, my plans. We must remember, the Christian walk is all about Jesus.

Sometimes we lose sight of that. We want to become like Jesus. We want to be led by Jesus. We want to treat others as Jesus did. We want to gain the mind, the personality, and the heart of Christ. We don't want to be like some high-powered preacher, as godly as that preacher may be. That mind-set was exactly what Paul was wrestling with in the Corinthian church. There were those in the church that thought only Paul had all the right answers. Then there were those that were convinced that it was Apollos who had the truth, the whole truth, and nothing but the truth. Added into the mix were those who were sure that Cephas, that is, the apostle Peter, was the one to follow. Then there was the voice of reason, "I follow Christ."

Friends, we must remember that no particular leader has all the truth. No particular denomination has all the truth. No one particular theology is the 100 percent pure theology. We can argue about who is right and who is wrong until we are blue in the face, and when Jesus comes again He will find us still arguing.

Paul reminds us that the arguments are worthless. There is no great merit in following any one particular teacher or one particular denomination. All the merit goes with following the One Particular Savior, Jesus Christ.

Remember, "It's not about you." The Christian walk is not about which particular theological persuasion a powerful man of God embraces. The Christian walk is not about our denominational stance on any particular issue. The Christian walk is about seeking the mind of Christ and doing the will of God. There is no reason to brag about how we got to Jesus. We just need to walk humbly in His way and try to show others that way as well.

STRAIGHT

1. What was Paul's purpose for writing this segment of Scripture to the Corinthians?
Paul heard that the Corinthians were divided, and he appealed to them to agree with one another.

2. Upon whose authority or in whose name was Paul asking the Corinthians to agree?
Paul asked them to agree in the name of Jesus, reminding them that he was representing Jesus.

3. What does Paul see as the outcome of disagreements in the church?
Paul notes that disagreements can lead to divisions.

4. What was Paul's (and ultimately Jesus') desire for the Corinthians?
That the Corinthians may be perfectly united in mind and judgments.

5. Why is it so important that any church be able to agree on the way we perceive things and the way we decide on things?
If folks in a church cannot agree on theology, the mind of Christ, or plans of action, little will ever get done for the Kingdom of God.

6. What seems to have been the source of the quarrels and contentions?
The Corinthians seem to have been split over the matter of which great teacher had been responsible for leading them to Christ.

7. What were the names of the leading disciples over whom the Corinthians were divided?
Paul, Apollo, and Cephas, meaning Peter. There were also those who claimed to follow Jesus Christ alone.

8. Paul implies believers should be baptized in whose name and under whose authority?
In the name and authority of Jesus Christ. The Christian walk is not about following a great earthly leader or teacher, but following Jesus.

9. Who does Paul list as believers he had baptized?
Paul says he baptized Crispus, Gaius, and those of the household of Stephanas.

10. What does Paul declare was the reason Christ sent Paul to the Corinthians?
Paul was sent not to baptize, but to preach the gospel of Jesus Christ.

I once read a story about a youth group somewhere in the northern states. We'll call their church Springdale Church. It seems the youth embarked upon a project to do kind deeds for people in need in the community. For these deeds the youth would accept no pay whatsoever. They were doing it out of their love for Jesus and their love for the community.

One group of the kids washed cars for free. Another group visited in a local nursing home. Still another group chose to do yard work for an elderly lady who could not get around well enough to do it herself and was too poor to pay someone to do it. The kids worked nearly all day.

That afternoon each team reported back to their youth leader. The group that did yard work told how, when they finished, the sweet lady brought them up on the porch for some lemonade. She said, "It is so good of you to do this. You Baptists at Springdale Church are such great Christians."

"Baptists!" the youth leader exclaimed. "I guess you told her we are the Springdale *Christian* Church."

"No," replied one of the kids, "we didn't think it mattered."

Of course, it doesn't matter. I think that is what Paul was trying to tell the Corinthians of yesterday and the Church of today. Labels just do not matter.

Of course, there are theological differences. I suspect those differences are healthy. Different denominations emphasize different aspects of the gospel. Yet, when we stand before the throne of grace, it will be of no importance at all whether we were Methodist or Baptist or Pentecostal or Catholic or of no denomination at all. What will be all important is whether or not we belonged to Jesus.

Christians disagree over many different things. Today, our churches are in great disagreement over homosexuality, abortion, what to do about the AIDS crisis, and what to do about terrorism in the world. Still, when people who have given their lives to Jesus Christ and have allowed Him to be their Lord get together, there is a kinship, brotherhood, and sisterhood that transcends all else.

There is unity in our diversity.

Lesson 2
Servants of Wisdom

1 Corinthians 2:1-2, 6-16

And I, brethren, when I came to you, came not with excellency of speech or of wisdom, declaring unto you the testimony of God.

2 For I determined not to know any thing among you, save Jesus Christ, and him crucified.

6 Howbeit we speak wisdom among them that are perfect: yet not the wisdom of this world, nor of the princes of this world, that come to nought:

7 But we speak the wisdom of God in a mystery, even the hidden wisdom, which God ordained before the world unto our glory:

8 Which none of the princes of this world knew: for had they known it, they would not have crucified the Lord of glory.

9 But as it is written, Eye hath not seen, nor ear heard, neither have entered into the heart of man, the things which God hath prepared for them that love him.

10 But God hath revealed them unto us by his Spirit: for the Spirit searcheth all things, yea, the deep things of God.

11 For what man knoweth the things of a man, save the spirit of man which is in him? even so the things of God knoweth no man, but the Spirit of God.

12 Now we have received, not the spirit of the world, but the spirit which is of God; that we might know the things that are freely given to us of God.

13 Which things also we speak, not in the words which man's wisdom teacheth, but which the Holy Ghost teacheth; comparing spiritual things with spiritual.

14 But the natural man receiveth not the things of the Spirit of God: for they are foolishness unto him: neither can he know them, because they are spiritually discerned.

15 But he that is spiritual judgeth all things, yet he himself is judged of no man.

16 For who hath known the mind of the Lord, that he may instruct him? But we have the mind of Christ.

Devotional Reading
Eph. 1:15-21

Background Scripture
1 Cor. 2

Memory Selection
1 Cor. 2:13

In Unit III of our Spring Quarter, several lessons explored the theme of "wisdom" in the book of Proverbs. Wisdom was still a much-discussed topic in the New Testament world. Like our own age, it was a time of religious ferment, with people seeking true wisdom in a variety of places for an increasingly complex world.

Today's lesson shows how the apostle Paul interpreted wisdom to the infant church at Corinth. He acknowledges, along with the "mystery cults" in Greece, the importance of wisdom—but with a fundamental difference. The cults held that wisdom was a secret given only to those admitted to their inner circle. Paul says that his message was based on a *revealed* secret, available through the Holy Spirit to all who had the willingness to accept it.

If the room where your group meets can be darkened, turn out the light. Note that reading and understanding study materials could be a problem without more light. Then, with available light, or a flashlight if necessary, make your way to the light switch. Turning on the light, comment on the importance of light for reading and understanding.

Now compare what you have just done to Paul's teaching on the nature of his own teaching. The basis for it was "Jesus Christ, and Him crucified." Jesus was "the light of the world." Yet people had to use "available light" to discover that divine Light. They had to admit their need for more light. They had to accept the guidance of the Holy Spirit to find the "switch" to flood their hearts with the true Light.

Teaching Outline	*Daily Bible Readings*
I. Wisdom of the Cross—1-2	Mon. Faith and Wisdom James 1:2-8
II. Wisdom for the Seeker—6-10	Tue. Two Kinds of Wisdom James 3:13-18
A. Hidden from the "wise," 6-8	Wed. A Spirit of Wisdom Eph. 1:15-21
B. Revealed to the seeker, 9-10	Thu. Teach with Wisdom Col. 1:24-29
III. The Spirit for the Spiritual—11-16	Fri. Faith vs. Human Wisdom 1 Cor. 2:1-5
A. Inner knowledge, 11	Sat. Speaking God's Wisdom 1 Cor. 2:6-10
B. Revelation by the Spirit, 12-13	Sun. Wisdom through the Spirit 1 Cor. 2:11-16
C. Knowing God's mind, 14-16	

Verse by Verse

I. Wisdom of the Cross—1-2

1 And I, brethren, when I came to you, came not with excellency of speech or of wisdom, declaring unto you the testimony of God.

2 For I determined not to know any thing among you, save Jesus Christ, and him crucified.

Paul first came to the city of Corinth after preaching in Athens, the center of Greek "wisdom" or philosophy (Acts 17:16; 18:1). He had few converts in Athens, whereas "*many* of the Corinthians hearing believed, and were baptized" (Acts 18:8). Some scholars say this was because Paul spoke to the Athenians in philosophical terms. It is possible that Paul revised his approach in Corinth, and relied more on the simple proclamation of Jesus as the Messiah instead of trying to couch the message in philosophical terms.

At any rate, Paul affirms here that he had not addressed the Corinthians with rhetorical or philosophical sophistication. Instead, he allowed the message of the Cross, "Jesus Christ, and him crucified," to stand alone in all its stark but compelling power.

Why does the apostle spend so much time on this point? Doubtless because the divisions that were fracturing the church at Corinth included differences in philosophy or human wisdom that had nothing to do with the basic message of the Cross—unless, God forbid, they included points of view that opposed the effects of "Christ crucified." Paul is calling the Corinthians (and us) back to the gospel in its simplest form, in part to avoid the divisive "spins" which differing philosophies would put on that message.

II. Wisdom for the Seeker—6-10

A. Hidden from the "wise," 6-8

6 Howbeit we speak wisdom among them that are perfect: yet not the wisdom of this world, nor of the princes of this world, that come to nought:

7 But we speak the wisdom of God in a mystery, even the hidden wisdom, which God ordained before the world unto our glory:

8 Which none of the princes of this world knew: for had they known it, they would not have crucified the Lord of glory.

Paul's having stuck to the simplicity of the gospel message does not mean that there is no wisdom in that message. "Christ crucified" has its own logic and wisdom, but it is perceived to be so only by those who are "mature" (NIV, for the KJV's "perfect") enough to see the emptiness of human philosophy when com-

403

pared with the gospel. .

The word "mystery" was a loaded word among the Greeks Paul addressed. A variety of "mystery cults" vied with each other for the hearts of people, promising that if they learned secret words or laid eyes on secret holy things they could gain "wisdom," or be enlightened. Some of these cults would flower into "Gnosticism" in the second century, and become a serious threat to the simplicity of the wisdom of "Christ crucified."

Paul uses wisdom and mystery almost interchangeably. He affirms that the wisdom of "Christ crucified" was not understood by the Jewish and Roman leaders who put Him to death. He implies that they failed to discern this wisdom because they thought themselves to be "princes," and above the needs which the Cross claims to meet. The wisdom of the Cross is more easily seen by the meek and simple than by those who cling to "the wisdom of this world."

B. Revealed to the seeker, 9-10

9 But as it is written, Eye hath not seen, nor ear heard, neither have entered into the heart of man, the things which God hath prepared for them that love him.

10 But God hath revealed them unto us by his Spirit: for the Spirit searcheth all things, yea, the deep things of God.

In verse 9 Paul quotes loosely from Isaiah 64:4 to show that the "wisdom" or "mystery" of the Good News is hidden from those who insist on finding their own way to God. Yet this does not mean that the gospel is hidden in the way that mystery cults hid their secrets. In fact the Holy Spirit had fully revealed this special wisdom to the apostles, and through their preaching to anyone else who would accept the authority of the Spirit. It is only that Spirit, and not the wisdom of men, who can probe "the deep things of God"—an assertion which the apostle will now illustrate with a human analogy.

III. The Spirit for the Spiritual— 11-16

A. Inner knowledge, 11

11 For what man knoweth the things of a man, save the spirit of man which is in him? even so the things of God knoweth no man, but the Spirit of God.

Paul's claim that only the Holy Spirit can know God's mind is compared with the way a person's own spirit is the only entity fully capable of knowing that person. For example, a person may look us straight in the eye and tell a lie which we believe, but which the liar knows to be false. Paul speaks here of a person's spirit as that part of the self that can be self-aware. This capacity of the human spirit is comparable to the way the Holy Spirit alone can know the mind of God. This is what makes possible the astounding affirmation in verse 10 that God has revealed His own mind to the apostles.

B. Revelation by the Spirit, 12-13

12 Now we have received, not

the spirit of the world, but the spirit which is of God; that we might know the things that are freely given to us of God.

13 Which things also we speak, not in the words which man's wisdom teacheth, but which the Holy Ghost teacheth; comparing spiritual things with spiritual.

"We" here seems to refer to the apostles and prophets in the early Church. Although all Christians have a measure of the Holy Spirit, Paul seems to speak of an even greater measure given to those whom "the Holy Ghost teacheth." The apostle argues that the Corinthians can count on his message being true because it was delivered by direct revelation of the Spirit, rather than any prompting by a "spirit of the world." Paul reserves this spirit for false teachers, as in the mystery cults, and for those who put Christ to death (as in vs. 8).

The last phrase of verse 13 is notoriously hard to translate. It can mean either "comparing spiritual things with spiritual people" or, as in the NIV, "expressing spiritual things in spiritual words." Paul's main point is clear, however: the truly spiritual person will attend to what the Holy Spirit teaches through the apostles.

C. Knowing God's mind, 14-16

14 But the natural man receiveth not the things of the Spirit of God: for they are foolishness unto him: neither can he know them, because they are spiritually discerned.

15 But he that is spiritual judgeth all things, yet he himself is judged of no man.

16 For who hath known the mind of the Lord, that he may instruct him? But we have the mind of Christ.

The "natural man" is literally the "soulful man," implying the person who only has the spark of life or soul (Grk. *psyche*), but not a *spirit* (*pneuma*) that is compatible with the Holy Spirit. At creation, God breathed into man the breath of life, enabling him to become a "living soul" (Gen. 2:7). That spark of life is shared by all living things. But only souls who are endowed with a "bent" or spirit toward God respond to the message of the Holy Spirit preached by the apostles. It is in this sense that spiritually-minded people can judge whether things are right or wrong, yet cannot be judged by unspiritual people (as in vs 15).

Again citing Isaiah (40:13), Paul asks a rhetorical question showing the impossibility of anyone but "the spiritual" knowing God's mind. Again the "we" here probably applies first to the apostles, although it is true in a secondary sense that those who heed their teaching also have, to a lesser degree, both the Spirit and "the mind of the Lord." Of course this does not mean that either the apostles or ordinary Christians know *all* of the Lord's mind, or are infallible, only that without a spiritually-oriented heart it is impossible to know His will.

Evangelistic Emphasis

It's hard to argue someone into the Christian faith. He has a question, then you give an answer, which leads to another question, which brings another answer, which elicits another question, and on and on.

There are some "why" questions about the Christian faith that cannot be reasoned out with pure logic. We need look no further than the life and death of Jesus Christ to be stumped by logic. The love, compassion, and concern Jesus showed for the people who killed Him, and for those not yet born, are illogical.

The fact that the human mind cannot fully comprehend the love of Jesus is related to why God chose to make the work of the Holy Spirit an essential factor in conversion. We can argue until we are blue in the face trying to convince an unbeliever to accept Christ, but if the Holy Spirit does not soften and penetrate a hardened heart, the unbeliever remains lost.

Yet the facts of the gospel are not hidden. The the story of Jesus was written about almost 2,000 years ago. Christians have been talking about His love for centuries. Never neglect to pray for the Holy Spirit's work in helping these facts to "make sense" to those with whom you share your faith.

ഇറങ്ങ

Which things also we speak, not in the words which man's wisdom teacheth, but which the Holy Ghost teacheth; comparing spiritual things with spiritual.—*1 Corinthians 2:13*

Paul reminds us that when he preaches the Good News of Jesus he is expressing spiritual truths in spiritual words. Further, the wisdom of humans, by itself, is not enough to understand completely the things of God.

Some years ago, when I was ministering in a nursing home, a resident gave me a phrase I pray I shall never forget. "The Christian faith is better caught than taught; better felt than 'telt,'" she said. I am convinced that this sister knew exactly what Paul was writing about in this verse. One does not come to salvation entirely by human reasoning. Of course, we are not required to check our minds at the door when we come into worship. Jesus told us we are to love God with our hearts and minds and strength. Yet, until we grasp the spiritual nature of Christianity—that unseen, unknowable aspect which only the Holy Spirit can reveal—we are lacking in our understanding.

Paul was a brilliant man, yet he fully understood that his wisdom had not come entirely as a result of his "book learning." The Holy Spirit teaches us things about God that cannot be learned or discerned any other way.

Weekday Problems

Ashley had listened to the discussion with great interest. A young man in the community wanted to be the youth leader of their church. This young man was a college graduate. He was raised in the church. He was very enthusiastic, and young people followed him as if he were the Pied Piper.

All the young people at the meeting were making impassioned pleas for the church to hire this young man. Most of youths' parents agreed. They recited a long list of his attributes. "He is impressive," Ashley found herself thinking. Yet, something in her heart said, *Don't jump into this.*

Ashley looked around the room. She studied the faces of those folks who were mature Christians. Most of them had looks of concern. She prayed a quick prayer for guidance, then asked to speak to the group. "I am sensing that we should not rush into this," she said. "Yet, I think this young man would do an incredible job with the youth. Why don't we allow him to come on staff part-time. Allow Pastor to mentor him. We can bring him on full-time when Pastor thinks it appropriate."

That did not go over well with the young man. He left the meeting, and shortly afterward took a position with another church in town. Most of the youth from Ashley's church followed him. After a few months, the young man was caught in an inappropriate relationship with one of the high school girls.

*In retrospect, was Ashley's suggestion a wise one?

*Share about a time you have been given wisdom by the Holy Spirit.

Daffy-nitions from Med School

Artery—The study of paintings.
Bacteria—The back door to a cafeteria.
Benign—What you be after you be 8.
Caesarean section—The area in Rome where the Emperor lived.
Cat scan—(1) A search for kitty. (2) What dogs do when they enter your yard.
Coma—A curly punctuation mark.
D & C—Where the city of Washington is located.
Dilate—To have a long life.
Enema—Not a friend.
GI series—Baseball between teams of soldiers.
Hangnail—A coat hook.
Labor pain—Getting hurt at work.
Medical staff—A lame doctor's cane.

This Lesson in Your Life

Webster's dictionary defines wisdom as "The power of judging rightly and following the soundest course of action based on knowledge and experience." That is an excellent definition according to the world. However, in the spiritual realm we sometimes have to make decisions and take particular courses of action without all the facts. For instance, although we cannot know a person's heart, in the spiritual realm we are often dealing with things of the heart. In addition, the human mind certainly cannot fully understand God, yet we are called to action based on our knowledge of Him.

Yet Scripture promises that we can discern the mind of God through the Holy Spirit—although thinking as God thinks, acting and reacting as Jesus would, is not necessarily viewed as wisdom in a worldly sense.

There once was a man who had been a reprobate and a drunkard. He had an encounter with Jesus and was radically and soundly converted. The guys at work used to try to shake him up by saying, "Surely a sensible man like you doesn't believe in those miracles the Bible tells about. You know Jesus didn't turn water into wine!"

"Whether he turned water into wine or not," said the man, "I do not know; but in my own house I have seen him turn whiskey into living room furniture."

You see, there are some things we will never understand about life until we give our own lives up to Jesus Christ. When we allow the presence of Jesus Christ through the Holy Spirit to live within us we begin to think thoughts He would think. That is what Paul calls "the mind of Christ."

Some Christ-like thinking is foolishness to the world. Generous giving comes to mind very quickly. How could it be wise to give a large percentage of income to the cause of Christ? The world would say, "Wouldn't it be smarter to invest that money, putting it toward your retirement, or making a payment on a boat?" God's wisdom tells us, "Give and it shall be given to you." God's wisdom tells us, "The one who sows sparingly will also reap sparingly."

Matters of the Spirit of God are spiritually discerned. They do not always make sense to the secular mind. I have a friend who at times will drop by my office with no prompting. Many times he has dropped by when I was wrestling with a problem or was just down in the dumps. I do not ask him to come by. God just lays it on his heart to come by. He always seems to come by with just what I need at the time.

Praise God that He enables us to think, act, and react as Jesus would!

STRAIGHT

1. What did Paul not rely on when he proclaimed the gospel to the Corinthians?
He came not with excellency of speech (eloquence) or superior wisdom.

2. Who can understand the message Paul shares about wisdom?
Paul reminds us that it is the mature, or perfect, among us who understand the message.

3. Who can*not* understand this message?
Paul says neither the princes, or rulers, of this world nor those who rely on worldly wisdom can grasp the message he shares.

4. If the rulers of Paul's age had understood God's message, what would they have refrained from doing?
If they had truly understood the Good News they would not have crucified Jesus Christ, the Lord of glory.

5. Who knows the thoughts of a person?
The only one on this earth who knows the thoughts of a person is that person himself.

6. Who imparts the ability to understand the deep things of God?
The Spirit of God reveals to us the deep things of God.

7. According to verse 12, what is one reason we are given God's Spirit?
The Spirit is given that we might know the things that are freely given to us by God.

8. Was Paul speaking knowledge he had gained by human wisdom?
No. Paul was speaking in words taught by the Spirit, expressing spiritual truths in spiritual words.

9. What does the natural man, or the man without the Spirit of God, think about the things of God?
The natural man cannot receive the things of God. They seem to be foolishness to the worldly mind.

10. How does the spiritual person make wise judgments about all things?
The spiritual person is able to do that because he has been given the mind of Christ. We are able to reason as Christ would have reasoned.

Paul reminds us in this passage that the only One who can tell us about God is the Spirit of God. He uses a human analogy.

Some feelings are so personal that only that particular person knows them. There are things that are so private that a person would never share them with anyone, even a spouse. There are things that are so intimate we would be embarrassed if anyone else knew them. The only person who knows all those things is that person himself.

Paul argues that the same is true of God. There are deep and intimate things about God that only His Spirit knows. That Spirit is the only Person who can lead us into really intimate knowledge of God.

Think of this. The God of the universe wants us to know as much about His feelings, His reasoning, His love, His will, and His way as we know about our own lives. Far back in Old Testament times God spoke to Jeremiah (33:3), saying, "Call to me and I will answer you and tell you great and unsearchable things you do not know." God wants us to know Him intimately. He has provided a way for us to do just that through His Holy Spirit.

Knowing God and the things of God intimately does not rest upon our human intellect. It really does not matter how smart we are. What matters is whether or not we have experienced the intimacy of the Holy Spirit.

There are those who do not want that. The person who lives as if there is nothing beyond physical life and there are no needs other than physical and material needs cannot understand spiritual things. A person who thinks there is nothing more important than the satisfaction of the sex urge cannot understand the meaning of chastity. A person who thinks amassing wealth is the most important thing in life cannot understand generosity. That type of person thinks spiritual things are foolishness.

But to those who desire to know God in His fullness, God gives His Holy Spirit; and the Holy Spirit gives us the mind of Christ.

Lesson 3
Servants Together

1 Corinthians 3:1-15

And I, brethren, could not speak unto you as unto spiritual, but as unto carnal, even as unto babes in Christ.

2 I have fed you with milk, and not with meat: for hitherto ye were not able to bear it, neither yet now are ye able.

3 For ye are yet carnal: for whereas there is among you envying, and strife, and divisions, are ye not carnal, and walk as men?

4 For while one saith, I am of Paul; and another, I am of Apollos; are ye not carnal?

5 Who then is Paul, and who is Apollos, but ministers by whom ye believed, even as the Lord gave to every man?

6 I have planted, Apollos watered; but God gave the increase.

7 So then neither is he that planteth any thing, neither he that watereth; but God that giveth the increase.

8 Now he that planteth and he that watereth are one: and every man shall receive his own reward according to his own labour.

9 For we are labourers together with God: ye are God's husbandry, ye are God's building.

10 According to the grace of God which is given unto me, as a wise masterbuilder, I have laid the foundation, and another buildeth thereon. But let every man take heed how he buildeth thereupon.

11 For other foundation can no man lay than that is laid, which is Jesus Christ.

12 Now if any man build upon this foundation gold, silver, precious stones, wood, hay, stubble;

13 Every man's work shall be made manifest: for the day shall declare it, because it shall be revealed by fire; and the fire shall try every man's work of what sort it is.

14 If any man's work abide which he hath built thereupon, he shall receive a reward.

15 If any man's work shall be burned, he shall suffer loss: but he himself shall be saved; yet so as by fire.

Devotional Reading
Matt. 13:3-9

Background Scripture
1 Cor. 3:1-15

Memory Selection
1 Cor. 3:9

411

This lesson shows the apostle Paul's continued concern over divisions in the church at Corinth. Earlier he had warned that human philosophy must not be allowed to divide Christians. Now his tone becomes sharper and more critical, accusing those who foster division of being "carnal"—worldly or fleshly.

This kind of language is usually reserved for condemning immorality, especially sexual sins. In this lesson, however, we see that being divisive is equally "fleshly." Further, those who divide the church by elevating one church leader leave the impression that there is more than one "Lord," since only He is "head of the body" (Eph. 1:22-23).

If we need evidence of the seriousness of divisiveness, Paul compares it to *carnality* and *idolatry*!

Ask group members how Paul's metaphor of the Church as a *building* might apply to your local congregation. *How can more of us get involved in "building" ministries in the church?. . . What specific areas of need in the church or the community need to be started, or expanded?. . . How do you think members would re-*

spond if they were to hear Paul preach the words of today's text to us?

Note how working together is a good way to unite members, regardless of their differences. For example Habitat for Humanity has built thousands of houses for low-income people. They draw together people from radically backgrounds, who find that wielding hammers and saws together takes precedence over the need to argue about their diverse viewoints.

Teaching Outline	Daily Bible Readings

I. Division is Carnal—1-4
  A. Immature believers, 1-2
  B. Carnality of strife, 3-4
II. Don't Follow Mere Men—5-8
  A. Sowing and reaping, 5-6
  B. Divine 'labor union,' 7-8
III. Division of Labor—9-15
  A. God's farm, 9a
  B. God's building, 9b-15
    1. Foundation and walls, 9b-10
    2. The one foundation, 11
    3. Materials that last, 12-13
    4. Builders' reward, 14-15
	Mon. Spreading the Word
	     Matt. 13:3-9
	Tue. Growing Together
	    Matt. 13:24-30
	Wed. Teachers Needed
	    Heb. 5:7-14
	Thu. Strength from the Spirit
	    Heb. 3:14-21
	Fri. Channels of Faith
	    1 Cor. 3:1-9
	Sat. Christ the Foundation
	    1 Cor. 3:10-15
	Sun. Don't Glory in Men
	    1 Cor. 3:16-23

Verse by Verse

I. Division is Carnal—1-4

A. Immature believers, 1-2

1 And I, brethren, could not speak unto you as unto spiritual, but as unto carnal, even as unto babes in Christ.

2 I have fed you with milk, and not with meat: for hitherto ye were not able to bear it, neither yet now are ye able.

Still concerned about divisions among the Corinthian Christians, Paul tackles the somewhat natural problem of converts tending to attach themselves to a favorite preacher. Natural or not, the apostle tells his audience bluntly that sectarianism, strife, and division are "carnal."

The NIV translation, "worldly," is not as graphic as the original, which literally means "fleshly." Because the word has its roots in the difference between an animal's soft flesh and hard bones, Paul brilliantly relates it to being "soft" in the sense of immature—an infant instead of an adult. While it is only appropriate to begin the Christian walk as babes, remaining at that level in how we get along with other Christians indicates stunted growth. Although Paul would like to teach them "meatier" topics, division among the Christians at Corinth indicates that they are still at the "pabulum" stage, spiritually.

B. Carnality of strife, 3-4

3 For ye are yet carnal: for whereas there is among you envying, and strife, and divisions, are ye not carnal, and walk as men?

4 For while one saith, I am of Paul; and another, I am of Apollos; are ye not carnal?

Now Paul spells out with painful clarity precisely what makes a fleshly Christian. Surprisingly he condemns *envy, strife,* and *division* in the same terms as adultery and fornication. A moment's reflection shows that one or another of these "fleshly" traits is at the core of almost every church squabble. One music leader envies another because she is used more. Strife develops when two people with sharp personality differences serve on the same committee, where both cannot get their way. Division crops up over whether church should be conducted in the way favored by this or that church leader (here, Paul and Apollos). Paul does not suggest that such issues aren't important, but that the spiritually mature can keep personal feelings for particular ministers from being divisive.

413

II. Don't Follow Mere Men—5-8
A. Sowing and reaping, 5-6

5 Who then is Paul, and who is Apollos, but ministers by whom ye believed, even as the Lord gave to every man?

6 I have planted, Apollos watered; but God gave the increase.

We recall that Paul first "planted" the church in Corinth by sowing the gospel there (Acts 18:1ff.) Later, the eloquent preacher Apollos came to "water" the tender shoots that were the results of Paul's sowing (18:24; 19:1). To stop the story there would be to omit the more basic involvement of *God*, who alone could bless Paul's sowing and Apollos' watering with numerical and spiritual growth. In effect Paul asks why anyone would follow the "servants"—sowers and reapers— instead of the One who enables the "plants" to grow.

B. Divine 'labor union,' 7-8

7 So then neither is he that planteth any thing, neither he that watereth; but God that giveth the increase.

8 Now he that planteth and he that watereth are one: and every man shall receive his own reward according to his own labour.

Persisting in his analogy of the church as a garden, Paul reminds us that he and Apollos, as well as the multitudes of ministers who have succeeded them in the worldwide church are not "any thing." "*Not any thing?*" we can hear a modern church member ask, if he is afflicted with the disease "preacheritis." "Why, Brother Jones was a far finer preacher than his successor, Brother Brown," etc. etc. Paul insists that however ministerial gifts differ, the ministers themselves are on the same team. God will reward them not on the basis of their popularity, but on how well they used their individual gifts.

III. Division of Labor—9-15
A. God's farm, 9a

9 For we are labourers together with God: ye are God's husbandry,

Paul momentarily stays with the imagery of proclaiming the Good News and nurturing the new seedlings as "planting" and "watering." The word "husbandry," which originally referred to a householder, came to mean a garden or farm (as in "animal husbandry"). The apostle paints a picture of the church as such a farm, and its ministers as husbandmen or farmers. This imagery now quickly gives way to another useful way of portraying the church and its leaders.

B. God's building, 9b-15
1. Foundation and walls, 9b-10

9b ye are God's building.

10 According to the grace of God which is given unto me, as a wise masterbuilder, I have laid the foundation, and another buildeth thereon. But let every man take heed how he buildeth thereupon.

Paul presses on with his appeal for church unity, switching the analogy of church as a farm to that of a building. As the first to enter Corinth with the gospel, Paul had laid the foundation of the church there. Then Apollos and other ministers built on it as stone masons laying rock walls on Paul's foundation.

In cautioning "every man [to] take heed how he buildeth," the apostle shifts subtly from addressing church members to their leaders. Given natural human weakness and the need for every "servant" to feel that his labors are not in vain, it is easy for leaders themselves to garner followers, with the dangerous potential of dividing the church. Sometimes this is as blatant as Absalom, David's son, who sat at the gate at Jerusalem and "stole the hearts of the men of Israel" by telling them how much better ruler he would be than his father (2 Sam. 15:2-6). It is a continuous challenge for a minister to exercise his gifts to the fullest without allowing himself to be elevated to the point of division.

2. The one foundation, 11

11 For other foundation can no man lay than that is laid, which is Jesus Christ.

Now Paul suggests that following one minister to the point of a church split is to build another foundation. In turn, another church is built on that foundation. This cannot rightly be done since "there is one body" or church (Eph. 4:4).

3. Materials that last, 12-13

12 Now if any man build upon this foundation gold, silver, precious stones, wood, hay, stubble;

13 Every man's work shall be made manifest: for the day shall declare it, because it shall be revealed by fire; and the fire shall try every man's work of what sort it is.

Focusing more specifically on the role of ministers in building a church, Paul warns that the material they use (the people they "build" into the church) will one day reveal the effectiveness of the minister/builder. In the context of church divisions, Paul apparently compares converts that follow the Lord over human leaders as "gold, silver, and precious stones," and those who allow partisan politics or "preacheritis" to rule as "wood, hay, and stubble." As Augustine would argue in his great work *City of God,* these two kinds of building materials often blend in during this life; but at the day of Judgment, their make-up—lasting or temporary—will be revealed as by the fires of a metal worker.

4. Builders' reward, 14-15

14 If any man's work abide which he hath built thereupon, he shall receive a reward.

15 If any man's work shall be burned, he shall suffer loss: but he himself shall be saved; yet so as by fire.

Finally Paul affirms that church planters and nurturers who build churches of long-lasting building materials—members taught not to quarrel and divide—will be rewarded for their wisdom and care. In other cases, when their churches are consumed by the fires of division, the ministers themselves will be saved, despite the inevitable sense of loss they will feel.

Evangelistic Emphasis

All of us who take seriously the Great Commission (Matt. 28: 18-20) understand that it is the work of the Christian to make disciples for Jesus Christ. Now, disciples of Jesus do not just appear. For one to become a Christian disciple one must first become a Christian. Then there is usually a process of Christian growth. This process involves listening to good biblical preaching. It involves spending time in prayer and Bible study. It involves service to others, and fellowship with other believers—that is, attending church and other fellowship opportunities.

Sometimes we get discouraged because we do not witness people "getting saved" under our ministry. Paul reminds us here that Christian discipleship is a process. In that process one may plant the seed of faith. Another may help that seed grow. Still another may encourage the plant of faith to grow into maturity and to produce fruit. Just because you may not be the first one to help another, or the last one to see the maturity, does not mean that God is not using you in the disciple-making process.

God uses all who are willing to be used by Him to bring others into mature faith in Jesus. It is all His work anyway, no matter where you or I may fit into the process.

ℰℴℭℛ

For we are labourers together with God: ye are God's husbandry, ye are God's building.—*1 Corinthians 3:9*

We are workers for God in His vineyard. None of us is boss. Paul was not. Apollos was not. Neither is Billy Graham or Pope John Paul II. We all work for God.

There was once a young man who went to work in the slums of Calcutta, when Mother Theresa was there. There were few visible results in his ministry. He went to Mother Theresa for counsel. He poured out his heart, "All I have ever wanted to do is serve the poor. I gave up everything to come here. Nothing is happening. They do not receive my ministry. They are not responding. Don't they know what I have given up to serve them?"

Mother Theresa replied, "I think I see what your problem is. You think you are serving the poor. When you serve people you will often be disappointed. Dear son, you are serving Christ. When you serve Christ, you will always be fulfilled."

Who is your boss? Is it your denomination? Is it your pastor? Is it your own ego? If we work for anyone other than God we will ultimately be disappointed.

Weekday Problems

The preparations for the church's anniversary celebration were going smoothly until Deacon Brown brought up the Christians Caring ministry. "We need to recognize this ministry. It is one of the most effective in our church. Who can give me the history of this ministry?"

Sister Smith spoke up, "Well, I began this ministry three years ago. We saw a need in our community. We prayed about it for awhile. My husband and I gave the seed money to get it started. Then we bought materials to do light home repairs for those who were unable to do for themselves. We . . . ."

Deacon Jones interrupted, "YOU started this ministry?! We had been doing that sort of thing before you and your husband ever came to this church. We have been building wheelchair ramps for five or six years now. All you did was change the name! My committee should get the credit. My committee should write the history!" Deacon Brown was sorry he brought it up. He had no idea such a ruckus would be raised over the Christian Caring ministry. He thought the work was being done for the Lord.

*If I seek credit for a ministry, for whom am I really doing it?

*Do you think giving more public recognition would reduce self-service?

Church Problems, Big and Small

Two boys were walking home from church after hearing a strong sermon on Satan. Said one to the other, "What do you think about all that. Do you believe the devil is real?

"Nah," said the other boy. "It's probably like Santa Claus turned out. It's probably just your dad."

***

Little Johnny had learned at Sunday School that God made woman out of Adam's rib. Later that week his mother noticed him lying down as though he were ill.

"What's the matter, Johnny?" she asked.

"I have this pain in my side," Johnny replied. "I think I'm going to have a wife."

***

The Sunday School teacher was teaching the Ten Commandments to 5- and 6-year-olds. After explaining the commandment to "Honor thy father and thy mother," the teacher asked if the Bible also taught the children how they should treat brothers and sisters.

Without missing a beat little Jimmy replied, "Thou shalt not kill."

This Lesson in Your Life

Not long ago I attended a funeral for a fellow who had died after a long illness. He had not lived the life of a believer. He had not gone to any church. Two pastors had visited him regularly in the hospital during his illness. Both were asked to preach at his funeral. As a pastor myself, I was embarrassed by what I witnessed at that service. It seemed to be a competition between the two as to who led the deceased to a death-bed conversion. We praised God that the man had come to saving faith, but it was ugly to see the two pastors almost arguing about who led the man to Christ.

In this passage of Scripture Paul reminds us that jealousy and ego within the Body of Christ only serve to damage the Body. There is no reason for one person to try to take credit over another. We are all on the same team anyway. Besides, nothing happens in the spiritual realm without God.

It is as if those of us in a Christian community are handling the oars on one of those sculling craft like you see in Olympic competition. Each person is on an oar. Each oarsman has a responsibility. The team rows in perfect unison. Each team member is perfectly synchronized with the other. If one person gets out of rhythm it throws the whole team off and slows the boat down. Of course, every person is rowing in the same direction. If one decided to go his own way, it would be disastrous for the team. Finally, when the boat crosses the finish line, no one asks which person won. You win or lose as a team.

The Kingdom of God is like that in some ways. Remember an earlier teaching, "It's not about me." The Kingdom of God is all about the Kingdom. It is not about personal egos or personalities. It's a God thing.

In the Kingdom there are individuals with differing skills and strengths. When we spend our time comparing our skills and strengths with another, we are just wasting time. God gives us differing skills so that we will complement each other, not compete with each other. We are workers together under the authority of God.

We are like farm implements. There is one tool for planting, another for keeping out the weeds. There is one system for irrigating the crop, and another for harvesting. Each tool is necessary. Although the combine cuts and gathers the wheat, it is certainly not the only machine responsible for the harvest.

We Christians must work much the same way for God's harvest. Each of us is equipped for one task or another. No one can do it all.

1. Why did Paul feel he could only "feed" the Corinthians with "milk" instead of "meat"?

Because they were unspiritual, worldly, and acting like babies in Christ.

2. What did Paul cite as the indication that the Corinthians were worldly and unspiritual?

Paul saw them as worldly because there was jealousy and they were quarreling among themselves.

3. In this passage, who is the one who planted the seed of the Word and who watered it?

Paul says he planted the seed and Apollos watered it.

4. Who is ultimately responsible for success in the spiritual realm? In other words, who makes the seed of the Word increase?

God is ultimately responsible. God makes the seed grow.

5. Who is most important—the one who plants the seed, the one who waters the seed, or the one who makes the seed grow?

Paul says neither he who plants nor he who waters is anything, but God who makes it grow is everything.

6. What are the three different ways Paul describes the Corinthian Christians in verse 9?

He says the Corinthians are laborers together (fellow workers); God's husbandry (God's field); and God's building.

7. In what practical way does Paul describe his ministry, in verse 10?

Paul says he laid the foundation for their faith as an expert builder might lay the foundation of a building.

8. What was the foundation Paul laid?

Jesus Christ.

9. In a spiritual sense, what tests the quality of any person's works?

The quality of a person's Christian spiritual work will be tested by fire and the quality revealed.

10. What happens if a person's work is burned up? What happens if it survives?

If a person's work is burned up, he will suffer loss, but that person will still be saved. If a person's work survives, that person will receive his reward.

Sometimes I get to thinking, "God must appreciate me a great deal." Of course, that really is a true statement. God does appreciate me. He appreciates you, too. He appreciates His children more than we may ever know. Still, we must handle those thoughts with a grain of grace. The fact that God through Jesus loves us enough to give His life for us is true, but it is not to become a source of selfish pride. God loves you no more than He loves me. God loves me no more than He loves you. God uses us both in His ministry to further His omnipotent plan.

If I get to thinking too highly of myself, or if my awareness of God's love and grace turns prideful, I only have to recall the story of Balaam. You may remember that Balaam was a prophet of sorts. King Balak asked Balaam to curse the Israelites. It would be good for you to read the whole story in Numbers chapter 22. As Balaam was going along the road, an angel of the Lord came to oppose him. Balaam could not see the angel, but Balaam's donkey could. The donkey shied away from the angel and Balaam beat her. Three times this happened. Balaam then told the donkey, "If I had a sword I would kill you right now." Then the donkey talked to Balaam! Basically, the donkey said, "I've always been good to you. Why are you beating me?" At this, God opened Balaam's eyes. Balaam saw the angel and realized the donkey had saved his life by veering away.

My point in recalling this story is this: When I begin to think I am so valuable to God and that nobody else is nearly as valuable as I am and that God is using me in mighty ways more than He is using anybody else, all I have to do is remember Balaam's donkey. You see, God used a donkey to do His will. He still can.

I know I am more to God than a donkey. Still, I have to remember that I am only a tool in God's hand. I know a hammer cannot begin to think it is most important in driving a nail. It is the hand that holds the hammer that makes the difference.

Paul planted. Apollos watered. God gives the increase. It still works that way today. It's all God's doing anyway.

Lesson 4

Servants in Ministry

1 Corinthians 4:1-13

Let a man so account of us, as of the ministers of Christ, and stewards of the mysteries of God.

2 Moreover it is required in stewards, that a man be found faithful.

3 But with me it is a very small thing that I should be judged of you, or of man's judgment: yea, I judge not mine own self.

4 For I know nothing by myself; yet am I not hereby justified: but he that judgeth me is the Lord.

5 Therefore judge nothing before the time, until the Lord come, who both will bring to light the hidden things of darkness, and will make manifest the counsels of the hearts: and then shall every man have praise of God.

6 And these things, brethren, I have in a figure transferred to myself and to Apollos for your sakes; that ye might learn in us not to think of men above that which is written, that no one of you be puffed up for one against another.

7 For who maketh thee to differ from another? and what hast thou that thou didst not receive? now if thou didst receive it, why dost thou glory, as if thou hadst not received it?

8 Now ye are full, now ye are rich, ye have reigned as kings without us: and I would to God ye did reign, that we also might reign with you.

9 For I think that God hath set forth us the apostles last, as it were appointed to death: for we are made a spectacle unto the world, and to angels, and to men.

10 We are fools for Christ's sake, but ye are wise in Christ; we are weak, but ye are strong; ye are honourable, but we are despised.

11 Even unto this present hour we both hunger, and thirst, and are naked, and are buffeted, and have no certain dwellingplace;

12 And labour, working with our own hands: being reviled, we bless; being persecuted, we suffer it:

13 Being defamed, we intreat: we are made as the filth of the world, and are the offscouring of all things unto this day.

Devotional Reading
Matt. 23:8-12
Background Scripture
1 Cor. 4:1-13
Memory Selection
1 Cor. 4:1

421

The focus of this lesson is capsuled neatly in 1 Corinthians 4:6, in the Contemporary English Version. Paul says that he has used himself and his co-worker Apollos as examples, because *"I want you to stop saying that one of us is better than the other."* This theme began in chapter 1, where Paul

Invite group members to recall what they like best about ministers they have known. Perhaps some will recall an especially powerful preacher. Others may remember when a godly minister provided comfort at the death of a loved one. Yet others may remember that "Bro. Smith" always had time to make home or hospital calls.

began a to attack the tendency of the Corinthian Christians to elevate one minister above another. Some were attaching themselves to their favorite preacher in sectarian zeal. As a result there were "Paul-ites" and "Apollos-ites," "Cephas-ites" and even exclusivist "Christ-ites." Now, to put all Christian leaders "in their place," Paul says that he and Apollos are the least of God's servants, and had no intention of starting their own sect.

Then bluntly ask whether any of these fondly remembered ministers should have established his own church. Most would be scandalized at the thought. Note that the problem Paul faces in this lesson is that some Christians at Corinth were playing ministerial favorites so zealously that the church faced just this danger. He will insist that the best ministers are not such "separatists" who glory in their own abilities. They find honor in being servants of Christ, not themselves.

Teaching Outline	*Daily Bible Readings*

I. Accountable to Christ—1-5
  A. Faithful stewards, 1-2
  B. Not judged by men, 3-5
II. Glorying in Christ—6-8
  A. Examples: Paul and Apollos, 6
  B. Gifts not of ourselves, 7
III. Fools for Christ—8-13
  A. To reign, serve, 8-9
  B. Apostles come last, 10-13
    1. "Fools," 10
    2. An "offscouring," 11-13
	Mon. Stewards of Grace
	    1 Peter 4:1-11
	Tue. Jesus Stoops to Serve
	    John 13:2-9
	Wed.Serve One Another
	    John 13:12-17
	Thu. Become a Servant
	    Mark 10:41-45
	Fri. Stewards of Mysteries
	    1 Cor. 4:1-7
	Sat. Fools for Christ
	    1 Cor. 4:8-13
	Sun. Fatherly Admonition
	    1 Cor. 4:14-21

Verse by Verse

I. Accountable to Christ—1-5
A. Faithful stewards, 1-2

1 Let a man so account of us, as of the ministers of Christ, and stewards of the mysteries of God.

2 Moreover it is required in stewards, that a man be found faithful.

Paul has been arguing that he and Apollos, along with others who had ministered among the Corinthians, were not to be followed as heads of conflicting sects. How then *should* they be viewed? His answer here is that they should be considered "ministers of Christ. " This time Paul does not use the term *diakonos* (servant) for "minister," but a word that meant literally an "under-rower." This was a slave made to labor at the bottom rank of oars in ancient warships. How could anyone think to elevate such a servant to be head of a church faction?

Yet God had entrusted certain "under-rowers" with the *mysteries* of God. We encountered this word in 2:7, and noted that it described secret objects and rites in various pagan cults. Paul "baptizes" the term and uses it for "Christ crucified," the center of the Christian faith. Although precisely how Christ's death purchased salvation was in one sense a mystery, unlike those in the mystery cults this "secret" had in fact been revealed, through the apostolic preaching—entrusted to faithful proclaimers charged not with starting new cults of their own but being good stewards in service to their master.

The word for "steward" gives us the term "economy," and referred in Paul's day especially to a household's system of operation. The head of the household often hired an "economist" or steward as a manager. Paul is saying that in Christ's "economy," the apostles must report faithfully to the "Head" of the household, Christ. Christians must not tempt them to set up their own "economy" by showing favoritism for one minister over another.

B. Not judged by men, 3-5

3 But with me it is a very small thing that I should be judged of you, or of man's judgment: yea, I judge not mine own self.

4 For I know nothing by myself; yet am I not hereby justified: but he that judgeth me is the Lord.

5 Therefore judge nothing before the time, until the Lord come, who both will bring to light the hidden things of darkness, and will make manifest the counsels of the hearts: and then shall every man have praise of God.

Showing sectarian preference for one minister over another also violates the very standard of judgment by which they were guided. In verse 3 Paul shows that he could not possibly allow himself to be put on a pedestal by being judged a favorite by divisive followers. Indeed, he was not even willing to judge himself. If he did that, he would perhaps have thought too little of himself to become a minister, having persecuted Christians. Fortunately, Christ was his judge.

"By" in verse 4 means "against," leading to the NIV's translation, "My conscience is clear." Paul had not wallowed in guilt for his past transgressions, but had by faith accepted the forgiveness Jesus offers. In fact, as verse 5 shows, Christians should be very slow to "judge" their leaders either positively or negatively. That is simply not their prerogative. Either elevating them as sectarian leaders or belittling them as unworthy servants is claiming authority that belongs to Christ, and is premature. Teir work will not be judged until the *Day* of Judgment (see also 3:13).

In our own day all this may raise the question about "Minister Appreciation Sunday" and other occasions when we honor faithful Christian leaders. Paul is not forbidding such gestures; giving a person a plaque or a gold watch (or even a trip to Israel!) is a far cry from making him a leader who causes division in the Body.

II. Glorying in Christ—6-8
A. Examples: Paul and Apollos, 6

6 And these things, brethren, I have in a figure transferred to myself and to Apollos for your sakes; that ye might learn in us not to think of men above that which is written, that no one of you be puffed up for one against another.

When he first raised the issue of dividing the church by placing leaders against each other, Paul used himself, Apollos, and "Cephas" as examples of men who had ministered among the Corinthians. Here he says he has done this, literally, as a "schema," an example. Appreciating their work without making them divisive leaders is a pattern Paul says should keep them from going beyond "that which is written." Since there is not single passage of Scripture that says, "Don't unduly lift up mere servants as leaders of separate churches," Paul is perhaps citing the general tone of Scripture, which condemns splitting the people of God by following opposing leaders, as was done in the case of Rehoboam and Jeroboam, sons of Solomon (1 Kings 12:16).

B. Gifts not of ourselves, 7

7 For who maketh thee to differ from another? and what hast thou that thou didst not receive? now if thou didst receive it, why dost thou glory, as if thou hadst not received it?

Paul seems to make a subtle but crucial shift from addressing church members to their leaders. It is a natural progression: undue praise easily "goes to the head" of a leader, who can easily begin to "believe his own press clippings." Here Paul warns against that very tendency. Regardless of the brilliance, leadership skills, or preaching ability of leaders among the Corinthians, they did not invent them. It is a misappropriation of gifts to take one's abilities and use them to divide the church as though those gifts were self-developed instead of God-given.

III. Fools for Christ—8-13

A. To reign, serve, 8-9

8 Now ye are full, now ye are rich, ye have reigned as kings without us: and I would to God ye did reign, that we also might reign with you.

9 For I think that God hath set forth us the apostles last, as it were appointed to death: for we are made a spectacle unto the world, and to angels, and to men.

Continuing to address unknown church leaders in Corinth, Paul compares the lowly place accorded even the apostles that resulted from their highly-visible leadership roles in the early Church. When a Roman ruler wanted to suppress the early Christian movement, he went to the "top" and imprisoned a Peter or a Paul, as though to cut off the head of the "viper" they considered the Church to be.

Paul's language is dripping with irony. Divisive church leaders in Corinth were accepting "kingly" treatment. Paul says that indeed he wished they *were* kings; instead, he knows that their self-glorification will come to an inglorious end when persecution arises and they are the first to be sought about by the authorities. Often imprisoned, tortured, even burned at the stake, they served as spectacles (lit. "theatre"), as the gladiators in the public arenas. Being willing to do this, Paul implies, is the mark of a true Christian leader— not accepting glory from schismatic Christians. One can only wonder how many of the bishops and other church leaders in the Middle Ages could have overlooked this warning as they began to assume the princely roles and opulent robes of church leaders in that day. (It was to protest such practices that St. Francis of Assisi stood before the bishop of Rome and calmly disrobed!)

B. Apostles come last, 10-13
1. "Fools," 10

10 We are fools for Christ's sake, but ye are wise in Christ; we are weak, but ye are strong; ye are honourable, but we are despised.

Continuing his tone of biting irony, Paul contrasts the "foolish" position of a genuine apostle or other church leader with the position held by divisive leaders who allowed their followers to push them to the forefront and to foster division in the church.

2. An "offscouring," 11-13

11 Even unto this present hour we both hunger, and thirst, and are naked, and are buffeted, and have no certain dwellingplace;

12 And labour, working with our own hands: being reviled, we bless; being persecuted, we suffer it:

13 Being defamed, we intreat: we are made as the filth of the world, and are the offscouring of all things unto this day.

The descriptive phrases Paul piles up here remind us of the hardships to which many early church leaders, especially the apostles, were subjected. The terms build up to a climax with the assertion that these leaders have been made the "filth" and "off-scouring" of the world. These terms were borrowed from the most menial of cleaning chores, referring to the scum discarded after scrubbing out a filthy container. They stand in stark contrast to church leaders who allow their followers to virtually idolize them, at the expense of church unity.

Evangelistic Emphasis

When Samuel was appointed by God to anoint a new king of Israel, God gave him these instructions, "Do not consider his appearance or his height, for I have rejected him. The LORD does not look at the things man looks at. Man looks at the outward appearance, but the LORD looks at the heart (1 Sam. 16:7)." Now, that is both good news and bad news.

The good news is that God looks at the intentions of our hearts. At some time in our lives, all of us have tried to do a good thing and it turned out bad. There are times we tried to say the right thing and it came out wrong, hurting someone's feelings. Those times are terrible, but God knows our hearts. God knows our intentions. God knows we meant well.

The bad news is also that God looks at the intentions of our hearts! Though our actions might look completely altruistic to another human being, God knows whether or not we are performing the act to gain some hidden advantage. Our words may be dripping with sweetness while our hearts are full of meanness and bitterness. God sees our motivations.

Therefore, our task is to keep our thoughts and motivations pure before the Lord, however our words and deeds appear to others.

❧

Let a man so account of us, as of the ministers of Christ, and stewards of the mysteries of God.— *1 Corinthians 4:1*

Paul urges the Corinthians not to think of Apollo and himself as great leaders. They are not to revered, but seen as men to whom the knowledge of the gospel was given. The Greek underlying the term "stewards" means "house manager." Paul understands that the "house" belongs to God, and that he has managerial responsibility.

The idea of stewardship and managing must be in the forefront of our thinking today, especially when it comes to the Church. Many times conflict occurs when we forget whose church it really is. We must understand the Church is God's Church. It does not belong to the pastor or to the deacons. The Church does not belong to the most influential family. The Church does not belong to the denominational headquarters.

The Church belongs to God through Jesus Christ. It was bought and paid for by the blood of Christ. The Church is only on loan to us from Him. We work for God through the Church as servants. We are servants together in God's Church for God's will in His way. If we remember that, we will get so much more done, and the Kingdom of God will grow.

Weekday Problems

"Whose project is this?" Al asked. Al is the owner of Computer Teacher, a software firm that supplies training programs to specialized businesses. The project was due next Monday. The company that ordered the new program wanted to make a change. Al needed to know how far along the project was.

"Well, actually, it's my project," Ben answered.

"How's it coming?" Al asked.

"I'm getting right on it," Ben replied.

"Ben, I need to see you in my office. Now," Al shot back.

Ben and Al are both Christians who go to the same church. The fact that Al knew Ben from church weighed heavily in Al's decision to hire him.

"Ben, what are you thinking?" Al exclaimed. "This project is due Monday! You should be almost through, not about to start!"

"Come on, Al. They'll give us more time," Ben answered. "I've been too busy lately to put the proper time into it."

"Ben, if you did not have the time to do it, you should not have volunteered to take it on," Al replied, exasperated.

*Was Ben wrong to count on the other company to extend the deadline?

*Was Al wrong to expect Ben to have higher standards of trust-worthiness and responsibility because Ben is a Christian?

Who's in Charge Here, Anyway?

And it came to pass that the lion walked grandly through the jungle taking a poll of who was the greatest among all the animals. When he saw the hippopotamus he inquired, "Who is the king of the jungle?"

"You are, O mighty one," said the hippo.

Next the lion met a giraffe and put the same question to the long-necked one. "You are king," the giraffe said.

Then the lion came upon a tiger, asked who was king, and received the same accolade.

Finally he met an elephant. He gave him a rap on the knee, looked up and demanded, "Who is king of the jungle?" Whereupon the elephant swept the lion up in the curl of his trunk and slammed him into a tree. He bounced off the tree, stunned, then struggled to his feet and was heard to mumble, as he dragged himself off to his lair, "You don't have to get so mad just because you don't know the right answer."

This Lesson in Your Life

The late theologian Dietrich Bonhoeffer once wrote about "the responsible man." I interpret what he says, basically, to mean that the Christian is supposed to be the most responsible person in the world.

The Christian is responsible to others. Though Paul says here that the opinion, or judgment, of others means nothing to him, the fact remains that we are responsible to others. In the long run the judgment of our fellow human beings is usually accurate. I have heard it said, "There are two people who will tell you the truth about yourself —an enemy who has lost his temper and a friend who loves you dearly." People admire honesty, reliability, trustworthiness, generosity, and love. We demonstrate these character traits (or our lack of them) in our relationships. People know who we are.

The Christian is responsible to God. In the final analysis, He is the only one to whom we are responsible, because God knows all the circumstances. He knows the struggles you are having. He knows the secrets in your heart that no one else knows. God also knows your motives. Humans see the deed, but God sees the intention. A deed that looks noble may have been done from self-promoting intent, while a deed that may have achieved very poor results may have been done with the highest motives. God knows. We are responsible to God.

We also would do well to remember that *all we are and all we have is a gift from God.* Paul asks, "What do you possess that you did not receive?" It is all about God's grace. William Barclay writes, "No man could ever have known Him unless God revealed Himself. No man could ever have won his own salvation. A man does not save himself, he is saved. When we think of what we have done and think of what God has done for us, pride is ruled out and only humble gratitude remains." As Andrae Crouch sang, "All that I am and ever hope to be, I owe it all the Thee."

We have no reason to boast of what we may have accomplished in the Kingdom of God. God has given us what we have. This brings us to another point. *It is our responsibility to use what God has given us to God's glory.* God did not give us gifts and graces in order for us to show off and bring attention to ourselves. God gives each of us certain gifts and graces in order that we may use those gifts to fulfill the Great Commandment and the Great Commission.

We use the abilities and talents God has given us to serve Him better. We are but stewards of those gifts. We are but servants of God.

1. In verse 1 Paul refers to himself, Apollos, and ultimately us in two ways. What does he call us?
Paul says that we are ministers (servants) of Christ and stewards of the mysteries of God.

2. What is required of stewards (vs.2)?
It is required that stewards, those in whom God's trust has been placed, prove themselves faithful.

3. Paul mentions three groups or individuals by whom we may be judged. Who are those groups or individuals?
Paul says other people may try to be our judges, that we may try to judge ourselves, but that ultimately God is our judge.

4. Though we may hide things from others and even from ourselves, are we able to hide things from God?
No. God will bring to light those things we try to hide in darkness, and He will expose the motives of our hearts.

5. Paul says in verse 4 that though his conscience may be clear, that does not make him innocent. What does he mean?
That our own hearts can even deceive us. As Jeremiah 17:9 says, "The heart is deceitful above all things, and desperately wicked: who can know it?"

6. Do we Christians have any reason to brag about our accomplishments or take pride in our own success?
No. All that we have has been given to us by God. Since we did nothing to earn what we have, we have no reason to boast or brag.

7. Paul uses irony to get the Corinthians to see how spiritually poor they really are. How does he communicate this in verse 8?
Paul says the Corinthians have all they want and that they are already rich. Paul ironically calls them "kings."

8. How does Paul refer to the apostles?
He refers to the apostles as gladiators God has sent to die in the arena. The apostles have been made a spectacle before the whole universe, angels and humans.

9. In reality, what were the apostles going through for the sake of the gospel of Jesus?
The apostles were going hungry and thirsty. They were in rags. They were homeless. They were brutally treated.

10. Paul reports how the apostles reacted to the horrible treatment they received. List the reactions Paul cites.
Paul says when they are cursed, they bless. When they are persecuted, they endure it. When they are slandered, they answer kindly.

 I remember a story I heard about our former president Jimmy Carter. If I recall the story correctly, President Carter was a midshipman at the U. S. Naval Academy. In that time he was required to appear for an interview before Admiral Hyman Rickover. The admiral questioned midshipman Carter on mathematics, physics, engineering, and military tactics and strategy. The interview was both exhaustive and exhausting. As the time drew to a close, Admiral Rickover looked at Jimmy Carter with a final question, "Did you always do your best?"

President Carter thought of all the tests and projects he had done. As he honestly evaluated each one, he had to admit that he had not always done his best. "No, sir," Carter answered. "Not every time."

"Why not?" the admiral asked. And the interview was over.

Paul writes, "Now it is required that those who have been given a trust must prove faithful (NIV)."

God has given us so much. God has given me so much. I must always keep in my heart that I must be a faithful steward of all that God has given me. I must always do my best with what I have.

There are always limitations on what we can do. We are limited by time. We are limited by ability. We are limited by intellect. We are limited by physical traits. However, we are only limited by our own wills if we do not do the best we can with what we have been given.

Jesus took 12 ordinary, unschooled men and poured Himself into them for three years. There was nothing remarkable about any one of those 12 men. They did not seem all that smart. They certainly did not hold any particular position of influence. They were not outstanding in any way, except that they were taught by Jesus. Then Jesus let those ordinary men, filled with the Holy Spirit, loose on the world, and the world was changed for the better.

Faithful men and women of God have always been able to change the world. We do it simply by faithfully doing our best with what God has given us.

Have you always done your best? Why not?

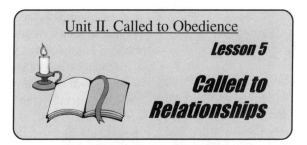

Unit II. Called to Obedience

Lesson 5

Called to Relationships

1 Corinthians 7:1-15

Now concerning the things whereof ye wrote unto me: It is good for a man not to touch a woman.

2 Nevertheless, to avoid fornication, let every man have his own wife, and let every woman have her own husband.

3 Let the husband render unto the wife due benevolence: and likewise also the wife unto the husband.

4 The wife hath not power of her own body, but the husband: and likewise also the husband hath not power of his own body, but the wife.

5 Defraud ye not one the other, except it be with consent for a time, that ye may give yourselves to fasting and prayer; and come together again, that Satan tempt you not for your incontinency.

6 But I speak this by permission, and not of commandment.

7 For I would that all men were even as I myself. But every man hath his proper gift of God, one after this manner, and another after that.

8 I say therefore to the unmarried and widows, It is good for them if they abide even as I.

9 But if they cannot contain, let them marry: for it is better to marry than to burn.

10 And unto the married I command, yet not I, but the Lord, Let not the wife depart from her husband:

11 But and if she depart, let her remain unmarried, or be reconciled to her husband: and let not the husband put away his wife.

12 But to the rest speak I, not the Lord: If any brother hath a wife that believeth not, and she be pleased to dwell with him, let him not put her away.

13 And the woman which hath an husband that believeth not, and if he be pleased to dwell with her, let her not leave him.

14 For the unbelieving husband is sanctified by the wife, and the unbelieving wife is sanctified by the husband: else were your children unclean; but now are they holy.

15 But if the unbelieving depart, let him depart. A brother or a sister is not under bondage in such cases: but God hath called us to peace.

Devotional Reading
1 John 4:7-16
Background Scripture
1 Cor. 7:1-20, 23-40
Memory Selection
1 Cor. 7:7

431

From teaching against division within the Church, the apostle Paul has turns to the topic of marriage, one of a variety of issues that had been raised by the Corinthians.

The relationship between the sexes has been at issue in virtually all religions. "Ascetism," the practice of avoiding sex and other practices that appeal to the "flesh," was popular among several religions in the world of the early Church. Since some thought that even marriage was wrong, some in the Corinthian church, especially with Greek backgrounds, asked Paul to explain how they should approach the issue. Paul himself was, at least when he wrote this letter, unmarried. Yet he views this as an exception to the general rule: "Marriage is honorable in all, and the bed undefiled" (Heb. 13:4).

With the help of a Bible dictionary, describe briefly marriage customs in Paul's day, and challenge group members to compare them with their own understanding of Jesus' teaching of "one man, on wife."

By the first century, most cultures in the Mediterranean world endorsed monogamy, as opposed to polygamy. Jesus taught that God had originally meant for marriage to be permanent (Matt. 19:8), but for obvious reasons (such as spouse abuse), the rabbis had developed many ways for Jewish men to obtain a divorce and to remarry. Greek and Roman law also allowed for women to sue for divorce.

Also, ascetism, in which marriage was viewed as too "worldly" for really holy people, was popular among some. Obviously, Paul's teaching met an audience as diverse as the people in your group.

Teaching Outline	*Daily Bible Readings*

I. Marriage is Honorable—1-2
II. Mutual Consideration—3-5
  A. Sexual consensus, 3-4
  B. Temporary abstinence, 5
III. Matter of Giftedness—6-9
  A. Temporary ideal, 6-8
  B. General rule, 9
IV. Marriage to Unbelievers—10-15
  A. Stability in marriage, 10-13
  B. Sanctified union, 14-15
	Mon. God Is Love
	    1 John 4:7-16
	Tue. To Husbands and Wives
	    1 Cor. 7:1-5
	Wed. To Single Persons
	    1 Cor. 7:6-11
	Thu. The Unbelieving Spouse
	    1 Cor. 7:12-16
	Fri. Live as God Called You
	    1 Cor. 7:17-24
	Sat. Remain as You Are
	    1 Cor. 7:25-31
	Sun. Unhindered Devotion
	    1 Cor. 7:32-40

Verse by Verse

I. Marriage is Honorable—1-2

1 Now concerning the things whereof ye wrote unto me: It is good for a man not to touch a woman.

2 Nevertheless, to avoid fornication, let every man have his own wife, and let every woman have her own husband.

Verse 1 indicates that marriage, in particular the sexual relationship, had excited particular interest among the new Christians in Corinth, and they had asked the apostle about it.

"To touch a woman" was a euphemism for sexual intercourse. This would not have been an issue for most *Jewish*-Christians, since their heritage had begun with God dealing with a sexual union between Abraham and his wife Sarah. In fact, the rabbis taught that "Any man who has no wife is no man." Given Paul's background as a rabbinically-trained Jew, many scholars believe he had been previously married, but that perhaps his wife had died, or left him when he converted to Christianity.

Thus it is not surprising that Paul's immediate response is in agreement with Hebrews 13:4: "Marriage is honorable in all, and the bed undefiled." Some Greek ideas that would develop into "Gnosticism" in the second century took is-

sue with this. Starting with the unbiblical premise that "flesh" is evil, these views could be expected to brand the union of flesh in marriage as evil also. The difficulty, as Paul states in verse 2, is that given natural human instincts, fornication (sex outside of marriage) is a common result of forbidding to marry. Paul's consistent teaching is that sex is good within marriage, but forbidden outside that relationship. The spread of disease and other physical and relational ills in our own times show the wisdom of this distinction.

II. Mutual Consideration—3-5

A. Sexual consensus, 3-4

3 Let the husband render unto the wife due benevolence: and likewise also the wife unto the husband.

4 The wife hath not power of her own body, but the husband: and likewise also the husband hath not power of his own body, but the wife.

Some "Gnostic-like" teachers held that, while a man and woman might marry, they should abstain from sex. For Paul, this is both unrealistic and unreflective of the beauty of sex within marriage. Given the male dominance in the culture about him, the apostle's teaching that both husband and wife have "power" over each other's body is remarkably progressive. This is part of the seriousness of taking the marriage vow: both husband and wife promise to give up total control over their bodies for the benefit of the other.

B. Temporary abstinence, 5

5 Defraud ye not one the other, except it be with consent for a time, that ye may give yourselves to fasting and prayer; and come together again, that Satan tempt you not for your incontinency.

Since the general rule is free and open sexuality in marriage, it "defrauds" a marriage partner to deny him or her sex. However, Paul allows that couples may abstain from sex temporarily in order to show, along with fasting and prayer, that the spirit and not only the flesh owes obedience to God. However, these periods of abstinence are to be brief, so that neither marriage partner is tempted to be unfaithful because of prolonged denial of sexual satisfaction.

III. Matter of Giftedness—6-9

A. Temporary ideal, 6-8

6 But I speak this by permission, and not of commandment.

7 For I would that all men were even as I myself. But every man hath his proper gift of God, one after this manner, and another after that.

8 I say therefore to the unmarried and widows, It is good for them if they abide even as I.

It is not clear what "this" refers to in verse 6. The best assumption seems to be that it refers to Paul's advice to stay single in the following verses. Perhaps he is saying that God's general "commandment" is that marriage is wholesome, but that he has been given special "permission" to recommend living alone as also worthy of consideration.

Being chaste but unmarried, however, is a special "gift" (*charisma*), Paul says. On the one hand, special circumstances prompt him to wish that all would remain single, as he was. In a time when persecution for being a Christian was always a threat, it would not inflict hardship on a family when a single Christian was arrested and jailed. Thus, in verse 26 Paul will say that it is good for a person not to marry in view of "the present distress."

B. General rule, 9

9 But if they cannot contain, let them marry: for it is better to marry than to burn.

Again recognizing that staying single is a "gift," Paul also recognizes the power of the sex drive. If a couple simply cannot resist this, it is better to marry than to "burn"—although exactly what this means is arguable. Some (including the NIV translators) believe that Paul is referring to the "burning" sexual passion that can consume a single person, or drive him or her to fornication. Others hold that Paul has in mind the burning fires of hell. Whichever is meant, the apostle is clear that marriage can be an aid to a pure life, and that no religious rules against it are to be allowed to tempt persons to impurity.

IV. Marriage to Unbelievers—10-15
A. Stability in marriage, 10-13

10 And unto the married I command, yet not I, but the Lord, Let not the wife depart from her husband:

11 But and if she depart, let her remain unmarried, or be reconciled to her husband: and let not the husband put away his wife.

12 But to the rest speak I, not the Lord: If any brother hath a wife that believeth not, and she be pleased to dwell with him, let him not put her away.

13 And the woman which hath an husband that believeth not, and if he be pleased to dwell with her, let her not leave him.

The marriage union is so all-consuming that the question arose whether it should be maintained in cases among pagans, when one spouse becomes a Christian and the other does not. Paul's reply is to keep the marriage together as long as the unbeliever is willing. Again his teaching is remarkably progressive, especially in verse 13 where he conceives it to be possible for a believing woman to leave an unbelieving husband who is *not* "pleased to dwell with her." Women could obtain a divorce under Greek and Roman law, but only men could sue for divorce under Jewish law.

B. Sanctified union, 14-15

14 For the unbelieving husband is sanctified by the wife, and the unbelieving wife is sanctified by the husband: else were your children unclean; but now are they holy.

15 But if the unbelieving depart, let him depart. A brother or a sister is not under bondage in such cases: but God hath called us to peace.

Paul anticipates (or perhaps responds to) the question, How can the marriage of a believer and an unbeliever be "sanctified" or approved by God? Furthermore, what about the children of such mixed unions? The question arises only when the marriage occurred before one of the spouses became a Christian. Elsewhere the apostle teaches to "be not unequally yoked together with unbelievers" (2 Cor. 6:14). Although he does not explicitly apply this principle to marriage, it is reasonable to assume that it might.

Paul's answer, however, is that the believing spouse's faith provides a holy sanction that covers both the unbelieving spouse and any children that might issue from the marriage. The exception to a believer's remaining in the marriage is when the unbeliever "departs." By saying that the believing spouse is "not under bondage," Paul apparently means that he or she is free to marry again.

The sum and tone of Paul's whole teaching on this issue is a sensitive awareness of the legitimate claims that marriage makes on a couple, and of the suffering that wives and children might endure if all believers broke up the homes they had established before conversion. Marriage is an older institution than the Church; and Paul's teaching is designed to preserve it if at all possible.

Evangelistic Emphasis

Quite often we Christians leave the impression with the secular world that the Bible teaches that sex is bad. If we took the time to read the Bible for ourselves, we would discover that this impression is a false one. It can be said that God invented sex, and that He meant for a husband and wife to enjoy sex together.

However, God set out some rules for humans to follow in the sexual arena. The rules God laid out are not designed to limit our enjoyment, but are for our own good. If we follow God's rules we are hurt emotionally less often. If we follow God's rules, we do not have to worry as much about sexually transmitted diseases. If we follow God's rules, we are able to live in mutually enriching relationships with members of the opposite sex in marriage.

God wants us to live significant, fulfilled lives in every area of life. Therefore, He gives us guidelines on how to do just that concerning our physical relationships with one another. He guides us in marriage. He guides us in singleness.

God gives us so many good things. When we give ourselves to Him, He gives Himself back to us. When God is in us, He empowers us to live significant, fulfilled lives in every area.

℘℧

For I would that all men were even as I myself. But every man hath his proper gift of God, one after this manner, and another after that.—*1 Corinthians 7:7*

At the time of this writing Paul is a single man. Some think that he suggests here that the single life is the best. I doubt it.

It was obvious that Paul was a focused, intense man. He was a focused, intense Jew. He now is a focused, intense Christian. Paul is consumed by his passion to spread Christianity throughout the world. Of course, in those days there were no television, no Internet, nor any satellite downlinks. If Paul was going to preach the gospel in a region, he personally had to travel to that place. Granted, his letters were very effective, too. Still, he traveled all over the area around the Mediterranean Sea to preach the gospel.

I suspect Paul knew he would not be treating a wife fairly if he was going to be the zealous evangelist that he was. For him, the spread of the gospel of Jesus was so consuming that marriage would have been a distraction; and he wished that there were more who would devote themselves entirely to the propagation of the gospel. He prayed that there would be more with that single-minded vision.

Weekday Problems

Susan and David had been married for six years. She had always known that he liked to flirt. She met him in a lounge and thought he was cute because he flirted with her. David assured her that all his interest in other women would stop when they got married, and Susan believed him.

Soon after they were married, however, Susan heard a rumor from one of David's co-workers that he was spending an inordinate amount of time with an attractive woman. When confronted by Susan, David assured her there was nothing going on. He had always worked irregular hours, and often needed to be away overnight. "It's this wretched job," he would tell her. Finally, one of Susan's friends told her she had seen David in a bar drinking and dancing with another woman. Susan remembered that it was one of the times he had to "work out of town overnight." She began asking around, and found that almost everyone else knew that David was sleeping with multiple partners.

Today, they are sitting across the dinner table from each other. David has told Susan that he has just found out he is HIV positive. She is stunned.

*What reaction that is in harmony with Scripture might Susan have to this news?

*What do you think Paul meant when he wrote, "the husband's body does not belong to him alone, but also to his wife"?

Marital (Martial?) Arts

Wife: Could I have some spending money, dear?
Husband: Money, money. If you ask me, I think you need brains more than money.
Wife (sweetly): I was just asking you for what I thought you might have the most of.

***

Husband: What? Beans again?!
Wife: I don't understand you. You liked beans fine on Monday, Tuesday, and Wednesday, but now all of a sudden you hate them.

***

Marriage, for men, is like a railroad sign. You see a girl, and you stop. Then you look. And after you're married, you listen.

***

Husband: Whatever became of those old-fashioned girls who fainted when a man kissed them?
Wife: Whatever happened to the old-fashioned men who made them faint?

This Lesson in Your Life

A person only has to turn on the television to get a glimpse of today's attitudes toward sex and sexual immorality. We are literally bombarded with images of immorality. In all this, Paul gives some practical Christian counsel about our relationships with those of the opposite sex.

Paul reminds us that married couples have a mutual responsibility to be faithful to each other. That is one of the things Paul means when he uses the phrase "has authority" over the other partner's body.

We know that Acquired Immune Deficiency Syndrome (AIDS) is primarily spread by sexual contact, and that many other sexually transmitted diseases can be passed around when one has multiple partners. An unfaithful partner exposes her/his spouse to the same risks. Thus, we do not have the authority selfishly to do what we want with our own bodies because what we do affects our spouses as well.

Paul also reminds us indirectly that marriage partners are not to use sex to manipulate each other. A marriage is in trouble when one or both of the partners offer or withhold sex in order to get what they want. He wants sex more often, using that to dominate his spouse. She withholds sex when it suits her mood in order to demonstrate her control in the relationship. Sex is a beautiful thing within marriage. God never intended sex to be used as a method of controlling one's spouse.

Sex outside of marriage seems to be becoming more and more commonplace in our society. Sexual encounters occur at younger and younger ages. Paul reminds us indirectly that sex outside of marriage is wrong. Adultery has been recorded as being against God's will ever since God gave Moses the seventh Commandment.

A piece of Scotch tape will illustate to us the danger of multiple partners. If you stick a piece of tape to something, pull it off, then stick it to another object, the tape will adhere less to the second object. With each additional sticking and re-sticking the tape loses more and more of its adhesive quality. In the same way, if a person bonds with another person in a physical sense, then pulls away and bonds with another, over and over again, that person eventually will lose her or his ability to bond with anyone. Multiple partners dulls our ability to commit to a lasting relationship. We lose our "stickiness." And lack of commitment to our spouses leads to all kinds of additional relational and family problems, as we are experiencing today.

Although Paul gave this teaching almost 20 centuries ago, it is as relevant as today's newspaper. God knows what He is doing!

GETTING THE FACTS STRAIGHT

1. Was Paul saying in verse 2 that every man and woman should be married? Explain.

No. Paul was simply referring to normal sexual relations between spouses. He was addressing the problem of being with more than one partner.

2. In Paul's day the culture generally accepted that the husband had sole authority over his wife in every way. What does Paul say?

Paul teaches that husbands and wives have authority over each other's body.

3. Does the Bible teach that sex is a sin?

Of course not. Sex within marriage is God's plan.

4. What does Paul suggest might be a valid reason for a Christian husband and wife to abstain from having sexual relations?

He says a couple should not deprive each other unless by mutual consent, and only temporarily, so that they may devote themselves to prayer.

5. In verse 5 Paul recommends normal, healthy sexual relations between a man and wife. Why?

The sex drive is a normal human function. Married couples with a healthy sex life are less likely to be tempted to look for relationships outside of marriage.

6. How do we know that Paul was unmarried when he wrote this letter?

He states that he is unmarried in verse 8.

7. What does Paul mean in verse 10 when he writes, "I command, yet not I, but the Lord?"

Paul means that Jesus, not just the apostle, taught that married couples should stay together (Matt. 5:32; Mark 10:2-12; Luke 16:18).

8. Paul later counsels in 2 Corinthians 6:14 for Christians not to be in relationships with non-Christians. What does he say here?

If a couple is already married and one becomes a Christian and the other does not, they should not divorce if the unbeliever is willing to continue to live with the Christian.

9. Why is it important for a couple to stay together when one is a believer and the other is not?

The godly influence of the believing spouse could have a great effect on the unbeliever.

10. What does Paul permit if one spouse becomes a Christian but the other does not, and the relationship becomes intolerable?

Paul says the believer is not bound to the marriage in such circumstances.

We all know that a person must make a personal decision to come to Christ. We do not become Christians by osmosis. Just because my mother is a Christian does not mean that I am a Christian. Each person comes to Christ on his own.

Still, Paul reminds us that a godly mother or father or spouse has great influence over an unbeliever in the family. A married couple in my church some years ago is a good example. I will call them Jack and Jill.

Jill was a committed Christian. Jack was not. Jill played the organ at the church. She sang in the choir. She attended Bible studies. And she loved her husband with a godly love.

Jack never attended church except for funerals. He was a heavy drinker. His language was coarse and crude. He was very uncomfortable around me, a minister. I think he was concerned he might say or do something that would be unChristian and embarrass both of us.

Jill continued to pray for her husband. She continued to serve the Lord. She encouraged Jack in every way she could think of to give his life to Christ. Somehow, she managed to nudge Jack without nagging him. Always, Jill lived out her Christian faith before Jack and everybody in a way that was pure and non-confronting.

Eventually Jack began to come to fellowship-type get-togethers at the church. Usually there was food involved when he came. Jack finally began to feel comfortable in the group of Christians. Later, he began to come to worship services. Still later, he began attending a small group Bible study that met in a home.

Finally, after years of being prayed for, Jack became a Christian. Though Jill takes no credit for Jack's commitment, I am convinced that the influence of her godly life and witness was instrumental in drawing Jack to Christ.

It doesn't always work. Sometimes unbelieving spouses never come to Christ. However, it happens often enough to keep us on our knees praying. If you have an unbelieving spouse or parent or child or friend, keep praying. Keep loving that person. Keep encouraging. Keep living a faithful life yourself. It may be your influence that draws that person into the Kingdom.

Lesson 6
Called to Help the Weak

1 Corinthians 8:1-13

Now as touching things offered unto idols, we know that we all have knowledge. Knowledge puffeth up, but charity edifieth.

2 And if any man think that he knoweth anything, he knoweth nothing yet as he ought to know.

3 But if any man love God, the same is known of him.

4 As concerning therefore the eating of those things that are offered in sacrifice unto idols, we know that an idol is nothing in the world, and that there is none other God but one.

5 For though there be that are called gods, whether in heaven or in earth, (as there be gods many, and lords many,)

6 But to us there is but one God, the Father, of whom are all things, and we in him; and one Lord Jesus Christ, by whom are all things, and we by him.

7 Howbeit there is not in every man that knowledge: for some with conscience of the idol unto this hour eat it as a thing offered unto an idol; and their conscience being weak is defiled.

8 But meat commendeth us not to God: for neither, if we eat, are we the better; neither, if we eat not, are we the worse.

9 But take heed lest by any means this liberty of yours become a stumblingblock to them that are weak.

10 For if any man see thee which hast knowledge sit at meat in the idol's temple, shall not the conscience of him which is weak be emboldened to eat those things which are offered to idols;

11 And through thy knowledge shall the weak brother perish, for whom Christ died?

12 But when ye sin so against the brethren, and wound their weak conscience, ye sin against Christ.

13 Wherefore, if meat make my brother to offend, I will eat no flesh while the world standeth, lest I make my brother to offend.

Devotional Reading
Mark 9:42-48

Background Scripture
1 Cor. 8:1-13; Rom. 14

Memory Selection
1 Cor. 8:8-9

Another question the Corinthian Christians had asked the apostle Paul was whether it was right to eat meat that had been offered to idols. The question arose when meat that had been offered as sacrifice in idol worship was then sold at the public market. Some Christians, knowing that the idols were not real, did not hesitate to buy and eat the meat. Others, however, whose belief in only one God was new or weak, saw this as partaking of "unholy meat," and therefore sinful. The "pro-meat" and "anti-meat" groups were dividing. Paul offers counsel on the problem here.

The apostle's reply applies to a great many more conscience-related issues than eating such meat. (The teacher is urged to read Romans 14 for "the other side of the coin" regarding matters of conscience.)

Challenge your group from the start by telling them that this lesson tells of a radical conclusion reached by the apostle Paul: *if eating meat that had been offered to idols was a problem for other Christians, he would become a vegetarian!*

You will want to indicate that you recognize that this issue probably isn't a point of contention for most Christians today. Yet ask how we might apply Paul's drastic decision to other issues that divide modern Christians. For example, Christians have argued over the morality of such practices as *drinking in moderation . . . smoking . . . movies . . . skimpy clothing for women . . . card-playing* and *gambling.* Your aim isn't to give any group member a platform for arguing his or her opinion on any one issue, but to test our own sensitivity, love, and tolerance in the light of Paul's own decision.

Teaching Outline	*Daily Bible Readings*

I. The Problem—1-3
   A. Idols vs. the market, 1a
   B. 'Too-smart' Christians, 1b-3
II. The Principles
   A. 'An idol is nothing,' 4-6
     1. Things 'called' gods, 4
     2. The One True God, 5-6
   B. The weak conscience, 7-8
   C. Liberty vs. license, 9-11
   D. Seriousness of the issue, 12-13
	Mon. Called to Life and Light
	       John 1:1-5
	Tue. Don't Tempt Others
	       Mark 9:42-48
	Wed. Love Neighbor as Self
	       Mark 12:28-34
	Thu. Don't Make Others Fall
	       Rom. 14:13-19
	Fri. There Is Really One God
	       1 Cor. 8:1-6
	Sat. Weak Consciences
	       1 Cor. 8:7-13
	Sun. Do All to God's Glory
	       1 Cor. 10:23–11:1

Verse by Verse

I. The Problem—1-3
A. Idols vs. the market, 1a
1 Now as touching things offered unto idols,

Once again Paul is responding to a question from the Christians at Corinth. A large trade center like Corinth naturally included a welter of pagan religions. Several such religions included animal sacrifices, both in formal temple worship and in private homes, where a bond with the god was thought to be struck by sharing the same meal. Since meat was not nearly so common in the daily diet as it is today, the leftover meat from many of these animal sacrifices was commonly taken to the public market and sold. One strand of strict Jewish tradition explicitly forbade Jews to partake of pagan animal sacrifices, so Jewish Christians would have been as concerned about this issue as those who had been converted from paganism.

B. 'Too-smart' Christians, 1b-3
1b we know that we all have knowledge.

2 And if any man think that he knoweth anything, he knoweth nothing yet as he ought to know.

3 But if any man love God, the same is known of him.

Paul was already known for advocating freedom from the Law, especially where Gentiles were concerned. Apparently he knew that some in the church at Corinth were heartily in agreement, and would be quick to join him in teaching that, as he will say below, idols are not real, and that eating leftovers from pagan sacrifices would not "taint" believers in the true God.

Here, however, Paul begins his counsel by discounting this knowledge *by itself*. Knowledge applied without love, and in this case without consideration for others, is dangerous and divisive. The apostle indicates in verse 2 that those who deal recklessly with the sensitivities of others out of "superior" intellectualism actually don't know as much as they think they do. They lack knowledge of human relationships, of the power of influence, and of the sometimes fragile nature of fellowship within the church. This question, he says, should be answered by starting not with bare facts, but with *love*—love for God, and for the people of God.

II. The Principles
A. 'An idol is nothing,' 4-6
1. Things 'called' gods, 4
4 As concerning therefore the eating of those things that are offered in sacrifice unto idols, we know that an idol is nothing in the world, and that there is none other God but one.

A delightful story in the book

called *Bel and the Dragon,* in the Apocrypha, illustrates Paul's point. When the Hebrew captive Daniel was in captivity, the Babylonians sought to prove that their god Bel was real. They pointed out that huge amounts of meat, flour, and wine were left on the altar each evening. Since it was all gone the next morning, the god had obviously eaten it, they said.

To show their folly, Daniel had flour sprinkled on the floor one evening, the usual food placed with the idol, and the doors locked. The next morning, footprints in the flour on the floor led to a secret door under the idol—showing that the pagan priests were coming into the Temple from within, each night, and feasting on the food themselves.

So "We know that an idol is nothing," Paul says. Again, however, something besides this insight is needed for the situation in Corinth, where not everyone knew this bare theological fact.

2. The One True God, 5-6

5 For though there be that are called gods, whether in heaven or in earth, (as there be gods many, and lords many,)

6 But to us there is but one God, the Father, of whom are all things, and we in him; and one Lord Jesus Christ, by whom are all things, and we by him.

Paul elaborates on the fact that gods are not real—and we can almost hear those in Corinth who share this "superior" knowledge cheering him on. The knowledge that pagan gods are not real had been drilled into ancient Israel. Indeed, their refusal to abstain from adopting the worship of false gods of Canaanite religion had resulted in the Babylonian captivity and the virtual destruction of the nation, so fiercely did the One God insist on their exclusive allegiance. The "to us" of verse 6 therefore includes both the Jews and the Christians, who worshiped the same God. There are as many Gods as there are Messiahs— only one.

B. The weak conscience, 7-8

7 Howbeit there is not in every man that knowledge: for some with conscience of the idol unto this hour eat it as a thing offered unto an idol; and their conscience being weak is defiled.

8 But meat commendeth us not to God: for neither, if we eat, are we the better; neither, if we eat not, are we the worse.

Now Paul turns to the point that made it unwise to roughly assert that gods are not real, and to partake openly and freely of meat that had been offered to them. Many among the Corinthian Christians who had been pagans no doubt still wondered whether the god Mithra, Isis, Osiris, or whatever god they had worshiped *might* be real. Thus, when they shared a meal with fellow Christians who enjoyed market-place meat left over from a pagan service, and partook of the very meat that before their conversion signified unity with the god, they had a definite conscience problem.

It is important to note that the problem at Corinth was not simply that former pagans were *offended* when "free" Christians who knew that gods "are nothing" ate the meat. The problem occurred when that freedom influenced the former pagan to actually join in eating the meat—then felt guilty and unfaithful about it.

Sometimes modern Christians who have many scruples try to bind their views on others on the basis of Paul's teaching here, simply because they disapprove of certain practices. For example, some rigid Christians have tried to make a church-wide rule against playing cards, since some people gamble with cards and they are against gambling. Paul's position here would apply only if those who believed cards are wrong actually joined in the games, and felt guilty. If this distinction is ignored, the level of fellowship in a congregation is reduced to that of those with the most scruples, whether biblical or not.

C. Liberty vs. license, 9-11

9 But take heed lest by any means this liberty of yours become a stumblingblock to them that are weak.

10 For if any man see thee which hast knowledge sit at meat in the idol's temple, shall not the conscience of him which is weak be emboldened to eat those things which are offered to idols;

11 And through thy knowledge shall the weak brother perish, for whom Christ died?

Paul agrees that Christians have the "liberty" to eat meat that had been offered to idols, but he warns against acting on that liberty if it causes fellow-Christians to stumble. Note that this entire passage both encourages respect for the conscience, and implies that it is not, of itself, the final arbiter of truth. The apostle is clear that those who believe that eating the meat is wrong have a weak conscience. However, "to him that esteemeth any thing to be unclean, to him it is unclean" (Rom. 14:14). We may wish that the conscience of an overly-scrupulous person were better instructed, but we do not want him to violate it, and be lost. Christ's death on the Cross is for all believers, not just those who have "superior" knowledge.

D. Seriousness of the issue, 12-13

12 But when ye sin so against the brethren, and wound their weak conscience, ye sin against Christ.

13 Wherefore, if meat make my brother to offend, I will eat no flesh while the world standeth, lest I make my brother to offend.

Paul's concept of the Church as the Body of Christ comes through clearly here. To sin against a member of the Christ's Body is to sin against Christ Himself. Paul feels so strongly about this that he says he is willing to become a vegetarian if eating meat cause another member to fall.

Evangelistic Emphasis

You may know that Mohandas Gandhi once sought Christianity. He eventually rejected Christianity and remained Hindu. I read that he once said something like, "I would be a Christian, if I ever saw one."

I wonder how many folks are turned away from Christianity by the conduct of so-called Christians. I know Christians cannot live absolutely perfect lives. I also know that Christians are "free indeed," that we do not have to live our lives in order to please or placate any human being. We live our lives entirely for an audience of one—God our Father through Jesus Christ.

Yet I am sure that the Kingdom of God would grow at a much greater clip if we Christians would consider more often how our words and deeds may be perceived by unbelievers. Of course, there are those who would be quick to pick apart anything we do that might be misconstrued as non-Christian. But others are earnestly seeking a way of life that is more significant than what they are presently living. It is this group of seekers who need to see a Christian whose love is evident. It is this group of seekers toward whom we must be sensitive, so that our words and actions will bring them closer to saving faith in Jesus Christ instead of pushing them farther away.

But meat commendeth us not to God: for neither, if we eat, are we the better; neither, if we eat not, are we the worse. But take heed lest by any means this liberty of yours become a stumblingblock to them that are weak.—*1 Corinthians 8:8-9*

Jesus said that "It is not what goes into the mouth that defiles a person, but it is what comes out of the mouth that defiles" (Matt. 15:11). Paul is saying somewhat the same thing. What a person eats is not all that important, unless it somehow detracts from the faith of a weaker brother or sister in Christ.

For instance, a person earnestly seeking God may be convinced that humans should never kill other animals for food. Therefore, that person becomes a strict vegetarian. We mature Christians know that it is permissible for Christians to eat meat. Yet, it would not be in the best interest of the Kingdom of God, nor of your vegetarian brother's faith, to invite him to a juicy steak dinner at Outback Steakhouse. To eat meat would not make him or you less Christian, but it may viewed so in his eyes. Therefore, in deference to our vegetarian brother, when we share a meal with him, we serve greens and cornbread and peas and carrots with a nice lettuce and tomato salad. We carnivores can do that out of Christian love.

Weekday Problems

"Mom! Can Ginny stay and eat with us tonight and sleep over? Please, please, please, please, please!" Sara could be a very insistent child.

"Sure," Mom answered. "Just call Ginny's mom and ask."

Sara and Ginny bounded off to use the phone. In just a minute Sara called out, "Mom! Ginny's mom wants to talk to you!"

Sara's mom picked up the phone. "Well, we were going to order pizza out. We have rented the video, "Finding Nemo," and we were going to pop some popcorn and watch the movie." However, Ginny's mom didn't want her daughter watching a movie.

"Well, we don't have to do that," Sara's mom said. "Could Ginny stay if we played Chutes and Ladders or some other board game? Great, the girls will be delighted." Then she told the girls.

"Yaaay!" the girls shouted, dancing around.

Sara's dad heard the conversation. "Why can't they watch the movie?," he asked. "It's rated G. It's a cute movie."

"Ginny's family's church forbids watching television or movies," Sara's mom answered. "But it will do us good to play some games together."

*Did Sara's mom do the right thing? Did Ginny's mom?

*Was that a good time for Sara's mom to lecture Ginny's mom on a Christian's freedom in Christ? Explain your answer.

Reflections on the Conscience

Conscience is merely our own judgment of the right or wrong of our actions, and so can never be a safe guide unless enlightened by the word of God.—*Tryon Edwards*

***

Tenderness of conscience is always to be distinguished from scrupulousness. The conscience cannot be kept too sensitive and tender; but scrupulousness arises from bodily or mental infirmity, and discovers itself in a multitude of ridiculous, superstitious, and painful feelings.—*Richard Cecil*

***

It is astonishing how soon the whole conscience begins to unravel if a single stitch drops. One single sin indulged in makes a hole you could put your head through.—*Charles Buxton*

***

Conscience is that still, small voice
That quells a wicked thought
Then adds this sequence,
"Besides, you might get caught."

This Lesson in Your Life

This passage of scripture is not just about eating meat that was offered to idols. If it were, it would have meaning for today only in cultures where idols are still worshiped. This passage is broader than that. It's about Christians steering away from activities that might cause someone to fall away from Christ.

In my community I have encountered an example of this. If we read our Bibles objectively we will discover that the Scripture condemns drunkenness, but does not condemn the consumption of alcoholic beverages, such as wine. As I read my Bible, when a person's vineyards are fruitful and the wine is plentiful, it is a blessing from God. Yet, we know the pain and suffering that alcoholism has inflicted on many families. We know the excruciating grief felt by those who have had a loved one killed by a drunk driver. We have tasted the tears of families in which a teenager or young person, experimenting with alcohol for the first time, crashes her or his car and kills all the occupants. Drinking within moderation may not be a sin, according to an objective interpretation of the Scripture. Still, alcohol consumption is dangerous.

When I was working in mid-management for a national drugstore chain, a group of supervisors had been invited to dinner by the top management team from the home office. Alcohol was served. I declined the offers. One of the men from the home office noticed I wasn't drinking. He made fun of me, "Is this some sort of religious belief?"

I answered, "Well, yes, it is. I have a personal conviction against drinking." He laughed and rolled his eyes as if I had just come in on a hay truck.

"Now, wait a minute," I said. If I had told you I was a recovering alcoholic and would not drink because of that, you would have thought I was courageous. You would have been proud of me. Instead, you think I'm some religious fanatic." He just rolled his eyes again.

We Christians must always be careful in our liberty. We do not want to do anything that will make a brother or sister in Christ stumble. We must also be careful in our restraint. Just because I may have a personal conviction against some activity might not mean everyone should, if that activity is not prohibited by Scripture.

All our activities, in liberty and restraint, must be tempered with *agape* love.

1. Paul says knowledge does one thing and love does another. What are those things?

Knowledge puffs up or makes us arrogant. Love builds up or edifies.

2. What does verse 2 say about our limited knowledge?

We may think we know a lot, but we really don't know anything at all, compared to God's knowledge.

GETTING THE FACTS STRAIGHT

3. What place or importance does Paul give to idols?

Paul says that an idol is nothing in the world. Idols are worthless. They are merely pretend-gods.

4. Although there are many so-called gods and lords, how many true gods and lords are there?

There is only one true God. His name is Yahweh, or Jehovah. There is only one true Lord. His name is Jesus and He is the Christ.

5. Do idols have any power except in the perception of idol worshipers?

No. Idols have no power as divine beings. The true God does not rely upon us to give Him power. He gives us power.

6. Does it matter greatly what kind of food a Christian eats?

Not really. Peter received a vision that all things were permissible to eat if eaten with thanksgiving (Acts 10). There is a prohibition against gluttony, which has to do more with the amount one eats than what one eats.

7. Who is hurt the worst when a Christian does something that could perceived as a sin?

The weaker brother or sister is hurt the worst.

8. Which is the greater witness: to demonstrate your superior knowledge of what is right and wrong in the faith or to build up another believer's faith?

The greater good is to build up a weaker Christian's faith. Helping another is greater than showing off our biblical or spiritual knowledge.

9. If you sin against a brother in Christ by wounding his weak conscience, whom are you really sinning against?

If you sin against the brethren, you sin against Christ. A sin against the Body of Christ is a sin against Christ Himself.

10. What should our attitude be toward things we do that may make a brother or sister in Christ stumble?

Our attitude should be the same as Paul's. If anything I do makes another stumble, I should quit doing it.

We Christians must be careful what we do. If someone copies what we do, it could be a stumbling block to that person.

When I was a youngster, Bob Pettit, the Hall of Fame basketball player, came to speak at my high school. He told this story. Early in his professional basketball career he was asked to do a television commercial for a cigarette company. He didn't think much about it. It was good money. "Besides," he thought, "it isn't as if I'm forcing somebody to smoke cigarettes." The filming went well. The tobacco company was pleased and the ad was a success.

Not long afterward, he was signing autographs after a game. There was a crowd of kids, but one waited until all the others had gone. He sidled up to Bob Pettit and with a sly grin whispered, "I smoked one of your cigarettes, Mr. Pettit." Bob Pettit told us he never again did an ad for anything that would not meet his approval for his own children.

We Christians must be aware that our actions can affect other people. There are those who are watching us. Of course our children are watching us. They see us all the time. They see us when we tell them they should always tell the truth, then ask them to tell somebody to whom we do not want to talk on the telephone that we are not at home. We must be careful of our actions.

Other Christians may be watching. There may be those who believe that you are a model Christian. There may be one or more who are watching you to see how you act and react in certain situations so that they can have guidance on how they should act and react in similar circumstances.

Such a thing is an awesome responsibility, but it is a reality in the community of believers. What we do affects others within the community, both positively and negatively. Because of our love for God and our love for our brothers and sisters, we accept and embrace that responsibility. We remain sensitive to our weaker brothers and sisters, aware always that our own actions can help build up their faith.

Lesson 7

Called to Win the Race

1 Corinthians 9:24–10:13

Know ye not that they which run in a race run all, but one receiveth the prize? So run, that ye may obtain.

25 And every man that striveth for the mastery is temperate in all things. Now they do it to obtain a corruptible crown; but we an incorruptible.

26 I therefore so run, not as uncertainly; so fight I, not as one that beateth the air:

27 But I keep under my body, and bring it into subjection: lest that by any means, when I have preached to others, I myself should be a castaway.

10:1 Moreover, brethren, I would not that ye should be ignorant, how that all our fathers were under the cloud, and all passed through the sea;

2 And were all baptized unto Moses in the cloud and in the sea;

3 And did all eat the same spiritual meat;

4 And did all drink the same spiritual drink: for they drank of that spiritual Rock that followed them: and that Rock was Christ.

5 But with many of them God was not well pleased: for they were overthrown in the wilderness.

6 Now these things were our examples, to the intent we should not lust after evil things, as they also lusted.

7 Neither be ye idolaters, as were some of them; as it is written, The people sat down to eat and drink, and rose up to play.

8 Neither let us commit fornication, as some of them committed, and fell in one day three and twenty thousand.

9 Neither let us tempt Christ, as some of them also tempted, and were destroyed of serpents.

10 Neither murmur ye, as some of them also murmured, and were destroyed of the destroyer.

11 Now all these things happened unto them for ensamples: and they are written for our admonition, upon whom the ends of the world are come.

12 Wherefore let him that thinketh he standeth take heed lest he fall.

13 There hath no temptation taken you but such as is common to man: but God is faithful, who will not suffer you to be tempted above that ye are able; but will with the temptation also make a way to escape, that ye may be able to bear it.

July 16

Devotional Reading
Heb. 12:1-2

Background Scripture
1 Cor. 9:24–10:13

Memory Selection
1 Cor. 9:24

The apostle Paul has told the Corinthians that those who knew the truth that "idols are nothing" still should not flaunt their freedom to eat meat from idolatrous sacrifices, lest "weaker brethren" be emboldened to join them against their conscience. In this lesson, Paul expands on this principle of being "free" from arbitrary and opinionated religious restrictions.

We learn here that freedom in Christ does not mean license. In fact there is no such thing as *absolute* freedom. As Paul also taught, we are only free to choose masters: *sin* or *Christ* (Rom. 6:16). He affirms in this lesson that choosing Christ frees us from sin, but not from being responsible and disciplined.

&)CR

Build a bridge between the previous lesson touching on idolatry and the present lesson on freedom vs. license by asking your group whether idolatry is a problem today.

Although Paul has said that "idols are nothing," he warns against idolatry in this lesson. Ask your group whether this warning has any relevance today. First, ask for definitions of idolatry. Note that *idolatry is giving anything or anyone beside God first place in our lives.* Of course this opens up a world of common practices. Some people put material gain before God. Others seek pleasure before submission to God's moral standards. Addictions are formed when we put any substance or other dependency before our dependency on God, and His call to serve Him and others. In other words, idolatry is still a common problem in our society today.

Teaching Outline	*Daily Bible Readings*

I. Race of Life—9:24-27
  A. Disciplined runners, 24-25
  B. Disciplined disciples, 26-27
II. Remembering Forefathers—10:1-11
  A. Blessed of God, 1-4
  B. Disobedient children, 5-11
    1. Lustful, 5-6
    2. Idolatrous, 7
    3. Sexually immoral, 8
    4. Tempters and murmurers, 9-10
    5. Examples for us, 11
III. Relying on God's Help—12-13
	Mon. Run with Perseverance
	    Heb. 12:1-12
	Tue. Stay Alert
	    Eph. 6:10-20
	Wed.Be Doers, not Just Hearers
	    James 1:19-27
	Thu. Press Toward Goal
	    Philip. 3:12-16
	Fri. Run for the Gospel's Sake
	    1 Cor. 9:22b-27
	Sat. Don't Follow Bad Examples
	    1 Cor. 10:1-7
	Sun. God Will Help Us Endure
	    1 Cor. 10:8-13

Verse by Verse

I. Race of Life—9:24-27

A. Disciplined runners, 24-25

24 Know ye not that they which run in a race run all, but one receiveth the prize? So run, that ye may obtain.

25 And every man that striveth for the mastery is temperate in all things. Now they do it to obtain a corruptible crown; but we an incorruptible.

Paul has just concluded a lengthy discourse affirming our freedom in Christ. As he also argues in the letters to the Romans and the Galatians, this freedom means that we are not bound by the Law of Moses or any other rule of life except the one taught by Christ. Now the apostle turns to the inevitable problem that some people will always treat *freedom* as *license.*

He draws his first argument from the ancient Greek games, especially the Olympics, which had begun in 776 B.C. His choice of metaphors in itself is a lesson for us. In verse 25, a single Greek word, which gives us our words "agony" and "agonize," is translated "striveth for the mastery" (NIV, "competes in the games"). This reminds us of the all-out, often agonizing effort it takes to be a champion in such contests. Paul is saying that the Christian life is like that, too. Despite the free-

dom from sin won by Jesus' work on the Cross, it requires disciplined effort for His followers to remain faithful.

Paul's argument is two-fold: (1) Although many contestants compete in the games, there is only one champion (vs. 24); and (2) such champions don't win without months of disciplined training beforehand, to build up their strength and hone their skills (vs. 25). "Temperate" here means "self-restraint," applied in the NT especially to disciplined eating, drinking, and sexual habits. It was this sort of discipline that Paul counted on when he exhorted those who knew very well that "an idol is nothing" to restrain from eating meat offered to idols if it caused a brother or sister to eat against their conscience (chap. 8). Surely if a contestant in a mere game can be so disciplined as to win a temporary crown, the Christian in life's race can be disciplined in striving for the eternal crown Christ promises the faithful.

B. Disciplined disciples, 26-27

26 I therefore so run, not as uncertainly; so fight I, not as one that beateth the air:

27 But I keep under my body, and bring it into subjection: lest that by any means, when I have preached to others, I myself should be a castaway.

Paul wisely shows that he takes the same medicine of self-discipline that he is prescribing for the Corinthians. Like a runner in the games, he is running not aimlessly but toward the finish line. As a boxer, he is not sparring but engaging the very real opponents of lethargy and fleshly temptation. To "keep under" one's body is to subject it to discipline. Even as an apostle, Paul is expected to be focused and faithful in the game of life, realizing that the laws of reward and punishment apply to him as well as those to whom he preaches.

II. Remembering Forefathers—10:1-11
A. Blessed of God, 1-4

1 Moreover, brethren, I would not that ye should be ignorant, how that all our fathers were under the cloud, and all passed through the sea;

2 And were all baptized unto Moses in the cloud and in the sea;

3 And did all eat the same spiritual meat;

4 And did all drink the same spiritual drink: for they drank of that spiritual Rock that followed them: and that Rock was Christ.

Now the apostle calls the Corinthians to remember the fate of their forefathers—a common theme in his letters that bases his argument on the solid ground of history. Just as many begin the Christian race, many Jews were among those whom Moses led out of Egypt. All saw the miracle of the parting of the waters, all were "baptized"—covered, referring to the ancient mode of baptism by immersion—by Moses' and God's leadership (the cloud by day, the fire by night), and all were given water when Moses struck the rock at Horeb (Exod. 17:6).

In typical rabbinic form, Paul now draws two "types" or metaphors from this Exodus experience. First, the water from Horeb did more than slake their thirst; it nourished their spirits. Second, and surprisingly, "that Rock was Christ." Yahweh Himself is called the Rock of salvation in the Old Testament (see Deut. 32:15, 18). It is possible that Paul only means that the rock from which water flowed was a "Messianic principle" in that it was "anointed" to save Israel. However, the fact that he makes the metaphor so personal as to *name* it seems to imply an affirmation of the fact that Christ the supreme "Deliverer" was an "ever-present help" even in the Wilderness. As the Word, He pre-existed His birth as a man (see John 1:1, 14, etc.).

B. Disobedient children, 5-11
1. Lustful, 5-6

5 But with many of them God was not well pleased: for they were overthrown in the wilderness.

6 Now these things were our examples, to the intent we should not lust after evil things, as they also lusted.

Although all of God's formerly enslaved people enjoyed the privileges of the exodus, Paul's reason for using this example is to show that, as in the races of a Greek Olympiad, not all "finished the race." In fact, all those age 40 and older died in the Wilderness (Num. 32:13), because after winning their freedom they did not discipline themselves in righteousness. Among other sins, they "lusted" after other gods, and after each other's spouses, serving as an eternal example of the

454

need for self-discipline, and for finishing the race.

2. Idolatrous, 7

7 Neither be ye idolaters, as were some of them; as it is written, The people sat down to eat and drink, and rose up to play.

Although worshiping the gods of the Canaanite was a constant shortcoming of many Israelites until the Captivity, the example Paul cites here is from the vivid picture of the idolatry of those who grew tired of waiting for Moses, when he went up to Sinai to receive the Law, and occupied themselves by making a golden calf around which they worshiped and frolicked (Exod. 32:4-6).

3. Sexually immoral, 8

8 Neither let us commit fornication, as some of them committed, and fell in one day three and twenty thousand.

The cult of the gods Israel was guilty of worshiping often included orgies, probably a part of an appeal for women to be fruitful in child-bearing. The incident Paul cites here is recorded in Numbers 25:1ff., where both "whoredom" and idolatry are mentioned—another example of the self-condemning nature of abandoning self-discipline.

4. Tempters and murmurers, 9-10

9 Neither let us tempt Christ, as some of them also tempted, and were destroyed of serpents.

10 Neither murmur ye, as some of them also murmured, and were destroyed of the destroyer.

The final sin Paul cites from the fathers was their continual tendency to "tempt" God to destroy them by murmuring and complaining about their lot. The most famous example is their complaint about the food God provided them in the wilderness (Num. 21:5). "Destroyer" is one of the Old Testament names for Satan, whom God used to destroy these complainers.

5. Examples for us, 11

11 Now all these things happened unto them for ensamples: and they are written for our admonition, upon whom the ends of the world are come.

Here Paul gives a good reason for studying the Old Testament. The fact that he points to such negative incidents shows how serious he is about the nature of immorality, faithlessness, and the general tendency to allow freedom to tempt us to excess and immorality.

III. Relying on God's Help—12-13

12 Wherefore let him that thinketh he standeth take heed lest he fall.

13 There hath no temptation taken you but such as is common to man: but God is faithful, who will not suffer you to be tempted above that ye are able; but will with the temptation also make a way to escape, that ye may be able to bear it.

Fortunately Paul does not remain on a note of judgment but of hope. No Christian need suffer the fate of the disobedient Israelites who died in the wilderness. All that is required is humility, realizing that all of us are capable of self-deceit and "falling" (vs. 12); and an eagerness to take the ways God provides to escape temptation— an eagerness that is more fervent than temptation to use freedom as an excuse for self-indulgence.

Evangelistic Emphasis

Paul says, "All the runners run, but only one gets the prize." In our day where building up one's self esteem seems to be a priority, this line grates on us. We want everybody to get a prize. We want everybody to be given an "attaboy" just for showing up and participating. Everybody wins.

Sadly, that's not necessarily the way things go in the Kingdom of God. Not everybody wins. Everybody *can* be a winner, but not everybody wins. There are losers. Some gain heaven. Some gain hell.

Listen carefully, please. Though there are winners and losers, Paul's analogy of a race isn't the whole story of salvation. We do not gain heaven by training harder or by trying harder. We actually gain heaven when we come to the realization that we cannot be winners by our own individual effort. We must admit defeat. We must admit we are sinners, ask Jesus to forgive us of our sin and to empower us to righteousness.

When we ask Jesus to be our Savior and Lord, then we are put in the winner's circle. It is by His merit and His effort that we become winners, that is, we gain our heavenly reward, certainly not out of our own power.

Winners or losers. There are only two categories in the Kingdom of God. Which one do you want to be?

ഭറ്റ.

Know ye not that they which run in a race run all, but one receiveth the prize? So run, that ye may obtain.—*Corinthians 9:24*

The NIV Study Bible tells us that the Corinthians were familiar with foot races in their own Isthmian games. These games occurred every other year and were second only to the Olympic games in importance. The Corinthians knew what it was to compete. They also knew what it took to win.

Some athletic contests are team sports. The team wins, or the team loses. All players work together for the advancement of the team. In this passage, however, Paul focuses on a sport that is entirely dependent upon individual effort. In individual sports we cannot blame others for our own failure.

In these individual sports, the spotlight is entirely upon the one competing. Oh yes, we have coaches and trainers and fans in the stands, but when it comes down to winning or losing, it comes down to the individual.

Paul reminds us that we are to strive to win. We are to strive for excellence. We are to strive to do our absolute best. Of course, our task in life is not to defeat others. Our task is to live a life of excellence, a life worthy of the calling of God, a life of moral and ethical purity. When we do, we are winners in God's eyes.

Weekday Problems

Ray and Lloyd were sitting in the stands at halftime at the Dallas Cowboys game. The Cowboys' cheerleaders were performing. Lloyd let out a low whistle, "Man, those girls sure are fine! Wouldn't it be something to be married to something like that?"

Ray answered back, "Well, I agree those are beautiful women. But, Lloyd, you're already married. You don't need to be thinking about trading your wife in on a newer model."

"Now, come on, Ray," Lloyd grinned, "you can't tell me you don't think about things like that. Every red-blooded American man has to notice those girls . . . even Christians like you and me."

"Lloyd, the 'everybody does it' argument really doesn't hold water. It's not the Christian's job to be like everybody else. The Christian is called to be like Christ. We are not supposed to be "just as good as." We aren't supposed to run with the crowd. We are supposed to run with Jesus. *He* is our standard.

"Maybe you're right, Ray," Lloyd muttered. "Maybe you're right."

*Is Ray just being a "stick-in-the-mud," or does he have a point?

*What are some methods we can employ to resist temptation?

Tempted and Tried

The road to success is dotted with many tempting parking places.

***

If God had believed in permissiveness, He would have given us the Ten Suggestions

***

People at the foot of Sinai: Moses, we're thinking of forming a union to protest all that stuff you say God wants to lay on us.
Moses: Sorry, guys. He said to tell you they're non-negotiable demands.

***

When a Sunday School teacher was asked to write out the Ten Commandments, one boy wrote down, for the Fifth Commandment, *"Humor thy father and thy mother."*

***

"Opportunity knocks only once," warned the preacher, "but temptation bangs on your door for years."

***

When you flee temptation, be sure you don't leave a forwarding address.

This Lesson in Your Life

The U.S. Army used to have a recruiting slogan, "Be all that you can be—in today's Army." They could have gleaned that idea from the apostle Paul. It seems that is what he is telling the Corinthians and us about our walk with Christ. Paul seems to be telling us to strive for excellence, to be the very best we can be.

Too often we Christians have taken the attitude that good enough is good enough. We attain a degree of respectability and we say, "That'll do." We think that God has called us simply to be good productive citizens and once we gain that status, we think we have arrived. We are willing to settle for much less than perfection in our lives. Of course no one is perfect, but that should not keep us from striving for holiness. Living the Christian life requires self-discipline and self-sacrifice. We cannot spend our lives in selfish indulgence, doing only what is comfortable and pleasurable for ourselves, and call that "living for Jesus."

According to one translation, Paul says he "buffets" his body. That is, he puts his own comfort and pleasure aside in order to seek first the things of God. Too often it seems we pronounce that word "buffet" wrong, pronouncing as if it were "boo-fay." As if we can be disciples of Jesus still picking and choosing the self-gratifying things from life's "buffet," as though our wants, needs, and enjoyment are primary.

To be a winner for Christ and not just one of the crowd, we must be willing to have discipline. Actually, the words *disciple* and *discipline* come from the same root. It is as though one cannot become a disciple of Jesus Christ without self-discipline.

We train ourselves and grow in discipleship by putting down the newspaper and those magazines and reading from God's Holy Word. We train ourselves and grow in discipleship by forcing ourselves out of bed on Sunday morning to get to Sunday School and church on time. We grow in discipleship by taking time out of our busy schedules to minister to others in the name of Jesus. We grow in discipleship when we swallow our fear and talk to someone who needs to hear about our Lord and Savior Jesus Christ. We grow in discipleship when we put away those activities or hobbies that do not glorify God, and when we break those bad habits with the help of the Holy Spirit.

The standard for holy Christian living is much higher than the standard the world has set as acceptable. We do not want to be accepted by the world. We want to be declared winners by Jesus.

Be all that you can be.

GETTING THE FACTS STRAIGHT

1. What does the analogy of the Christian life as a race say about the way we should live?
It reminds us to do our very best in life. We are to live out our Christianity striving for excellence.

2. In 9:26-27 Paul reminds us that the effective Christian life requires *focus*. What metaphor does he use to make his point?
He says that he does not run like a man running aimlessly, nor as a boxer merely sparring.

3. Contrast the prize for an earthly race and the prize for living for Christ.
The prize for an earthly race was simply a crown, or wreath, that will soon fade. The prize for the Christian walk is an eternal crown.

4. What figurative language is used in 10:1-2 concerning the pillar of cloud, the Red Sea, and Israel under Moses' leadership?
Paul says they were all baptized into Moses in the cloud and in the sea. They also ate the same spiritual food and drank the same drink.

5. How does Paul describe Christ's abiding presence with the people of Israel in the desert?
Paul calls Christ the Rock from which the water came. The Rock (Jesus Christ) followed God's people in their journeys.

6. What happened when some of God's people became involved in sexual immorality or fornication?
Paul tells us that 23,000 of them fell dead in one day.

7. What happened when some of God's people tested or tempted Christ?
Those people were killed by serpents or snakes.

8. What happened when they murmured or grumbled against the Lord?
The complainers were struck down by the destroying angel.

9. Why did these terrible things happen?
These things happened as an example to the people of Israel and were written down as warnings to Christians.

10. What promises do we have when strong temptation comes to us?
We have the promise that God will not allow us to be tempted beyond what we can bear. Further, when we are tempted, God will provide a way out so that we do not have to succumb to that temptation (vs. 13).

You may remember Mary Lou Retton. She was the gymnast who was catapulted to international fame at the 1984 Olympic Games in Los Angeles. Mary Lou was the first American woman ever to win the gold medal in the all-around women's gymnastics. As a member of the silver medalist team from the United States, she also won an individual silver medal in the pole vault, as well as bronze medals in the uneven bars and floor exercise. Her five medals were the most won by any athlete at the 1984 Olympics. Mary Lou Retton was only 15 years old at the time.

Somebody gave Mary Lou a brand new Corvette automobile as a gift rewarding her achievements. It had to sit dormant for several months. She was too young to drive it.

In an interview after the Olympics, Mary Lou Retton was asked what it was like to be an Olympic champion at such a young age. Her answer was revealing. First, she said, she loved gymnastics. The sport of gymnastics was her life. Then she talked a moment about her life. She got up every morning and went to the gym before going to her high school classes. After class, she went back to the gym. While other girls were out with boys, she was in the gym. While other girls ate whatever they wanted, she watched her diet. While other girls were staying up until all hours of the night, she was getting to bed at a decent hour in order to get enough rest to keep her body in Olympic shape. She gave up a lot in order to gain Olympic gold.

I cannot help but compare this to Christian discipleship. When we say Yes to Jesus Christ, we are automatically saying No to things that do not honor Him. We focus upon those things that glorify Him. The writer of Hebrews says, "Let us throw off everything that hinders and the sin that so easily entangles, and let us run with perseverance the race marked out for us. Let us fix our eyes on Jesus, the author and perfecter of our faith . . . ."

Mary Lou Retton received several medals for her focus and training. We will receive the Crown of Life.

Lesson 8

Called to the Common Good

1 Cor. 12:1-13

Now concerning spiritual gifts, brethren, I would not have you ignorant.

2 Ye know that ye were Gentiles, carried away unto these dumb idols, even as ye were led.

3 Wherefore I give you to understand, that no man speaking by the Spirit of God calleth Jesus accursed: and that no man can say that Jesus is the Lord, but by the Holy Ghost.

4 Now there are diversities of gifts, but the same Spirit.

5 And there are differences of administrations, but the same Lord.

6 And there are diversities of operations, but it is the same God which worketh all in all.

7 But the manifestation of the Spirit is given to every man to profit withal.

8 For to one is given by the Spirit the word of wisdom; to another the word of knowledge by the same Spirit;

9 To another faith by the same Spirit; to another the gifts of healing by the same Spirit;

10 To another the working of miracles; to another prophecy; to another discerning of spirits; to another divers kinds of tongues; to another the interpretation of tongues:

11 But all these worketh that one and the selfsame Spirit, dividing to every man severally as he will.

12 For as the body is one, and hath many members, and all the members of that one body, being many, are one body: so also is Christ.

13 For by one Spirit are we all baptized into one body, whether we be Jews or Gentiles, whether we be bond or free; and have been all made to drink into one Spirit.

July 23

Devotional Reading
1 Cor. 12:27-31

Background Scripture
1 Cor. 12:1-26

Memory Selection
1 Cor. 12:7

Apparently the Corinthians had also asked Paul about "spiritual gifts." This lesson is taken from the beginning of three chapters (12–14) the apostle devoted to the subject.

Not long after the outpouring of the Holy Spirit at Pentecost (Acts 2), the apostles were called on to lay hands on new Christians to bestow spiritual gifts such as speaking in tongues (Acts 8:14-17). Unfortunately, this sensational gift had become so prized that there was something of a competition for it in the church at Corinth. In this lesson, Paul affirms the value of all the gifts, even those that attracted less attention. He also points out that the gifts were for the purpose of building up the Body of Christ, the Church, and that it was divisive and destructive to be jealous of others' gifts.

ഇ**ര**

Before class, ask four different readers to be prepared to read these four lists of spiritual gifts: **1 Corinthians 12:8-10; 12:28; Eph. 4:11**; and **Romans 12:6-8**. Tell your group that the lesson today is on the apostle Paul's appeal for spiritual gifts to be allowed to build up the Church. Tell them also that the four readers will read different lists of these gifts, and invite group members to listen carefully and to *single out which gifts they would consider most valuable in the church today.* After the readings, lead a brief discussion on this topic.

Note that there are various views on whether all these gifts are still active among Christians today. You can also note that all gifts, whether "spiritual" or "natural" (such as "talents") are God-given.

Teaching Outline	*Daily Bible Readings*

I. Paganism vs. Spirituality—1-3
  A. Former ignorance, 1-2
  B. Present understanding, 3
II. Plural Gifts, One Lord—4-7
  A. Structure of gifts, 4-6
  B. One purpose, 7
III. Partial List of Gifts—8-11
  A. Diverse gifts, 8-10
  B. One Spirit, 11
IV. Place Unity First!—12-13
	Mon. Excel in Gifts
	    1 Cor. 14:6-12
	Tue. Rich in Good Works
	    1 Tim. 6:13-19
	Wed. Varieties of Gifts
	    1 Cor. 12:1-6
	Thu. All of One Spirit
	    1 Cor. 12:7-11
	Fri. One Body, Many Members
	    1 Cor. 12:12-20
	Sat. Shared Suffering
	    1 Cor. 12:21-26
	Sun. The Greater Gifts
	    1 Cor. 12:27-31

Verse by Verse

I. Paganism vs. Spirituality—1-3

A. Former ignorance, 1-2

1 Now concerning spiritual gifts, brethren, I would not have you ignorant.

2 Ye know that ye were Gentiles, carried away unto these dumb idols, even as ye were led.

Paul's usual term for "spiritual gifts" is *charismata*. Here, however, he calls them *pneumatica*, because he wants to relate them to the One *"pneuma"* or Spirit that was poured out on the Church's "birthday" (Acts 2). Why does Paul begin with a reference to the pagan background? Possibly because some pagan religions practiced ecstatic speech and "faith healing" in ways at least somewhat similar to these gifts as they were manifested among Christians. If this is the right train of thought, Paul wants them to be able to make a distinction between gifts that proclaim Jesus as Lord, and the apparent gifts that resulted in allegiance only to "dumb" or mute idols.

B. Present understanding, 3

3 Wherefore I give you to understand, that no man speaking by the Spirit of God calleth Jesus accursed: and that no man can say that Jesus is the Lord, but by the Holy Ghost.

Again, there is a question about what raised the issue about calling Jesus "accursed" (Grk. *anathema*). It is possible that someone, while speaking in tongues, had referred to Christ as being "cursed" by "dying on a tree" (the Cross), instead of allowing it to fall on us (Gal. 3:13). Of course such a radical description of Jesus' work on the Cross might easily have been misunderstood, prompting others in the congregation to accuse the tongue-speaker of being under Satan's power. Obviously someone speaking hypocritically could mouth "Jesus is Lord" without the aid of the Spirit. Paul is speaking of a genuine confession, which can only be of the Spirit—thus hopefully easing the way for the falsely-accused tongue-speaker to be accepted by the congregation.

II. Plural Gifts, One Lord—4-7

A. Structure of gifts, 4-6

4 Now there are diversities of gifts, but the same Spirit.

5 And there are differences of administrations, but the same Lord.

6 And there are diversities of operations, but it is the same God which worketh all in all.

Here is one of the carefully structured and balanced statements for which Paul's writings are well-known. The formula is:

Many gifts / one Spirit
Many "administrations" / one Lord
Many "operations" / one God

It is important for Paul that we understand that the *true* spiritual gifts (as distinguished from pagan practices) all come from one source: the Trinity. This establishes a foundation of *unity* for the entire discussion to follow. It calls for the Corinthians to unite because the many gifts; the several "administrations" (NIV "service"); and the many "operations" (NIV "working") are all from the One God, and are given for the purpose of building up the One Body, the Church. Whatever our opinion about the continued presence of such gifts today, if they are allowed to divide the Body they are not being practiced in the way Paul envisioned.

B. One purpose, 7

7 But the manifestation of the Spirit is given to every man to profit withal.

To argue over who has the "best gift," or to allow jealousy over the gifts to strain relationships in the church, is decidedly *unprofitable,* while the Spirit's diverse manifestations distributed to a variety of people are intended to *profit* all the Body. The Corinthians (and many Christians today) were therefore in the ironic position of allowing what God intended to be a source of strength and power to make them weak and divisive.

III. Partial List of Gifts—8-11
A. Diverse gifts, 8-10

8 For to one is given by the Spirit the word of wisdom; to another the word of knowledge by the same Spirit;

9 To another faith by the same Spirit; to another the gifts of healing by the same Spirit;

10 To another the working of miracles; to another prophecy; to another discerning of spirits; to another divers kinds of tongues; to another the interpretation of tongues:

What, precisely, are we talking about when we refer to "spiritual gifts"? These verses give a partial list of them. That it is not intended to be a complete list can be seen by comparing it with similar lists in 12:28; Ephesians 4:11; and Rom. 12:6-8. (Prophecy is the only gift common to all four lists.) Experience has also shown that the Spirit is free to gift people in ways not listed here, as when a person is musically gifted, and uses that gift to build up the Body.

The **word of wisdom** and the **word of knowledge** (vs. 8) were apparently gifts enabling certain Christians to know, and to know how to apply, Christian truths, and to distinguish them from error.

Faith (vs. 9) is of course required of all who come to Christ. As a spiritual gift, it must have had a special dimension such as that granted to some in the Church who were granted the faith to perceive which ill persons would be healed (as in

James 5:15, "the prayer of faith shall save the sick").

Healing was one of the most sought after, yet elusive gifts. Paul himself apparently had the gift in some circumstances, as when he withheld it from Elymas the sorcerer, striking him temporarily blind (Acts 13:11), and when he and his missionary partner Silas healed some at Iconium (Acts 14:3). Yet Paul could not heal himself of his famous "thorn in the flesh" (see 2 Cor. 12:7-9).

Verse 10 lists several gifts, some of which are not clearly defined. **Miracles** (lit. "powers") cover several gifts. **Prophecy**, the gift of "speaking forth" the word, seems virtually the same as the word of wisdom and word of knowledge in verse 8. **Discerning of spirits** was important in distinguishing truth from error before the apostolic doctrine was drawn together in the "canon," or officially approved list of inspired writings we have in our Bibles today.

Different **tongues** obviously meant *languages* when the gift was first manifest in Acts 2. Some believe this was different from the "tongues of angels" (1 Cor. 13:1), which they define as ecstatic utterances given as a "praise-language" but not spoken by any particular ethnic group. **Interpretation of tongues** was a gift necessary for the edification of those in the congregation who did not speak the language in which the Spirit gave His message to the speaker (see 14:27).

B. One Spirit, 11

11 But all these worketh that one and the selfsame Spirit, dividing to every man severally as he will.

Paul goes to the trouble of listing these gifts for the express purpose of affirming that they all come from the Holy Spirit, who is in charge of which Christians get which gifts. This should put to rest any wrangling and jealousy over who gets which gift.

IV. Place Unity First!—12-13

12 For as the body is one, and hath many members, and all the members of that one body, being many, are one body: so also is Christ.

13 For by one Spirit are we all baptized into one body, whether we be Jews or Gentiles, whether we be bond or free; and have been all made to drink into one Spirit.

Here Paul's concept of the Church as the Body of Christ is pressed into the important service of illustrating church unity. Just as Jesus had arms and legs, feet and hands, so His spiritual Body, the Church, has many members. Later (vss. 21-22) Paul will paint an almost comical picture of the eye telling the hand, "I have no need of thee." Paul compares this picture to the equally ridiculous squabbles among some Corinthians over who gets the most sensational or visible gifts. The fact is that the One Spirit decides this without regard for race or other background, for the benefit of the Church, not for the gifted member. Gifts are for the larger Body.

Evangelistic Emphasis

Just before Jesus physically left this earth He gave Christians this assignment, "Therefore go and make disciples of all nations, baptizing them in the name of the Father and of the Son and of the Holy Spirit, and teaching them to obey everything I have commanded you." (Matthew 28:19-20a, NIV) We know that Jesus would not give us a job without giving us the tools needed to complete the task. Jesus made available to us the tools needed to carry out this assignment. We call these "tools" the gifts of the Holy Spirit.

The Spirit gives us knowledge to know how to lead someone to Christ. The Spirit gives us wisdom to know when to speak to someone about Christ. There are the spiritual gifts of preaching and prophecy. The Holy Spirit empowers some to be evangelists to share the Good News effectively. The Spirit enables some to be caring pastors and some to be teachers that communicate well.

All these gifts are given not so that the gifted one can be proud and show off her or his gifts. Indeed not! The gifts are given in order that God's work may be done. The gifts are given so that God's will may be manifest. The gifts are not given so that they may be hidden away.

God has given us the tools needed to make disciples of all nations. Are we using our tools?

ജാരു

Memory Selection

But the manifestation of the Spirit is given to every man to profit withal.—*1 Corinthians 12:7*

When Paul says the gifts are given "to profit withal," he means that the gifts of the Spirit are given for the common good. That is, the gifts are given in order that the Body of Christ might be built up, not one individual.

I wish the King James Version did not have the word "profit" in this verse. I am convinced there are those who have used the manifestations of the Holy Spirit for personal profit. Some have become materially wealthy by exploiting a spiritual gift they claim God gave them.

There are those who have put their own personal gain before the common good. There are those who have exploited the gift of healing and have become as rich as kings. There are those who have used the gift of prophecy for their own advantage, gaining great personal wealth and power.

God never intended that. When the gifts of the Spirit are used properly, in God-honoring ways, the Body of Christ is built up, not just one individual. The gifted individual must be careful that she/he always uses God's gifts to benefit the Body of Christ first and foremost.

Weekday Problems

Bert was muttering to himself as he drove home from the meeting of the church's Board of Trustees, "I should have said something weeks before! I should have listened to God!" Bert's church was in a building campaign. They had architect's drawings for their new multipurpose hall.

Some months before, they had asked several local building contractors to bid on the project. One other contractor from out of town heard about their building program and asked if he could bid. "Sure," they all agreed, "there's no harm in letting him bid." When the bids came in, the out-of-town contractor had the best price. Although the other trustees were cautiously optimistic, Bert still felt uneasy.

"He gave us references," Bert said. "I'll call them and report back." All the references came back positive. They were not glowing reports, but the contractor had done a decent job. The worst one simply said the man was slow getting the work done. Despite his gnawing uneasiness, Bert reasoned, "Well, we checked his references." Now, at this last meeting, the trustees have discovered that the contractor has taken their initial payment and skipped the country.

*What would you have done in Bert's case?

*Could Bert's uneasiness been a manifestation of the gift of discerning of spirits? Discuss responses.

Out of the Mouths of Babes

A mother was teaching her 3-year-old the Lord's Prayer. For several evenings at bedtime the little girl repeated it after her mother. One night she said she was ready to "solo." The mother listened with pride as her daughter carefully said each word, right up to the end when she said, "And lead us not into temptation, but deliver us some e-mail."

***

A Sunday School teacher asked her children, as they made their way to the church service, "Now, why must we be quiet in church?"

Chirped one bright little girl, "Because people are sleeping!"

***

When asked who she was, little Jane would reply, "I'm Mr. Brown's daughter." Her mother suggested it would be better just to say, "I'm Jane Brown."

The next Sunday the family's minister said to Jane, "Aren't you Mr. Brown's daughter?"

"Well, I thought I was," Jane replied, "but Mother says I'm not."

One of the most useful airplanes in the general aviation world has been the Boeing 747. When the first 747s went into service in early 1970, they revolutionized the airline industry. These giant, hump-backed airplanes are still being used extensively around the world.

One of the newest models, the 747-400, has 6 million parts, half of which are fasteners. A 747-400 has 171 miles of wiring and 5 miles of tubing. It consists of 147,000 pounds of high-strength aluminum. The 747-400 has 16 main landing-gear tires and two nose landing-gear tires.

For the 747 to function at its peak effectiveness and safety, those six million parts, miles of wiring and tubing, sheets and sheets of aluminum, and the tires all have to do what they are designed to do in order for the jumbo jet to fly. All have to work properly.

When a 747 flies over, nobody says, "Look at those rivets fly." Nobody says, "Boy, I would like to fly on those miles of wires." Folks don't see the parts, they see the airplane.

I think the 747 illustrates simply what Paul is teaching us in this passage. Every Christian has some ability that God can use in His Kingdom. When each one exercises that ability the Body of Christ, the Church, functions at peak efficiency. When one or more refuses to exercise his abilities, the Body of Christ suffers.

As we continue to examine the illustration, we note that each part of the airplane works for the good of the airplane. When everything works properly, the whole airplane flies properly. When the pins that hold the bolts that hold the engines onto the wings work, nobody notices the pins. We only notice that the airplane flies.

In the same sense, God has given each Christian a function in the Body of Christ. When everything goes as God designed, each Christian exercises her/his ability or gift in a way that builds up the whole Body. The spiritual gifts, abilities, and talents are given by God not to make superstars out of the one who receives the gift, but to enable the Body of Christ to function at a higher peak of efficiency.

When folks use their spiritual gifts and God-given abilities in the manner God intended, then the focus is upon God, not upon the individual to whom the gift was given. We do not want people to see a Christian disciple and say, "What a great guy he is!" We want people to see the Christian disciple utilizing his gift and say, "What a great God he serves!"

You see, it's all about Him. It's not about us.

1. In this passage, what subject does Paul want the Corinthians to understand, or not be ignorant about?

Paul wants them to understand about spiritual gifts.

2. Before the Corinthians had become Christians what was the object of their worship (vs. 2)?

They had been influenced and led astray to worship "dumb" or mute idols.

3. No one can say, "Jesus is Lord," and mean it from the heart, unless that person is empowered by whom?

Only those empowered by the Holy Spirit, or the Spirit of God, can make that testimony truthfully.

4. Although there are different kinds of gifts, administrations, and operations, what is their common bond?

Though gifts differ, they come from the same Spirit. Though service differs, we serve the same Lord. Though operations differ, it is the same God who works all of them in all believers.

5. The manifestation of the Spirit of God is given for what purpose?

The manifestation of the Spirit of God is given for the common good. That is, that the Body of Christ profits, not just one member.

6. What gifts of the Spirit does Paul list here?

Word of wisdom; word of knowledge; faith; healing; working of miracles; prophecy; discerning of spirits; speaking in tongues; interpretation of tongues.

7. These gifts are all ministries of what person of the Godhead?

These are all workings of the Spirit of God or the Holy Spirit.

8. How does a believer decide which one of these gifts she/he wants?

We don't decide. The Holy Spirit gives the gifts as He determines.

9. In verse 12 Paul uses what physical illustration to communicate that although Christians are diverse, all function as one?

Paul uses the human body and its different members functioning as a unified whole.

10. How does Paul illustrate that there should be no racial, cultural, or social distinctions within the Body of Christ?

He says that everyone who has been regenerated by the Holy Spirit becomes part of the whole, whether that person is a Jew or Gentile, slave or free.

Rick Warren is pastor of Saddleback Valley Community Church in California. Rick Warren is a marvelous communicator of the gospel. One of his major contributions is the idea that the Christian works within the Body of Christ according to that person's SHAPE.

SHAPE is a simple acrostic for five areas of our lives that help us discover our ministry. Our SHAPE also helps us function effectively in that ministry. In SHAPE . . .

The "S" is for our *spiritual gifts*. Spiritual gifts are those Holy Spirit-given abilities that are given to each of us as a means of helping the entire Church.

The "H" is for our *heart*. The heart is our passion, our desire—those things that really get our motors running. Heart describes those things that we love to do.

The "A" is for our *abilities*. Ability describes the natural talents we were born with. We probably have noticed that some people are just naturally better at some things than others.

The "P" is for our *personalities*. We have different personalities. Some folks are gregarious, others prefer to be alone. Some folks seem to be bubbly all the time, while others are much more low key.

The "E" is for our *experience*. This describes the things we have been through in our lives.

Warren reminds us that God uses our SHAPE—our spiritual gifts, our heart, our ability, our personality, and our experiences—to do His will by edifying the Church. When each Christian uses her or his SHAPE to determine her or his ministry, the Body of Christ begins to function as an automobile motor firing on all cylinders.

When we use what God has given us we find ourselves fulfilling the Great Commandment (Matt. 22:37-40) and the Great Commission (Matt. 28:19-20). May our desire be to obediently carry out God's will in His way.

1 Corinthians 13

Though I speak with the tongues of men and of angels, and have not charity, I am become as sounding brass, or a tinkling cymbal.

2 And though I have the gift of prophecy, and understand all mysteries, and all knowledge; and though I have all faith, so that I could remove mountains, and have not charity, I am nothing.

3 And though I bestow all my goods to feed the poor, and though I give my body to be burned, and have not charity, it profiteth me nothing.

4 Charity suffereth long, and is kind; charity envieth not; charity vaunteth not itself, is not puffed up,

5 Doth not behave itself unseemly, seeketh not her own, is not easily provoked, thinketh no evil;

6 Rejoiceth not in iniquity, but rejoiceth in the truth;

7 Beareth all things, believeth all things, hopeth all things, endureth all things.

8 Charity never faileth: but whether there be prophecies, they shall fail; whether there be tongues, they shall cease; whether there be knowledge, it shall vanish away.

9 For we know in part, and we prophesy in part.

10 But when that which is perfect is come, then that which is in part shall be done away.

11 When I was a child, I spake as a child, I understood as a child, I thought as a child: but when I became a man, I put away childish things.

12 For now we see through a glass, darkly; but then face to face: now I know in part; but then shall I know even as also I am known.

13 And now abideth faith, hope, charity, these three; but the greatest of these is charity.

July 30

Devotional Reading
John 3:16-21
Background Reading
1 Cor. 13
Memory Selection
1 Cor. 13:13

471

First Corinthians 13, an "ode to love," has been called the foundation of the Christian doctrine. It has become immortalized even in the minds of many who are not Christians, especially because of its frequent use at weddings. Unfortunately, the use of the KJV term "charity" sometimes leaves the impression that the chapter is about doing good for the poor. Even the English word "love" is inadequate, since we can use it both to say "love your enemies" and "I'd love to strangle him"!

Paul chooses the Greek word *agape* (a-GAH-pay) from several other possible words for love in Greek. This is the highest form of love, the kind that acts selflessly in behalf of others, and therefore the kind that God showed to us in giving us His Son Jesus. Now our task is to show how we can express it concretely to others.

෨ා෨

Ask group members to scan 1 Corinthians 12 for the topic that forms the background to chapter 13. Lead a discussion that shows that this famous chapter was prompted by the jealousy and envy shown by Christians over who had received the "best" spiritual gifts—traits that actually undermined the *love* that prompted God to give these gifts.

Note that the apostle now pens this famous chapter to focus our attention on the best "gift," love. Although its immediate application was that the Corinthians should love each other instead of coveting each other's gifts, the chapter also forms a kind of "constitution" against which we are to measure everything we do as Christians. Spiritual gifts would pass away, while love endures forever.

Teaching Outline	Daily Bible Readings

I. The Importance of Love, 1-3
  A. Over other gifts, 1-2
  B. Over other giving, 3
II. The Nature of Love, 4-7
III. The Endurance of Love—8-13
  A. Beyond other gifts, 8-10
  B. Into maturity, 11
  C. Into the light, 12
  D. Into eternity, 13
	Mon. God So Loved
	     John 3:16-21
	Tue. God's Love in Jesus
	     Rom. 8:31-39
	Wed. Love One Another
	     John 13:31-35
	Thu. Love Fulfills the Law
	     Rom. 13:8-14
	Fri. From the Beginning: Love!
	     1 John 3:11-18
	Sat. Definition of Love
	     1 Cor. 13:1-7
	Sun. The Greatest Gift
	     1 Cor. 13:8-13

Verse by Verse

I. The Importance of Love, 1-3
A. Over other gifts, 1-2

1 Though I speak with the tongues of men and of angels, and have not charity, I am become as sounding brass, or a tinkling cymbal.

2 And though I have the gift of prophecy, and understand all mysteries, and all knowledge; and though I have all faith, so that I could remove mountains, and have not charity, I am nothing.

Paul's reference to "tongues" (Grk. *glossais*, from which we get the term "glossolalia") ties this chapter to the one preceding, which rebukes jealousy toward those in the early Church who had been given the gift of tongues-speaking. Paul closed chapter 12 with a reference to a "better way" than coveting each other's gifts. That better way is love.

The original display of "tongues" in the New Testament consisted of languages actually spoken by various ethnic groups (Acts 2:4-8). Some distinguish between such "tongues of men" and those "of angels," here, holding that angelic tongues were ecstatic speech given for the edification of the speaker rather than the hearer (see 14:4). It is this kind of "tongue-speaking" usually referred to by Pentecostal believers who continue the practice today.

Paul insists that a more important "language" is the language of love. The Greeks used the term *philos* for friendship, *eros* for attraction (including sexual love), and *storge* for the love among family members. Paul chooses a fourth word, *agape,* which, although sometimes used interchangeably with the other terms, speaks especially of the kind of refined love that puts the needs of others above one's own—like the love God had for the world when He sent His only-begotten Son. Actually, the KJV "charity" captures the concrete dimension of *agape*, although Paul is speaking of a love beyond that which prompts us to give to the needy.

Some pagan rituals were accompanied by blaring trumpets and banging cymbals, often to frighten away evil spirits. Paul implies that speaking in tongues without a spirit of love is as useless as these pagan practices. Of course the principle applies to any supposedly charitable or religious act that is done without heartfelt love.

In verse 2, the "understanding and communication" gifts are also said to be of less value than love. *Prophecy* meant not only fore-telling, but *forth*-telling; and Paul says this is not as valuable as love. The same is said of special insights, understanding, and faith—all of which can actually make the gifted person arrogant instead of loving.

B. Over other giving, 3

3 And though I bestow all my goods to feed the poor, and though I give my body to be burned, and have not charity, it profiteth me nothing.

Ananias and Sapphira made an impressive financial gift for charitable work (Acts 5:1-11). They gave for show, however, which made the gift null and void. The reference to giving one's body to be burned may be a clue that Rome was already burning Christians at the stake. At least we know that only a few years later some believers begged for martyrdom, believing, like some Muslims today, that this "gift" would usher them immediately into heaven. Paul indicates that even martyrdom may be motivated by self-gratification.

II. The Nature of Love, 4-7

4 Charity suffereth long, and is kind; charity envieth not; charity vaunteth not itself, is not puffed up,

To be long-suffering means literally to be a "slow-burner"—not quick to show anger. Love does not "envy"—the sin committed by those in Corinth who were jealous of each other's gifts. Those who truly love are secure enough in God's love that they do not need to boast or "vaunt" themselves. Also, as Paul said in 8:1, mere knowledge "puffs up" a person with arrogance, while the truly loving person does not need to be inflated by the acclaim of others.

5 Doth not behave itself unseemly, seeketh not her own, is not easily provoked, thinketh no evil;

"Unseemly" means indecently or

shamefully. The truly loving young man courting his true love does not act indecently toward her. To "seek one's own" is to be self-centered instead of other-centered (see Philip. 2:4). Love means not having "hot buttons" so touchy that we fly off the handle at the least provocation. Love is not suspicious of others, always expecting, and looking for, the worst of people and charging them with evil without real evidence.

6 Rejoiceth not in iniquity, but rejoiceth in the truth;

7 Beareth all things, believeth all things, hopeth all things, endureth all things.

Just as love does not quickly think evil of others, it does not rejoice even when they are clearly shown to be evil. Verse 6 can therefore describe a law officer whose job satisfaction is in getting at the truth, not in hurting the evil person. Verse 7 speaks of the strength and endurance of true love, as against the flightiness and self-centered nature of mere infatuation.

III. The Endurance of Love—8-13

A. Beyond other gifts, 8-10

8 Charity never faileth: but whether there be prophecies, they shall fail; whether there be tongues, they shall cease; whether there be knowledge, it shall vanish away.

Although the apostle does not say precisely when these spiritual gifts will cease, he clearly says that, unlike love, they will not last forever. As early as the second century, some Christian leaders would hold that the gifts died out with the death of the last apostle, since they seem to require the laying on of an apostle's hands to be transmitted to others (as in Acts 8:14-17). Others believe that with the compilation of the Gospels the early Church would simply outgrow its need for such evidence of God's power through Christ, while still others think the gifts' "vanishing" will not be until the next life.

9 For we know in part, and we prophesy in part.

10 But when that which is perfect is come, then that which is in part shall be done away.

Although this is a difficult passage, it begins plainly enough with the assertion that the miraculous gifts of the Spirit were given "piecemeal"—here and there, now and then, and not intended to "perfectly" supply the Church with all knowledge. There is a question, however, over just what is meant by saying that these gifts of "planned obsolescence" would in fact disappear when "that which is perfect is come." The term translated perfect (*telos*) can also means "mature," or "consummated." This may mean that the gifts would disappear when the Church grows to sufficient spiritual maturity. Some think it refers to the completion of the New Testament canon, but that was a gradual, uncertain, and controversial process that does not seem to fit the idea of "perfection" or maturity. Others say the word refers to "perfect love," since this is the subject of the chapter. Just when that was to ar-

rive, however, is also arguable.

B. Into maturity, 11

11 When I was a child, I spake as a child, I understood as a child, I thought as a child: but when I became a man, I put away childish things.

The possibility that the "perfect" in verse 10 means maturity is strengthened by this comparison of spiritual growth with a child's development. At least we can understand that Paul is urging us to grow past the spiritually childish need to vie with each other over the "best" or most visible gifts. However, when might this occur, this side of heaven?

C. Into the light, 12

12 For now we see through a glass, darkly; but then face to face: now I know in part; but then shall I know even as also I am known.

Even in the presence of miraculous gifts, no gifted Christian saw God's entire plan clearly or in its entirety; and this verse supports those who believe that the gifts would cease only when the Church is called up to heaven, and we are privileged to know God as He now knows us.

D. Into eternity, 13

13 And now abideth faith, hope, charity, these three; but the greatest of these is charity.

In sum, Paul says, faith and hope, like love, are more essential for the Church than the more sensational spiritual gifts. Of all these traits, love stands out as the greatest, tougher than either faith or hope. Without love, faith wilts and hope wanes.

Evangelistic Emphasis

Paul seems to tell us that you can have every gift and ability available. But if you do not have love, the rest is really not worth much. On the other side of that, you can have few or none of the more spectacular Christian gifts, but if you have love for others, your life will have great effectiveness in winning others to Jesus.

When I was a young man, I was obsessed with saving souls. "Just get 'em saved," tended to be my motto. I learned the "Roman Road" method of soul winning and I utilized it every opportunity I had. I even forced some opportunities to witness.

I was counting souls as a professional bass fisherman might count his catch. "Another one in the live well, Lord," and I would be off to win another soul for Jesus. One day the Lord revealed to me exactly what was going on. I did not love the people to whom I was witnessing. It was almost as if I simply viewed them as a job to be done, a task to be completed. I thank God for that revelation.

Yes, God wants each of us to be a soul winner. He also wants us to love our fellow human beings. When we love another, we validate that person's worth to the Master.

Loving the people around me made me a better and more effective witness for Jesus, too.

℘℘

And now abideth faith, hope, charity, these three; but the greatest of these is charity.— *1 Corinthians 13:13*

"Whoever does not love does not know God, because God is love" (1 John 4:8). "This is love: not that we loved God, but that he loved us and sent his Son as an atoning sacrifice for our sins" (1 John 4:10). "A new command I give you: Love one another. As I have loved you, so you must love one another. By this all men will know that you are my disciples, if you love one another" (John 13:34-35).

These three scriptures reinforce what Paul writes in 1 Corinthians 13. Love is the greatest gift because God *is* love, He has communicated His love to us, and He commands us to love one another. Love supersedes the gifts of the Holy Spirit because it outlasts them all. Long after these sought-after gifts are no longer necessary, love will still be the governing principle that controls all that God and His redeemed people are and all they do.

Of course we have to have faith. We cannot even become a Christian without faith. "For it is by grace you have been saved, through faith . . . ." (Ephesians 2:8a). We must have hope for we cannot look toward better times without hope. But it is love that makes heaven and earth go 'round.

Weekday Problems

Jeff watched the man cross the street and come toward his shop. Jeff had not seen this man before. The man was not clean. He looked as if he had not seen a razor in several days. He was carrying a crumpled paper bag. "Heaven only knows what is in that bag," Jeff thought. Jeff noticed the way the man kind of shuffled along, keeping his head down. The bell on the door bonged once when the man came in.

"Can you help me, sir?" the man asked softly. "I'm trying to get back home. My car broke down this morning. I had been driving every day as long as I could stay awake, then I would find a rest stop and sleep in my car. I'm not on drugs. I don't drink alcohol or smoke. I'm willing to hitch-hike the rest of the way home, but nobody will pick me up because of the way I look. Could you help me with a bus ticket? I would be glad to repay you when I get home. My sister called me and said I have a job there if I can get there before Friday. I need $23 more for the ticket."

Jeff reached for his wallet. "I really hate to do this," he said to himself. "First thing you know every bum will be coming in." Yet he pulled out a twenty and a five. As he handed it over to the man, Jeff was thinking, "You better use this for a bus ticket, fella." But what Jeff said was, "Have a nice day."

*Did Jeff really help the man? Explain.

*Did Jeff get any spiritual reward for what he did? Explain.

Second Thoughts About Love

We owe to the Middle Ages the two worst inventions of humanity—romantic love and gunpowder.—*Andrew Maurois*

***

By the time you swear you're his, shivering and sighing,
And he vows his passion is infinite, undying—
Lady, make a note of this: one of you is lying.
—*Dorothy Parker*

***

I am not one of those who believes in love at first sight, but I believe in taking a second look.—*Henry Vincent*

***

Bill: Isn't she a little small for you, Will?
Will: Better to have loved a short girl than never to have loved a-tall.

***

Love looks not with the eyes, but with the mind.—*Shakespeare*

This Lesson in Your Life

Love. The word has been overused and abused. In English we have only one word for love. We use that word to describe how we feel about our pets, a good steak, our alma mater, and our spouses.

Most believe 1 Corinthians 13 is the ultimate teaching on Christian love. Of course, this lesson is about *God's* kind of love. The Greek word for that is *agape*. God's kind of love might be defined as this: *to seek the well-being of the beloved, regardless of the action or response of the beloved.* This is what Paul is addressing.

First, Paul teaches that religious practices devoid of love are hollow, futile, and meaningless. You see, a person can be in church every time the door opens, pray for an hour a day, and go on mission trips to the jungles of the Amazon every year, but if that person does not have love in his heart for people and for Christ, all that means nothing.

You may know someone who is great about doing Christ-like things, but never seems to be happy. I have known people who were excellent at church work, but were just mean. I know it was because they never caught on to what Paul meant when he wrote, "if I have not love, I am nothing."

Paul also reminds us that we must never confuse personal sacrifice with love. One cannot love without giving. However, one can give without loving. I've seen that in the church. Folks may give in order to manipulate a situation, not for the well-being of the Body of Christ.

We must be lovers. It's all about the heart. If the heart truly loves, the actions will follow. Paul tells us in this passage how to relate to one another. He tells us how to develop deep, significant, fulfilling love relationships with other human beings. I read 1 Corinthians 13:4-8a at every wedding I do. However, these verses should not limited to the relationship between husband and wife. Paul's teaching on love can be applied to every relationship between two human beings, not just romantic relationships. Paul tells us how to love each other.

Last, Paul tells us that love is the greatest Christian character trait. He also lists faith and hope, but says that love is the greatest. In Galatians 5:22-23 (NIV) Paul lists love, joy, peace, patience, kindness, goodness, faithfulness, gentleness, and self-control as character traits that grow in the Christian's life. Love is the first.

Paul reminds us that it is greater to have a heart filled with pure love than it is to have the more spectacular spiritual gifts of the Spirit. God has given us many gifts and abilities to help us serve Him and minister to others. He expects us to use them all. Yet, if you had to throw them all away except one, keep love. The greatest trait is love.

GETTING THE FACTS STRAIGHT

1. What does Paul say about the gift of speaking in tongues if the gift is used without love?
Paul says, basically, that you are just making noise.

2. What does Paul say about the gifts of prophecy and knowledge if they are exercised without love?
Paul reminds us that they are good for nothing. He says that the gifts are worthless without love.

3. What does Paul say about the one who performs sacrificial giving, even to the point of death, if there is no love?
The person who sacrifices gains nothing if the sacrificial act is not motivated by love.

4. List the character traits of the loving person from verse 4.
The loving person is patient and kind. The loving person is not envious, boastful, or proud.

5. List the character traits of the loving person from verse 5.
The person who loves with agape love is not rude, self-seeking, nor easily angered, and thinks the best of another person.

6. Would a person whose heart is filled with love be glad when something bad happens to another person?
No, the loving person does not rejoice when bad things happen to others.

7. List the "all things" love does, from verse 7.
Love bears all things, believes all things, hopes all things, and endures all things. The NIV puts it, "loves always protects, always trusts, always hopes, and always perseveres."

8. Why will love prevail even when prophecies cease, tongues are stilled, and knowledge has passed away?
Love will outlive all these because these gifts are only partial in nature. When the perfect (love) comes, the imperfect will be done away with.

9. Paul tells us that though we do not completely understand the things of God, one day we will. How does he describe that?
Now we see through a glass, darkly, but then face to face: now our knowledge is partial, but then we will know the things of God as He knows us.

10. What is the greatest character trait of the Christian?
Though faith, hope, and love (charity) are all important, the greatest of all is love.

There is an old saying, "People don't care how much you know until they know how much you care." We Christians must remember that. Sometimes we evangelical Christians get so caught up in trying to bring others to the saving knowledge of Jesus Christ that we forget that we are supposed to love them in the process.

I realized that bringing someone into the Kingdom of God is the most loving thing one person can do for another. Yet, sometimes we get so zealous to get that person saved that we come across as rude. Paul teaches us that love is not rude.

Sometimes we get so zealous that the unbeliever perceives we think we are better than he is. This ultimately forms a barrier between the Christian and the unbeliever. This must never be. Remember, love is not proud.

So, we love. We love folks enough to tell them about Jesus. We love folks enough to share that Pearl of Great Price with them. We love others enough to go the second mile with them.

Love is one of the greatest of all evangelistic tools. Love can soften a hardened heart. Of course, when we speak of love we are not speaking of some kind of sappy, sentimental emotion. To love someone into the Kingdom of God requires more than just sentiment. It takes work. Love is not only a sentiment, it is an action.

To love someone into the Kingdom of God usually takes time. That's why Paul reminds us that love perseveres. I have heard testimony given by a godly mother as she shared that she prayed for her lost son for over 40 years. She loved him, so she kept on, regardless of whether or not she actually saw any spiritual progress. Finally, the son came around. He gave his life to Christ and is now serving God along with his whole family. Oh no, my friends, loves does not give up easily.

We must be God-lovers, and then we must love others as God loves us. Love makes a world of difference.

Unit III. The Spirit of Giving

Lesson 10

Giving Forgiveness

2 Corinthians 2:8-11; 7:2-12

But if any have caused grief, he hath not grieved me, but in part: that I may not overcharge you all.

6 Sufficient to such a man is this punishment, which was inflicted of many.

7 So that contrariwise ye ought rather to forgive him, and comfort him, lest perhaps such a one should be swallowed up with overmuch sorrow.

8 Wherefore I beseech you that ye would confirm your love toward him.

9 For to this end also did I write, that I might know the proof of you, whether ye be obedient in all things.

10 To whom ye forgive any thing, I forgive also: for if I forgave any thing, to whom I forgave it, for your sakes forgave I it in the person of Christ;

11 Lest Satan should get an advantage of us: for we are not ignorant of his devices.

7:2 Receive us; we have wronged no man, we have corrupted no man, we have defrauded no man.

3 I speak not this to condemn you: for I have said before, that ye are in our hearts to die and live with you.

4 Great is my boldness of speech toward you, great is my glorying of you: I am filled with comfort, I am exceeding joyful in all our tribulation.

5 For, when we were come into Macedonia, our flesh had no rest, but we were troubled on every side; without were fightings, within were fears.

6 Nevertheless God, that comforteth those that are cast down, comforted us by the coming of Titus;

7 And not by his coming only, but by the consolation wherewith he was comforted in you, when he told us your earnest desire, your mourning, your fervent mind toward me; so that I rejoiced the more.

8 For though I made you sorry with a letter, I do not repent, though I did repent: for I perceive that the same epistle hath made you sorry, though it were but for a season.

9 Now I rejoice, not that ye were made sorry, but that ye sorrowed to repentance: for ye were made sorry after a godly manner, that ye might receive damage by us in nothing.

10 For godly sorrow worketh repentance to salvation not to be repented of: but the sorrow of the world worketh death.

11 For behold this selfsame thing, that ye sorrowed after a godly sort, what carefulness it wrought in you, yea, what clearing of yourselves, yea, what indignation, yea, what fear, yea, what vehement desire, yea, what zeal, yea, what revenge! In all things ye have approved yourselves to be clear in this matter.

12 Wherefore, though I wrote unto you, I did it not for his cause that had done the wrong, nor for his cause that suffered wrong, but that our care for you in the sight of God might appear unto you.

Aug. 6

Devotional Reading
Matt.18:21-35
Background Scripture
2 Cor. 2:5-11; 7:2-15
Memory Selection
2 Cor. 7:10

481

As indicated by the title of Unit III, the final lessons of this quarter deal with "The Spirit of Giving." They are drawn from 2 Corinthians, which, along with other topics, reflects some difficulties in Paul's relationship with some in the church at Corinth. In dealing with these strained relationships, Paul shows in this first lesson that a "spirit of giving" has to do with "giving *forgiveness*," not just money.

Paul warns that withholding forgiveness provides Satan with a prime opportunity to create division (2 Cor. 2:11). Yet merely pretending the difficulty doesn't exist is not constructive either. Paul models the more fruitful course of "gentle confrontation," genuine repentance, and full restoration of the relationship.

problems that may be real are "swept under the rug" and thus never dealt with . . . withholding forgiveness models the exact opposite of God's attitude toward us. Although we often sin against Him, He stands, like the Prodigal Son's father, ready to forgive.

Ask group members what happens when church members hold grudges and allow strained relationships to fester. Incorporate their responses, in a discussion that includes the following ideas:

The church's witness to outsiders is damaged . . . people may live for years nursing hurt feelings, and are therefore emotionally damaged . . .

Note that feelings were also hurt in Paul's often stormy relationship with the church at Corinth; but that in this lesson he presents important principles of healing from which we can benefit today.

Teaching Outline	*Daily Bible Readings*

I. Forgive the Penitent—2:5-11
  A. Sorrowful sinner, 5-7
  B. 'Comfirm your love,' 8-11
II. Fruits of Conflict—7:2-7
  A. Joy in tribulation, 2-4
  B. Comfort in Concern—5-7
IV. Godly Sorrow—8-11
V. Church's Stake—12
	Mon. Forgive Others
	     Matt. 6:9-15
	Tue. Jesus on Forgiveness
	     Matt. 18:21-35
	Wed. Circle of Forgiveness
	     Mark 11:20-25
	Thu. 'You Must Also Forgive'
	     Col. 3:12-17
	Fri. Console the Offender
	     2 Cor. 2:5-11
	Sat. Paul's Pride in Corinth
	     2 Cor. 7:2-7
	Sun. Paul's Joy at Repentance
	     2 Cor. 7:8-16

Verse by Verse

I. Forgive the Penitent—2:5-11
A. Sorrowful sinner, 5-7

5 But if any have caused grief, he hath not grieved me, but in part: that I may not overcharge you all.

6 Sufficient to such a man is this punishment, which was inflicted of many.

7 So that contrariwise ye ought rather to forgive him, and comfort him, lest perhaps such a one should be swallowed up with overmuch sorrow.

Someone in the church at Corinth had been guilty of such a public sin that Paul had urged the church to confront and discipline him. This may have been the man who was apparently committing fornication with his step-mother (1 Cor. 5:1). Paul had commanded that the man be "delivered to Satan"—probably meaning that his immorality was to be publicly denounced and the man shunned (see 1 Cor. 5:9).

Apparently this action had had the desired effect—not to humiliate the man but to reclaim him to the fellowship. It appears that the offender had repented of his sin; yet some in the church were continuing to shun him, showing a reluctance to forgive him despite his penitence. Paul therefore exhorts the church to forgive the man, probably in a way as public as the ban they had administered, lest he be "overwhelmed by excessive sorrow" (vs. 7, NIV).

B. 'Confirm your love,' 8-11

8 Wherefore I beseech you that ye would confirm your love toward him.

9 For to this end also did I write, that I might know the proof of you, whether ye be obedient in all things.

10 To whom ye forgive any thing, I forgive also: for if I forgave any thing, to whom I forgave it, for your sakes forgave I it in the person of Christ;

11 Lest Satan should get an advantage of us: for we are not ignorant of his devices.

Now that the man had repented, it was time for the church, composed of sinners who had been forgiven, to confirm their love and forgiveness to him. The reference to having written about this to the Corinthians opens up the fact that we have only part of the "Corinthian correspondence"—1 and 2 Corinthians. We have noted in previous lessons that the Corinthians had written at least one letter to Paul (1 Cor. 7:1). In turn, Paul had also written at least two letters to them. Some scholars think that the content of these letters has since been folded into 2 Corinthians, but we cannot be sure. Whatever they contained, they included Paul's urging for the Corinthian church not only to forgive the penitent sinner they had disciplined, but to convey to him that Paul, through the church, also forgave him.

Otherwise, as verse 11 indicates, Satan would gain a foothold in the church. Nothing is a clearer Satanic "device" than a church that remains embroiled in enmity and hard feelings, with members refusing to extend the very forgiveness to others that they expect to receive from Christ.

II. Fruits of Conflict—7:2-7
A. Joy in tribulation, 2-4

2 Receive us; we have wronged no man, we have corrupted no man, we have defrauded no man.

3 I speak not this to condemn you: for I have said before, that ye are in our hearts to die and live with you.

4 Great is my boldness of speech toward you, great is my glorying of you: I am filled with comfort, I am exceeding joyful in all our tribulation.

Not only had some in the Corinthian church remained angry and aloof from the sinner they had disciplined, they had also nursed hard feelings toward Paul. Although we are not told just why this occurred, it may have simply been from the fact that he dared to correct their disunity and other difficulties in 1 Corinthians. We know that some had decided, from Paul's bold letters, that

"his letters . . . are weighty and powerful; but his bodily presence is weak, and his speech contemptible" (2 Cor. 10:10).

Here Paul protests that he holds no personal animosity or ulterior motives for anyone at Corinth. He is ready to die for them. His boldness was for their own good, and even in the midst of the strained relationship that had resulted, the changed life of many had been a cource of joy for the apostle.

B. Comfort in Concern—5-7

5 For, when we were come into Macedonia, our flesh had no rest, but we were troubled on every side; without were fightings, within were fears.

6 Nevertheless God, that comforteth those that are cast down, comforted us by the coming of Titus;

7 And not by his coming only, but by the consolation wherewith he was comforted in you, when he told us your earnest desire, your mourning, your fervent mind toward me; so that I rejoiced the more.

In verse 5 Paul returns to a recounting of his travels and travails in behalf of the Corinthians and others. In Troas, on the west coast of Asia Minor, he had been disappointed by not finding Titus, who may have taken the "severe" letter to the Corinthians (2 Cor. 2:12-13). Paul may have been anxious to hear how the Corinthians received his correctives. Finally, as these verses indicate, Titus and Paul met up in

Macedonia. Amid his concern about how the Corinthians might receive his strong language, Titus' report enabled Paul to rejoice at their positive attitudes. It is with attitudes like this that mutual forgiveness can occur, and amid attitudes of resentment and hostility, which Paul feared Titus might report, that reconciliation can be neither given nor received.

IV. Godly Sorrow—8-11

8 For though I made you sorry with a letter, I do not repent, though I did repent: for I perceive that the same epistle hath made you sorry, though it were but for a season.

9 Now I rejoice, not that ye were made sorry, but that ye sorrowed to repentance: for ye were made sorry after a godly manner, that ye might receive damage by us in nothing.

10 For godly sorrow worketh repentance to salvation not to be repented of: but the sorrow of the world worketh death.

11 For behold this selfsame thing, that ye sorrowed after a godly sort, what carefulness it wrought in you, yea, what clearing of yourselves, yea, what indignation, yea, what fear, yea, what vehement desire, yea, what zeal, yea, what revenge! In all things ye have approved yourselves to be clear in this matter.

Paul goes to great lengths here to tell the Corinthians of his initial sorrow over having to write harsh, corrective letters to them, then how that sorrow had been replaced by joy because of their positive response. They modeled "godly sorrow," which leads to repentance and salvation, as opposed to "the sorrow of the world," which works death.

These contrasting kinds of sorrow are illustrated in the contrast between the apostles Judas and Peter, when confronted with sin in their lives. Judas, overwhelmed by "the sorrow of the world," committed suicide. Peter, struck to the heart by "godly sorrow," repented of denying His Lord and was then restored to useful ministry. The Corinthians exhibited this latter kind of sorrow by the "carefulness," "indignation," and "zeal" Paul describes in verse 11.

V. Church's Stake

12 Wherefore, though I wrote unto you, I did it not for his cause that had done the wrong, nor for his cause that suffered wrong, but that our care for you in the sight of God might appear unto you.

Finally, Paul serves notice that the tempest caused by his calling for discipline against the sinful brother was not just for the sinner's benefit, but for the entire church. Concerned that the man's blatant and public immorality would infect the entire church, he was equally concerned that the corrective measures be taken as "medicine for the Body" (of Christ), not just for the man. Paul was convinced that both the Church's defense of morality, and the acceptance of the penitent, has repercussions in the larger culture about it.

Evangelistic Emphasis

Some time ago I read an account written by a man who had a pet boa constrictor. He kept the boa in a glass tank, the bottom of which was covered with cedar shavings. Periodically he would drop a live mouse into the glass box to feed the snake.

The man once fed the snake when it wasn't immediately hungry, and it just lay there. The mouse, on the other hand, sensed the imminent danger it was in. It cowered in the corner away from the snake for just a little while. Then the mouse seemed to have an idea.

The mouse began to paw and dig in the shavings, throwing the cedar shavings over the snake's body. After a time of frantic effort, the mouse succeeded in covering up a large portion of the snake. Satisfied that the snake was no longer a threat, the mouse relaxed. The snake was out of sight, out of mind, so to speak. But we know that the snake was really just postponing lunch.

Don't we sometimes think that way about sin in our lives? We think if we can cover it up, it will never bite us. That thinking is "mouse thinking." We do not relieve ourselves from the dangers and consequences of sin by covering it up. To get ourselves out of reach of sin, we must repent and ask forgiveness. Then God will remove our sin as far from us as the east is from the west.

~

Memory Selection

For godly sorrow worketh repentance to salvation not to be repented of: but the sorrow of the world worketh death.—*2 Corinthians 7:10*

There is a huge difference between sorrow for sin and sorrow for getting caught. Suppose a married man is having an affair. It goes along for awhile, but the man always feels guilty. Finally, he is convicted in his heart of the damage he is doing to his wife and family, the other woman's family, and to his own soul. He breaks off the affair, repents, and asks the Lord for forgiveness. He confesses to his wife and asks her for forgiveness. They go to counseling together to move on.

Now, suppose another married man is having an affair. His wife begins to suspect, so she hires a private investigator. The private eye takes pictures of the two unfaithful partners together. The wife confronts the man. He weeps pitifully and asks her forgiveness. He is terribly sorry for his indiscretion.

Man number one was sorry for the affair. He repented and asked forgiveness. He had what Paul might call "godly sorrow."

Was man number two sorry for the affair, or sorry that he got caught? One will only know if he had "godly sorrow" by the final outcome of his actions. Does he stay faithful? Only then will we know whether his penitence is real.

Weekday Problems

Jim could hardly believe his eyes. There before him was the résumé of Brett Smith. "The very idea!" Jim thought. Jim was now Vice President of Human Resources for the Trinity Company. It had taken him several years to work his way to this position in the corporation. It had taken so long because Brett Smith had betrayed him some years ago.

Brett and Jim had been assigned a project to work on together. They both had put many days and after-hours' work into the joint effort. All along, Brett was feeding their immediate supervisor false information about the project. According to Brett's reports, Jim was merely loafing along. In the end, Brett got all the credit for the project, leaving Jim looking as if he was incompetent and lazy. Brett was very quickly promoted. Not long afterward, Brett left Trinity for a much higher paying position in another company.

Jim had been very bitter, but he soon realized that his unforgiveness was getting him nowhere. He forgave Brett and began to work hard again. Eventually, Jim worked his way up to Vice President of Human Resources. Now, Brett was looking for a job. Jim invited him in.

"Jim," Brett began, "I'm so sorry for what I did to you. It has haunted me ever since. I won't blame you if you don't give me a job. Still, I wanted to come in here and apologize face to face."

*What do you think you would do if you were in Jim's position?

*How might Jim be able to tell if Brett is sincere in his apology?

Curious Classifieds

Free puppies. Part German Shepherd, part dog.
Free puppies. Half Cocker Spaniel, half sneaky neighbor dog.
German Shepherd, 85 lbs. Speaks German. Free.
2 wire-meshed butchering gloves, one 5-finger, one 3-finger.
    Pair, $15.
Tickle-Me-Elmo, new in box. Hardly tickled. $700.
1983 Toyota Hunchback, $2,000.
Whirlpool built-in oven. Frost free!
Nordic Track, $300. Hardly used. Call "Chubbie," at . . . .
Found: Dirty white dog, looks like a rat. Been out awhile.
    Better be a reward.
Georgia peaches. California grown. 89 cents lb.
Nice parachute. Never opened, used once. Slightly stained.

This Lesson in Your Life

We discover in our two passages of scripture that Paul had had to rebuke a man in the church at Corinth for some sin. He was glad that the man had repented. Folks do not always repent when someone in authority rebukes or corrects them. I remember an incident that happened some years ago that illustrates several different reactions to correction. A young lady who played the organ in the church was about to get married. Some of her friends wanted to throw her a "bachelorette" party. There were several hostesses. One of the hostesses was a Sunday School teacher at our church. Another was our nursery keeper.

Many friends were invited, including several from our congregation. There were some junior high age girls present. The entertainment for the party got very risque. One of the saints of our church called me, weeping. She did not want to tattle, but she felt I needed to know what went on. She and several others had gone to the party expecting a wedding shower, not an X-rated performance.

That Sunday I called the three in: the honoree, who was our organist; one hostess, who was a Sunday School teacher; and another who was our nursery keeper. I told them that their behavior was wrong. I told them that, as leaders of the church, they had to contact the ladies and teenagers and apologize for the party.

I got three reactions. One lady said, "There's nothing wrong with having a little fun!" She said I had no right to talk to them like that. When she walked out that day, she never came back to our church.

One lady became embarrassed and angry. She began to make excuses. Then she began to tell me it wasn't as bad as I had heard. Then she shifted and told me it was somebody else's fault. After she left the meeting she called others in the church and told gave them an inaccurate account of what happened. She tried to turn folks against me.

The honoree, the young lady who played the church organ, began to weep. "You're right, Pastor," she cried. "I know better than that. I was raised better than that. I know God doesn't approve of that kind of conduct. I am so sorry I didn't have the courage to stop things that night."

Only one of those ladies remains strong in the Lord to this day. Can you tell which one it might be? When we repent rather than try to justify our actions or excuse our sin, our relationship with the Lord is restored. If we refuse to repent, our relationship is forever damaged.

I want to be as close to God as I can. When I do wrong I want to repent quickly and ask forgiveness. When I do, God restores our relationship.

488

STRAIGHT

1. What is one reason the church should forgive a person who is truly repentant (2 Cor. 2:7)?
So the person will not be overwhelmed by excessive sorrow.

2. What is the next step one should take after forgiveness (2:6-7)?
The group or individual should comfort, reaffirm their love, and restore the person into fellowship.

3. Why did Paul write the Corinthians a letter of correction (see 2:9)?
Paul wrote to see if the Corinthians would stand the test and be obedient in everything.

4. In chapter 7, Paul apologizes somewhat for his harsh letter. He says he should be received by the Corinthians for what three reasons?
He has wronged no one. He has corrupted no one. He has neither defrauded nor exploited anyone.

5. In what two ways was Paul comforted while in Macedonia (7:6-7)?
He was comforted by the visit from Titus, and by the news Titus had: that the Corinthians were sorry for the grief they had caused Paul.

6. Though Paul's letter caused the Corinthians sorrow, what good came out of it (7:9-10)?
Their godly sorrow led them to repentance. Godly sorrow brings repentance that leads to salvation and leaves no regrets.

7. Godly sorrow leads to repentance. What does worldly sorrow bring?
Worldly sorrow brings death. This kind of self-centered sorrow comes from the consequences of sin, not sorrow for the sin itself.

8. What are some of the things godly sorrow produced in the Corinthians?
Earnestness, eagerness to clear themselves, righteous indignation, alarm at sin, longing, concern, and readiness to see justice done.

9. Were the Corinthians the ones at fault in this matter about which Paul wrote them the earlier letter?
No. Paul says that they proved at every point that they were innocent in that matter.

10. What caused Titus' affection for the Corinthian church to grow?
His affection became more abundant when he found that the Corinthians were obedient and that they received Paul's correction with fear and trembling.

Once upon a time there were two sisters, young married women, who lived side-by-side. They decided to plant a rose garden right on the property line between their places. They both tended the beautiful garden. They weeded. They pruned. They watered. They fertilized. Neither of them every really gave it a thought as to who was doing the most work. They never thought about whose garden it was.

That is, they never thought about it until one of the bushes began to produce the most beautiful blooms one had ever seen in that area. People walking by on the sidewalk would stop and stare. Some would come in their yards to smell the roses.

A friend suggested to one of the sisters, "Why don't you enter your rose in the County Fair competition. I know it would win."

Well, the sister decided to do just that. The next morning she took her pruning snips out to cut the rose.

The other sister saw her through the window. "Just what do you think you're doing?" she asked.

"I'm cutting my rose for the County Fair competition," she replied.

"*Your* rose! That's *my* rose," her sister shot back.

"Oh, no, it's mine!" the other sister shouted as she snipped the beautiful flower.

That was 23 years ago. The sisters haven't spoken to each other since. They put up a fence in the middle of the garden. Each tended her side only. But the roses never seemed to produce quite as much beauty.

Finally, one morning one sister walked around the fence and up to her sister's door. "What do you want," her sister snapped.

With tears in her eyes, she replied, "Sis, I want to be your sister again. Would you please forgive me? I should have never clipped that rose. I can't believe I valued a rose over your love."

Her sister burst into tears. "Of course, I forgive you. I should never have been mad in the first place."

Most of the time, all it takes when a relationship is breached, is for one party to ask forgiveness.

Is there someone to whom you need to go today and say, "I'm sorry. Please forgive me?" Try it. It will do your soul good.

490

2 Corinthians 8:1-15

Moreover, brethren, we do you to wit of the grace of God bestowed on the churches of Macedonia;

2 How that in a great trial of affliction the abundance of their joy and their deep poverty abounded unto the riches of their liberality.

3 For to their power, I bear record, yea, and beyond their power they were willing of themselves;

4 Praying us with much intreaty that we would receive the gift, and take upon us the fellowship of the ministering to the saints.

5 And this they did, not as we hoped, but first gave their own selves to the Lord, and unto us by the will of God.

6 Insomuch that we desired Titus, that as he had begun, so he would also finish in you the same grace also.

7 Therefore, as ye abound in every thing, in faith, and utterance, and knowledge, and in all diligence, and in your love to us, see that ye abound in this grace also.

8 I speak not by commandment, but by occasion of the forwardness of others, and to prove the sincerity of your love.

9 For ye know the grace of our Lord Jesus Christ, that, though he was rich, yet for your sakes he became poor, that ye through his poverty might be rich.

10 And herein I give my advice: for this is expedient for you, who have begun before, not only to do, but also to be forward a year ago.

11 Now therefore perform the doing of it; that as there was a readiness to will, so there may be a performance also out of that which ye have.

12 For if there be first a willing mind, it is accepted according to that a man hath, and not according to that he hath not.

13 For I mean not that other men be eased, and ye burdened:

14 But by an equality, that now at this time your abundance may be a supply for their want, that their abundance also may be a supply for your want: that there may be equality:

15 As it is written, He that had gathered much had nothing over; and he that had gathered little had no lack.

Aug. 13

Devotional Reading
Luke 20:45–21:4
Background Scripture
2 Cor. 8:1-15
Memory Selection
2 Cor. 8:9

491

After dealing with several points of contention between himself and the Corinthian, Paul must have welcomed the subject matter shift here. He is concerned now to enlist the Corinthians' cooperation in an inter-church campaign to help Christians in Jerusalem cope with a serious famine.

This critical food shortage had been predicted by a relatively unknown prophet named Agabus in Acts 11:27-28. Paul saw it not only as an opportunity to help the needy, but to cement relationships between Jewish and Gentile churches. The result is a classic passage on Christian giving that is based on the greatest gift—the self-giving of God's only-begotten Son.

෨෦ᏨᏜ

The informal setting of your Bible study group offers a good opportunity to involve rank-and-file church members in a discussion of church programs that rely on their financial contributions. Sometimes church members feel in the dark about such works, and can therefore be resentful when church leaders ask for increased contributions. Thus it is common to hear statements such as "All the church ever talks about is money," and "What happens to all the money they're always begging for?"

You can deal with this issue both by emphasizing the reasons for giving that this lesson provides, and by doing some research in order to discuss how members' contributions are being used. Note that quite apart from specific needs that require funding, Christians need to give as a response to the self-giving of Christ Himself, which this lesson emphasizes.

Teaching Outline

I. Responding to Needs—1-4
  A. Example of others, 1-2
  B. Immediate need, 3-4
II. Giving as a 'Grace'—5-8
  A. The gift of self, 5-7
  B. Proving sincerity, 8
III. The Imitation of Christ—9-12
  A. Christ's example, 9
  B. 'Do As You Said,' 10-11
IV. Fair-Share Giving—12-15
  A. A willing mind, 12
  B. Two-way giving, 13-15

Daily Bible Readings

Mon.	Widow's Offering	Luke 20:45–21:4
Tue.	Chosen to Serve	Acts 6:1-6
Wed.	Generosity: A Gift of God	Rom. 12:3-8
Thu.	Collection for the Saints	1 Cor. 15:58–16:4
Fri.	Generosity: A Fruit of the Spirit	Gal. 5:16-26
Sat.	Excel in Generosity	2 Cor. 8:1-7
Sun.	Guidelines for Giving	2 Cor. 8:8-15

Verse by Verse

I. Responding to Needs—1-4
A. Example of others, 1-2

1 Moreover, brethren, we do you to wit of the grace of God bestowed on the churches of Macedonia;

2 How that in a great trial of affliction the abundance of their joy and their deep poverty abounded unto the riches of their liberality.

It has often been noted that more space is devoted to the Christian attitude toward wealth than to any other single topic. This is no doubt grounded in the very nature of God and the Church. Since "God is love," He seeks to help the needy, and gave His only-begotten Son to the spiritually poor; and since the Church is the Body of Christ, Christians are Christ's hands and we are to open them to the poor. Indeed, in Jesus' first sermon He applied a Messianic prophecy from Isaiah to His mission to preach Good News to the poor and the needy (Luke 4:18; Isa. 61:1).

Thus Paul had no doubt already laid the foundation for appealing for funds when he first preached to the Corinthians. Now he seeks to impart a spirit of cooperation between them and churches in Macedonia, who had already committed to a project of helping the poor (see vs. 4, below). This would have included the churches in Thessalonica, Philippi, and Berea. Note that these churches were not filled with wealthy people who could give without making a sacrifice. Christians there gave out of their "deep poverty"—and, significantly, felt that it was a joy instead of a sacrifice. Little wonder that Paul urges the Corinthian to follow their example. This "reciprocal" principle means that benevolence is never "paternalistic." Christians need to give as much as the poor need to receive.

B. Immediate need, 3-4

3 For to their power, I bear record, yea, and beyond their power they were willing of themselves;

4 Praying us with much intreaty that we would receive the gift, and take upon us the fellowship of the ministering to the saints.

The ordinary and even poverty-stricken Christians in Macedonia had set an example of Christian charity by giving beyond their ability to do so, trusting God to supply funds for needs that they denied themselves in order to give to "the saints."

This term, originally meaning all Christians as those "set apart" for service to God, refers especially in this context to Christians in Judea. Apparently the immediate need here was a series of famines that had created special hardships there. The prophet Agabus had predicted that such a disaster would strike the area during the reign of the Emperor Claudius (Acts11:27-28). Secular historians of the day record at least four such famines during Claudius' reign. Paul had already been sent to Jerusalem with relief during one of these famines, bringing funds from Christians in Antioch of Syria, which for years was the center of Gentile Christianity (Acts 11:29-30).

There was more than one reason for Paul's making another collection. First, the Macedonians themselves had "entreated" the apostle to accept their contributions, realizing that being a part of the Church meant seeking "fellowship" in such a ministry. Second, Paul hoped that relief sent from Gentile churches would help heal tensions between them and Jewish Christians in Judea. He told the Romans that "If the Gentiles have been made partakers of their (the Jews') spiritual things, their duty is also to minister unto them in carnal things [money]" (Rom. 15:27).

II. Giving as a 'Grace'—5-8
A. The gift of self, 5-7

5 And this they did, not as we hoped, but first gave their own selves to the Lord, and unto us by the will of God.

6 Insomuch that we desired Titus, that as he had begun, so he would also finish in you the same grace also.

7 Therefore, as ye abound in every thing, in faith, and utterance, and knowledge, and in all dili-gence, and in your love to us, see that ye abound in this grace also.**

Three times in these three verses alone (plus several other verses), contributing to others' needs is called a "giving" or a "grace." Paul has involved Titus in the process of coordinating the contributions of the churches of Macedonia and Corinth. The Corinthians (in Achaia) needed to "finish" the plan of giving to which they had committed a year earlier (8:10; 9:2).

In verse 7 Paul makes an almost sly reference to the Corinthians' competition among themselves for the "best" spiritual gifts, dealt with in 1 Corinthians 12–14. He insists that they should give at least as much effort to receive the gift of giving as they had to obtain the more sensational gifts of tongue-speaking ("utterance") and "knowledge."

B. Proving sincerity, 8

8 I speak not by commandment, but by occasion of the forwardness of others, and to prove the sincerity of your love.

Despite the many exhortations in the New Covenant Scriptures for Christians to give generously to meet the needs of others, a consistent effort is made to distinguish these admonitions from *law*. Thus Paul says here that his appeal for funds is not a "commandment" which, upon being obeyed, earns them salvation. Instead it is to "prove the sincerity" of the love they profess to have for God and His children. Again, giving is shown to be a grace—a *fruit* of salvation showing that we already have the Holy Spirit, not a *work* that earns it. Christian giving is not "of necessity: for God loveth a cheerful giver" (9:7).

III. The Imitation of Christ—9-12

A. Christ's example, 9

9 For ye know the grace of our Lord Jesus Christ, that, though he was rich, yet for your sakes he became poor, that ye through his poverty might be rich.

Again the term "grace" appears, this time referring to the self-giving act of Jesus in the Incarnation. Giving would never be a problem for Christians if we realized that being able to give is a "grace." When the Macedonians gave of themselves (vs. 5), they emulated the way Jesus left His rightful place at the right hand of God to take on human flesh or "become poor" for our sake, that we might become spiritually rich by taking on His likeness (see Philip. 2:5-7).

B. 'Do As You Said,' 10-11

10 And herein I give my advice: for this is expedient for you, who have begun before, not only to do, but also to be forward a year ago.

11 Now therefore perform the doing of it; that as there was a readiness to will, so there may be a performance also out of that which ye have.

Again declining to "command" the Corinthians to give, Paul says his exhortation is "advice" (Grk. *gnome*, "opinion" or "counsel"). It is one thing to broadcast a "plan" to give generously, and quite another to follow through and *do* it.

IV. Fair-Share Giving—12-15

A. A willing mind, 12

12 For if there be first a willing mind, it is accepted according to that a man hath, and not according to that he hath not.

This restates the principle that Christian giving, as distinguished from that under the Law, is a matter not of command but of a "willing mind." Paul also makes it clear that he is not asking the Corinthians to give more than they were able (even though, living in a wealthy city, they were probably much better off financially than the Macedonians). Yet this does not remove the challenge of giving sacrificially.

B. Two-way giving, 13-15

13 For I mean not that other men be eased, and ye burdened:

14 But by an equality, that now at this time your abundance may be a supply for their want, that their abundance also may be a supply for your want: that there may be equality:

15 As it is written, He that had gathered much had nothing over; and he that had gathered little had no lack.

Paul cites God's provision for His people in the wilderness after the exodus from Egypt, when *enough* manna was preserved until eaten, but a *surplus* spoiled. He is not asking that the Corinthians bear an undue proportion of the burden of giving, but, again, to treat it as a privilege or gift to be caught up in a cooperative effort of giving proportionately.

Evangelistic Emphasis

The teaching of the Cross is central to the Christian faith. Among the implications of this teaching is that the Cross is about sacrifice. It is about giving of ourselves. We cannot even become a Christian without giving ourselves to Jesus Christ. We die to self and live for Christ. We give up our lives to save them.

The Christian life is one of giving. We give ourselves to others. We visit in the hospitals. We provide food for those who have none. We give of our time to teach Sunday School, lead a small group, work around the church, and sing in the choir. We give of our time to the Lord in personal devotion, Bible study, and prayer.

Christians also give of their material goods. Jesus said, "I was hungry and you gave me something to eat, I was thirsty and you gave me something to drink. I needed clothes and you clothed me" (Matt. 25:35-36a). All those ministries take financing. Thus, for the Christian to be in those ministries, one has to give from one's own material goods and finances.

We give of our finances in order that the good news of Jesus Christ might be spread around the world. Most of us are not called by God to be missionaries in foreign countries. Yet God calls us to sacrifice in order to send those missionaries to the places we are unable to go ourselves.

ഇൟ

For ye know the grace of our Lord Jesus Christ, that, though he was rich, yet for your sakes he became poor, that ye through his poverty might be rich.—*2 Corinthians 8:9*

When Jesus was in heaven He had everything. Jesus was with God and He was God. John 1:3 (NIV) tells us, "Through him all things were made; without him nothing was made that has been made." Jesus was omnipotent, all powerful; omnipresent, able to be everywhere at once; and omniscient, knowing everything, even the thoughts of men. Jesus gave up all that to become a little baby born in a feed trough to a nondescript Jewish couple. He lived a life with the same human limitations we endure. He was confronted with the same types of human problems we face. He was executed in a cruel and painful manner by the government authorities of His day.

He embraced all that because of you and me. He gave up His glory. He took up human limitations. He endured the Cross. He did it all for us.

Jesus came and lived with us in order that one day we will go to live with Him. He became poor that we may become rich. He gave it all up in order that we may gain it all. Don't you just love Him?

Weekday Problems

Jane read the letter from the church about the upcoming mission trip to Mexico. The purpose of the trip was to build concrete block houses for the working poor. There were pictures. Some of the people were living in hovels made of cardboard nailed to wooden shipping pallets. The houses had no floors, only hard, packed dirt. One picture showed a family of six standing before a 16 x 20-foot shack. "My, my," Jane thought, "my closet is that big. Honey!" she shouted at her husband who was out washing their new Lexus, "do you think we can give something to this Mexico mission?"

"I don't see how," he shouted back. "Remember the storm blew some shingles off our country home. The insurance won't cover it, so we've got to replace that roof. Plus we want to remodel the cabinets in the motor home. That's going to cost $1,200. And Susan wants that $1,900 dress for her sorority ball. I just don't see how we can afford to give to the Mexico mission."

Jane sighed as she sat down on her leather-covered sofa, "One day we'll have enough to help those poor people in Mexico."

*Just from this scenario, do you think Jane's family's problem is that they don't have enough money to give?

*Finish this statement: "From whom much is given, much is _____ ."

The Gift of Giving

One reason there are so many pennies in the collection basket is that it's the smallest coin we have.

***

When the usher came up the aisle with the collection basket, a five-year-old boy whispered excitedly to his dad, "Here comes the pennyman!"

***

Three men decided at the last minute to go to church. When it came time to pass the plate, they realized they had no money. Not wanting to be embarrassed by putting nothing in the plate, they quickly hatched a plan. One of them fainted and the other two carried him out.

***

Some people who give the Lord credit are reluctant to give Him cash.

This Lesson in Your Life

The late Flip Wilson used to do a comedy routine in which he played a pastor named Rev. Leroy. "The Lord wants this church to RUN!" he would say. "He wants this to be a running church! But before the church can run, it has to learn to crawl!"

The congregation comes back, "Let it crawl, Rev., let it crawl!"

Rev. Leroy is getting wound up, "And once the church has learned to crawl, it has to learn to stand up on its own two feet, to rise up and walk!"

"Let it walk, Rev., let it walk!"

By now Rev. Leroy is thundering away, "And once the church is walking well, if it *realllllly* wants to run, you got to give your money!"

The congregation shot back, "Let it crawl, Rev., let it crawl!"

Flip Wilson got a big laugh from that routine. In real life, it's not all that funny—because our level of generosity is usually a relatively accurate gauge of our spiritual commitment.

Some years ago as I was preaching a series of messages on stewardship I made the statement, "I can look at your check register and tell if you are a Christian or not."

The very next morning a lady was at my office. "Preacher," she said, "I think that's a pretty bold statement to make. There's no way you can tell if a person is a Christian or not by looking at that person's check register!"

I then tried to explain that how the Christian manages money is a spiritual issue. The things upon which we spend our money are often determined by our spiritual depth. The amount of money we give away (translate that "generosity") is a barometer of our love for Christ. I closed my remarks by saying, "Let's take a look at your checkbook and mine."

This lady reacted noticeably by clutching her wallet closer to her body. She said, "That's private!" She left in a huff.

Generosity of spirit is a character trait of God. God is always giving to us. The spirit in which we give back to God reflects our willingness to become more like Him.

When we were in need, God gave His Son to us. God always provides for us. One of our tasks as Christians is to provide for others who are in need. As God blesses us, we are to bless others.

Remember what Paul wrote in Philippians 4:19 (NRSV): "And my God will fully satisfy every need of yours according to his riches in glory in Christ Jesus." God meets our needs. We must help others who are in need. Sometimes that costs us money.

GETTING THE FACTS STRAIGHT

1. What does Paul write that reminds us that we do not have to be wealthy to be generous?

He tells us that the Macedonian churches were generous even though they were in poverty.

2. Did Paul have to beg or manipulate the Macedonians in order to entice them to give generously? Explain.

No. The Macedonians begged Paul for the privilege of sharing in the service to the saints.

3. Does giving generously make us Christians?

No. Paul reminds us in verse 5 that the Macedonians gave themselves first to the Lord. We cannot buy our way into the Kingdom of God.

4. Who was Paul's friend who became the emissary between Paul and the Corinthians?

It was Titus who relayed messages and carried letters back and forth.

5. Paul brags on the Corinthians for their excellence in everything, yet he specifies four things (vs.7). What are the four things?

They abounded in faith, utterance (speech), knowledge, all diligence (complete earnestness), and in their love for Paul and his companions.

6. According to verse 9, why did Jesus, who was rich in heaven, leave those riches to come to earth?

Jesus became poor for our sakes, so that we through His poverty might become rich in spiritual blessings, and gain the riches of heaven.

7. What advice does Paul give the Corinthians in verses 10-11?

He reminds them (and us) that the willingness to do a good work should be matched with the doing or the completion of the work.

8. Does God want us to do without to give to others in order that they might have plenty?

No. God does not want us to give if we have too little to give, but out of what we have, not what we do not have.

9. What is the goal of giving in this situation as stated in verses 13-14?

The goal of giving was equality, that those with plenty would share with those who were in need. In this manner, both groups will have enough.

10. Paul refers to the time when the Israelites were gathering manna in the desert. Which is the reference verse?

Verse 15: "He that had gathered much had nothing over; and he that had gathered little had no lack."

Maybe you have heard this old joke. Once upon a time a $100 bill, a $20 bill, and a $1 bill were talking together. The $100 bill bragged about where it had been, as the other two bills listened intently.

"I've been to the finest restaurants in Paris. I have been to Broadway musicals. I have been to the most beautiful ski resorts in Colorado," the $100 bill boasted. "I guess I have been to the finest places in the world."

Then the $20 bill chimes in, "Well, I've been to some very interesting places, too. I have been to the San Diego Zoo. I have been to Las Vegas. I have been to Disney World. I get around some myself."

The $100 and the $20 looked at the $1 bill. "How about you? Have you been anyplace interesting?"

"No," the dollar bill sighed, "but I've been to church a hundred times."

Isn't that the way it is? Quite often, we give our best to ourselves. So many folks spend most of their money on their own comfort, pleasure, or entertainment. Then they give their leftovers to benevolent causes, such as for the work of the church.

Paul bragged on the Macedonians because they gave generously out of their extreme poverty. They did not give only when they had plenty of money. I have discovered that folks who wait to give until they have enough money almost never get around to being generous—because, in their eyes, they never feel as if they have enough.

I remember a story of a man who lost a $1 dollar bet to a millionaire miser. As the man was paying up he jokingly asked, "How many dollars do you need before you have enough?"

The millionaire miser answered back with a forced smile, "Always one more, son, always one more."

We Christians cannot be like that. We seek first the Kingdom of God, knowing that God will take care of us. We do not need to be greedy. In fact, if we are going to be imitators of God, then we must duplicate His generous Spirit with generosity of our own.

Remember Jesus said in Luke 6:38, "Give, and it will be given to you. A good measure, pressed down, shaken together and running over, will be poured into your lap. For with the measure you use, it will be measured to you."

2 Corinthians 9:1-15

For as touching the ministering to the saints, it is superfluous for me to write to you:

2 For I know the forwardness of your mind, for which I boast of you to them of Macedonia, that Achaia was ready a year ago; and your zeal hath provoked very many.

3 Yet have I sent the brethren, lest our boasting of you should be in vain in this behalf; that, as I said, ye may be ready:

4 Lest haply if they of Macedonia come with me, and find you unprepared, we (that we say not, ye) should be ashamed in this same confident boasting.

5 Therefore I thought it necessary to exhort the brethren, that they would go before unto you, and make up beforehand your bounty, whereof ye had notice before, that the same might be ready, as a matter of bounty, and not as of covetousness.

6 But this I say, He which soweth sparingly shall reap also sparingly; and he which soweth bountifully shall reap also bountifully.

7 Every man according as he purposeth in his heart, so let him give; not grudgingly, or of necessity: for God loveth a cheerful giver.

8 And God is able to make all grace abound toward you; that ye, always having all sufficiency in all things, may abound to every good work:

9 (As it is written, He hath dispersed abroad; he hath given to the poor: his righteousness remaineth for ever.

10 Now he that ministereth seed to the sower both minister bread for your food, and multiply your seed sown, and increase the fruits of your righteousness;)

11 Being enriched in every thing to all bountifulness, which causeth through us thanksgiving to God.

12 For the administration of this service not only supplieth the want of the saints, but is abundant also by many thanksgivings unto God;

13 Whiles by the experiment of this ministration they glorify God for your professed subjection unto the gospel of Christ, and for your liberal distribution unto them, and unto all men;

14 And by their prayer for you, which long after you for the exceeding grace of God in you.

15 Thanks be unto God for his unspeakable gift.

Devotional Reading
Ps. 37:16-24

Background Scripture
2 Cor. 9:1-15

Memory Selection
2 Cor. 9:8

Aug. 20

501

Today's lesson can be considered "Part 2" of Lesson 11. The apostle Paul continues to set out principles of giving, with special emphasis on the need for the Corinthians to coordinate their contributions with those of the churches of Macedonia. Together, they will form a network of support to meet emergency needs of Christians in Jerusalem and Judea, who are suffering from the effects of famine (Rom. 15:25-26).

Of course the mechanics of this collection are far less important than the spirit behind the gifts that the Corinthians are collecting. Paul lays down principles and attitudes that are still fundamental to instructing modern Christians both on how to give, and the blessing of giving liberally.

Sharing anecdotes that show how God often blesses those who give is an inspirational way to begin this lesson. You might share one to "prime" the discussion. 'Way out west a young Christian couple were struggling to get through college. There came a time when they had to choose between buying groceries and giving to their church the amount they had pledged. They decided to make their regular church check, and let God take care of the groceries. When grocery-buying day came, a check for $50 showed up in their mailbox. An uncle had sold the young man's saddle, and God had known just when to send the money.

Many other similar stories have been shared by missionaries and other ministers. Perhaps members of your group can share some of these as well as their own.

Teaching Outline	Daily Bible Readings
I. Contagious Zeal—1-5 A. Provinces involved, 1-2 B. Advance preparation, 3-5 II. Sowing and Reaping—6-11 A. Built-in principle, 6 B. The generous heart, 7-9 C. Giving to give more, 10-11 III. Glorifying God—12-15 A. Serving God and man, 12-13 B. Prayer for givers, 14-15	Mon. Prompted from Above 　　　 James 1:12-17 Tue. Give and You Shall Receive 　　　 Luke 6:32-38 Wed. Giving Quietly 　　　 Matthew 6:1-6 Thu. Pleased to Share 　　　 Romans 15:25-29 Fri. Arranging to Give 　　　 2 Cor. 9:1-5 Sat. A Cheerful Giver 　　　 2 Cor. 9:6-10 Sun. Generosity Glorifies God 　　　 2 Cor. 9:11-15

Verse by Verse

I. Contagious Zeal—1-5

A. Provinces involved, 1-2

1 For as touching the ministering to the saints, it is superfluous for me to write to you:

2 For I know the forwardness of your mind, for which I boast of you to them of Macedonia, that Achaia was ready a year ago; and your zeal hath provoked very many.

Because Paul had previously mentioned that the churches of Macedonia had originated a plan to contribute to the famine-stricken Christians in Jerusalem and Judea (2 Cor. 8:1-5), further teaching might be considered "superfluous." Yet he must refer again to the arrangements. As a part of the Balkan peninsula of southeastern Europe, Macedonia presented problems to travelers ("Balkan" means "mountain" in Turkish). Paul had given Titus and another brother the challenge to serve as administrators of the project (8:16, 22-23). They would have had to retrace Paul's steps to such Macedonian cities as Berea, Thessalonica, and Philippi.

The "forwardness" (NIV "eagerness") of mind of the Corinthians refers to their previously expressed eagerness to join the Macedonian churches in this unprecedented collection. Paul had already bragged on this

eagerness to Christians in Macedonia.

B. Advance preparation, 3-5

3 Yet have I sent the brethren, lest our boasting of you should be in vain in this behalf; that, as I said, ye may be ready:

4 Lest haply if they of Macedonia come with me, and find you unprepared, we (that we say not, ye) should be ashamed in this same confident boasting.

5 Therefore I thought it necessary to exhort the brethren, that they would go before unto you, and make up beforehand your bounty, whereof ye had notice before, that the same might be ready, as a matter of bounty, and not as of covetousness.

Paul is extremely eager for the often tense relationships he had with the church at Corinth not to interfere with the collection. "The brethren" refers again to Titus and "the brother" of 8:18, and perhaps a third unnamed "brother" mentioned in 8:22. Together they comprised a team of "messengers of the churches" (8:23), appointed for the express purpose of collecting and managing the funds from Corinth and Macedonia for the poverty-stricken Christians in Judea. The whole scene has elements that could have been explosive: mixed races, especially Jews and Gentiles, mixed backgrounds, and unknown "fund-raisers."

All this helps explain why Paul makes this rather elaborate explanation of why he is sending the delegation to Corinth. The Corinthians had previously indicated their willingness to assist with this rather large project, and Paul does not want any surprises, or leftover animosity between himself and the Corinthians, to interfere with the smooth collection of the funds. He wants the Corinthians to have their contribution ready, and to be immediately available as a surplus ("bounty" or "blessing)" rather than conducting a surprise emergency fund drive that may create hard feelings, not to say embarrass both Paul and the Corinthians for their lack of preparedness.

II. Sowing and Reaping—6-11
A. Built-in principle, 6

6 But this I say, He which soweth sparingly shall reap also sparingly; and he which soweth bountifully shall reap also bountifully.

Paul has been careful to say that giving to this significant project is a matter of choice, not commandment (8:8). Now, however, he states a basic principle of contributing to the Lord's work: God blesses us in proportion to our willingness to give. When one person commented on how a brother had prospered after giving a large gift to his church, he put it this way: "God just has a bigger shovel than I do." A basic principle is at work here: "For whosoever hath, to him shall be given, and he shall have more abundance: but whosoever hath not, from him shall be taken away even that he hath" (Matt. 13:12).

Unfortunately, this principle of generosity coming to those with generous hearts is sometimes reduced in our day to what has been called a "prosperity gospel." The term refers to the theory that growing wealthy because we give liberally is somehow guaranteed. In fact, the blessings God has for those who are generous are often spiritual, not financial, in nature. The "return" on an investment placed with God may even come in the form of an even more generous heart, not monetary wealth after all.

B. The generous heart, 7-9

7 Every man according as he purposeth in his heart, so let him give; not grudgingly, or of necessity: for God loveth a cheerful giver.

8 And God is able to make all grace abound toward you; that ye, always having all sufficiency in all things, may abound to every good work:

9 (As it is written, He hath dispersed abroad; he hath given to the poor: his righteousness remaineth for ever.

Now Paul lays down further general principles on giving that apply to the Christian life today as much as they did to the Corinthians. Again, no fixed amount to be given is prescribed under the New Covenant. Instead, the amount is to be what one purposes in his own heart. Otherwise the gift would be "of necessity," and liable to be given with anything but a cheerful heart.

Again, in verses 8-9, the principle that God will reward givers is laid down, but not as a "prosperity gospel." God simply promises to care for those who put Him first. Paul's teaching echoes that of Christ when He said, "Seek ye first the kingdom of God and his righteousness; and all these things [the necessities of life] will be added unto you" (Matt. 6:33). This principle is reinforced here by a loose quotation from Psalm 112:9.

C. Giving to give more, 10-11

10 Now he that ministereth seed to the sower both minister bread for your food, and multiply your seed sown, and increase the fruits of your righteousness;)

11 Being enriched in every thing to all bountifulness, which causeth through us thanksgiving to God.

Yet another reason for giving liberally is to be able to give more. Those who scatter liberally the seeds of generous giving will find even more seed in their bins, from which they can sow again, in an unending circle. God does not bless us for giving just in order for us to boast, or to grow fat on His blessings. He blesses us in order for us to be able to bless others again. The same is true in human relationships. Those with a "giving spirit" or openness to others will find others opening up their spirits to them, too (see Luke 6:32-38, a passage that refers primarily to relationships and only secondarily to financial giving).

Verse 11 shows that the whole point of our giving is not to just to bless the needy, and even less to draw attention to ourselves; it is to bless God. The One from whom all blessings flow blesses a giver with a generous heart; and in turn this giving causes the recipients to glorify Him.

III. Glorifying God—12-15

A. Serving God and man, 12-13

12 For the administration of this service not only supplieth the want of the saints, but is abundant also by many thanksgivings unto God;

13 Whiles by the experiment of this ministration they glorify God for your professed subjection unto the gospel of Christ, and for your liberal distribution unto them, and unto all men;

Elaborating on the purpose of giving as glorifying God, Paul speaks of such projects as the one for which he is raising funds as a "ministry" (the term "administration" is from *diakonia*). Also, it is significant that the term translated "service" in verse 12 is in other contexts translated *worship*—not that humanistic works such as giving to the poor can take the place of worship, but that they serve people in a way similar to the way our worship serves, or blesses, God.

Believers should be eager to broadcast a picture of the God they worship as a generous God, the giver of "every good and perfect gift" (James 1:17). Paul indicates that there is no better way to paint a portrait of Him whom we worship than to give generously to programs that bless the needy.

B. Prayer for givers, 14-15

14 And by their prayer for you, which long after you for the exceeding grace of God in you.

15 Thanks be unto God for his unspeakable gift.

A final way Paul mentions that blessings will come to those who give generously is that others, particularly those who receive gifts, will pray for the givers, thanking God for unfathomable "gift of giving."

Evangelistic Emphasis

To a person who has absolutely no money with which to buy groceries, a $20 bill is good news. To a person whose water will be turned off if his $53 water bill is not paid, $53 is that person's salvation. To a mother with a crying baby and nothing in her wallet with which to buy Pampers, $12 is a Godsend.

Of course money is not the gospel in a theological sense. Neither is paying a bill for someone else going to get us into heaven. Still, helping others financially in the name of Jesus is connected to sharing the good news of Jesus Christ with them.

Perhaps God has blessed most of those who read this with a way to earn a living. We, in turn, being children of Abraham, are blessed to be a blessing just as Abraham was.

Just after the Day of Pentecost, the believers had everything in common. Some sold their possessions and gave the proceeds to anyone who had a need. I am not convinced God wants us to live today in such a communal society, but I am convinced God wants us to give of what we have to help others in need. We can do that through the church or personally. Just as long as it is done in Jesus' name.

ഓന്ദ

Memory Selection

And God is able to make all grace abound toward you; that ye, always having all sufficiency in all things, may abound to every good work:
—2 Corinthians 9:8

Do you realize what this Scripture says? God, through His grace, will provide everything we need to do His good work. Think of that! God will give us plenty of money to do what He has called us to do, both personally and as a church . . . *if* we use those resources to do God's good work.

I'm not sure all of us are willing to claim that promise. Maybe it is because we do not have enough faith. Maybe it is because we are not sure what we are doing is God's good work. I have heard it many times in church board meetings. Some in the group feel God's leading to embark upon some new ministry. Then another in the group comes up with something like, "We don't have enough money to do that! What if the roof gets blown off by a tornado! What if the air conditioners all give out at the same time! We couldn't do those repairs and finance this ministry at the same time!"

Too often the voice of the concerned one wins out. We begin to say, "We don't have enough money if all those bad things happen," and we shelve the ministry. Paul reminds us that God will provide plenty of everything we need to do God's good work. We can take that to the bank.

Weekday Problems

"Now is a fine time to be thinking about this!" Sara mused as she sat in the automobile dealer's showroom. Sara needed a new car. She had been saving for several years. Her old car really was shot. The old car had left her stranded on the highway twice in the last month. That was a dangerous predicament for a single mother with a toddler in tow.

She had enough money saved for the economy model. It was a nice little four-door model with air conditioning and a stereo radio/tape deck/CD player. It got good gas mileage. It was just what she needed. But what she wanted was the SUV. It was beautiful. It had every option imaginable—even a drop-down DVD player for the back-seat passengers. It had leather interior and even seat warmers. Sara knew she had only enough cash to make a sizable down payment on the big vehicle. She would have to take out a note for the rest.

That's where the problem came in. She would have to reduce her giving to the Lord through her church in order to make the payments. Her church supported a food pantry in her community as well as sending money to agricultural missionaries overseas. Sara had a decision to make.

*Which decision do you think most Christians would make?

*Does God promise He will give us everything we want? Explain.

The Ideal Preacher

The congregation was searching for a new minister when the following piece mysteriously appeared on a bulletin board in the foyer:

We have heard about a minister who preaches exactly 20 minutes, and then sits down. He condemns sin, but never hurts feelings. He works from 8 a.m. to 10 p.m., doing everything from working up sermons to giving taxi service to the elderly. He wants a salary of only $60 a week, wears good clothes, buys good books, drives a nice car, and gives $30 a week back to the church

This man is 30 years old, and has been preaching for 35 years. He is short enough to talk at eye-level to children, yet has a tall, commanding presence in the pulpit. He has one brown eye and one blue, and parts his hair in three places: left, right, and center. He has a burning desire to convert the lost, but spends all his time comforting church members. He smiles all the time but with a serious cast to his face because he has a sense of humor that keeps him seriously dedicated.

He is truly a remarkable person . . . and he doesn't exist.

This Lesson in Your Life

The apostle Paul gives us two goals of giving in verses 11-13: (1) helping people grow spiritually through their financial giving, and (2) providing sufficient resources for the Church's mission and ministries.

Jesus said, "Where your treasure is, there will be your heart also" (Luke 12:34). I used to think people gave generously to the Lord's work through the church because they had plenty of money. I have since changed my view. People do not give because they have money. People give because they love the Lord. Better incomes do not produce better givers. Faith determines what we give. The stronger the faith, the higher the percentage of giving. The weaker the faith, the lower the percentage. God promises we will always have enough to give back to Him and His work.

People give generously because they are grateful to God. When we stop to think what Jesus did for us on the Cross when He gave His life in a painful manner, we cannot help but be grateful. He asks from us total commitment back to Him. Total commitment means 100 percent. If we give 100 percent of ourselves to Him, it's not so hard for us to let go of 10 percent of our finances.

People see their giving as part of their spiritual relationship with God. John 3:16 tells us, "For God so loved the world that He gave His only begotten Son . . . ." God gave, and is giving to us, so we give back to Him.

People give because they see a connection between their giving and their service to God. St. Francis of Assisi once said, "Preach the gospel at all times. If necessary, use words." In a sense, people can also preach the gospel with their dollars. Christians know they are serving God with their financial gifts as much as if they were preaching sermons from behind a pulpit.

Giving brings us joy. We certainly enjoy seeing positive effects occur in the Kingdom of God as a direct result of our giving.

Giving helps us grow spiritually. I know when we first began to tithe, it was a leap of faith to believe that God could stretch 90 cents as far or farther than we could stretch a dollar.

God has always been faithful to us. We have never missed a meal because of money we gave to God's work. We have never been thrown out of our house because we gave money to the church and did not have any to pay rent. We have never had to go without proper clothing because we gave 10 percent of our income to Christ.

God is faithful. He will provide. Trust Him in everything. Especially in the area of your finances.

1. Why was Paul sending brethren to Corinth ahead of himself?

He wanted the brothers to make sure the Corinthians finished the arrangements for the generous gift they had promised to the Christians in Jerusalem.

2. Why would Paul be ashamed of the Corinthians if they did not have the offering ready?

Because he had boasted about the Corinthians' willingness to give, and did not want to be embarrassed.

3. According to the law of sowing and reaping (vs. 6), what determines our harvest of crops or finances?

Our harvest is largely determined by the amount we sow. If we sow little, we reap little. If we sow generously, we reap generously.

4. What attitude does God want us to have toward giving for His work?

God wants us to give without reluctance. He does not want us to be forced to give. He wants us to give cheerfully.

5. In which verse does Paul say that God will give us everything we need to do His good work?

Verse 8: "And God is able to make all grace abound toward you; that ye, always having all sufficiency in all things, may abound to every good work."

6. It is God who supplies seed to the sower and bread for food. What does God do for the one who gives to God's work?

God will multiply the seed sown and increase the fruits of righteousness.

7. According to verse 11, who should receive the thanksgiving for a gift given to others?

Thanksgiving should go to God. A Christian's gift should always bring glory to God, not to the person who gives it.

8. What are two results of the Corinthians giving this offering to the Lord's work?

The offering will supply the needs of God's people in Jerusalem, and it will result in many expressions of thanks to God.

9. What reason for the Corinthians' giving generously is given in verse 13?

Because their obedience supported their confession of the gospel.

10. Paul closes with, "Thanks be unto God for His unspeakable gift." What might the "unspeakable gift" be?

He could be talking about the generosity that God placed in the hearts of the Corinthians. However, most scholars believe that Paul is speaking of the perfect gift, the gift of God's own son, Jesus Christ.

I heard a story some years ago about a church in Louisiana that was trying to raise a huge amount of money for a missions project in Russia. A new congregation had begun there as a result of this particular church helping to support a missionary. Now the Russian congregation had outgrown the pastor's living room. They desperately needed a building, a sanctuary, in which to hold services.

The Louisiana church felt God's leading to tackle that project. However, the funds were not coming in at the level needed. So the pastor called the church together to fast and pray for one week. They were to seek God's will in the matter to see if they were to abandon the project or move forward. They were to come back together in seven days to see if God had given anybody a revelation.

When they came back together, the pastor stood up and said, "I have received a word from the Lord. He has given me good news and bad news." The room hushed.

The pastor continued, "The good news is, God told me that He has provided the money for the whole project." The room erupted with shouts of "Hallelujah!" and "Praise the Lord!"

When things quieted down the pastor said, "Now the bad news is, *the money is still in your pockets!"*

God will provide all the resources to do His will. If we give to Him and to His work, He will see to it that we have enough of what we need. I have heard many people say, "You can't out-give God," but I have witnessed very few people try it. Quite often we hang on to our offerings until we are certain we can meet all our own needs. Seldom do we give out of faith, counting on God to supply our needs.

We must remember that God is faithful. He will not let us down. I love what David said in Psalm 37:25: "I have been young, and now am old, yet I have not seen the righteous forsaken or their children begging bread."

God will provide. As we provide for His work, He will provide for us.

Lesson 13

The Giving of Sufficient Grace

2 Corinthians 12:1-10

It is not expedient for me doubtless to glory. I will come to visions and revelations of the Lord.

2 I knew a man in Christ above fourteen years ago, (whether in the body, I cannot tell; or whether out of the body, I cannot tell: God knoweth;) such an one caught up to the third heaven.

3 And I knew such a man, (whether in the body, or out of the body, I cannot tell: God knoweth;)

4 How that he was caught up into paradise, and heard unspeakable words, which it is not lawful for a man to utter.

5 Of such an one will I glory: yet of myself I will not glory, but in mine infirmities.

6 For though I would desire to glory, I shall not be a fool; for I will say the truth: but now I forbear, lest any man should think of me above that which he seeth me to be, or that he heareth of me.

7 And lest I should be exalted above measure through the abundance of the revelations, there was given to me a thorn in the flesh, the messenger of Satan to buffet me, lest I should be exalted above measure.

8 For this thing I besought the Lord thrice, that it might depart from me.

9 And he said unto me, My grace is sufficient for thee: for my strength is made perfect in weakness. Most gladly therefore will I rather glory in my infirmities, that the power of Christ may rest upon me.

10 Therefore I take pleasure in infirmities, in reproaches, in necessities, in persecutions, in distresses for Christ's sake: for when I am weak, then am I strong.

Devotional Reading
James 4:1-10

Background Scripture
2 Cor. 12:1-10

Memory Selection
2 Cor. 12:9

Aug. 27

511

The final chapters of the letter we call 2 Corinthians contain some of the most intensely passionate language of all of Paul's letters. This is because he is trying to make peace with those in the Corinthian church who had opposed him. They have challenged his authority as an apostle, questioned his sincerity and his capacity as a leader, and said that while his letters were powerful he was a woefully weak preacher (10:10)!

Now he feels the need to defend himself. He says he is forced to boast of some "mountaintop experiences" God has given him, while at the same time having to accept limitations God has placed on him. In short, he has had to rely on God's grace—and he appeals to his opposition to join him on that firm ground.

Ask group members to share testimonials of strength coming out of difficulty, blessings out of the crucible of suffering. The teacher can elicit such testimonials by asking such questions as: *Has there ever been a time in your life when you felt you were at the end of your rope, but suddenly something unexpected seemed to rescue you? . . . Do you have to live with some ailment or illness you'd just as soon do without? How do you handle it? Does God seem to give you strength you didn't know you had? . . . What advice would you give someone who is faced with an issue for which there doesn't seem to be a good answer?*

Note that today's Memory Selection summarizes the lesson: *"My grace is sufficient for thee: for my strength is made perfect in weakness."*

Teaching Outline	Daily Bible Readings
I. Inexpressible Experience—1-4	Mon. When Grace Abounds Rom. 5:12-21
A. A time for boasting?, 1	Tue. Grace for the Humble James 4:1-10
B. Mysterious vision, 2-4	Wed. The God of Grace 1 Pet. 5:5-10
II. Infirmities as 'Boasting'—5-6	Thu. Paul Receives God's Grace 1 Cor. 15:3-10
III. Impatience vs. Grace—7-9	Fri. Paul's Need for Grace 2 Cor. 11:23-29
A. Thorn in the flesh, 7	Sat. Deep Spiritual Experience 2 Cor. 12:1-7
B. Grace all-sufficient, 8-9	Sun. Grace All-Sufficient 2 Cor. 12:8-13
IV. In Weakness, Strength, 10	

Verse by Verse

I. Inexpressible Experience—1-4

A. A time for boasting?, 1

1 It is not expedient for me doubtless to glory. I will come to visions and revelations of the Lord.

Earlier lessons have found the apostle Paul responding to attacks by some in the church at Corinth. Who was this man who claimed to be an apostle? Who gave him authority to rebuke one of their number for living in fornication (1 Cor. 5), and to call on them to take up a collection (Lessons 11 and 12)? Some even said "His letters . . . are weighty and powerful; but his bodily presence is weak, and his speech contemptible" (2 Cor. 10:10).

Beginning in chapter 10, Paul had begun to defend himself and to try to establish his apostolic authority. He argued that not asking for a salary while preaching among them showed his sincerity (11:7-9). He cited the hardships and dangers he had been willing to undergo in his travels (11:24-28). Now, in chapter 12, he bases his authority on the fact that *God had favored him with visions*.

Verse 1 is hard to translate, but comparing various version it seems to mean, "Although boasting is not expedient, I feel that it's necessary in this case to show that God has entrusted me with revelations." The vision Paul cites here is only one of several. The most spectacular was the one on the Damascus Road that led to his salvation (Acts 9; 22; 26). He could also have cited the one in which the man from Macedonia plead for Paul to bring the gospel to them (Acts 16:9), and the times of revelation when Christ Himself taught Paul the elements of Christianity (Gal. 1:11-12). This revelation, however, is different from the others in that it brought Paul up close to the heart of the mystery that is God Himself—a mystery so profound that it was inexpressible.

B. Mysterious vision, 2-4

2 I knew a man in Christ above fourteen years ago, (whether in the body, I cannot tell; or whether out of the body, I cannot tell: God knoweth;) such an one caught up to the third heaven.

3 And I knew such a man, (whether in the body, or out of the body, I cannot tell: God knoweth;)

4 How that he was caught up into paradise, and heard unspeakable words, which it is not lawful for a man to utter.

In his reluctance to boast, Paul switches to the third person, as though the vision he is about to refer to happened to someone else. This literary device can be compared to the "plural of royalty" when the Queen of England refers to herself as *We* (as in "We are not amused.") Verse 5a, below, strengthens this probability. Paul can bring himself to boast of visions given to him as an apostle, but not to himself as a person.

People in Paul's time had several views of heaven, speaking of three, five, or seven "levels." Paul apparently viewed "the third heaven" as equivalent to paradise, the place the Jews of his day believed the souls of the departed awaited final release into an afterlife with God (see also "Abraham's bosom," Luke 16:22). He had been caught up into this celestial realm either "in the body" (physically), or "in the spirit," as though dreaming—he could not tell which.

The purpose of this mysterious blessing was apparently for Paul's own edification, since the message he had been given there was "unspeakable"—literally "unwordable words"—that is, a message incapable of being put into human language.

Although we are tantalized to know more about this vision, Paul ceases his reference to it almost as soon as he brings it up. Although the Corinthians have "forced" him to boast, he will only go so far. It was enough for them to know that, unworthy as he was, Paul had been graced with the privilege of hearing some secret that was at the heart of the Mystery that is God. His audience's familiarity with this principle in the "mystery" religions among pagans probably gave the apostle's argument weight.

II. Infirmities as 'Boasting'—5-6

5 Of such an one will I glory: yet of myself I will not glory, but in mine infirmities.

6 For though I would desire to glory, I shall not be a fool; for I will say the truth: but now I forbear, lest any man should think of me above that which he seeth me to be, or that he heareth of me.

Paul continues to indicate embarrassment over being driven to "boast." If he must do so, however, he will confirm his apostleship by the way God has undergirded and strengthened him amid otherwise impossible trials. This turns the tables on those in Corinth who pointed to the "weakness" of Paul's bodily presence as evidence that he could not be a "glorious and victorious" apostle. Those very weaknesses, Paul will argue, would have defeated anyone but a person God had commissioned and supported. Thus Paul "forbears" or resists boasting in personal strengths such as his rabbinic training in argumentation, or his extensive knowledge of the Law.

III. Impatience vs. Grace—7-9
A. Thorn in the flesh, 7

7 And lest I should be exalted above measure through the abundance of the revelations, there was given to me a thorn in the flesh, the messenger of Satan to buffet me, lest I should be exalted above measure.

The "abundance of revelations" that included the vision in which Paul was caught up to the third heaven (vs. 2) were accompanied by the risk that the person so blessed would become arrogant. To forestall this, God gave Paul something painful to keep him humble. Just what this was has been a subject of wide (and wild!) speculation. All we really know is that it was a "thorn *in the flesh*," or apparently a bodily ailment. Some connect this with the apostle's reference to writing with a "large hand" (Gal. 6:11), and suppose the ailment was poor eyesight. Others suggest that "in the flesh" refers to fleshly desires, and that Paul struggled with lust or some other such spiritual affliction.

It is also noteworthy that Paul attributes this ailment to Satan, being careful to distance it from God himself. As in the case of Job, God *allowed* affliction, but kept a tight reign on the afflictor, Satan.

B. Grace all-sufficient, 8-9

8 For this thing I besought the Lord thrice, that it might depart from me.

9 And he said unto me, My grace is sufficient for thee: for my strength is made perfect in weakness. Most gladly therefore will I rather glory in my infirmities, that the power of Christ may rest upon me.

Verse 8 confronts us with the mystery of the instances of miraculous healing, and the times it was withheld. Even in Scripture it occurred only at the sovereign decision of God, and was not under unfailing and immediate command even of the apostles. There was the time when Christ's disciples returned with the report that they could not cast out a particular kind of demon (Matt. 17:14-20). Jesus Himself understood that His opponents would accuse Him of being unable to heal Himself (Luke 4:23). And here, even while trying to establish his authority as an apostle, Paul has to admit that he was unable to have his "thorn in the flesh" removed.

Many a modern Christian, praying without apparent effect to be released from suffering, has memorized the lesson Paul takes away from this disappointing experience: *"My grace is sufficient for thee."* Paul uses God's presence in His life, and the work he was able to do *despite* suffering or perhaps even *because* of suffering, as sufficient evidence of his apostleship. Paul seems to say that if being afflicted brings more of God's grace, "Bring it on!"

IV. In Weakness, Strength, 10

10 Therefore I take pleasure in infirmities, in reproaches, in necessities, in persecutions, in distresses for Christ's sake: for when I am weak, then am I strong.

The great paradox of strength-in-suffering remains as Paul's strongest defense against his enemies. It "pulls the teeth" from any who would maintain the position of Job's friends: *You are suffering because of sin in your life.* Paul turns this around and says *Because of my inadequacies and suffering, God's strength is more apparent in me.* This faith-filled position is to be compared to Paul's teaching in 4:16: "Though our outward man perish, yet the inward man is renewed day by day"; and with Peter's affirmation that suffering is a sign that "the spirit of glory and of God resteth upon you" (1 Pet. 4:14).

Evangelistic Emphasis

Once upon a time a man decided he would swim nonstop from Miami, Florida, to the west coast of England. His friends told him, "Please don't try this! It's humanly impossible."

"I can do it," he replied with conviction. So he began to swim.

After several miles, an oceangoing ship pulled alongside him. "Ahoy," the captain shouted over the bullhorn, "can we give you a lift?"

"No," the man replied. "I'm swimming nonstop to England."

The ship stayed alongside. The captain called again, "Sir, you cannot make it on your own. Please, I'm begging you. Get in the ship!"

"No!" the man stubbornly replied, "I can do it on my own."

As the hours went by the man got weaker. Finally, he slipped beneath the waves, exhausted, and drowned.

Now, that's just a story I made up—a parable to illustrate that it is imposible for a person to get to heaven under her/his own power. Just as the man needed to get into the ship, so we need to get into the "Old Ship of Zion."

We cannot get to heaven on our own. We need Jesus. "For by grace you have been saved through faith, and this is not your own doing; it is the gift of God—not the result of works, so that no one may boast" (Eph. 2:8-9, NRSV). Only by God's grace are we saved.

ℰℭ

Memory Selection

And he said unto me, My grace is sufficient for thee: for my strength is made perfect in weakness. Most gladly therefore will I rather glory in my infirmities, that the power of Christ may rest upon me.—*2 Corinthians 12:9*

A line in an old song goes, "When you've tried everything and everything has failed, try Jesus." Personally I think a person would be wise to try Jesus first and not have to bother with searching around, but the line makes a good point.

Many obstacles in life are just too big for us to handle on our own. When we come upon one of those problems—a rebellious teenager, an alcoholic husband, a gambling-addicted wife—we must realize we are powerless to effect permanent change by ourselves. If we are wise, at that time we will recognize our weakness, our impotence, and our limitations, and call on Jesus Christ to help us.

And help He will. He will never leave us nor forsake us. He is always ready to pick us up when we are down. He is our strength when we are weak. We don't have to climb every mountain, swim every sea, nor solve every problem on our own. Ask for God's help. He is grace-filled. His grace is enough.

Weekday Problems

It was 2:30 a.m. Jacob was determined he was going to finish his term paper that night. He had never turned in a paper late, and this was not going to be the first one. He poured himself another cup of coffee, and massaged his own neck as he sat back down to the computer. "Professor Jones asked for twelve pages and he is getting twelve pages," Jacob thought with a smile as he finished. He returned to the start of his paper and began to proofread it. "This is good," he gloated.

"Whoa! What's this?" Jacob was shocked as he realized that what should have been page 6 was a repeat of page 5. He looked for page 7, but it was not to be found. Jacob's stomach began to churn. Apparently his computer had crashed, deleting over half of his paper. Jacob was sick at his stomach. "Why hadn't I saved it page by page!" he wept.

Jacob spent the next two hours trying to recover his paper. It was no use. It was gone. He went to bed with hot tears on his cheeks. The next morning Jacob was at Professor Jones' office at 8 a.m. "Professor, I know you've heard every excuse in the book about late papers," Jacob began, "but please give me an extension. My computer crashed and I lost it."

"Jacob," Professor Jones replied, "you've always turned your work in on time. I'll give you three more days without penalty."

*Would you call Professor Jones' response "grace"? Why or why not?

*Share a time when you received grace from another person.

Faith from the Fire

As in nature, as in art, so in grace; it is rough treatment that gives souls, as well as stones, their luster. The more the diamond is cut, the brighter it sparkles.—*Thomas Guthrie*

***

There is no merit where there is no trial; and till experience stamps the mark of strength, cowards may pass for heroes, and faith for falsehood.—*Aaron Hill*

***

Suffering accepted and vanquished . . . will give you a serenity which may well prove the most exquisite fruit of your life.—*Cardinal Mercer*

***

By afflictions God is spoiling us of what otherwise might have spoiled us. When He makes the world to hot for us to hold, we let it go.—*Sir John Powell*

This Lesson in Your Life

To me, one of the greatest moments in sports occurred in the 1992 Olympic Games in Barcelona, Spain. It all happened in a semifinal heat involving Derek Redmond, a 400-meter British runner.

Picture the scene. The stadium is packed with 65,000 fans bracing themselves for one of sport's greatest and most exciting events. The runners are off. Redmond breaks from the pack and quickly seizes the lead. He runs well. Down the backstretch, with less than 200 meters to go, Redmond is a shoo-in to make the finals. Suddenly, he hears a pop. It's his right hamstring. He goes down as if he'd been shot.

Redmond realizes his dream of an Olympic medal is gone. Tears run down his face. As the medical crew arrives with a stretcher, Redmond tells them, "No, there's no way I'm getting on that stretcher. I'm going to finish my race." Then, in a moment that will live forever in my mind, Redmond struggles to his feet. He begins to hobble painfully down the track toward the finish line. Nobody sees it right then, but from the top of the stands an older man heads down toward the track. Redmond struggles on. The older man finally gets to the bottom of the stands, leaps over the railing, and avoids a security guard with the words, "That's my son out there, and I'm going to help him."

Finally, Jim Redmond reaches his son Derek. "I'm here, son," Jim says softly, hugging his boy. "We'll finish together."

Together, arm in arm, with 65,000 people cheering, clapping, and crying, father and son finish the race. A couple of steps from the finish line, with the crowd in an absolute frenzy, Jim Redmond releases his grip on his son, so Derek can cross the finish line by himself.

I could not believe the determination of that young man. He had not come to *start* a race, but to finish it. Yet something happened he could not control. He may have been able to hobble across the finish line unassisted, but, in reality he made it with the help of his father.

The story of Derek Redmond and his father is also the story of the Christian and our heavenly Father. There are times in our lives when we are unable to finish the race. There are times when we fall on the track, injured. There are times when the pain is too great to bear.

During those times, our heavenly Father comes to us quickly with the words, "That's my child out there. I'm going to help." Sure enough, the Father reaches us, puts his arms around us and says, "I'm here, child. We'll finish the race together."

God's grace. It truly is amazing.

1. What is Paul talking about in verse 1?
Paul writes about visions and revelations from the Lord.

2. How long ago did this man of which Paul speaks experience being caught up to the third heaven?
It was 14 or more years ago.

3. Was this event a vision or an out-of-body experience?
Paul was not sure whether it was a vision or an out-of-body experience. However, he knew that God knows what kind of experience it was.

4. In verse 2 Paul uses the phrase, "third heaven." What word does Paul use in verse 4 to describe the same place?
Paul uses the word "paradise" to describe the place to which the man was caught up.

5. If Paul chose to boast, would he have to exaggerate to make himself look better?
No, even if Paul were to brag, the facts of God's revelations to him would still be true.

6. What happened to keep Paul from becoming conceited because of the revelations he received?
He was given a thorn in the flesh.

7. Do we know exactly what Paul's "thorn in the flesh" was?
No, we know only that it was a messenger of Satan sent to torment Paul.

8. How many times did Paul ask the Lord to take this thorn in the flesh away from him?
Paul asked the Lord three times to relieve him of this tormenting factor.

9. What was God's answer when Paul asked Him to remove this "thorn"?
God said, "My grace is sufficient for thee, for my strength is made perfect in weakness."

10. What was Paul's reaction to God's answer?
Paul says that he takes pleasure in infirmities, in reproaches, in distresses for Christ's sake. Paul knows that in his weakness, Christ would make him strong.

God said to Paul, "My grace is sufficient for you." God's grace is enough. It is always enough.

Some years ago I read a testimony that came out of the Pacific Garden Mission in Chicago. One evening at the services a prostitute wandered in. She listened to the message. It touched her heart and she was saved. She began to come regularly to the Mission. She gave up her life of prostitution and began to live a productive, decent life.

Later, she was given an opportunity to share what God had done for her at one of the services. As she began to testify, she was overcome with gratitude for what Jesus had done and was doing for her. She thought she would have greater impact on the congregation if she described the life from which she had been saved. She began to recount her days of prostitution in detail. Things became a little too graphic, so the pastor interrupted her and called her to the side.

"You cannot say those things like that, sister," the pastor counseled.

Through her tears she replied, "I just want people to know the hell God saved me from!"

The pastor replied, "Sister, we're all going to hell without Jesus."

That's the truth. We're all going to hell without Jesus. Whether we live a life of prostitution, drugs, and murder; or we go to work every day in a three-piece suit, we're all going to hell without Jesus.

Yet God's grace can get us out of any state in which we can get ourselves. There is no work we can do for ourselves to earn His grace. Because we are so fallen, good folks and bad folks included, we could never find the strength to turn back to God. God comes to get us . . . by His grace.

" 'Twas grace that taught my heart to fear,
And grace my fears relieved.
How precious did that grace appear
The hour I first believed."